Applied Behavior Analysis for Teachers

Fourth Edition

Paul A. Alberto
Georgia State University

Anne C. Troutman
University of Memphis

Merrill,
an imprint of Prentice Hall
Englewood Cliffs, New Jersey   Columbus, Ohio

Library of Congress Cataloging-in-Publication Data

Alberto, Paul.
    Applied behavior analysis for teachers / Paul A. Alberto, Anne C. Troutman.
—4th ed.
        p. cm.
    Includes bibliographical references and indexes.
    ISBN 0-02-301264-1
    1. Behavior modification. 2. Students—Psychology. 3. Human
behavior.   I. Troutman, Anne C. II. Title.
LB1060.2.A43   1995
371.1'024—dc20

94-19320
CIP

Cover art: Bryan Lysaght, Indian Mound Elementary, Marion, Ohio
Editor: Ann C. Davis
Production Editor: Mary M. Irvin
Text Designer: Ed Horcharik
Cover Designer: Gryphon III
Production Buyer: Laura Messerly
Electronic Text Management: Marilyn Wilson Phelps, Matthew Williams, Jane Lopez,
   Karen L. Bretz

This book was set in Souvenir by Prentice Hall and was printed and bound by R. R.
Donnelley/Virginia. The cover was printed by Phoenix Color Corp.

© 1995 by Prentice-Hall, Inc.
A Simon & Schuster Company
Englewood Cliffs, New Jersey 07632

Earlier editions © 1990, 1986, 1982 by Merrill Publishing Company.

Printed in the United States of America

10 9 8 7 6 5 4 3 2 1

ISBN: 0-02-301264-1

Prentice-Hall International (UK) Limited, *London*
Prentice-Hall of Australia Pty. Limited, *Sydney*
Prentice-Hall of Canada, Inc., *Toronto*
Prentice-Hall Hispanoamericana, S. A., *Mexico*
Prentice-Hall of India Private Limited, *New Delhi*
Prentice-Hall of Japan, Inc., *Tokyo*
Simon & Schuster Asia Pte. Ltd., *Singapore*
Editora Prentice-Hall do Brasil, Ltda., *Rio de Janeiro*

Preface

We prepared the first edition of *Applied Behavior Analysis for Teachers* because we needed a technically sound, systematically organized, and readable text for our own students. We want students to understand concepts of applied behavior analysis and also to know how to apply those concepts in classrooms and other settings. Applied behavior analysis can make a difference; its principles can be used to teach academic skills, functional skills, and appropriate social behavior. Applied behavior analysis is an overall management system, not a collection of tricks for keeping students under control.

This is not a cookbook providing simple step-by-step directions for solving every possible problem an educator might encounter. That would be impossible in any event—what makes working with children and young adults so much fun is that every one is different and no one procedure will be effective for all of them. We want students to be able to use the principles to create their own recipes for success. Successful application of the principles requires the full and active participation of a creative educator. Because we believe so strongly that applied behavior analysis is the most powerful teaching tool available, we stress learning to use it appropriately and ethically.

Instructors will be interested in knowing that the text is as technically accurate and as well documented as we could make it. At the same time, we've tried to enliven it with examples students will enjoy reading. Our examples describe students from preschool through young adulthood functioning at various levels of ability. We describe poor teachers as well as excellent ones. Many of our examples describe the kind of teachers we think we are and hope your students will be—good teachers who learn from their inevitable mistakes.

In preparing this fourth edition, we took to heart suggestions from colleagues and thoughtful letters from students using the book. We did, however, consider the mousetrap example in Chapter 11 sufficiently valuable to retain in spite of a letter from an irate animal rights activist. We have added a new chapter, "Functional Analysis and Assessment" (Chapter 9), and greatly expanded the chapter on "Putting It All Together" to include settings other than traditional classrooms.

Finally, the text remains organized to allow instructors to assign students a behavior-change project concurrently with lectures and readings. The text progresses from identifying a target behavior to collecting data, selecting an experimental design, arranging consequences, arranging antecedents, and generalizing the behavior change. Chapters 12 and 13 provide suggestions for teaching behavioral procedures to others. We've tried to provide students with the basics of a teaching technology that will serve as a solid foundation for other methods courses.

We welcome your continued personal response to our book. We hope you enjoy reading it as much as we enjoyed writing it.

ACKNOWLEDGMENTS

We would like to thank all the people who helped us in the process of producing the fourth edition of *Applied Behavior Analysis for Teachers,* including all the editors at Prentice Hall with whom we worked. We appreciate the suggestions provided by those who reviewed the text, including Linda K. Elksnin, The Citadel; Nancy J. Fenrick, Mankato State University; Tom McFarland, Lewis Clark State College; and Ronald B. Straub, Mansfield University. We thank Nancy Wilder again for word processing, editing, verifying references, indexing, and prodding.

We would also like to acknowledge B. F. Skinner, who died shortly after the publication of the third edition of this text. What started with teaching pigeons tricks on a windowsill has changed the lives of millions of people: children and adults, typical people, and those so physically and mentally challenged that they could not, before applied behavior analysis, take care of their most basic needs. Neither of us ever met Skinner, but our teachers were taught by him. We are grateful for his legacy and for the opportunity to share his work with the next generation of teachers.

Contents

Section One
Behavior Modification in Perspective   1

1
Roots of Applied Behavior Analysis   **3**

4

Collecting and Graphing Data   *101*

5

Single-subject Designs   *153*

Section Three
Applying Learning Principles   205

6
Arranging Consequences That Increase Behavior   207

7
Differential Reinforcement: Stimulus Control and Shaping   257

8

Arranging Consequences That Decrease Behavior   *295*

9

Functional Assessment and Analysis   *347*

10

Putting It All Together   *369*

Section Four

Maintaining Behavior Change   393

11

Providing for Generalization of Behavior Change   *395*

12

Teaching Students to Manage Their Own Behavior   *431*

13

Teaching Behavior-Change Procedures to Others   *457*

Section One
Behavior Modification in Perspective

1

Roots of Applied Behavior Analysis

Did you know that . . .

- There may be some validity in your mother's claim that "You're just like your father"?
- Chemicals in your brain may affect your behavior?
- Apes can have insight?
- Pretzels preceded M&Ms as rewards for good behavior?
- Benjamin Franklin knew about applied behavior analysis?

Why do people behave as they do? Why do some people behave in socially approved ways and others in a manner condemned or despised by society? What can be done to predict what people are likely to do? What can be done to change behavior that is harmful to an individual or destructive to society?

In an effort to answer questions like these, human beings have offered explanations ranging from possession by demons to abnormal quantities of chemicals in the brain. Suggested answers have been debated, written about, attacked, and defended for centuries and continue to be offered today. There are good reasons for continuing to investigate human behavior. Information about the development of certain behaviors in human beings may help parents and teachers find the best way of child-rearing or teaching. If we know how people are likely to behave under certain conditions, we can decide whether to provide or avoid such conditions. Those of us who are teachers are particularly concerned with changing behavior; that is, in fact, our job. We want to teach our students to do some things and to stop doing others.

In order to understand, predict, and change human behavior, we must first understand how human behavior works. In short, we must answer as completely as possible the "why" questions asked above. Therefore, Alexander Pope's dictum that "the proper study of mankind is man" (perhaps rephrased to "the proper study of humanity is people") needs no other revision; it is as true in the 20th century as it was in the 18th.

This chapter discusses the requirements for meaningful and useful explanations of human behavior. It then describes several interpretations of human behavior that have influenced large numbers of practitioners, including teachers. The discussion concludes by tracing the historical development of a way of understanding and predicting human behavior called *applied behavior analysis*.

THE USEFULNESS OF EXPLANATIONS

If a way of explaining behavior is to be useful for the practitioner, it must meet four requirements. First, it should be *inclusive*. It must account for a substantial quantity of behavior. An explanation has limited usefulness if it fails to account for the bulk of human behavior and thus makes prediction and systematic change of behavior impossible. Second, an explanation must be *verifiable*; that is, we should be able to test in some way that it does account for behavior. Third, the explanation should have *predictive utility*. It should provide reliable answers about what people are likely to do under certain circumstances, thereby giving the practitioner the opportunity to change behavior by changing conditions. Fourth, it should be *parsimonious*. A parsimonious explanation is the simplest one that will account for observed phenomena. Parsimony does not guarantee correctness (Mahoney, 1974)—because the simplest explanation may not always be the correct one—but it prevents our being so imaginative as to lose touch with the reality of observed data. When the bathroom light fails to operate at

3:00 A.M., one should check the bulb before calling the electric company to report a blackout. There may be a blackout, but the parsimonious explanation is a burned-out bulb.

In examining some of the theories developed to explain human behavior, we shall evaluate each explanation for its inclusiveness, verifiability, predictive utility, and parsimony.

A useful theory has inclusiveness, verifiability, predictive utility, and parsimony.

BIOPHYSICAL EXPLANATIONS

Since physicians of ancient Greece first proposed that human behavior was the result of interactions among four bodily fluids or "humors"—blood, phlegm, yellow bile (choler), and black bile (melancholy)—theorists have searched for explanations for human behavior within the physical structure of the body. Such theories have included those based on genetic or hereditary factors, those that emphasize biochemical influences, and those that suggest aberrant behavior is caused by some damage to the brain. The following anecdote offers an explanation for behavior that indicates a belief in hereditary influences on behavior.

Some theorists state that human behavior is controlled by physical influences.

Professor Grundy Traces the Cause

Having observed an undergraduate student's behavior for some time, Professor Grundy noticed that the student was consistently late for class (when he came at all), invariably unprepared, and frequently inattentive. Since Grundy was certain his dynamic, meaningful lectures were not related to this behavior, he decided to investigate the matter. He paid a visit to the high school attended by the student and located his 10th-grade English teacher, Ms. Marner. "Yes, DeWayne was just like that in high school," said Ms. Marner. "He just didn't get a good background in junior high."

Professor Grundy then went to visit the junior high school. "You know," said the guidance counselor, "a lot of our kids are like that. They just don't get the foundation in elementary school." At the elementary school, Professor Grundy talked to the principal. "DeWayne was like that from day one. His home situation was far from ideal. If we don't have support from the home, it's hard to make much progress."

Professor Grundy, sure that he would at last find the answer, went to talk to DeWayne's mother. "I'll tell you," said his mother, "he takes after his father's side of the family. They're all *just like that*."

Genetic and Hereditary Effects

DeWayne's mother explained his inappropriate behavior by referring to hereditary influences. Could she have been right? The effects of heredity on human behavior, both normal and atypical, have been investigated extensively. There is little question that mental retardation (which results in significant deficits in a wide range of behaviors) is sometimes associated with chromosomal abnormalities or with the inheritance of recessive genes (Achenbach, 1974). There is some evidence that other behavioral characteristics have some hereditary basis as well. Although few can be as explicitly identified as the syndromes resulting in some mental retardation, we can learn about hereditary influences through other types of investigation.

Researchers studying heredity often compare the characteristics of sets of twins.

Most studies investigating the hereditary components of behavior have been carried out by comparing identical twins with fraternal twins. Identical twins have exactly the same genetic inheritance; fraternal twins are no more alike genetically than any other siblings. Thus, if behavioral characteristics occur more consistently in both of a number of pairs of identical twins than in pairs of fraternal twins, we can assume that the behavioral characteristics result from some inherited factor. Serious behavior disorders, such as that labeled *schizophrenia*, occur more frequently in both members of a pair of identical twins than in both members of a pair of fraternal twins (Kallmann & Roth, 1956). Some less dramatic behavioral characteristics, such as those labeled *social introversion* or *extroversion, depression* (Eysenck, 1956; Vandenburg, 1967), and *reading difficulty* (Bannatyne, 1971; Hallgren, 1950), apparently also have some hereditary component.

Inheritance appears, in addition, to affect some behavioral characteristics that are not labeled *deviant* or *atypical*. Thomas, Chess, and Birch (1968) conducted a study of 136 children whose development has been closely monitored for a number of years. Each child was observed shortly after birth and then frequently throughout childhood. Interviews were held with parents and teachers. The authors identified nine categories of behavior that they labeled *temperament*. Each characteristic could be reliably observed and was consistent throughout childhood. The categories of temperament included

1. *Activity level*—the degree to which the child moves around
2. *Rhythmicity*—the child's regularity with regard to sleep patterns, eating, and bowel and bladder functions
3. *Approach or withdrawal*—the child's reaction to any new stimulus including people, food, and places
4. *Adaptability*—the child's ability to adapt to a new situation even if the initial response was withdrawal
5. *Intensity of reaction*—the child's tendency to scream or whimper when hungry, shriek with laughter or smile when amused
6. *Threshold of responsiveness*—the degree of sensitivity to stimuli and to changes in the environment
7. *Quality of mood*—the child's overall disposition whether pleasant and friendly or grumpy and unfriendly
8. *Distractibility*—the ease with which the child can be interrupted in an ongoing activity

9. *Attention span and persistence*—the length of time a child pursues an activity or persists despite interruptions

Since several sets of twins were included in the sample, it was possible to determine by the method described earlier that characteristics 1–7 appear to be more similar in identical than in fraternal twins. Not enough data were available for characteristics 8 and 9. However, only activity level and approach or withdrawal remained more similar for identical twins than for fraternal twins after the first year (Rutter, Korn, & Birch, 1963). The fact that all the characteristics listed show such consistency over time indicates that they have some constitutional, if not genetic, basis.

When DeWayne's mother explained her son's behavior to Professor Grundy, her claim that DeWayne takes after his father's family may have involved a degree of truth. It is possible that certain genetic characteristics may increase the probability of certain behavioral characteristics.

Biochemical Explanations

Some researchers have suggested that certain behaviors may result from excesses or deficiencies of various substances found in the body. These chemical substances are labeled differently from those hypothesized by the ancient Greeks. Some theorists who propose a biochemical basis for behavior hold that brain injury, which we will discuss later, contributes to the biochemical dysfunction (Rimland, 1964).

Some children with disabilities show biochemical abnormalities.

Biochemical abnormalities have been found in some children with serious disturbances of behavior labeled *autism* or *childhood psychosis* (Boullin, Coleman, O'Brien, & Rimland, 1971). Investigation of such factors, however, has established only that biochemical abnormalities exist, not that they cause the disorder.

Other behavior disturbances characterized as hyperactivity, learning disability, or mental retardation have been linked to biophysical factors such as hypoglycemia (Cott, 1972; Wunderlich, 1977), malnutrition (Cott, 1972; Cravioto & DeLicardie, 1975; Morgane, Stern, & Resnick, 1974; Vitale & Velez, 1968; Wunderlich, 1977), and allergic reactions (Feingold, 1975; Wunderlich, 1977). Feingold's is the best known of such theories. His theory suggests that food containing natural salicylates, artificial flavorings and colorings, and certain antioxidant preservatives contribute to hyperactivity in children. Although Feingold (1975) attributes dramatic effects to removal of such additives from the diet of hyperactive children, most studies that report such findings have been poorly controlled and have relied heavily on such questionable data as parent reports. Some controlled studies using unbiased observers, where neither parents, children, nor teachers were aware of the presence or absence of additive substances, indicate a tentative relationship between hyperactivity and certain foods (Conners, 1975; Rose, 1978). Recent reviews of research (Mattes, 1983; Pruess, Fewell, & Bennett, 1989) report a lack of evidence of any dietary effect on hyperactivity. Another bio-physical abnormality is used to explain the behavior in Professor Grundy's next adventure.

Studies relating hyperac-tivity to food additives have been inconclusive.

Professor Grundy Learns to Think in Circles

Professor Grundy, as part of his instructional duties, visited student teachers. On his first trip to evaluate Ms. Harper, in a primary resource room, he observed that one student, Ralph, wandered continuously about the room. Curious about such behavior, since the other students remained seated, Professor Grundy inquired, "Why is Ralph wandering around the room? Why doesn't he sit down like the others?" Ms. Harper was aghast at such ignorance on the part of a professor.

"Why, Ralph is hyperactive, Professor Grundy. That's why he never stays in his seat."

"Ah," replied the professor. "That's very interesting. How do you know he's hyperactive?"

With barely concealed disdain, Ms. Harper hissed, "Professor, I know he's hyperactive because *he won't stay in his seat.*"

After observing the class for a few more minutes, he noticed Ms. Harper and the supervising teacher whispering and casting glances in his direction. Professor Grundy once again attracted Ms. Harper's attention. "What," he inquired politely, "causes Ralph's hyperactivity?"

The disdain was no longer concealed. "Professor," answered Ms. Harper, "hyperactivity is caused by brain damage."

"Indeed," responded the professor, "and you know he's brain damaged because . . . "

"Of course I know he's brain-damaged, Professor. He's hyperactive, isn't he?"

Brain Damage

The circular reasoning illustrated by Ms. Harper is, unfortunately, not uncommon. Many professionals explain a great deal of students' inappropriate behavior similarly. The notion that certain kinds of behavior result from brain damage has its roots in the work of Goldstein (1939), who studied soldiers returning from World War I having suffered head injuries. He identified certain behavioral characteristics, including distractibility, perceptual confusion, and hyperactivity. Observing similar characteristics in some retarded children, some professionals concluded that the children must also be brain-injured (Strauss & Werner, 1942; Werner & Strauss, 1940) and that the brain injury was the cause of the behavior. This led to the identification of a hyperkinetic behavior syndrome (Strauss & Lehtinen, 1947), assumed to be the result of brain injury. This syndrome included such characteristics as hyperactivity, distractibility, impulsivity, short attention span, emotional lability (changeability), perceptual problems, and clumsiness. Studying a group of children known to be brain-injured because of cerebral palsy, Cruickshank, Bice, and Wallen

Hyperactivity is not necessarily caused by brain dysfunction.

(1957) reported the existence of similar behavioral characteristics in children with normal intelligence. Subsequently, the term *minimal brain dysfunction* was used to describe a disorder assumed to exist in children who, although they had no history of brain injury, behaved similarly.

There is, however, little empirical support of using the theory of brain injury to account for problem behavior in all children who show such behavioral characteristics. Even when brain damage can be unequivocally shown to exist, there is no proof that it causes any particular behavior (Pond, 1961). And, finally, "there is good evidence to show that when psychopathology is associated with brain damage it can take any form, the *least* common of which is the hyperkinetic syndrome" (Werry, 1972, p. 97).

Large numbers of children are presently being defined as "at risk" for the development of academic and social problems because of the effects of both influences before birth (such as parental malnutrition or substance abuse) and environmental factors (Davis & McCaul, 1991). Although there are clear indications that these factors result in biochemical, central nervous system, and other physiological abnormalities, no specific behavioral deficit or excess is directly attributed to any specific factor (Gelfand, Jenson, & Drew, 1988).

The Usefulness of Biophysical Explanations

The search for explanations of human behavior based on physiological factors has important implications. As a result of such research, the technology for preventing or lessening some serious problems has been developed. The best known example of such technology is perhaps the routine testing of all infants for phenylketonuria (PKU), a hereditary disorder of metabolism. Placing infants with PKU on special diets can prevent the mental retardation formerly associated with this disorder (Berry, 1969). It is possible that future research may explain a good deal more human behavior on a biological or hereditary basis. Currently, however, only a small part of the vast quantity of human behavior can be explained in this way, so that such biophysical explanations fail to meet our criterion of inclusiveness.

Some biophysical explanations are testable, meeting the second of our four requirements for usefulness. For example, scientists can definitely establish the existence of Down syndrome by observing chromosomes. Some metabolic or biochemical disorders can also be scientifically verified. Verification of such presumed causes of behavior as minimal brain dysfunction, however, is not dependable (Werry, 1972).

Even with evidence of the existence of some physiological disorder, it does not follow that any specific behavior is automatically a result of the disorder. For the teacher, explanations based on presumed physiological disorders have very little predictive utility. To say that Rachel can't walk, talk, or feed herself because she is retarded as a result of a chromosomal disorder tells us nothing about the conditions under which Rachel might learn to perform these behaviors. For Ms. Harper to explain Ralph's failure to sit down on the basis of hyperactivity caused by brain damage does not provide any useful information about what might help Ralph learn to stay in his seat. To say that Harold can't read because he is an at-risk child is to put Harold at the greater risk of not learning because we have low expectations for him. Even apparently constitutional differences in temperament are so vulnerable to environmental influences (Thomas & Chess, 1977) as to provide only limited information about how a child is apt to behave under given conditions.

The final criterion, parsimony, is also frequently violated when physical causes are postulated for student behaviors. Searching for such causes often distracts teachers from simpler, more immediate factors that may be controlling behaviors in the classroom. Perhaps the greatest danger of such explanations is that some teachers may use them as excuses not to teach: Rachel can't feed herself because she's retarded, not because I haven't taught her. Ralph won't sit down because he's brain-damaged, not because I have poor classroom management skills. Irving can't read because he has dyslexia, not because I haven't figured out a way to teach him. Biophysical explanations may also cause teachers to have low expectations for some students. When this happens, teachers might not even try to teach things students are capable of learning. The following chart summarizes the usefulness of biophysical theory.

The Usefulness of Biophysical Theory	Good	Fair	Poor
Inclusiveness			✓
Verifiability		✓	
Predictive Utility			✓
Parsimony			✓

DEVELOPMENTAL EXPLANATIONS

Observation of human beings confirms that many predictable patterns of development occur. Physical growth proceeds in a fairly consistent manner. Most children start walking, talking, and performing some social behaviors like smiling, in fairly predictable sequences and at generally predictable chronological ages (Gesell & Ilg, 1943). Some theorists have attempted to explain many aspects of human behavior—cognitive, social, emotional, and moral—based on fixed, innate developmental sequences. Their proposed explanations are meant to account for normal as well as "deviant" (other than the accepted or usual) human behavior. The following sections review three of the numerous developmental theories and examine their usefulness in terms of inclusiveness, verifiability, predictive utility, and parsimony.

A Freudian by the Garbage Can

Upon returning to the university after observing student teachers, Professor Grundy prepared to return to work on his textbook manuscript, now at least 7 months behind schedule. To his horror, his carefully organized notes, drafts, and revisions were no longer "arranged" on the floor of his office. Professor Grundy ran frantically down the hall, loudly berating the custodial worker who had taken advantage of his absence to remove what he considered "that trash" from the floor so that he could vacuum.

"Well, well, Professor Grundy, did you lose something or are you just doing 'research' on the things you professors throw away?"

As Grundy pawed through the outside garbage can, a colleague offered sympathy. "That's what happens when an anal-expulsive personality conflicts with an anal-retentive." Grundy's regrettably loud and obscene response to this observation drew the additional comment, "Definite signs of regression to the oral-aggressive stage, there, Grundy."

Psychoanalytic Theory

Although many different explanations of human behavior have been described as psychoanalytic, all have their roots in theories of Sigmund Freud (Fine, 1973), who described human behavior in an essentially developmental manner (Kessler, 1966). Freud's assertion that normal and aberrant human behavior may be understood and explained on the basis of progression through certain crucial stages (Hall, 1954) is perhaps the most commonly accepted and most widely disseminated of his theories.

Freud postulated the existence of certain biologically based drives, specifically a sex drive and an aggressive drive. These drives provide a source of energy referred to by Freud as the *id*, the part of human personality that seeks gratification of desires without reference to any external controls. A second part of personality, the *ego*, develops as an infant learns to relate to his or her environment. The ego includes such processes as motility, memory, judgement, reasoning, language, and thought (Kessler, 1966). A third component of personality, the *superego*, develops as a function of parental training. The superego includes conscience, morals, ethics, and aspirations. Anxiety-arousing conflict results when the drives of the id encounter the standards of the superego. Freud suggested that these conflicts are mediated by the ego.

The id says "I wanna"; the superego says "I ought." The ego is the umpire.

The hypothesized energy of the id centers in different parts of the body during the various stages suggested by Freud. Freud's stage theory was subsequently elaborated by Abraham, whose modifications were incorporated into the theory by Freud (Hall, 1954). The stages are

1. *Oral stage.* In this stage, which lasts from birth through about the second year, gratification is centered around the mouth. The stage is subdivided into oral-dependent and oral-aggressive stages, before and after the acquisition of teeth.

2. *Anal stage.* This stage, from the second to fourth years of life, centers around the elimination of feces. It may be subdivided into an anal-expulsive stage and an anal-retentive stage. The anal-retentive stage, when the child derives gratification from withholding and controlling feces, corresponds to the years when toilet-training is a major parental concern.

3. *Phallic stage.* Gratification in this stage centers around the genitalia. It is during this stage, from ages 4 to 6, that the so-called Oedipus complex (named for a mythical Greek who killed his father and married his mother) arises. During the oedipal stage, the child becomes very attached to the parent of the opposite sex and develops hostility to the parent of the same sex.

4. *Latency stage.* This stage represents a sort of rest-stop after the tumultuous development of the first three stages. If the child has mastered the complexes of the prelatency stages, he or she has identified with the parent of the same sex. Children of this stage, from age 6 to puberty, play primarily with other children of the same sex in sex-stereotyped activities.

5. *Genital stage.* At puberty, the child becomes interested in members of the opposite sex.

This theory suggests that people who progress through the stages successfully become relatively normal adults. In Freud's view, problems arise when a person fixates at a certain stage because that person's ego cannot resolve conflicts, or when anxiety causes a regression to a previous stage. People who fixate at or regress to the oral-dependent stage may merely be extremely dependent, or they may seek to solve problems by oral means such as overeating, smoking, or alcohol or drug abuse. A person fixated at the oral-aggressive stage may be sarcastic or verbally abusive. Fixation at the anal-expulsive stage results in messiness and disorganization; at the anal-retentive stage, in compulsive orderliness. Freud suggested that failure to resolve oedipal problems results in sexual identification difficulties.

Theories of Cognitive and Moral Development

Psychoanalytic theory is not the only explanation of human behavior that suggests the existence of developmental stages. Other theories have been proposed that describe stages related to cognitive and moral development.

Cognitive Development

Jean Piaget was a biologist and psychologist who proposed a stage theory of human development. Piaget's descriptions of the cognitive and moral development of children have had extensive impact among educators. Like Freud, Piaget theorized that certain forces, biologically determined, contribute to development (Piaget & Inhelder, 1969). The forces suggested by Piaget, however, are those enabling the organism to adapt to the environment—specifically, *assimilation*, the tendency to adapt the environment to enhance personal functioning; and *accommodation*, the tendency to change behavior to adapt to the environment (Achenbach, 1974). The process of maintaining a balance between these two forces is called *equilibration*. Equilibration facilitates growth; other factors that also do so are organic maturation, experience, and social interaction.

When assimilation and accommodation are balanced, a state of equilibration exists.

The cognitive stages suggested by Piaget are

1. *Sensorimotor intelligence* (from birth to 1 1/2 years). During this state, the infant is preoccupied with differentiating himself from the rest of the world and establishing representations of the objects in his world. He learns how to get to things and how to get things to him. He learns object constancy, that things exist even when he can't see them.

2. *Preoperational thought, representational thinking* (from age 1 1/2 years to 4 or 5). This stage includes the development of language. Piaget postulates, however, that private symbols and representations precede the development of language. Some limitations still exist; children at this stage are still unable to take another person's point of view—even in the very concrete sense of What would this room look like if you were standing over here? Children's thinking at this stage is typified by their reaction to the familiar conservation experiments: the child who agrees that two glasses hold exactly equal amounts of liquid will insist there are unequal amounts when the contents of one glass are poured—while he is watching—into a wider or narrower glass.

3. *Preoperational thought, intuitional thinking* (from 5 to 7 years). During this stage, the child begins to understand conservation of amount, quan-

tity, number, and weight. She is able to attend to more than one aspect of an object at a time and is less a victim of her immediate perceptions. She begins to understand the reversibility of some operations, but cannot always justify or explain her conclusions. The conclusions may be intuitively correct, but the child lacks the ability to systematize them.

4. *Concrete operations* (from 7 to 11 years). During this stage, the child organizes his perceptions and symbols; he becomes able to classify and categorize along several dimensions simultaneously. He can also describe verbally what he is doing, but will not be able to solve problems presented in a purely abstract manner.

5. *Formal operations* (from 12 years through adulthood). Once she has reached this stage, the child no longer needs concrete referents in order to solve problems. The formal-operational thinker can deal with abstractions and with hypothetical situations and can think logically (Dember & Jenkins, 1970).

Moral Development

A theory of moral development with stages parallel to those of Piaget's cognitive theory has been described by Kohlberg (1964, 1969) and Turiel (1974). The stages of moral development include

1. *Punishment and obedience orientation*. In this stage, children behave because of externally imposed rules. Appropriate behavior is performed to avoid punishment.

2. *Naive instrumental hedonism*. This stage emphasizes satisfying personal needs and, to some extent, others' needs. Children begin to view "fairness" as important.

3. *Good-boy morality of maintaining good relations and approval of others*. In this stage, children are attuned to gaining the approval of others. Great emphasis is placed on intentions. "I didn't mean to do it" is a common defense.

4. *Authority-maintaining morality*. In this stage, appropriate behavior is based on respect for authority. Personal values are not an important factor. Such orientation may provide little guidance in situations where authority and fixed rules are absent.

5. *Morality of contract and of democratically accepted law*. At this stage, people show concern for individual rights within the context of societal standards. There is an emphasis on procedures for establishing rules that are fair for the individual as well as being good for society.

6. *Morality of individual principles of conscience*. By this stage, the individual has developed a consistent, logical, personal ethical system. Decisions about right and wrong are based on universal principles, not concrete moral rules.

Stage Theories and Intelligence

Piaget and others who propose stage theories of human development have been primarily interested in describing and explaining normal human behavior. Consequently, the chronological age ranges offered in the two previous lists of stages are approximate indicators of when proponents of each theory would expect normal people to develop certain characteristics. It is frequently assumed, however, that cognitive developmental stages are closely tied to mental age rather than to chronological age (Achenbach, 1974), thus leading to the conclusion that persons with mental retardation reach each stage later than do people with normal intelligence. Studies concerning moral development (Hoffman, 1970) relate intelligence also to moral development.

The Usefulness of Developmental Theories

Both developmental theories we have discussed are inclusive; they apparently explain a great deal of human behavior, cognitive and emotional, normal and deviant. Verifiability, however, is another matter. Although Piagetian theorists have repeatedly demonstrated the existence of academic and preacademic behaviors that appear to be age-related (Piaget & Inhelder, 1969), attempts to verify psychoanalytic explanations have not been very successful (Achenbach & Lewis, 1971; Rapaport, 1959). Indeed, considerable resistance to verifying theoretical constructs seems to exist among those who accept the psychoanalytic explanation of human behavior (Schultz, 1969). Although it can be verified that many people act in certain ways at certain ages, this does not prove that the cause of such behavior is an underlying developmental stage or that failure to reach or pass such a stage causes inappropriate or maladaptive behavior. There is little evidence to verify that the order of such stages is invariant, or that reaching or passing through earlier stages is necessary for functioning at higher level stages (Phillips & Kelly, 1975). The following chart summarizes the usefulness of developmental theories.

The Usefulness of Developmental Theory	Good	Fair	Poor
Inclusiveness	✓		
Verifiability			✓
Predictive Utility		✓	
Parsimony			✓

Some developmental theories have enough predictive utility to predict what some human beings will do at certain ages; not all of them, however, do even that. Kurtines and Greif (1974) have suggested that "individuals at different stages [of Kohlberg's hierarchy] can exhibit the same types of behavior using different types of reasoning, whereas individuals at the same stage can exhibit different behaviors using the same types of reasoning" (p. 459). They provide data that support this concern. Another concern is that, by their nature, these theories offer general information about average persons. However, "a prediction about what the average individual will do is of no value in dealing with a particular individual" (Skinner, 1953, p. 19). Marx and Hillix (1963) directed a criticism toward psychoanalytical theory: "The unfortunate thing is that the analysts' statements are so general that they can explain whatever behavior occurs. A genuine scientific explanation cannot do this; it must predict one behavior to the exclusion of all other behaviors" (p. 231). Developmental theories do not provide information about what conditions predict an individual's behavior in specific circumstances. The practitioner who wishes to change behavior by changing conditions can expect little help from developmental theories.

Developmental explanations of behavior are equally inadequate when judged by the criterion of parsimony. To say that a child has temper tantrums because he has a weak ego or is fixated at the oral stage of development or to attribute his behavior to his being at the naive instrumental hedonism stage of moral development is seldom the simplest explanation available. Because of their lack of parsimony, developmental explanations may lead the teacher to excuses as unproductive as those prompted by biophysical explanations. Teachers, particularly teachers of students with disabilities, may wait forever for a student to become developmentally ready for each learning task. An explanation that encourages teachers to take students from their current levels to subsequent levels is clearly more useful than a developmental explanation—at least from a practical point of view. We might expect Professor Grundy's developmental colleagues, for example, to explain Grundy's difficulty with the concept of hyperactivity on the basis of his failure to reach the level of formal operational thinking required to deal with hypothetical constructs. Might there be a more parsimonious, more useful explanation of his behavior? Professor Grundy continues to collect theories of behavior in the following episode.

Professor Grundy Gains Insight

Having been thoroughly demoralized by his interaction with his student teacher, Professor Grundy decided to pay another surprise visit that afternoon. He was determined to avoid subjecting himself to further ridicule. He did not mention Ralph's hyperactivity but instead concentrated on observing Ms. Harper's teaching. Her lesson plan indicated that she was teaching math, but Professor Grundy was confused by the fact that her group was playing with small wooden blocks of various sizes. Ms. Harper sat at the table with the group but did not interact with the students.

At the conclusion of the lesson, Professor Grundy approached Ms. Harper and asked her why she was not teaching basic addition and subtraction facts as she had planned.

"Professor," stated Ms. Harper, "I conducted my lesson exactly as I had planned. The students were using the blocks to gain insight into the relationship among numbers. Perhaps you are not familiar with the discovery approach, but everyone knows that true insight is vital to the learning process."

Professor Grundy, knowing better but unable to help himself, asked, "Have they discovered yet that $2 + 2 = 4$?"

"Professor," hissed Ms. Harper, "that's not the point. Rote learning is meaningless. I don't care if the children know that $2 + 2 = 4$. I want them to comprehend the meaning of the numerical system."

COGNITIVE EXPLANATION

The educational theory espoused (in a somewhat exaggerated form, to be sure) by Ms. Harper is based on an explanation of human behavior first described in Germany in the early part of the 20th century. The first major proponent of this explanation was Max Wertheimer (Hill, 1963), who was interested in people's perception of reality.

Wertheimer suggested it was the relationship among things perceived that was important rather than the things themselves. People, he said, tend to perceive things in an organized fashion, so that what is seen or heard is different from merely the parts that compose it. He labeled an organized perception of this type a *gestalt*, using a German word for which there is no exact English equivalent but which may be translated as "form," "pattern," or "configuration." The word *gestalt* has been retained by English-speaking advocates of this view, and we call this explanation Gestalt psychology.

The gestaltist seeks to impose structure on chaos to obtain meaning.

Koffka (1935) applied Wertheimer's theories to learning as well as perception. He concluded that learning in human beings is also a process of imposing structure on perceived information.

The basic principles applied by gestalt psychologists to both perception and learning are referred to as *principles of organization* (Schultz, 1969). These principles are

1. *Proximity.* Parts that are close together in time or space tend to be grouped together. Examples: The x's in Figure 1–1a are seen in three groups. Similarly, when listening to Morse code, the receiver is able to perceive patterns of dots and dashes as letters because they are close together in time.

2. *Similarity.* Parts that are similar tend also to be grouped. Example: The x's in Figure 1–1b are seen in rows rather than columns.

3. *Closure.* Incomplete figures tend to be seen as wholes. Most people would describe what they see in Figure 1–1c as a circle, even though it is not complete.

4. *Pragnanz.* Figures tend to be seen as correct or simple. Example: Many people have difficulty proofreading because they "see" words spelled correctly even when they are not.

FIGURE 1–1
Perceptual
Organization.

(a)
Proximity

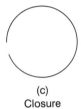

(b)
Similarity

(c)
Closure

Gestalt psychology's emphasis, then, is upon the tendency of human beings to impose structure on their environment and to see relationships rather than individual objects or events as separate entities. This tendency was further described by Kohler (1927) in terms of insight. Kohler was conducting research in the Canary Islands when World War I began and was unable to leave for 7 years. He spent these years studying the apes on the island and formulating theories about behavior. His best known experiment involved an ape named Sultan.

Sultan was put in a large cage with a variety of objects including some short sticks. He discovered that he could use a stick to rake things toward him when he was feeling lazy. One day Kohler put a banana and a very long stick outside the cage; both objects were too far for Sultan to reach with his arm, but the stick was closer than the banana. Sultan first picked up one of the short sticks in the cage and tried to rake in the banana. The stick wasn't quite long enough, and he threw it down and stomped off to another part of the cage in a fit of pique. As he sat brooding, his eyes suddenly focused on the two sticks and the banana, all arranged in a row. He jumped up, ran over to the small stick, used it to rake in the larger stick, and triumphantly raked in the banana. Kohler showed that the learning experience involved a rearrangement of Sultan's pattern of thought. The ape had previously raked things, but the idea of using one stick to rake another and then the banana involved a new application of his prior activity. (Biehler, 1974, p. 238)

According to Kohler, Sultan solved the problem of getting the banana by rearranging in his mind the gestalt of the situation and thus gaining insight.

Wertheimer (1959) extended gestalt theory into human problem solving. He studied children's and adults' insights into geometric problems and concluded that meaningful solutions depended on insight, and that rote learning—even if it led to correct solutions to problems—was less useful.

Gestalt psychology has had considerable influence on education. The best-known educator to espouse this approach to understanding behavior is Jerome Bruner (1960). What has come to be called the *cognitive theory of education* places an emphasis on rearranging thought patterns and gaining insight as a basis for learning new academic and social behaviors. The resulting teaching practices are called *discovery learning*. Learning is explained on the basis of insight, pattern rearrangement, and intuitive leaps. Teachers do not impart knowledge; they merely arrange the environment to facilitate discovery. Motivation is presumed to occur as a result of innate needs that are met when organization is imposed on objects or events in the arrangement. Motivation is thus intrinsic and need not be provided by the teacher.

Educators who espouse gestalt theory encourage "discovery learning."

Principles derived from Gestalt psychology have also been applied to social behavior, notably in the work of Lewin (1951). His approach has been called *field theory* or *cognitive field theory*. Lewin described human social behavior as based on factors within the person's "life space," the environment as it is perceived by the person and as it affects the person's behavior. He asserts that different people perceive and value environmental objects and events in different ways and that forces exist within people that move them toward or away from these objects or events. Based on a complex procedure for "mapping" or drawing diagrams of people's life spaces, Lewin stated that predictions could be made about what people would do based on the value of the events and the strength of the force. Changing behavior thus depends on changing people's perceptions of their life space and the relationships among the various events and objects in it.

The Usefulness of Cognitive Theory

Cognitive theory explains a great deal of human behavior. Theorists can account for both intellectual and social behavior. Virtually all behavior can be explained as the result of imposing structure on unstructured environmental events or of perceiving the relative importance of such events. Cognitive theory, then, meets the criterion of inclusiveness.

The theory lacks verifiability, however. Since all of the processes that take place occur internally, there is no way to confirm their existence. Although Kohler, for example, explained Sultan's banana-retrieving behavior based on insight and pattern rearrangement and his stomping as a "fit of pique," none of these processes can be verified. Only the outcome is verifiable—the process is assumed.

The predictive utility of cognitive theory is also extremely limited. In academic areas, the teacher who uses a discovery approach has very little control over what his or her students will discover. Indeed, most advocates of this approach would insist that they do not want to predict outcomes of learning. Unfortunately, this unwillingness to control the outcome of the teaching-learning process has led to rather poor results. In general, educational practices based on a cognitive approach have been less successful than those emphasizing direct instruction (De Cecco, 1968; Engelmann & Carnine, 1982).

The predictive utility of cognitive field theory is somewhat greater than that of cognitive theory. If we know enough about the objects and events in a person's life space, the value that she assigns them, and her motivation to approach or avoid them, we may be able to predict behavior. Given all this information, of course, we could almost certainly predict behavior without recourse to theory.

The Usefulness of Cognitive Theory	**Good**	**Fair**	**Poor**
Inclusiveness	✓		
Verifiability			✓
Predictive Utility			✓
Parsimony			✓

Addressing our final criterion, we must conclude that cognitive theory is not parsimonious. In neither intellectual nor social areas are the explanations necessary to understanding or predicting behavior.

Although all of the theories described so far provide information about human behavior, none of them meets all four of our criteria. The explanations we have provided are very general, and our conclusions about their usefulness should not be taken as an indication that they have no value. We simply believe they provide insufficient practical guidance for classroom teachers. After the following vignette, we shall describe a behavioral explanation of human behavior that we believe most nearly reaches the criteria of inclusiveness, verifiability, predictive utility, and parsimony.

Professor Grundy Takes Action

Professor Grundy had had an absolutely rotten day. A number of the students in his 8 A.M. class—including, of course, DeWayne—had come in late, disrupting his lecture. He had been ridiculed by a student teacher; his precious manuscript had been retrieved from the dumpster in a sadly wrinkled and malodorous condition; his colleague had made repeated references to "anal-expulsive" and "oral-aggressive" tendencies during the day in spite of Grundy's protests.

After arriving at home and pouring himself a large drink for medicinal purposes, Grundy decided something must be done. He made several detailed plans and retired for the evening, confident he was on the right track. The next morning, he arose enthusiastically determined, in spite of a slight headache, to put his plans into action.

His first step was to arrive at his 8 A.M. class 5 minutes early—somewhat of a novelty since he usually arrived several minutes after the bell. He spent the extra 5 minutes chatting affably with students and clarifying points from the previous day's lecture when asked to do so. When the bell rang, he presented each of the five students present with an "on-time slip" worth 2 points on the next exam.

"The librarian sent me over to pick up one of your 48 overdue books . . . if you're . . . uh . . . done with it."

After the morning lecture, Professor Grundy proceeded to his office, where he affixed to the door a large sign reading "PLEASE DO NOT CLEAN THIS OFFICE TODAY." He then opened the window, wondering just what the biology department had deposited in the dumpster to cause so strong a smell. He spent an hour reorganizing his notes.

Next, Grundy once again visited Ms. Harper, this time suggesting that she would receive a failing grade for student teaching unless she learned to control Ralph's behavior and to teach basic math facts. Her habitual expression of disdain changed to one of rapt attention.

Professor Grundy had observed that Ralph, since he was too "hyperactive" to remain in his seat, spent the time while other students worked wandering from toy to toy in the free-time area of the classroom. He suggested that Ms. Harper allow Ralph to play with the toys only after remaining in his seat for a specified length of time: very short periods at first, gradually increasing in length.

Grundy further suggested the student teacher make flash cards of basic addition and subtraction facts and allow the students to play with the colored blocks after they had learned several combinations.

Returning happily to his office, the professor encountered his psychoanalytically oriented colleague, who once again jocularly repeated his insights into Grundy's character. Ignoring the comments, the professor began an animated conversation with his secretary, praising the rapidity with which she was retyping his manuscript. She assured him it had first priority, since she couldn't wait to dispose of the stinking pages. She did suggest that if he had written his original draft on the available word processor, it would be safely stored on a disk.

Within a short time, Professor Grundy felt that he had things under control. Most of the students enrolled in his 8 A.M. class were present and on time every morning, even though Grundy had begun to give "on-time slips" only occasionally. Ms. Harper had stopped sneering and started teaching. Ralph's wandering had decreased dramatically, and the math group had learned to add and subtract. Grundy continued to ignore his colleague's comments, which gradually ceased when no response was forthcoming, and the fresh copy of his manuscript was typed in record speed. The only negative outcome was a sharp note from campus security stating that the condition of his office constituted a fire hazard and that it must be cleaned immediately.

 ## BEHAVIORAL EXPLANATION

In the preceding vignette, Professor Grundy emerged as the behaviorist that he is. To solve some of his problems, he used techniques derived from yet another explanation of human behavior. The behavioral explanation states that human behavior, both adaptive and maladaptive, is learned. Learning occurs as a result of the consequences of behavior. To put it very simply, behavior that is followed by pleasant consequences tends to be repeated and thus learned. Behavior that is followed by unpleasant consequences tends not to be repeated and thus not learned. By assuming that his students, including DeWayne, came to class late, that the custodian cleaned, that the student teacher ridiculed, that Ralph wandered, and that his psychoanalytic colleague teased because they had learned to do so, Professor Grundy was able to teach them to do other things instead. In doing so, he applied several learning principles (Homme, C'deBaca, Cottingham, & Homme, 1970) underlying the behaviorists' view of human behavior. The following sections introduce these principles, each of which will be discussed in detail in later chapters.

Positive Reinforcement

Positive reinforcement[*] describes a functional relationship between two environmental events: a **behavior** (any observable action) and a **consequence** (a result of that act). Positive reinforcement is demonstrated when a behavior is followed by a consequence that increases the behavior's rate of occurrence.

Many human behaviors are learned as a result of positive reinforcement. Parents who praise their children for putting away toys may teach the children to be neat; parents who give their children candy to make them stop

---

[*]Words printed in **boldface** in the text are defined in the Glossary at the end of the book.

screaming in the grocery store may teach the children to scream. The cleaning behavior of Professor Grundy's custodian undoubtedly was learned and maintained through positive reinforcement, as was the wit of Grundy's psychoanalytic colleague. Grundy used positive reinforcement (on-time tickets, conversation, and time with toys) to increase his students' rate of coming to class on time and the amount of time Ralph stayed in his seat.

Negative Reinforcement

Chapter 6 describes reinforcement in detail.

Negative reinforcement describes a relationship among events in which the rate of a behavior's occurrence increases when some (usually aversive or unpleasant) environmental condition is removed or reduced in intensity. Human beings learn many behaviors when acting in a certain way results in the termination of unpleasantness. Professor Grundy, for example, had learned that opening windows results in the reduction of unpleasant odors in closed rooms. Similarly, his secretary typed rapidly, because, when she finished, she could throw away the smelly papers.

Punishment

Punishment also describes a relationship: a behavior is followed by a consequence that decreases the behavior's future rate of occurrence. An event is described as a **punisher** only if the rate of occurrence of the preceding behavior decreases. Behaviorists use the word **punishment** as a technical term to describe a specific relationship; confusion may arise because the same word is used in a nontechnical sense to describe unpleasant things done to people in an effort to change their behavior. To the behaviorist, punishment occurs only when the preceding behavior decreases. In the technical sense of the term, something is not necessarily punishment merely because the consequent event is perceived by someone as unpleasant. A behaviorist can never say, "I punished him, but it didn't change his behavior," as do many parents and teachers. It's punishment *only* if the functional relationship can be established. We could say that Professor Grundy's verbal threat to Ms. Harper, for example, was apparently a punisher: her ridiculing comments to him stopped. We wish, of course, that he had used a more positive approach.

Extinction

Chapter 8 describes punishment and extinction in detail.

When a previously reinforced behavior is no longer reinforced, its rate of occurrence decreases. This relationship is described as **extinction**. Recall from our vignette that when Grundy no longer reacted to his colleague's ridicule, the behavior stopped. For a behaviorist, all learning principles are defined on the basis of what actually happens, not what we think is happening. Grundy may have thought he was punishing his colleague by yelling or otherwise expressing his annoyance. In reality, the rate of the behavior increased when Grundy reacted in this way; the real relationship was that of positive reinforcement. The behavior stopped when the positive reinforcer was withdrawn.

Stimulus Control

Stimuli, such as environmental conditions or events, become linked to particular behavior over time. Any behavior is more likely to occur in the presence of those stimuli that have accompanied the behavior when it was reinforced in the past. This is the principle of **stimulus control**, which describes a relationship between behavior and an **antecedent stimulus** (an event or condition occurring before the behavior is performed) rather than behavior and its consequences. The consequences must have been present during the development of the relationship, but the antecedent condition or event now serves as a signal or cue for the behavior. In our vignette, the custodian's adherence to posted notices had apparently been reinforced in the past, so Professor Grundy's sign was effective even in the absence of a reinforcer or punisher on this occasion.

Stimulus control is the focus of Chapter 7.

Other Learning Principles

In addition to these major learning principles, Professor Grundy illustrated the use of several other influences on human behavior described by behaviorists. These influences include modeling and shaping. **Modeling** is the demonstration of behavior. The professor had been modeling inappropriate behavior—coming to class late—and his students had apparently been imitating that behavior. Many behaviors, both appropriate and inappropriate, are learned by imitation of a model. Infants learn to talk by imitating their parents; adults can learn to operate complex machinery by watching a demonstration.

Shaping uses the reinforcement of successive approximations to a desired behavior to teach new behavior. Grundy suggested that Ms. Harper use shaping to teach Ralph to stay in his seat. She initially reinforced sitting behavior when it occurred for short periods of time and gradually increased the sitting time required for Ralph to earn the reinforcer. Many behaviors are taught by shaping. Parents may praise a young child effusively the first time she dresses herself, even if her blouse is on inside-out and her shorts are on backward. Later, she may earn a compliment only if her outfit is perfectly coordinated and her shoes are polished.

The Task of the Behaviorist

Behaviorists explain the development of both typical and atypical human behavior in terms of the several principles just described. An important aspect of this approach is its emphasis on behavior (Ullmann & Krasner, 1965). To qualify as a behavior something must be *observable* and *quantifiable* (Baer, Wolf, & Risly, 1968). We must be able to see (or sometimes hear, feel, or even smell) the behavior. In order to make such direct observation meaningful, some way of measuring the behavior in quantitative terms (How much? How long? How often?) must be established. Behaviorists cannot reliably state that any of the relationships described as learning principles exist unless these criteria are met.

If you can see it, hear it, feel it, or smell it, it's observable. If you can count it or measure it, it's quantifiable.

Skinner (1953) has suggested that behaviorists are less concerned with explaining behavior than with describing it. The emphasis, he says, is on which environmental factors increase, decrease, or maintain the rate of occurrence of specific behaviors. Although it may be an interesting exercise to speculate on what environmental consequences in the distant past have led to the development of certain behaviors, it is much more important to determine what factors in the immediate environment have a functional relationship to the behaviors in question. The reinforcers or punishers that led to the acquisition or suppression of behaviors in the past cannot be observed in the present and may not be the events that currently maintain it (Ullman & Krasner, 1965). The child who learned to scream in the supermarket because his parent gave him candy may well scream in school when asked to do arithmetic. There may be no candy around in the classroom, but careful observation of the environment will probably help his teacher locate some environmental condition reinforcing this behavior. We cannot go back into the past and remove the candy or other past reinforcers; we must be concerned with present rather than past events.

It is important to note that behaviorists do not deny the existence of physiological problems that may contribute to some behavioral problems. Nor do most behaviorists deny the effects of heredity (Mahoney, 1974) or even developmental stages (Ferster, Culbertson, & Boren, 1975). Their primary emphasis, however, is on present environmental conditions maintaining behavior and on establishing and verifying functional relationships between such conditions and behavior.

The Usefulness of Behavioral Explanation

One of the most common criticisms of the behavioral approach is that it leaves much of human behavior unexplained (Schultz, 1969). Emphasis on observable behavior has led many to assume that behavioral principles cannot account for any but simple motor responses. However, Skinner (1953, 1957, 1971) applied basic learning principles to explain a wide variety of complex human behavior, including verbal behavior and sociological, economic, political, and religious beliefs.

The fact that behavioral principles have not accounted for all aspects of human behavior should not lead to the assumption that they cannot. Skinner (1966) had an interesting reaction to assumptions about the limitations of behavioral principles:

Patience with respect to unexplored parts of a field is particularly important in a science of behavior because, as part of our own subject matter, we may be overwhelmed by the facts that remain to be explained. Subtle illusions, tricks of memory, the flashes that solve problems—these are fascinating phenomena, but it may be that genuine explanations, within the framework of a science of behavior, as distinguished from verbal principles or "laws" or neurological hypotheses, are out of reach at the present time. To insist that a science of behavior give a rigorous account of such phenomena in its present state of knowledge is like asking the Gilbert of 1600 to explain a magnetic amplifier or the Faraday of 1840 to explain superconductivity. Early physical scientists enjoyed a natural simplification of their subject matters. Many of the most subtle phenomena were to come into existence only through technical advances in the sciences themselves. . . . The behavioral scientist enjoys no such natural protection. He is faced with the full range of the phenomena he studies. He must therefore more explicitly resolve to put first things first, moving on to more difficult things only when the power of his analysis permits. (p. 218)

Many advances have been made since Skinner's 1966 statement. Many phenomena have yet to be explained. Because behaviorists refuse to theorize about what they have not observed, explanation must await verification. Behaviorists are ready temporarily to sacrifice some degree of inclusiveness for verifiability.

Verifiability is the essence of the behavioral explanation. Other theorists posit a theory and attempt to verify it through experimental investigation. Behaviorists, on the other hand, investigate before formulating what may be described as generalizations rather than theories. That adult attention serves as a positive reinforcer for most children (Baer & Wolf, 1968; Harris, Johnston, Kelley, & Wolf, 1964) is an example of such a generalization. This statement was made only after repeated observations established a functional relationship between children's behavior and adult attention. The following chart summarizes the usefulness of behavioral theory.

The Usefulness of Behavioral Theory	Good	Fair	Poor
Inclusiveness		✓	
Verifiability	✓		
Predictive Utility	✓		
Parsimony	✓		

The focus of the behavioral approach is changing behavior (Ullmann & Krasner, 1965). Predictive utility is an essential part of any behavioral explanation. Functional relationships are established and generalizations are made precisely so that they can be used to change maladaptive or inappropriate behavior and increase appropriate behavior. Behaviorists are reinforced by changing behavior, not by discussing it. Unless it is possible to use generalizations to predict what people will do under certain conditions, behaviorists see little point in making the statements. An enormous body of evidence exists representing the application of learning principles to human behavior. The *Journal of Applied Behavior Analysis*, from 1968 to the present, attests to this wealth of evidence. Such data make possible the prediction of behavior under a wide variety of conditions.

Behavioral explanations are parsimonious, satisfying our fourth criterion for usefulness. Describing behavior solely in terms of observable, verifiable, functional relationships avoids the use of "explanatory fictions" (Ullmann & Krasner, 1969). Such fictions are defined only in terms of their effects, resulting in the circular reasoning we discussed earlier. Rather than invoking "hyperactivity"—an example of an explanatory fiction—to explain Ralph's out-of-seat behavior, Professor Grundy chose a behavioral approach, to look at what happened before and after Ralph left his seat. In this way, behaviorism avoids explanations distant from observed behavior and its relationship to the environment. It is unacceptable to explain out-of-seat behavior by labeling the cause as hyperactivity or to explain messiness as fixation at or regression to the anal-expulsive stage of behavior. Neither explanation adds anything useful to our information about the problem.

"Explanatory fictions" explain nothing. Behaviorists explain behavior on the basis of observation, not imagination.

Haughton and Ayllon (1965) offer one example of the fluency with which many professionals are willing to invoke unparsimonious explanations of behavior. The authors were working with a hospitalized mental patient whose behavior for many years had been limited to sitting and smoking cigarettes. After a period during which smoking was limited, the patient was given cigarettes only when standing up and holding a broom. The patient began carrying the broom most of the time. Two psychiatrists were asked to observe and evaluate the patient's behavior. The report of the first psychiatrist read:

> The broom represents to this patient some essential perceptual element in her field of consciousness. How it should have become so is uncertain; on Freudian grounds it could be interpreted symbolically, on behavioral grounds it could perhaps be interpreted as a habit which has become essential to her peace of mind. Whatever may be the case, it is certainly a stereotyped form of behavior such as is commonly seen in rather regressed schizophrenics and is rather analogous to the way small children or infants refuse to be parted from some favorite toy, piece of rag, etc. (Haughton & Ayllon, 1965, p. 97)

The second psychiatrist theorized:

> Her constant and compulsive pacing holding a broom in the manner she does could be seen as a ritualistic procedure, a magical action. When regression conquers the association process, primitive and archaic forms of thinking control the behavior. Symbolism is a predominant mode of expression of deep-seated unfulfilled desires and instinctual impulses. By magic, she controls others, cosmic powers are at her disposal and inanimate objects become living creatures.

Her broom could be then

1. a child that gives her love and who she gives in return her devotion;

2. a phallic symbol;

3. the scepter of an omnipotent queen.

Her rhythmic and prearranged pacing in a certain space are not similar to the compulsions of a neurotic, but because this is a far more irrational, far more controlled behavior from a primitive thinking, this is a magical procedure in which the patient carries out her wishes, expressed in a way that is far beyond our solid, rational and conventional way of thinking and acting. (Haughton & Ayllon, 1965, pp. 97–98)

When staff members stopped giving cigarettes to the woman while she was carrying the broom, she stopped carrying the broom. Although we stated earlier that the parsimonious explanation may not always be correct, in this case it was. Even when the development of unusual behavior is not as easy to trace as in this example, the assumption that such behaviors are being maintained by current environmental conditions and that the behavior may be changed by changing the environment is not merely parsimonious, it is supremely optimistic. The teacher who concentrates on discovering and changing the environmental conditions maintaining students' inappropriate or maladaptive behavior does not give up on them because they are retarded, brain-damaged, emotionally disturbed, hyperactive, at-risk, or developmentally unready to learn; she or he teaches them. If students' behavior is described in terms of behavioral excesses (too much moving around) or deficits (too little reading) as suggested by Gelfand and Hartmann (1975) and Hersen and Bellack (1977) rather than in terms of explanatory fictions, the teacher can go about the business of teaching—decreasing behavioral excesses and remediating behavioral deficits.

HISTORICAL DEVELOPMENT OF BEHAVIORISM

Behaviorism as a science has roots in philosophical and psychological traditions dating from the 19th century. However, the learning principles described earlier certainly existed before being formally defined. People's behavior has been influenced since people existed. In the following section, we will examine several historical descriptions of how people have used the relationship between behavior and its consequences. Then, we will trace the development of behaviorism as a formal way of explaining, predicting, and changing human behavior.

Historical Precedents

The arrangement of environmental conditions in order to influence behavior is by no means a recent invention. It is said that the ancient Romans put eels in the bottom of wine cups in order to decrease excessive drinking. Not all examples are so negative. Birnbaum (1962) provides the following more positive example:

> A parable comes down to us across the centuries, which are but a moment in God's eye. It tells us that when a teacher wishes a young boy to study the Torah, a boy too young to understand how meaningful a thing this is to do, the teacher says to him: "Read, and I shall give you nuts, and figs, and honey." And the boy makes an effort, not because of the sweetness of reading, but because of the sweetness of the eating. As the boy grows older, no longer tempted by sweets, his teacher says to him: "Read, and I shall buy you fine shoes and garments." Again the boy reads, not for the fine text, but for the fine clothing. As the boy reaches young manhood, and the new clothes become less important to him, his teacher now tells him: "Learn this paragraph, and I shall give you a dinar, or perhaps even two dinars." The young man studies now to attain not the learning, but the money. And still later, as his studies continue into his adult life, when even a bit of money comes to mean less to him, his teacher will now say to him: "Learn, so that you may become an elder and a judge, that the people honor you and rise before you, as they do before this one and that." Even at this stage of life, then, this student learns, not in order to exalt the Lord, but so that he himself will be exalted by other men. (p. 32)

Crossman (1975) provides another example of the use of positive reinforcement.

> There is a fascinating history behind the pretzel. About 610 A.D. an imaginative Alpine monk formed the ends of dough, left over from the baking of bread, into baked strips folded into a looped twist so as to represent the folded arms of children in prayer. The tasty treat was offered to the children as they learned their prayers and thereby came to be called "pretiola"—Latin for "little reward." [From the back of a Country Club Foods pretzel bag, Salt Lake City.] (p. 348)

Several innovative educators developed elaborate programs of rewards and punishment to manage their students' behavior. In the early 19th century, Lancaster (Kaestle, 1973) instituted a system in Great Britain that was later also used in the United States. Students earned tickets that could be exchanged for prizes or money. They lost tickets when they misbehaved. A similar program, the Excelsior School system (Ulman & Klem, 1975), was marketed and used in several states.

Benjamin Franklin demonstrated that adults' behavior could also be changed, using a rather different positive reinforcer.

Educators used behavioral principles long before the principles were formally identified.

> We had for our chaplain a zealous Presbyterian minister, Mr. Beatty, who complained to me that the men did not generally attend his prayers and exhortations. When they enlisted, they were promised, besides pay and provisions, a gill of rum a day, which was punctually serv'd out to them, half in the morning, and the other half in the evening; and I observ'd they were as punctual in attending to receive it; upon which I said to Mr. Beatty: 'It is, perhaps, below the dignity of your profession to act as steward of the rum, but if you were to deal it out and only just after prayers, you would have them all about you.' He liked the tho't, undertook the

office, and, with the help of a few hands to measure out the liquor, executed it to satisfaction, and never were prayers more generally and more punctually attended; so that I thought this method preferable to the punishment inflicted by some military laws for non-attendance on divine service. [From: Franklin, Benjamin, American Philosophical Society.] (Reprinted in Skinner, 1969, p. 247)

Parents and teachers have likewise applied the principles of learning in their efforts to teach children. "Clean up your plate and then you can have dessert," says the parent hoping for positive reinforcement. "When you finish your arithmetic, you may play a game," promises the teacher. Parents and teachers, whether they are aware of it or not, also use punishment: the child who runs into the street is spanked; the student who finishes his assignment quickly is given more work to do. All of us have heard "Just ignore him and he'll stop—he's only doing it for attention." If he does stop, we have an example of extinction.

Behavioral principles operate whether or not anyone is consciously using them.

Of course, many parents and teachers extinguish appropriate behavior as well, paying no attention to children who are behaving nicely. Negative reinforcement is demonstrated in many homes every day: "You don't play outside until that room is clean." Teachers also use negative reinforcement when they require students, for example, to finish assignments before going to lunch or to recess. Kindergarten teachers who ask their charges to use their "inside voices" are trying to establish stimulus control. Whenever teachers show their students how to do something, they are modeling.

It becomes apparent that a person does not need to know the names of the relationships involved to use them. Indeed, applying behavioral learning principles sounds a lot like common sense. If it is so simple, why must students take courses and read books? Why have such quantities of material been written and so much research conducted?

The answer is that it is inefficient to fail to arrange environmental conditions so that functional relationships are established, or to allow such relationships to be randomly established, or to assume that such relationships have been established based only on common sense. This inefficiency has resulted in high levels of maladaptive behavior in schools as well as sometimes frighteningly low levels of academic and preacademic learning. It is our aim in writing this book to help teachers become applied behavior analysts. The derivation and definition of the term *applied behavior analysis* will be discussed in the remaining sections of this chapter.

Philosophical and Psychological Antecedents

The roots of the behavioral viewpoint are firmly planted in a 19th-century philosophical movement known as *positivism*. Its earliest proponent, Auguste Comte (Schultz, 1969), emphasized that the only valid knowledge was that which was objectively observable. Comte apparently arrived at such a standard as a result of his attempt to make a systematic survey of all knowledge. In order to limit his task, he decided to accept only facts or knowledge that resulted from direct observation.

A second important contribution came from *animal psychology*, influenced by the work of Charles Darwin (Boring, 1950), which emphasized the continuity between animal and human behavior and thus suggested that something about human beings could be learned through the careful observation of lower animals. Animal psychology focused on the adaptation of physical structures in the body to the environment. This focus led to consideration of mental processes in the same light and to a psychological movement known as *functionalism* (Schultz, 1969).

Functionalism was a third important influence on the development of a behavioral approach to explaining human behavior. William James, whose work was a precursor of behaviorism (Boring, 1950), emphasized that Dewey and James Angell were also influential in turning the emphasis in American psychology from an introspective, theorizing model to one emphasizing a practical, observational approach.

Respondent Conditioning

A famous physiologist who had won a Nobel Prize for his studies of digestion in dogs noticed a curious thing in his laboratory. If the attendant who ordinarily fed the dogs came into the room when he was studying a dog's stomach, he observed that the dog began to secrete gastric juices, just as if it had been given some food. The physiologist called this *psychic secretion* and noted that it affected the whole digestive system, starting the flow of saliva in the mouth as well as the secretion of acids in the stomach.

The advice of his friends and colleagues in physiology was to forget the whole mysterious business. He was assured that he had nothing to gain and everything to lose by getting associated with something so unscientific, so insubstantial, and so unphysiological as "psychic secretions." From the point of view of mechanistic physiology, there was every reason to avoid these intangible sources that supposedly produced tangible secretions. The "mind," the "life force," and the emergent spirit had all been swept back via psychic secretions. His friends thought that his observations were probably in error in some way. And even if there were such secretions, the whole matter would be cleared up when the nervous system was completely explored.

After a good deal of soul-searching, the physiologist made the painful decision to desert the work that had brought him fame and turn to the pursuit of the nature and origins of psychic secretions. He embarked on a career of studies that was to last 30 years and provide support for theories of learning unformulated at that time. Thus, Ivan Pavlov committed himself to his classic research on the conditioned reflex. (Dember & Jenkins, 1970, p. 3)

Pavlov's work has been extremely influential in the development of contemporary psychology and education. His precise observation and measurement have served as a model for experimental research to this day (Schultz, 1969). Pavlov is best known for the model of behavior derived from his observations of the salivation of dogs, a study inspired by the chance observation described in the preceding extract. Pavlov ultimately did come to discuss his observations in terms of observed behavior rather than "psychic secretions." His classic experiment involved pairing food powder (which elicits salivation—an automatic reflex) with a tone that would normally have no effect on dogs' salivation. The presentation of the tone preceded the presentation of the food powder; and after repeated pairings, salivation occurred when only the tone was presented. The food powder was labeled the *unconditioned stimulus* (UCS); the tone, the *conditioned stimulus* (CS). Salivation is an unconditioned response to food powder and a conditioned response to the tone. The relationship may be represented as shown in the accompanying diagram showing two stages.

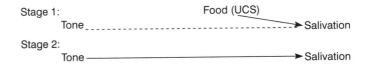

The term *conditioning*, often used to describe any form of learning, came to be attached to this process of *respondent*, or *classical, conditioning* by a quirk of translation. Pavlov had used the terms *conditional* and *unconditional* stimuli. The words were then translated from Russian as "conditioned" and "unconditioned," and thus conditioning was applied as a label for this learning process and, ultimately, for others as well (Hill, 1970).

The process of pairing stimuli so that an unconditioned stimulus elicits a response is known as *Pavlovian, classical*, or *respondent conditioning*. Such conditioning is the basis of a method of behavior change known as *behavior therapy*. Behavior therapists concentrate on breaking up maladaptive, conditioned reflexes and building more adaptive responses. These therapists often work with people who have problems such as irrational fears or phobias. They also help those who want to change habits like smoking, overeating, or excessive alcohol consumption. A detailed discussion of behavior therapy is beyond the scope of this text. For the student who is interested in learning more about it, we recommend texts by Lazarus (1971, 1976), Ross (1981), Wolpe (1958, 1969), and Wolpe and Lazarus (1966).

Associationism

Another influential experimenter whose research paralleled that of Pavlov was Edward Thorndike. Thorndike studied cats rather than dogs, and his primary interest was discovering associations between situations and responses (Thorndike, 1931). He formulated two laws that profoundly influenced the subsequent development of behavioral science. The Law of Effect (Thorndike, 1905) states that "any act which in a given situation produces satisfaction becomes associated with that situation, so that when the situation recurs the act is more likely than before to recur also" (p. 203). Second is the Law of Exercise, which states that a response made in a particular situation becomes associated with the situation. The relationship of the Law of Effect with the principle of positive reinforcement is obvious. The Law of Exercise is similarly related to the stimulus control principle discussed earlier.

Behaviorism

The use of the term *behaviorism* was originated by John Watson (1914, 1919, 1925). Watson advocated the complete abolition of any datum in psychology that did not result from direct observation. He considered such concepts as mind, instinct, thought, and emotion both useless and superfluous. He denied the existence of instinct in human beings and reduced thought to subvocal speech, emotion to bodily responses. A Watsonian behaviorist of our acquaintance once responded to a question by saying "I've changed my mind (you should excuse the expression)." The true Watsonian does not acknowledge the existence of any such entity as "mind."

If we were all Watsonians, we couldn't say, "She hurt my feelings," "My mind wandered," or "Use your imagination."

Watson and Raynor (1920) conditioned a startle response in a baby, Albert, by pairing a white rat (CS) with a loud noise (UCS). Watson contended that all "emotional" responses such as fear were conditioned in similar ways. In an interestingly related procedure, Jones (1924) desensitized a 3-year-old child who showed a fear response to white rabbits and other white furry objects by pairing the child's favorite foods with the rabbit. This procedure was unfortunately not carried out with Albert, who moved away before his conditioned fear could be eliminated. Albert may still be scared of white rats, which may have created a number of problems in his life, including preventing his employment as a behavioral psychologist.

Operant Conditioning

The learning principles described at the beginning of this section are those suggested by proponents of an operant conditioning model for explaining, predicting, and changing human behavior. The best known operant conditioner is B. F. Skinner (1938, 1953), who first distinguished operant from respondent conditioning.

Respondent conditioning, you will remember, deals with behaviors elicited by stimuli that precede them. Most such behaviors are reflexive; that is, they are not under voluntary control. *Operant conditioning* (sometimes called *instrumental conditioning*), on the other hand, deals with behaviors usually thought of as voluntary rather than reflexive. Operant conditioners are concerned primarily with the consequences of behavior and the establishment of functional relationships between behavior and consequences. The behavioral view described earlier is that of operant conditioning, which will be the emphasis of the entire text.

Operant behaviors are emitted voluntarily; respondent behaviors are elicited by stimuli.

Skinner's early work was with animals, primarily white rats. In this, he followed in the tradition of earlier behaviorists, to whom this particular animal was so important that one researcher (Tolman, 1932) dedicated a major book to *Mus norvegious albinius*, a strain of white rats. Bertrand Russell, the philosopher, is said to have suggested facetiously that the different emphases in European (primarily gestalt, introspective, and theorizing) and American (primarily behavioral, active, observational) studies may have resulted from differences in the breeds of rats available. Whereas European rats sat around quietly waiting for insight, American rats were active go-getters, scurrying around their cages and providing lots of behaviors for psychologists to observe.

Skinner also worked with pigeons. He explained (1963) that, while in the military, he was assigned to a building whose window sills were frequented by these birds. Because there was very little to do, he and his colleagues began to train the pigeons to perform various behaviors.

Early application of operant conditioning techniques to human beings was directed toward establishing that the principles governing animal behavior also govern human behavior. The use of these principles to change human behavior—usually called *behavior modification*—did not really emerge in nonlaboratory settings until the 1960s. One of the authors remembers being told in an experimental psychology course in 1961 that there was some indication operant conditioning could be applied to simple human behavior. As an example, the instructor laughingly described college students' conditioning their professor to lecture from one side of the room simply by looking interested only when he stood on that side. The instructor insisted that it would not be possible to modify his behavior in this way, because he was aware of the technique. He was wrong; he ended up backed into one corner of the room by the end of the next lecture.

At that time, however, in spite of Skinner's (1953) theoretical application of operant conditioning techniques to complex human behavior, and pioneer studies like those of Ayllon and Michael (1959) and Birnbrauer, Bijou, Wolf, and Kidder (1965), few people anticipated the enormous impact that the use of such principles would have on American psychology and education as well as on other disciplines, including economics (Kagel & Winkler, 1972). The application of behavior modification in real-life settings had become so prevalent by 1968 that a new journal, the *Journal of Applied Behavior Analysis*, was founded to publish the results of research. In Volume 1, Number 1, of the journal, Baer, Wolf, and Risley (1968) defined applied behavior analysis as the "process of applying sometimes tentative principles of behavior to the improvement of specific behaviors, and simultaneously evaluating whether or not any changes noted are indeed attributed to the process of application" (p. 91).

Baer and his colleagues (1968) suggest that in order for research to qualify as applied behavior analysis, it must change socially important behavior, chosen because it needs change, not because its study is convenient to the researcher. It must deal with observable and quantifiable behavior, objectively defined or defined in terms of examples, and clear evidence of a functional relationship between the behavior to be changed and the experimenter's intervention must exist. In a recent retrospective analysis of the progress of applied behavior analysis since 1968, the same authors (Baer, Wolf, & Risley, 1987) suggest that in spite of considerable opposition and in light of many failures of the procedures in real settings, applied behavior analysts should persevere. They state that "current theory has worked far too well to be abandoned in the face of what are more parsimoniously seen as technological rather than theoretical failures" (p. 325). In other words, we are still not always able to make what we know ought to work actually work, but that is a problem of implementation not an indication of the inadequacy of applied behavior analysis as a discipline. Applied behavior analysis is more rigorously defined than behavior modification. In our earlier vignette, Professor Grundy did succeed in modifying behavior, but he failed to meet the criterion of analysis—he had no way of knowing for sure whether his techniques changed behavior or whether the change was more coincidence. This book is designed to help teachers become applied behavior analysts—effective modifiers of behavior and efficient analyzers of the principles of learning involved in all aspects of their students' performance.

Applied behavior analysis must deal with socially important, observable behaviors. Relationships between behaviors and interventions must be verified.

SUMMARY

In this chapter, we described a number of approaches to explaining human behavior. We evaluated these approaches in terms of their inclusiveness, verifiability, predictive utility, and parsimony. We also described an explanation of human behavior that appears to us to be the most useful—the behavioral explanation.

In tracing the history of the behavioral approach to human behavior, we emphasized the development of a science of applied behavior analysis. We discussed the necessity for concentrating on socially useful studies of human behavior as well as careful observation of the establishment of functional relationships. In Chapter 2, we will describe the difficulty of defining the term *socially useful* and the related ethical and professional concerns about applied behavior analysis. We will also address other issues concerning the responsible use of the technology.

DISCUSSION QUESTIONS

1. Why do applied behavior analysts consider biophysical, developmental, and cognitive explanations of behavior less useful than a behavioral explanation?

2. What useful information might teachers gain from biophysical, developmental, or cognitive information about their students?

3. What differentiates the historical examples of the use of consequences to change behavior from applied behavior analysis?

4. What is the difference between operant and respondent conditioning? Why, in a text for teachers, have we chosen to emphasize operant conditioning?

REFERENCES

Achenbach, T.M. 1974. *Developmental psychopathology*. New York: Ronald Press.

Achenbach, T.H., & Lewis, M. 1971. A proposed model for clinical research and its application to encopresis and enuresis. *Journal of American Academy of Child Psychiatry, 10*, 535–554.

Ayllon, T.A., & Michael, J. 1959. The psychiatric nurse as a behavior engineer. *Journal of the Experimental Analysis of Behavior, 2*, 323–334.

Baer, D.M., & Wolf, M.M. 1968. The reinforcement contingency in preschool and remedial education. In R.D. Hess & R.M. Bear (Eds.), *Early education: Current theory, research, and action*, Chicago: Aldine.

Baer, D.M., Wolf, M.M. & Risley, T.R. 1968. Some current dimensions of applied behavior analysis. *Journal of Applied Behavior Analysis, 1*, 91–97.

Baer, D.M., Wolf, M.M., & Risley, T.R. 1987. Some still-current dimensions of applied behavior analysis. *Journal of Applied Behavior Analysis, 20*, 313–327.

Bannatyne, A. 1971. *Language, reading and learning disabilities*. Springfield, Ill.: Charles C Thomas.

Berry, H.K. 1969. Phenylketonuria: Diagnosis, treatment and long-term management. In G. Farrell (Ed.), *Congenital mental retardation*. Austin: University of Texas Press.

Biehler, R.F. 1974. *Psychology applied to teaching*. Boston: Houghton Mifflin.

Birnbaum, P. (Ed.). 1962. *A treasury of Judaism*. New York: Hebrew Publishing.

Birnbrauer, J.S., Bijou, S.W., Wolf, M.M. & Kidder, J.D. 1965. Programmed instruction in the classroom. In L.P. Ullmann & L. Krasner (Eds.), *Case studies in behavior modification*. New York: Holt, Rinehart & Winston.

Boring, E.G. 1950. *A history of experimental psychology*. New York: Appleton-Century-Crofts.

Boullin, D.J., Coleman, M., O'Brien, R.A., & Rimland, B. 1971. Laboratory predictions of infantile autism based on 5-hydroxytryptamine efflux from blood platelets and their correlation with the Rimland E-2 score. *Journal of Autism and Childhood Schizophrenia, 1*, 63–71.

Bruner, J.S. 1960. *The process of education*. Cambridge, Mass.: Harvard University Press.

Conners, C.K. 1975. *Food additives and hyperkinesis: A controlled double-blind experiment*. Pittsburgh: University of Pittsburgh. (ERIC Document Reproduction Service No. ED 117 877.)

Cott, A. 1972. Megavitamins: The orthomolecular approach to behavior and learning disabilities. *Therapy Quarterly, 7*(3), 245–258.

Cravioto, J., & Delicardie, E. 1975. Environmental and nutritional deprivation in children with learning disabilities. In W.M. Cruickshank and D.P. Hallahan (Eds.), *Psychoeducational practices: Perceptual and learning disabilities in children* (vol. 1). Syracuse, N.Y.: Syracuse University Press.

Crossman, E. 1975. Communication. *Journal of Applied Behavior Analysis. 8*, 348.

Cruickshank, W.M., Bice, H.V., & Wallen, N.E. 1957. *Perception and cerebral palsy*. Syracuse, N.Y.: Syracuse University Press.

Davis, W.E., & McCaul, E.J. 1991. *The emerging crisis: Current and projected status of children in the United States* (monograph). Orono, Maine: Institute for the Study of At-Risk Students.

De Cecco, J.P. 1968. *The psychology of learning and instruction: Educational psychology*. Englewood Cliffs, N.J.: Prentice-Hall.

Dember, W., & Jenkins, J. 1970. *General psychology: Modeling behavior and experience*. Englewood Cliffs, N.J.: Prentice-Hall.

Engelmann, S., & Carnine, D.. 1982. *Theory of instruction: Principles and applications*. New York: Irvington.

Eysenck, H.H. 1956. The inheritance of extroversion-introversion. *Acta Psychologica, 12*, 95–110.

Feingold, B.F. 1975. *Why your child is hyperactive*. New York: Random House.

Ferster, C.B., Culbertson, S., & Boren, M.C.P. 1975. *Behavior principles* (2nd ed.). Englewood Cliffs, N.J.: Prentice-Hall.

Fine, S. 1973. Family therapy and a behavioral approach to childhood obsessive-compulsive neurosis. *Archives of General Psychiatry, 28*, 695–697.

Gelfand, D.L., & Hartmann, D.P. 1975. *Child behavior analysis and therapy.* New York: Pergamon Press.

Gelfand, D.M., Jenson, W.R., & Drew, C.J. 1988. *Understanding children's behavior disorders.* New York: Holt, Rinehart, & Winston.

Gesell, A., & Ilg, F.L. 1943. *Infant and child in the culture of today.* New York: Harper.

Goldstein, K. 1939. *The organism.* New York: American Book

Hall, C.S. 1954 *A primer of Freudian psychology.* Cleveland: World Publishing.

Hallgren, B. 1950. Specific dyslexia (congenital word blindness): A clinical and genetic study. *Acta Psychiatriea et Neurologica, 65.* 1–287.

Harris, F.R., Johnston, M.K., Kelley, C.S., & Wolf, M.M. 1964. Effects of social reinforcement on repressed crawling of a nursery school child. *Journal of Educational Psychology, 55*, 34–41.

Haughton, E., & Ayllon, T. 1965. Production and elimination of symptomatic behavior. In L.P. Ullmann & L. Krasner (Eds), *Case studies in behavior modification* (pp. 94–98). New York: Holt, Rinehart & Winston.

Hersen, M., & Bellack, A.S. 1977. Assessment of social skills. In A.R. Ciminero, K.S. Calhoun, & H.E. Adams (Eds.), *Handbook for behavioral assessment.* New York: Wiley.

Hill, W.F. 1963. *Learning: A survey of psychological interpretations.* San Francisco: Chandler.

Hill, W.F. 1970. *Psychology: Principles and problems.* Philadelphia: Lippincott.

Hoffman, M.L. 1970. Moral development. In P.H. Mussen (Ed.), *Carmichael's manual of child psychology* (3rd ed., vol. 2, pp. 261–359). New York, Wiley.

Homme, L., C'Debaca, P., Cottingham, L., & Homme, A. 1970. What behavioral engineering is. In R. Ulrich, T. Stacknik, & J. Mabry (Eds.), *Control of human behavior* (vol. 2, pp. 17–23). Glenview, Ill.: Scott, Foresman.

Jones, M.C. 1924. A laboratory study of fear: The case of Peter. *The Pedagogical Seminary and Journal of Genetic Psychology, 31*, 308–315.

Kaestle, C.F. (Ed.). 1973. *Joseph Lancaster and the monitorial school movement: A documentary history.* New York: Teachers College Press.

Kagel, J.H., & Winkler, R.C. 1972. Behavioral economics: Areas of cooperative research between economics and applied behavior analysis. *Journal of Applied Behavior Analysis, 5*, 335–342.

Kallmann, F.J., & Roth, B. 1956. Genetic aspects of preadolescent schizophrenia. *American Journal of Psychiatry, 112*, 599–606.

Kessler, J.W. 1966. *Psychopathology of childhood.* Englewood Cliffs, N.J.: Prentice-Hall.

Koffka, K. 1935. *Principles of Gestalt psychology.* New York: Harcourt, Brace & World.

Kohlberg, L. 1964. Development of moral character and moral ideology. In M. Hoffman & L.W. Hoffman (Eds.), *Review of child development research* (vol. 1). New York: Russell Sage.

Kohlberg, L. 1969. *Stage and sequence: The developmental approach to morality.* New York: Holt, Rinehart & Winston.

Kohler, W. 1927. *The mentality of apes* (E. Winter, Trans.). New York: Humanities Press.

Kurtines, W., & Greif, E.B. 1974. The development of moral thought: Review and evaluation of Kohlberg's approach. *Psychological Bulletin, 81*, 453–470.

Lazarus, A.A. 1971. *Behavior therapy and beyond.* New York: McGraw-Hill.

Lazarus, A.A. 1976. *Multimodal behavior therapy.* New York: Springer.

Lewin, K. 1951. *Field theory in social science.* New York: Harper & Row.

Mahoney, M.J. 1974. *Cognition and behavior modification.* Cambridge, Mass.: Ballinger.

Marx, M.H., & Hillix, W.A. 1963. *Systems and theories in psychology.* New York: McGraw-Hill.

Mattes, J.A. 1983. The Feingold diet: A current reappraisal. In G.M. Senf & J.K. Torgensen (Eds.). *Annual review of learning disabilities* (vol. 1), 127–131.

Morgane, P.J., Stern, W., & Resnick, O. 1974. Early protein lack: Malevolent effects. *Science News, 106*, 229.

Phillips, D.C., & Kelly, M.E. 1975. Hierarchical theories of development in education and psychology. *Harvard Educational Review, 45*, 351–375.

Piaget, J., & Inhelder, B. 1969. *The psychology of the child*. New York: Basic Books.

Pond, D. 1961. Psychiatric aspects of epileptic and brain-damaged children. *British Medical Journal, 2*, 1377–1382, 1454–1459.

Pruess, J.B., Fewell, R.R., & Bennett, F.C. 1989. Vitamin therapy and children with Down syndrome: A review of research. *Exceptional Children, 55*(4), 336–341.

Rapaport, D. 1959. The structure of psychoanalytic theory: A systematizing attempt. In J.S. Koch (Ed.), *Psychology: A study of science*. New York: McGraw-Hill.

Rimland, B. 1964. *Infantile autism*. New York: Appleton-Century-Crofts.

Rose, T.L. 1978. The functional relationship between artificial food colors and hyperactivity. *Journal of Applied Behavior Analysis, 11*, 439–446.

Ross, A.O. 1981. *Child behavior therapy*. New York: McGraw-Hill.

Rutter, M., Korn, S., & Birch, H.G. 1963. Genetic and environmental factors in the development of primary reaction patterns. *British Journal of Social and Clinical Psychology, 2*, 161–173.

Schultz, D.P. 1969. *A history of modern psychology*. New York: Academic Press.

Skinner, B.F. 1938. *The behavior of organisms*. New York: Appleton-Century-Crofts.

Skinner, B.F. 1953. *Science and human behavior*. New York: Macmillan.

Skinner, B.F. 1957. *Verbal behavior*. New York: Appleton-Century-Crofts.

Skinner, B.F. 1963. Operant behavior. *American Psychologist, 18*, 503–515.

Skinner, B.F. 1966. What is the experimental analysis of behavior? *Journal of the Experimental Analysis of Behavior, 9*, 213–218.

Skinner, B.F. 1969. Communication. *Journal of Applied Behavior Analysis, 2*, 247.

Skinner, B.F. 1971. *Beyond freedom and dignity*. New York: Knopf.

Strauss, A.A., & Lehtinen, L.E. 1947. *Psychopathology and education of the brain-injured child*. New York: Grune & Stratton.

Strauss, A.A., & Werner, H. 1942. Disorders of conceptual thinking in the brain-injured child. *Journal of Nervous and Mental Disease, 96*, 153–172.

Thomas, A., & Chess, S. 1977. *Temperament and development*. New York: Brunner/Mazel.

Thomas, A., Chess, S., & Birch, H.G. 1968. *Temperament and behavior disorders in children*. New York: New York University Press.

Thorndike, E.L. 1905. *The elements of psychology*. New York: Seiler.

Thorndike, E.L. 1931. *Human learning*. New York: Appleton-Century-Crofts.

Tolman, E.C. 1932. *Purposive behavior in animals and men*. New York: Appleton-Century-Crofts.

Turiel, E. 1974. Conflict and transition in adolescent moral development. *Child Development, 45*, 14–29.

Ullmann, L.P., & Krasner, L. (Eds.). 1965. *Case studies in behavior modification*. New York: Holt, Rinehart & Winston.

Ullmann, L.P., & Krasner, L. 1969. *A psychological approach to abnormal behavior*. Englewood Cliffs, N.J.: Prentice-Hall.

Ulman, J.D., & Klem, J.L. 1975. Communication. *Journal of Applied Behavior Analysis, 8*, 210.

Vandenburg, S.G. 1967. Hereditary factors in normal personality traits as measured by inventories. In J. Wortis (Ed.), *Recent advances in biological psychiatry* (vol. 9). New York: Plenum Press.

Vitale, J.J., & Velez, H. 1968. In R.A. McCance & E.M. Widdowson (Eds.), *Calorie deficiencies and protein deficiencies*. London: Churchill.

Watson, J.B. 1914. *Behavior: An introduction to comparative psychology*. New York: Holt, Rinehart & Winston.

Watson, J.B. 1919. *Psychology from the standpoint of a behaviorist*. Philadelphia: Lippincott.

Watson, J.B. 1925. *Behaviorism*. New York: Norton.

Watson, J.B., & Raynor, R. 1920. Conditioned emotional reactions. *Journal of Experimental Psychology, 3*, 1–4.

Werner, H., & Strauss, A.A. 1940. Causal factors in low performance. *American Journal of Mental Deficiency, 45*, 213–218.

Werry, J.S. 1972. Organic factors in childhood psychopathology. In H.G. Quay & J.S. Werry (Eds.), *Psychopathological disorders of childhood*. New York: Wiley.

Wertheimer, M. 1959. *Productive thinking.* New York: Harper & Row.

Wolpe, J. 1958. *Psychotherapy by reciprocal inhibition.* Palo Alto, Calif.: Stanford University Press.

Wolpe, J. 1969. *The practice of behavior therapy.* New York: Pergamon Press

Wolpe, J., & Lazarus, A.A. 1966. *Behavior therapy technique.* New York: Pergamon Press.

Wunderlich, R.C. 1977. The hyperactivity complex. *Journal of Optometric Vision Development, 8*(1), 8–45.

2

Responsible Use of Applied Behavior Analysis Procedures

Did you know that . . .

- Some people think that behavior modification and brain surgery are the same thing?
- It's possible to be both a humanist and a behaviorist?
- It isn't always ethical to follow the rules?
- Effective procedures scare some people?
- Applied behavior analysis can make students more creative?

The use of applied behavior analysis in classrooms and other environments has engendered considerable controversy. The debate has not been limited to professionals: arguments about the use of operant principles to change behavior have appeared in popular magazines and newspapers as well as in scholarly journals. Discussion occurs on social occasions as well as at conventions and symposia. Psychiatrists, psychologists, social workers, and teachers weigh the merits of behavioral procedures, as do judges, lawyers, legislators, parents, and students themselves. Much of the discussion, however, has come from applied behavior analysts (cf. Wood, 1975). In addition to defending applied behavior analysis, professionals have felt it necessary to clarify ethical issues and suggest guidelines for the responsible use of the technology.

This chapter addresses many of the issues raised by the current popular interest. First, we'll consider some of the concerns often expressed and some possible causes of these concerns. Then we'll examine and respond to some of the specific criticisms of behavioral procedures, particularly as these methods are used in educational settings. We will suggest ethical guidelines for using procedures, Professor Grundy will answer some common questions asked by uninformed people, and we will suggest reasons for thoroughly understanding procedures and principles.

CONCERNS ABOUT APPLIED BEHAVIOR ANALYSIS

Resistance to the use of operant procedures to change behavior has come from several sources. The term *behavior modification*, which is most commonly used to describe such techniques, has caused some confusion. Because the word *modification* is synonymous with *change*, the term *behavior modification* has often been misused to refer to any procedure that has the potential to change behavior. This contamination of the term is one reason that this book uses the term *applied behavior analysis*.

Other objections to operant procedures have come from those who feel that any systematic effort to change behavior is coercive and, thus, inhumane. Those who take this position often describe themselves as "humanists." Their objections are based on a rejection of a deterministic viewpoint and advocacy of free will and personal freedom. The intuitive appeal of these humanistic values makes humanists' rejection of behavioral procedures a formidable objection, although, as we shall see, such objections frequently rely on a rather shaky logical foundation.

Some people believe that changing behavior invariably infringes on personal freedom.

The very effectiveness of applied behavior analysis procedures is one source of much concern about this approach. It is ironic that many people are very comfortable with ineffective techniques or with techniques whose effectiveness at least lacks verification. The same people often reject other procedures—such as those based on applied behavior analysis—because their use results in predictable, consistent behavior change.

Confusion with Other Procedures

Much of the public outcry against what is popularly called *behavior modification* results from the use of this term to describe procedures that are totally unrelated to applied behavior analysis. Popular journalists (Holden, 1973; Mason, 1974; Wicker, 1974) and even behavior modification professionals (McConnell, 1970) have done incalculable harm to the image of applied behavior analysis by including unrelated treatment procedures under the heading of behavior modification. Hypnosis, psychosurgery, brain implants, drug therapy, and electroconvulsive shock treatment have all been lumped under this label. Such procedures undoubtedly change behavior, but they are not related to the systematic changing of behavior by application of behavioral principles. It would be equally logical and equally erroneous to list under the title of behavior modification the entire array of therapeutic interventions including "psychoanalysis, Gestalt therapy, primal screams, lectures, books, jobs and religion" (Goldiamond, 1975, p. 26).

Applied behavior analysis is not hypnosis, prefrontal lobotomy, brain implants, drug therapy, or shock treatment.

Applied behavior analysis certainly does not include such treatments as electroconvulsive therapy or brain surgery; neither does it involve the use of drugs. Indeed, the effective application of appropriate behavioral procedures often reduces the need for such drastic interventions. This has been strongly demonstrated in studies using positive reinforcement as an alternative to medication for children labeled *hyperactive* (Ayllon, Layman, & Kandel, 1975). It is possible that behavior modification, in the proper sense of the term, will ultimately diminish the use of surgery, drugs, and other such behavior-change techniques. It is, therefore, particularly unfortunate that the improper use of the term has caused so much public hostility to a technology that is so potentially benign.

Used correctly, the term *behavior modification* refers only to procedures derived from the experimental analysis of human behavior. Unfortunately, the term has become so unalterably linked with other procedures in the minds of the public that its use is best avoided. The teacher who tells parents that he or she uses behavior modification must be prepared for negative reactions. By no means do we advocate abandoning the technology of behavior modification: we simply suggest that teachers avoid using the term with uninformed or misinformed people. In many cases, other professionals, including administrative staff and fellow teachers, may be as confused as parents and school board members. Indeed, some textbooks and other materials widely used in preservice teacher education programs may well contribute to this confusion (Cooke, 1984). It may be as necessary to educate fellow professionals as it is to teach children. The use of terminology has consistently caused problems for behaviorally oriented practitioners. It may be that it is not what behaviorists do that disturbs people but the way they refer to it. Teachers should be careful how they talk about procedures, even among themselves. Problems may arise because of the way programs are described even when the programs themselves are appropriate.

Risley (1975) describes a *time-out* procedure that was disallowed primarily because staff members referred to the free-standing structures built for short-term exclusion as "boxes" and to the procedure as "putting him (the resident) in the box." That the "boxes" were large, adequately lighted structures made no difference. The use of the wrong words resulted in withdrawal of approval for the program. Those of us who tend toward flippant labels would be especially wise to guard our tongues when discussing procedures with people who might misunderstand.

Reaction to Controversial Procedures

Not all of the misunderstanding or hostility has resulted from those outside the field. Procedures derived from the experimental analysis of behavior are frequently rejected by professionals as well as the public. Such procedures include, among others, the use of contingent electric shock or other procedures that cause pain or discomfort (Lovaas & Simmons, 1969; Risley, 1968) for suppressing certain extremely maladaptive behaviors and the use of exclusion (Bostow & Bailey, 1969; Wolf, Risley, & Mees, 1964). Although these procedures are only a few of the tools of the applied behavior analyst, their use has received a disproportionate share of attention from the press, the public, and the judiciary (Stolz, 1977). It is sufficient to note that aversive or exclusionary procedures may create problems in two ways:

Guidelines for the use of aversive and exclusionary procedures are provided in Chapter 8.

1. Their misuse is common and often described by the users as behavior modification.
2. Their use, even when appropriate, causes more concern than other behavioral procedures.

Unfortunately, there have been many abuses. Risley (1975) describes a "behavior modification" program in a Florida institution where bizarre punishments were used. The mildest of these was washing residents' mouths out with detergent when they spoke, in the staff members' opinions, inappropriately. One of us was recently asked to work with a student who, while a resident in a "behavior modification unit" in a private facility, had been in what was called *time-out* for several weeks. Time-out, used properly, is measured in minutes. Isolation for days or weeks is more properly called *solitary confinement* and is certainly not an applied behavior analysis procedure. It is fully understandable that procedures causing pain or discomfort to children or young people, particularly those who are disabled, cause concern. Many, but not all, professionals, however, believe certain controversial procedures are sometimes justified, just as many, but not all, parents believe spanking children is sometimes appropriate. The controversy over aversive procedures will be discussed in Chapter 8.

Concerns About Coercion

The notion that applied behavior analysis is inhumane rests on the assumption that each human being should be free to choose a personal course of behavior. It follows, for those who criticize behavioral procedures, that any systematic attempt to alter the behavior of another human being is coercive and thus inhumane.

A belief that behavior is lawful does not imply that human beings are not free to choose what they will do.

This criticism of behavioral techniques is based on the philosophic concept of free will. Advocates of the assumption of free will tend to attribute human behavior to forces arising from within the individual and, thus, not subject to prediction or control. In other words, people just do what they do because they decide to do it. A deterministic position, on the other hand, holds that behavior is "lawful" (subject to lawful prediction) and its causes can be identified in environmental events. A determinist recognizes systematic relationships among such events (Mahoney, Kazdin, & Lesswing, 1974) and considers human behavior as part of the system. This contrasting view concludes, then, that human behavior is subject to lawful prediction. People do things, or decide to do things, because of past events and present circumstances. It is important to distinguish between the use of the term *lawful*, in the sense of an orderly relationship between events, and any implication of authoritarian control (Becker, Engelmann, & Thomas, 1975). Lawful, in the sense used here, refers simply to relationships among events that occur naturally, not to attempts to legislate human behavior.

Applied behavior analysts, by definition, are also determinists. Their position is predicated on solid evidence that "the assumption of determinism is both justified and essential in dealing with human behavior" (Craighead, Kazdin, & Mahoney, 1976, p. 172). This confirmation has come from a large body of psychological research, some but by no means all of it conducted by those who call themselves applied behavior analysts. The assumption of lawful relationships among events and behavior does not imply a rejection of human freedom. For the applied behavior analyst, "freedom is defined in terms of the number of options available to people and the right to exercise them" (Bandura, 1975, p. 865). The goal of the behavior analyst is to increase, not decrease, such options (Bandura, 1975) and thus to increase the freedom of the individual. The high-school student who repeatedly fails English is not free to attend college. The child who is afraid to interact with peers is not free to make friends. People who have severe behavioral deficits may have no options at all; they cannot move around, take care of their basic needs, or control their environment in any way.

Behaviorists define freedom in terms of a person's ability to make choices and to exercise options.

The last example points out a crucial concept in understanding the deterministic position. The relationship between behavior and the environment is reciprocal (Bandura, 1969; Craighead, Kazdin, & Mahoney, 1976). Environmental events control behavior, but behavior also inevitably alters the environment as well. This reciprocal relationship exists between people. The behavior modifier's behavior is changed by the actions of the subject of the modification. Thus, everyone influences and controls others' behavior. It is impossible to abandon control; we inevitably influence the behavior of other people (Bandura, 1975; Rogers & Skinner, 1956). For example, a child who seldom smiles is not very pleasant to be around so he may be avoided by teachers and other children. If his teacher systematically reinforces his occasional happy facial expressions he will smile more. Because a smiling child is pleasant to be around and to interact with he will himself become more reinforcing to others, including his teacher. She will then have more opportunities to reinforce smiling.

Seen in this context, behavioral technology is neither dehumanizing nor inhumane. When goals are humane, we must offer the most effective means available to reach them. In many cases, the proven effectiveness of applied behavior analysis procedures makes them the most humane choice.

The following anecdote illustrates a clash between humanists and behaviorists. We urge you to consider the values being practiced on each side of this particular example.

A colleague at a different university showed us a deeply moving film. The heroine was an institutionalized primary-grade girl. She was a head-banger, so a padded football helmet was put on her head. Because she could take it off, her hands were tied down in her crib. She kept tossing her neck and tore out her hair at every opportunity. She accordingly had a perpetually bruised face on a hairless head, with a neck almost as thick as that of a horse. She was nonverbal.

My colleague and his staff carefully planned a program for her, using all kinds of reinforcers. She was remanded to their program, but persisted in her typical behavior. In desperation, the ultimate weapon was unwrapped. When she tossed her head, my colleague yelled "Don't!" simultaneously delivering a sharp slap to her cheek. She subsided for a brief period, tossed again, and the punishment was delivered. My colleague reports that less than a dozen slaps were ever delivered and the word "Don't!" yelled even from across the room was effective. Its use was shortly down to once a week and was discontinued in a few weeks. In the meantime, the football helmet was removed and the girl began to eat at the table. She slept in a regular bed. Her hair grew out, and she turned out to be a very pretty little blond girl with delicate features and a delicate neck. In less than a year, she started to move toward joining a group of older girls whose behavior, it was hoped, she would model. She smiled often.

The initial institution and her parents discovered that she had been slapped. They immediately withdrew her from the custody of my colleague's staff. The last part of the film shows her back at the institution. She is strapped down in her crib. Her hands are tied to a side. She is wearing a football helmet. Her hair is torn out, her face is a mass of bruises and her neck is almost as thick as that of a horse. (Goldiamond, 1975, pp. 62–63)

ETHICAL USE OF APPLIED BEHAVIOR ANALYSIS PROCEDURES

All teachers—whether or not they are also applied behavior analysts—are concerned with ethics. Before describing ways in which teachers can behave ethically, we will discuss the concept of ethics itself. A decision or action is ethical if it is right. That, of course, is a deceptively simple statement. The determination of what is right, according to whom it is right, and how we decide it is right has occupied philosophers and others since the days of Aristotle. Very simply stated, a teacher who is doing the right thing is behaving ethically. Doing the right thing, however, means far more than avoiding censure or even complying with some set of ethical guidelines. We are not "more concerned that . . . teachers follow the rules than that . . . teachers become ethical beings" (Watras, 1986, p. 14). Simply because something is accepted practice does not assure that it is right (Kitchener, 1980). People following rules have done some very wrong things over the centuries, and no set of rules can ever cover every eventuality. Teachers must be prepared to act ethically in the absence of guidelines and even when their actions are in conflict with guidelines or instructions.

The ways prospective teachers become ethical beings is currently the subject of intense interest among teacher educators. A volume of the *Journal of Teacher Education* (1986) was almost entirely devoted to the issue. The consensus appears to be that ethical reasoning is best developed by discussing ethical dilemmas in a forum of other interested prospective and practicing professionals. Ethics should not be addressed in a single course but should permeate all courses. If ethical issues do not arise and are not discussed in your classes, we suggest you bring them up.

Awareness of potential criticism may help avert interference from uninformed persons.

Although the primary reason to behave ethically is to act consistently with what one believes is right, there is another reason. Teachers must always be aware that other people are concerned with teachers' doing the right thing. Previous sections have acknowledged that people are especially apt to worry about ethics when behavioral techniques are used. Unless teachers take particular care to act ethically and to assure others that they do, they may find noneducators seeking and acquiring more and more control over what may and may not be done in classrooms.

A number of factors must be considered when attempting to determine whether a proposed intervention is ethical. These include "community standards, laws, prevailing philosophies, individual freedom and responsibility of the clients through informed consent as well as the clients' attitudes and feelings" (Sulzer-Azaroff, Thaw, & Thomas, 1975). In the case of schoolchildren or residents of an institution, it is important to seek the opinions of the parents or guardians of the students to ask them how they feel about procedures being used or proposed for use with their children. It may seem strange for behaviorists to concern themselves with such subjective criteria as attitudes and feelings, but Wolf (1978) makes a strong case for considering these factors. If participants do not like a program, he says, "They may avoid it, or run away, or complain loudly" (p. 206). Wolf suggests that social validity should be established for goals, procedures, and outcomes. Social validity, or consumer satisfaction (Holman, 1977), is simply the acceptability of a program or procedure to its consumers. Assessing social validity requires applied behavior analysts to rely on sources of data that have not traditionally been used in this field—questionnaires, interviews, surveys. It is possible that reliance on such data makes many conclusions about social validity invalid. However, "it is entirely possible that even quite invalid queries into social validity are better than no queries at all: Giving consumers any opportunity to express complaints and discontents that otherwise would go unnoticed may save at least some programs from fatal backlashes, at least if the offended consumer is moved enough by simply the existence of an otherwise inadequate social-validity assessment form to write in its margins or talk to the appliers" (Baer, Wolf, & Risley, 1987, p. 323).

Stainback and Stainback (1984) suggest that increased attention be given to qualitative research methods that provide "more attention to the social and educational relevance of research efforts" (p. 406). Simpson and Eaves (1985) urge that attempts be made to quantify such subjective measurements. It is clear that teachers using behavioral procedures must concern themselves with factors in addition to those within their classrooms. Goals, procedures, and outcomes must be acceptable to the consumers of education—students, parents, and the community.

Misunderstanding of behavioral procedures, as well as concern about their misuse, has resulted in increasing pressure for mandatory guidelines for the use of applied behavior analysis procedures. Such mandatory guidelines and restrictions are becoming increasingly common, especially in institutional settings (Martin, 1975). Particularly likely to be restricted are aversive or exclusionary procedures and items or events that may be used as positive reinforcers. It is not generally permissible, for example, to require residents of institutions to earn the right to food, privacy, or basic activities (Wyatt v. Stickney, 1972).

We hope we have convinced you that it is in your best interests to behave ethically. Although we acknowledged earlier that guidelines are necessarily incomplete, we believe it would be unethical not to provide some. It would be difficult to imagine an ethical position that did not focus on protecting students' rights. A recent statement, approved by the Executive Council of the Association for Behavior Analysis (ABA) includes a list of individual rights that provides teachers with the basis for making ethical decisions about many issues. We will elaborate on each part of the statement in an effort to give concrete examples of instances in which each individual right should be protected.

The statement begins: "We propose that individuals who are recipients or potential recipients of treatment designed to change their behavior have the right to (1) a therapeutic environment, (2) services whose overriding goal is personal welfare, (3) treatment by a competent behavior analyst, (4) programs that teach functional skills, (5) behavioral assessment and ongoing evaluation, and (6) the most effective treatment procedures available" (Van Houten et al., 1988, p. 111).

A Therapeutic Environment

A therapeutic environment is "safe, humane, and responsive to individual needs" (Van Houten et al., 1988, p. 111). It is also enjoyable. It seems sad that in the recent "back to basics" school reform movements we have lost sight of the notion that school should be fun and children should have some choices about their activities. The environment for students with disabilities must also be the least restrictive environment for those individuals. The least restrictive environment is not necessarily the regular classroom or even a regular school for all students. It is that environment that "imposes the fewest restrictions necessary, while insuring individual safety and development. Freedom of individual movement and access to preferred activities, rather than type or location of placement, are the defining characteristics of a least restrictive environment" (p. 112). Given the current emphasis in increasing inclusion of individuals with disabilities in activities with their typical peers, sometimes called the Regular Education Initiative (Gartner & Lipsky, 1989), educators will need to become increasingly vigilant about environments to which these individuals are exposed.

Providing a safe environment is unarguably necessary. Doing so requires such simple and obvious, but too often neglected, steps as removing any potentially dangerous items or storing them so students do not have access to them. When a student stabs another student with the teacher's four-inch pointed scissors, our first question is why, in a classroom where some students are known to have violent outbursts, the scissors were not locked away.

Students' safety outside the classroom must also be assured. Students with disabilities are especially vulnerable, for example, to verbal, physical, and sexual abuse from their peers. Students' safety must be monitored in halls, restrooms, cafeterias, playgrounds, and busses. It is not only peers who may abuse or neglect students. Recently, in the city in which one of us lives, a student living in a residential treatment facility was left on a school bus overnight. His parents thought he was at the facility and the staff at the facility assumed his parents had taken him home for a visit, as they sometimes did. Someone should have checked.

Providing a humane environment means more than refraining from neglecting or abusing students. Every human being has a right to be treated with dignity. "Minimally dignified treatment requires sanitation, cleanliness, comfort, and attempts at respectful communication and consent" (Schroeder, Oldenquist, & Rohahn, 1990, p. 105). This means, among many other things, not talking about students' problems in front of them, even if they are too young or too low-functioning to understand. It means not having a student "do his thing" for visitors, even if his "thing" is funny. It also means not treating older students with disabilities like babies by, for example, changing their clothing in front of others.

An environment sensitive to individual needs provides each individual with a comfortable place or places to sit, interesting things to look at and do, and access to those things for all students. It allows students some choices about what they will do, when they will do it, and how they will do it. Of course, children will inevitably have to do things they don't want to do. These should lead to positive reinforcement and a feeling of accomplishment. Adults, after all, often do things they dislike doing but they are glad they have done. For example, we, like Dorothy Parker, loathe writing but love having written.

Services Whose Overriding Goal Is Personal Welfare

It may seem obvious that the behaviors targeted for change should be those whose change will benefit the student. Nevertheless, accusations have been made that residential institutions (Wyatt v. Stickney, 1972) and schools (Winett & Winkler, 1972) use behavior-change programs primarily to reduce behaviors that disrupt the smooth functioning of the institution or school but are not detrimental to residents or students. Winett and Winkler examined articles detailing behavior-change programs in the *Journal of Applied Behavior Analysis* from 1968 through 1970. They stated that the majority of the articles concerned the attempted suppression of talking, moving around, and such disruptive behaviors as whistling, laughing, and singing. Winett and Winkler concluded that the technology of applied behavior analysis was being used merely to establish "law and order" (p. 499) rather than to serve the best interests of students. They further mentioned that similar goals were set in residential institutions.

Although O'Leary (1972) agreed with Winett and Winkler that careful examination of goals is important, he disagreed with their conclusions. He cited numerous studies that demonstrated the researchers' concern with such behaviors as academic response rates (Lovitt & Curtiss, 1969), talking (Reynolds & Risley, 1968), prosocial interactions (O'Connor, 1969), and language and reading skills (Bereiter & Engelmann, 1966). O'Leary did agree with Winett and Winkler's call for "extensive community dialogues concerning those behaviors and values we wish to develop in our children" (p. 511).

Applied behavior analysis procedures may be abused if students' rights and best interests are not considered.

Applied behavior analysis procedures may be used to decrease or increase any behavior. Even such behaviors as creativity (defined in terms of observable behavior, of course) have been increased using this technology (Goetz & Baer, 1973; Goetz & Salmonson, 1972; Maloney & Hopkins, 1973; Reese & Parnes, 1970). There is no justification for asserting that the procedures, in and of themselves, contribute to maintenance of behaviors for the convenience of those other than students. Appropriate goal selection should prevent the use of such institution-oriented criteria for change as "be still, be quiet, be docile" (Winett & Winkler, 1972, p. 499).

For selected goals to be in the best interests of the students, they and/or their parents must voluntarily agree to the goals. Federal legislation requires that parents consent to programs planned for their children with disabilities. If parents are not available, an advocate must be named to determine that any proposed program is in the best interests of the child. Such a requirement is intended to ensure that participation in programs is voluntary. It is not necessary to acquire parental consent for all aspects of a teaching program, however. Martin (1975) suggests that widely accepted strategies for overall classroom management and student motivation do not require anyone's consent, even if the teacher decides to change from one strategy to another. Consent is required for procedures not yet widely accepted and for those applied only to individual students.

The consent that ensures voluntary participation in behavior-change programs must be both informed and voluntary. *Informed consent* is based on full understanding of the planned program. Informed consent does not occur unless parents or other advocates demonstrate they comprehend all aspects of the program, including possible risks. If necessary, information must be provided in the native language of those involved.

Voluntary consent may be obtained only if neither threats nor rewards are used to acquire such consent (Martin, 1975). It is not acceptable, for example, to tell parents that unless a particular procedure is used, their child will have to be institutionalized. Nor is it ethical to assure parents that if a procedure is used, their child will no longer require placement in a special class.

Sulzer-Azaroff and Mayer (1977) suggest that the voluntariness of students' participation in behavior-change programs should also be considered. Voluntary participation is facilitated by avoiding threats and incentives that are too powerful and by involving the subjects of the programs in selecting as many aspects of the program as possible. Such involvement leads naturally to eventual self-management—the ultimate goal for most students.

Treatment by a Competent Behavior Analyst

Because many applied behavior analysis procedures seem so simple, they are often misused by persons who do not adequately understand them. A common example is the teacher who attends a short workshop on applied behavior analysis techniques, buys a bag of candy, and proceeds to hand out "reinforcement" indiscriminately. A common result is that the teacher in question concludes, as have many others, that behavior modification doesn't work. An unfortunate side effect is that the children treated in this manner may become more disruptive than ever because they understand neither why they got candy nor why they stopped getting it. Moreover, parents become upset because their children's teeth are decaying and their appetites are spoiled; the principal expresses annoyance because she receives numerous irate phone calls from those parents; other teachers become enraged because their students demand candy, too; and the escutcheon of applied behavior analysis receives another blot.

Implementing these procedures is not always as easy as it sounds.

It is not possible to learn, in a few days, enough about applied behavior analysis to implement ethical, effective programs (Franks & Wilson, 1976). One of the authors attended a seminar several years ago during which she was asked to develop a packet for other faculty members that would enable them, after a few hours' reading, to include behavior management techniques in their methods courses. When she retorted that she had taken eight courses in applied behavior analysis, had a background in animal research, had been practicing the procedures for 17 years, and was still learning, the reaction was the usual: "But behavior mod is so simple!"

The principles of applied behavior analysis are, indeed, easy to understand. Their effective implementation, however, is not so easy. In addition to a thorough understanding of the principles, acquired from qualified instructors, supervised practice is desirable. This is particularly important for difficult procedures, such as shaping, or procedures subject to abuse, such as aversive or exclusionary techniques.

Some professionals within the field who are concerned about adequate training have suggested that some licensing procedures be implemented. Most applied behavior analysts, however, reject a plan for licensing practitioners of applied behavior analysis unless the same standards are imposed on practitioners of other types of intervention procedures. Licensing applied only to behavior analysts implies that this group is less responsible than other practitioners (Kazdin, 1978).

In addition to ensuring personal competence, a responsible teacher makes certain others who interact with students understand the principles and techniques of applied behavior analysis. Chapter 13 describes programs for training parents, paraprofessionals, and classroom volunteers to use these principles efficiently and responsibly.

Good supervision includes training, observation, and evaluation.

Initial training must always be followed by adequate supervision. Martin (1975) suggests that such supervision include formal and informal in-service training and regular evaluation. Ongoing supervision will continuously upgrade the performance of competent staff. It is equally important to ensure that incompetent staff members do not implement procedures that may be detrimental to students or fail to follow through with procedures that are in the students' best interests.

Programs That Teach Functional Skills

Students need to learn skills that will enable them to function effectively in their environment. Teaching those skills should be the primary focus of every student's educational program. What skills are functional will be different for each student. It is functional for some students to learn algebra so they can learn geometry and trigonometry. It is functional for others to learn household skills so they are an asset to their families and thus less likely to be institutionalized. In every case the choice of skills must be based on the assumption that "unless evidence clearly exists to the contrary, an individual is . . . capable of full participation in community life and [has] a right to such participation" (Van Houten et al., 1988, p. 113). This assumption is a cornerstone for educators. It means, in our opinion, that it is unethical to believe any young child, even if she is poor, at risk, or even disabled, is not capable of learning academic and preacademic skills. As a resource teacher-friend said, "I teach as if every one of my 6-year-olds will be going to Harvard." We believe equally strongly that it is unethical to waste the time of students for whom there is clear evidence that they are not capable of full comprehension in continued attempts to teach them the alphabet, color and shape names, and other traditional skills. An individual with a disability who can take care of her personal needs, help around the house, do simple shopping, entertain herself, behave appropriately in public, and perform routine tasks with sufficient instruction has functional skills. Skills like these should be the focus of her education. It is of great importance that the particular environment in which an individual lives be considered when decisions about functional skills are made (Schroeder, Oldenquist, & Rohahn, 1990). The customs and values of a given community are as important as the resources available.

It is sometimes necessary to eliminate or reduce the rate of some student behaviors. A child who bites himself must be stopped from doing so. A student who hurts others cannot be allowed to continue. Students who are so disruptive that they cannot be maintained in a classroom must learn to stop running, screaming, or destroying property. Merely eliminating such behavior, however, is indefensible in the absence of a plan to develop constructive behavior. A student who just sits quietly doing nothing is not much better off than she was before intervention. Teachers must pay attention to developing behaviors in the student that will lead to improved learning or social interaction.

In some cases, inappropriate behavior may be decreased by reinforcing constructive behavior rather than by directly attempting to decrease destructive behavior. For example, decreasing disruptive behavior does not automatically result in improved academic performance (Ferritor, Buckholdt, Hamblin, & Smith, 1972), whereas increasing academic output may result in decreased inappropriate behavior (Ayllon & Roberts, 1974; Kirby & Shields, 1972). In general, for students who display any appropriate behavior at all, the teacher should try reinforcing such behavior and monitoring the effects of this procedure on the inappropriate behavior. Some students' repertoires of appropriate behavior are so limited and their performance of inappropriate behavior so continuous that there is little or no opportunity for a positive-reinforcement approach. In such cases, the teacher may first have to undertake elimination of the maladaptive behavior. This should be only a first step, however. As soon as possible, the student must be taught to substitute constructive behaviors that lead to the acquisition of functional skills.

Behavioral Assessment and Ongoing Evaluation

Ethical teachers cannot and do not arbitrarily decide what to teach students to do or to stop doing. Goals and objectives for each student must be based on careful observation of what the student does under a variety of conditions. After goals are selected and programs implemented, the ethical teacher keeps track of how the program is going. It is wrong to make statements like "I started using counters to help Ben with his math and he seems to be doing better." We want you to be able to say, "I observed that for four days Ben got only two to three of ten one-digit addition problems right. I gave him 20 bottle caps and showed him how to use them as counters. He got six right that day, seven yesterday, and nine today. When he gets all ten right for three days in a row, I'll go on to subtraction." We'll teach you how to say that in "behaviorese" in Chapter 4, which covers using data collection to assess and evaluate the results of procedures.

*Information for goal set-
ting comes from many
sources: tests, records,
observation, parents,
teachers, and the stu-
dents themselves.*

The Most Effective Treatment Procedures Available

A primary consideration that guides professionals and parents in designing a
program to change a student's behavior is the proven effectiveness of a technique in changing similar behaviors in similar students. In general, the most
ethical and responsible procedure to use in changing behavior is one that has
been established as most effective. Throughout this text, we shall review literature related to changing specific behaviors and provide suggestions about
effective procedures. Teachers who plan behavioral programs should also continually review current professional journals in order to keep abreast of new
developments. The *Journal of Applied Behavior Analysis* is an excellent source
of information for teachers as well as professionals in other fields. Many other
journals also provide information on behavior-change procedures for use with
students who have specific handicapping conditions and with students in regular classes who display certain deficits or excesses.

In some cases, it may not be possible or ethical to use a procedure that has
been proven effective. The use of aversive procedures—specifically including
contingent electric shock—though proven effective in eliminating some very
maladaptive behaviors such as self-mutilation (Bucher & Lovaas, 1968; Lovaas,
Freitag, Gold, & Kassorla, 1965; Wolf, Risley, & Mees, 1964)—has been
restricted (Wyatt v. Stickney, 1972). Such procedures may now be used only if
consent has been obtained from the subject (or parents or advocate) and a
supervisory committee has confirmed that less drastic procedures have not eliminated or sufficiently decelerated the maladaptive behavior (Martin, 1975). Limitations have also been placed on the use of **time-out** from positive reinforcement, a technique that may involve seclusion (confining a student in an isolated
area) or exclusion (removing a student from a potentially reinforcing situation).
Seclusionary time-out is particularly subject to regulation (Morales v. Turman,
1974). Before using any aversive or seclusionary procedure, teachers should
examine their employers' guidelines or regulations pertaining to such procedures, as rules may vary considerably. The unauthorized use of even short-term
seclusion, a relatively mild but effective technique (Birnbrauer, Wolf, Kidder, &
Tague, 1965; Madsen & Madsen, 1970; Wolf, Risley, & Mees, 1964; Zeilberger,
Sampen, & Sloane, 1968), may result in criticism or misunderstanding.

*Techniques for decreas-
ing behavior will be
described in Chapter 8.*

The use of aversive or seclusionary interventions should, in any event, be
reserved for severely maladaptive behaviors that have not been successfully
modified using positive means. Many behaviors targeted for deceleration
may be eliminated using reinforcement of incompatible behavior, differential
reinforcement of other behavior (DRO), or extinction. More information
about the appropriate use of procedures to reduce inappropriate behaviors
will be provided in Chapter 8.

ACCOUNTABILITY

Accountability implies publication of goals, procedures, and results so that
they may be evaluated. Applied behavior analysis lends itself easily to such

TABLE 2–1
Suggestions for ethical use of applied behavior analysis.

Assure competence of all staff members.
Choose appropriate goals.
Ensure voluntary participation.
Be accountable.

accountability. Goals are stated behaviorally, procedures described clearly, and results defined in terms of direct, functional relationships between interventions and behaviors. It is, indeed, impossible to conduct applied behavior analysis as described by Baer, Wolf, and Risley (1968) without being accountable. The entire process is visible, understandable, and open to evaluation. The result of such accountability is that parents, teachers, administrators, and the public can judge for themselves whether an approach is working or whether a change is needed.

Accountability is a major benefit of applied behavior analysis.

Teachers should not view the requirement of accountability as negative or threatening. It is to a teacher's advantage to verify the effectiveness of his or her teaching. This approach enables teachers to monitor their own competence and to demonstrate this competence to others. It is much more impressive to face a supervisor at a yearly evaluation conference armed with charts and graphs showing increases in reading ability and decreases in disruptive behavior than it is to walk in with only vague statements about a pretty good year.

To whom are teachers accountable? In terms of ethical behavior, we're afraid the answer is everyone. Teachers are accountable to their profession, the community, their administrative superiors, the parents of their students, those students, and themselves.

The teacher who follows the suggestions provided in this chapter should avoid many problems associated with the use of applied behavior analysis procedures in the classroom. Table 2–1 summarizes these suggestions. No amount of prevention can forestall all criticism; nor can a teacher avoid making mistakes. Systematic attention to the ethical standards in the ABA's statement, however, can minimize criticism and enable teachers to learn from mistakes rather than become discouraged by them.

In the final section of this chapter, let's listen in on Professor Grundy, whose workshop discussion may address concerns you have. All the questions the professor answers here are inevitably addressed to everyone who undertakes a career as an applied behavior analyst.

Professor Grundy Conducts a Workshop

The superintendent of schools in a large metropolitan area near the university asked Professor Grundy to conduct a one-day workshop on behavior modification for elementary and secondary teachers. Although aware of the limitations of such short-term workshops (Franks & Wilson, 1976), Grundy concluded, if he confined himself to a description of basic learning principles, no harm would be done. On the appointed day, Grundy, dressed in his best tweed coat with leather elbow patches, stood before 700 teachers, wondering how he got himself into this mess.

After a slow start, during which several teachers fell asleep and numerous others openly graded papers, Grundy hit his stride. He delivered a succinct, snappy talk full of humorous anecdotes and sprinkled with just enough first-name references to his friends, all "biggies" in applied behavior analysis and all totally unfamiliar to the teachers. As Grundy reached the conclusion of his presentation, glowing with satisfaction, he noticed to his horror that he was coming up about 45 minutes short of the amount of time agreed to in his contract. Over the thunderous applause (resulting at least partially from the fact that the teachers thought they were going to be released early), Grundy called faintly for questions. There was considerable rumbling and shifting about, but when the superintendent mounted the stage and glared fixedly at the audience, the hands began to go up. The nature of the questions made Grundy vow never to be caught short again, but he did his best to answer each.

Question: Isn't what you're suggesting bribery?

Answer: I'm glad you asked that question. *Webster's Third New International Dictionary* (1986) defines a bribe as something given to pervert the judgment or corrupt the conduct of a person. In that sense, the use of the principles I have described is certainly not bribery. Teachers use the principles of learning to motivate their students to do things that will benefit them—things like reading, math, and social skills.

A second definition is that a bribe is anything promised or given to induce a person to do something against his or her wishes. Some people might say that's exactly what I'm advocating. As a behaviorist, I have some difficulty with the word *wishes*, since I cannot see wishes but only actions. It appears to me that students have a free choice as to whether they will perform a behavior for which they know they will receive a reinforcer. My interpretation is that if Joanie, for example, chooses to perform the behavior, she has demonstrated her "wishes."

The word *bribery* definitely implies something underhanded. I prefer to think of applied behavior analysis procedures as open, honest attempts to change students' behavior in a positive direction. Any other questions? If not . . .

Question: But shouldn't children be intrinsically motivated? Surely they don't have to be rewarded for learning. They should want to learn.

Answer: Madam, why are you here today? I'm sure that given the choice of spending the day at the beach or coming to an in-service session, your intrinsic motivation for learning might have wavered just a little. All of us here are being paid to be here; most adults, even those who enjoy their work enormously, would not continue to perform it in the absence of some very concrete application of the law of positive reinforcement. Why should we expect children to perform difficult tasks for less than we expect of ourselves?

Question: But won't our students expect rewards for everything they do?

Answer: Certainly. And why not? However, as your students become more successful, they will begin to respond to the reinforcers available in the natural environment—the same reinforcers that maintain the appropriate behavior of students who are already successful. Good students do not work without reinforcers; their behavior is reinforced by good grades, by parental approval and, yes, by the love of learning. When doing good work has been consistently reinforced, it eventually does become a secondary, or conditioned, reinforcer. We cannot, however, expect this to happen overnight with students who have had very little experience with success in learning tasks. Does that answer your questions? Thank . . .

"With automotive 'behavior,' prof, you gotta get right to the cause. Now, after you had the oil changed in 1953 . . . "

Question: Doesn't this kind of behavior management just suppress the symptoms of serious emotional problems without getting at the root cause?

Answer: Oh, my. That's a very complicated question. Behaviorists don't accept the concept of emotional problems caused by some underlying root cause. We have found that if we deal with the problem behaviors the roots just seem to die out. Human beings are not like weeds whose roots lurk under the surface of the ground waiting to send up shoots as soon as it rains.

Question: "Yes, but everyone knows if you suppress one symptom, a worse one will take its place. Doesn't that prove there are underlying problems?"

Answer: No, sir, everyone does not know that. Human beings are no more like piston engines than like weeds. Just because one symptom "goes down" another one will not necessarily "pop up." My colleagues (Baer, 1971; Bandura, 1969; Rachman, 1963; Yates, 1970) have reported extensive research indicating that removal of so-called symptoms does not result in the development of new ones. As a matter of fact, when children's inappropriate behaviors are eliminated, they sometimes learn new, appropriate behaviors without being taught (Chadwick & Day, 1971; Morrow & Gochros, 1970; O'Leary, Poulos, & Devine, 1972). Even if new maladaptive behaviors do occur—and they sometimes do (Balson, 1973; Schroeder and MacLean, 1987)—there is no evidence to show they are alternative symptoms of underlying deviance. Such behaviors may be easily eliminated using applied behavior analysis procedures. Now if . . .

Question: Isn't what you're talking about based on the behavior of animals like rats and monkeys? Isn't it unethical to treat our kids like animals?

Answer: Early research studying the laws of behavior was conducted with animals. This doesn't mean we control human beings as if they were nothing but white rats or pigeons. Such animal research—also called *analogue research* (Davison & Stuart, 1975)—provides only a basic foundation for studying human behavior. The applied behavior analyst uses procedures tested with human beings in real-world conditions—not in laboratories. These procedures take into account the complexity of human behavior and the undeniable freedom of human beings to choose their course of action. What's unethical is not learning and applying all we can from whatever source.

Question: This stuff may work on those special education kids, but my students are smart. Won't they catch on?

Answer: Good heavens; of course they'll catch on. The laws of behavior operate for all of us. We can change behavior in youngsters with very severe disabilities, but it's a very complex process. With your students, you can shorten and simplify the procedure. You just tell them what the contingencies are. You don't have to wait for the students to learn from experience. Applied behavior analysis procedures work on everyone, even professors. Take punishment, for example. If I ever agree to do another workshop, it'll be a cold day in. . . . Pardon me. Any more questions?

Question: But how can behavior mod work with my kids? I don't care how much candy you gave them, they still couldn't read.

Answer: Perhaps, madam, you missed some of my presentation during your nap. Applied behavior analysis is not just giving students candy. If your students do not respond verbally to the written word, then you must bring their responses under stimulus control. That's applied behavior analysis. If they have no vocal language, you shape it; that's applied behavior analysis. If they just sit there and do nothing, you get their attention. AND THAT'S APPLIED BEHAVIOR ANALYSIS! ARE THERE ANY MORE QUESTIONS?

Question: I think the whole thing sounds like too much trouble. It seems awfully tedious and time-consuming. Is it really worth the trouble?

Answer: If . . . it's . . . not . . . worth . . . the . . . trouble, . . . don't . . . do . . . it. Behaviors that are serious enough to warrant more complicated procedures take up an enormous amount of your time. You don't use a complicated procedure to solve a simple problem. Try timing yourself with a stopwatch. How much time is this problem taking the way you're handling (or not handling) it now? Try applying systematic contingencies and keeping records. Then compare the amount of time you've spent. You might be surprised! Now, I really must . . .

Question: I have only one student with really serious problems. If I use some systematic procedure with him, won't the others complain? What do I say to them?

Answer: The problem will not occur as often as you think. Most students know that a student who is not performing well needs extra help and are neither surprised nor disturbed when he gets it. Few students will even ask why that student is treated differently. If they do, I suggest you say to them, "In this class everyone gets what he needs. Harold needs a little extra help remembering to stay in his seat." If you consistently reinforce appropriate behavior for all your students, they will not resent it when a more systematic procedure is implemented for a student with special problems. If that's all, I . . .

Question: Most of my students with problems can't learn much because they come from very bad home situations. There's just nothing you can do in such cases, is there?

Answer: Madam, pigeons can learn to discriminate between environments and to perform the behaviors that will be reinforced in each. Are you implying your students are less capable than birds? Such an assumption is inhumane. Blaming poor learning or inappropriate behavior on factors beyond your control is simply a refusal to accept responsibility. You may have very little influence on your students' environment outside your classroom, but you have an enormous influence on that classroom environment. It is your job to arrange it so your students learn as much as possible, both academically and socially. What do you think teaching is, anyway? *Teach* is a transitive verb. You're not teaching unless you're teaching somebody something.

Question: Have you ever taught school?

At this point Professor Grundy became incoherent and had to be helped from the podium by the superintendent. As he drove home, he realized he had made a number of mistakes, the first of which was agreeing to do the workshop. He had assumed that teachers expecting to receive concrete help with classroom management problems would be interested in a theoretical discussion of learning principles. He had also assumed that the teachers would immediately see the relationships between these principles and the behaviors of their students. Grundy realized it was unreasonable of him to expect this. He did decide, however, that he needed to include more practical applications in his courses on applied behavior analysis.

THEORY OR RECIPES

Professor Grundy was undoubtedly correct in his belief that the effective use of applied behavior analysis requires a knowledge of the basic principles. Teachers often reject theory and seek immediate practical solutions to specific problems. Such a cookbook approach, however, has serious limitations. Although students supplied with cookbook methods may acquire competencies more quickly, the students who are required to spend more time on basic principles tend to show more competence in the long run (White, 1977).

To this point we have spent considerable time discussing definition, historical background, basic principles, and ethical concerns of applied behavior analysis. It is now finally time to go on to what teachers call "the good stuff." In succeeding chapters, we shall discuss practical procedures for changing behavior in classroom settings and provide a more thorough discussion of basic learning principles. By striking a balance, we hope to offer not only a review of tried-and-true solutions to classroom problems, but also the knowledge to enable teachers to develop their own solutions.

SUMMARY

This chapter described several objections to the use of applied behavior analysis techniques. These techniques have been criticized on the basis that they interfere with personal freedom and that they are inhumane. We have described our reasons for disagreeing with these objections. Properly used, applied behavior analysis procedures enhance personal freedom by increasing options. Applied behavior analysis procedures are humane because they are an effective tool for increasing options and teaching appropriate skills.

Applied behavior analysis procedures will be used ethically if the program includes a therapeutic environment, services whose overriding goal is personal welfare, treatment by a competent behavior analyst, programs that teach functional skills, behavioral assessment and ongoing evaluation, and the most effective treatment procedures available. Teachers who choose applied behavior analysis procedures and consider these factors know they are acting in the best interests of their students.

DISCUSSION QUESTIONS

1. If, as a teacher, you decided to use applied behavior analysis procedures to teach your students, how would you justify or describe their use to parents? to school administrators? to students?

2. Would changing the terminology—avoiding the word *punishment*, for example—change the acceptability of applied behavior analysis to professionals and the public? Can you think of alternative terms?

3. Is it ever ethical to use aversive procedures? If so, under what circumstances is their use justified? (Review this question and your answer after you have read and studied Chapter 8.)

4. At what point should the attempt to teach academic or preacademic skills to students with disabilities be abandoned? Should the attempt even be made with some students?

REFERENCES

Ayllon, T., Layman, D., & Kandel, H.J. 1975. A behavioral-educational alternative to drug control of hyperactive children. *Journal of Applied Behavior Analysis, 8,* 137–146.

Ayllon, T., & Roberts, M.D. 1974. Eliminating discipline problems by strengthening academic performance. *Journal of Applied Behavior Analysis, 7,* 71–76.

Baer, D.M. 1971. Behavior modification: You shouldn't. In E.A. Ramp and B.L. Hopkins (Eds.), *A new direction for education: Behavior analysis* (vol. 1). Lawrence: University of Kansas Support and Development Center for Follow Through.

Baer, D.M., Wolf, M.M., & Risley, T.R. 1968. Some current dimensions of applied behavior analysis. *Journal of Applied Behavior Analysis, 1*, 91–97.

Baer, D.M., Wolf, M.M., & Risley, T.R. 1987. Some still-current dimensions of applied behavior analysis. *Journal of Applied Behavior Analysis, 20*, 313–327.

Balson, P.M. 1973. Case study: Encopresis: A case with symptom substitution. *Behavior Therapy, 4*, 134–136.

Bandura, A. 1969. *Principles of behavior modification.* New York: Holt, Rinehart & Winston.

Bandura, A. 1975. The ethics and social purposes of behavior modification. In C.M. Franks and G.T. Wilson (Eds.), *Annual review of behavior therapy, theory & practice* (vol. 3, pp. 13–20). New York: Brunner/Mazel.

Becker, W.C., Engelmann, S., & Thomas, D.R. 1975. *Teaching 1: Classroom management*, Chicago: Science Research Associates.

Bereiter, C., & Engelmann, S. 1966. *Teaching disadvantaged children in the preschool.* Englewood Cliffs, N.J.: Prentice-Hall.

Birnbrauer, J.S., Wolf, M.M., Kidder, J.D., & Tague, C.E. 1965. Classroom behavior of retarded pupils with token reinforcement. *Journal of Experimental Child Psychology, 2*, 219–235.

Bostow, D.E., & Bailey, J. 1969. Modification of severe disruptive and aggressive behavior using brief timeout and reinforcement procedures. *Journal of Applied Behavior Analysis, 2*, 31–37.

Bucher, B., & Lovaas, O.I. 1968. Use of aversive stimulation in behavior modification. In M. R. Jones (Ed.), *Miami Symposium on the Prediction of Behavior, 1967: Aversive Stimulation.* Coral Gables, Fla.: University of Miami Press.

Chadwick, B.A., & Day, R.C. 1971. Systematic reinforcement: Academic performance of underachieving students. *Journal of Applied Behavior Analysis, 4*, 311–319.

Cooke, N.L. 1984. Misrepresentation of the behavioral model in preservice teacher education textbooks. In W.L. Heward, T.E. Heron, D.S. Hill, & J. Trap-Porter (Eds.), *Focus on behavior analysis in education*, Columbus, OH, Merrill.

Craighead, W.E., Kazdin, A.E., Mahoney, M.J. 1976. *Behavior modification: Principles, issues, and applications.* Boston: Houghton Mifflin.

Davison, G.C., & Stuart, R.B. 1975. Behavior therapy and civil liberties. *American Psychologist, 30*(7), 755–763.

Ferritor, D.E., Buckholdt, D., Hamblin, R.L., & Smith, L. 1972. The noneffects of contingent reinforcement for attending behavior on work accomplished. *Journal of Applied Behavior Analysis, 5*, 7–17.

Franks, C.M., & Wilson, G.T. (Eds.). 1976. *Annual review of behavior therapy, theory & practice.* New York: Brunner/Mazel.

Gartner, A., & Lipsky, D.K. 1989. *The yoke of special education: How to break it.* Rochester, NY: National Center on Education and the Economy.

Goetz, E.M., & Baer, D.M. 1973. Social control of form diversity and the emergence of new forms in children's blockbuilding. *Journal of Applied Behavior Analysis, 6*, 209–217.

Goetz, E.M., & Salmonson, M.M. 1972. The effect and general and descriptive reinforcement on "creativity" in easel painting. In G. Semb (Ed.), *Behavior analysis and education—1972.* Lawrence: University of Kansas Department of Human Development.

Goldiamond, I. 1975. Toward a constructional approach to social problems: Ethical and constitutional issues raised by applied behavior analysis. In C.M. Franks & G.T. Wilson (Eds.), *Annual review of behavior therapy, theory & practice* (vol. 3, pp. 21–63). New York: Brunner/Mazel.

Holden, C. 1973. Psychosurgery: Legitimate therapy or laundered lobotomy? *Science, 173*, 1104–1112.

Holman, J. 1977. The moral risk and high cost of exological concern in applied behavior analysis. In A. Rogers-Warren & S. Warren (Eds.) *Ecological perspectives in behavior analysis* (pp. 63–100). Baltimore, Md.: University Park Press.

Journal of Teacher Education. 1986. *37*(1).

Kazdin, A.E. 1978. *History of behavior modification.* Baltimore, Md.: University Park Press.

Kirby, F.D., & Shields, F. 1972. Modification of arithmetic response rate and attending behavior in a seventh-grade student. *Journal of Applied Behavior Analysis, 5*, 79–84.

Kitchener, R.F. 1980. Ethical relativism and behavior therapy. *Journal of Consulting and Clinical Psychology, 48*, 1–7.

Lovaas, O.I., Freitag, G., Gold, V.J., & Kassorla, I.C. 1965. Experimental studies in childhood schizophrenia: Analysis of self-destructive behavior. *Journal of Experimental Child Psychology, 2*, 67–84.

Lovaas, O.I., & Simmons, J.Q. 1969. Manipulation of self-destruction in three retarded children. *Journal of Applied Behavior Analysis, 2*, 143–157.

Lovitt, T.C., & Curtiss K.A. 1969. Academic response rate as a function of teacher- and self-imposed contingencies. *Journal of Applied Behavior Analysis, 2*, 49–53.

Madsen, C.K., & Madsen, C.H. 1970. *Parents-children-discipline: A positive approach.* Boston: Allyn & Bacon.

Mahoney, M.J., Kazdin, A.E., & Lesswing, N.J. 1974. Behavior modification: Delusion or deliverance? In C.M. Franks & G.T. Wilson (Eds.), *Annual review of behavior therapy, theory & practice* (vol. 2, pp. 11–40). New York: Brunner/Mazel.

Maloney, K.B., & Hopkins, B.L. 1973. The modification of sentence structure and its relationship to subjective judgements of creativity in writing. *Journal of Applied Behavior Analysis, 6*, 425–433.

Martin, R. 1975. *Legal challenges to behavior modification: Trends in schools, corrections, and mental health.* Champaign, Ill.: Research Press.

Mason, B. 1974. Brain surgery to control behavior. *Ebony, 28*(4), 46.

McConnell, J.V. 1970. Stimulus/response: Criminals can be brain-washed now. *Psychology Today, 3*, 14–18, 74.

Morales v. Turman, 383 F. Supp. 53 (E.D. Tex., 1974).

Morrow, W.R., & Gochros, H.L. 1970. Misconceptions regarding behavior modification. *The Social Service Review, 44*, 293–307.

O'Connor, R.D. 1969. Modification of social withdrawal through symbolic modeling. *Journal of Applied Behavior Analysis, 2*, 15–22.

O'Leary, K.D. 1972. The assessment of psychopathology in children. In H.C. Quay & J.S. Werry (Eds.), *Psychopathological disorders of childhood* (pp. 234–272). New York: Wiley.

O'Leary, K.D., Poulos, R.W., & Devine, V.T. 1972. Tangible reinforcers: Bonuses or bribes? *Journal of Consulting and Clinical Psychology, 38*, 1–8.

Rachman, S. 1963. Spontaneous remission and latent learning. *Behavior Research and Therapy, 1*, 3–15.

Reese, H.W., & Parnes, S.J. 1970. Programming creative behavior. *Child Development, 41*, 413–423.

Reynolds, N.J., & Risley, T.R. 1968. The role of social and material reinforcers in increasing talking of a disadvantaged preschool child. *Journal of Applied Behavior Analysis, 1*, 253–262.

Risley, T.R. 1968. The effects and side effects of punishing the autistic behaviors of a deviant child. *Journal of Applied Behavior Analysis, 1*, 21–34.

Risley, T.R. 1975. Certified procedures not people. In W.S. Wood (Ed.), *Issues in evaluating behavior modification* (pp. 159–181). Champaign, Ill.: Research Press.

Rogers, C.R., & Skinner, B.F. 1956. Some issues concerning the control of human behavior: A symposium. *Science, 124*, 1057–1066.

Schroeder, S.R., & MacLean, W. 1987. If it isn't one thing, it's another: Experimental analysis of covariation in behavior management data of severely disturbed retarded persons. In S. Landesman & P. Vietze (Eds.) Living environments and mental retardation (pp. 315–338). Washington, DC: AAMD Monograph.

Schroeder, S.R., Oldenquist, A., & Rohahn, J. 1990. A conceptual framework for judging the humaneness and effectiveness of behavioral treatment. In A.C. Repp & N.N. Singh (Eds.) *Perspectives on the use of nonaversive and aversive interventions for persons with developmental disabilities.* New York: Sycamore.

Simpson, R.G., & Eaves, R.C. 1985. Do we need more qualitative research or more good research? A reaction to Stainback and Stainback. *Exceptional Children, 51*, 325–329.

Stainback, S., & Stainback, W. 1984. Broadening the research perspective in special education. *Exceptional Children, 50*, 400–408.

Stolz, S.B. 1977. Why no guidelines for behavior modification? *Journal of Applied Behavior Analysis, 10*, 541–547.

Sulzer-Azaroff, B., & Mayer, G.R. 1977. *Applying behavior-analysis procedures with children and youth.* New York: Holt, Rinehart & Winston.

Sulzer-Azaroff, B., Thaw, J., & Thomas, C. 1975. Behavioral competencies for the evaluation of behavior modifiers. In W.S. Wood (Ed.), *Issues in evaluating behavior modification* (pp. 47–98). Champaign, Ill.: Research Press.

Van Houten, R., Axelrod, S., Bailey, J.S., Favell, J.E., Foxx, R.M., Iwata, B.A., & Lovaas, O.I. 1988. The right to effective behavioral treatment. *The Behavior Analyst, 11,* 111–114.

Watras, J. 1986. Will teaching applied ethics improve schools of education? *Journal of Teacher Education, 37,* 13–16.

Webster's third new international dictionary. 1986. Springfield, Mass.: Merriam-Webster.

White, O.R. 1977. Behaviorism in special education: An arena for debate. In R.D. Kneedler & S.G. Tarber (Eds.), *Changing perspectives in special education,* Columbus, Ohio: Merrill.

Wicker, T. February 8, 1974. A bad idea persists. *The New York Times,* p. 31.

Winett, R.A., & Winkler, R.C. 1972. Current behavior modification in the classroom: Be still, be quiet, be docile. *Journal of Applied Behavior Analysis, 5,* 499–504.

Wolf, M.M. 1978. Social validity: The case for subjective measurement or how applied behavior analysis is finding its heart. *Journal of Applied Behavior Analysis, 11,* 203–214.

Wolf, M.M., Risley, T.R., & Mees, H.L. 1964. Application of operant conditioning procedures to the behavior problems of an autistic child. *Behavior Research and Therapy, 1,* 305–312.

Wood, W.S. (Ed.). 1975. *Issues in evaluating behavior modification.* Champaign, Ill.: Research Press.

Wyatt v. Stickney, 344 F. Supp. 373, 344 F. Supp. 387 (M.D. Ala., 1972) affirmed sub nom. Wyatt v. Aderholt, 503 F. 2nd 1305 (5th Cir., 1974).

Yates, A.J. 1970. *Behavior therapy.* New York: Wiley.

Zeilberger, J., Sampen, S.E., & Sloane, H.N., Jr. 1968. Modification of a child's problem behaviors in the home with the mother as therapist. *Journal of Applied Behavior Analysis, 1,* 47–53.

Section Two
Technology of Behavior-Change Programs

3

Preparing Behavioral Objectives

Did you know that . . .

- If you don't know where you're going, you'll probably never get there?
- There are reasons for writing behavioral objectives besides satisfying legal or administrative requirements?
- Even professors write behavioral objectives?
- 90% may not be a passing grade?
- IEP does *not* stand for Idiotic Educational Plot?

Definition
A behavioral objective is a statement that communicates a proposed change in behavior. It describes a level of performance and serves as a basis for evaluation.

This chapter discusses the first step in carrying out a program for behavior change—defining the target behavior; that is, the behavior to be changed. As Chapter 1 stated, a target behavior may be selected because it represents either a behavioral deficit (such as too few math skills) or a behavioral excess (such as too much screaming). After the behavior to be changed has been identified, teachers formulate a written **behavioral objective**.

A behavioral objective for a student who demonstrates a deficit in math skills would describe the level of math performance the student should reach. A behavioral objective for a student who screams excessively would describe an acceptable level of screaming. Anyone reading a behavioral objective should be able to understand exactly what a student is working to accomplish. Because behavioral objectives are such an integral part of planning for student behavior change, they are required as part of the IEP for students with disabilities. The relationship between objectives and the IEP will be discussed later in the chapter.

In this chapter, you'll also meet some teachers who are learning to use a behavioral approach in their teaching. Through them, you'll encounter some of the difficulties of putting behavioral programs into effect. Consider the plight of Ms. Samuels, the resource teacher, in the following vignette.

Are We Both Talking About the Same Thing?

Ms. Wilberforce, the third-grade teacher, was in a snit.

"That resource teacher," she complained to her friend, Ms. Folden, "is absolutely useless. I asked her two months ago to work on vowels with Martin and he still doesn't know the short sounds."

"You're absolutely right," agreed Ms. Folden, "I told her last September that Melissa Sue had a bad attitude. The longer Melissa Sue goes to see the resource teacher, the worse it gets. All she does is giggle when I correct her. It seems to me that we were better off without resource teachers."

Meanwhile, Ms. Samuels, the resource teacher, was complaining bitterly to her supervisor.

"Those regular classroom teachers are so uncooperative. They don't seem to appreciate what I'm doing at all. Just look at what I've done with Martin. He can name all the vowels when I ask him, and he even knows a little song about them. And Melissa Sue, who used to pout all the time, smiles and laughs so much now. I've done exactly what the teachers asked—why don't they appreciate it?"

DEFINITION AND PURPOSE

Behavioral objectives improve communication.

The preceding vignette illustrates one of the most important reasons for writing behavioral objectives: to clarify the goals of a behavior-change program and thus to facilitate communication among people involved in the program. Because it is a written statement targeting a specific change in behavior, the objective serves as an agreement among school personnel and parents about the academic or social learning goals for which school personnel are taking responsibility. The statement may also serve as a vehicle for informing the student of the goals he or she is expected to reach.

A second important reason for writing behavioral objectives is that a clearly stated target for instruction facilitates effective programming by the teacher and ancillary personnel. A clearly stated instructional target provides a basis for selecting appropriate materials and instructional strategies. Mager (1962) pointed out that "a machinist does not select a tool until he knows what operation he intends to perform; a composer does not orchestrate a score until he knows what effects he wishes to achieve; a builder does not select his materials or specify a schedule until he has his blueprints" (p. 3). Clearly written behavioral objectives should prevent the classroom teacher from using materials simply because they are available or strategies simply because they are familiar. The selection of materials and teaching strategies is more likely to be appropriate if goals are clearly defined.

There is yet another excellent reason for writing behavioral objectives. Consider the following account.

A Matter of Opinion

Mr. Henderson, the teacher of a self-contained class for students with severe disabilities, hurried to the principal's office in a state of complete panic. The parents of Alvin, one of his students, had just threatened to remove the boy from school. They insisted Mr. Henderson was not teaching Alvin anything. Mr. Henderson had agreed in August to work on toilet training with Alvin and felt the boy had made excellent progress. Alvin's parents, however, were upset because Alvin still had several accidents a week. They insisted Mr. Henderson had not reached his stated goal.

"I have toilet trained Alvin," howled Mr. Henderson. "Wouldn't you consider only two or three accidents all right?"

Behavioral objectives help evaluate progress.

Mr. Henderson's problem could have been prevented if a clearly written objective statement had come out of the August meeting. If a definition of *toilet trained* had been stated at the beginning of the year, there would have been no question as to whether the goal had been achieved. Behavioral objectives provide for precise evaluation of instruction. When a teacher identifies a deficit or an excess in a student's behavioral repertoire, he or she has identified a discrepancy between current and expected levels of functioning. If the teacher states a performance criterion (the ultimate goal) and records ongoing progress toward this goal, both formative (ongoing) and summative (final) evaluation of intervention procedures become possible for program alteration and future planning. Such ongoing evaluation and measurement enable the teacher, the student, or a third party to monitor the student's progress continuously and to determine when goals have been reached. Continuous monitoring ensures that individual interpretations or prejudices in judgment are minimized in the evaluation of an instructional procedure or a student's performance.

Pinpointing Behavior

Before initiating a behavior-change program for a student, it is necessary to describe the target behavior clearly. Referral information may often be vague and imprecise. In order to write effective objectives for guiding educational programs, the applied behavior analyst must refine broad generalizations into specific, observable, measurable behaviors. This process is frequently referred to as **pinpointing** behavior.

Pinpointing may be accomplished by asking a series of questions, usually including "Could you please tell me what he *does*?" or "What exactly do you want her to *do*?" For example, teachers often refer students to a behavior analyst because of "hyperactivity." The referring teacher and the applied behavior analyst must define this hyperactive behavior by describing exactly what is occurring. Is it that the student, like Ralph in Ms. Harper's class, wanders around the room? Does he tap his pencils on the desk? Does he weave back and forth in his chair?

There are many categories of behavior that may result in referrals and require pinpointing. Here are a few examples, with some questions that may help to refine the definition:

- *Jeff can't do math*: Is the problem that he doesn't have basic arithmetic computation skills or that he can't finish his problems within the time limit set?
- *Virginia is always off-task*: Is the problem that she stares out the window, or is it that she talks to her neighbor, or is it that she scribbles in her book instead of looking at the chalkboard?
- *Arthur is always disturbing others*: Is he grabbing objects from someone, or talking to others during lessons, or hitting his neighbor, or knocking neighbors' books off the desk, or pulling someone's hair?
- *Nancy's lab projects are a mess*: Is it that she can't read the instructions in the lab manual, or that her handwriting is sloppy, or that she does not do the prescribed steps in the right order, or that she can do the experiments but can't write the results coherently?
- *Lauren throws tantrums*: Is she crying and sobbing, or is she throwing herself on the floor, or is she throwing objects around the room?

A teacher may ask a similar series of questions in describing more complex or abstract categories of behaviors. If the referring teacher said "Carol doesn't use the critical thinking skills in reading," the applied behavior analyst would want to know if Carol

1. distinguishes between facts and opinions;
2. distinguishes between facts and inferences;
3. identifies cause-effect relationships;
4. identifies errors in reasoning;
5. distinguishes between relevant and irrelevant arguments;

6. distinguishes between warranted and unwarranted generalizations;
7. formulates valid conclusions from written material;
8. specifies assumptions needed to make conclusions true. (Gronlund, 1985, p. 14)

With certain behaviors, questioning or redefining may need to go a step further. If a student is often out of his chair, the teacher's concern may be either the number of times he gets out of his chair or the length of time he stays out. The student who gets up only once, but stays up all morning is doing something quite different from the student who hops in and out of his seat every few minutes. Each of these students will require different intervention strategies and data collection techniques. In the case of broad behavior categories, such as temper tantrums for which a teacher must pinpoint multiple behaviors occurring simultaneously, it will be necessary to list the behaviors in some order of priority. For instance, they might be listed in order from least-to-most interference to the child or to the environment. After referral information has been refined so that target behaviors can be clearly described, educational goals and eventually behavioral objectives can be written.

EDUCATIONAL GOALS

Goals precede objectives. Behavioral objectives should not be created on the spur of the moment. Objectives should be derived from a set of **educational goals** that provide the framework for the academic year. These goals should evolve from an accumulation of evaluation information and should be correlated with curriculum planning. Goals define the anticipated academic and social development for which the school is taking responsibility. During goal selection, educators estimate what proportion of the student's educational potential is to be developed within the next academic year. Thus, educational goals (long-term objectives) are statements of annual program intent whereas behavior objectives (short-term or instructional objectives) are statements of actual instructional intent, usually for a three- to four-month period (quarterly) for individuals with more severe disabilities and for the length of time of the school's grading period for students with mild disabilities.

Establishing Goals

A staffing committee or multidisciplinary team usually is responsible for setting goals for students who need special services and have been formally referred. When gathering data on which to base a student's educational program, the staffing committee (or an equivalent group of professionals from various disciplines and the student's parent) will review the results of various evaluations. These evaluations represent information that has been generated (often by educational specialists and consultants) to determine the student's current levels of functioning. These data may include reports from

Formal sources of information for goal setting.

1. *School psychology*: scores on the third edition of the Wechsler Intelligence Scale for Children (Wechsler, 1991), Bayley Scales of Infant Development (Bayley, 1984), or Behavior Problem Checklist (Quay & Peterson, 1975)

2. *Education*: scores from the Wide Range Achievement Test—Revised (Jastak & Wilkinson, 1984), KeyMath Diagnostic Arithmetic Test, Revised (Connolly, 1988), Woodcock Reading Mastery Tests—Revised (Woodcock, 1987), Brigance Inventory of Basic Skills (Brigance, 1977), or Behavioral Characteristics Progression (Santa Cruz County, 1973)

3. *Medicine*: neurological, pediatric, vision, hearing screenings

4. *Therapeutic services*: results of physical therapy, occupational therapy, speech pathology, recreation therapy evaluations

5. *Adaptive behavior*: scores on the AAMD (American Association on Mental Deficiency) Adaptive Behavior Scale—School Edition (Lambert, Windmiller, Tharinger, & Cole, 1981), or the Vineland Adaptive Behavior Scales (Sparrow, Balla, & Ciccetti, 1984).

Informal sources of information for goal setting.

In addition to these more formal sources, the goal-setting group should also consider the concerns of the parent who is automatically included in such meetings. Recommendations from previous teachers will be considered as well. The social and academic environmental demands of the present classroom, the home, the projected educational placement, or a projected work site should also be examined.

These data reveal the student's current functioning in the various areas, certain deficits defined by chronological-age or mental-age expectancies, or specific behavior excesses, any of which may become likely targets for a behavior-change program. Based on this accumulated information, the committee proposes a set of educational goals for the student. An estimate of progress is then included in the long-term objectives prepared for the student's Individualized Education Program (IEP).

A promising new technology for assisting teachers to set appropriate goals, derive instructional objectives, and monitor students' progress is Curriculum-Based Measurement (CBM) (Fuchs, Deno, & Mirkin, 1984). CBM uses the computer for data management, including record keeping, trend analysis, and making decisions about changes in goals or procedures. Students also work directly on the computer to practice skills and take tests. Computer managed and assisted instruction also allows the process of goal setting and monitoring to be directly based on student achievement across curriculum areas.

In many regular classrooms, the establishment of educational goals may not involve such an extensive accumulation of information. Assessment may be limited to group achievement tests supplemented by informal teacher-made assessments. Goal setting may also be constrained by the adopted grade-level curriculum guide. For example, the school board and district administrators or curriculum coordinators usually provide a standard set of educational goals for each class of fourth-graders. Such goals assume equal background and achievement. Under a standard curriculum, for example, all students at a certain grade level are to be instructed in the natural resources of Peru, the excretory system of the earthworm, multiplication of fractions, and reading comprehension. The teacher's task, then, becomes translating these goals into reasonable objectives for each member of a particular class. The teacher may write behavioral objectives for the class as a whole, giving consideration to the general characteristics of the group. In addition, if the teacher is to help a particular student who is having problems or to teach a reading group that is progressing slowly, that teacher may need to write additional behavioral objectives to prescribe a course of instruction that will facilitate learning.

Educational goals for individual students must be developed on the basis of evaluation data but should also consider other factors:

1. The student's past and projected rate of development compared with long-range plans for his or her future
2. The presenting physical and communicative capabilities of the student
3. Inappropriate behaviors that must be brought under control because they interfere with learning
4. Skills the student lacks for appropriate functioning in the home, school, and social environments
5. The amount of instructional time available to the student within the school day and within the total school experience
6. The prerequisites necessary for acquiring new skills
7. The functional utility of the skills (what additional skills may be built on these?)
8. The availability of specialized materials, equipment, or resource personnel (speech pathologist, remedial reading teacher, and so on).

Because educational goals are projected over long periods of time, they are written in broad terms. For practical application, however, they need to be written in terms that are observable and quantifiable. As you learned in Chapter 1, applied behavior analysts deal only with observable behaviors.

Write goals in observable and quantifiable terms.

For students who are not disabled or who have mild disabilities, goals are needed only for each curriculum area. For very young students or those with severe disabilities, goals should be written in a number of *domains* of learning:

1. Cognitive
2. Communication
3. Motor
4. Social
5. Self-help
6. Vocational
7. Maladaptive behavior

Hypothetical long-term goals for Bill, a student with learning problems in math, and for Thom, a student with severe disabilities, are listed below.

Bill will

Arithmetic: Master basic computation facts at the first-grade level.

Social studies: Demonstrate knowledge of the functions of the three branches of the federal government.

Reading: Be able to identify relevant parts of a story he has read.

Science: Demonstrate knowledge of the structure of the solar system.

Language arts: Increase the creative expression of his oral language.

Physical education: Increase his skills in team sports.

Bill's regular classroom teacher will be responsible for setting all goals except the one in arithmetic. Bill will probably go to a part-time special education class (resource room) for arithmetic. Compare Bill's goals with Thom's.

Thom will

Cognitive: Categorize objects according to their function.

Communication: Demonstrate increased receptive understanding of functional labels.

Motor: Develop gross motor capability of his upper extremities.

Social: Learn to participate appropriately in group activities.

Vocational: Complete assembly tasks for a period of at least one hour.

Maladaptive behavior: Decrease out-of-seat behavior.

Self-help: Demonstrate the ability to dress himself independently.

The teacher must convert these broad goals into statements of instructional intent (behavioral objectives) for actual classroom use. A behavioral objective is not a restatement of a goal; instead it breaks a goal into instructional components. Because of the complexity of certain goals, a given goal may have more than one objective. A goal that states a student will learn to play cooperatively with other children, for example, may require individual objectives identifying the need to share with others, to take turns, and to follow the rules of the game.

Components of a Behavioral Objective

In order to communicate all of the intended information and provide a basis for evaluation, a complete behavioral objective should

1. Identify the learner.
2. Identify the target behavior.
3. Identify the conditions under which the behavior is to be displayed.
4. Identify criteria for acceptable performance.

Identify the Learner

Use the student's name.

Behavioral objectives were initially designed to promote individualization of instruction (Gagne, 1970). As part of the continuing effort to emphasize the process of individualization, in each objective statement the teacher must reidentify the specific student or students for whom the objective has been developed. Restatement reinforces the teacher's focus on the learner in question and communicates this focus to others who may become involved in the intervention program. Thus, we include in a behavioral objective statements such as

- John will . . .
- The fourth-graders will . . .
- The participants in the training program will . . .

Identify the Target Behavior

State what the student will do.

After pinpointing and goal setting have resulted in agreement on the deficient or excessive target behavior, the teacher must state what the student will be doing when the desired change has been achieved. This statement must identify a precise response that is representative of the target behavior.

There are three basic purposes for including this component in the behavioral objective:

1. It ensures that the teacher is consistently observing the same behavior. The observation and recording of the occurrence or nonoccurrence of exactly the same behavior allow for an accurate and consistent reflection of the behavior in the data to be collected.
2. The statement of the target behavior allows for confirmation by a third party that the change observed by the teacher has actually occurred.
3. The precise definition of the target behavior facilitates continuity of instruction when people other than the teacher are involved.

In order to achieve these three purposes, the target behavior must be described so that its occurrence is verifiable. Precise description will minimize differing interpretations of the same behavior. A student's performance of a given behavior can best be verified when the teacher is able to see or hear the behavior or to see or hear a direct product of the behavior. To attain this precision and clarity in an objective, the verb used to delineate the behavioral response should describe a behavior that is directly *observable*, *measurable*, and *repeatable*.

Though teachers of the gifted would like students to "discover" and art teachers would like students to "appreciate," objectives described in this manner are open to numerous interpretations. For example, it would be difficult for a third party to decide whether a student were performing the following behaviors:

- will *recognize* the difference between big and little
- will *understand* the value of coins
- will *develop* an appreciation of Chaucer
- will *remain* on-task during reading group

Using such broad terms, any individual who works with a student is, at best, inferring the existence of some behavior (guessing). These four descriptions would require yet another step to increase their specificity: the use of an **operational definition**. Operationally defining a vague term provides examples of what action(s) would confirm that the student is exhibiting the target behavior. In other words, the observer would look to the operational definition to determine the observable action(s) the student would perform to indicate he or she was "understanding" or "on-task." There is no one proper definition of a term like *on-task*. The definition for each student should be derived from the student's current behavior, the behavior the student should be engaged in, and the classroom setting. For example, Bryant and Budd (1982) recorded a student as on-task when she "engaged in motor task-related actions . . . or was looking at the teacher or task material during teacher's explanation" (p. 263). In contrast, Fielding and O'Leary (1979) recorded that students were on-task "when they worked on their assigned task for seven consecutive seconds" (p. 213).

The need for added explanation through an operational definition is reduced when the behavior analyst uses more precise verbs *in the objective*. Increased precision also promotes more accurate recording of data. A precise behavioral description such as "will circle," "will state orally," or "will point to" is less likely to be interpreted differently. With such a description, individuals can agree on whether an action did or did not take place without calling for a conference or lengthy written explanation. Here are some examples of precise behavioral descriptions:

- will point to the largest item in an array.
- will verbally count the equivalent in dimes.
- will write a translation of the prologue to *The Canterbury Tales*.
- will look at his book or the speaker.

One guide for selecting appropriate verbs has been offered by Deno and Jenkins (1967). Their classification of verbs is based on agreement of occurrence between independent classroom observers. They arrived at the three sets of verbs shown in Table 3–1, categorized as *directly observable action verbs*, *ambiguous action verbs*, and *not directly observable action verbs*.

TABLE 3-1
Observability classification of verbs.

Action Verbs That Are Directly Observable

to cover with a card	to draw	to place
to mark	to lever press	to cross out
to underline	to point to	to circle
to repeat orally	to walk	to say
to write	to count orally	to read orally
to shade	to put on	to name
to fill in	to number	to state
to remove	to label	to tell what

Ambiguous Action Verbs

to identify in writing	to check	to construct
to match	to take away	to make
to arrange	to finish	to read
to play	to locate	to connect
to give	to reject	to select
to choose	to subtract	to change
to use	to divide	to perform
to total	to add	to order
to measure	to regroup	to supply
to demonstrate	to group	to multiply
to round off	to average	to complete
to inquire	to utilize	to summarize
to acknowledge	to find	to borrow
to see	to convert	to identify

Action Verbs That Are Not Directly Observable

to distinguish	to be curious	to solve
to conclude	to apply	to deduce
to develop	to feel	to test
to concentrate	to determine	to perceive
to generate	to think	to create
to think critically	to discriminate	to learn
to recognize	to appreciate	to discover
to be aware	to become competent	to know
to infer	to wonder	to like
to realize fully	to analyze	to understand

Note: From "Evaluating preplanned curriculum objectives" by S. Deno and J. Jenkins (Philadelphia, Research for Better Schools, 1967). Reprinted by permission.

In addition to these verbs, which are appropriate for more general areas of instruction, individual discipline specialists may derive observable verbs specific to their needs and activities, as in these examples:

Fine Arts

blend, brush, carve, drill, fold, hammer, heat, melt, mix, paste, flour, roll, sand, saw, shake, sketch, trace, trim, varnish

Drama

clasp, cross, direct, display, enter, exit, move, pantomime, pass, perform, sit, start, turn

Laboratory Science

calibrate, connect, convert, dissect, feed, insert, lengthen, limit, manipulate, operate, plant, remove, (re)set, straighten, time, transfer, weigh

Language

abbreviate, accent, alphabetize, capitalize, define, edit, hyphenate, indent, print, pronounce, punctuate, recite, sign, spell, state, summarize, syllabicate, translate

Music

blow, bow, clap, compose, finger, harmonize, hum, mute, play, pluck, practice, sing, strum, tap, whistle

Physical Education

catch, climb, float, grasp, hit, jump, kick, lift, pitch, pull, push, run, skip, somersault, swim, swing, throw

In order to evaluate a description of a target behavior, Morris (1976) suggests using his IBSO (Is the Behavior Specific and Objective?) Test questions:

1. Can you count the number of times the behavior occurs in, for example, a 15-minute period, a one-hour period, or one day? Or, can you count the number of minutes it takes for the child to perform the behavior? That is, can you tell someone the behavior occurred "X" number of times or "X" number of minutes today? (Your answer should be yes.)

2. Will a stranger know exactly what to look for when you tell him/her the target behavior you are planning to modify? That is, can you actually see the child performing the behavior when it occurs? (Your answer should be yes.)

3. Can you break down the target behavior into smaller components, each of which is more specific and observable than the original target behavior? (Your answer should be no.) (p. 19)

Identify the Conditions of Intervention

Conditions are antecedent stimuli related to the target behavior.

The statement of conditions, the third component of a behavioral objective, is a description of the antecedent (behavior-preceding) stimuli in the presence of which the target behavior is expected to occur. This part of the objective affirms that the learning experience can be consistently reproduced.

The teacher may set the occasion for an appropriate response using any or all of several categories of antecedent stimuli:

1. Verbal requests or instructions

   Sam, point to the little car.

   Debbie, add these numbers.

   Jody, go back to your desk.

2. Written instructions or format

   Diagram these sentences.

   Find the products.

   Draw a line from each word to its definition.

3. Demonstration

   This is how you use litmus paper.

   This is how to operate . . .

4. Materials to be used

   A worksheet with 20 single-digit addition problems

   A tape recorder with the "play" button colored green and the "stop" button colored red

5. Environmental setting or timing

   In the vocational workshop

   In the cafeteria

   On the playground

   During independent study period

   During transition between classes

Providing appropriate antecedent stimuli will be discussed in Chapter 7.

6. Manner of assistance

   Independently

   With the aid of a number line

   With partial physical assistance from the teacher

   Receiving only verbal prompts

The teacher must be sure that the verbal or visual cue planned does in fact provide an opportunity for the desired response in the student. That is, a teacher should deliver an unambiguous request or instruction to the student. The teacher who holds a flashcard with the word *get* and says, "Give me a sentence for get," is likely to hear, "I for get my milk money," or "I for get my homework."

The materials described in the objective should ensure stimulus consistency for the learner and reduce the chance for inadvertent, subtle changes in the learning performance being requested. For example, presenting a red, a blue, and a green block and asking the student to "point to red" is a less complex task than presenting a red car, a blue sock, and a green cup and making the same request. Giving the student a page with written instructions to fill in the blanks in sentences is less complex when a list of words that includes the answers is provided. Asking the student to write a story based on a stimulus picture is different from asking the student to write a story without visual stimulus.

The following are examples of condition statement formats:

- Given an array of materials containing . . .
- Given a textbook containing 25 division problems with single-digit divisors . . .
- Given the manual sign for toilet . . .
- Given the use of a thesaurus and written instructions . . .
- Given a pullover sweater with the label cued red and the verbal cue . . .
- Given a ditto sheet with 20 problems containing improper fractions having unlike denominators and the written instruction to "Find the products" . . .
- Without the aid of . . .

Careful statement of the conditions under which the behavior is to be performed may prevent problems like the one encountered by Ms. Samuels in the vignette that follows.

Ms. Samuels Teaches Long Division

Ms. Samuels was once again in trouble with a regular classroom teacher. She and Mr. Watson, the sixth-grade math teacher, had agreed she would work on long division with Harvey. Ms. Samuels had carefully checked to be sure the method she taught Harvey to use in the resource room was the same as Mr. Watson's. She made dozens of practice worksheets, and Harvey worked long-division problems until he could do them in his sleep. Ms. Samuels was predictably horrified then when Mr. Watson asked her if she ever planned to start working on division with Harvey. Investigation revealed that in the regular classroom, Harvey was expected to copy the problems from the math book to notebook paper; and that he made so many copying errors, he seldom got the correct answer. The conditions under which the task was to be performed were thus significantly different.

As part of a plan of instruction for students with learning problems, teachers may need to include extra support in the form of supplementary cues, such as a model of a completed long-division problem for the student to keep at his desk. It is important to include a description of such supplementary cues in the condition component of the behavioral objective so that no misunderstanding will occur. When the cue is no longer needed, the objective may be rewritten.

Identify Criteria for Acceptable Performance

Criterion statements set minimum performance standards.

In the criterion statement included in a behavioral objective, the teacher sets the standard for minimally acceptable performance. This statement indicates the level of performance the student will be able to achieve as a result of the intervention. The performance itself has been defined; the criterion sets the standard for evaluation. Throughout the intervention process, this criterion is used to measure the effectiveness of the intervention strategy selected to meet the behavioral objective.

The basic criterion statement for initial learning or **acquisition** indicates the *accuracy* of a response or the response's *frequency of occurrence*. Such statements are written in terms of the number of correct responses, the student's accuracy on trial presentations, the percentage of accurate responses, or some performance within an error of limitation. Here are some sample criterion statements:

> *17 out of 20 correct responses.*
>
> *label all 10 objects correctly.*
>
> *with 80% accuracy.*
>
> *20 problems must be answered correctly (100% accuracy).*
>
> *four out of five trials correct.*
>
> *on five consecutive successful trials.*
>
> *complete all steps in the toilet training program independently.*
>
> *list all four of the main characters in a book report of no less than 250 words.*
>
> *with no more than five errors in spelling.*
>
> *on each occasion.*

See Chapter 4 for an extended discussion of duration and latency.

Two additional types of criteria may be included when time is a critical dimension of the behavior. *Duration* is a statement of the length of time the student performs the behavior. *Latency* is a statement of the length of time that elapses before the student begins performing the behavior.

- *Criterion statements addressing duration:*
  will complete within one hour.
  for at least 20 minutes.
  for no more than 1/2 hour.
  will return within 10 minutes.

within two weeks.

- *Statements addressing latency:*
  within 10 seconds after the flashcard is presented.

  within one minute after a verbal request.

Writing criterion statements in terms of percentage requires care. How many problems, for example, would a student have to solve correctly to satisfy a 90% criterion on a 5-item math quiz?

When setting criteria for acceptable performance, teachers must be careful to set goals that are sufficiently ambitious, yet reasonable. Selection should be based on the nature of the content, the abilities of the students, and the learning opportunities to be provided. The criterion should provide for the development of a functional skill. There is no sense in teaching a student to play a game only so well that he gets beaten every time he plays or in teaching a student to do math problems only well enough to earn a high F in the regular classroom. There is evidence (Fuchs, Fuchs, & Deno, 1988) that setting ambitious goals results in more learning, but teachers should not set unobtainable goals that will result in frustration for students.

Certain types of content require particular criterion levels. When a student is acquiring basic skills on which other skills will be built, a criterion of 90% may not be high enough. For example, learning "almost all" of the multiplication facts may result in a student's going through life never knowing what 8×7 is. There are other skills as well that require 100% accuracy. Remembering to look both ways before crossing the street only 90% of the time may result in premature termination of the opportunity for future learning!

For certain students, a disability may influence the force, direction, or duration of the criterion set by the teacher. For example, a student may not be able to hammer a nail all the way into a piece of wood; range-of-motion limitations may influence motor capability for reaching; hypotonic muscles (those with less-than-normal tone) may limit the duration of walking or sitting; or a spastic condition may limit the perfection of cursive handwriting.

In addition to considering the number or percentage correct and the accuracy of response, writers of behavioral objectives must also determine the number of times a student must meet a criterion to demonstrate mastery. For example, how often must Jane perform a behavior successfully on 8 out of 10 trials before the teacher will be convinced of mastery and allow her to move on to the next level of learning or to the next behavioral objective?

It may be inferred from an open-ended criterion statement that the first time a student reaches 85% accuracy, the skill will be considered "learned" or that from now until the end of the school year, the teacher will continually test and retest to substantiate the 85% accuracy. Either inference could be false. Therefore, a statement such as one of the following should be included in the behavioral objective to provide a point of closure and terminal review:

85% accuracy for four consecutive sessions.

85% accuracy for three out of four days.

on 8 out of 10 trials for three consecutive teaching sessions.

will return within 10 minutes on three consecutive trips to the bathroom.

FORMAT FOR A BEHAVIORAL OBJECTIVE

A management aid for the teacher in writing behavioral objectives is the adoption of a standard format. A consistent format helps the teacher include all the components necessary for communicating all intended information. No single format is necessarily superior to others; a teacher should simply find one that is compatible with his or her writing style. Here are two such formats:

Format 1

Conditions: Given 20 flash cards with preprimer sight words and the instruction "Read these words,"

Student: Sam

Behavior: will read the words orally

Criterion: within two seconds for each word with 90% accuracy on three consecutive trials.

Format 2

Student: Marvin

Behavior: will write in cursive handwriting 20 fourth-grade spelling words

Conditions: from dictation by the resource teacher

Criterion: with no more than two errors for 3 consecutive weeks.

The following behavioral objectives may be derived from the educational goals previously set for students Bill and Thom:

Arithmetic

See page 74 for Bill's and Thom's long-term goals.

Goal: Bill will master basic computation facts at the first-grade level.

Objective: Given a worksheet of 20 single-digit addition problems in the form $6 + 2$ and the written instruction "Find the sums," Bill will complete all problems with 90% accuracy for three consecutive math sessions.

Social Studies

Goal: Bill will demonstrate knowledge of the functions of the three branches of the federal government.

Objective: After reading pages 23–26 in the text *Our American Heritage*, Bill will list the 10-step sequential process by which a bill becomes a law. This list will have no more than one error of sequence and one error of omission. This will be successfully accomplished on an in-class exercise and on the unit-end test.

Reading

Goal: Bill will be able to identify relevant parts of a story he has read.

Objective: Given the short story "The Necklace," Bill will write a minimum 200-word paper that (1) lists all the main characters and (2) lists the sequence of main actions, with no more than two errors.

Science

Goal: Bill will demonstrate knowledge of the structure of the solar system.

Objective: Given a map of the solar system, Bill will label each planet in its proper position from the sun with 100% accuracy on two consecutive sessions.

Language Arts

Goal: Bill will increase the creative expression of his oral language.

Objective: Given an array of photos of people, objects, and locations, Bill will tell a 5-minute story to the class that makes use of a minimum of seven items, on three out of five days.

Physical Education

Goal: Bill will increase his skills in team sports.

Objective: Given a basketball, Bill will throw the ball into the hoop from a distance of 10 feet, 8 out of 10 trials for four consecutive gym classes.

Recall from our earlier discussion that although Bill has mild learning problems, Thom has much more severe disabilities. Here are some objectives and corresponding goals for Thom:

Cognitive

Goal: Thom will be able to categorize objects according to their function.

Objective: Given 12 Peabody cards (4 foods, 4 clothing, 4 grooming aids), a sample stimulus card of each category, and the verbal cue "Where does this one go?", Thom will place the cards on the appropriate category pile with 100% accuracy, for 17 out of 20 trials.

Communication

Goal: Thom will demonstrate increased receptive understanding of functional labels.

Objective: Given an array of three objects found in his environment (cup, spoon, dish) and the verbal cue "Give me the . . . ," Thom will hand the teacher the named object 9 out of 10 times for four consecutive sessions.

Motor

Goal: Thom will develop gross motor capability of his upper extremities.

Objective: Given a soft rubber ball suspended from the ceiling and the verbal cue "Hit the ball," Thom will hit the ball causing movement 10 out of 10 times for five consecutive days.

Social

Goal: Thom will learn to participate appropriately in group activities.

Objective: When sitting with the teacher and two other students during story time, Thom will make an appropriate motor or verbal response to each of the teacher's questions when called upon a minimum of three times in a 10-minute period for five consecutive days.

Self-help

Goal: Thom will demonstrate the ability to dress himself independently.

Objective: Given a pullover sweater with the back label color-cued red and the verbal cue "Put on your sweater," Thom will successfully complete all steps of the task without physical assistance 2 out of 3 trials for four consecutive days.

Vocational

Goal: Thom will complete assembly tasks for a period of at least one hour.

Objective: Given the four parts of a plumbing "U" in sequential order, Thom will assemble at a rate of one per 3 minutes without error during three vocational periods for 4 weeks.

Maladaptive Behavior

Goal: Thom will decrease out-of-seat behavior.

Objective: Given the period from 9:00 to 9:20 A.M. (functional academics), Thom will remain in his seat, unless given permission by the teacher to leave, for five consecutive days.

Professor Grundy's Class Writes Behavioral Objectives

It was the time of the semester for Professor Grundy's 8 o'clock class to learn about behavioral objectives. After presenting a carefully planned lecture (remarkably similar to the first part of this chapter), Grundy asked if there were any questions. Dawn Tompkins stopped filing her nails long enough to ask, with a deep sigh, "Yes, Professor, would you please tell me what a behavioral objective is, exactly?"

"I was under the impression, young lady, that I had done just that," replied Grundy. "Is anyone else confused?"

A chorus of muttering and rumbling ensued from which Grundy was able to extract clearly only two questions.

"Is this covered in the book?" and "Will it be on the test?"

After once more presenting a drastically abbreviated description of the components of a behavioral objective, Grundy announced that each member of the class was to write a behavioral objective for the curriculum area of science and present it to him for checking before leaving class. This announcement, followed by a chorus of groans and considerable paper shuffling, also brought forth a flurry of hands:

"You mean list the components?"

"No," said Grundy, "Write an objective."

"You mean define a behavioral objective?"

"No," said Grundy, "Write one."

"But you never *said* anything about writing them."

"What," Grundy retorted, "did you think was the purpose of the lecture?"

After everyone who lacked these tools had been provided with paper and pencil, silence descended upon the class. DeWayne was the first one finished and proudly presented his objective to the professor:

To understand the importance of the digestive system.

"Well, DeWayne," said the professor, "that's a start, but do you not remember that a behavioral objective must talk about *behavior*? Remember the list of verbs I gave you . . ." When DeWayne continued to look blank, Grundy rifled through his briefcase and found a copy. (See Table 3–1.)

"Look here," the professor said, "use one of these directly observable verbs." DeWayne returned some time later with his rewritten objective:

To label the parts of the digestive system.

"Good, DeWayne," sighed the professor, "that's a behavior, all right. Now, do you recall the components of a behavioral objective?" Once again, DeWayne looked blank. Grundy carefully wrote:

Conditions   Student Behavior   Criteria

across the top of the gasoline credit card receipt DeWayne had evidently found in his wallet. DeWayne returned to his desk.

An hour and a half later, as Grundy was regretting ever having made this assignment, DeWayne returned again:

Given an unlabeled diagram of the human digestive system, 4th-grade students will label the major parts of the digestive system (mouth, esophagus, stomach, small intestine, large intestine) with no errors.

Grundy read DeWayne's objective with interest, because his own digestive system was beginning to be the major focus of his attention. "Excellent, DeWayne," said the professor, "I suppose it's too late to get lunch in the cafeteria. Why didn't you do this in the first place?"

"Well, Professor," answered DeWayne, "I didn't really understand what you wanted. I'm still not sure I could do another one."

After getting some crackers from the vending machine, Grundy returned meditatively to his office. He found a piece of paper and began to write as he munched:

Given a worksheet listing appropriate verbs and the components of a behavioral objective, students enrolled in Education 411 will write five behavioral objectives including all components.

"Do you have any idea what his objective for this class is?"

After musing for a few minutes, he added:

. . . in less than half an hour.

"Perhaps," Grundy muttered to himself, "if I had been sure what I wanted and told the students at the front end, they would have had less trouble figuring it out."

EXPANDING THE SCOPE OF THE BASIC BEHAVIORAL OBJECTIVE

Earlier discussion in this chapter outlined the process of developing a standard behavioral objective for acquiring a new behavior. In this process, the teacher describes a behavior that had not previously been in the student's repertoire. Mastery of such a behavior is admirable, but the teacher has yet to provide the student with a functional response; that is, one that can be used outside the confines established in the objective as written. The student has demonstrated the behavior only under controlled conditions. Many teachers select new target behaviors as soon as this degree of mastery is demonstrated. Moving on to a new objective at this point is often inappropriate and may interfere with or halt learning at a critical stage. Before replacing one objective with the next one in the learning sequence, the teacher should *ensure the student's functional use of the behavior.* Two possible perspectives on expanded use are

1. Programming according to a hierarchy of response competence
2. Programming according to a hierarchy of levels of learning

Hierarchy of Response Competence

A measure of response accuracy (8 out of 10 correct, for example) is only one dimension for evaluating performance. It represents the acquisition level of response competence. At this level, we merely verify the presence of the ability to do something the student wasn't previously able to do and the ability to do it with some degree of accuracy. Moving to measures of competence in performance beyond accuracy, beyond this acquisition level, requires alterations or additions to the statements of criteria and conditions. Such alterations reflect a hierarchy of response competence. Once a child can perform the behavior, we are then concerned with fluency, or rate, of performance, as well as performance under conditions other than those imposed during the initial teaching process.

A response hierarchy should contain the following minimum levels:

As an example of the use of this hierarchy, let us assume John has reached the acquisition level on the following objective:

> Given one quarter, two dimes, two nickels, and one penny and the verbal cue "John, give me your bus fare," he will hand the teacher coins equaling 35 cents 8 out of 10 trials for three consecutive sessions;

and that Lauren has reached acquisition on this objective:

> Given a worksheet with 20 division problems with two-digit dividends and single-digit divisors, Lauren will write the correct answer in the appropriate place on the radical with 90% accuracy for four consecutive days.

After John and Lauren have met these stated criteria for their performances, the teaching concern should turn to their fluency of performance, or the rate at which they perform the behavior. **Fluency** refers to the appropriateness of the rate at which the student is accurately performing this newly acquired response. In John's case, we know that he can select the appropriate coins to make 35 cents, but this does him little good if when we take him to the bus, it takes him five minutes to do it. The bus driver cannot wait this long. In Lauren's case, we know she can now solve division problems, but it takes her so long that either we interrupt her when her reading group is scheduled or she misses part of her reading lesson so she can finish her problems.

In both instances, the students are demonstrating accurate performance at an inappropriate rate. Recognizing the necessity for an appropriate rate of performance, a teacher can indicate an acceptable fluency when the behavioral objective is written. This is accomplished by adding a time limit to the statement of criteria, as found in parentheses, in the following objectives:

> Given one quarter, two dimes, two nickels, and one penny and the verbal cue "John, give me your bus fare," he will hand the teacher coins equaling 35 cents (within 30 seconds) 8 out of 10 trials for three consecutive sessions.

> Given a worksheet with 20 division problems with two-digit dividends and single-digit divisors, Lauren will write the correct answer in the appropriate place on the radical (within 20 minutes) with 90% accuracy for four consecutive days.

In cases of typical or high-functioning learners, the rate is often included in the initial objective, thus combining acquisition and fluency in a single instructional procedure.

Programming for maintenance will be discussed in Chapter 12.

It is not necessary to adjust the original behavioral objective to include the level of competence labeled *maintenance*. **Maintenance** is the ability to perform a response over time without reteaching. Maintenance-level competence is confirmed through the use of postchecks or probes, during which the teacher rechecks the skill to be sure the student can still do it. Maintenance may be promoted through building in the opportunity for overlearning trials and distributed practice (Biehler, 1974; Denny, 1966; Gruenenfelder & Borkowski, 1975). *Overlearning* refers to repeated practice after an objective has been initially accomplished. An optimum number of overlearning opportunities is approximately 50% of the number of trials required for acquisition of the behavior. If it takes John 10 teaching sessions to learn to tie his shoes, we should ideally provide 5 additional sessions for overlearning. *Distributed practice* is practice that is spread out over time (as opposed

Distributed practice is a more efficient way of learning for long-term maintenance.

to *massed practice*, which is compressed in time). An example of massed practice familiar to college students is cramming for an exam. The material may be learned between 10 P.M. and 6 A.M. the night before the test, but most of it will be rapidly forgotten. If maintenance is desired, the preferable approach is studying for short periods every evening for several weeks before the exam, using distributed practice. Another means of providing for maintenance, alteration of schedules of reinforcement (Skinner, 1968), will be discussed in Chapter 6.

The level of response competence labeled **generalization** is of great importance in assuring that a behavior is functional. A student has a generalized response if she can perform, and adapt if necessary, the behavior under conditions different from those in place during acquisition. An acquired response may be generalized across at least four basic dimensions. The condition statement may be written to reflect the student's ability to perform the behavior in response to various verbal or written instructions, with various materials, for or with various persons, and in various environments (settings). The following examples illustrate this point.

Various Instructions

Given an array of coins and the verbal instruction, "Give me bus fare" ("Give me 75 cents," "Give me what you need for the bus") . . .

Given a worksheet with 30 one-digit subtraction problems and the verbal (or written) instruction, "Find the difference" ("Solve these problems," "Write the answers to these problems") . . .

Various Materials

Will write his name, address, phone number, and birth date in the appropriate blanks on at least three different job application forms . . .

Will demonstrate the multiplicative principle of math using counting chips (a number line, paper and pencil) . . .

Various Persons

Will use the sign for "toilet" as a signal of need to her teacher (parent) . . .

Will comply with instructions from his math (English, social studies, science) teacher (mother, father, coach, piano teacher) . . .

Various Settings

Will pull up his pants after toileting in the restroom in the special class (in the restroom near the class he joins for art) . . .

Will remain in his seat and complete assignments in math (English, social studies, science) class . . .

Hierarchy of Levels of Learning

It may seem that writing behavioral objectives inevitably focuses teacher attention on very concrete, simple forms of learning. Indeed, this has been one of the most frequent criticisms of a behavioral approach. It is not necessary, however, to confine behavioral objectives to lower levels of learning. Bloom (1956) has proposed hierarchies of learning in cognitive, affective, and psychomotor areas. These hierarchies classify possible learning outcomes in terms of increasingly abstract levels. They are helpful in writing objectives in behavioral terms because they suggest observable, measurable behaviors that may occur as the result of both simple and complex learning. The cognitive hierarchy, which will serve as our example, contains six levels of learning, as shown in the following diagram (Bloom, 1956).

Many behavioral objectives are written in terms of the knowledge level of the hierarchy—we simply want students to demonstrate they know or remember something we have taught them. Once the student has achieved mastery on the lowest of the six levels, the teacher can shift programming toward higher levels of learning by preparing subsequent objectives that alter the target behavior and criterion statements. As an aid in this process, Gronlund (1985) prepared a table that illustrates behavioral terms appropriate to describe target behaviors at each level of learning. (See Table 3–2.)

Knowledge

Bloom (1956) defines learning at the *knowledge level* as the recall or recognition of information ranging from specific facts to complete theories. These memory functions are the only behavior to be demonstrated at this basic level of cognitive learning. The following acquisition objectives are examples written for students at this level:

After reading *Biology for Your Understanding* and completing the exercise in Chapter 2, Virginia will list the biological categories of the Linnaean system, in their order of evolutional complexity, without error during two class sessions and on a unit-end exam.

Given the symbols for the arithmetic processes of addition, subtraction, multiplication, and division, Danny will respond with 90% accuracy on a multiple-choice test of their labels and basic functions.

Given a list of Shakespearean plays, Deborah will underline the names of the tragedies with no more than one error.

TABLE 3–2
Examples of general instructional objectives and behavioral terms for the cognitive domain of the taxonomy.

Illustrative General Instructional Objectives	Illustrative Behavioral Terms for Stating Specific Learning Outcomes
Knows common terms Knows specific facts Knows methods and procedures Knows basic concepts Knows principles	Defines, describes, identifies, labels, lists, matches, names, outlines, reproduces, selects, states
Understands facts and principles Interprets verbal material Interprets charts and graphs Translates verbal material to mathematical formulas Estimates future consequences implied in data Justifies methods and procedures	Converts, defends, distinguishes, estimates, explains, extends, generalizes, gives examples, infers, paraphrases, predicts, rewrites, summarizes
Applies concepts and principles to new situations Applies laws and theories to practical situations Solves mathematical problems Constructs charts and graphs Demonstrates correct usage of a method or procedure	Changes, computes, demonstrates, discovers, manipulates, modifies, operates, predicts, prepares, produces, relates, shows, solves, uses

Comprehension

Once the student has reached the performance criterion at the knowledge level, the teacher moves to the *comprehension level*, the understanding of meaning. The student may demonstrate comprehension by paraphrasing and providing examples. Here are some sample objectives at this level:

Given the Linnaean system of biological classification, Virginia will provide a written description of an organism in each category. The description will include at least one factor that distinguishes the category from others.

Given a worksheet of 40 basic arithmetic examples requiring addition, subtraction, multiplication, and division, Danny will complete the sheet with 90% accuracy.

Illustrative General Instructional Objectives	Illustrative Behavioral Terms for Stating Specific Learning Outcomes
Recognizes unstated assumptions Recognizes logical fallacies in reasoning Distinguishes between facts and inferences Evaluates the relevancy of data Analyzes the organizational structure of a work (art, music, writing)	Breaks down, diagrams, differentiates, discriminates, distinguishes, identifies, illustrates, infers, outlines, points out, relates, selects, separates, subdivides
Writes a well-organized theme Gives a well-organized speech Writes a creative short story (or poem, or music) Proposes a plan for an experiment Integrates learning from different areas into a plan for solving a problem Formulates a new scheme for classifying objects (or events, or ideas)	Categorizes, combines, compiles, composes, creates, devises, designs, explains, generates, modifies, organizes, plans, rearranges, reconstructs, relates, reorganizes, revises, rewrites, summarizes, tells, writes
Judges the logical consistency of written material Judges the adequacy with which conclusions are supported by data Judges the value of a work (art, music, writing) by use of internal criteria Judges the value of a work (art, music, writing) by use of external standards of excellence	Appraises, compares, concludes, contrasts, criticizes, describes, discriminates, explains, justifies, interprets, relates, summarizes, supports

Note: Reprinted with permission of Macmillan Publishing Co., Inc., from Stating objectives for classroom instruction by Norman E. Gronlund. Copyright ©1985. Norman E. Gronlund.

Given the metaphoric passage, "Oh that this too, too solid flesh would melt . . ." from *Hamlet*, Deborah will write an essay describing the literal intent of the passage. The essay will be a minimum of 300 words.

Application

Programming at Bloom's *application level* requires the student to use the method, concept, or theory in various concrete situations. Consider these objectives:

Given the names of five organisms and the Linnaean system, Virginia will place each in its proper category and write a list of rationales for placement. Each rationale will contain a minimum of two reasons for placement.

Given a set of 10 paragraphs that present problems requiring an arithmetic computation for solution, Danny will write the correct answer, showing all computations with 100% accuracy.

After reading *Hamlet*, Deborah will be able to explain the parallels between Hamlet's ethical dilemma and the problem of abortion and to cite an additional current parallel example of her own choosing.

Analysis

Analysis is the ability to break down material into its constituent parts in order to identify these parts, discuss their interrelationship, and understand their organization as a whole. The following objectives are analytically oriented:

Given a list of five organisms, Virginia will use appropriate references in the library to investigate and report to the class the role of the organisms in either the food chain or in the ecological stability of their habitat.

Given a written statement of the associative property, Danny will be able to explain accurately to the class, using examples at the chalkboard, the property's relation to the basic additive and multiplicative functions.

After having read *Hamlet* or *Macbeth*, Deborah will guide the class in a discussion of the play's plot development. This discussion will be based upon a schematic representation of each scene that she will provide in written form.

Synthesis

At the cognitive level of *synthesis*, the student should demonstrate the ability to bring parts together resulting in a different, original, or creative whole:

Given a list of reference texts, Virginia will write a 1,000-word summary explaining the biological classifications in Darwin's theory of evolution. The paper will be evaluated on the basis of accuracy, completeness, organization, and clarity.

Given the numerical systems of base 10 and base 2, Danny will orally demonstrate the use of the functions of addition, subtraction, multiplication, and division within each system.

Given the study of the Shakespearean tragedy *Macbeth*, Deborah will rewrite the end of the play in iambic pentameter, assuming that the murder of the king was unsuccessful.

Evaluation

The highest level of learning demonstrated in this hierarchy is *evaluation*. The student is asked to make a judgment of value:

Based on the principles of mutual exclusion, Virginia will devise a taxonomy for the classification of means of transportation and provide a justification for the categories created and their constituent parts.

Given a set of unknown values and a given arithmetic computational function, Danny will explain the probability of differing answers that may be correct.

Given plays by Shakespeare and Bacon, Deborah will state a preference for one and justify her preference in a 500-word essay based on some element(s) of style.

Learning Levels for the Limited Learner

In most instances of planning for expanded instructional intent, we tend to focus on a hierarchy-of-response competence for the more limited learner and a hierarchy of levels of learning for the typical or above-average learner. This dichotomy is not necessarily warranted simply by the level of the student's functioning. Consider the following examples of how we may write behavioral objectives for the limited learner in conjunction with levels of learning:

Knowledge:	Given a common coin and the verbal cue, "What is the name of this," George will state the appropriate label on 18 out of 20 trials for five consecutive sessions.
Comprehension:	Given a common coin and the verbal cue "What is this worth," George will count out the coin's equivalent in pennies and state something to the effect that "A dime is worth 10 pennies" on 8 out of 10 trials for each coin.
Application:	When presented with 10 pictures of food items, each with its cost written on it, George will count out coins equal to the amount written upon the verbal cue "Show me the amount" on 18 out of 20 trials.
Analysis:	When presented with pictures of items each with its cost printed on it, a $1 bill, and a verbal cue such as "Can you buy a pencil and a newspaper?" George will respond correctly on 18 out of 20 trials.
Synthesis:	Given a $1 bill and the instruction to buy various priced items, George will simulate the buying exchange and decide whether he was given correct change without error on 10 trials.
Evaluation:	Given a $1 bill and a 5-mile ride from the sheltered workshop to his home, George will use the $1 for the bus ride rather than a candy bar.

Even learners with limitations can acquire higher-level cognitive skills.

BEHAVIORAL OBJECTIVES AND THE IEP

IDEA requires an IEP for every student with a disability.

The development of educational goals (long-term objectives) and behavioral objectives (short-term objectives) for students in need of special education services was included as one of the mandates of the Education for All Handicapped Children Act of 1975 (P.L. 94–142) and its successor, the Individuals with Disabilities Education Act of 1990 (P.L. 101-476, IDEA). Among the results of this legislation have been the formalization of the planning aspects inherent in the writing of goals and objectives and the provision for active parental participation in the educational planning process for their child. This planning process ultimately results in the development of an Individualized Education Program (IEP).

The rules and regulations require five elements to appear as part of the IEP:

The individualized education program for each child must include:
1. A statement of the child's present levels of educational performance;
2. A statement of annual goals, including short-term instructional objectives;
3. A statement of the specific special education and related services to be provided to the child, and the extent to which the child will be able to participate in regular education programs;
4. The projected dates for initiation of services and the anticipated duration of the services; and
5. Appropriate objective criteria and evaluation procedures and schedules for determining, on at least an annual basis, whether the short-term instructional objectives are being achieved.

This excerpt shows the parallel in procedural format between the development of behavioral objectives and the content of the IEP adopted by the legislative authors. Both processes include the accumulation of data to determine the student's current levels of functioning, the development of behavioral objectives (short-term objectives) for attaining the goals, and the review of objective mastery.

On the sample form (see Figure 3–1), the components that state the target behavior and the conditions are placed in the column labeled *Short-term instructional objectives*. The component that states the criteria for mastery is placed in the correspondingly labeled column. Because each IEP is developed for an individual student, the student's identity need not be restated for each objective on the form.

The following behavioral objective has been transferred onto the sample form in Figure 3–1:

Given a worksheet of 20 single-digit addition problems in the form $6 + 2$ and the written instruction, "Find the sums," Bill will complete all problems with 90% accuracy for three consecutive math sessions.

In order to manage an IEP and monitor its constituent objectives, teachers should observe the following recommendations:

Student: _____	Person to provide service to: _____			
Short-Term Instructional Objectives	Person Responsible	Criteria for Mastery	Date Reviewed	Mastery Yes No
1. Complete single-digit addition problems in the form 6 + 2 given written instructions to "find the sum."		90% accuracy for 3 consecutive math sessions.		

FIGURE 3–1
Sample IEP.

When Bill's math skills are at grade level, he no longer has a disability.

Thom's objectives should be reviewed frequently so that he will make the maximum possible progress.

1. Short-term objectives should be sequentially related to goal statements (long-term objectives).

2. In the case of students with mild disabilities, the short-term objective should deal directly with the reason for their referral for special education services.

3. For students with moderate and severe disabilities, two or three short-term objectives per learning domain should be placed on the IEP.

4. New short-term objectives should not be added until maintenance has been achieved on current objectives and generalization instruction has begun. Once the planned generalizations have been reached, the objective may be removed from the IEP.

5. Management of the IEP should be a continuing process. Teachers and administrators should not overlook the regulations stating that a review should be conducted "on at least an annual basis," not "only on an annual basis." The annual review should include the full committee.

   a. The objectives for students with mild disabilities should be reviewed as soon as achievement has been verified to assess whether or not the original need for special education services still exists.

   b. Reasonable review dates should be set for objectives of students with moderate and severe disabilities. As objectives are met, the teacher should add new short-term objectives and notify the committee chairperson and parent(s) in writing, with full data justification made at the annual review. Such a procedure will foster the student's progress, while prohibiting stagnation of instruction until the full committee can be gathered.

6. Review dates should be set bearing in mind the need for instruction at the higher levels of learning in order to promote full functional use of the skill.

7. If personnel other than the special education teacher (such as the physical therapist, speech pathologist, or regular class teacher) take part in the instruction of a particular objective, each individual's name and signature should appear on the IEP along with that of the teacher.

SUMMARY

In this chapter, we described the process of writing behavioral objectives and the relationship between such objectives and the IEP required for students with disabilities. This process is an integral part of any program for behavior change, whether the program is directed toward academic or social behavior. A program for changing behavior is unlikely to be successful unless we are sure what constitutes success. Behavioral objectives facilitate communication, so that everyone knows the goal of instruction. They also provide for evaluation, so that everyone knows whether the goal has been reached.

DISCUSSION QUESTIONS

1. Most teachers are required to write objectives as a part of lesson planning or in IEPs. Many teachers consider writing objectives as unnecessary paperwork. Does the time taken to write objectives improve instruction or are those teachers right?

2. What is the significance of a criterion statement? For what kinds of objectives are criterion statements more or less important?

3. Should teachers of students with disabilities be required to write daily objectives as well as IEPs? Why or why not?

REFERENCES

Bayley, N. 1984. *Bayley scales of infant development*. New York: The Psychological Corporation.

Benderesky, M. (Ed.) 1978, *Uniform performance assessment system*. Seattle: University of Washington.

Biehler, R.F. 1974. *Psychology applied to teaching*. Boston: Houghton Mifflin.

Bloom, B.S. (Ed.). 1956. *Taxonomy of educational objectives handbook I: Cognitive domain*. New York: David McKay.

Brigance, A. 1977. *Inventory of basic skills*. Newton, Mass.: Curriculum Associates.

Bryant, L., & Budd, K. 1982 Self-instructional training to increase independent work performance in preschoolers. *Journal of Applied Behavior Analysis, 15*, 259–271.

Connolly, A. 1988. *KeyMath Diagnostic Arithmetic Test. Revised*. Circle Pines, Minn.: American Guidance Service.

Denny, M.R. 1966. A theoretical analysis and its application to training the mentally retarded. In N. R. Ellis (Ed.), *International review of research in mental retardation* (vol. 2). New York: Academic Press.

Deno, S., & Jenkins, J. 1967. *Evaluating preplanning curriculum objectives*. Philadelphia: Research for Better Schools.

Fielding, C., & O'Leary, K. 1979. Effects of self-instructional training on second- and third-grade hyperactive children: A failure to replicate. *Journal of Applied Behavior Analysis, 12*, 211–219.

Fuchs, L., Deno, S.L., & Mirkin, P.K., 1984. The effects of frequent curriculum-based measurement and evaluation on pedagogy, student achievement, and student awareness of learning. *American Educational Research Journal, 21*, 449–460.

Fuchs, L., Fuchs, D., & Deno, S. 1988. Importance of goal ambitiousness and goal mastery to student achievement. *Exceptional Children, 52*, 63–71.

Gagne, R. 1970. *The conditions of learning*. New York: Holt, Rinehart & Winston.

Gronlund, N. 1985. *Stating objectives for classroom instruction*. New York: Macmillan.

Gruenenfelder, T., & Borkowski, J. 1975. Transfer of cumulative rehearsal strategies in children's short-term memory. *Child Development, 46*, 1019–1024.

Jastak, K., & Wilkinson, G. 1984. *Wide Range Achievement Test—Revised*. Wilmington, Del.: Jastak Assessment Systems.

Lambert, N.M., Windmiller, M., Tharinger, D., & Cole, L. (1981). *AAMD adaptive behavior scale—school edition*. Monterey, Calif.: CTB Macmillan/McGraw Hill.

Mager, R. 1962. *Preparing instructional objectives*. Palo Alto, Calif.: Fearon Publishers.

Morris, R. 1976. *Behavior modification with children*. Cambridge, Mass.: Winthrop Publications.

Quay, H.C., & Peterson, D.R. 1975. *Manual for the behavior problem checklist*. Champaign, Ill.: Children's Research Center, University of Illinois.

Santa Cruz County. 1973. *Behavioral characteristics progression*. The Office of the Santa Cruz County Superintendent of Schools. Palo Alto, Calif.: Vort Corporation.

Skinner, B.F. 1968. *The technology of teaching*. New York: Appleton-Century-Crofts.

Sparrow, S.S., Balla, D.A., & Ciccetti, O.V. 1984. *Vineland adaptive behavior scales*. Circle Pines, Minn.: American Guidance Service.

Wechsler, D. 1991. *The Wechsler Intelligence Scale for children*, 3rd ed. New York: The Psychological Corporation.

Woodcock, R. 1987. *Woodcock Reading Mastery Tests—Revised*. Circle Pines, Minn.: American Guidance Service.

4

Collecting and Graphing Data

Teachers react strongly to suggestions that they collect data in their classrooms:

- "I don't have time to write down everything anyone does."
- "I just don't think I can manage shuffling all those sheets of paper, handling stopwatches, wrist counters, giving proper cues. When am I supposed to concentrate on teaching?"
- "This data collection adds an extra hour a day, at least, in summarizing the data, putting the data on graphs, and so on. Where's that time supposed to come from?"
- "Give me a break."

Most teachers regard the kind of data collection procedures that we shall discuss in this chapter with the same enthusiasm they reserve for statistics. In some cases, their comments are thoroughly justified. Some of the systems we are going to discuss are not practical for everyday classroom use. Classroom teachers may never use some of the more complex systems. Understanding how these systems work, however, helps in understanding the research published in this area. That teachers read research and attempt to apply it in their classrooms is a fond belief we are unwilling to abandon. This chapter does describe, then, the most common systems and shows how many of them can be adapted for classroom use. Because these systems require collecting and graphing data, the chapter focuses on both tasks.

A RATIONALE

Even after accepting the feasibility of data collection in the classroom, many teachers see very little value in it. Beyond recording grades on tests, most teachers have traditionally kept very few records of their students' academic and social behaviors. There are, nevertheless, two excellent reasons for collecting classroom data. The first is that precise observation and measurement of behavior may enable teachers to determine the best way to change it. The second is that observation and measurement enable very accurate determination of a particular intervention's effect.

By writing behavioral objectives, teachers communicate their intent to change particular behaviors. They also state the criteria they will use to judge whether change procedures have been successful. In many classroom situations, the intervention's effect on the students' original level of performance would be evaluated by administering a pretest and posttest. However, the precision desired within a behavioral approach to instruction and in program evaluation necessitates additional data.

Behavioral evaluation requires observation of students' current functioning and ongoing progress.

Behavioral evaluation has two requirements. First, a detailed observation of a student's current functioning is needed. This observation should reflect the conditions and description of the behavior stated in the objective. For example, a behavioral objective stating that students should solve 25 long-division problems in 30 minutes requires that the teacher determine how many long-division problems the students can already solve in 30 minutes. Second, evaluation of an instructional program must facilitate ongoing monitoring of the teaching/learning process as well as provide a system for terminal evaluation. Thus, evaluation must be continuous so that programs can be adjusted as instruction progresses. As the students in our example receive instruction in long division, for instance, the teacher could record daily how many problems they could solve in 30 minutes, thus providing continuous evaluation. The monitoring process can provide guidelines for continuing or altering the application of instructional techniques and help avoid false assumptions about student progress. Such false assumptions are unfortunately very common, as illustrated by the following vignette.

Ms. Waller Goes Electronic

Ms. Waller was ecstatic. After months of complaining that she had no materials to use to teach reading to her most challenging reading group, she had received a computerized teaching machine. The salesman proudly demonstrated the machine and pointed out the features that justified the hundreds of dollars invested.

"All you have to do," he assured her, "is hook the little, er, students up to these here headphones, drop in a cassette, and turn this baby on. Everything else is taken care of . . . you don't do a thing."

Ms. Waller briskly administered the pretest included in the materials, scheduled each student for 15 minutes a day on the machine, and assumed that her worries were over.

At the end of the school year, Ms. Waller administered the posttest. Imagine her distress when, although several members of the group had made remarkable progress, some students had made none at all.

"I don't understand," she wailed. "The machine was supposed to do everything. How was I supposed to know it wasn't working?"

"Perhaps," suggested her principal kindly, as he wished her success in her career as an encyclopedia salesperson, "you should have checked before now."

CHOOSING A SYSTEM

Dimensions for observation of behavior

The first step in the evaluation of ongoing measurement of behavior is the selection of a system of data collection. The characteristics of the system selected must be appropriate to the behavior being observed and to the kind of behavior change desired.

Behavior may be measured and changed on a number of dimensions (White & Haring, 1980):

1. *Rate.* When frequency data are expressed in a ratio with time, we have a measure of rate.

   John made seven trips per hour to the bathroom.

   Harold did 11 math problems per minute.

   Marvin had eight tantrums per week.

2. *Duration.* When we describe how long a behavior lasts, we are measuring duration.

   John stayed in the bathroom for 30 minutes.

   Harold worked on his math for 20 minutes.

   Marvin's tantrum lasted for 65 minutes.

3. *Latency.* A measure of how long it takes a student to start performing a behavior is a measure of latency.

   After I told John to come out of the bathroom, it took him 5 minutes to appear at the door.

After the teacher said, "Get to work," Harold stared into space for 5 minutes before he started his math.

It took 20 minutes for Marvin to stop having a tantrum after I put him in the time-out room.

4. *Topography.* Topography refers to the "shape" of the behavior—what it looks like.

Harold writes all the 4's backward on his math paper.

Marvin screams, kicks his heels on the floor, and pulls his hair during a tantrum.

5. *Force.* When we are concerned with how strongly (loudly, for example) a behavior is performed, we measure force.

Harold writes so heavily that he makes holes in his math paper.

Marvin screams so loudly that the teacher three doors down the hall can hear him.

6. *Locus.* A concern with where a behavior occurs is described as locus.

I refused to let John go to the bathroom, so he wet his pants.

Harold wrote the answers to his math problems in the wrong spaces.

Marvin had a tantrum in the lunchroom.

The decision to use a particular system of data collection will be based partly on the dimension of behavior that is of concern, as well as on the convenience. Systems for collecting data can be classified into three general categories. First is the recording and analysis of written reports that ideally include a full record of behaviors emitted during the observation period. Second is the observation of tangible products resulting from a behavior. Third is the recording of a sample of the behavior as it occurs. These systems may be categorized as shown in the accompanying table.

Analyzing written records:	Anecdotal reports
Observing tangible products:	Permanent product recording
Observing a sample of behavior:	Event recording
	Interval recording
	Time sampling
	Duration recording
	Latency recording

ANECDOTAL REPORTS

Anecdotal reports are written to provide as complete a description as possible of a student's behavior in a particular setting or during an instructional period. Anecdotal reports do not identify a predefined or operationalized target behavior. Rather, this approach anticipates that, as an end product of writing and analyzing anecdotal data, a specific behavior may be identified as the source of a general disturbance or lack of learning by the student that requires some modification. Anecdotal reports are useful primarily for analysis, not for evaluation.

An anecdotal system of data collection is frequently used by teachers, parents, and therapists to describe some general disturbance that is taking place or a lack of academic progress for a reason that cannot be determined. For example, it might be reported that "Sheila constantly disrupts the class and does not complete her own work," or "During therapy sessions, I cannot seem to get Sheila under control in order to do the needed speech remediation," or "Sheila keeps getting up from the dinner table and throwing her food."

Reports such as these are common and should prompt the applied behavior analyst to ask the series of questions offered on page 70 in Chapter 3. Should the specific behavior continue to elude identification, even after those questions have been asked, the analyst will have to further isolate and identify a target behavior that may be the source of the complaint in the natural setting of the behaviors—such as at the dinner table, in the schoolyard during recess, in the classroom during reading period—and attempt to write down everything that occurs.

This system of data collection produces a written description of nearly everything that occurred in a specific time period or setting. Therefore, this procedure does not yield isolated markings on a data sheet (such as + and –), but rather a report or narrative, written in everyday language, describing individuals and interactions. Wright (1960) has provided some suggested guidelines for the writing of anecdotal reports:

Guide to writing anecdotal records

1. Before beginning to record anecdotal data, write down the setting as you initially see it, the individuals in the setting and their relationships, and the activity occurring as you are about to begin recording (for example, lunch, free play).

2. Include in your description everything the target student(s) says and does and to whom or to what.

3. Include in your description everything said and done to the target student(s) and by whom.

4. As you write, clearly differentiate fact (what is actually occurring) from your impressions or interpretations of cause or reaction.

5. Provide some temporal indications so as to be able to judge the duration of particular responses or interactions.

Structuring an Anecdotal Report

After observations have been made, an anecdotal report must be analyzed to determine the behavior(s), if any, that should be the subject of a behavior-change program. The observations in this initial anecdotal format are dif-

FIGURE 4–1
Excerpt from an anecdotal report.

9:40 A.M.: Brian is walking around the room, touching various things such as plants on the windowsill. Teacher says, "It's now time for reading group. Everybody bring your books to the round table. You too, Brian." Teacher goes to table. Brian continues to wander. Teacher, in louder voice, "I'm still waiting." She goes and puts her hand on his shoulder. Brian pulls his shoulder out from under her hand. She takes him by the hand to the group of four other students. Brian sits. Teacher says, "Open your books. Where is your book, Brian?" Brian says, "Back there." "Back where, Brian?" "In my desk." "Go get it." "I will read from her book." "No, Brian, please go get your own book" (about 15 seconds pass). "Now, Brian, we are all waiting for you." Brian says, "So wait, we have plenty of time." Teacher stands. Brian gets up, goes to his desk (where he sits). When first student, Larry, is finished reading, teacher says, "Brian, come back here. It's almost your turn to read." Brian comes back to the table. Carl is reading. Brian makes a noise with his nose. Karen, sitting to his left, giggles and says, "Yuk." Teacher tells Karen to stop talking. Brian makes nose noise again. Karen, "Oh, yuk, yuk." Teacher says, "Brian, I see you. Stop it. Do we all see Brian? That is no way to behave when we are learning." Brian drops his book, bends down to get it, his chair falls. Teacher tells him to "come sit next to me." Brian moves his chair and begins to hum quietly. Teacher stands, moves three feet away from table, and tells Brian to move his chair "over here away from the group." Back at table she says, "Do we all see Brian and what happens when you disturb the group?" Larry raises his hand. "Yes, Larry." Larry says, "They don't get to read." Teacher says, "Yes, very good, Larry. Now let's read again: your turn, Mary." Mary starts reading. Brian is rocking in his chair, Karen looks and giggles. Brian continues to rock: his chair falls backward. Teacher reprimands him, takes him to front of room, and puts him in chair facing blackboard. Brian is singing. Larry yells, "Stop singing. You're disturbing me." Brian quiets down, begins drawing on blackboard (teacher is seated with her back to him). Brian intermittently sings loud enough to be heard. Twice teacher says, "Quiet down, Brian." Reading group ends (17 minutes later). Students are told to line up at the door. On way out teacher tells Brian how good he was while separated from the group. "But tomorrow you will have to read first in group." 10:35 A.M.: Brian is sent to P.E. with classmates.

ficult to separate into individual behaviors and relationships, so it is helpful to present the anecdotal data in a more schematic manner for review. Bijou, Peterson, and Ault (1968) employed a system for sequence analysis in which they redrafted an anecdotal report into a form that reflects a behavioral view of environmental interactions. By this system, the contents of the report are arranged into columns divided to indicate antecedent stimuli, specific responses, and consequating stimuli. This table format clearly represents the temporal relationship among individual behaviors, the antecedents that stimulate them, and the consequences that maintain them.

The anecdotal report in Figure 4–1 was taken in an elementary classroom. It records a period of interaction between a student named Brian, his teacher, and the members of his reading group.

Using the approach suggested by Bijou and his colleagues, the beginning of this report could be transposed into columns as begun in Figure 4–2. The antecedents, behaviors, and consequences are numbered to indicate the time sequence. Note that transposing the report makes it apparent that, in several instances, consequences of a given response can become the antecedents for a succeeding response.

When the content of an anecdotal report has been arranged in a format that clearly presents the sequence of and the relationships among behavioral events, the source of the problem behavior may be determined. The following questions help in analysis:

Questions for analyzing anecdotal information

1. What are the behaviors that can be described as *inappropriate*? The behavior analyst should be able to justify labeling the behaviors *inappropriate* given the setting and the activity taking place.

2. Is this behavior occurring frequently, or has a unique occurrence been identified?

3. Can reinforcement or punishment of the behavior be identified? The reinforcement may be delivered by the teacher, parent, another child, or some naturally occurring environmental consequence.

4. Is there a pattern to these consequences?

5. Can antecedents to the behavior(s) be identified?

FIGURE 4–2
Structure of an anecdotal report.

Time	Antecedent	Behavior	Consequence
9:40 A.M.		1. Brian is walking around room.	
	2. Teacher: "Time for group....You too, Brian." T moves to table.		
		3. B continues to walk.	
	5. T puts hand on B's shoulder.		4. T: "I'm still waiting."
		6. B pulls shoulder.	7. T takes B's hand and leads him to table.
	9. T: "Where is your book, B?"	8. B sits.	
		10. B: "Back there."	
		12. B: "In my desk."	11. T: "Back where?"
		14. B: "I will read from her book."	13. T: "Go get it."

6. Is there a pattern that can be identified for certain events or stimuli (antecedents) that consistently precede the behavior's occurrence?

7. Are there recurrent chains of certain antecedents, behaviors, and consequences?

8. Given the identified inappropriate behavior(s) of the student and the patterns of antecedents and consequences, what behavior really needs to be modified, and who is engaging in the behavior (for example, the referred student, or the teacher, or the parent)?

The use of anecdotal reports is seldom practical for regular classroom teachers. However, special education teachers who work with students only part of the day in a special classroom or resource room may be called upon to observe referred students in the regular classroom. For such observation, skill in recording and analyzing anecdotal data is extremely valuable. Anecdotal reports can enable these teachers to determine accurately what factors in the classroom are occasioning or maintaining appropriate and inappropriate behaviors.

PERMANENT PRODUCT RECORDING

Teachers have been using permanent product recording since the first time a teacher walked into a classroom. A teacher uses **permanent product recording** to grade a spelling test, check arithmetic problems, verify the creation of a chemical emulsion, or count the number of pegs a student has placed in a container. *Permanent products* are tangible items or environmental effects that result from a behavior. Permanent products are outcomes of behavior; thus, this method is sometimes called *outcome recording*. This type of recording is an *ex post facto* method of data collection, meaning it takes place after the behavior has occurred.

Permanent product recording is the easiest to use, but not all behaviors leave a permanent product.

To collect permanent product data, the teacher reviews the statement of the behavior as written in the behavioral objective and determines what constitutes an acceptable outcome of the behavior. For example, if the behavior is building a tower of blocks, the objective will state whether the student is required to place one block on top of another or whether the blocks should be arranged in a certain color sequence. If the behavior is academic, conditions will also be specified. For example, the objective may specify the number of spelling errors permitted in a written paragraph, or the number of references required in a term paper. If the behavior is vocational, quality may be specified as well as the number of widgets to be assembled. In each case, the teacher reviews the operational definition of the behavior. After evaluating the products of the required behavior, the teacher simply notes how many of the products were produced and how many were acceptable according to the definition.

Because the concrete results of a behavior are being evaluated and recorded, the teacher does not have to observe the student directly engaged in the behavior. Nor does the teacher have to sit and watch while the student takes a spelling test, writes a composition, or reads a language sample into a tape recorder. Convenience is the explanation for the frequent use of permanent product recording in the classroom—it causes minimal interference with a classroom schedule.

Applications of permanent product recording

The versatility of permanent product recording makes it useful in a variety of instructional programs and settings. In the home, permanent product recording has been used to record data on bedwetting (Hansen, 1979) and encopresis (O'Brien, Ross, & Christophersen, 1986)—some permanent products are less appealing than others—dental flossing (Dahlquist & Gil, 1986), and room cleaning (Wood & Flynn, 1978). In vocational settings, this method has been used to record increases in work production (Martin, Pallotta-Cornick, Johnstone, & Goyos, 1980). In educational settings, it has been employed to monitor academic progress in spelling accuracy (Greenwood et al., 1987; Stevens & Schuster, 1987) and completion and accuracy of arithmetic problems (Howell, Sidorenko, & Jurica, 1987; Roberts, Nelson, & Olson, 1987; Stern, Fowler, & Kohler, 1988). It has also been used to record the expanded complexity of sentence writing (Heward & Eachus, 1979) and to note development of fine motor control in cursive writing (Trap, Milner-Davis, Joseph, & Cooper, 1978). McDonnell and Ferguson (1989) used it to monitor the progress of student learning of banking skills; Williams and Cuvo (1986) used it to record upkeep of home appliances. More generally, permanent product recording has been used in such diverse public policy concerns as controlling blood pressure (Cincirpini, Epstein, & Martin, 1979); modifying purchases of foods with high fat content (Winett, Kramer, Walker, Malone, & Lane, 1988); assessing litter-control techniques (Bacon-Prue, Blount, Pickering, & Drabman, 1980); using seat belts with children (Sowers-Hoag, Thyer, & Bailey, 1987), college students (Rudd & Geller, 1985), and the general adult population (Williams, Thyer, Bailey, & Harrison, 1989); and even selectively using seat belts for children in shopping carts (Ferrari & Baldwin, 1989).

The main advantage of permanent product recording is the durability of the sample of behavior obtained. The permanent product is not apt to disappear before its occurrence can be recorded. In light of this, the teacher may keep an accurate file of the actual products of certain target behaviors (such as test papers) or a report of the products for further review or verification later.

With the increased availability of audiovisual equipment in schools and institutions, permanent product recording may include the use of audiotape and videotape systems. With such devices, the teacher can take samples of specific transitory behaviors that would not ordinarily produce permanent products, such as a child's gait or a student's social interactions in play group. Expressive language, for example has been audiotaped (Matson, Sevin, Fridley, & Love, 1990) and videotaped (Knapszyk, 1989; Watkins, Sprafkin, & Krolokowski, 1990). Taping makes a permanent record of a behavior sample that might otherwise have been transitory.

*Behavioral dimensions
for which permanent
product recording may
be used*

What permanent products or outcomes might be observed for each of the behavioral dimensions discussed in the section on choosing a system of data collection?

Rate:	number of written products of any academic behavior per unit of time
Duration or latency:	Unfortunately, do not lend themselves to permanent product recording unless recording equipment is available
Topography:	The correct formation of letters or numerals
	Following a pattern in such activities as pegboard designs, block-building, or vocational assemblies
Force:	Too light, too heavy, or uneven pressure when writing or typing
	Holes kicked in a classroom wall by a student having a tantrum

This list of examples is by no means exhaustive. Because permanent product recording is relatively simple and convenient, teachers can be imaginative in defining behaviors in terms of their outcomes. We have known teachers who operationally defined

- Test anxiety as the number of visible erasures on a test paper
- Sloppiness as the number of pieces of scrap paper on the floor within two feet of a student's desk
- Hyperactivity as the number of table tennis balls still balanced in the pencil tray of a student's desk (the classroom was carpeted, which reduced the noise).

The following vignette examines one use of permanent product recording.

Mr. Martin Observes Room Cleaning

Mr. Martin, while majoring in special education, was a night-shift assistant at a residential institution for students with severe emotional and behavioral problems. One of his duties was to see that each bedroom (shared by two residents) was cleaned before bedtime. He had decided that he would establish some system for reinforcing room cleaning but was uncertain about what he should measure. When he tried measuring and reinforcing the time students spent cleaning their rooms, he found that, although there was a great deal of scurrying around, the rooms were still very messy. Because the major problem appeared to be clothes, toys, and trash scattered on the floors, beds, and other furniture, he decided to use the number of such objects as his measure. Each evening before lights-out, he stood at the door of each bedroom with a clipboard containing a sheet of paper with each pair of residents' names and a space for each day of the week. He rapidly counted the number of separate objects scattered in inappropriate places and entered the total in the space on his data sheet.

FIGURE 4–3
Observational data collection systems as related to the basic behavioral paradigm.

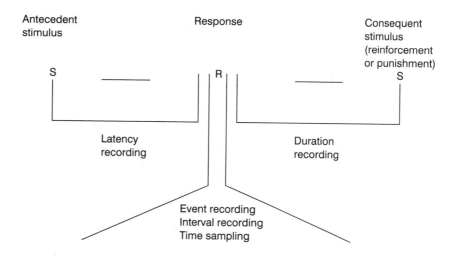

OBSERVATIONAL RECORDING SYSTEMS

Whereas the permanent product method of data collection records the outcome of a behavior, **observational recording systems** are used to record behavior samples as the behavior is actually occurring. A data collector may choose from several basic observational recording systems. Teachers who are interested in recording the number of times a behavior is occurring may select **event recording**. Those who want to find the proportion of a specified time period during which the behavior occurs may select **interval recording** or **time sampling**. **Duration recording** allows the teacher to determine the length of time the student spends performing some behavior. **Latency recording** measures the length of time it takes a student to start doing something. An illustration of the relationship between observational recording procedures and the components of a behavioral, stimulus-response sequence is shown in Figure 4–3.

Event Recording

Event recording provides an exact count of how many times a behavior occurs.

Event recording is a frequently used observational recording procedure because it most directly and accurately reflects a behavior's frequency. In event recording, a notation is made every time the student engages in the target behavior. The tally data give an exact record of how often the behavior occurred. A count of the target behavior is made within a specified sample observation period—for example, during the reading period from 10:00–10:30 A.M., or during lunch in the cafeteria. Recording how often the behavior occurs in this time period documents its **frequency** or rate of occurrence.

Event recording is usually the method of choice when the objective is to increase or decrease the number of times a student engages in a certain behavior. Event recording may be used to record an increase in an appropriate social behavior (raising hands prior to talking in the classroom) or an increase in an academic response (number of correctly identified sight vocabulary words) or a decrease in an inappropriate behavior (hitting other children, cursing, or spitting).

Event recording can be used only for discrete behaviors.

Because the teacher attempts to record exactly the number of times the behavior occurs, event recording must be used with behaviors that are discrete. **Discrete behaviors** have an obvious beginning and an obvious end. With such a behavior, the teacher can clearly judge when one occurrence ends and the next begins, thus enabling an accurate frequency count. Event recording has been used in counting and recording a range of discrete behaviors, such as the number of correctly spelled words (Gettinger, 1985), the number of manual signs a student used (Carr, Binkoff, Kologinsky, & Eddy, 1978; Duker & Morsink, 1984), letter recognition and labeling (Kincaid & Weisberg, 1978), sight work recognition (Cuvo & Klatt, 1992), number of oral reading errors (Singh, 1987), identification of words and counting of coins (Valcante, Roberson, Reid, & Wolking, 1989), picture naming (Olenick & Pear, 1980), use of adjectives in verbal sentence production (Brody, Lahey, & Combs, 1978), frequency of responses during small group conversations (Gajar, Schloss, Schloss, & Thompson, 1984), use of yes or no responses (Neef, Walters, & Egel, 1984), correct coin selection (Browder, Snell, & Wildonger, 1988), echolalic responses (Schreibman & Carr, 1978), self-bites (Luiselli, 1989), spoon banging (Horton, 1987), and nondelusional responses by schizophrenic children (Schraa, Lautmann, Luzi, & Screven, 1978).

Some labels for behavior may be used to describe what is actually a number of different behaviors, each of which may or may not occur each time the so-called behavior occurs. Examples that many teachers try to target for change are on-task or off-task behavior, appropriate or inappropriate verbalizations, in-seat or out-of-seat behavior, or disturbing one's neighbor. For accurate event recording, a standard definition, with an agreed upon beginning and end, is necessary. In other words, such behaviors can be made discrete by operationally defining them (see Chapter 3).

Certain behaviors, however, may not be adequately measured using event recording. This data collection procedure is not appropriate in the following instances:

1. *Behavior occurring at such a high frequency that the number recorded may not reflect an accurate count.* Certain behaviors, such as the number of steps taken while running, some stereotypic behaviors (such as hand flapping or rocking by students with severe disabilities), and eye blinking may occur at such high frequencies that it is impossible to count them accurately (especially if the data collector blinks).

2. *Cases in which one behavior or response can occur for extended time periods.* Examples of such behaviors might be thumb sucking or attention to task. If out-of-seat behavior were being recorded, for instance, a record showing that the student was out of her seat only one time during a morning would give an inaccurate indication of what the student was actually doing if this one instance of the behavior lasted from roll call to lunchtime.

FIGURE 4–4
Basic data sheet
for event recording.

Event Recording Data Sheet

Student: _PATRICIA_
Observer: _MRS. COHEN_

Behavior: _INAPPROPRIATE TALK-OUTS (NO HAND RAISED)_

	Time Start Stop	Notations of occurrences	Total occurrences
5/1/95	10:00 10:20	++++ ++++ //	12
5/2/95	10:00 10:20	++++ ////	9

An advantage of event recording, in addition to accuracy, is the relative ease of the data collection itself. The teacher does not need to interrupt the lesson to take data. The teacher may simply make a notation on an index card or paper on a clipboard, make slash marks on a piece of tape around a wrist (requiring stoicism upon removal), or transfer paper clips from one pocket to another. Following the lesson, this information may be tallied and transferred to a data sheet similar to the one presented in Figure 4–4.

FIGURE 4–5
Adapted data sheet
for event recording.

Student: _JEREMY_
Observer: _MS. GARWOOD_

Behavior: _Errors in oral reading_

	CAROL	5/1/95	EXERC. #2	READER PG. 7
SUBSTITUTIONS				
MISPRONOUNCIATIONS				
INSERTIONS				
REPETITIONS				

FIGURE 4–6
Adapted data sheet
for event recording.

Event Recording Data Sheet

Student: _GAIL_

Observer: _MRS ELLIOT_

Behavior: _VERBALLY STATING SIGHT WORDS_

	1	2	3	5/1	5/2	CAROL	ROBERT
OUT							
IN							
GIRL							
BOY							
EXIT							

Event recording is also easily used for many academic behaviors. Figure 4–5 is a data sheet used for recording the errors made during an oral reading exercise. The teacher simply places a mark in the appropriate row as a particular error is made. The column heads may record the day of week, child's who's reading, dates, page number from the reader where the mistake was made, and so on.

On the data sheet in Figure 4–6, the teacher can record the correct oral naming of sight words (listed in the left column) during or following instruction. A simple method for recording mistakes is to mark directly on the back of the flashcard being used. Marks can later be tallied on a summary data sheet.

For the more mechanically inclined, counting devices are commercially available. Although these make data collection easier and more accurate, they entail some expense and may break. An inexpensive counter sold for tallying purchases in a grocery store may be useful, but it is noisy and possibly distracting. Stitch counters designed to fit on the end of a knitting needle come in sizes large enough to fit on a pen. Drash, Ray, & Tudor (1989) describe a four-step procedure for using a simple calculator to record event data. Other commercial devices include

Wrist golf-counters or Wrist Tally Board

Behavior Research Company

P.O. Box 3351

Kansas City, KS 66103

Hand Tally Digital Counters (counter for single behavior)

Cambosco Scientific Co., Inc.
342 Western Ave.
Boston, MA 01235

Hand Tally Digital Counters (counter for multiple behaviors)
Lafayette Radio & Electronics
111 Jerico Turnpike
Syosset, Long Island, NY 11791

The Wrist Tally Board is an arrangement of beads on a leather strap that functions as an abacus. It is a rather attractive device somewhat reminiscent of jewelry made at summer camp.

Recording Controlled Presentations

One variation on the event-recording technique is the use of **controlled presentations** (Ayllon & Milan, 1979). In this method, the teacher structures or controls the number of opportunities the student will have to perform the behavior. Most often this method consists of presenting a predetermined number of opportunities or trials in each instructional session. A **trial** may be viewed as a discrete occurrence because it has an identifiable beginning and ending. A trial is defined by its three behavioral components: an antecedent stimulus, a response, and a consequating stimulus (S-R-S). The delivery of the antecedent stimulus (usually a verbal cue) marks the beginning of the trial, and the delivery of the consequating stimulus (reinforcement or punishment) signifies the termination of the trial. For example, in a given session the teacher may decide that a student will be given 10 opportunities, or trials, to respond by pointing to a specified object upon request. Each trial is then recorded as correct or incorrect. Controlled presentation allows the teacher to monitor progress simply by looking at the number of correct responses for each session.

Figures 4–7, 4–8, and 4–9 present three variations of data sheets used in the collection of trial or controlled presentation data. The data sheet in Figure 4–7 (Saunders & Koplik, 1975) is arranged to allow for up to 20 trials per instructional session. The teacher records dichotomous data (correct or incorrect) using the following simple procedure:

After each trial

1. Circle the trial number that corresponds to a correct response.
2. Slash (/) through the trial number that corresponds to an incorrect response.

After each session

1. Total the number of correct trials (those circled).

FIGURE 4-7

Data collection sheet for use with controlled presentations.

Note: From a "A multi-purpose data sheet for recording and graphing in the classroom," by R. Saunders and K. Koplik. AAESPH Review, 1975. Copyright 1975 by the Association for the Severely Handicapped. Reprinted with permission

FIGURE 4-8
Data collection sheet for use with controlled presentations.

Note: From Vocational habilitation of severely retarded adults: A direct service technology, by
G. Bellamy, R. Horner & D. Inman (Baltimore: University Park Press, 1979). Copyright © 1979
University Park Press, Baltimore. Reprinted by permission.

S^D		Response
13	Parts in bin	Pick up bearing and place on table
12	Bearing on table	Place hex nut in one bearing corner
11	Nuts in one corner	Place hex nut in second corner
10	Nuts in two corners	Place hex nut in third corner
9	Nuts in three corners	Place cam base in bearing
8	Cam in bearing	Place roller in bearing
7	Roller in bearing	Place red spring in bearing
6	Red spring placed	Rotate bearing and cam 180°
5	Bearing rotated	Place roller in bearing
4	Roller in bearing	Place green spring in bearing
3	Green spring placed	Wipe bearing with cloth
2	Bearing cleaned	Place cammed bearing in bag
1	Cam in bag	Place bag in box

FIGURE 4-9

Data collection sheet for use with controlled presentations.

Note: Adapted from "An instructional interaction pattern for the severely handicapped," by P. A. Alberto and P. Schofield, Teaching exceptional children, 1979. Copyright 1979 by the Council for Exceptional Children. Reprinted with permission.

Student: _____Baxter_____ Staff: _____Mr. McCorkel_____

		Trials
Cue	1 2 3 4 5 6 7 8 9 10	1 2 3 4 5 6 7 8 9 10	1 2 3 4 5 6 7 8 9 10
Verbal	1 2 3 4 5 6 7 8 9 10	1 2 3 4 5 6 7 8 9 10	1 2 3 4 5 6 7 8 9 10
Gesture	1 2 3 4 5 6 7 8 9 10	1 2 3 4 5 6 7 8 9 10	1 2 3 4 5 6 7 8 9 10
Partial physical	1 2 3 4 5 6 7 8 9 10	1 2 3 4 5 6 7 8 9 10	1 2 3 4 5 6 7 8 9 10
Full physical	1 2 3 4 5 6 7 8 9 10	1 2 3 4 5 6 7 8 9 10	1 2 3 4 5 6 7 8 9 10

Date   4-18

Time start/stop   9:15 - 9:30

Task/step   4

Cue(s)   "HAND ME"   CUP
                        SPOON
          ARRAY = DISH
                   FORK

Criterion   8/10 Trials

Observation
Comments

2. Place a square around the corresponding number in the session column that corresponds to the number of correct trials.

3. To graph directly on the data sheet, connect the squared numbers across the sessions to yield a learning curve.

Figure 4–8 (Bellamy, Horner, & Inman, 1979) is arranged for recording dichotomous data on the instruction of complex tasks. One column is provided for listing antecedents to be provided (S^D) and another for a description of the subbehaviors or steps being requested (response). Each trial consists of an opportunity for the student to perform the entire chain of steps (1–13) that make up the complex behavior. For each trial, the teacher may record the accuracy of the student's performance of each step within the chain, using the same circle and slash procedure. As with Figure 4–7, this format also allows for graphing directly on the raw data sheet. (*Raw data* means the original record taken by the observer that has not yet been converted or processed.) The number corresponding to the number of correctly performed steps is indicated by a square, and the squares are connected across trials.

Figure 4–9 (Alberto & Schofield, 1979) is systematized to permit recording of the type of interactions between teacher and student. The data sheet depicts five sessions, each containing 10 trials. For each trial, the teacher can indicate the type of assistance that was necessary to enable the student to perform the response. Following each trial, the trial number is marked on the row corresponding to the type of assistance provided (for example, the use of a gesture or a physical prompt). This data sheet may also serve as a self-graphing sheet if the marked trial numbers are connected within and across sessions, thus yielding a curve that displays the increasing independence of the student's performance of the response.

Classroom teachers can improve instruction by using controlled presentations. For example, a teacher might want to be sure to ask each member of a seminar group five questions during a discussion on early Cold War events and the Berlin Wall. A very simple data sheet with the names of the students and a space to mark whether answers were correct or incorrect would provide valuable information for analysis and evaluation.

Behavioral dimensions appropriate to event recording

Event recording (including controlled presentation) lends itself to the observation of the rate or frequency of behavior, for example:

- Number of times Mel talks out in an hour
- Number of times Charlie hits another student in a 20-minute recess
- Number of questions Melissa answers correctly during a 15-minute world geography review
- Number of times Sam answers questions in a whisper
- Number of times Mary throws trash on the floor
- Number of stairs Eliot climbs putting only one foot on each step

---

Ms. Stallings Counts Tattling

Four of the students in Ms. Stallings' third-grade class seemed to spend most of their time telling her what other students were doing wrong. Ms. Stallings was worried about this for two reasons: The students were not working efficiently and they were driving her up the wall. When she asked her colleague Ms. Barbe for advice, Ms. Barbe suggested that the first thing to do was to find out how often each of the students was tattling.

"Otherwise," she said, "you won't know for sure whether whatever you do to stop them is working."

Ms. Stallings decided to count an instance of tattling each time a student mentioned another student's name to her and described any number of inappropriate behaviors. Thus, "Johnny's not doing his work and he's *bothering* me," was counted as one instance, but "Harold and Manolo are talking," was counted as two instances. She then went back to Ms. Barbe.

"How can I write it down every time they do it?" she asked. "I move around my room all the time and I don't want to carry paper and pencil."

Ms. Barbe laughed. "No problem," she answered, "I'm sure that's why dry beans come in so many sizes and shapes. I just pick a different bean for each student, put a handful of each in my right pocket, and transfer by feel to my left pocket when I observe the behavior. Just be sure you get them out before your slacks go into the washer."

INTERVAL RECORDING AND TIME SAMPLING

The observer counts intervals, not discrete behaviors.

The data collection systems of interval recording and time sampling are means of recording an estimate of the actual number of times behavior occurs. Instead of counting each occurrence of the behavior, the teacher counts the number of intervals of time within a sample observation period in which the behavior has occurred. With these methods, it is possible to record continuous behaviors, as well as high-frequency behaviors that may be incompatible with event recording.

In terms of making the closest representation of the actual occurrence of the behavior, event recording is the most accurate, interval recording is the next, and time sampling the least exact (Repp, Roberts, Slack, Repp, & Berkler, 1976). Each system, however, has its own advantages and disadvantages.

Interval Recording

In interval recording, the teacher defines a specific time period in which the behavior will be observed. This observation period is then divided into equal intervals. Typically, the intervals are no longer than 30 seconds (Cooper, 1981). To record these data, the teacher draws a series of boxes representing the intervals of time. In each box or interval the teacher simply notes whether the behavior occurred (+) or did not occur (–) *at any time*

FIGURE 4–10
Interval recording
for one minute.

Note: From Measurement
and analysis of behavioral
techniques, by J. Cooper.
(Columbus, Ohio: Merrill,
1974), p. 48. Reprinted by
permission.

*Interval recording does
not provide an exact
count of behaviors, but is
especially appropriate for
continuous behaviors.*

during the interval. Therefore, each interval has only one notation. The example of a 1-minute observation period shown in Figure 4–10 has been divided into 10-second intervals. The sample target behavior occurred during two of the intervals in this observation period, namely the second and third 10-second intervals.

Because of the manner in which these interval data are recorded, only limited conclusions can be drawn from the record of the behavior's occurrence. Regardless of whether the behavior occurred once or five times during the interval, it is recorded by a single notation. Therefore, the actual number of occurrences is not included in the record. If, in the preceding example, cursing was being recorded, all the teacher could say was that, during two of the intervals, the student cursed. There were at least two instances of this behavior, but there may have been more. Even if the student cursed 11 times during the second interval, only one notation would have been made. Recording occurrences of discrete behaviors, such as cursing or hitting, is known as *partial-interval* recording (the behavior does not consume the entire interval).

Behaviors like walking around the room or being off-task may begin in one interval and continue unbroken into the next interval. Such timing would appear as two instances, because it would be recorded in two intervals in this instance, but the same duration of behavior would appear as only one instance if it fell within a single interval. Recording ongoing behaviors that may continue for several intervals is known as *whole-interval* recording (the behavior consumes the entire interval).

An additional problem encountered with interval data collection is created by the shortness of each interval in which the notation is to take place. It is very difficult to teach and collect interval data simultaneously. The teacher must keep an eye on a student or students, observe a stopwatch or second hand on a watch, and note the occurrence or nonoccurrence of the target behavior all within matters of seconds; therefore, a third-party observer is often required.

Even with an observer, however, the necessity of looking down at the data sheet to make a recording might cause an observer to miss an occurrence of the behavior, thus resulting in inaccurate data. A cassette tape with timed beeps for the chosen intervals at least eliminates the timing difficulty. Another way of simplifying the task is to allow for recording interludes as part of the data collection schedule. In this system, a specific time is allotted

FIGURE 4–11
Interval recording with five-second scoring interludes.

10"	5"	10"	5"	10"	5"	10"	5"	10"	5"	10"
Observe	Score	Observe	Score	Observe	Score	Observe	Score	Observe	Score	Observe

for observation and scoring, as seen in the sample row from a data collection sheet shown in Figure 4–11.

Figures 4–12 and 4–13 are examples of interval recording sheets for a 15-minute period divided into 10-second intervals. Looking at the notations of occurrence and nonoccurrence, the data collector can infer certain information:

1. Approximate number of occurrences of the behavior
2. Approximate duration of the behavior within the observation period
3. Distribution of the behavior across the observation period

Assuming that off-task behavior during a written arithmetic assignment is recorded in both examples, the behavior appears to have occurred in 38 of the 90 intervals (see Figure 4–12). When looking at the successive intervals in which the behavior occurred, it can be seen that the off-task behavior occurred over long durations (3 minutes each) but it appears to have been confined primarily to two periods. When reviewing such data, teachers should analyze the situation for some indication of what seem to be the immediate precipitating factors. In this example, off-task behavior may have been due to the two sets of written instructions on the worksheet, which prompted the student to ask a neighbor what to do.

In Figure 4–13, the off-task behavior is distributed throughout the time period. The teacher might find that the off-task behavior coincided with times when another student asked a question. Therefore, this student's problem may be distractibility rather than inability or unwillingness to read instructions.

Time Sampling

Time sampling allows for only one observation per interval.

In order to use time sampling, the data collector selects a time period in which to observe the behavior and divides this period into equal intervals. This process is similar to that employed with interval recording; however, the intervals in time sampling are usually minutes rather than seconds. Such a format allows for observing the behavior over longer periods of time (Ayllon & Michael, 1959). To record these data, the observer draws a series of boxes representing the intervals. The observer simply notes in each box (interval) whether the behavior was occurring (+) or not (–) when the student was observed *at the end of the interval*. Each interval therefore has only one notation. Note that the time sampling procedure differs from interval recording in that the student is observed only at the end of the interval rather than throughout it.

The observation period in Figure 4–14 is divided into 10-minute intervals. The exact observation period was 90 minutes. The target behavior was occurring at the end of five of the intervals: the first, second, fourth, fifth, and ninth. A fairly simple way of recording time sampling data is to set a kitchen timer to ring next at the end of the interval and to observe the behavior when the timer rings. To prevent students' figuring out the schedule and performing (or not performing) some behavior only at the end of the

FIGURE 4–12
Interval recording of off-task behavior.

Student __MALCOLM__

Date __2/2/95__

Observer __MR. RILEY__

Time Start __9:15__

Time End __9:30__

Behavior __OFF-TASK__

Note occurrence within the 10-second interval.

X = occurrence
O = nonoccurrence

Data summary

Number of intervals of occurrence: 38
Percent of intervals of occurrence: 42%
Number of intervals of nonoccurrence: 52
Percent of intervals of nonoccurrence: 58%

FIGURE 4–13
Interval recording of off-task behavior.

10-second intervals

	1	2	3	4	5	6
1	X	X	X	X	O	X
2	O	X	X	O	O	O
3	O	O	O	O	X	O
4	O	O	X	X	X	O
5	O	X	O	O	O	O
6	X	X	O	X	X	O
7	O	O	X	O	O	O
8	O	O	O	X	X	X
9	X	O	O	O	O	X
10	O	O	X	O	O	X
11	O	O	O	X	X	O
12	X	X	X	X	O	O
13	O	O	O	O	O	X
14	X	O	X	O	O	O
15	O	X	X	X	X	X

Minutes

Student   LEROY

Date   9/18/95

Observer   MS HEILBRUNER

Time Start   11:00

Time End   11:15

Behavior   OFF-TASK

Note occurrence within
the 10-second interval.

X = occurrence
O = nonoccurrence

Data summary

Number of intervals of occurrence: 38
Percent of intervals of occurrence: 42%
Number of intervals of nonoccurrence: 52
Percent of intervals of nonoccurrence: 58%

interval, the intervals may be of varying lengths. For example, a 10-minute time sampling recording system might have intervals of 8, 12, 6, 14, 9, and 11 minutes. The average interval duration would be 10 minutes, but the students would never know when they were about to be observed. Common sense indicates the need to hide the face of the timer.

An observer may miss a lot of behavior when using time sampling.

Because of the method of recording time sampling data, only limited conclusions can be drawn about the behavior recorded. As with interval recording, the behavior may have occurred more than once within the 10-minute observation interval. A particularly serious drawback with time sampling occurs when a single instance of a behavior occurs just before or just after

The longer the time sam-
pling interval, the less
accurate the data will be.

the observer looks up to record the occurrence, resulting in a record of nonoccurrence.

When time sampling intervals are divided into segments by minutes as opposed to seconds, the procedure allows for longer periods between observations. It is, therefore, more practical for simultaneous teaching and data collection. Indeed, the interval may be set at 15, 30, 45 minutes or more, allowing for observation throughout an entire day or class period. As the interval gets longer, however, the similarity between the data recorded and the actual occurrence of the behavior probably *decreases* (Saudargas & Zanolli, 1990).

FIGURE 4–14
Time sampling at 10-minute intervals.

Student _____   Behavior *Walking around room without permission*

Date   _____   Time start   *9:15*

Observer_____   Time stop   *10:45*

                                     Total period *90 minutes*

	10'	20'	30'	40'	50'	60'
1 hour	X	X	O	X	X	O

	10'	20'	30'	40'	50'	60'
1 hour	O	O	X	▌		

	10'	20'	30'	40'	50'	60'
1 hour						

X = occurrence   O = nonoccurrence

Data summary
Number of intervals of occurrence: 5
Percent of intervals of occurrence: 55%
Number of intervals of nonoccurrence: 4
Percent of intervals of nonoccurrence: 45%
Symbol for minutes: '

Time sampling, therefore, is suitable primarily for recording behaviors that are frequent or of long duration: for example, attention to task, out-of-seat behavior, or thumb sucking.

Although time sampling is practical for classroom use, its usefulness may diminish as a behavior change program progresses successfully. For example, if Barry's teacher decides to use time sampling to record his out-of-seat behavior, she may observe that during baseline almost all of her observations indicate that Barry is out of his seat when she records at 15-minute intervals during the first 90 minutes of school. However, when a contingency is applied—Barry, you will receive one token for each 15 minutes that you stay in your seat—the procedure will become less useful. Barry will assume that his teacher is visually impaired or terribly inattentive if she holds to her recording procedure, records only out-of-seat behavior at the end of the interval, and provides the reinforcer if Barry beats the clock to his seat. If the procedure is successful in spite of this assumption, the data may reflect a complete absence of the behavior long before it has really been eliminated. Barry may be out of his seat for a short while a number of times that do not happen to coincide with the end of intervals. At this point, because the behavior is occurring less frequently and for shorter durations, event recording may be as practical and much more accurate.

Behavioral dimensions appropriate to interval and time sampling recording

Data collected using interval recording or time sampling can be used to measure behavior along the frequency dimension but *cannot be converted to rate.* You cannot say that a certain behavior occurred at the rate of two per minute when what you have recorded is behavior occurring during two 10-second intervals in a 60-second period. Interval and time sampling data are most often expressed in terms of the percentage of intervals during which the behavior occurred. The procedure for converting raw data into percentages will be discussed later in this chapter.

Measurement of duration can be approximated using interval recording, but this procedure does not lend itself to measures of latency. Force, locus, and topography may be measured, as with event recording, if they are included in the operational definition.

Ms. Simmons Observes Pencil Tapping

Ms. Simmons is an elementary-school resource teacher for students with learning disabilities. One of her students, Arnold, tapped his pencil on the desk as he worked. He completed a surprising number of academic tasks but tapped whenever he was not actually writing. Ms. Simmons's concern was that this behavior would make it difficult for Arnold to be accepted in a regular classroom. She had tried counting pencil taps but found that Arnold tapped so rapidly that the pencil was a blur.

She was working with another student, Shane, on paying attention and concentrating. She decided that recording interval data would be an excellent task for Shane. She carefully defined the behavior, provided Shane with a recording sheet on a clipboard, gave him a stopwatch, and told him to mark a + in the box if Arnold tapped during a 10-second interval and a – if he didn't. She left Shane to observe and went to teach a small group. Very soon, she heard the sound of the clipboard hitting the floor and an expression of annoyance totally unacceptable in the classroom.

"I'm sorry, Ms. Simmons," said Shane, "but how the [expletive deleted] am I 'posed to watch the kid, the watch, and the sheet at the same time?"

Realizing that she had asked too much of a student who had difficulty concentrating, Ms. Simmons revised her procedure. She took her cassette recorder home and prepared to make a tape that would "bleep" every 10 seconds. She set up the recorder next to her new electronically controlled microwave oven and touched the "clear" button every 10 seconds as she watched the stopwatch. She had to start over only once when her teenage son, who had learned to expect dinner after a small number of "bleeps" (see Chapter 7 for a discussion of stimulus control), came in to ask when and what he was going to be fed.

The next day Ms. Simmons provided Shane with earphones and a 20-minute tape divided into 10-second intervals. Shane was able to record pencil tapping this way very efficiently, even though he couldn't hear it.

After several days of observation and analysis of data, it occurred to Ms. Simmons that she might have used time sampling to observe Arnold's pencil tapping, because it occurred so frequently.

Variations on the Collection Sheet

The basic data collection sheet format for interval recording and time sampling is an extremely flexible tool that can easily be adapted to meet a variety of instructional situations that arise in the classroom.

Multiple Students

These data collection procedures are very flexible. They can be used to record data on several students simultaneously.

In many instances, a teacher encounters several students in the same classroom who exhibit the same behavior within the same observation period. In such cases, data may be collected for each student. The basic data collection can be adapted to meet this need by adding additional row(s) of intervals for each student, as shown in Figure 4–15.

FIGURE 4–15
Data sheet for multiple students.

Symbol for seconds: "

FIGURE 4–16
Round-robin format
of interval record-
ing.

	1st 15-sec. interval	2nd 15-sec. interval	3rd 15-sec. interval	4th 15-sec. interval
	Kate	Michael	Harry	Jody
1				
2				
3				
4				

Another way of adapting the system for use with a group is a round-robin format (Cooper, 1981) of interval recording or time sampling. With this format, the behavior of a single group member per interval is observed and recorded. For example, when instructing a group of students in a DISTAR language lesson, the teacher might choose to monitor each student's attending behavior. The language period would then be divided into equal 15-second intervals to accommodate a group of four students, with the name of each group member assigned to an interval. As shown in Figure 4–16, Kate was observed for occurrence or nonoccurrence of attending during the first 15-second interval of each minute; Michael's attending was observed and recorded during the second; Harry's, during the third; and Jody's, during the fourth. Lloyd, Bateman, Landrum, & Hallahan (1989) used this adaptation when recording attentive behavior of five elementary aged students with learning and behavior disabilities.

A method of data collection similar to time sampling and useful for recording group behavior is **PLACHECK**—Planned Activity Check (Doke & Risley, 1971). Doke and Risley (1972) used the PLACHECK procedure to measure and record participation of children in a day-care center in required-versus-optional activities. At 3-minute intervals, observers recorded the number of children participating in an appropriate manner in the alternative activities.

The PLACHECK procedure is similar to time sampling except that several students are observed at the end of the interval. The number of students engaged in an activity can be compared to the number of students present.

A classroom teacher might use a PLACHECK procedure to record how many of her students were actively engaged, for example, in an art activity. She could set the timer, in a manner similar to that used in time sampling, and then count the number of participants each time the timer rang.

Multiple Behaviors

They can be used to record data on several behaviors simultaneously.

In some instances, a teacher may be focusing on a behavior that has a number of possible responses. The crucial task in this case is recording, with some detail, the nature or topography of the behavior as it occurs. Such a refinement of the recording system is possible using a coding procedure (Bijou, Peterson, & Ault, 1968).

FIGURE 4–17
Recording multiple
behaviors using
codes.

Interval Recording

Student_____   Time Start_____   H = hitting
Date_____   Time End _____   T = talking
Observer_____   P = pinching

	10"	20"	30"	40"	50"	60"
1	H	—	T	T	T	—
2	—	P	H	—	—	—
3	—	—	—	T	T	—
4	H	—	—	—	—	—
5	—	H	—	T	T	—

(row labels = Minutes)

    A data collection sheet for coding has a legend at the top indicating the behaviors being observed and their codes. The example in Figure 4–17 shows a few rows of data from an observation period in which occurrences of "disturbing one's neighbor" were recorded. The legend includes hitting (H), talking (T), and pinching (P).

    When the behaviors to be coded occur during the observation period (interval recording) or at the end of the interval (time sampling), the code for the behavior is recorded for that interval. Coding enables the observer to record a category of behavior or several different behaviors.

    An alternative system for coding more than one behavior or for coding a behavior whose topography ("shape") varies is the use of a tracking format (Bijou, Peterson, & Ault, 1968). In this format, each interval is divided into the number of rows corresponding to the possible behaviors or operationally

FIGURE 4–18
Coding form for four behaviors.

H = head rolling
F = hand flapping
C = finger contortions
V = high-pitched vocalizations

FIGURE 4-19
Coding form with additional rows for nontarget behaviors.

Note: From Measurement and analysis of behavioral techniques, 2nd ed., by J. Cooper (Columbus, Ohio: Merrill 1981).

defined responses that are to be recorded. Each row is reserved for the notation of that behavior. Figure 4–18 shows an example of data collected on stereotypic behavior where the exact responses to be recorded were head rolling, hand flapping, finger contortions, and high-pitched vocalizations, behaviors sometimes observed in people with autism, severe or profound mental retardation, or other severely disabling conditions.

The format in Figure 4–18 targets specific responses for observation; it is also possible, however, to track occurrences of more general behaviors. The data sheet (Cooper, 1981) in Figure 4–19 tracks on-task behavior. The teacher also wanted to know, however, the general nature of any off-task behavior. Therefore, in addition to noting the occurrence or nonoccurrence of an on-task behavior, she provided track rows to indicate the general nature of any off-task behavior that occurred. The observer would simply put a check mark in the appropriate box(es) to indicate which behavior(s) occurred in which intervals.

A third type of coding, represented in Figure 4–20 (Alberto, Sharpton, & Goldstein, 1979), uses letter codes for specific responses within each interval. With this prepared format the observer simply places a slash through the

FIGURE 4-20
Format for coding specific behaviors within intervals.

Note: From Teaching exceptional children, by P.A. Alberto, W. Sharpton, & D. Goldstein (Atlanta: Georgia State University, 1979).

	10"	20"	30"	40"	50"	60"
1 min.	WG AI / A / CG NI	WG AI / A / CG NI	WG AI / A / CG NI	WG AI / A / CG NI	WG AI / A / CG NI	WG AI / A / CG NI
2 min.	WG AI / A / CG NI	WG AI / A / CG NI	WG AI / A / CG NI	WG AI / A / CG NI	WG AI / A / CG NI	WG AI / A / CG NI
3 min.	WG AI / A / CG NI	WG AI / A / CG NI	WG AI / A / CG NI	WG AI / A / CG NI	WG AI / A / CG NI	WG AI / A / CG NI

appropriate letter(s) indicating the behavior that occurred. During the observation period, the student's social interactions were monitored for within-group interaction (WG), cross-group interaction (CG), adult interaction (AI), no interaction (NI), or aggressive behavior (A).

DURATION AND LATENCY RECORDING

Duration and latency recording emphasize measures of time rather than instances of behavior.

Event recording, interval recording, and time sampling collection techniques focus primarily on exact or approximate counts of the occurrence of a behavior. Duration and latency recording differ from these systems in that the focus is on a temporal rather than a numerical dimension of the behavior.

Duration Recording

See pages 111–113.

Duration recording is used when the primary concern is the length of time a student engages in a particular behavior. For example, if a teacher wants to know about a student's out-of-seat behavior, either event recording or duration recording might be appropriate. Event recording would provide information about the number of times a student left her seat. If, however, the teacher's concern is *how long* she stays out of her seat, the most appropriate data collection method would be duration recording. In this example, event recording would mask the temporal nature of the target behavior. Although event data might indicate, for example, that the number of times the student got out of her seat had decreased substantially, it would not reveal that the length of time spent out-of-seat might actually have increased.

Duration recording, like event recording, is suitable for discrete behaviors—those that have an easily identifiable beginning and end. It is important to define clearly the onset of the behavior and its completion. The observer may time the duration of the behavior using the second hand of a watch or wall clock, but a stopwatch makes the process much simpler. For certain behaviors like seizures or tantrums, an observer may use a tape recorder. The duration of the episode may be determined later using the resulting permanent product.

You could measure average duration of tantrums, of time spent on-task, of recreational reading.

There are two basic ways to collect duration data: by recording average duration or total duration. The *average duration* approach is used when the student performs the target behavior routinely or with some regularity. In a given day, the teacher measures the length of time consumed in each occurrence (its duration) and then finds the average duration for that day. If the behavior occurs at regular but widely spaced intervals (for example, only once per day or once per class period), the data may be averaged for the week. One behavior that can be measured by duration data is time spent in the bathroom. Perhaps his teacher feels that each time John goes to the bathroom he stays for an unreasonable length of time. To gather data on this behavior, she decides to measure the amount of time he takes for each trip. On Monday, John went to the bathroom three times. The first trip took him

FIGURE 4–21
Basic formats for latency and duration recording data sheets.

Latency Recording Data Sheet	Duration Recording Data Sheet

Student ___EDITH___ Observer _MR. HALL_

Behavior _TIME ELAPSED BEFORE_
TAKING SEAT

Student ___SAM___ Observer _MS. JAMES_

Behavior _TIME SPENT IN BATHROOM_

Operationalization of behavior initiation ————

Behavior initiation ————————

Behavior termination ————————

Date	Time		Latency	Date	Time		Duration
	Delivery of S^D	Response initiation			Response initiation	Response termination	

7 minutes, the second 11 minutes, and the third 9 minutes. If she continued to collect data in this manner during the rest of the week, the teacher would be able to calculate John's average duration of bathroom use for the week.

Total duration recording measures how long a student engages in a behavior in a limited time period. This activity may or may not be continuous. As an example, the target behavior "appropriate play" might be observed over a 15-minute period. The observer would record the number of minutes the student was engaging in appropriate play during this period. The child might, for example, have been playing appropriately from 10:00–10:04 (4 minutes), from 10:07–10:08 (1 minute), and from 10:10–10:15 (5 minutes). Although such a behavior record is clearly noncontinuous, these notations would yield a total duration of 10 minutes of appropriate play during the 15-minute observation period.

Total duration could be used to record the time spent talking, reading, or playing with toys.

Latency Recording

Refer to Figure 4–3.

Latency recording measures how long a student takes to begin performing a behavior once its performance has been requested. This procedure measures the length of time between the presentation of an antecedent stimulus and the initiation of the behavior. For example, if a teacher says, "Michael, sit down" (antecedent stimulus) and Michael does, but so slowly that 5 minutes elapse before he is seated, the teacher would be concerned with the latency of the student's response.

As seen in Figure 4–21, a basic collection sheet for duration or latency data should provide information on the temporal boundaries that define the procedures. A duration recording data collection sheet should note the time the student began the response and the time the response was completed. A latency recording data collection sheet should note the time the student was given the cue to begin a response (antecedent stimulus) and the time he actually began to respond.

Duration and latency recording are closely matched to the behavioral dimensions of duration and latency. Consideration of topography, locus, and force, however, may also apply here. For example, a teacher might want to measure

- How long Calvin can maintain perfectly a position in gymnastics
- How long Roberta talks to each of a number of other students
- How long after being given a nonverbal signal to lower her voice Ellen actually does so
- How long David maintains sufficient pressure to activate a microswitch

The five observational systems available to the data collector are *event recording, interval recording, time sampling, duration recording,* and *latency recording.* Figure 4–22 summarizes the decision making involved in selecting the system appropriate for a particular target behavior. This process is based on a series of questions to be answered by the data collector:

Questions for the data collector. How to choose a recording system.

1. Is the target behavior numerical or temporal?
2. If it is numerical
   a. Is the behavior discrete or continuous?
   b. Is the behavior expected to occur at a high, moderate, or low frequency?
   c. Will I be able to collect data during intervention/instruction, or will I need a third party to collect the data so as not to interrupt instruction?
3. If it is temporal, do I want to measure the time before initiation of the response or time elapsed during performance of the response?

RELIABILITY

Computing reliability for permanent product data

When data collection depends on human beings (teachers are included within this category), there is always the possibility of error. Even in the case of permanent product data, which are easiest to record, mistakes may hap-

FIGURE 4–22
Selected observational recording procedures.

pen. Teachers occasionally count math problems as incorrect even when they are correctly done, or overlook a misspelled word in a paragraph. Because there is something tangible, however, the teacher can easily recheck the accuracy or **reliability** of her observations of the behavior. In using an observational recording system, however, the teacher does not have this advantage. The behavior occurs and then disappears, so she cannot go back and check her accuracy. To be sure the data are correct, or reliable, it is wise to periodically have a second observer record the same behavior of the same student(s) at the same time. When this is done, the two observations can be compared and a coefficient or percent of *interobserver reliability* or *interobserver agreement* may be computed.

Computing reliability for event recording

To check event recording, the teacher and a second observer, a paraprofessional or another student, simultaneously watch the student and record each instance of the target behavior. After the observation period, the teacher calculates the coefficient of agreement or reliability by dividing the smaller number of recorded instances by the larger number of recorded instances. For example, if the teacher observed 20 instances of talking-out in a 40-minute session, and the second observer recorded only 19, the calculation would be 19/20 = 95. Therefore, the coefficient of interobserver agreement would be .95. Coefficients of agreement are often reported as *percent of agreement*. The percent of agreement is calculated by multiplying the coefficient by 100. So, in this example, the percent of agreement is .95 × 100 = 95%.

However, this method of calculating reliability for research purposes lacks a certain amount of precision and has, therefore, been referred to as a gross method of calculation. "The problem is that this method does not permit the researcher to state that both observers saw the same thing or that the events they agreed on were all the same events" (Tawney & Gast, 1984, p. 138). In other words, there is no absolute certainty that the 19 occurrences noted by the paraprofessional were the same ones noted by the teacher.

Computing reliability for duration and latency recording

The reliability of duration and latency data is determined by a procedure similar to that of event recording, except that the longer time is divided into the shorter, as in the following equation:

$$\frac{\text{Shorter number of minutes}}{\text{Longer number of minutes}} \times 100 = \text{percent of agreement}$$

When using interval recording or time sampling, the basic formula for calculating reliability is as shown below:

$$\frac{\text{Agreements}}{\text{Agreements} + \text{Disagreements}} \times 100 = \text{percent of agreement}$$

If the data below represent 10 intervals during which the teacher and the paraprofessional were recording whether or not Lauren was talking to her neighbor, we see that their data agree in 7 intervals (that is, intervals 1, 2, 3, 4, 6, 7, and 8); their data are not in agreement in 3 intervals (that is, 5, 9, and 10). Therefore, using the basic formula the calculation for reliability would be as follows:

$$\frac{7}{7 + 3} \times 100 = 70\%$$

	1	2	3	4	5	6	7	8	9	10
Teacher	×	×	-	-	×	×	-	-	×	-
Paraprofessional	×	×	-	-	-	×	-	-	-	×

Under certain research circumstances an additional, more rigorous determination of reliability should be considered. This should be a calculation of *occurrence reliability* or of *nonoccurrence reliability*. When the target behavior is recorded to have occurred in *less* than 75% of the intervals, occurrence reliability should be calculated. When the target behavior is recorded to have occurred in *more* than 75% of the intervals, nonoccurrence agreement should be computed (Tawney & Gast, 1984). These coefficients are determined with the same basic formula (agreements/agreements + disagreements × 100) except only those intervals in which the behavior occurred (or did not occur) are used in the computation.

In general, applied behavior analysts aim for a reliability coefficient of around .90. Anything less than .80 is a signal that something is seriously wrong. The problem is most often in the definition of the behavior; sloppy definitions result in low reliability because the observers have not been told with sufficient exactitude what they are observing.

Kazdin (1977) has suggested four additional sources of bias that can affect interobserver agreement. First, just knowing another person is present collecting reliability data can influence the accuracy of the primary observer. Such knowledge has influenced reliability data by as much as 20–25%. It is suggested that reliability checks should be unobtrusive or covert or that the second observer collect data on several students including the target student. These suggestions may not be practical in the classroom. However, limiting communication between the teacher and the second observer during the observation period can reduce their influence on one another's observations. The presence of an observer can also affect the behavior of the student being observed and of the teacher. This is known as reactivity (Repp, Nieminen, Olinger, & Brusca, 1988). Some teachers give more prompts to the target student when an observer is present (Hay, Nelson, & Hay, 1977), and some increase their rate of instruction and positive feedback (Hay, Nelson, & Hay, 1980).

The second concern is referred to as *observer drift*. This is the tendency of observers to change over time the stringency with which they apply the operational definitions of behavior. They may begin to record as "instances" behaviors that do not exactly conform to the operational definition. It is recommended that the observers periodically review definitions together and practice during the course of the program.

Kazdin (1977) provides suggestions for limiting complexity bias in research studies.

A third influence on the reliability of data concerns the complexity of the observational coding system. The more complex the system, the more the reliability is in jeopardy. Complexity refers to either the number of different types of a response category being recorded (for example, types of disruptive behavior), the number of different students being observed, or the number of different behaviors being scored on a given occasion. In a classroom, the teacher might mitigate the effects of complexity by limiting the number of behaviors or students observed at any given time. The fourth bias is that of expectancy. Observers who look for behavior change are likely to find it. The reverse is also true; a teacher who has decided that nothing can be done with a student is not likely to find a behavior change. Observers may be biased because of the student's sex, race, appearance, or previous history. In addition, a bias may be based on the purpose of the observation (Repp et al., 1988). Teachers may be biased data collectors if the failure of a behavior change strategy results in a problem student being moved to a special class.

The procedures just described are adequate for determining reliability for most teachers. More stringent standards are sometimes applied in research studies. The student who is interested in learning more about interobserver reliability should consult Hawkins and Dotson (1975) and the series of invited articles on this topic in Volume 10 (1977) of the *Journal of Applied Behavior Analysis*.

FUNDAMENTALS OF GRAPHING DATA

To be useful, data obtained through observational techniques must be easily readable. Tallies or coded entries on data collection forms (raw data) are difficult if not impossible to interpret for information about what is happening to the target behavior. The most common method of data presentation used by applied behavior analysts is graphing. The translation of raw data into a graph is not difficult. It may involve two important steps: conversion of data or calculation of rate and plotting the graph.

Conversion of Data

Before data can be graphed, they must be converted into a consistent graphing form. The data may be reported as a number correct, as a percentage, or as a rate. The measurement conversion used depends on the collection system employed and the data obtained.

Converting permanent product data

Permanent product data are reported as a number of items or a percentage of items resulting from the behavior. For example, a teacher might record the number of math problems completed, the percentage of correctly spelled words, the number of beads strung, or the number of dirty clothes placed in the hamper. If the number of opportunities for responding remains constant—as in spelling tests that always have 20 items or in a series of math worksheets that always have 10 problems—the data may be graphed simply as the number of items. If, on the other hand, the number of opportunities varies—different numbers of test items or math problems—the analyst will need to calculate percentages (see Figure 4–23).

FIGURE 4–23
Choosing measurement conversion for permanent product data.

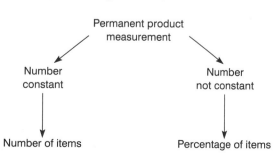

Calculating percentages of correct responses requires only dividing the number of correct responses by the total number of responses and multiplying the result by 100, as shown:

$$\frac{\text{Number of correct responses}}{\text{Total number of responses}} \times 100 = \text{percentage of correct responses}$$

Percentages do not take time (speed) into account as a factor in describing the behavior.

Calculation of Rate

Calculating rate

A conversion to rate data is required when the behavior analyst is concerned with the occurrence of the target behavior *within a certain time period* and the number and accuracy of responses. Rate data reflect accuracy and speed, or fluency of performance, and thereby allow judgments about the development of proficiency. It is important to note that if the time allowed for the response(s) is the same across all sessions, a simple reporting of frequency is all that is necessary. Such is the case where each day the student has 20 minutes to complete a set of math problems. However, in instances where the time allocated for responding, or that required by the student to complete a task, varies from session to session, a rate calculation is needed for comparison.

A *rate of correct responding* is computed by dividing the number of correct responses by the time taken for responding:

$$\text{Correct rate} = \frac{\text{Number correct}}{\text{Time}}$$

For example, if on Monday Kevin completed 15 problems correctly in 30 minutes, his rate of problems correct would be .5 per minute. If, on Tuesday, he completed 20 correct problems in 45 minutes, his rate per minute would be .45. If Kevin's teacher had merely recorded that Kevin completed 15 problems on Monday and 20 problems on Tuesday, the teacher might think that Kevin's math was improving. In reality, though the number of math problems increased, the rate decreased, and Kevin did not do as well on Tuesday as on Monday.
Monday:

$$\frac{\text{15 correct problems}}{\text{30 minutes}} = .5 \text{ correct problems per minute}$$

Tuesday:

$$\frac{20 \text{ correct problems}}{45 \text{ minutes}} = .45 \text{ correct problems per minute}$$

Calculating and plotting a rate of error may be done by dividing the number of errors by the time:

$$\text{Error rate} = \frac{\text{Number of errors}}{\text{Time}}$$

These calculations will provide the teacher with the numbers of correct and incorrect behaviors per minute (or second, or hour).
Session 1:

$$\frac{12 \text{ spelling errors}}{20 \text{ minutes}} = .60 \text{ errors per minute}$$

Session 2:

$$\frac{10 \text{ spelling errors}}{30 \text{ minutes}} = .33 \text{ errors per minute}$$

Converting other kinds of data

Event recording data may be presented in terms of the number of occurrences if the opportunities for responding are consistent each time data are collected. If opportunities for responding are not consistent—as might happen if we were counting the number of times a student followed an instruction from the teacher—the data may be converted to a percentage. Controlled presentation would eliminate this necessity. For example, the teacher might decide to issue exactly 10 instructions in a one-hour period. If the fluency of responding is an issue, conversion may also be made to rate.

Interval or time sampling data are reported as the number or percent of intervals in which the behavior occurred. They are most often presented as percentages.

Duration data are reported as the number of minutes or seconds during which the behavior occurred within a specified period of time.

Latency data are reported as the number of minutes that lapsed prior to the initiation of the behavior following a request. A summary of data conversion procedures appears in Table 4–1.

TABLE 4–1
Summary of data conversion procedures.

Type of Recording	Data Conversion	
Permanent product recording Event recording	Report number of occurrences...	if both time and opportunities to respond are constant.
	Report percentage...	if time is constant (or not of concern) and opportunities vary
	Report rate...	if both time (which is of concern) and opportunities vary, OR if time varies and opportunities are constant.
Interval recording Time sampling	Report number of intervals... Report percentage of intervals...	if constant.
		during or at the end of which behavior occurred.
Duration	Report number of seconds/minutes/hours...	for which the behavior occurred.
Latency	Report number of seconds/minutes/hours...	between antecedent stimulus and onset of behavior.

Plotting Basic Components of a Graph

The basic model for graphing is a simple *line graph*, drawn to include two *axes*. The horizontal axis is the **abscissa** or x-axis. The vertical axis is the **ordinate** or y-axis. Each data point is placed at the intersection of the session during which the behavior was recorded and the quantity or level of the behavior performance (see Figure 4–24).

The time dimension is indicated along the abscissa. Each unit on this axis often represents an observation period during which data were collected. The observation period might be units of days or sessions (of 15 minutes, from 10:00–10:30), or sets of trials (one session equaled 20 trials), or opportunities for response. The first principle of graphing, then, is that *behavior* goes on the ordinate, *time* on the abscissa.

A more specific description of the time units and behavior is included in each axis title. It is a challenge to include as much information as possible without crowding the graph. For example, see the labeling on the graphs in Figure 4–25.

After labeling, the lines on the graph are then numbered in equal increments to show the passage of time and the number, percentage, or rate of the behavior. Notice in Figure 4–26 that the intersection of the axes is the zero point—the numbers start on the first line of the graph.

Each data point, converted from the record sheets, is next plotted with a dot at the appropriate intersection of the two points on the axes. If Harold

FIGURE 4–24
Basic line graph.

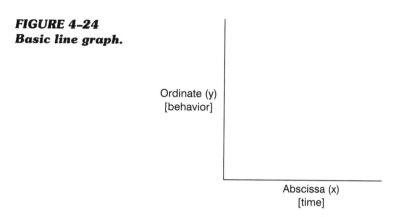

completed five problems the first day, ten the second, and five the third, the graph would look like the one in Figure 4–27. To complete the graph, the dots are connected with a solid line, as in Figure 4–28. This is the basic form for presenting applied behavior analysis data.

Alternative Graphing Formats

Several alternative methods are used for displaying data graphically: cumulative graphs, ratio graphs, and bar graphs.

FIGURE 4–25
Sample graph labeling.

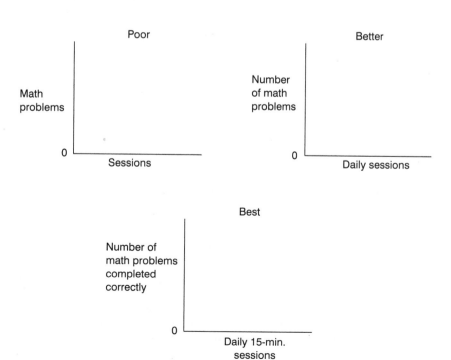

FIGURE 4–26
Sample graphs with
units numbered.

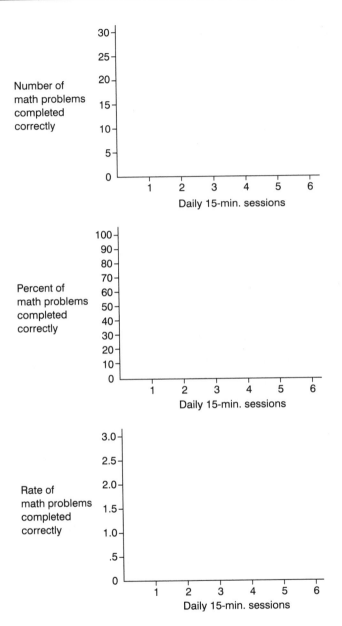

*A cumulative graph
shows the total number
of responses for all ses-
sions including the one
being plotted.*

Cumulative Graph.   On a line graph, data points are plotted at the appropriate intersections without regard to the performance level of the previous
session. For a **cumulative graph**, on the other hand, the number of occurrences observed in a given session are graphed *after being added* to the
number of occurrences of the previous session. This approach provides a
count of the total number of responses. Such graphs must always demonstrate an upward curve provided that any behavior at all is being recorded

FIGURE 4–27
Data points plotted
on graph.

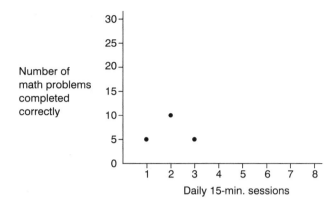

(Ferster, Culbertson, & Boren, 1975). A cumulative graph presents an additive view of a behavior across the intervention sessions.

This form of data illustration provides a continuous line with a slope that indicates the rate of responding. A steep slope indicates rapid responding, a gradual slope indicates slow responding, and a plateau or straight line indicates no responding (see Figure 4–29).

A teacher might want to use a cumulative graph to trace a student's progress toward performing a predetermined number of behaviors. For example, in a prevocational class, the teacher might decide that students should assemble the parts of a simple appliance 50 times in order to demonstrate mastery. A cumulative graph would show clearly when this objective had been accomplished. The slope of the graph would also give the teacher informal data about how rapidly students were moving toward mastery. The hypothetical graphs in Figure 4–30 show the same raw data plotted on a line graph (a) and a cumulative graph (b).

Ratio Graph.   A form of graphing particularly suited to charting rate data has been described by White and Haring (1980). Their **ratio graphs** are designed to show proportional change. The procedure for plotting data points for this

FIGURE 4–28
Completed graph.

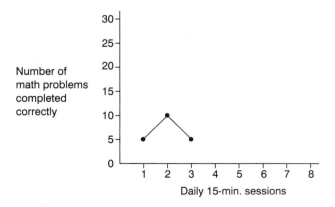

FIGURE 4–29
Slope and rate of
responding.

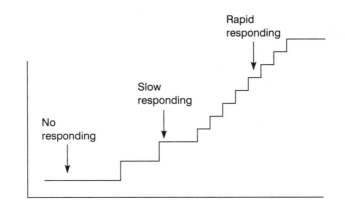

FIGURE 4–30
Comparing line and cumulative graphs.

Raw Data	
Session	Occurrences
1	1
2	1
3	1
4	2
5	0
6	0
7	1
8	3
9	3
10	1

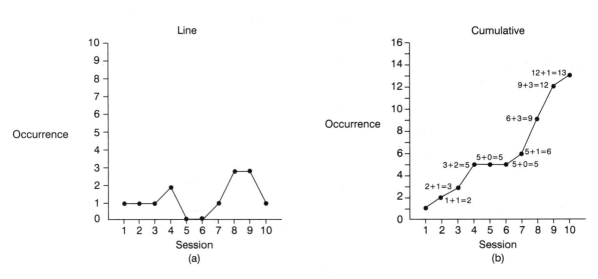

kind of graph is the same as that for line graphs; only the form of the chart or graph itself is different. All data for ratio graphing are converted to rate per minute, and the chart can be used to plot behaviors that occur at the rate of 1,000 per minute down to behaviors that occur at the rate of .000695 per minute (once in 24 hours). Such graphs are a major tool in an outgrowth of applied behavior analysis known as *precision teaching*. Precision teaching involves recording students' responses during a specified time period and plotting these data in the form of rate of responding. The usual procedure is to plot a performance rate and an error rate so the teacher will not be misled into thinking that is effective if an increasing performance rate is accompanied by an even more rapidly increasing error rate.

Teachers may initially be put off by the appearance of a ratio or logarithmic graph, but with a little practice, these tools are easy to use and interpret. Ratio graphs provide the basis for making decisions about teaching based on students' rate of performance. Figure 4–31 shows an example of a ratio or logarithmic chart.

FIGURE 4–31
Chart for recording ratio data.

FIGURE 4–32
Comparing line and bar graph.

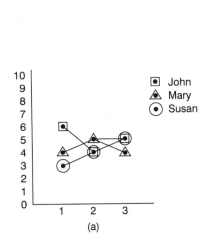

(a)

(b)

Bar Graph. A **bar graph**, or **histogram**, is yet another means of displaying data. As its name implies, a bar graph uses vertical bars rather than horizontal lines to indicate performance levels.

A bar graph may be the preferred means of displaying data in situations where clear interpretation of the pattern of behavior plotted on a line graph is difficult. Such confusion may result when several lines are plotted on a single line graph, as when a teacher chooses to include data from several students or from multiple behaviors. In such cases, plotted lines may overlap or appear extremely close together because data points fall at the same intersections. Figure 4–32 offers an example of the same data plotted on a line graph and on a bar graph. The bar graph is plainly much clearer. A classroom teacher might use a bar graph to display daily the number of correct responses from each member of a small group.

DATA COLLECTION AND THE IEP

Teachers often wonder how daily direct data collection relates to the development of statements to be included in students' Individualized Education Plans. One requirement for every IEP, of course, is a statement of current levels of functioning. The teacher who collects, analyses, and graphs data is in a position to make simple, accurate, and helpful statements, as illustrated by the following anecdote.

It's That Time of Year Again

When others think of spring they may associate it with budding flowers, soft rains, warm weather, or even romance. For Ms. Taber, along with most special education teachers, spring means the annual renewal of the IEP. In preparation for meetings about each of the students in her resource program Ms. Taber must prepare brief, understandable statements of the student's current level of functioning. This year she starts with Russell's folder. Russell has annual and short-term objectives in the areas of math, written English, on-task behavior, and appropriate social behavior.

Ms. Taber first makes sure that data sheets and graphs of Russell's performance are separated by the appropriate objective. She pauses a few minutes to appreciate the progress Russell has made this year, then checks her graphs and formulates the following simple, but meaningful statements:

- On timed tests of multiplication facts Russell completes an average of 85 problems correct over 5 days with a range of 78 to 90.

- On seven in-class compositions within the last 20 school days, 60% of Russell's sentences have shown subject-verb agreement.

- Over seven 15-minute observation sessions during the last 10 school days, Russell attended to task (as defined in his present IEP) 67% of the time.

- During physical education and lunch periods over the last 5 school days Russell has cursed out loud an average of 11 times per period, with a range of 7 to 24 instances.

The cursing, she reminded herself, still needs work.

A Day in the Life of Professor Grundy

6:30 A.M. The alarm clock beside Professor Grundy's bed rang loudly. He groped for the off button and silenced the noise. He put the pillow over his head and contemplated his day. He remained prone for several minutes, then sat up, turned on the bedside lamp, and swung his feet to the floor. On the alarm clock was taped a data record sheet on which he recorded the latency of his getting up behavior.

"Ten minutes," he groaned. "Yesterday, I made it in five, but that was before behavioral objectives. Oh Lord, today I have to do observational procedures with the graduate class." Professor Grundy felt himself pulled again toward the pillow but forced himself into the bathroom instead, where he shed his pajamas and stepped on the scale. He noted the (very) permanent product thus measured on a graph handily placed on the bathroom wall.

"Oh well," sighed Professor Grundy, "I have big bones."

He then proceeded to the kitchen where his wife, Minerva, was preparing breakfast. He watched his stopwatch carefully.

"I compliment you, my dear," he exclaimed, when she served him. "Your facial twitch is much better. It occurred in only 35% of the 10-second intervals during the 15 minutes it took you to cook today. That's down 12% from yesterday."

Professor Grundy proceeded to the university. During the day, he picked up the phone in his office at 15-minute intervals, recording a time sample of his garrulous colleague's talking on the party line they shared.

"Just as I thought," he gloated. "That psychoanalytic fruitcake is on the phone 65% of the time. I knew he was hogging the line."

At 4:30, Professor Grundy went to teach his graduate class. All the students were employed as teachers during the day, and it was a challenge merely to keep them awake. He presented a crisp, factual description of behavioral observation procedures (remarkably similar to the one presented in this chapter) and then assigned an observation project.

"Which data sheet is it, Oliver?"

One of the students still awake snorted, "How utterly ridiculous . . .," apparently waking the rest of the class, all of whom chimed in: "Yes, I have to teach, I don't have time . . .," "You must be kidding. . . ."

Professor Grundy had activated his stopwatch when the first comment was made. He waited calmly until the uproar ceased, then made a notation in his grade book.

"Eleven minutes this semester," he told the class. "Last semester the duration of complaints was only eight minutes."

After repeating the instructions for the assignments, Professor Grundy returned home where he recorded and graphed

- The latency of Minerva's getting dinner on the table after he announced that he was hungry

- The rate per hour of television commercials

- The fact that once again Minerva went to bed early with a blinding headache, brought on, she announced, by the sight of graph paper all over the house

SUMMARY

This chapter described procedures for collecting data that will form the basis for decisions about intervention strategies. We discussed a number of types of data collection such as anecdotal reports, permanent product recording, and observational recording. One section examined basic procedures for determining interobserver reliability. The chapter concluded with information on graphing data, including a description of line graphs, cumulative graphs, bar graphs, and ratio graphs. You'll find the tools presented in this chapter very useful in working with data.

DISCUSSION QUESTIONS

1. Jerry's behavior in his 5th-grade class was reported as "disruptive." The consulting teacher visited his classroom to collect some initial referral data. (a) She went into his class for 30 minutes on three days to count instances of "disruptive" behavior. (b) On three days she checked every 20 minutes between 9 A.M. and noon to see if he was being disruptive. (c) For one hour on Tuesday morning and a Thursday afternoon, she sat in Jerry's class and wrote down everything he did, his teacher did, and significant actions of other students. What observational recording system did she use in each instance?

2. Susan never gets her math problems done before the end of class. To help determine the nature of her problems, the teacher could (a) give her a set of problems and record how long it was before she began to work, or (b) record how long it took her to complete the set of problems once she had begun. What recording system is being used in each instance?

3. Four student data collectors were observing John, a fourth-grade student. John was doing poorly in spelling. Observer 1 divided his observational time into 15-second intervals and noted whether John was working in his spelling workbook during each interval. Observer 2 went to John's desk at the end of the spelling period and counted the number of answers John had written in his spelling workbook. Observer 3 counted each time John put his pencil on the workbook and wrote something. Observer 4 divided the period into 5-minute intervals and recorded whether John was working in his spelling workbook at the end of each interval. What recording procedure is each observer employing?

4. Mrs. Carrington wanted the students to help her check their knowledge of multiplication facts. The students were divided into pairs in order to ask each other the 7, 8, and 9 multiplication table facts, and record their accuracy. Each student was given a packet of flashcards that had the problem statement on one side and the answer on the back of the card. Also, on the back was a place to mark whether the answer given by his or

her partner was correct or incorrect. What recording procedure is being used by the students?

5. What steps should Ms. Tabor, described in the next to last anecdote, take to determine what to do about Russell's cursing?

REFERENCES

Alberto, P.A., & Schofield, P. 1979. An instructional interaction pattern for the severely handicapped. *Teaching exceptional children, 12*, 16–19.

Alberto, P.A., Sharpton, W., & Goldstein, D. 1979. *Project Bridge: Integration of severely retarded students on regular education campuses.* Atlanta: Georgia State University.

Ayllon, T.A., & Michael, J. 1959. The psychiatric nurse as a behavior engineer. *Journal of the Experimental Analysis of Behavior, 2*, 323–334.

Ayllon, T., & Milan, M. 1979. *Correctional rehabilitation and management: A psychological approach.* New York: Wiley.

Bacon-Prue, A., Blount, R., Pickering, D., & Drabman, R. 1980. An evaluation of three litter control procedures: Trash receptacles, paid workers, and the marked item technique. *Journal of Applied Behavior Analysis, 13*, 165–170.

Bellamy, G., Horner, R., & Inman, D. 1979. *Vocational habilitation of severely retarded adults: A direct service technology.* Baltimore: University Park Press.

Bijou, S.W., Peterson, R.F., & Ault, M.H. 1968. A method to integrate descriptive and experimental field studies at the level of data and empirical concepts. *Journal of Applied Behavior Analysis, 1*, 175–191.

Brody, G.H., Lahey, B.B., & Combs, M.L. 1978. Effects of intermittent modelling on observational learning. *Journal of Applied Behavior Analysis, 11*, 87–90.

Browder, D., Snell, M., & Wildonger, B. 1988. Simulation and community-based instruction of vending machines with time-delay. *Education and Training of the Mentally Retarded, 23*, 175–185.

Carr, E.G., Binkoff, J.A., Kologinsky, E., & Eddy, M. 1978. Acquisition of sign language by autistic children. I: Expressive labelling. *Journal of Applied Behavior Analysis, 11*, 489–501.

Cinciripini, P.M., Epstein, L.H., & Martin, J.E. 1979. The effects of feedback on blood pressure discrimination. *Journal of Applied Behavior Analysis, 12*, 345–353.

Cooper, J. 1981. *Measurement and analysis of behavioral techniques.* Columbus, Ohio: Merrill.

Cuvo, A., & Klatt, K. 1992. Effects of community-based, videotape, and flash card instruction of community-referenced sight words on students with mental retardation. *Journal of Applied Behavior Analysis, 25*, 499–512.

Dahlquist, L., & Gil, K. 1986. Using parents to maintain improved dental flossing skills in children. *Journal of Applied Behavior Analysis, 19*, 255–260.

Doke, L., & Risley, T.R. 1971. The PLACHECK evaluation of group care. Unpublished paper presented at Annual Meeting of the Kansas Psychological Association, Overland Park, Kan., April.

Doke, L.A., & Risley, T.R. 1972. The organization of day-care environments: Required vs. optional activities. *Journal of Applied Behavior Analysis, 5*, 405–420.

Drash, P., Ray, R.,L, Tudor, R. 1989. An inexpensive event recorder. *Journal of Applied Behavior Analysis, 22*, 453.

Duker, P., & Morsink, H. 1984. Acquisition and cross-setting generalization of manual signs with severely retarded individuals. *Journal of Applied Behavior Analysis, 17*, 93–103.

Ferrari, J., & Baldwin, C. 1989. From cars to carts. *Behavior Modification, 13*, 51–64.

Ferster, C.B., Culbertson, S., & Boren, M.C.P. 1975. *Behavior principles* (2nd ed.). Englewood Cliffs, N.J.: Prentice-Hall, Inc.

Gajar, A., Schloss, P., & Thompson, C. 1984. Effects of feedback and self-monitoring on head trauma youths' conversational skills. *Journal of Applied Behavior Analysis, 17*, 353–358.

Gettinger, M. 1985. Effects of teacher-directed versus student-directed instruction and cues versus no cues for improving spelling performance. *Journal of Applied Behavior Analysis, 18*, 167–171.

Greenwood, C., Dinwiddie, G., Bailey, V., Carta, J., Dorsey, D., Kohler, F., Nelson, C., Rotholz, D., & Schulte, D. 1987. Field replication of classwide peer tutoring. *Journal of Applied Behavior Analysis, 20,* 151–160.

Hansen, G.D. 1979. Enuresis control through fading, escape, and avoidance training. *Journal of Applied Behavior Analysis, 12,* 303–307.

Hawkins, R.P., & Dotson, V.S. 1975. Reliability scores that delude: An Alice in Wonderland trip through the misleading characteristics of inter-observer agreement scores in interval recording. In E. Ramp & G. Semb (Eds.), *Behavior analysis: Areas of research and application* (pp. 359–376). Englewood Cliffs, N.J.: Prentice-Hall.

Hay, L., Nelson, R., & Hay, W. 1977. Some methodological problems in the use of teachers as observers. *Journal of Applied Behavior Analysis, 10,* 345–348.

Hay, L., Nelson, R., & Hay, W. 1980. Methodological problems in the use of participant observers. *Journal of Applied Behavior Analysis, 13,* 501–504.

Hersen, M., & Barlow, D.H. 1976. *Single-case experimental designs: Strategies for studying behavior change.* New York: Pergamon Press.

Heward, W.L., & Eachus, H.T. 1979. Acquisition of adjectives and adverbs in sentences written by hearing impaired and aphasic children. *Journal of Applied Behavior Analysis, 12,* 391–400.

Horton, S. 1987. Reduction of disruptive mealtime behavior by facial screening. *Behavior Modification, 11,* 53–64.

Howell, R., Sidorenko, E., & Jurica, J. 1987. The effects of computer use on the acquisition of multiplication facts by a student with learning disabilities. *Journal of Learning Disabilities, 20,* 336–341.

Kazdin, A. 1977. Artifact, bias, and complexity of assessment: The ABCs of reliability. *Journal of Applied Behavior Analysis, 10,* 141–150.

Kincaid, M.S., & Weisberg, P. 1978. Alphabet letters as tokens: Training preschool children in letter recognition and labelling during a token exchange period. *Journal of Applied Behavior Analysis, 11,* 199.

Knapczyk, D. 1989. Generalization of student question asking from special class to regular class settings. *Journal of Applied Behavior Analysis, 22,* 77–83.

Lloyd, J., Bateman, D., Landrum, T., & Hallahan, D. 1989. Self-recording of attention versus productivity. *Journal of Applied Behavior Analysis, 22,* 315–323.

Luiselli, J. 1989. Contingent glove wearing for the treatment of self-exoriating behavior in a sensory-impaired adolescent. *Behavior Modification, 13,* 65–73.

Martin, G., Pallotta-Cornick, A., Johnstone, G., & Goyos, A.C. 1980. A supervisory strategy to improve work performance for lower functioning retarded clients in a sheltered workshop. *Journal of Applied Behavior Analysis, 13,* 183–190.

Matson, J., Sevin, J., Fridley, D., & Love, S. 1990. Increasing spontaneous language in three autistic children. *Journal of Applied Behavior Analysis, 23,* 227–233.

McDonnell, J., & Ferguson, B. 1989. A comparison of time delay and decreasing prompt hierarchy strategies in teaching banking skills to students with moderate handicaps. *Journal of Applied Behavior Analysis, 22,* 85–91.

Neef, N., Walters, J., & Egel, A. 1984. Establishing generative yes/no responses in developmentally disabled children. *Journal of Applied Behavior Analysis, 17,* 453–460.

O'Brien, S., Ross, L., & Christophersen, E. 1986. Primary encopresis: Evaluation and treatment. *Journal of Applied Behavior Analysis, 19,* 137–145.

Olenick, D.L., & Pear, J.J. 1980. Differential reinforcement of correct responses to probes and prompts in picture-name training with severely retarded children. *Journal of Applied Behavior Analysis, 13,* 77–89.

Repp, A.C., Nieminen, G., Olinger, E., & Brusca, R. 1988. Direct observation: Factors affecting the accuracy of observers. *Exceptional Children, 55,* 29–36.

Repp, A.C., Roberts, D.M., Slack, D.J., Repp, C.F., & Berkler, M.S. 1976. A comparison of frequency, interval, and time-sampling methods of data collection. *Journal of Applied Behavior Analysis, 9,* 501–508.

Roberts, R., Nelson, R., & Olson, T. 1987. Self-instruction: An analysis of the differential effects of instruction and reinforcement. *Journal of Applied Behavior Analysis, 20,* 235–242.

Rudd, J., & Geller, E. 1985. A university-based incentive program to increase safety belt use. *Journal of Applied Behavior Analysis, 18,* 215–226.

Saudargas, R., & Zanolli, K. 1990. Momentary time sampling as an estimate of percentage time: A field validation, *Journal of Applied Behavior Analysis, 23,* 533–537.

Saunders, R., & Koplik, K. 1975. A multi-purpose data sheet for recording and graphing in the classroom. *AAESPH Review, 1*, 1.

Schraa, J.C., Lautmann, L., Luzi, M.K., & Screven, C.G. 1978. Establishment of nondelusional responses in a socially withdrawn chronic schizophrenic. *Journal of Applied Behavior Analysis, 11*, 433–434.

Schreibman, L., & Carr, E.G. 1978. Elimination of echolalic responding to questions through the training of a generalized verbal response. *Journal of Applied Behavior Analysis, 11*, 453–463.

Singh, N. 1987. Overcorrection of oral reading errors. *Behavior Modification, 11*, 165–181.

Sowers-Hoag, K., Thyer, B., & Bailey, J. 1987. Promoting automobile safety belt use by young children. *Journal of Applied Behavior Analysis, 20*, 133–138.

Stern, G., Fowler, S., & Kohler, F. 1988. A comparison of two intervention roles: Peer monitor and point earner. *Journal of Applied Behavior Analysis, 21*, 103–109.

Stevens, K., & Schuster, J. 1987. Effects of constant time delay procedure on the written spelling performance of a learning disabled student. *Learning Disability Quarterly, 10*, 9–16.

Tawney, J., & Gast, D. 1984. *Single-subject research in special education*. Columbus, Ohio: Merrill.

Trap, J.J., Milner-Davis, P., Joseph, S., & Cooper, J.O. 1978. The effects of feedback and consequences on transitional cursive letter formation. *Journal of Applied Behavior Analysis, 11*, 381–393.

Valcante, G., Roberson, W., Reid, W., & Wolking, W. 1989. Effects of wait-time and intertrial interval durations on learning by children with multiple handicaps. *Journal of Applied Behavior Analysis, 22*, 43–55.

Watkins, L., Sprafkin, J., & Krolikowski, D. 1990. Effects of video based training on spoken and signed language acquisition by students with mental retardation. *Research in Developmental Disabilities, 11*, 273–288.

White, O.R., & Haring, N.G. 1980. *Exceptional teaching* (2nd ed.). Columbus, Ohio: Merrill.

Williams, G., & Cuvo, A. 1986. Training apartment upkeep skills to rehabilitation clients. *Journal of Applied Behavior Analysis, 19*, 39–51.

Williams, M., Thyer, B., Bailey, J., & Harrison, D. 1989. Promoting safety belt use with traffic signs and prompters. *Journal of Applied Behavior Analysis, 22*, 71–76.

Winett, R., Kramer, K., Walker, W., Malone, S., & Lane, M. 1988. Modifying food purchases in supermarkets with modeling, feedback, and goal-setting procedures. *Journal of Applied Behavior Analysis, 21*, 73–80.

Wood, R., & Flynn, J.M. 1978. A self-evaluation token system *versus* an external evaluation token system alone in a residential setting with predelinquent youth. *Journal of Applied Behavior Analysis, 11*, 503–512.

Wright, H. 1960. Observational study. In P.H. Mussen (Ed.), *Handbook of research methods in child development*. New York: Wiley.

CHAPTER 5

Single-Subject Designs

Did you know that . . .

- There's no such thing as an average student?
- What you think is working may not be?
- Classroom teachers can conduct research?
- Classroom teachers *must* conduct research if their instruction is to be effective?

When teachers collect data on student progress, they can make systematic observations of student behavior change. Data collection and observation certainly make statements about the direction and magnitude of behavioral changes possible. They do not, however, provide sufficient information to indicate a cause-effect relationship between an intervention and the behavior in question.

To make assumptions about cause and effect, teachers must carry out data collection and recording under rigorous conditions. There are certain patterns, or *designs*, for collecting data that enable professionals to determine the relationship between an intervention and a behavior. Only when such a relationship can be established may teachers make confident statements about the effect of an intervention on behavior.

In this chapter we will describe a number of designs that enable teachers and researchers to determine the relationship between intervention procedures and behaviors. We include research designs for two reasons: (1) to enable teachers to design classroom intervention procedures that can be systematically evaluated, and (2) to familiarize teachers with experimental designs used in applied behavior analysis. Actual research applications, taken from professional journals, accompany the text describing each research design. Each design discussed in the chapter is also applied to a classroom problem to stress the utility of applied behavior analysis designs in the classroom. After reading this chapter, teachers should be able to conduct simple research and to read and understand experimental research reported in professional journals.

VARIABLES

Before discussing specific designs, we shall define some terms basic to an understanding of experimental investigation. The term **variable** may be used to refer to any number of factors involved in research. These may include attributes of the individual being studied or conditions associated with the setting in which the study is done. Experimental design differentiates between two types of variables: dependent and independent. The term **dependent variable** refers to the behavior targeted for change. The term **independent variable** refers to the treatment or procedure that the experimenter controls—the treatment or procedure being used to change behavior. In the following sentences from a research synopsis, the independent variable is italicized and the dependent variable appears in parentheses.

> *Verbal praise* is contingently presented when (oral questions are answered correctly).
> *Time-out* is contingently presented when (a temper tantrum occurs).

If a design is able to demonstrate that manipulation of the independent variable results in changes in the dependent variable, a tentative cause-effect relationship may be assumed. This link is termed a **functional relation-**

ship. There is a functional relationship, in other words, if it can be demonstrated that the dependent variable systematically changes as a result of changes in the independent variable. The changes in the dependent variable "depend" on changes in the independent variable.

BASIC CATEGORIES OF DESIGNS

Group designs versus single-subject designs

Two major categories of designs are **group designs** and **single-subject**, or single-case, **designs**. As indicated by the names, group designs focus on data related to a number of individuals, whereas single-subject designs focus on a single individual in a research sample. Group designs are used to compare the performance of groups of people (or subjects) on some dependent variable. The comparison is most often made using an average of each group's performance. Most applied behavior analysts prefer to record specific information about an individual rather than information about the average performance of a group. The use of averages may obscure important information as illustrated in the following anecdote.

Ms. Witherspoon Orders Reading Books

Ms. Witherspoon, a third-grade teacher, was urged by her principal to order new reading books at the beginning of the school year. Being unfamiliar with her class, Ms. Witherspoon decided to use a reading test to determine which books to order. She administered the test and averaged the scores to determine the most appropriate reader. She came up with an exact average of third grade, first month, and ordered 30 readers on that level.

When the books arrived, she found that the reader was much too hard for some of her students and much too easy for others. Using an average score had concealed the fact that, although the class average was third grade, some students were reading at first-grade and others at sixth-grade level.

Single-Subject Designs

Single-subject designs compare the effects of different conditions on the same individual.

To avoid the problems associated with the use of averages, most applied behavior analysis researchers prefer to use single-subject designs. These designs monitor the performance of individual subjects during manipulation of the independent variable(s). Certain techniques, which will be described later in the chapter, are used to ensure that changes in the dependent variable result from experimental manipulations and not from chance or coincidental factors.

Single-subject designs require repeated measures of the dependent variable. The performance of the individual whose behavior is being monitored (the subject) is recorded weekly, daily, or even more frequently over an extended period of time. That subject's performance can then be compared under different *experimental conditions*, or manipulations of the independent variable. Each subject is compared only to himself or herself, an approach that contrasts with group-design research, in which groups of subjects are compared to each other. Certain components are common to all single-subject designs. These include a measure of baseline performance and at least one measure of performance under an intervention or treatment condition.

Baseline Measures

The first phase of single-subject design involves the collection and recording of **baseline data**. Baseline data are measures of the level of behavior (the dependent variable) as it occurs naturally, before intervention. Kazdin (1982) states that baseline data serve two functions. First, baseline data serve a *descriptive function*. These data describe the existing level of student performance. When data points are graphed, they provide a picture of the student's behavior—his current ability to solve multiplication problems or his current rate of talk-outs. This objective record can assist the teacher in verifying the existence, and extent, of the behavior deficit (lack of ability to do multiplication) or behavior excess (talking-out) that she has decided to alter.

Second, baseline data serve a *predictive function*. "The baseline data serve as the basis for predicting the level of performance for the immediate future if the intervention is not provided" (Kazdin, 1982, p. 105). To evaluate the success of an intervention (the independent variable), the teacher must know what student performance was like before the intervention. Baseline data serve a purpose similar to that of a pretest. "The predication is achieved by projecting or extrapolating into the future a continuation of baseline performance" (p. 105). It is against this projection that the effect of an intervention is judged.

The baseline phase continues for several days before beginning the intervention phase(s). In most instances, at least five baseline data points are collected and plotted. The extent of baseline data collection, however, is affected by certain characteristics of these data points.

Baselines should be stable.

Because baseline data are to be used to judge the effectiveness of the teacher's intervention, it is important that the baseline be *stable*, providing a representative sample of the natural occurrence of the behavior. The *stability* of a baseline is assessed by two characteristics: variability of the data points and trends in the data points.

See Chapter 3 for suggestions on writing operational definitions.

Variability of data refers to fluctuations in the student's performance. "As a general rule, the greater the variability in the data, the more difficult it is to draw conclusions about the effects of the intervention" (Kazdin, 1982, p. 109) and to make projections about future performance. When baselines are unstable, the first thing to examine is the definition of the target behavior. A lack of stability in the baseline may suggest that the operational definition of the target behavior is not sufficiently descriptive to allow for accurate and consistent recording or that the data collector is not being consistent in the procedure used for data collection.

In laboratory settings, other sources of variability can very often be identified and controlled. In classrooms, attempts to control variability are desirable if the sources of variability can be identified—for example, if fluctuations are caused by inconsistent delivery of medication. In cases of temporary fluctuations caused by such unusual events as a fight or a problem at home, the teacher may just wait for the fluctuation to pass. However, in classrooms, unlike laboratories, "variability is an unavoidable fact of life," and in such settings there are seldom "the facilities or time that would be required to eliminate variability" (Sidman, 1960, p. 193).

Where variables can be rigorously controlled, a research-oriented criterion for the existence of variability would be data points within a 5% range of variability (Sidman, 1960). A therapeutic criterion of 20% has been suggested (Repp, 1983). However, in classrooms where pure research concerns might be less important than rapid modification of the behavior, we suggest a more lenient parameter of 50% variability. If variability exceeds 50%, statistical techniques for performance comparisons must be used (Barlow & Hersen, 1984). A baseline is often considered stable if no data point of the baseline varies more than 50% from the mean, or average, of the baseline. Figure 5–1 illustrates a procedure for computing the stability of a baseline based on this criterion.

A trend in the data refers to an indication of a distinctive direction in the performance of the behavior. A trend is defined as three successive data points in the same direction (Barlow & Hersen, 1984). A baseline may show no trend, an increasing trend, or a decreasing trend. Figures 5–2 and 5–3 illustrate two types of trends—increasing and decreasing.

An ascending baseline denotes an increasing trend. Teachers should initiate intervention on an ascending baseline only if the objective is to decrease the behavior. Because the behavior is already increasing, the effects of an intervention designed to increase behavior will be obscured by the baseline trend.

FIGURE 5–1
Computing baseline stability.

Session	Data Points
1	14
2	10
3	20
4	16
5	11

Baseline mean (arithmetic average) = 14.2 = 14
50% of mean = 7
Acceptable range of data points = 7 – (14 ± 7)
This baseline is stable because no data point varies more than 50% from the mean.

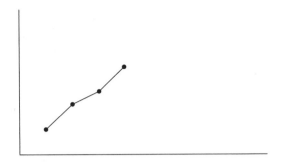

FIGURE 5–2
Increasing trend
(ascending base-
line).

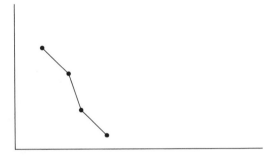

FIGURE 5–3
Decreasing trend
(descending base-
line).

Take baseline trends into account before intervention.

A *descending baseline* includes at least three data points that show a distinctive decreasing direction or trend in the behavior. Teachers should initiate intervention on a descending baseline only if the objective is to increase the behavior.

Intervention Measures

The second component of any single-subject design is a series of repeated measures of the subject's performance under a treatment or intervention condition. The independent variable (treatment or intervention) is introduced and its effects on the dependent variable (the subject's performance) are monitored. Trends in treatment data indicate the effectiveness of the treatment and provide the teacher or researcher with guidance in determining the need for changes in intervention procedures.

Experimental Control

Professor Grundy encounters a confounding variable when he again visits Ms. Harper in this chapter.

Experimental control refers to the researcher's efforts to ensure that changes in the dependent variable are in fact related to manipulations of the independent variable—that a functional relationship exists. The researcher wants to eliminate to the greatest extent possible the chance that other, confounding variables are responsible for changes in the behavior. *Confounding variables* are those environmental events or conditions that are not controlled by the researcher but may affect behavior. For example, if a teacher institutes a behavioral system for reducing disruptive behavior in a class after the three most disruptive students have moved away, she really cannot be sure that the new system is responsible for the lower levels of disruption. Removal of the three students is a confounding variable.

The designs discussed in this chapter provide varying degrees of experimental control. Some, called here *teaching designs*, do not permit confident assumption of a functional relationship. They may, however, provide sufficient indication of behavior change for everyday classroom use, particularly if the teacher remains alert to the possibility of confounding variables. Other designs, called *research designs*, provide for much tighter experimental control and allow the teacher or researcher to presume a functional relationship. Experimental control is most often demonstrated by repeating an intervention several times and observing its effect on the dependent variable each time it is repeated. Research designs may be used in classrooms when a teacher is particularly concerned about possible confounding variables and wants to be sure that intervention has the desired effect on behavior. The teacher who is interested in publishing or otherwise sharing with other professionals the results of an intervention would also use a research design if at all possible. In the following sections on specific research designs, both a research and a classroom application are described for each design whenever possible.

AB DESIGN

The AB design is a teaching design.

The **AB design** is the most basic of all single-subject designs. Each of the more complex designs is actually an expansion on this simple one. The designation *AB* refers to the two phases of the design: the A, or baseline, phase and the B, or intervention, phase. During the A phase, baseline data are collected and recorded. Once a stable baseline has been established, the intervention is introduced, and the B phase begins. In this phase, intervention data are collected and recorded. The teacher can evaluate increases or decreases in the amount, rate, percentage, or duration of the target behavior during the intervention phase and compare them to the baseline phase. Using this information to make inferences about the effectiveness of the intervention, the teacher can make decisions about continuing, changing, or discarding the intervention.

Implementation

Table 5–1 shows data collected using an AB design. The teacher in this instance was concerned about the few correct answers a student gave to questions about a reading assignment. For five days, she collected baseline data. She then made 2 minutes of free time contingent on each correct answer and continued to record the number of correct responses. As shown

TABLE 5-1
Sample data from
an AB design.

Baseline Data	
Day	Number of Correct Responses
Monday	2
Tuesday	1
Wednesday	0
Thursday	2
Friday	1

Intervention Data	
Day	Number of Correct Responses
Monday	5
Tuesday	6
Wednesday	4
Thursday	8
Friday	6

in Table 5-1, the number clearly increased during the intervention phase. The teacher could make a tentative assumption here that her intervention has been effective.

Graphic Display

Data collected using an AB design are graphed in two phases: A, or baseline, and B, or intervention. The two phases are separated by a broken vertical line on the graph, and data points between phases are not connected. The graph (Figure 5–4) shows a clearer picture of the effectiveness of the intervention than do the data in table form.

FIGURE 5–4
Graph of AB design
data from Table
5–1.

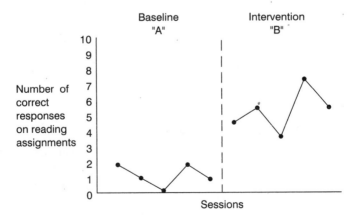

Design Application

The basic AB design is not often found in the research literature because it is the weakest of the single-subject designs. The following example demonstrates the use of an AB design in a classroom setting.

Jack Learns to Do His French Homework

Mr. Vogl had difficulty working with Jack, a student in the fourth-period French class. Jack was inattentive when homework from the previous evening was reviewed. Closer investigation revealed that Jack ignored the review sessions because he was not doing the assignments. To increase the amount of homework completed, Mr. Vogl decided to use positive reinforcement. To evaluate the effectiveness of the intervention, he selected the AB design using the number of homework questions completed correctly as the dependent variable.

Over a baseline period of 5 days, Jack did 0 out of 10 (0/10) homework problems correctly each day. Since Jack frequently asked to listen to tapes in the French lab, Mr. Vogl decided to allow Jack to listen to tapes for 2 minutes for each correct homework question. Data collected during the intervention phase indicated an increase in the number of questions Jack answered correctly. Data analysis suggested that the intervention technique was effective.

Advantages and Disadvantages

The primary advantage of an AB design is its simplicity. It provides the teacher with a quick, uncomplicated means of comparing students' behavior before and after implementation of some intervention or instructional procedure, making instruction more systematic.

Many teachers use AB designs to evaluate their students' progress.

The disadvantage of the AB design is that it cannot be used to make a confident assumption of a functional relationship. Although the data may show an increase or decrease in the behavior during the intervention phase, thus indicating effectiveness of the intervention, this design does not provide for a replication of the procedure. Therefore, the AB design is very vulnerable to confounding variables or coincidental events. This is illustrated in the following example.

Ms. Harper Conducts Research

As part of her student teaching assignment, Ms. Harper was required to carry out a simple research project using an AB design. She decided to use Ralph's staying in his seat as her dependent variable. (Remember Ralph from Chapter 1?) Ms. Harper collected baseline data for several days and determined that Ralph stayed in his seat for periods varying from 20 to 25 minutes during the one-hour reading class. She prepared to intervene, choosing as her independent variable points exchangeable for various activities that Ralph enjoyed.

When Professor Grundy made a visit soon after intervention began, Ms. Harper met him at the door in a state of high excitement.

"It's working, Professor!" gloated Ms. Harper. "Look at my graph! Ralph was absent the first two days of this week, but since he's been back and I've been giving him points, he's been in his seat 100% every day. Do you think I'll get an A on my project?"

Professor Grundy inspected Ms. Harper's graph and agreed that her procedure appeared to be effective. He then sat down in the rear of the classroom to observe. After a few minutes, during which Ralph indeed stayed in his seat, Professor Grundy attracted Ms. Harper's attention and called her to the back of the room.

"Ms. Harper," he asked gently, "did it not occur to you that the heavy cast on Ralph's leg might have some effect on the amount of time he spends in his seat?"

"Its working, professor. He's staying in his seat!"

REVERSAL DESIGN

ABAB is a research design. A functional relationship can be demonstrated.

The **reversal design**, another type of single-subject design, is used to analyze the effectiveness of a single independent variable. Commonly referred to as the *ABAB design*, this design involves the sequential application and withdrawal of an intervention to verify the intervention's effects on a behavior. By repeatedly comparing baseline data to data collected after application of the intervention strategy, the researcher can determine whether a functional relationship exists between the dependent and independent variables.

Implementation

The reversal design has four phases: A, B, A, and B:

FIGURE 5–5
Reversal design graph that demonstrates a functional relationship between variables.

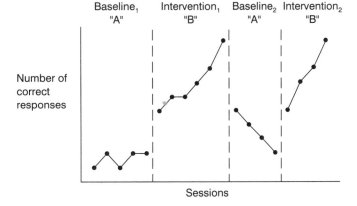

FIGURE 5–6
Reversal design graph that does not demonstrate a functional relationship between variables.

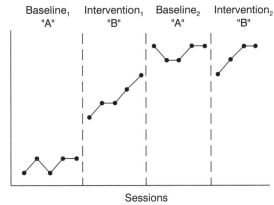

- A *(baseline 1)*: the initial baseline during which data are collected on the target behavior under conditions existing before the start of the study.
- B *(intervention 1)*: the initial introduction of the intervention selected to alter the target behavior. Intervention continues until the criterion for the target behavior is reached or a definite trend in the desired direction of behavior change is noted.
- A *(baseline 2)*: a return to original baseline conditions, accomplished by withdrawing or terminating the intervention.
- B *(baseline 2)*: the reintroduction of the intervention procedure.

Data collected using a reversal design should be examined for a functional relationship between the dependent and independent variables. The data in Figure 5–5 demonstrate a functional relationship between the dependent and independent variables, said to exist if the second set of baseline data returns to a level close to that in the original A phase or if a trend is evident in the second A phase in the opposite direction of the first B phase. Figure 5–6 graphs data that do not demonstrate the existence of a functional relationship.

It must be noted that a second B phase (intervention phase) is also desirable for verification of a functional relationship. Cooper (1981, p. 117) states that researchers need three pieces of evidence before they can say that a functional relationship is demonstrated: (1) *prediction*: the instructional statement that a particular independent variable will alter the dependent variable, for example, the contingent use of tokens to increase the number of math problems Michael completes; (2) *verification of prediction*: the increase (or decrease) in the dependent behavior during the first intervention phase, and the approximate return to baseline levels of performance in the second A phase; and (3) *replication of effect*: the reintroduction of the independent variable during a second B phase resulting again in the same desired change in behavior.

The reversal design is a research design that allows the teacher to assume a functional relationship between independent and dependent variables. The second baseline and intervention phases, with conditions identical to those of the first, provide an opportunity for replication of the effect of the intervention on the target behavior. It is unlikely coincidental confounding variables would exist simultaneously with repeated application and withdrawal of the independent variable. The reversal design, however, is not always the most appropriate choice. The reversal design should not be used in the following cases:

It would be unethical to withdraw, for purposes of research, an intervention that stopped a student with severe disabilities from banging her head on the floor.

1. When the target behavior is dangerous, for example, aggressive behavior directed toward other students (hitting) or self-injurious behavior. Because the reversal design calls for a second baseline condition to be implemented after a change in the target behavior rate, ethical considerations would prohibit withdrawing a successful intervention technique.

2. When the target behavior is not reversible. Many academic behaviors, for example, are not reversible, because the behavior change is associated with a learning process. Under such conditions, a return to baseline performance is not feasible: information cannot be "unlearned."

Graphic Display

The reversal design calls for four distinct phases of data collection. Figure 5–7 illustrates the basic reversal design. (Note that ABAB is derived from the labeling of each baseline period as an A phase and each intervention period as a B phase.)

Design Variations

Variations of the reversal design can be found in the literature. The first such variation does not involve a change in the structure of the design, but simply

FIGURE 5-7
Basic reversal
design format.

"A" Baseline₁	"B" Intervention₁	"A" Baseline₂	"B" Intervention₂

shortens the length of the initial baseline (A) period. This format of the design is appropriate when a lengthy baseline period is unethical or not called for, as in the case of a student who is not capable of performing the target behavior to any degree.

A second variation of the reversal design omits the initial baseline entirely. This BAB variation is considered if the target behavior is obviously not in the student's repertoire. When this design is used, a functional relation between the dependent and independent variables can be demonstrated only in the second intervention (B) phase.

Research Application

There are many examples of the ABAB design applied to research. An ABAB design was employed by Carr, Newsom, and Binkoff (1980) as a means of determining the variables controlling the severely aggressive behavior of two children with mental retardation. The experiment examined the effects of a simple "demand" situation: demands were alternately presented and withheld. Under the two demand conditions, the children's teacher selected problem situations as the dependent variable.

Figure 5–8 displays in graph form the results of this experiment. In Bob's case, the verbal cue "sit down" was chosen to require in-seat behavior. The demand situation for Sam involved practicing buttoning skills on an appropriate board with verbal cues provided at 10-second intervals. No demand situations imitated the nonstructured portions of a typical day. Note the clear relationship between the use of a verbal cue and the compliance of each child. More frequent demands resulted in more aggressive behavior.

Piggott, Fantuzzo, and Clement (1986) used an ABAB design to evaluate an intervention designed to improve the arithmetic performance of fifth-grade students. The study examined the effects of peer tutoring, including peer instruction, observation, evaluation, and reinforcement. Figure 5–9 displays in graph form the results of this experiment for students giving and receiving peer tutoring (tx group) and their classmates who were doing well without any special intervention. The data recorded are the average number of arithmetic problems

FIGURE 5–8
Research application of the reversal design.

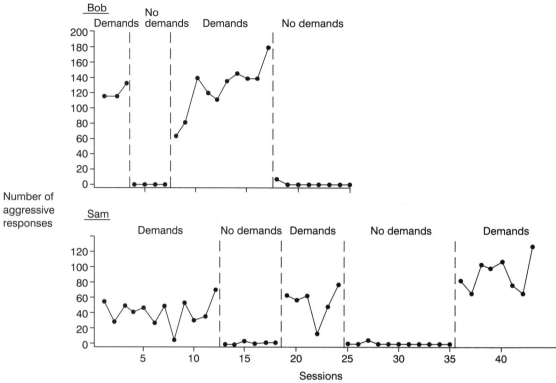

Note: From "Escape as a factor in the aggressive behavior of two retarded children," by E. Carr, C. D. Newsom, & J. A. Binkoff, Journal of Applied Behavior Analysis, 1980. Copyright 1980 by the Society for the Experimental Analysis of Behavior, Inc. Reprinted by permission.

accurately completed during a 7-minute drill. There is clearly a relationship between the intervention and the performance of the targeted students. Each time the intervention was implemented, the target students performed as well as their classmates. Each time the intervention was withdrawn, their performance fell below acceptable levels. During the maintenance phase, materials for the arithmetic drill were set out and students were allowed to tutor if they asked to. No reinforcement contingencies were in effect.

Teaching Application

The following vignette illustrates the use of an ABAB design in the classroom.

Jill Learns Not to Suck Her Thumb
Ms. Kimball, a kindergarten teacher with 27 pupils, recently designed an effective intervention program to reduce her student Jill's thumb sucking. She

decided that a reversal design would allow her to determine the existence of a functional relation between the change in behavior and the selected intervention procedure. Ms. Kimball chose a time sampling observation procedure. She looked at Jill every 10 minutes and marked a + on the data sheet if Jill was sucking her thumb and a – if she wasn't.

During the baseline condition (the first A phase), Ms. Kimball noted that Jill had her thumb in her mouth an average of 8 out of the 12 observations during a 2-hour period. Ms. Kimball decided to make a chart for Jill and to put a "smelly sticker" on the chart whenever Jill was not sucking her thumb at the end of an interval. After the intervention was applied (the first B phase), thumb sucking occurred at the end of only three intervals, on the average. To determine if a causal relation existed between the intervention and the behavior, Ms. Kimball returned to baseline (A) conditions. Jill no longer got smelly stickers, and the target behavior immediately returned to its previous level. Reinitiating the B condition immediately brought the behavior back to the lower level. Ms. Kimball felt confident the intervention had changed Jill's behavior.

Advantages and a Disadvantage

ABAB designs allow for precise analysis, but require an effective intervention to be withdrawn.

As the preceding applications show, the reversal design offers the advantages of simplicity and experimental control. It provides for precise analysis of the effects of a single independent variable on a single dependent variable.

FIGURE 5–9
Research application of the reversal design.

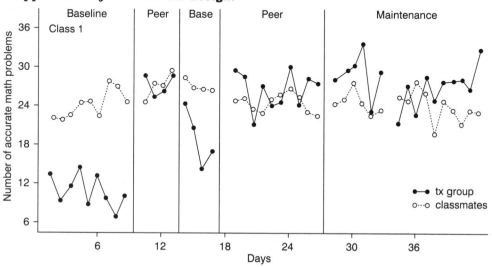

Note: From the "The effects of reciprocal peer tutoring and group contingencies on the academic performance of elementary school children," by H. Piggott. J. Fantuzzo, & P. Clement, *Journal of Applied Behavior Analysis, 1986. Copyright 1986 by the Society for the Experimental Analysis of Behavior, Inc. Reprinted by permission.*

The primary disadvantage of this design is the necessity for withdrawing an effective intervention in order to determine whether a functional relationship exists. Even if the target behavior is neither dangerous nor irreversible, it often seems foolish to teachers to stop doing something that is apparently working.

CHANGING CRITERION DESIGN

The **changing criterion design** is used to evaluate a gradual and systematic increase or decrease in the student's performance level by changing the criterion for reinforcement in a stepwise fashion (Hartmann & Hall, 1976). This design includes two major phases, much like the AB design. In the changing criterion design, however, the intervention phase is divided into subphases. Each subphase requires a closer approximation of the terminal behavior than the previous one. The student's performance thus moves gradually from the baseline level to the terminal objective.

This design is particularly appropriate when the terminal goal of the behavior-change program requires a considerable length of time to reach. The changing criterion design is well suited for measuring the effectiveness of a shaping procedure (see Chapter 7). This design is also useful when the teacher wants to accelerate or decelerate behaviors measured in terms of frequency, duration, latency, or force.

Implementation

The first step in implementing the changing criterion design is to gather baseline data in the same manner used in other single-subject designs. After a stable baseline has been established, the teacher must determine the level of performance change that will be required for each subphase during intervention. The overall or terminal level of performance becomes the goal for the first subphase of intervention. The choice of the first interim level of performance may be determined using one of several techniques:

1. The interim criterion for performance can be set at, and then increased by, an amount equal to the mean of the stable portion of the baseline data. This technique is appropriate when the goal of the behavior-change program is to increase a level of performance and when the student's present level is quite low. For example, if a teacher wanted to increase the number of questions a student answered and the student's mean baseline level of correct responses was two, that teacher might set two correct answers as a first interim criterion. Each subsequent subphase would then require two additional correct answers.

2. Interim levels of performance can be determined by taking 50% of the computed mean of baseline data (or the stable portion of the baseline

data). For example, suppose that a student's number of problems correct was noted for one week and that the following data were recorded:

Monday	9
Tuesday	10
Wednesday	7
Thursday	6
Friday	8

3. Interim criteria can be based on selecting the highest (or lowest, depending on the terminal objective) level of baseline performance. This is probably most appropriate for use with social behavior, for example, out-of-seat, positive peer interactions, rather than for an academic behavior. The assumption is that if the student were able to perform at that high (or low) level once, the behavior can be strengthened (or weakened) and maintained at that level.

4. Interim criteria can be based on a professional estimate of the student's ability. This procedure is particularly appropriate when the student's present level of performance is zero.

Regardless of the technique a teacher uses to establish the initial criterion, the data collected should be used to evaluate whether the amount of criterion change for each subphase is appropriate for a particular student.

The next step in implementing the changing criterion design is to begin the intervention phases. In each phase, if the student performs at least at the level of the interim criterion, the teacher provides reinforcement. It is important for the teacher to analyze the appropriateness of the selected interim level of performance during the initial intervention phase. If the student does not meet the criterion after a reasonable number of trials, the teacher should consider decreasing the interim level of performance required for reinforcement. Conversely, the teacher should consider adjusting the interim level of performance required for reinforcement if the goal was reached too easily.

The teacher as our example would require 16, then 20, then 24 correct problems for reinforcement.

After the student has reached the established level of performance in a predetermined number of consecutive sessions (usually two), or in two out of three consecutive sessions of a subphase, the level of performance required for reinforcement should be adjusted in the direction of the desired level of performance for the overall behavior-change program. Each successive interim level of performance should be determined using the same mathematical difference established at the first interim level of performance. That is, the behavior-change program should reflect a uniform step-by-step increase or decrease in criterion level. This process is continued until

1. The behavior is increased to a 100% or decreased to a 0% level of performance; or

FIGURE 5–10
Basic changing criterion design format.

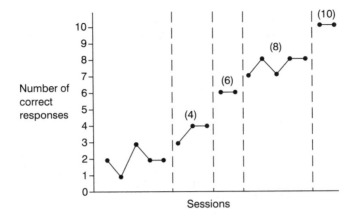

2. The final goal established by the teacher in the behavioral objective is attained.

Changing criterion designs enable teachers and researchers to establish functional relationships.

A functional relationship between the dependent and independent variables can be demonstrated in the changing criterion design if the student's performance level consistently changes when the criterion for reinforcement is adjusted. Generally, a student must meet the established criteria in at least three consecutive phases before the assumption of a functional relationship is valid.

Graphic Display

The basic changing criterion design format is similar to the one used for the AB design. A baseline phase is followed by the intervention phase, with a dashed vertical line separating the two conditions and each subphase. As shown in Figure 5–10, the data for the intervention phase are identified according to the level of performance selected for reinforcement. The procedure for graphing the data calls for connecting data points within each subphase. Data points collected in different interim phases or subphases are never connected. The magnitude of student behavior necessary for consequation (delivery of reinforcement) should be clearly identified at each level of the intervention phase (see Figure 5–10).

Research Application

The changing criterion design was utilized by Hall and Fox (1977) to increase the number of math problems correctly solved by a child with a behavior disorder. Under baseline conditions, the student demonstrated a mean level of performance of one math problem.

The first interim level of performance was established at the next whole number greater than the mean baseline performance (2). If the student met this level of performance, he was allowed to play basketball. If the student

FIGURE 5–11
Research applica-
tion of the changing
criterion design.

Note: From "Changing crite-
rion designs: An applied
behavior analysis proce-
dure," by R. V. Hall & R. G.
Fox, in B. C. Etzel, J. M.
LeBlanc, & D. M. Baer
(Eds.), New developments in
behavioral research: Theory,
method and application.
Copyright 1977 by Lawrence
Erlbaum Associates, Inc.,
Publishers. Reprinted with
permission of the authors
and the publishers.

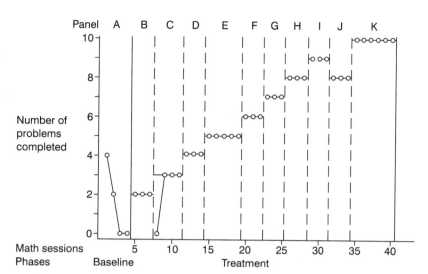

failed to reach the criterion, he had to stay in the math session until the problems were solved correctly. As shown in Figure 5–11, this process was continued until 10 math problems were solved correctly.

Bates, Renzaglia, and Clees (1980) used a changing criterion design to increase the rate at which Lucy, a worker with severe mental retardation, assembled drapery pulleys. Following a traditional baseline phase and a phase during which an unsuccessful self-reinforcement system was used, the researchers implemented a changing criterion procedure using positive reinforcement. Lucy received one cent for each two units completed and could use the money she earned to buy a snack during her break.

The first interim criterion was determined by averaging Lucy's work rate across the sessions of self-reinforcement; her average rate was .07 units per minute. "The following four criterion changes also involved small increases over previous criteria so as to acquaint Lucy with the program and to maximize her possibilities for success. However, after Lucy had demonstrated success with the initial criterion increases, it was decided that larger incremental increases were feasible and would demonstrate more clearly the effects of the changing criterion design" (p. 97). As shown in Figure 5–12, Lucy's improvement continued until she was producing drapery pulleys at a rate of at least 2.2 units per minute, well above the minimum rate required for maintenance of employment.

Certain procedural elements may be included in the changing criterion design to increase its research credibility. In Figure 5–11, three sessions at each criterion were generally included; however, this number of sessions was altered in some cases. Varying the increase (or decrease) in performance required in subphases provides a more credible demonstration of experimental control than requiring the same performance level change across all subphases (Cooper, 1981). Finally, note that in panel J a change in the crite-

FIGURE 5-12
Application of the changing criterion design.

Note: from "Improving the work performance of severely/profoundly retarded young adults: The use of a changing criterion procedural design," by P. Bates, A. Renzaglia, & T. Clees. Education and Training of the Mentally Retarded, 15, 1980. Reprinted by permission.

172

rion for reinforcement was made in the direction opposite to the terminal objective. Returning the student's performance level to a previously mastered criterion demonstrates a reversal effect similar to that of a return to baseline conditions in an ABAB design.

Teaching Application

Here's a teaching application of a changing criterion design to compare with the research application.

Claudia Learns to Sort by Color

Claudia was a student in Mr. Carroll's intermediate class for students with moderate mental retardation. Mr. Carroll was trying to teach Claudia to sort objects rapidly by color. Claudia could perform the task, but she did it too slowly. Mr. Carroll decided to use a changing criterion design to evaluate the effectiveness of a positive reinforcement procedure. He established that Claudia's average baseline rate of sorting was 4 objects per minute. He set 6 per minute as the first interim criterion and 30 per minute as the terminal goal. Claudia earned a poker chip exchangeable for a minute's free time when she met the criterion. When Claudia met the criterion on two consecutive trials or opportunities, Mr. Carroll raised the criterion required for reinforcement by 2. He continued to do this until Claudia sorted 30 objects per minute in order to earn her poker chip. Mr. Carroll concluded that there was a functional relationship between the dependent and independent variables, because Claudia's behavior changed quickly each time the criterion was changed but did not change until then.

Advantage and Disadvantage

The advantage of the changing criterion design is that it can establish a functional relationship while always changing the behavior in a positive direction. There is no need to withdraw a successful intervention. Using the changing criterion design, however, necessitates very gradual behavior change. It may, therefore, be inappropriate for behaviors that require or lend themselves to rapid modification.

MULTIPLE BASELINE DESIGN

As indicated by its name, the **multiple baseline design** permits simultaneous analysis of more than one dependent variable. A teacher may experimentally test the effects of intervention (the independent variable) on

1. Two or more behaviors associated with one student in a single setting: for example, John's out-of-seat and talking-out behaviors in social studies class (*multiple baseline across behaviors*).

2. Two or more students exhibiting the same behavior in a single setting: for example, the spelling accuracy of Sara and Janet in English class (*multiple baseline across individuals*).

3. Two or more settings in which one student is exhibiting the same behavior: for example, Kurt's cursing during recess and also in the school cafeteria (*multiple baseline across settings*).

When to use a multiple baseline design

The multiple baseline is the design of choice when the teacher is interested in applying an intervention procedure to more than one individual, setting, or behavior. The multiple baseline design does not include a reversal phase; therefore, it may be used when the reversal design is not appropriate: when the target behavior includes aggressive actions or when academic learning is involved.

Implementation

A teacher using the multiple baseline design takes data on each dependent variable simultaneously. The teacher collects data under baseline conditions for each student, on each behavior, or in each setting. In setting up the data collection system, the teacher should select an ordinate scale that is appropriate for each of the variables involved in the program. To make data analysis possible, the same scale of measurement (for example, minutes involved in appropriate play, number of math problems completed correctly, percent of on-task behavior) should be used for each dependent variable.

"Baseline, directionality, stability, control—is this teaching or tennis?"

After a stable baseline has been achieved on the first variable, intervention with that variable can be initiated. During the treatment period, baseline data collection continues for the remaining variables. Intervention on the second variable should begin when the first variable has reached the criterion established in the behavioral objective or when the data for the first variable show a trend in the desired direction as indicated by three consecutive data points. The intervention condition should be continued for the first variable, and baseline data should still be collected for any additional variables. This sequence should be continued until the intervention technique has been applied to all the variables identified for the behavior-change program.

The data collected in a multiple baseline design can be examined for a functional relation between the independent variable and each of the dependent variables. The introduction of the intervention with the second and subsequent dependent variables constitutes a replication of effect. The functional relationship is assumed if each dependent variable in succession shows a change when, and only when, the independent variable is introduced. Adjacent graphs should be examined to be sure that each successive intervention has an independent treatment effect on the appropriate dependent variable. Only the first independent variable should be affected by the first intervention. A change in the second and succeeding dependent variables should be seen only when the intervention is applied to them as well. Figure 5–13 shows an example of a functional relation, whereas Figure 5–14 does not. In Figure 5–14 the second dependent variable begins an upward trend when the intervention is introduced for the first variable, showing that the relationships between variables are not discrete, or independent.

Graphic Display

When using the multiple baseline design, the teacher should plot the data collected using a separate axis for each of the dependent variables to which

FIGURE 5–13
Data from a multiple baseline design that reflect a functional relation.

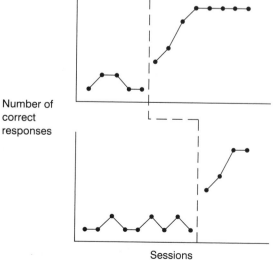

FIGURE 5–14
Data from a multiple baseline design that do not reflect a functional relation.

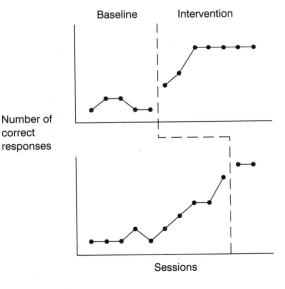

intervention was applied (individuals, behaviors, or situations). Figure 5–15 shows a composite graph of a multiple baseline design.

FIGURE 5–15
Basic multiple baseline design format.

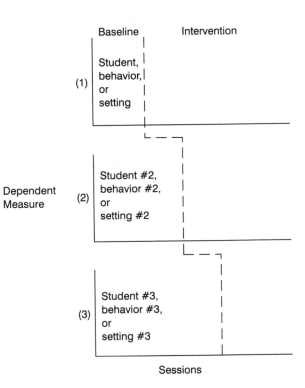

Design Variation

A problem with the multiple baseline design— and a suggested solution

One problem associated with the multiple baseline design is the necessity for collecting baseline data over extended periods, particularly baseline data for the second and subsequent dependent variables. When the student cannot perform the behavior at all or access to additional settings is not available, collecting daily baseline data may take more time than is actually warranted. The *multiple-probe technique*, as illustrated in Figure 5–16, has been suggested as a reasonable solution to this situation (Horner & Baer, 1978; Murphy & Bryan, 1980). In this variation of the multiple baseline design, data are not continuously collected on the behaviors (or students, or settings) on which intervention is not being conducted. Rather, a probe trial (a trial under baseline conditions) or a probe session (more than one trial) is conducted *intermittently* on these subsequent behaviors to verify that the student can perform the behavior (following intervention), or that he still cannot perform the behavior, or to record any changes in his ability before intervention. While intervening on behavior 1 (or with student 1 or in setting 1), the teacher intermittently probes behaviors 2 and 3. When behavior 1 reaches the criterion, one or more probe sessions are conducted on all three behaviors. Then intervention is begun on behavior 2, while postcheck probes are conducted on behavior 1, and probes continue on behavior 3. When behavior 2 reaches the criterion, one or more probe sessions are conducted on all three behaviors. Then intervention is begun on behavior 3, while postcheck probes are conducted on behaviors 1 and 2.

FIGURE 5–16
Hypothetical data using a multiple-probe design across spelling word groups: (1) initial probe, (2) probe after criterion, (3) consecutive probe (baseline) sessions before intervention, (4) review probes, (5) continuous training data.

Note: From Measuring behavior (2nd ed.), by J. O. Cooper (Columbus, Ohio: Merrill, 1981), pp. 144–145. Reprinted with permission.

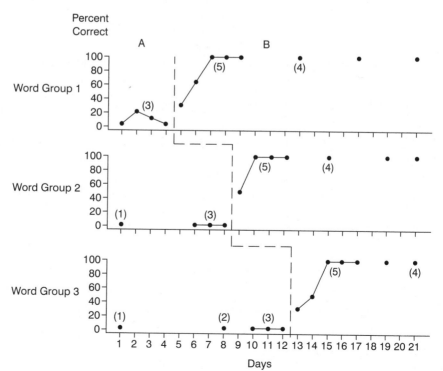

Research Applications

Across Behaviors

Test, Grossi, and Keul (1988) used a multiple baseline design across behaviors in a research study. The authors identified three sets of janitorial tasks—cleaning restrooms, detail cleaning of desks, and daily office cleaning—for community-based vocational training in an office building. The client was a 19-year-old woman with severe disabilities. Figure 5–17 demonstrates the effect of the intervention (training by a job coach using task analyses) on each of the three sets of behaviors. Each set of behaviors reached acceptable levels only after the intervention was applied. The results demonstrate a functional relationship between the intervention provided by the job coach and the acquisition of the janitorial skills by the client.

Across Individuals

Caron and Ladouceur (1989) used a multiple baseline design across individuals to evaluate the effectiveness of a multidimensional behavioral treatment package (modified regulated breathing method, easy speech, and modified parental attitudes) for children who stuttered. Figure 5–18 on page 180 displays the graph for the four children in the study. Data are presented in terms of the main dependent variable, percentage of stuttered syllables in each of three 1-minute samples randomly taken in each session. A functional relationship can be shown; each individual's stuttering decreased only when the intervention was applied to that individual.

White and Bailey (1990) used a multiple baseline design across individuals in which an entire class of students was considered "an individual." They assessed the effectiveness of a "sit and watch" procedure, a form of time-out, on the disruptive behavior (noncompliance, aggression, and throwing objects) of 30 regular fourth-grade students and 14 students in an alternative education class for fourth- and fifth-grade boys with severe behavior problems. Students who engaged in disruptive behavior were required to sit and watch the other students playing for 3 minutes. During each observation interval, the observers recorded each instance of disruptive behavior on hand counters. Figure 5–19 on page 181 displays the graph showing data for both classes. The numbers above the data points represent the number of times "sit and watch" was implemented. A functional relationship is assumed because the disruptive behavior decreased for each group of students when the intervention began.

Across Settings

Knapczyk (1988) used a multiple baseline design across settings to analyze the effects of a video training program on the verbally and physically aggressive behaviors of a student in his special education class, his regular education class in shop, and his regular education class in physical education.

FIGURE 5-17
Graphs of a multiple baseline design across behaviors.

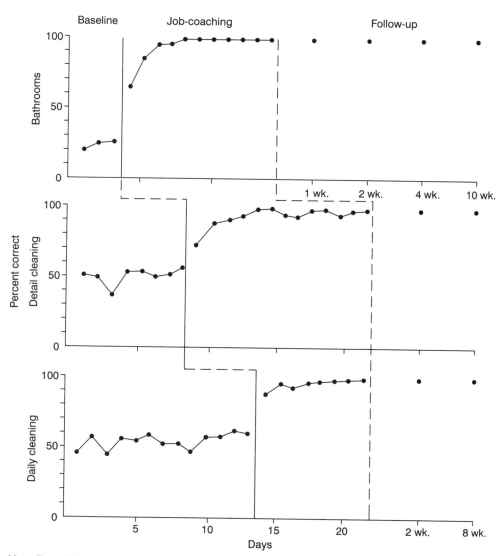

Janitorial skills

Note: From "A functional analysis of the acquisition and maintenance of janitorial skills in a competitive work setting," by D. Test, T. Grossi, P. Keul, Journal of the Association for Persons with Severe Handicaps, 13, 1988. Reprinted by permission.

FIGURE 5–18
Graph of a multiple baseline design across individuals.

Note: From C. Caron & R. Ladouceur, "Multidimensional behavior treatment for child stutterers," Behavior Modification, 1989. Copyright © 1989 by Sage Publications, Inc. Reprinted by permission of Sage Publications, Inc.

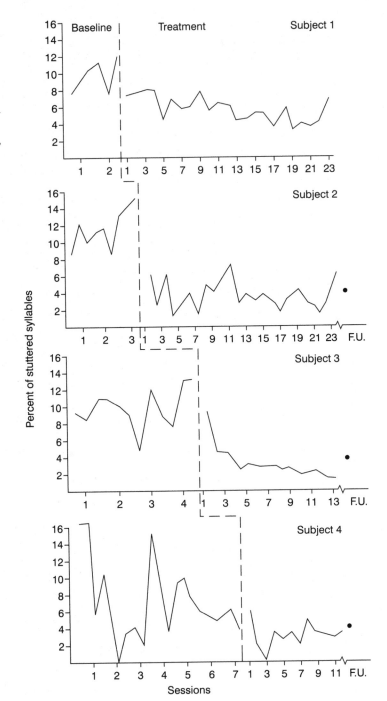

FIGURE 5–19

***Use of a multiple baseline design across individuals in which an
entire class was considered "an individual."***

Note: From "Reducing disruptive behaviors of elementary physical education students with sit
and watch," by A. White & J. Bailey. Journal of Applied Behavior Analysis, 1990. Copyright
1990 by The Society for the Experimental Analysis of Behavior, Inc. Reprinted by permission.

FIGURE 5–20
Graph of a multiple baseline design across settings.

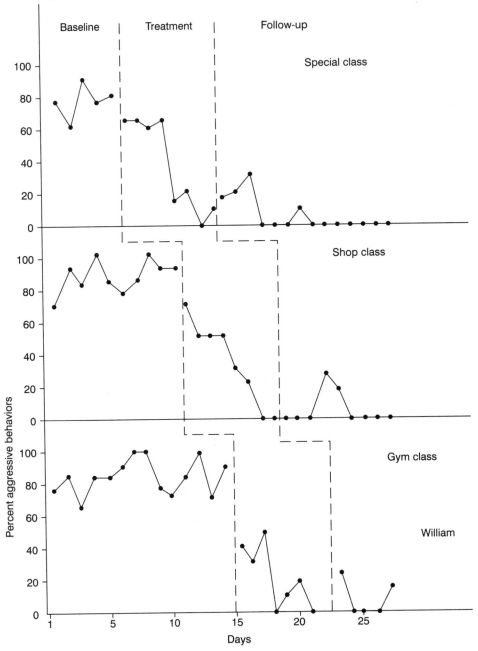

Note: From "Reducing aggressive behaviors in special and regular class settings by training alternative social responses," by D. Knapczyk, Behavior Disorders, 14, 1988. Reprinted by permission.

Intervention consisted of showing the student videotapes from each setting, showing the student's typical behavior, and demonstrating alternative responses. Figure 5–20 displays the clear and rapid change in the percent of aggressive behaviors by the student when the intervention was applied in each setting. There is clearly a functional relationship between the dependent and independent variables.

Teaching Application

The following vignette illustrates a classroom application of a multiple baseline design.

Students Learn to Come to Class on Time

Ms. Raphael was a junior-high-school English teacher. The students in all three of her morning classes consistently came late. She began to record baseline data on the three classes. She recorded the number of students in their seats when the bell rang. She found that an average of five students in the first class, four in the second, and seven in the third class were in their seats. Ms. Raphael then began recording an extra-credit point in her grade book for each student in the first class who was in his or her seat when the bell rang. Within a week, 25 students were on time and in their seats. The baseline data for the other classes showed no change during this first intervention. When she began giving extra-credit points in the second class, the number of students on time increased immediately and dramatically. After a week, she applied the intervention in the third class with similar results. Ms. Raphael had accomplished two things: she had succeeded in getting her classes to arrive on time and she had established a functional relationship between her intervention (the independent variable) and her students' behavior (the dependent variable).

Advantages and Disadvantages

The multiple baseline design can establish a functional relationship without withdrawing the intervention, as is necessary in a reversal design, and without gradual alteration, as is required in a changing criterion design. These advantages make it a particularly useful design for classroom use. The multiple baseline design does, however, have some limitations. This design requires that the researcher apply the intervention to several students, behaviors, or settings, which may not always be practical.

Furthermore, the multiple baseline design is inappropriate in two specific situations:

1. When the target behavior calls for immediate action. The multiple baseline design calls for a considerable delay in delivery of the intervention procedure for the second and subsequent dependent variables.

2. When the behaviors selected for intervention are not independent. In such a case, intervention with one behavior will bring about a change in the related behavior; therefore, the teacher will be unable to evaluate clearly the effects of the procedure. For example, if two behaviors targeted for a student are cursing and fighting, the teacher might find that after the student's cursing decreases, there are fewer fights. In this case, the two behaviors are clearly not independent.

ALTERNATING TREATMENTS DESIGN

In contrast to the multiple baseline design that uses a single independent variable and multiple dependent variables, the **alternating treatments design** (Barlow & Hayes, 1979) allows comparison of the effectiveness of more than one treatment or intervention strategy on a single dependent variable. For example, using this design the teacher can compare the effects of two reading programs on a student's reading comprehension ability or the effects of two behavior reduction procedures on a student's talking-out. The teacher can also examine the efficiency of three different types of symbols on a student's communication board. A number of different terms have been used to describe this design: **multiple schedule design** (Hersen & Barlow, 1976), **alternating conditions design** (Ulman & Sulzer-Azaroff, 1975), and **multi-element baseline design** (Sidman, 1960).

Implementation

The first step in setting up an alternating treatments design is to select the target behavior and two or more potential treatments. If the target behavior is social (for example, asking appropriate questions or remaining on task), it should be operationally defined. If the target behavior is academic, two or more representative samples of the behavior (for example, two or more equally difficult sets of division problems) should be selected, each designated for one of the intervention or treatment strategies.

As the name of this design implies, the treatments will be implemented alternately or in rotation. The presentation of the treatments may be in random order, for example ABABBAABABBA. When two treatments are used, the student should be exposed to each an equal number of times. If there are three treatments, a block rotation may be used. Each block consists of one presentation of each treatment; for example, ABC, BCA, CAB, ACB, BAC, CBA. If data are collected long enough, each possible order of presentation should be used at least once.

The alternating treatments can be used sequentially within a single session (A followed by B), or from one session to the next (A in the morning, B in the afternoon of the same day), or on successive days (A on Monday, B on Tuesday). The scheduling should be counterbalanced; that is, the treatment that was employed first in one session should be used second in the next session; the treatment employed in the morning on the first day should be used in the afternoon on the second day; and the treatment that was used on Monday the first week should be used on Tuesday of the second week of treatment. (In research situations, similar counterbalancing is used to minimize the effects of other potential confounding variables like the person administering the treatment and the location of the treatment.) This counterbalancing should control for the possibility of carry-over and sequencing effects (Barlow & Hayes, 1979). In other words, by presenting the treatments in random order the possible effects each treatment may have on the other(s) will be minimized.

A distinctive discriminative stimulus, signal, or cue immediately preceding each treatment will make the differential effects of each treatment more noticeable. For example, the teacher might say, "This is treatment A," or "This is treatment B," or "Now we are going to use a number line," or "Now we are going to use counting chips." The teacher might also color-coded worksheets to indicate a particular condition is in effect.

Graphic Display

The basic form of graphing the alternating treatments design is shown in Figure 5–21. As in all designs, baseline data are plotted first and separated from intervention data by a vertical broken line. The graph for the alternating treatments design differs from others in that several curves may be shown on each graph. The points for each treatment are connected only to other points for that treatment so that the data for each are displayed as separate lines, or curves.

If the data curve of one treatment is vertically separated from the other curves, it is said to be *fractionated*. This fractionation indicates that the treatments are differentially effective (Ulman & Sulzer-Azaroff, 1975).

The top graph in Figure 5–21 shows data that demonstrate an effective treatment. Treatment A is the more effective of the two treatments. The data curves are separated; they do not cross at any point other than at the very beginning of the intervention phase. The two curves are fractionated. Figure 5–21 also shows data that are not significantly different from one another. The middle graph shows two treatments, neither of which demonstrates control over the dependent variable—neither is effective. The bottom graph shows two treatments that both demonstrate control over the dependent variable—either is equally effective.

By visual inspection of the graphs, we may infer experimental control between one or more of the independent variables and the dependent variable.

> Because confounding factors such as time of administration have been neutralized (presumably) by counterbalancing, and because the two treatments are readily discriminable by subjects through instructions or other discriminative stimuli, differences in the individual plots of behavior change corresponding with each treatment should be attributable to the treatment itself, allowing a direct comparison between two (or more) treatments. (Barlow & Hayes, 1979, p. 200)

FIGURE 5–21
Graphs of data collected using an alternating treatments design. Top graph indicates treatment A is the more effective treatment. Middle and bottom graphs indicate no difference between treatments.

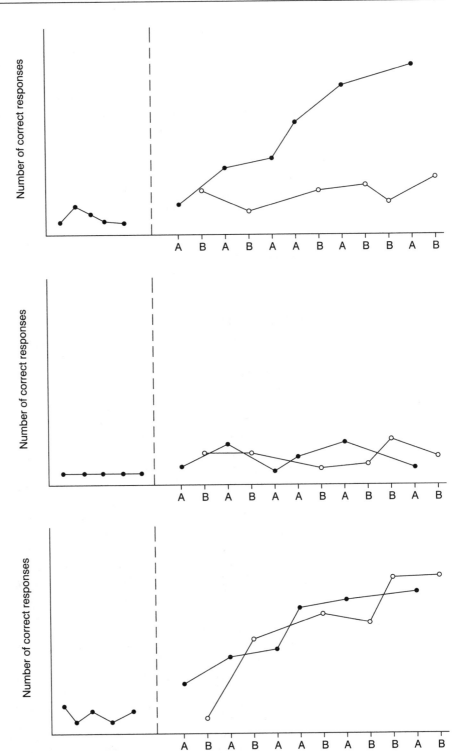

As described until now, the alternating treatments design does not include a replication phase. Therefore, the case for the existence of a functional relationship is relatively weak. To make a stronger case a third phase can be instituted. In this phase only the most effective of the treatments is applied to the behavior (or behavior sample) that was treated with the ineffective treatment during the intervention phase. Figure 5–22 shows such a three-phase variation of the design.

To provide even stronger evidence of a functional relationship, Higgins-Hain and Baer (1989) suggest using the alternating treatments design within a conventional reversal design. An example may be seen in the study of aggressive play by Sherburne, Utley, McConnell, and Gannon (1988). An example of the alternating treatments and reversal designs within a multiple baseline design may be seen in Charlop, Kurtz, and Milstein's (1992) study of task acquisition by children with autism. Students interested in an in depth discussion of the alternating treatments design for research purposes are directed to Higgins-Hains and Baer (1989) and Higgins-Hains (1991).

Research Application

Singh (1990) used an alternating treatments design to measure the comparative effectiveness of two error correction procedures in reducing oral reading errors of students with moderate mental retardation. Students read an unfamiliar 100-word passage orally three times each day. The correction procedures were

FIGURE 5–22
Three-phase alternating treatments design demonstrating functional relationship.

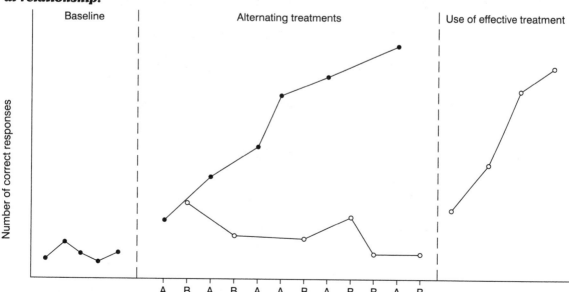

FIGURE 5–23
Use of an alternating treatments design.

Note: From "Effects of two error-correction procedures on oral reading errors," by N. Singh. Behavior Modification, 1990. Copyright 1990 by Sage Publications, Inc. Reprinted by permission.

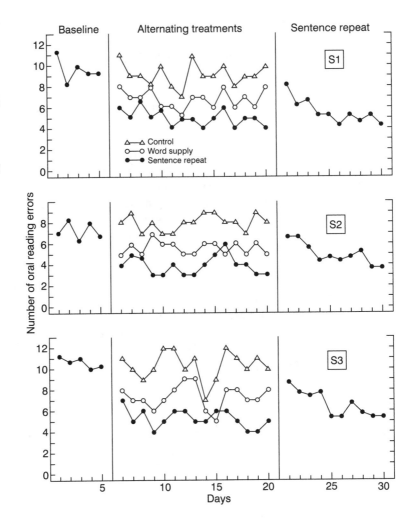

word supply—the teacher supplied the correct word, the student repeated it once and continued to read; and sentence repeat—the student repeated the correct word after the teacher, read the rest of the sentence, then reread the entire sentence. As shown in Figure 5–23 the sentence-repeat procedure was more effective than the word-supply procedure (or a control—no correction) for each of the three students. In the third phase of the design the more effective procedure was used in all three daily sessions.

Ollendick, Matson, Esveldt-Dawson, and Shapiro (1980) used an alternating treatments design to examine the effectiveness of spelling remediation procedures. Figure 5–24 shows the data reported for one of the students, a 13-year-old girl. Three treatments were used in an effort to improve her spelling accuracy: (1) positive practice overcorrection plus positive reinforcement, (2) a correction procedure in which the teacher identified spelling errors for her to study plus positive reinforcement, and (3) the same traditional procedure without positive reinforcement. Positive practice plus positive reinforcement, initially applied to words in Set A, was clearly the most effective remediation form. In the third phase, this successful treatment was applied to the other sets of words. The increase in spelling accuracy of these sets replicates that seen with Set A, thus providing evidence of a functional relationship.

Teaching Application

For teachers, the alternating treatments design can provide rapid and accurate feedback about the comparative effectiveness of various teaching techniques, as the following example shows.

Marcia Learns Sight Vocabulary

Using an alternating treatments design can help teachers individualize instruction.

Mr. Hagan was a resource teacher for elementary students. He wanted one of his students, Marcia, to learn basic sight vocabulary on a first-grade level. He chose 15 words and established that Marcia's baseline rate for reading them was zero. Mr. Hagan then divided the words into three sets of five. One set he printed on cards accompanied by an audio recording tape that Marcia could use to hear the words pronounced. He assigned a peer tutor to work with Marcia on the second set, and the teacher worked on the third set. Mr. Hagan recorded and graphed the number of words Marcia pronounced correctly each day for each set. Within a week, Marcia was pronouncing correctly the group of words learned with the peer tutor at a higher rate than either of the other sets. Mr. Hagan concluded that, for Marcia, peer tutoring was the most efficient way to learn sight vocabulary.

Advantages and Disadvantages

The alternating treatments design is an efficient way for teachers to answer one of the most important instructional questions: Which method is most likely to be successful with this student? Once clear fractionation appears, the teacher can select the most successful method using as few as three to five data points. One disadvantage is the necessity to institute a replication phase in order to establish a clear functional relationship. This, however, is likely to be of little practical importance to teachers.

CHANGING CONDITIONS DESIGN

The changing conditions design reflects reality—teachers keep trying different techniques until they find one that works.

A **changing conditions design** is used to investigate the effect of two or more treatments (independent variables) on the behavior of a student (dependent variable). Unlike the alternating treatments design, the treatments in a changing conditions design are introduced consecutively.

This design is ideal for the teacher who finds it necessary to try a number of interventions before finding one that is successful. The changing condi-

FIGURE 5-24
Alternating treatments design in a research application for behavior increase.

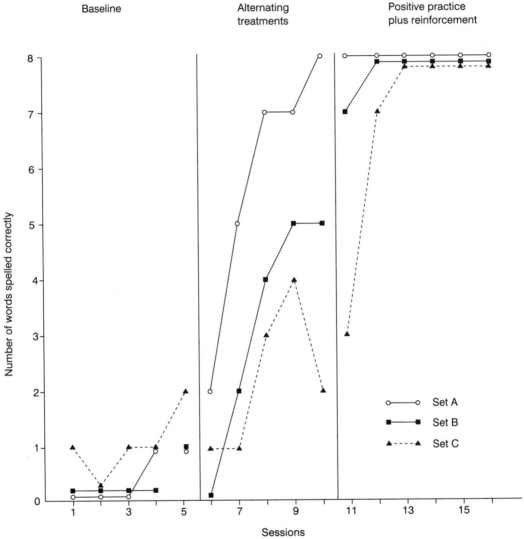

Note: From "Increasing spelling achievement: An analysis of treatment procedures utilizing an alternating treatments design," by T. Ollendick, J. Matson, K. Esveldt-Dawson, & E. Shapiro, Journal of Applied Behavior Analysis, 1980. Copyright 1980 by the Society for the Experimental Analysis of Behavior, Inc. Reprinted by permission.

tions design is also referred to as an **ABC design**, because each treatment phase is labeled with a different letter of the alphabet.

The data resulting from a changing conditions design cannot be used to determine the existence of a functional relationship between the dependent variable and any of the tested independent variables. As is the case with an AB design, the data can give only an indication of the effectiveness of a particular procedure.

The changing conditions design can, however, be altered to meet the qualifications of a research design by increasing the number of baselines. This modification calls for a return to baseline conditions before the initiation of a different intervention technique.

Implementation

The first step in implementing a changing conditions design is to collect data under baseline conditions in order to assess the student's present level of performance. Once a stable baseline is established, the teacher can introduce the selected treatment and measure its effectiveness through data collection.

If the data for the first intervention period do not demonstrate a change in the student's performance, or if the change in performance is not of a sufficient magnitude or in the desired direction, the teacher may design a second treatment. This second treatment can be either a complete change in strategy or a slight modification of the earlier treatment. A broken line should be drawn on a graph of both sets of data to indicate the session on which the second treatment was initiated.

This process of redesigning treatment conditions is repeated until the desired effect on the student's behavior is achieved. Generally, the teacher should expect to see some evidence of a change in the student's behavior within five intervention sessions.

Graphic Display

The format for the changing conditions design is similar to the one used for the basic AB design. A baseline phase is followed by the intervention phases, with a dashed vertical line separating the data associated with each specific treatment. Figure 5–25 illustrates this basic format. Figure 5–26 illustrates the format for a changing conditions design with repeated baselines (ABAC).

Research Application

Smith (1979) used a changing conditions design to measure the effect of a number of teaching conditions on a 12-year-old boy's oral reading (see Figure 5–27). The dependent variable measured was the number of words read orally by the student (per minute) and the number of reading errors made. (Note that the numbers in the circles represent the average number of words

FIGURE 5–25
Changing condi-
tions design basic
format.

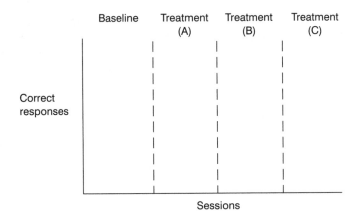

read per phase. The numbers in the rectangles represent the average number of errors per phase.) Figure 5–27 presents the data recorded under each
of the following conditions:

1. Baseline. John was asked to read from his book.

2. Modeling. The teacher read the first page of a new story from the child's
   text. John was then asked to read orally.

3. Modeling plus correction. The previous condition was altered by adding a
   correction procedure. The teacher corrected John when he made an
   error and offered the correct word if he did not know it.

4. Modeling plus previewing, and correction. After the teacher read, John
   reread the same passage and continued reading until the instructional
   time (5 minutes) elapsed. The correction procedure remained in effect.

FIGURE 5–26
Changing condi-
tions design with
repeated baselines.

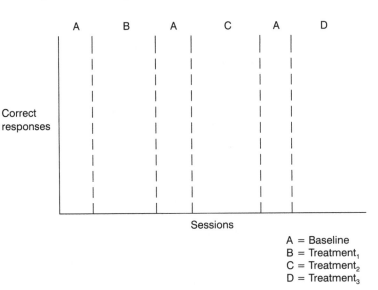

FIGURE 5–27
Research applica-
tion of a changing
conditions design.

Note: From "The improve-
ment of children's oral reading through the use of
teacher modeling," by D. D.
Smith, Journal of Learning
Disabilities, 1979. Copyright
1979 by the Journal of
Learning Disabilities.
Reprinted by permission

5. Follow-up. Baseline conditions were reinstituted.

Handen, Parrish, McClung, Kerwin, and Evans (1992) used a changing
conditions design with repeated baseline to examine the relative efficacy of
guided compliance and time-out as a method of increasing adherence to
adult requests by young children with mild mental retardation. The following
conditions (phases) were included in the study. In all phases each child was
presented with ten requests (five targeted and five generalization probes).
Compliance within 10 seconds was followed by praise. Figure 5–28 presents
the data recorded for one of the children.

1. Baseline. Noncompliance was ignored and compliance praised.
2. Guided compliance. Noncompliance within 10 seconds resulted in the
   adult's guiding the child to complete the task using hand-over-hand assistance. Praise was withheld if assistance was provided.
3. Baseline condition.
4. Time-out. Noncompliance within 10 seconds resulted in placement of the
   child in a chair facing a corner of the room for 30 seconds (the child was
   held gently in the chair if he or she refused to remain seated).
5. Baseline condition.

It should be noted that with the changing conditions design with repeated
baselines in Figure 5–28, the teacher may determine the existence of a
"weak" functional relationship. To strengthen this determination, a replication phase of one or more of the interventions would have to be included.

FIGURE 5-28
Use of a changing conditions design.

Note: from "Using guided compliance versus time out to promote child compliance: A preliminary comparative analysis in an analogue context," by B. Handen, J. Parrish, T. McClung, M. Kerwin, & L. Evans. Research in Developmental Disabilities. Copyright 1992 with kind permission from Elsevier Science Ltd, The Boulevard, Langford Lane, Kidlington OX5 1GB, UK.

For additional sophisticated variants of the changing conditions design, the reader is referred to the discussion of multitreatment designs by Tawney and Gast (1984).

Teaching Application

Here's how a changing conditions design can be used in the classroom.

Roberta Learns to Shoot Baskets

Baseline

Mr. Woods was recently hired to teach physical education at an elementary school. When he arrived at work, Mr. Woods was approached by the special education teacher, Ms. Jones. She was concerned about Roberta, a student with physical disabilities who would be in Mr. Woods's gym class. Roberta, who used a wheelchair, had difficulty with eye-hand coordination. Ms. Jones hoped the student could learn to throw a basketball. Learning to play basketball would provide coordination training and a valuable leisure skill for Roberta. Mr. Woods agreed that the basketball skill seemed appropriate.

First condition

Mr. Woods decided to use a systematic approach to instruction. He asked Roberta to throw the basketball 20 times to see how often she could place the ball through a lowered hoop. This procedure was followed for five gym periods with no additional instruction until a baseline performance rate was determined. Mr. Woods then decided to use a modeling technique; he showed Roberta how to throw the ball and asked her to imitate him. Very little improvement was noted in five class periods. Mr. Woods met with the special education teacher to determine what could be done.

Second condition

Ms. Jones carefully reviewed all the data and suggested changing the conditions. She explained that a change in intervention seemed necessary and that a modeling procedure could be used in combination with keeping score on a chart.

Third condition

Mr. Woods agreed to try this. In 2 weeks, Roberta showed improvement but still missed more baskets than she hit. A final condition was implemented using modeling, scorekeeping, and a correction procedure. Mr. Woods now showed Roberta how to throw, recorded her score, and showed her exactly what she did wrong when she missed. This combination of procedures resulted in Roberta's being able to throw a basketball through a hoop 15 out of 20 times. A suggestion was made to Roberta's parents that a hoop be constructed at her home so that she could enjoy her new skill after school.

Advantages and Disadvantages

Changing conditions is a teaching design.

The changing conditions design with a single baseline allows the teacher to compare the effects of a number of interventions on student behavior. Although no functional relationship can be established, recording data in this format allows the teacher to monitor the effects of various procedures on student behavior. The teacher should be aware, however, that what she may be seeing is the cumulative effects of the interventions rather than the effects of any one intervention in isolation. Individual analysis of the effects of the interventions can be made using the repeated baselines format of the changing conditions design. The teacher who records data systematically in a changing conditions design will have a record of the student's progress and a good indication of what procedures are effective with that student.

EVALUATING SINGLE-SUBJECT DESIGNS
Statistical Analysis

The purpose for using behavior modification and applied behavior analysis techniques in the classroom is to achieve, and verify, meaningful changes in a student's behavior. The effectiveness of an intervention is commonly judged against both an experimental criterion and a therapeutic criterion. The *experimental criterion* verifies that an independent variable (an intervention) was responsible for the change in the dependent variable (a behavior). Single-subject designs demonstrating within-subject replications of effect satisfy this criterion (Baer, Wolf, & Risley, 1968; Barlow & Hersen, 1984 Kazdin, 1977).

The *therapeutic criterion* is a judgment as to whether the results of the teacher's intervention are "important or of clinical or applied significance" (Kazdin, 1982, p. 47). For example, the teacher should ask herself whether it is truly meaningful to increase a student's grade from a D- to a D (Baer, Wolf, & Risley, 1968) or to decrease a child's self-destructive behavior from 100 to 60 instances per hour (Kazdin, 1977) or to reduce a student's off-task behavior in a resource room while it remains at high in the regular classroom. Kazdin (1977) suggests a third evaluation criterion: *social validation*, the "social acceptability of an intervention program" (p. 430). Social validation was discussed at length in Chapter 2.

Intervention effects in applied behavior analysis are usually evaluated through *visual inspection* of the graph displaying the plotted data points of the various phases (conditions). Interpretation of data based on visual inspection sounds unrefined and may certainly be subjective. It may therefore be viewed by some as a weak form of evaluation. Evaluation resulting from visual inspection, however, reveals only strong intervention results, and that is what teachers are seeking.

The grossness and subjectivity of visual inspection are somewhat modified by common agreement that certain characteristics of the graphed data should be evaluated. These characteristics include the *means* of the data in the phases, the *levels* of performance in the phases, the *trends* in performance, and the *rapidity* of behavior change (Kazdin, 1982).

Evaluation of changes in means focuses on the change in the average rate of student performance across the phases of a design. Within each phase, the mean (average) of the data points is determined and may be indicated on the graph by drawing a horizontal, dashed line corresponding to the value on the ordinate scale. Visual inspection of the relationship of these means will help determine if the intervention resulted in consistent and meaningful changes in the behavior in the desired direction of change. In Figure 5–29, Fox and Shapiro (1978) have supplied such indicators of means. The viewer can easily see the relative position of the students' disruptive behavior across the various design phases.

Evaluation of the level of performance refers to the increase or decrease in student performance from the end of one phase to the beginning of the next phase. The teacher wants to evaluate the magnitude and direction of this change. "When a large change in level occurs immediately after the introduction of a new condition, the level change is considered abrupt, which is indicative of a powerful or effective intervention" (Tawney & Gast, 1984, p. 162). Tawney and Gast suggest the following steps to determine and evaluate a level change between two adjacent conditions: (1) identify the ordinate value of the last data point of the first condition and the first data point value of the second condition, (2) subtract the smallest value from the largest, and (3) note whether the change in level is in an improving or decaying direction (p. 162). In Figure 5–29, the arrows have been added to indicate level changes.

Evaluation of a trend in performance focuses on systematic and consistent increases or decreases in performance. Data trends are most often evaluated using a procedure known as the *quarter-intersect method* (White & Liberty, 1976). Evaluation of trends is based on lines of progress developed from the median value of the data points in each phase. The use of a trend line increases the reliability of visual analysis among people looking at a graph (Bailey, 1984; Ottenbacher & Cusick, 1991). This is of particular importance as teams of teachers, students, parents, and other concerned

FIGURE 5–29
Mean percent of time spent in disruptive classroom behavior by four students.

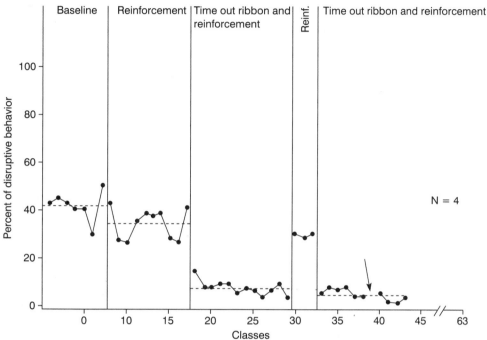

Note: The horizontal broken lines indicate the mean for each condition. The arrow marks a one-day probe (Day 39) during which the time-out contingency was suspended. A follow-up observation of the teacher-conducted program occurred on Day 63. Source: "The timeout ribbon: A nonexclusionary timeout procedure," by R. Foxx & S. Shapiro, Journal of Applied Behavior Analysis, 11, 1978, p. 131. Reproduced by permission.

individuals review student data to assess progress and make decisions about future instruction or intervention. Steps for computing lines of progress are illustrated in Figure 5–30. Trend lines can provide (1) an indication of the direction of behavior change in the past and (2) a prediction of the direction of behavior change in the future. This information can help the teacher determine whether to change the intervention.

Taking this process one step further will yield a split-middle line of progress (White & Haring, 1980). This line of progress is drawn so that an equal number of data points fall on and above the line as fall on and below the line. As illustrated in Figure 5–31, if the data points do not naturally fall in such a pattern, the line is redrawn higher or lower, parallel to the original line, until the balance of data points is equal.

A fourth characteristic that may be evaluated through visual inspection is the rapidity of the behavior change. This refers to the length of time between the onset or termination of one phase and changes in performance. The sooner the change occurs after the intervention has been applied (or with-

FIGURE 5–30
Steps for computing lines of progress.

1. Divide the number of data points in half by drawing a vertical line down the graph.

In this example, there are 10 data points: therefore, the line is drawn between sessions 5 and 6. If there had been an odd number of data points, this would have been drawn through a session point.

2. On the left half of the graph, find the mid-session and draw a vertical line.

In this example, there are five data points; therefore, the line is drawn at session 3. If there had been an even number of sessions, this line would have been drawn between two session points.

3. On the left half of the graph, find the mid-performance point and draw a horizontal line.

In this example, the data point at performance value 6 is the mid-performance point because there are two data points below it and two data points above it. If there had been an even number of data points, this line would have been drawn between the two media points.

4. Repeat steps 2 and 3 on the right half of the graph.

In this example, session 8 is the mid-session, and the data point at performance value 10 is the mid-performance point.

5. Draw a line connecting the intersections of both halves of the graph. This is the trend line for the data.

FIGURE 5–31
Split-middle line of
progress.
Source: O. White and N.
Haring, Exceptional teach-
ing (Columbus, Ohio:
Merrill, 1980), p. 118.
Reproduced by permission.

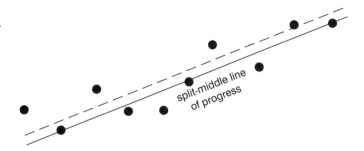

drawn), the clearer the intervention effect. It should be noted that "rapidity of change is a difficult notation to specify because it is a joint function of changes in level and slope (trend). . . . A marked change in level and in slope usually reflects a rapid change" (Kazdin, 1982, p. 316).

Although visual inspection is useful, convenient, and basically reliable for identifying or verifying strong intervention effects, much of the current published research using single-subject designs has accompanied visual inspection with statistical verification of effects (for example, t test, F test, R test, time series analysis). Kazdin (1976) offers three reasons to support the use of statistical techniques:

1. To assist in distinguishing subtle effects from chance occurrence
2. To analyze the effects of a treatment procedure when a stable baseline cannot be established
3. To assess the treatment effects in environments that lack control

More information about advanced uses of visual inspection and especially about statistical evaluation in single-subject designs can be found in Barlow and Hersen (1984), Kazdin (1982), and Tawney and Gast (1984).

Replication

A frequently asked question regarding the use of single-subject designs for research is whether the results can be generalized. If a study shows that a procedure is effective with a single subject, does this mean that it will be effective with others? Applied behavior analysts do not assume generalizability of research results based on a single successful intervention. Instead, they depend on *replication*—the repeated application of the same intervention with different subjects. That systematic teacher praise increases one student's rate of doing math problems may not be a convincing argument for the use of praise. However, documentation that such praise has increased production of not only math problems but also many other academic and social behaviors with dozens of students at many different ages is convincing. By replication, applied behavior analysts gradually identify procedures and techniques effective with many students. These procedures and techniques can then be adopted by others with considerable confidence that they will work.

SUMMARY

In this chapter we have discussed a number of single-subject designs for research and teaching. We have described procedures for implementation, graphic representation, and data analysis for each design. It is the systematic analysis of data collected in a planned and organized form that distinguishes the applied behavior analyst from the mere behavior modifier. The teacher who is familiar with design can quickly evaluate the results of his or her own instruction and ultimately share these results with others. The continuing process of applied behavior analysis results in more effective teaching that is ultimately reflected in more adaptive academic and social behaviors of students.

DISCUSSION QUESTIONS

1. Draw a graph of the following baseline data that: (a) displays a reporting of the duration of each trip to the bathroom and (b) displays the average time spent in the bathroom per day.

Day	Trip Number	Duration
Monday	1	12 minutes
	2	8 minutes
	3	7 minutes
Tuesday	1	11 minutes
	2	10 minutes
	3	9 minutes
	4	10 minutes
Wednesday	1	14 minutes
	2	11 minutes
	3	8 minutes
Thursday	1	9 minutes
	2	9 minutes
Friday	1	6 minutes
	2	10 minutes
	3	8 minutes
	4	12 minutes

2. The data in the chart on page 201 represent baseline data on George's disruptive behavior in class during a 2½-hour observation period, from 9:00 A.M. to 11:30 A.M. His disruptive behavior was defined as occurrences of throwing objects (e.g., paper, pencils) and being out of his seat without permission. On the data sheet, throwing objects is coded T, and out-of-seat is coded S. Data were collected using time sampling. Intervals were 15 minutes

in length. Draw a baseline graph of these data that: (a) reports number of intervals of occurrence and (b) reports percent of intervals of occurrence.

Student   George

Date   January 6–10

Behavior   T = throwing objects   S = out of seat

Observation period   9:00–11:30 A.M.

Observer   Ms. Calloway

	15'	30'	45'	60'	15'	30'	45'	60'	15'	30'
Monday	—	T	—	S	T S	S	—	S	T	—
Tuesday	—	—	S	—	T	T	—	S	S	—
Wednesday	S	S	—	T S	S	—	—	—	S	T
Thursday	S	—	S	S	T	—	T S	—	S	T S
Friday	—	—	T S	T S	S	—	T	T	—	S

3. Gary, a first-grader, does not seem to be understanding the concept of subtraction. Mr. Robertson, his teacher, wants to determine which of two alternative approaches to teaching subtraction would be potentially most effective to use with Gary. Select two instructional methods. Outline the steps Mr. Robertson must follow to make this determination.

4. Outline a procedure that will demonstrate the generalization of an intervention across settings in a high school—for example, a student who arrives late to history, English, and biology classes.

REFERENCES

Baer, D., Wolf, M., & Risley, T. 1968. Some current dimensions of applied behavior analysis. *Journal of Applied Behavior Analysis, 1*, 91–97.

Bailey, D. 1984. Effects of lines of progress and semilogarithmic charts on ratings of charted data. *Journal of Applied Behavior Analysis, 17*, 359–365.

Barlow, D., & Hayes, S. 1979. Alternating treatments design: One strategy for comparing the effects of two treatments in a single subject. *Journal of Applied Behavior Analysis, 12*, 199–210.

Barlow, D., & Hersen, M. 1984. *Single-case experimental designs: Strategies for studying behavior change*, New York: Pergamon Press.

Bates, P., Renzaglia, A., & Clees, T. 1980. Improving the work performance of severely/profoundly retarded young adults: The use of the changing criterion procedural design. *Education and Training of the Mentally Retarded, 15*, 95–104.

Caron, C., & Ladouceur, R. 1989. Multidimensional behavioral treatment for child stutterers. *Behavior Modification, 13*, 206–215.

Carr, E.G., Newsom, C.D., & Binkoff, J.A. 1980. Escape as a factor in the aggressive behavior of two retarded children. *Journal of Applied Behavior Analysis, 13*, 101–117.

Charlop, M., Kurtz, P., & Milstein, J. 1992. Too much reinforcement, too little behavior: Assessing task interspersal procedures in conjunction with different reinforcement schedules with autistic children. *Journal of Applied Behavior Analysis, 25*, 795–808.

Cooper, J. 1981. *Measuring behavior* (2nd ed.). Columbus, Ohio: Merrill.

Foxx, R., & Shapiro, S. 1978. The timeout ribbon: A nonexclusionary timeout procedure. *Journal of Applied Behavior Analysis, 11*, 125–136.

Hall, R.V., & Fox, R.G. 1977. Changing-criterion designs: An applied behavior analysis procedure. In B.C. Etzel, J.M. LeBlanc, & D.M. Baer (Eds.), *New developments in behavioral research: Theory, method and application.* Hillsdale, N.J.: Lawrence Erlbaum Associates, Inc., Publishers. (In honor of Sidney W. Bijou.)

Handen, B., Parrish, J., McClung, T., Kerwin, M., & Evans, L. 1992. Using guided compliance versus time out to promote child compliance: A preliminary comparative analysis in an analogue context. *Research in Development Disabilities, 13*, 157–170.

Hartmann, D.P., & Hall, R.V. 1976. The changing criterion design. *Journal of Applied Behavior Analysis, 9*, 527–532.

Hersen, M., & Barlow, D.H. 1976. *Single-case experimental designs: Strategies for studying behavior change.* New York: Pergamon Press.

Higgins-Hains, A. 1991. Multi-element designs for early intervention research: Some considerations. *Journal of Applied Behavior Analysis, 15*, 57–69.

Higgins-Hains, A., & Baer, D. 1989. Interaction effects in multielement designs: Inevitable, desirable, and ignorable. *Journal of Applied Behavior Analysis, 22*, 57–69.

Horner, R.D. & Baer, D.M. 1978. Multiple-probe technique: A variation on the multiple baseline. *Journal of Applied Behavior Analysis, 11*, 189–196.

Kazdin, A.E. 1976. Statistical analyses for single-case experimental designs. In M. Hersen & D. Barlow (Eds.), *Single-case experimental designs: Strategies for studying behavior change* (pp. 265–316). New York: Pergamon Press.

Kazdin, A.E. 1977. Assessing the clinical or applied importance of behavior change through social validation. *Behavior Modification, 1*, 427–451.

Kazdin, A.E. 1982. *Single-case research designs.* New York: Oxford University Press.

Knapczyk, D. 1988. Reducing aggressive behaviors in special and regular class settings by training alternative social responses. *Behavioral Disorders, 14*, 27–39.

Murphy, R., & Bryan, A. 1980. Multiple-baseline and multiple-probe designs: Practical alternatives for special education assessment and evaluation. *The Journal of Special Education, 14*, 325–335.

Ollendick, T., Matson, J., Esveldt-Dawson, K., & Shapiro, E. 1980. Increasing spelling achievement: An analysis of treatment procedures utilizing an alternating treatments design. *Journal of Applied Behavior Analysis, 13*, 645–654.

Ottenbacher, K., & Cusick, A. 1991. An Empirical investigation of interrater agreement for single-subject data using graphs with and without trend lines. *Journal of the Association for Persons with Severe Handicaps, 16. 48–55.*

Piggott, H., Fantuzzo, J., & Clement, P. 1986. *The effects of reciprocal peer tutoring and group contingencies on the academic performance of elementary school children. Journal of Applied Behavior Analysis, 19,* 93–98.

Repp, A. 1983. *Teaching the mentally retarded.* Englewood Cliffs, N.J.: Prentice-Hall.

Sherburne, S., Utley, B., McConnell, S., & Gannon, J. 1988. Decreasing violent or aggressive theme play among preschool children with behavior disorders. *Exceptional Children, 55,* 166–172.

Sidman, M. 1960. *Tactics of scientific research.* New York: Basic Books.

Singh, N. 1990. Effects of two error-correction procedures on oral reading errors. *Behavior Modification, 14,* 188–199.

Smith, D. 1979. The improvement of children's oral reading through the use of teacher modeling. *Journal of Learning Disabilities, 12,* 172–175.

Tawney, J., & Gast, D. 1984. *Single-subject research in special education.* Columbus, Ohio: Merrill.

Test, D., Grossi, T., & Keul, P. 1988. A functional analysis of the acquisition and maintenance of janitorial skills in a competitive work setting. *Journal of the Association for Persons with Severe Handicaps, 13,* 1–7.

Ulman, J.D., & Sulzer-Azaroff, B. 1975. Multi-element baseline design in educational research. In E. Ramp & G. Semb (Eds.), *Behavior analysis: Areas of research and application* (pp. 377–391). Englewood Cliffs, N.J.: Prentice-Hall.

White, A., & Bailey, J. 1990. Reducing disruptive behaviors of elementary physical education students with sit and watch. *Journal of Applied Behavior Analysis, 23,* 353–359.

White, O., & Haring, N. 1980. *Exceptional teaching.* Columbus, Ohio: Merrill.

White, O., & Liberty, K. 1976. Evaluation and measurement. In N.G. Haring & R.L. Schielfelbusch (Eds.), *Teaching special children.* New York: McGraw-Hill.

Section Three

Applying Learning Principles

Arranging Consequences That Increase Behavior

Did you know that . . .

- Behaviorists did not invent positive reinforcement?
- Candy may not be a positive reinforcer?
- Sometimes it's better not to reinforce every instance of appropriate behavior?
- Negative reinforcement is not punishment?
- You don't need a lawyer to write a contract?

The term *reinforcement*, used to describe pleasant events or rewards given to a person who complies with the demands of some behavior-change agent, has become part of the vocabulary of the general public. It has thus become associated with a stereotypic, manipulative view of behavior modification, conceptualized as an artificial tool created to make people engage in behaviors chosen by others. Although many applied behavior analysts use the principles of reinforcement to change behavior, it is not true that reinforcement is an invention of behaviorists. Reinforcement is a naturally occurring phenomenon. Behaviorists have simply applied the effects of reinforcement in a thoughtful and systematic manner.

As Chapter 1 stated, reinforcement describes a relationship between two environmental events, some behavior (response), and some event or consequence that follows the response. The relationship is termed *reinforcement* only if the response increases or maintains its rate as a result of the consequence. Chapter 1 described two types of reinforcement: positive reinforcement—the *contingent presentation* of a consequence that increases behavior—and negative reinforcement—the *contingent removal* of some unpleasant stimulus that increases behavior. Both positive and negative reinforcement increase the future probability of the event that they follow.

We do a lot of things we do because of the consequences of doing them. Every action we engage in results in some consequence. When our behavior results in a naturally occurring, desirable consequence, this experience motivates us to continue behaving that way. Consider these examples:

- An office worker goes to work each day expecting to receive a check at the end of the week. If the check is delivered on Friday in an amount the individual finds satisfying, it increases the probability that the person will return to work on Monday.
- A little leaguer hits a double and is applauded by fans and teammates. This motivates her to play again next Saturday.
- A baby coos at his mother's approach so she cuddles him and spends more time playing with him. The mother's response increases the frequency of the baby's cooing, which increases the time spent playing, which increases . . .
- A student spends 45 minutes each night for a week studying for a history exam. If the student makes an A on the exam, this consequence will motivate her to study just as hard for her next exam.

Although many appropriate behaviors are maintained by naturally occurring reinforcers, this natural process may be insufficient to maintain all desirable behaviors. Teachers often find students for whom naturally occurring reinforcers currently fail to maintain appropriate behavior. Some students may see little immediate benefit from learning plane geometry or applied behavior analysis. Some students may be motivated by stronger competing reinforcers than those being offered by the teacher. These students may find the laughter of other students more reinforcing than the teacher's approval. Some students may not value the reinforcers the teacher offers. Grades, for example, may have little meaning to them. In such instances, the teacher must develop an interim program to systematically arrange opportunities for students to earn valued reinforcers. When naturally occurring reinforcers are not sufficiently powerful, the wise teacher looks for more powerful ones.

In this chapter, we shall describe procedures for the effective use of reinforcement procedures in changing classroom behavior. The majority of the chapter examines the use of positive reinforcement, while the final section describes classroom applications of negative reinforcement. Suggested categories and examples of potential reinforcers are summarized in Table 6-1. This table is not designed as a scheme for ordinal selection of reinforcement categories on a contrived to natural continuum. One might be tempted to identify, for example, the use of edible reinforcers as contrived or artificial in the classroom. Such a designation, however, depends on the target behavior, the setting, and the age of the student.

Any category or specific stimulus could be described as a contrived or natural reinforcer. Food as a reinforcer while teaching a student to feed himself or access to the water fountain as a reinforcer for properly lining up after a PE period may be considered natural consequences of the target behav-

TABLE 6-1
Categories and examples of reinforcers for classroom use.

Class		Category	Examples
Primary reinforcers	1.	Edible reinforcers	Foods, liquids, e.g., pieces of cracker, sips of juice, pudding
	2.	Sensory reinforcers	Exposure to controlled visual, auditory, tactile, olfactory, or kinesthetic experience, e.g., face stroked with furry puppet, taped music through headphones
Secondary reinforcers	3.	Tangible (material) reinforcers	E.g., certificates, badges, stickers, rock star posters, balloons
	4.	(a) Privilege reinforcers	E.g., monitorships, team captain, excused from homework
		(b) Activity reinforcers	E.g., play activities, special projects, access to media, extra math problems to do (yes there is such a student!)
	5.	Generalized reinforcers	E.g., tokens, points, credits
	6.	Social reinforcers	E.g., expressions, proximity, contact, words and phrases, feedback, seating arrangements

iors. It may be helpful to distinguish among items or events ordinarily available in a given environment (that is, natural) and those temporarily added to the environment for increased consequence intensity (that is, contrived).

POSITIVE REINFORCEMENT

Positive reinforcement(S^{R+}) is the contingent presentation of a stimulus, immediately following a response, that increases the future rate and/or probability of the response. There are three operative words in this definition. The word _increases_ makes it clear we are dealing with some form of reinforcement, for the stimulus will have the effect of increasing the probability that the response will reoccur. The second operative word is _presentation_. When we use positive reinforcement, we intentionally present the student with a stimulus following the production of a response. The third operative word is _contingent._ The teacher will not present the consequence to the student unless and until the requested response is produced. If a teacher states the contingency, "Bill, when you finish all your math problems, you may play with the airplane models," the teacher is using positive reinforcement (if airplane models are reinforcing to Bill). The reinforcing stimulus (playing with airplane models) will be presented to the student contingent on production of the requested behavior (completion of math problems). The examples in Table 6-2 illustrate the principle of positive reinforcement.

Whereas _positive reinforcement_ refers to the relationship between a behavior and a consequence, the term _positive reinforcer_ describes the consequent event itself. A positive reinforcer is a consequential stimulus (S^R) that

1. Increases or maintains the future rate and/or probability of occurrence of a behavior

TABLE 6–2
Examples of positive reinforcers.

	Stimulus	Response	S^{R+}	Effect
Example 1	Statement of the contingency and availability of appropriate materials.	Bill completes math problems.	He is allowed to play with model planes.	Increased probability that Bill will complete next set of problems on time.
Example 2	—	John sits upright in his seat.	Teacher presents him with a smile and words of praise.	Increased likelihood that John will continue to sit appropriately.
Example 3	—	Sara brings in her homework each day this week.	She is appointed board monitor for next week.	Increased probability that Sara will continue to bring her homework every day.

2. Is administered contingently upon the production of a desired or requested behavior

3. Is administered immediately following the production of the desired or requested behavior.

Choosing Effective Reinforcers

The reinforcing potential of an item or event depends on reinforcement history and deprivation.

Because a stimulus is defined as a positive reinforcer only as a result of its effect on behavior, no item or event can be termed a positive reinforcer until this relationship has been established. It follows, therefore, that a teacher cannot state with any real degree of certainty—in advance of evidence of such a relationship—what will or will not be a reinforcing consequence for any given student. What serves as a reinforcer for a particular student depends on several factors, including the student's reinforcement history (what has motivated her in the past), the student's deprivation state (what she wants but does not get easily or frequently), the perceived value of the reinforcer (whether it is worth performing the behavior to get it), consistency (whether reinforcers have been reliably delivered in the past), and age-appropriateness (whether the reinforcer, even if the student might enjoy it, is more suitable for a younger child and thus embarrassing to her).

What will serve as a reinforcer may be different for each student. Preconceived notions of what should be reinforcing are frequent reasons for the failure of intervention programs. When the desired behavior change does not occur, the teacher's first reaction is often to assume the reinforcement procedures have not worked, when in fact one of the fundamental notions of reinforcement has been violated: the *individualization of reinforcers*.

Ms. Ledbetter Wastes Silli-Circles

Ms. Ledbetter, who had been a second-grade teacher for 27 years, read about positive reinforcement in a newspaper article. The article described a program designed to teach children with disabilities self-care skills such as dressing themselves. The researchers had used presweetened cereal as a positive reinforcer. Ms. Ledbetter was very excited about the prospect of motivating her students to do better in school. She therefore purchased a large, economy-size box of Silli-Circles, the newest sweetened oat cereal, and prepared to reinforce appropriate behavior.

Her lowest reading group included several students who lacked any reading skills whatever, as well as any apparent interest in acquiring such skills. When she called them to the reading circle, she announced, "Boys and girls, today when you answer a question correctly, you'll get a Silli-Circle. Won't that be nice?"

Ms. Ledbetter then proceeded with her lesson. She was disappointed to find the students seemed no more interested in reading than before and the few students who earned cereal either dropped it on the floor or attempted with little success to give it away.

"Well!" snorted Ms. Ledbetter, "I should have known. These newfangled ideas. . . . That positive reinforcement stuff just doesn't work."

Ms. Ledbetter's conclusion that positive reinforcement doesn't work was based on her assumption that because cereal was a reinforcer for some students, it would be a reinforcer for all. Apparently, members of her reading group did not like Silli-Circles, or they had eaten a bowl for breakfast, or they couldn't read well enough to answer the questions. Therefore, Silli-Circles were not a positive reinforcer.

An aid in determining the potential effectiveness of reinforcers is reinforcer sampling. Systematic sampling has been found to be more reliable than teachers' predictions or guesses for identifying items that will function as reinforcers when applied contingently (Daly, Jacob, King, & Cheramie, 1984; Green, Reid, White, Halford, Brittain, & Gardner, 1988). The sampling method will vary depending on students' level of functioning. Students can often simply be asked what they would like to have as a result of their effort or achievement. Ms. Ledbetter could have saved a lot of grief if she had simply asked, "Do you like Silli-Circles?"

Another strategy for reinforcer sampling is using a prepared reinforcer menu like the one shown in Figure 6–1. Students would be asked to list the potential reinforcers in order of preference. A reinforcer menu should include a variety of potential reinforcers that teachers can reasonably make available. The presentation of limited choices will prevent unrealistic selections (such as stereos, video game machines, and trips to Acapulco) that students might suggest. Teachers, however, may still wish to offer the opportunity for an open-ended response following some forced choices.

Reinforcer sampling for students with severe disabilities must be concrete.

To determine reinforcer preference with students whose abilities to respond are more limited, it may be necessary to conduct the reinforcer sampling with actual objects or events. It is usually best to bring to a sampling session up to five items the teacher thinks are potential reinforcers. These may include edible items, sensory items, and toys. The student should be allowed to experience each of the items and then to select from an array of three. The teacher should keep a tally of the student's choice on each trial. Once an item has been selected a predetermined number of times, another item should be substituted. Various systematic approaches to reinforcer sampling have been suggested by Datilo (1986); Green et al. (1988); Green, Reid, Canipe, & Gardner, (1991); and Pace, Ivancic, Edwards, Iwata, and Page (1985). For students with physical limitations, microswitches may be used to enable them to access the array of items (Wacker, Berg, Wiggins, Muldoon, & Cavanaugh, 1985). As noted by Ayllon and Azrin (1968):

> The sampling of the event does not guarantee that the event will, in fact, be reinforcing to the individual; rather, the sampling allows any reinforcing properties to be exhibited if the event has any potential reinforcing properties. If the individual does not seek the event after it has been sampled, it will not be because of a lack of familiarity with it. (p. 92)

FIGURE 6-1
Reinforcer menu.

It's your choice:

"I would most like to earn" = 1
"I would least like to earn" = 9

Candy bar	Flag monitor for a week	Extra dessert at lunch
Pinwheel	Poster	Use of the computer
Captain of softball team for a week	Extra time in the gym	No homework one night next week

or

Hall and Hall (1980, pp. 15–17) suggest the following nine-step sequence for selecting potential reinforcers:

Step 1: "Consider the age, interests and appetites of the person whose behaviors you wish to strengthen." The teacher should select potential consequences that attempt to correspond to the student's chronological age and social background. Fruit Loops or an opportunity to work puzzles will probably have little motivational value to an adolescent.

Step 2: "Consider the behavior you wish to strengthen through reinforcement." The teacher should select potential consequences that attempt to correspond to the value, or effort required to produce the response. "If an employer offered to buy an employee a cup of coffee for working all weekend on a special job it would be unlikely that any worker would accept the offer." Similarly, offering a student five additional minutes of free time for completion of an entire day's written assignment is an opportunity the student will probably pass up.

Step 3: "List potential reinforcers considering what you know of the person, his or her age, interests, likes and dislikes and the specific behavior you have defined." This step allows the teacher to organize the potential reinforcers she is considering in an orderly and objective manner. Hall and Hall suggest that the potential reinforcers be organized according to categories, such as material reinforcers, activity reinforcers, and social reinforcers.

Step 4: "The Premack Principle." When selecting potential reinforcers, the teacher should consider watching the student and noting activities in which he likes to engage. The use of preferred activities as reinforcers was systematized by David Premack (1959). A discussion of the Premack Principle follows later in this chapter.

Step 5: "Consider asking the person." The teacher should remember that the best authority on the likes and dislikes of a student is that student. The mechanism most often used to determine a student's potential reinforcers is the previously mentioned reinforcer menu. For alternative forms of reinforcer menus, see Raschke (1981).

Step 6: "Consider novel reinforcers." With this step Hall and Hall remind teachers that "varying the reinforcers is more effective than using the same reinforcers over and over." Repeated use of the same reinforcer can lead to boredom and satiation, lessening the motivating effectiveness of a consequence.

Step 7: "Consider reinforcers that are natural." Hall and Hall suggest three advantages to the use of natural reinforcers. First, natural reinforcers such as recognition and privileges can be provided more easily and at lower cost than most edible and material consequences. Second, natural reinforcers are more likely to be available to the student after the behavior has been established. "In a natural situation, even though you discontinue to systematically reinforce the behavior you wanted to strengthen, the natural positive consequence you provided is more likely to be available on at least some occasion in the future." Third, natural reinforcers automatically occur on a contingent basis. Praise for a homework assignment well done will not naturally occur unless the behavior was performed.

Step 8: "Select the reinforcer or reinforcers you will use." Once the teacher has considered Steps 1-7, Hall and Hall suggest he or she now select the reinforcers that will most likely have the desired effect on the target behavior.

Step 9: "Make a record of the behavior." The teacher is reminded that the only way to confirm a consequence as a reinforcer is to observe its effect on the behavior. To verify this effect the teacher should systematically document the change, if any, in the production of the behavior. Various methods for providing such documentation are presented in Chapter 4 of this text.

Periodic reassessment of any reinforcer is important (Mason, McGee, Farmer-Dougan, & Risley, 1989). This is especially true if a single item or small set of items is used. When behavior change slows down, it may simply be because a student is tired of the reinforcer.

Making Reinforcers Contingent

It may also be necessary to be sure parents or other caregivers don't make potential reinforcers available noncontingently.

If reinforcement is to be effective, the student must receive the reinforcer only after performing the target behavior. An "if . . ., then . . ." statement is in place. Such a statement establishes a clear and explicit relationship between performing the behavior and receiving the reinforcer. If Clara finds, regardless of whether she has performed the target behavior, she can get a lollipop at the end of the day when the teacher is tired and has a few pops left over, Clara may decide the teacher does not mean business: no contingency is actually in force. Implied in such a contingency and explicit in reinforcer delivery is that the teacher or some other specifically designated person is the source of the reinforcer. If the student can go to the classroom assistant or some other adult during the day and get the same promised reinforcer without having performed the desired behavior, that student will quickly determine there is no need to comply with the contingency.

Making Reinforcement Immediate

To be effective, a reinforcer should initially be delivered immediately after the target behavior is performed. This timing convinces the student of the veracity of the contingency and underlines the connection between a particular behavior and its consequence. Immediacy of delivery is also necessary to avoid the hazard of inadvertently reinforcing an intervening behavior. The longer the delay between the desired behavior and receipt of the reinforcer, the greater the possibility the student may engage in a behavior not under the contingency or not desired. If the reinforcer is delivered following any intervening behavior, it is the latter whose probability will be increased. Eventually the teacher will want to introduce a delay between the behavior and the reinforcer. This systematically arranged delay is known as a *schedule of reinforcement* and is dealt with later in this chapter.

Ms. Troutman Reinforces Chaos

Ms. Troutman was a teacher of students with severe social maladjustments. She taught in a self-contained special class. It was the first week of her first year in this setting, and she was determined to make it a success. She had taken a course in applied behavior analysis and decided to set the following contingency for her students:

If you complete at least 20 assignments during the week, *then* you may participate in a class party at 2:15 on Friday.

The students worked busily, and Ms. Troutman glowed with satisfaction as she wondered why people thought these students were difficult to teach. At 11:00 on Friday morning, the first student completed his 20th assignment. By noon, all seven students had fulfilled the contingency. The remaining hours before 2:15 were among the longest Ms. Troutman had ever spent. Even though the students yelled, fought, cursed, ran around, and generally created havoc, the party was held as scheduled. (Ms. Troutman at least had sense enough to know that if she failed to live up to her end of the contingency, the students would never believe her again.) Monday morning the class came in yelling, fighting, cursing, and running around. Ms. Troutman had reinforced chaos, and that's what she got.

Types of Reinforcers

Two major varieties of reinforcers are available to teachers: *primary reinforcers* and *secondary reinforcers*.

Primary Reinforcers

Primary reinforcers can be powerful tools for changing behavior.

Primary reinforcers are stimuli that have biological importance to an individual. We can assume that they are innately motivating because they are necessary to the perpetuation of life. Therefore, primary reinforcers are described as *natural, unlearned,* or *unconditioned reinforcers*. Given their biological importance, we may expect that they will be highly motivating to individual students. The major types of primary reinforcers include foods, liquids, sleep, shelter, and sex (the last reinforcer is most commonly used as entry to social activities that include both males and females). Obviously, the two most common and appropriate primary reinforcers for the classroom are food and liquids.

Edible reinforcers are used mainly when teaching new behaviors to younger students and students with severe disabilities. Because of their high motivational value, they quickly affect behavior.

Different strokes for different folks.

In spite of the almost mystical association between behavior modification and M&M candy, teachers rarely find it necessary to use edible reinforcers with older students students with mild disabilities. An imaginative teacher can choose from a great many other potential reinforcers. Reinforcing these students' behavior with candy or other treats is an example of behavioral overkill. Besides being unnecessary, primary reinforcers may be perceived by students as insulting. A ninth-grader could hardly take seriously a teacher who said, "Great job on that algebra assignment, Casey. Here's your cookie." This is not to imply that teachers of older students should never use food as a reinforcer. An occasional treat may be very effective, when appropriately presented. For example, a popcorn party for students who have met some contingency may be perfectly appropriate. It is amazing to observe how rapidly second- or third-graders complete assignments once the smell of the popping corn begins wafting about the room.

Deprivation is a condition that must be met if primary reinforcers are to be effective.

For primary reinforcers to be effective, the student whose behavior is to be reinforced must be in a state of deprivation in relation to that reinforcer. Using an edible reinforcer with a student who has just returned from lunch is less likely to be effective because the student is not hungry. This by no means suggests that students should be starved so that food will be an effective reinforcer, but the necessity for a state of deprivation is a major drawback to the use of primary reinforcers. A student need not be hungry, however, for limited amounts of special foods such as potato chips, raisins, ice cream, or candy to be effective reinforcers.

The opposite of deprivation is satiation. Satiation occurs when the deprivation state that existed at the beginning of an instructional session no longer exists, and the student's cooperation and attention have worn thin. A teacher of students with severe disabilities who conducts a training session lasting perhaps 30 minutes may come to a point in the session when the primary reinforcer loses its effectiveness. The teacher will know this when the student's rate of correct responding slows down or—in the case of more assertive students—when the student spits the no-longer-reinforcer at the teacher. There are at least six ways a teacher may plan to prevent or delay satiation:

1. Assign a particular reinforcer to each instructional task. There is no need to use a single reinforcer all day, in all subject areas, with any given student. To do so is to build in the potential danger of satiation. As a result of the reinforcer sampling that was conducted, an ordered list of several potential reinforcers is available so that more than one can be used during the day.

2. Shorten the instructional session in which the edible reinforcer is being used. Shorter sessions with fewer trials (controlled presentations) decrease the chances of satiation. Several short sessions may be held during the day.

3. If satiation occurs, try switching to an alternate reinforcer. Alternating salty foods and sips of liquid may be a very effective way of delaying satiation.

4. Decrease the size of the pieces of the edible reinforcer given for correct responses. Smaller portions also disappear more quickly, thus not creating artificially long periods between trials as the student continues to "savor" his raisin.

5. Have an array of edible reinforcers available for the student to select from following each correct response. In this way, the teacher may say, "Good, that's right. What would you like to eat?" She has a plate next to her with pieces of three or four different foods the student likes (Lovaas, 1977).

6. Reinforce after approximately every third correct response using one of three reinforcers identified through sampling. Such reinforcer variation has been found to produce more stable responding than constant use of the same reinforcer (Egel, 1981).

Carr, Binkoff, Kologinsky, and Eddy (1978) delayed the onset of satiation and tied their use of reinforcers directly to the concepts they were teaching to a group of students with autistic behaviors. While teaching the students manual signs for the words *milk, apple, cookie, candy,* and *banana,* the teacher reinforced a correctly formed sign with a piece of the food indicated. By this method, the students received only a small amount of the reinforcer requested, and the reinforcer was varied according to the randomization of the trial presentations. A problem with satiation is illustrated by the following story.

Mr. Alberto Eats Ice Cream

Jeff was a student with severe retardation whose behavioral repertoire seemed to consist mainly of throwing materials and chairs. He sometimes varied this by hitting teachers and other students. In an effort to control this behavior, Mr. Alberto had tried more than a dozen potential primary reinforcers—from potato chips to candy—with no success whatsoever. Appropriate behavior stayed at a low rate and inappropriate behavior at a high rate.

In desperation, Mr. Alberto asked Jeff's mother if there was *anything* Jeff liked. (It occurred to him that this might have been a good thing to have done in the first place.)

"Of course," said Mother, "Jeff loves butter-pecan ice cream."

One quick trip to the grocery store later, Mr. Alberto began to make progress with Jeff. By the end of a week, the behavior was under reasonable control, and Mr. Alberto thought his troubles were over. Before long, however, the inappropriate behavior was back in full force. Once again, Mr. Alberto questioned Jeff's mother. Could she explain why butter-pecan ice cream wasn't working any more?

"Well, maybe," said Mother, "it's because he gets so much at home. I learned long ago that it was the only way to make him behave. I give him a whole carton some days."

As Mr. Alberto solaced himself with the remaining pint of butter-pecan, he prepared once again to go in search of the elusive reinforcer.

Edibles provide the teacher with a wide range of potential reinforcers—for example, cereal (Alberto, Jobes, Sizemore, & Doran, 1980), ice cream and soda (Newsom & Simon, 1977), diet chocolate (Olenick & Pear, 1980), chips and pieces of cookie (Parrish, Cataldo, Kolko, Neef, & Egel, 1986), and grapes and raisins (Egel, 1981). Certain precautions, however, are necessary. A review of medical records or consultation with parents is advisable. A student may have allergies to certain foods, be on a special diet, have a lactose intolerance, or be susceptible to diabetic reactions. When using edible reinforcers with younger students, teachers should be aware of the danger of choking, particularly with foods like raisins and grapes. The teacher should also take into account the relative nutritional value of corn chips and raisins.

Common sense also suggests some precautions in selecting reinforcers. A teacher conducting language training would not use peanut butter as a reinforcer, because it is difficult to imitate sounds with your tongue stuck to the roof of your mouth. Liquid reinforcers may increase the number of toileting breaks necessary, unduly delaying the session.

Teachers should also note that the strong motivational property of certain reinforcers, especially edible reinforcers, has the potential to encourage responses that are incompatible with the target response. Balsam and Bondy (1983) illustrate this point with the example of using ice cream as a reinforcer for a young child. They suggest that the ice cream itself might stimulate so much approach behavior (that is, staring, reaching) that it interferes with the child's attending to the relevant antecedent and response requirement of the contingency. Similarly, if a teacher tells the students if they are good they will be allowed a special treat at lunch time, they may become increasingly fidgety and inattentive in anticipation of the reinforcement. (For a full discussion of the theoretical and operant negative side effects of reinforcement, see Balsam and Bondy, 1983.)

A sixth reinforcer often included as a primary reinforcer is a sensory reinforcer. Sensory reinforcers include:

Auditory: tones, voices, music, environmental (music through headphones)

Visual: black/white, color, lights (with and without blinking), movement (pictures, books, magazines, slide videos, battery operated toys, bubbles)

Olfactory: sweet, pungent (cinnamon, clove, orange, inexpensive perfume)

Taste: solids or liquids (sweet, sour, salty, sharp, bitter)

Tactile: soft/rough, soft/hard, warm/cold, wet/dry, movement (vibrators, fans, various textures such as fur)

Proprioceptive: bounce, swing, rock (trampolines, swings, rocking chairs, rocking horses)

These events can be used individually or in combination (Dewson & Whiteley, 1987). When implementing sensory reinforcers one can and must be sure to select events that are age-appropriate (Gutierrez-Griep, 1984). Sensory reinforcers have been successfully used with nondisabled persons (Sigueland, 1968; Stevenson & Odom, 1964) and disabled persons (Rincover, Cook, Peoples, & Packard, 1979), though most often with populations of students with severe disabilities (Datilo, 1986; Dewson & Whitely, 1987; Fehr, Wacker, Trezise, Lennon, & Meyerson, 1979; Rincover, Newsom, Lovaas, & Koegel, 1977; Wacker, Berg, Wiggins, Muldoon, & Cavanaugh, 1985). With these students they have often been used as competing sensory input for decreasing stereotypic behaviors (Favell, McGimsey, & Schell, 1982; Rincover et al., 1979). There are indications that naturally occurring sensations may be reinforcing stimuli for stereotypic or self-injurious behavior (Durand, 1990; Durand & Crimmins, 1988).

Secondary Reinforcers

No teacher wants to make students dependent on primary reinforcers for working or behaving appropriately. Primary reinforcers, even for very young or severely disabled students, are temporary measures to enable rapid acquisition of appropriate behavior. The teacher cannot send a student back into a regular classroom expecting a Tootsie Roll each time that he can identify the word *dog* or to work expecting a chocolate cake or side of beef at the end of the work week. Primary reinforcers, if used, should eventually be replaced by secondary reinforcers. **Secondary reinforcers** include social stimuli, such as words of praise or the opportunity to engage in preferred activities; and a symbolic representation, such as a token, exchangeable for another reinforcer. Unlike primary reinforcers, secondary reinforcers do not have biological importance to individuals. Rather, their value has been learned or conditioned. Thus, secondary reinforcers are often called *conditioned reinforcers*. Some students have not learned to value secondary reinforcers and must be taught to do so before secondary reinforcers will be effective.

Pairing teaches students to value secondary reinforcers.

Pairing.   Students for whom secondary reinforcers have no value often need primary reinforcement to acquire appropriate behavior. To avoid dependence upon primary reinforcers, however, their use should always be in conjunction with some secondary reinforcer. The combined use of primary and secondary reinforcers is known as **pairing**. (The primary reinforcer is paired with a secondary reinforcer.) For example, when Jake behaves appropriately, his teacher may give him a bite of food and simultaneously tell him what a good job he has done. Through pairing we condition or teach the student to be motivated by the secondary reinforcer alone. Once this association has been established, the secondary reinforcer may be as effective as the primary reinforcer. The teacher may then gradually withdraw the primary reinforcer. Some students, of course, have a reinforcement history including paired association, allowing for the use of secondary reinforcers without the need for primary reinforcers.

Tangible reinforcers and privileges are concrete and can have immediacy. There is a great range of potential tangible reinforcers, from awards, such as certificates and badges of merit, to age-appropriate items like small toy figures, balloons, and stickers (Dunlap, Koegel, Johnson, & O'Neill, 1987; Guevremont, Osnes, & Stokes, 1986) for very young children; and posters of rock stars, sports magazines, and cosmetics for adolescents. Sometimes not knowing exactly what the reinforcer is can be enticing. Baer, Blount, Detrich, and Stokes (1987) and Dahlquist and Gil (1986) successfully used a grab bag. Privileges such as monitorships, being team captain, being excused from homework, collecting milk money, or caring for a class pet can earn status among the student's peers (Sainato, Maheady, & Shook, 1986).

Activity Reinforcers.   An activity is the secondary reinforcement perhaps most often used by teachers. The systematic use of such activity reinforcers was described by Premack (1959) and is referred to as the **Premack principle**. The Premack principle states that individuals engage in certain behaviors at low frequencies, so these behaviors have a low probability of occurrence. Other behaviors are engaged in at high frequencies and therefore have a high probability of occurrence. When low-frequency behaviors are followed by high-frequency behaviors, the effect is to increase the probability of the low-frequency behavior. In other words, any activity a student voluntarily performs frequently may be used as a reinforcer for any activity he seldom performs voluntarily. When a teacher tells a student she may work on her airplane model in the back of the room when she has finished the math assignment, or when a mother tells her child he may play outside when he has finished eating his brussels sprouts, they are using the Premack principle. (Table 6-3 offers suggestions for secondary reinforcers.)

Kazdin (1975) suggests some limitations to the use of activity reinforcers. First, access to some high-preference activities cannot always immediately follow the low-preference behavior, thereby reducing the effectiveness of the high-preference behavior as a reinforcer. For example, scheduling problems might prevent students' using the gym right after doing their math. Second, an activity may often be an all-or-none enterprise. It is either earned or not earned. This may limit flexibility in administration of the reinforcer. For example, a student either earns the right to go on a field trip or make a Halloween mask or he doesn't earn it. Such activities cannot be proportionally

TABLE 6–3
Examples of secondary reinforcers.

Manage the class store for a week or two
Decorate a bulletin board
Select and plan next field trip or holiday party
Lead a class activity (making popcorn, singing
  songs)
Put on a skit or direct next class play
Use media equipment (videotape machine, tape
  recorder)
Set schedule of day's activities and lessons
Take part in a tutoring program
Conduct a class lesson on topic of your choice
Learn to drive
Be excused from homework
Be excused from a test
Become a member of the safety patrol
Be a monitor (of chalkboard, messages, pets, plants,
  paper, playground equipment, flag, milk)
Be a class officer
Be a team captain
Go to the gym, library
Play with games or toys
Get a citation
Wear a badge
Use paints or craft materials
Get free time
Operate equipment

awarded depending on the degree of acceptable performance. This limitation, however, is not invariably true with activity reinforcers. Some activities may be earned in increments of time. For example, the consequence of one minute of shooting baskets in the gym for each correctly spelled word is easily administered.

A third limitation on activities as reinforcers is that many activities must be freely available to students without reference to their performance. Examples include lunch periods, physical education, or art and music classes. Finally, the use of an activity reinforcer may cause an interruption in the continuous performance of the target behavior. For example, a teacher would not want to allow a student to go to the gym and shoot a basket after each correctly spelled word. Some students, however, may not continue to perform the target behavior unless some reinforcement is available after each response. In cases where the effectiveness of activity reinforcers seems lessened by such factors, the use of generalized conditioned reinforcers may be considered.

Generalized Conditioned Reinforcers.   When a reinforcer has been associated with a variety of behaviors or with access to a variety of other primary or secondary reinforcers, it may be termed a **generalized conditioned reinforcer** or simply a *generalized reinforcer.* For example, a smile or words of praise are reinforcing following a variety of behaviors: praise from the boss after a particularly difficult work assignment, or from a spouse for a delicious dinner; a smile from a teacher following a clever verbal response in class, or a hug from Mother for picking up dirty clothes.

A second type of generalized reinforcer includes those that are exchangeable for something of value. Money is the most obvious example. Money, which has little or no intrinsic value, can be earned in a variety of ways, and is associated with access to many types of reinforcers: food, shelter, or clothing; admission to a concert; a ticket to the Super Bowl; or a Mercedes. The effectiveness of generalized conditioned reinforcers is not dependent on a single type of deprivation (Ferster & Culbertson, 1982), and they are less susceptible to satiation than other types of reinforcers.

The use of generalized reinforcers has a number of advantages. Kazdin and Bootzin (1972) suggest that

1. As opposed to certain edible or activity reinforcers, generalized reinforcers permit the reinforcement of a response at any time and allow sequences of responses to be reinforced without interruption.

2. Generalized reinforcers may be used to maintain performance over extended periods of time and are less subject to satiation effects due to their reinforcing properties and their relative independence of deprivation states.

3. Generalized reinforcers provide the same reinforcement for individuals who have different preferences.

Token Reinforcers.   Because the use of money is unrealistic in most school settings, a generalized reinforcer known as a *token reinforcer* has become widely used. Token reinforcers are simply symbolic representations exchangeable for some reinforcer of value to students. Originally, Ayllon and Azrin (1968) described procedures for using a token reinforcement system in a mental hospital ward. Although token systems are still used in hospital settings (Magrab & Papadopoulou, 1977; Nelson & Cone, 1979), variations have been used in residential settings for disturbed and delinquent adolescents (Cohen & Filipczak, 1971; Wood & Flynn, 1978), sheltered workshops (Welch & Gist, 1974), and high-school and college classes (Keller & Sherman, 1974; Kulik, Kulik, & Carmichael, 1974). Today, token systems are used in most special education and many regular education classes. They are used by teachers, aides, and parents in teaching specific skills (Goldstein & Wickstrom, 1986; Heward & Eachus, 1979; Van Hasselt, Hersen, Egan, McKelvey, & Sisson, 1989); in self-instruction (Roberts, Nelson, & Olson, 1987); in tutoring situations (Schwartz, 1977); in managing the integration of disabled students into regular classes (Russo & Koegel, 1977); and in coordinating behavior-change programs between school and home (Trovato & Bucher, 1980). Peers have even been taught to evaluate behavior and distribute tokens (Stern, Fowler, & Kohler, 1988).

The use of tokens is analogous to the use of money in the general society. Token reinforcers are exchangeable for a wide variety of primary and secondary reinforcers. They are used as a transition between primary reinforcers and the natural community of secondary reinforcers. A token system may be adapted for use with a single student and a single behavior, one student and several behaviors, groups of students and a single behavior, and groups of students and several of the same or different behaviors.

Tokens won't work unless they can be exchanged for something.

A token reinforcement system requires two components: the token itself and a back-up reinforcer. The token itself is delivered immediately on the desired response. This token can be an object, such as a poker chip, button, sticker, star, play money, paper clip, or metal washer. It can also be a symbol, such as check marks, a hole punched in a card, points, or the ubiquitous happy face. In general, tokens should be portable, durable, and easy to handle.

The teacher and the student should keep an accurate record of the number of tokens earned. When the token is an object, such as a chip, a token box or some other receptacle can be designated for storing the tokens in an assigned location or at the student's desk. With younger students, chaining necklaces with tokens or building towers will help in control of token loss. A dot-to-dot representation of the back-up reinforcer may be drawn. In this system, as each response occurs, two dots are connected. When all dots are connected, the picture is complete and the student has earned the back-up reinforcer (Trant, 1977). Students may accumulate puzzle pieces that depict the back-up reinforcer when all have been earned. Token cards with blank circles to be filled in with a smiley face for each point earned (Odom & Strain, 1986) may be used, or holes may be punched in a card (Maher, 1989). When the token is points earned, stamps, or check marks, a chart in the front of the classroom or some recording card similar to those displayed in Figure 6–2 may be used.

FIGURE 6–2
Point cards for the use with token reinforcement systems.

Note: From It's positively fun: Techniques for managing learning environments, by P. Kaplan, J. Kohfeldt, & K. Sturla (Denver: Love Publishing, 1974). Copyright 1974 by Love Publishing. Reprinted by permission.

The use of token systems requires precautions against counterfeiting or theft. Any student with 30 cents can buy 100 paper clips, thus debasing the value of paper clip tokens and thereby the effectiveness of the system. A simple preventive measure is to mark tokens, objects, or symbols with a code that allows validation of their source or confirmation of their ownership by a particular student. If check marks on a card are used, the teacher can randomly use different-colored markers on different days. The chances of a student's having a puce-colored marker in school on the day the teacher chooses that color are minimal.

Birnbrauer, Wolf, Kidder, and Tague (1965) point out that tokens in and of themselves are unlikely to have reinforcing power. They attain their reinforcing value by being exchangeable for items that are reinforcing. Therefore, the students must clearly understand they are working for these tokens to exchange them, at some point, for the second component of the token system, the **back-up reinforcer**.

The selection of the back-up reinforcer is probably the most difficult aspect of the token system, especially if the system is being used with a group of students or an entire class. The teacher must select a wide enough variety of back-up reinforcers to provide a motivating item for each member of the class. Therefore, teachers should try to include an assortment, such as edibles (cereals, crackers, cookies, juice), activities (going to the library, earning project time, listening to record player), objects (earning a game, notebook, or crayons), and privileges (being first in line, being collector of lunch money).

What students need to know about a token system

When a teacher announces the initiation of a token system to a class or to an individual, students will want to know at least four things immediately. First, they will want to know what behaviors are required. As always, the contingency (if . . . , then . . .) should be clearly stated by the teacher and understood by the students. The description of each behavior to be performed and the parameters of acceptability should be clearly stated or posted.

Second, the students will want to know what back-up reinforcers their tokens will buy. It is a good idea to keep representations of the back-up reinforcers, if not the items themselves, in full view in the classroom.

The third question might involve the cost of each back-up reinforcer in tokens. Based on their evaluation of the expense and desirability of the back-ups, the students will decide whether the reinforcer is worth the required behavior change. To get the process working initially, the teacher may price reinforcers to allow everyone to quickly acquire some. Students should learn at this very first exchange that if they earn a certain number of tokens, they may trade them for a certain back-up reinforcer. Stainback, Payne, Stainback, and Payne (1973) suggest that prices of items, such as edibles, posters, and toy soldiers, should be in proportion to their actual monetary value. The pricing of activities and privileges is difficult to judge. Students should neither earn backups too quickly nor should they be required to work inordinately hard. It will take a while for the teacher to judge the value of back-up reinforcers based upon their perceived desirability among class members.

Finally, the students will want to know when they can exchange the tokens for the back-up reinforcers. It is most common for an exchange period to take place at the end of each day or week. In the early stages of a token system, especially with young or disabled students, the period before the first exchange should be very short. It would be unwise to start a token system on Monday and schedule the first exchange period on Friday. Students need to see quickly how the exchange process works and that the teacher is indeed telling the truth. Therefore, we suggest that the first exchange period be either at lunch, at the end of school, or even at the morning break (using a cookie exchange, for example). Stainback et al.

(1973) suggest that tokens be paid frequently in the early stages and that exchange times be held once or twice a day for the first three to four days and then gradually decreased in frequency until they are held only once a week by the third week.

Exchanging tokens for back-up reinforcers may take place in a variety of formats. The most common is the classroom store (Nelson & Cone, 1979; Stainback et al., 1973). In this format, the price-labeled back-up reinforcers are located on shelves in a corner of the classroom. During the designated exchange period, students may enter the store and purchase any item they can afford. An interesting variation on the exchange is the class auction (Polloway & Polloway, 1979). In this format, the students are allowed to bid for each of the back-up reinforcers. Students may bid as high as they choose, up to the number of tokens they have earned.

One potential impediment to an effective token system occasionally arises as a result of exchange procedures. It is illustrated by the following case.

The Case of Charlie the Miser

Charlie was a student in Mr. Thomas's class for children with learning disabilities. He was a very intelligent boy with severe reading problems and many inappropriate behaviors. He, like Mr. Thomas's other students, responded well to a token reinforcement system. The students earned check marks on a card exchangeable for a variety of back-up reinforcers, including toys and privileges. The most expensive item cost three cards and many were available for one or two cards.

After several months, Mr. Thomas noticed that both Charlie's behavior and his academic work had deteriorated drastically. This deterioration seemed to have happened overnight. Mr. Thomas could see no reason for it so he decided to do a very sensible thing. He asked Charlie what had happened. Charlie grinned and opened his work folder. "Look here," he chortled. "I got 11 cards saved up. I don't have to do anything for weeks, and I can still get anything I want from the store."

It is wise, as Mr. Thomas learned, to think through your token system to prevent the accumulation of tokens as Charlie demonstrated. There are various strategies for avoiding this problem. For example:

1. Instead of having a designated day for exchanging tokens, an exchange may be allowed as soon as the student has earned enough tokens for a particular item. This ongoing exchange will encourage students to plan for specific items and exchange their tokens rather than save them.

2. Immediate and delayed exchange may be combined. Students are allowed immediate exchange when they have earned sufficient tokens for a particular reinforcer. They may bank all tokens earned or tokens left over after an exchange for major items or events in the future. There should be a substantial penalty for early withdrawal of banked tokens.

3. The color or some other characteristic of tokens can be changed monthly or quarterly. All students understand that when the tokens change old tokens become worthless. This is a variant of a strategy sometimes employed by fiscally embarrassed governments.

4. Extremely well organized managers can limit the number of tokens a student can accumulate and enforce this limit. This requires very careful and accurate record keeping. You would be wise to remember that few school systems are willing to employ an independent bookkeeper to assist you. Any token system that takes too much of a teacher's time and energy to implement and maintain is doomed to be abandoned.

See pages 55 to 59 for Professor Grundy's advice.

It is feasible to use token systems with an entire class or only with selected members of a class. If only some children earn tokens, others may question this. Professor Grundy's advice in Chapter 2 should help the teacher deal with this problem.

When using a system with an entire class, it is easiest to begin with some behavior that is a target for change for the entire class. For example, the teacher might initially give points for academic assignments finished or hands raised during class discussions. Once students have become familiar with the exchange system, the program can be individualized. While still distributing tokens for the initially targeted behavior, the teacher can integrate many academic tasks and social behaviors into the system. For example, Marty might earn tokens for neatness, Debbie for increased speed, and Sara for speaking loudly enough to be heard. Or, instead of this individual focus, the teacher might expand the initial system for classroom behavior management to include additional behaviors that are appropriate for all class members. The following is an example of a teacher's criteria for classroom points (Schumaker, Hovell, & Sherman, 1977, p. 453).

When a discussion is held

4 pts.: Student listens and contributes three times to discussion.

3 pts.: Student listens and contributes twice to discussion.

2 pts.: Student listens and contributes once to discussion.

1 pt.: Student pays attention and listens to discussion.

0 pt.: Student does not listen to discussion.

When in-class assignment is given

4 pts.: Student works all of class time on assignment.

3 pts.: Student works 3/4 of class time on assignment.

2 pts.: Student works 1/2 of class time on assignment.

1 pt.: Student starts work on assignment.

0 pt.: Student does no work on assignment.

In classes where there is no opportunity for participation (reading on own, movie, lecture)

4 pts.: Student is extremely attentive to subject (movie, teacher, guest lecturer) throughout class.

2 pts.: Student is generally attentive to subject.

0 pt.: Student does not attend to subject.

A token system can also be used for teaching complex academic tasks. For instance, if a teacher is trying to teach a class of students to write appropriate paragraphs, instead of awarding 20 points for writing a paper on "How I Spent My Summer Vacation," the teacher might use the token system by awarding points for the following behaviors:

1 point for bringing pen and paper to class

1 point for beginning the writing assignment on time

1 point for completing the writing assignment on time

1 point for each sentence that begins with a capital letter

1 point for each sentence that ends with a period

Once the students have begun to master these items, the teacher can replace them with a point system for a more complex writing task. For example, by the fourth or fifth writing lesson, instead of awarding points for bringing paper and pen, the teacher might begin to award points for sentences using the appropriate plural suffix. Providing many alternative ways to earn a few points can be important in a token system. Some students find working toward several relatively simple objectives less frustrating and easier to undertake than attempting to earn many points for a long assignment that they may feel inadequate to complete. This approach also builds some measure of assured success into the assignment. Token exchange time can be used for direct or incidental teaching or for review and practice (Fabry, Mayhew, & Hanson, 1984; Kincaid & Weisberg, 1978). The teacher may place letters, words, numbers, math problems, social studies, or science questions on each back-up reinforcer. Students would respond to a stimulus or solve a problem before receiving the reinforcer. Be sure that students understand this contingency and perhaps even know what the question will be before the exchange takes place. Imagine your reaction if your employer suddenly refused to hand over your salary check until you named the Supreme Court Justices in order of appointment.

Token reinforcers can be very useful in management of a classroom. Ayllon and Azrin (1968, p. 77) suggest there are advantages to using tangible reinforcers (tokens) that may make them more effective than generalized social reinforcers (smiles and praise).

1. The number of tokens can bear a simple quantitative relation to the amount of reinforcement.

2. The tokens are portable and can be in the student's possession even when he or she is in a situation far removed from the classroom.

3. No maximum exists on the number of tokens a subject may possess.

4. Tokens can be used directly to operate devices for the automatic delivery of reinforcers.

5. Tokens are durable and can be continuously present during the period prior to exchange.

6. The physical characteristics of the tokens can be easily standardized.

7. The tokens can be made fairly indestructible so they will not deteriorate during the period prior to exchange.

8. The tokens can be made unique and nonduplicable so that the experimenter can be assured that they are received only in the authorized manner.

9. The use of tokens provides the student with a tangible means of continuous feedback. By having custody of the token objects or point card, the student can follow personal progress toward the criterion set in the contingency—whether it is for a behavior to be brought under control or for the acquisition of an academic objective.

10. The use of tokens enables more precise control by the teacher over administration of reinforcers. As noted by Kazdin (1977), a teacher's vocal tone will differ each time she or he says "Good work," as will the exact phrasing of "good," "pretty good," "very good," although in each instance the teacher means to convey an equal praise statement. Token reinforcement does not suffer from this subjective influence.

11. Tokens can be carried by the teacher and delivered unobtrusively. Thus, the administration of a token can be immediate without interfering with the student's performance of the target response or with other students' work.

12. A system of token reinforcement allows for differential valuing of performance. It does not require an all-or-nothing delivery of reinforcement. The student may initially be given a token for each correctly spelled word and later earn reinforcement for a 20-out-of-20 performance. The criterion for performance can be changed as performance improves.

13. A system of token reinforcement allows the student to become accustomed to delayed gratification of wants.

14. The use of a token system allows for greater versatility than is possible with other reinforcement systems. This versatility is related to the wide variety of back-up reinforcers that may be selected and to the variety of behaviors that may be placed under a contingency for earning tokens.

15. The most important advantage a token system provides is its ease of generalizability. Unlike primary reinforcers or certain activity reinforcers,

tokens can easily be used across settings (in other classrooms, in the cafeteria, on field trips) and with different behaviors simultaneously (in-seat behavior *and* correct spelling). They can also easily be administered by more than one teacher and by parents.

16. Tokens can often maintain behavior at a higher level than other secondary reinforcers such as praise, approval, and feedback (Birnbrauer, Wolf, Kidder, & Tague, 1965; Kazdin & Polster, 1973; O'Leary, Becker, Evans, & Saudargas, 1969).

Many residential and self-contained programs for students with behavior disorders use an adaptation of a token economy usually referred to as a *levels system*. Students on the lowest level, often identified by having to wear, for example, a particular color shirt, have very basic privileges, little freedom of choice or activity, and earn limited reinforcers. After a period of acceptable behavior, students move up a level, must meet higher expectations, can earn more varied and valuable reinforcers, and may even get to wear a shirt of a more prestigious color. As students progress through levels, they have increased responsibility for their own behavior, more rigorous standards to meet, access to more kinds of back-up reinforcers, and progressively better shirts. Some programs include aspects of a psychoeducational model like log or journal keeping and personal goal setting as requirements for reinforcement (Bauer, Shea, & Keppler, 1986; Mastropieri, Jenne, & Scruggs, 1988).

Social Reinforcers.   A category of secondary reinforcers that teachers use almost unconsciously includes demonstrations of approval or attention. There is a wide variety of verbal or physical interactions associated with a job well done. As seen in the following list, the range of potential social reinforcers includes various nonverbal expressions, teacher proximity to the student, physical contact between teacher and student, and words and phrases that convey pleasure and approval of the student's performance. Social reinforcers have proved effective not only for teachers in changing and maintaining student behavior (for example, Kirby & Holborn, 1986; Nutter & Reid, 1978), but also for students in changing and maintaining teacher behavior (see Polirstok & Greer, 1977).

Expressions

smiling, winking, laughing, nodding, clapping

Proximity

sitting next to the student at lunch, sitting next to the student on bus trips, placing the student's desk next to the teacher's, sitting on teacher's lap during storytime, being teacher's partner in a game

Contact

hugging, touching, shaking hands, holding hands, patting head or back

Privileges

having good work displayed, being leader of an activity, being classroom monitor, being team captain

Words and Phrases

"I like the way you are sitting." "That is excellent work." "You should be proud of what you have done." "That is just what I wanted you to do." "You should show this to your parents."

Of these social reinforcers, words and phrases are the most often deliberately used by teachers. Words and phrases used by teachers may be affirmatively described as forms of teacher *praise*. O'Leary and O'Leary (1977) have stated that teacher praise must have certain qualities to function effectively as reinforcement:

1. Praise must be delivered contingent on performance of the behavior to be reinforced. Noncontingent delivery of praise violates one of the essentials of the operational definition of reinforcement. Noncontingent delivery of praise removes the dependent relationship between student performance and teacher's affirmative attention and therefore does not increase the future probability of the behavior.

2. Teacher praise should specify the behavior or particulars of the behavior being reinforced. There should be no confusion on the part of the student as to why he is receiving the teacher's affirmative attention.

3. The praise should sound sincere. This means the teacher should avoid the use of stock phrases. The praise statement should vary in content and tone according to the situation and the preference of the student being praised. Just as a student can satiate on the unrelenting delivery of primary reinforcers, students can satiate on the unrelenting delivery of certain phrases. Such stock phrases soon lose their reinforcing quality, deteriorate into teacher patter, and are soon ignored or even resented by the student.

Clinton and Boyce (1975) differentiate the words and phrases used by teachers into two types. They refer to *affirmative reinforcers*, which are characterized by words such as *good* and *fine*, and *informative reinforcers*, which are characterized by words such as *right* and *correct*. Informative reinforcers would commonly be referred to as *constructive feedback*. When feedback is used as a reinforcer, it is almost always prefaced with an affirmative, followed by a specific praise statement that focuses on the accuracy or appropriateness of the behavior, as in "That's it, you put the puzzle piece on the table" (Parrish et al., 1986). Verbal feedback may also be used to reinforce an attempt or approximation (Hall, Sheldon-Wildgen, & Sherman, 1980); for example, "Good try, you got two out of three right. Now do this one the same way." This form of feedback has been used in such diverse situations as a teaching strategy for students with multiple disabilities (Valcante, Roberson, Reid, & Wolking, 1989); a coaching strategy in football, gymnastics, and tennis (Allison & Ayllon, 1980); and a supervisory strategy in sheltered workshops (Martin, Pallotta-Cornick, Johnstone, & Goyos, 1980). Table 6–4 offers examples of constructive verbal feedback. Some forms of feedback provide the student with a more tangible measure of accuracy, as in Cronin and Cuvo's (1979) use of various-colored stars (red stars equal a performance better than last time; gold stars equal 100% accuracy). Graphs and charts alone have been used as a means of feedback and reinforcement. Young children may be reinforced simply by seeing their individual bar graphs grow. Line or cumulative graphs may be used as visual reinforcers for older students (Jens & Shores, 1969). People have used graphs to reinforce themselves. See Chapter 12. Feedback alone, however, may not be a reinforcer for all students in all situations. Depending on a student's previous experience it may serve as a reinforcer, a punisher, or as a powerless antecedent that does not alter inappropriate behavior or result in the continuation of desired behavior (Brophy, 1981; Peterson, 1982).

Contracting

It can be difficult for a teacher to use a reinforcement system serving a number of students and having a variety of objectives for managing behavior and instruction. On a hectic day, a teacher might offhandedly state a contingency for a student without thinking it through. Later the teacher may not remember the details of what was said and thus not be in a position to enforce the contingency. To complicate this uncertainty, students tend to rewrite reality to suit themselves: "You said I could go outside if I finished my math. You didn't *say* I had to get them right." A simple way to systematize the use of reinforcement is

TABLE 6–4
Constructive verbal feedback.

Affirmative	Feedback
"Great!	(Description of correct response) You finished your work on time."
"Good try!	(Reinforcement of approximation) You almost got finished this time."
"Much better!	(Suggestion for modification) If you keep trying not to make careless mistakes, you'll finish all of them next time."

contracting. **Contracting** is placing the contingency for a reinforcement into a written document. In the contract itself, the teacher creates a permanent product that can be referred to if questions arise.

As with any contract, the classroom contract should be the product of reasonable negotiations between the parties involved—namely, the teacher and the student. Though the exact wording of a written contract will depend on the sophistication of the student for whom it is designed, each will contain some form of the basic "if . . ., then . . ." statement, as shown in Figure 6–3. A written contract should always contain those elements minimally necessary for any reinforcement contingency: the behavior, the conditions, the criterion, the reinforcer.

To avoid later disagreement about what was really meant, the contract should contain precisely written statements describing the behavior required. This description should include the parameters within which the behavior is to be performed and the criterion level for meeting the contract terms. After discussion of the criterion, the student should understand the method or instruments that will be used to evaluate performance. The contract should also include the type, amount, and method of delivery of the reinforcement.

In addition to these basic items, dates for an interim and final review should appear in the contract. The interim date reminds the teacher of the need to monitor progress and allows renegotiation if the behavior required is unrealistic or if there is an instructional component to be added. Listing the final review date sets the student's time limit for fulfilling the terms of the contract.

Once the terms of the contract have been discussed and written down, the teacher should answer all questions the student may have. To ensure that the student understands the terms of the contract, he or she should read it back to the teacher and then restate the terms in different words. If this process results in a very different statement, the contract should be rewritten in easier language. Once a contract is finalized, the teacher and the student should both sign it, and each should have a copy.

Homme, Csanyi, Gonzales, and Rechs (1970, pp. 18–20) suggest basic rules for the use of reinforcers in contracting (number 1–5) as well as characteristics of proper contracting (6–10):

1. "The contract payoff (reward) should be immediate." This rule follows what has been stated as one of the essential elements of an *effective reinforcer*: it must be administered immediately upon performance of the target behavior.

2. "Initial contracts should call for and reward small approximations." This form of *successive approximations*—that is, progressive steps toward the target behavior—is particularly useful for behaviors the student has never performed before, a criterion level set too high, or a behavior category that is too broad (such as "clean your room").

3. "Reward frequently with small amounts." Homme states that experience has shown that "it is far more effective to give frequent, small reinforcements than a few large ones." Frequent delivery of reinforcement allows

FIGURE 6–3
Formats used in contracting.

I've Got An Offer You Can't Refuse

If_____

_____ by _____

Then _____

_____

_____

| date | student | witness | Teacher |

_____'s
Good Citizen Contract

I think I can _____

_____ by _____

If I do, I will be able to _____

_____

Teacher will help by _____

_____

| student | Teacher | date |

Note: From It's positively fun: Techniques for managing learning environments. by P. Kaplan, J. Kohfeldt, & K. Sturla (Denver: Love Publishing, 1974). Copyright 1974 by Love Publishing. Reprinted by permission.

for closer monitoring of the progress of the behavior change by both the teacher and the student.

See Chapter 7 for more about reinforcement of small approximations.

4. "The contract should call for and reward accomplishment rather than obedience." Homme suggests that contracts focusing on accomplishments lead to independence. Therefore, appropriate wording should be, "If you accomplish such and such, you will be rewarded with such and such," as opposed to "If you do what I tell you to do, I will reward you with such and such."

5. "Reward the performance after it occurs." This rule restates an essential element of a reinforcer: it must be administered contingently. Inexperienced teachers sometimes state contingencies as, "If you get to go on the field trip today, you must do all your work next week." They are usually disappointed with the effects of such statements.

6. "The contract must be fair." The "weight" of the reinforcement should be in proportion to the amount of behavior required. The ratio set up in the contract should be fair to both the teacher and the student. Asking the student to finish 2 out of 20 problems correctly for 30 minutes free time is just as unfair as requiring 20 out of 20 problems correct for 2 minutes free time.

7. "The terms of the contract must be clear." Ambiguity causes disagreement. If the teacher and the student do not agree on the meaning of the contract, the teacher may decide contracting is more trouble than it is worth. The student may decide neither the teacher nor the system can be trusted.

8. "The contract must be honest." According to Homme, an honest contract is one that is (a) "carried out immediately", and (b) "carried out according to the terms specified in the contract." This can be assured if the teacher and the student have freely engaged in the contract negotiation. Teachers should avoid imposing a "contract" on the student.

9. "The contract must be positive."

    Appropriate: "I will do . . ., if you do. . . ." Inappropriate: "I will not do . . ., if you do. . . ." "If you do not . . ., then I will. . . ." "If you do not . . ., then I will not. . . ."

10. "Contracting as a method must be used systematically." As with any form of reinforcement strategy, if contracting is not done systematically and consistently, it becomes a guessing game: "Does she really mean it this time?"

Writing contracts brings added advantages to a reinforcement system:

1. A written contract is a permanent document that records the variables of the original contingency for consultation by the teacher and the student.

2. The process of negotiation that leads to the contract enables students to see themselves as active participants in their learning as they each take part in setting their own expectations or limitations.

3. The writing of a contract emphasizes the individualization of instruction.

4. Contracting provides interim documents that state current objectives between IEP meetings. Such information may be shared with parents.

Variations in Administration of Reinforcers

A basic reinforcement system has the following design:

- The teacher presents the antecedent discriminative stimulus.
- The student performs the requested response.
- The teacher presents the student with an appropriate reinforcer.

This basic scheme focuses on the administration of an individually selected reinforcer designed for the particular student. Reinforcement is, however, a flexible strategy that can be adapted to a number of situations that arise in the management of a classroom. Based on the type of contingency and manner of administering consequences, Kazdin (1977) devised a matrix to represent these variations (see Figure 6–4). Although the matrix was originally proposed for variation in use of token systems, it is equally appropriate with any reinforcement system.

As Figure 6–4 shows, there are two options for administering consequences. First, reinforcement can be administered individually: the particular student who has performed the requested response is given the cereal, free time, or the appropriate number of tokens. Second, reinforcement can be administered to students as a group: given an acceptable performance by the whole class, for example, all 30 students will earn extra time for crafts on Wednesday afternoon.

There are three options for the type of contingency a teacher may establish for receipt of reinforcement. These are represented at the top of the matrix in Figure 6–4. For the first one, *individualized contingencies*, the behavior requested and the criterion of performance required are specific to the behavior or instructional needs of a particular student. Under the second

FIGURE 6–4
Variations in administration of consequences.

Note: From The token economy: A review and evaluation, by A. E. Kazdin (New York: Plenum Press, 1977). Reprinted by permission.

Type of contingencies

Manner of administering consequences		Individualized	Standardized	Group
	Individual	1	2	3
	Group	4	5	6

option, *standardized contingencies*, the teacher sets a requirement that is applied equally to all members of a class or to several class members. Using the third alternative, *group contingencies*, some behavior is required of a group of students and reinforcement is based on performance of the group as a whole.

Interaction among the two manners of administration and the three types of contingencies yields the six-celled matrix in Figure 6–4.

Cell 1 shows a system in which both the contingency for reinforcement and the manner of its delivery are individualized. The behavior and criterion are specific to a particular student, and the reinforcement is delivered only to that student.

1. Randy, if you complete 17 of your 20 arithmetic problems correctly, then you may have 10 minutes extra use of the computer terminal.
2. Randy, for each arithmetic problem you solve correctly, you will receive one token.

Cell 2 shows a system that provides the same contingency for reinforcement for all class members (standard) but individualizes the manner of delivery to each student.

1. Class, each of you who completes 17 of your 20 math problems correctly may have an extra 10 minutes at the computer terminal.
2. Class, each of you may earn one token each time you raise your hand before asking a question.

Cell 3 shows a system that sets the same contingency for reinforcement for a particular group of students, but individualizes the manner of reinforcer delivery to each group member.

1. Math Group B, if you students can develop 10 original problems that require multiplication for their solution, you all may have 10 extra minutes at the computer terminal when you choose and with whichever program you wish.
2. Each boy in the class may earn a token for placing his tray on the cart when he has finished eating his lunch.

Cell 4 shows a system that requires each member of a group to perform a specific behavior in order for the group as a unit to be reinforced.

1. Math Group B, you are to present a 15-minute program to the class concerning the use of multiplication. Randy, you are responsible for an explanation of the basic computation procedure; Carol, you are to explain the relationship between multiplication and addition; Nicholas, you are to

demonstrate how to work problems from our math workbooks; and Sandy, you are to pose three original problems for the class to solve. At the end of the presentation, the four of you may use the computer terminal together for one of the game programs.

2. The following students may go to the gym to play basketball if they write an essay on basketball: Gary, your essay must have at least 4 sentences; Jamie, your essay must have at least 6 sentences, and Cory, your essay must have at least 10 sentences.

Cell 5 shows a system that sets the same contingency for reinforcement for all class members and allows each individual who has met this standard criterion to become a member of a group to be jointly reinforced.

1. Class, for homework you are to develop a problem that requires multiplication for its solution. All students who bring an appropriate problem will be allowed to go to the math lab tomorrow morning from 10:00 to 10:30.

2. All students who receive a grade of 100 on the geography test today will be exempt from geography homework tonight.

Cell 6 shows a system that sets the same contingency for reinforcement and same manner of reinforcer delivery for a group of class members.

1. Math Group B, here are 20 problems. If you get the correct answers for all 20, you may go to the math lab for 30 minutes.

2. Redbirds, if you all remember to raise your hand before speaking during our reading lesson, you may select your own books to take home this weekend.

Following a review of studies in which contingencies were applied to more than one individual at a time, Litow and Pumroy (1975) delineated three administrative systems. They categorized these as dependent, independent, and interdependent group-oriented contingency systems.

In *dependent group-oriented contingency systems*, "the same response contingencies are simultaneously in effect for all group members, but are applied only to the performances of one or more selected group members. It is the performance of the selected group members that results in consequences for the whole group" (p. 342). This contingency system is illustrated by Litow and Pumroy as the teacher who makes reinforcement for the entire class contingent on the performance of (a) particular student(s). The remaining class members are *dependent* on the targeted student's performance for the reinforcement.

1. The opportunity for the class to have an extra session of physical education depends on Robert and Caroline passing Friday's spelling test.

2. The opportunity for the class to have an extra session of physical education depends on Samuel and Lorelei completing 90% of their written assignments.

3. The opportunity for the class to have an extra session of physical education depends on William and Bernice having talked-out without raising their hands no more than seven times during math class.

In *independent group-oriented contingency systems*, "the same response contingencies are simultaneously in effect for all group members, but are applied to performances on an individual basis. . . . In this type of contingency system, each member's outcomes are not affected (are *independent* of) the performances of the other group members" (p. 342). This contingency system is illustrated by the teacher who makes reinforcement for each class member contingent on that class member being able to meet the contingency criterion level of performance. Those who fail to achieve the performance criterion will not receive the reinforcer.

1. The opportunity for an extra session of physical education is available to each student who passes Friday's spelling test.
2. The opportunity for an extra session of physical education is available to all students who complete 90% of their written assignments.
3. The opportunity for an extra session of physical education is available to each student who talks out no more than three times.

In *interdependent group-oriented contingency systems*, "the same response contingencies are simultaneously in effect for all group members, but are applied to a level of group performance. . . . Consequently, in this type of contingency system each member's outcome depends ([is] *interdependent*) upon a level of group performance" (p. 343).
Litow and Pumroy (1975) list three types of group performance levels:

1. The contingency is stated so that each group member must achieve a set criterion level. Failure to achieve this criterion level by the class results in no class member receiving the reinforcer. For example, the opportunity for an extra session of physical education is contingent on each member of the class earning at least 90% on Friday's spelling test.
2. The contingency is stated such that each group member's performance meets a criterion *average* for the entire group. For example, the opportunity for an extra session of physical education is contingent on a class average of 90% of written work completed.
3. The contingency is stated so the class, as a group, must reach a single highest or lowest level of performance. For example, the opportunity for an extra session of physical education is contingent on the class as a whole having engaged in no more than 12 talk-outs.

Always use the simplest effective system.

By using these variations of the reinforcer delivery system, the teacher can tailor a reinforcement system to a particular classroom. Every classroom is different: some groups, even in regular classrooms, need a formal token system; other groups may have members who need contracting or individual systems; many regular classrooms can be managed using relatively informal arrangements of social and activity reinforcers. In general, teachers should use the simplest, most natural system that will be effective.

Group Contingencies and Peer Pressure

Group contingencies, as described above, can be an extremely effective means of managing some students' behavior. Adolescents, particularly, may find working as a group more reinforcing. There is some evidence that both typical and disabled students rank academic work with peers very highly (Martens, Muir, & Meller, 1988). Group contingencies can foster interdependence and may result in increasing cooperative behavior among students (McCarty, Griffin, Apolloni, & Shores, 1977). Group contingencies can be accomplished through peer mediation as well as teacher-managed intervention. Pigott, Fantuzzo, and Clement (1986) successfully arranged peer tutoring and group contingencies for the academic performance of underachieving fifth-grade students. The students were divided into arithmetic drill teams. Each member of the team was assigned a role. The coach reminded the team of their group goal for the number of correct answers, the strategy they had selected (for example, "work fast," "work carefully," "don't talk"), and selected back-up reinforcers from a reinforcer menu. The scorekeeper counted the number of correct answers on individual team members' papers. The referee served as the reliability checker, and the team manager compared the total team score with the goal and decided if the goal was met. In all three classes the students' math performance improved and was maintained during the 12-week follow-up when students were allowed to use teams if they wished, but no reinforcement contingency was in place.

Peer pressure is a powerful tool in group contingencies. Indeed, it is so powerful that group contingencies should be used with caution to avoid the negative side effect of undue pressure on some members of a group (Balsam & Bondy, 1983). Consider the following example.

Ms. Montgomery Teaches Spelling

Ms. Montgomery, a fifth-grade teacher, was concerned about her students' grades on their weekly spelling test. Some students did very well, but others spelled only a few words correctly. Ms. Montgomery thought for some time and came up with what she felt was a brilliant plan. She divided the students into pairs—one good speller and one poor. She then announced, "The grade that I enter in my grade book on Friday will be an average of what you and your partner make on the test." She sat back and watched the students busily drilling one another and assumed that her troubles were over. (The astute reader will have noticed by now that teachers who assume their troubles are over usually find that they are just beginning.)

She first began to see a flaw in her plan when she observed LeeAnn chasing Barney around the playground during recess, slapping him with her speller and yelling, "Sit down, dummy, you've got to learn these words." She knew she had blown it when she got a phone call at home that night from LeeAnn's mother protesting that LeeAnn was going to fail spelling because that dumb Barney couldn't learn the words, and one from Barney's mother asking if Ms. Montgomery had any idea what might have caused Barney to spend the entire afternoon crying in his room.

Teachers sometimes think these procedures work only on American children. Saigh and Umar (1983) report that they are also effective for Sudanese students.

Ms. Montgomery violated one of the most important rules about setting group contingencies: *be absolutely sure each member of the group is capable of performing the target behavior.* If this rule is violated, the teacher risks subjecting students to verbal and physical abuse by their peers.

Another important caution is being sure some member does not find it reinforcing to sabotage the group's efforts. Barrish, Saunders, and Wolf (1969) arranged a group contingency to modify disruptive out-of-seat and talking-out behavior in a class of 24 fourth-grade students. The class was divided into two teams during reading and math periods. Each instance of out-of-seat behavior or talking-out by an individual team member resulted in a mark against the entire team. The team with the greatest number of marks would lose certain privileges. Although this procedure was successful, an important modification was implemented. Two members of one of the teams consistently gained marks for their team. During one session, one of the members "emphatically announced" that he was no longer going to play the game. The teacher and the children felt the consistent behavior of one student should not further penalize the entire team. The saboteur was removed from the team (and the group contingency) and made into a one-person team, thus applying an individual-consequences procedure until his behavior was brought under control and he could then be returned to one of the class teams. The authors stated that it appeared the expected effects of peer pressure, instead of bringing individual behavior under group control, may have served as a social reinforcer for the student's disruptive behavior.

Finally, the system must minimize the possibility of some members' performing the target behavior for others. If these factors are taken into account, group contingencies can be a very useful management device.

Schedules of Reinforcement

Schedules of reinforcement refer to patterns of timing for delivery of reinforcers. Until now, we have described the delivery of reinforcers for each occurrence of the target behavior. Delivery of reinforcement on a continuous basis is referred to as a **continuous schedule of reinforcement (CRF)**. That is, each time the student produces the target response she or he immediately receives a reinforcer. This schedule may be seen as having a one-to-one ratio—Response:Reinforcement (R:S^R).

Because of this dense ratio of response to reinforcement, CRF schedules are most useful in teaching new behaviors (acquisition), especially to young children and individuals with disabilities. It is necessary to ensure that a student who is learning a new behavior will receive a reinforcer for each response that is closer to a correct response. The process of reinforcing such successive approximations to the target behavior is called *shaping* and will be discussed in Chapter 7. For now, it is sufficient simply to be aware that a CRF schedule is usually used in shaping procedures. A CRF schedule may also be used when the target behavior initially has a very low frequency. It may be most effective during the early stages of any reinforcement system. There are, however, certain problems in using a CRF schedule.

Problems with CRF schedules

1. A student whose behavior is on a CRF schedule may become satiated on the reinforcer, especially if a primary reinforcer is being used. Once correct responding is frequent, the continuous receipt of an edible will reduce the deprivation state and thereby reduce motivation for correct responding.

2. Continuous delivery of reinforcers may lead to accusations that teachers are leading students to expect some type of reinforcement every time they do as they are told.

3. CRF schedules are not the most efficient way to maintain a behavior following its initial acquisition or control. First, once a behavior has been acquired, or its frequency increased, by reinforcement on a CRF schedule, teachers may terminate the intervention program. The transfer from continuous reinforcement to no reinforcement results in a rapid loss of the behavior. This rapid loss of behavior when reinforcement is withdrawn is called *extinction* and will be discussed in Chapter 8. Second, CRF schedules may interfere with classroom routine. How long could (or would) a teacher continuously reinforce 4, 6, 8, or 30 students for raising their hands before speaking or for making the letter *a* correctly?

The problems caused by continuing the use of CRF schedules beyond the point of effectiveness may be solved by using a variety of less-than-continuous schedules.

Intermittent Schedules

In the real world, the ability to delay gratification is necessary.

In **intermittent schedules**, reinforcement follows some, but not all, correct or appropriate responses (Skinner, 1953). Because each occurrence of the behavior is no longer reinforced, intermittent schedules put off satiation effects. Behaviors maintained on intermittent schedules are also more resistant to extinction. Intermittent schedules require greater numbers of correct responses for reinforcement. The student learns to delay gratification and to maintain appropriate behavior over longer periods of time.

The two categories of simple intermittent schedules most often used to increase frequency of response are **ratio schedules** and **interval schedules** (Ferster & Skinner, 1957; Skinner, 1953). To increase the duration of a response, the teacher may use *response-duration schedules* (Stevenson &

Clayton, 1970). For a discussion of multiple, compound, and concurrent schedules, consult Reynolds (1975).

Ratio Schedules.   Under ratio schedules, the number of times a target behavior occurs determines the timing of reinforcer delivery. Under a *fixed-ratio schedule (FR)*, the student is reinforced on completion of a specified number of correct responses. A behavior on an FR3 schedule would be reinforced immediately following the occurrence of every third correct response, a contingent ratio of three correct responses to each reinforcer (R, R, R:S^R). A student who must complete eight math problems correctly to earn the right to work the puzzles or who must correctly point to the blue object on eight trials before getting a bite of pretzel, would be on an FR8 schedule of reinforcement.

Behaviors placed on FR schedules have particular characteristics. The student generally has a higher rate of responding than on CRF schedules because increases in rate result in increases in the frequency of reinforcement. Because the time it takes the student to perform the specified number of correct responses is not considered when delivering reinforcers, FR schedules may result in inappropriate fluencies for a given behavior. For example, to earn a reinforcer a student may work math problems so rapidly that he makes more mistakes and his handwriting deteriorates. In addition to inappropriate fluency, FR schedules may cause another type of problem. As the schedule ratio increases (from FR2 to FR10, for example) the student will often stop responding for a period of time following delivery of the reinforcer, taking what is termed a *postreinforcement pause.*

The problems of fluency and postreinforcement pause are eliminated by transition to a *variable-ratio schedule (VR)*. Under a VR schedule, the target response is reinforced on the *average* of a specified number of correct responses. A behavior on a VR10 schedule would be reinforced on the average of every 10th correct response. Therefore, in a teaching or observation session, the student may be reinforced following the 2nd, 4th, 8th, 9th, 12th, 16th, and 19th correct responses.

After the occurrence of a behavior on the FR schedule has been established at the criterion level (as stated in the behavioral objective), the VR schedule will maintain the desired level or rate of responding. The unpredictability of reinforcer delivery on a VR schedule causes the student's rate of responding to even out, with little or no postreinforcement pausing. "The probability of reinforcement at any moment remains essentially constant and the 'student' adjusts by holding to a constant rate" (Skinner, 1953, p. 104).

Interval Schedules.   Under interval schedules, the occurrence of at least one correct or appropriate response plus the passage of a specific amount of time are the determinants for delivery of the reinforcer. Under a *fixed-interval schedule (FI)*, the student is reinforced the first time he or she performs the target response following the elapse of a specified number of minutes. A behavior on an FI5 schedule may be reinforced five minutes after the last

"No, Mrs. Cole, a VR10 schedule does not mean 10 cookies every time Ralph gets it right."

reinforced response. The first correct response that occurs after the five minutes has passed is reinforced. Following the delivery of that reinforcer, the next five-minute cycle begins.

Behaviors placed on FI schedules also have particular characteristics. Because the only requirement for reinforcement on an FI schedule is that the response occur at least once following each specified interval, behaviors occur at a relatively low rate as compared with behaviors on ratio schedules. This is especially true if and when the student becomes aware of the length of the interval and, therefore, aware of when reinforcement is possible. This rate of responding will be affected by the length of the interval (Skinner, 1953). If reinforcement is available every minute, responding will be more rapid than if it is available every 10 minutes. Behaviors on FI schedules also have a characteristic that parallels the postreinforcement pause of FR schedules. A student eventually realizes additional correct responses before the interval ends do not result in reinforcement. It also becomes apparent responses immediately after reinforcement are never reinforced. The rate of responding eventually is noticeably lower (or ceases) for a short time after each reinforcement (the initial portion of the next interval). This decrease in correct responding is termed a *fixed-interval scallop*, because of the appearance of the data when plotted on a cumulative graph.

The effects on rate of responding resulting from FI schedules are eliminated by transition to a *variable-interval schedule (VI)*. Under a VI schedule, the intervals are of different lengths, while their average length is consistent. A behavior on a VI5 schedule would have a reinforcer available for the target response on the average of every five minutes. As in use of VR schedules, the unpredictability levels out student performance. Behaviors under a VI schedule are performed at higher, steadier rates without the appearance of fixed-interval scallops, because the student can no longer predict the length of the interval following delivery of a reinforcer and therefore cannot predict which response will be reinforced.

A technique for increasing the rate of responding under an interval schedule is use of a **limited hold (LH)** contingency. A limited hold restricts the time the reinforcer is available following the interval. That is, when the interval has elapsed and the next correct response will be reinforced, the reinforcer will remain available for only a limited time. In this case, students must respond quickly to earn reinforcers, whereas under a simple interval schedule they may delay responding and still be reinforced. An F15-min/LH5-sec schedule would make a reinforcer available for 5 seconds following each 5-minute interval. For example, when a student is being trained to ride a bus, he learns that the bus comes every 15 minutes and that he must step in quickly when the doors open (naturally occurring reinforcement) as they stay open for only 30 seconds (FI15 min/LH30 sec).

Response-duration Schedules.   Under **response-duration schedules**, the continuous amount of time of a target behavior is the determinant for delivery of the reinforcer. Under a *fixed-response-duration schedule (FRD)*, the student is reinforced following completion of a specified number of minutes (or seconds) of appropriate behavior. A behavior on an FRD10 schedule would be reinforced immediately at the end of each 10 minutes of continuous appropriate behavior. A student whom the teacher wants to remain seated during reading period and whom the teacher verbally praises for in-seat behavior every 10 minutes is under an FRD10 schedule. If the behavior stops occurring at any point during the time period, the timing is restarted.

As in FR and FI schedules, a pause following reinforcement may be seen under FRD schedules. In this case, the pause appears to be related to the length of the required time period for appropriate behavior. The longer the time period, the longer the pause. It may be expected if the time period is too long or is increased too rapidly, the behavior will either decrease or stop occurring altogether. These problems are minimized by varying the length of the time periods required for reinforcement, using a *variable-response-duration schedule (VRD)*. Under a VRD schedule, continuous appropriate behavior is reinforced on the average of a specified time period. A behavior on a VRD10 schedule would be reinforced on the average of every 10 minutes.

Thinning Schedules of Reinforcement

A formal classroom reinforcement system should be viewed as a temporary structure used to produce rapid behavior change. Most teachers eventually plan to bring students' behavior under the control of more natural reinforcers. Schedule **thinning** helps decrease dependence on artificial reinforcers. In thinning, reinforcement gradually becomes available less often, or, in other words, becomes contingent on greater amounts of appropriate behavior.

In thinning reinforcement schedules, the teacher moves from a dense schedule (continuous) to a sparse schedule (variable). The ratio between correct responding and reinforcement is systematically increased. The following examples illustrate this concept.

1. A student may be on a CRF schedule (1:1) for correctly identifying vocabulary words on flashcards. As the student approaches the criterion of 90% accuracy, the teacher may move the student to an FR3 schedule (R, R, R:S) and then to an FR6, to a VR8, and to a VR10. With each schedule shift, the teacher requires the student to perform more correct responses in order to receive a reinforcer.

2. A student may be on an FRD5 for sitting in her seat during the time she is to work in a workbook. Once the student has been able to meet this criterion, the teacher may move her to an FRD10, FRD20, and FRD30 schedule. With each schedule shift, the teacher is requiring the student to maintain longer periods of appropriate behavior to earn reinforcement.

Figure 6–5 presents an elemental scheme for schedule thinning. As schedule shifts are made from a continuous schedule to a fixed schedule to a variable schedule, a point is finally reached where predetermined timing of

FIGURE 6–5
Schedules for delivery of reinforcers.

reinforcer delivery is no longer required. At this point the behavior is under the control of naturally occurring reinforcers.

Thinning schedules of reinforcement should result in the following:

1. Higher, steadier levels of responding as a result of moving to variable schedules

2. Decreasing expectation of reinforcement

3. Maintenance of the behavior over longer periods of time as the student becomes accustomed to delayed gratification

4. Removal of the teacher as a necessary behavior monitor

5. Transfer of control from the reinforcer to more traditional methods, such as teacher praise and attention (O'Leary & Becker, 1967), especially if schedule thinning is done in conjunction with pairing social reinforcers with tokens or primary reinforcers

6. An increase in persistence in responding toward working for goals (reinforcers) that require greater amounts of correct responding (work)

One caution should be considered when thinning schedules. Behaviors are subject to an effect known as **ratio strain**. Ratio strain occurs when the schedule has been thinned so quickly that the ratio for correct responding and reinforcement is too large. In such instances, the student doesn't earn reinforcement often enough to maintain his or her responding, and there is a marked decrease in rate. The student may stop responding altogether. If teachers see this effect occurring, they should return to the last schedule that resulted in an acceptable rate of responding and then thin again, but in smaller schedule shifts.

Professor Grundy Goes to Las Vegas

As Professor Grundy prepared to leave the house one morning, Mrs. Grundy handed him a stack of envelopes.

"Oliver, dear," she asked, "would you mind putting these in the mail for me?"

"More contests?" sneered Professor Grundy. "You've entered every contest, every sweepstakes, bought every raffle ticket ever offered. And how often have you won?"

"Well," answered Mrs. Grundy, "there was the pickle dish six years ago, the steak knives the year after that, and last year . . ."

"Minerva," scolded the Professor, "I've heard of resistance to extinction, but your behavior is being maintained on a V13 *year* schedule. I'd think that was a little lean, even for you."

Imagine the professor's surprise when he received a phone call later that morning. "Oliver," bubbled Mrs. Grundy, "I've won a trip for two to Las Vegas! How's that for a reinforcer?"

The very next weekend, the Grundys flew off to claim their prize. As they walked into the lobby of their hotel, they passed a bank of slot machines.

"Just one moment, my dear," said Professor Grundy. "Let me try a couple of quarters in one of these. After all, when in Las Vegas . . ."

"Humph! Just as I thought—primary and secondary reinforcers galore!"

An hour later, Mrs. Grundy checked into their room. Three hours later, she ate a solitary dinner. At midnight, she returned to the lobby where the professor was still pulling the handle on the slot machine.

"Oliver," she insisted, "you must stop this."

"Just a few more minutes, Minerva," pleaded the professor, "I know a few more quarters will do it."

Mrs.Grundy watched for a few minutes as Professor Grundy pulled the handle. Occasionally, the machine paid off with a few quarters.

"Oliver," snorted Mrs. Grundy, as she turned on her heel and stalked off, "I've heard of resistance to extinction, but your behavior is being maintained on a VR27 schedule of reinforcement. How utterly ridiculous!"

NEGATIVE REINFORCEMENT

Although positive reinforcement is most often used when the teacher's goal is to increase the rate or frequency of a target behavior, another procedure is available. *Negative reinforcement* (S^{R-}) is the contingent removal of an aversive stimulus immediately following a response that increases the future rate and/or probability of the response.

The first operative word in this definition is, once again, *increases*, which implies that some form of reinforcement is taking place. The second operative word is *removal*. Whereas in positive reinforcement a stimulus is *pre-*

sented to the student, in negative reinforcement something is removed from the student's environment. The third operative word is *contingent*. The teacher will not remove the aversive condition (negative reinforcer) unless and until the requested response is produced. If a teacher states the contingency, "Bill, you must stay in the room and finish all your math problems before you may join the rest of the class in the gym," that teacher is using negative reinforcement. The aversive condition of being left behind in the classroom while the rest of the class goes to the gym will be removed contingent on completion of the math assignment Bill should have completed earlier. Further, it is to be expected that Bill's rate of completion of math problems will increase today to get to the gym and may well increase tomorrow to avoid a similar circumstance.

Negative reinforcement works because the student performs the behavior to *escape* the aversive stimulus. It is not necessary, however, for an aversive stimulus to be present for negative reinforcement to work. Negative reinforcement also works when a student performs some behavior in order to *avoid* an aversive stimulus. The disruptive behavior of a student who joins in to avoid the ridicule of his classmates is maintained by negative reinforcement.

Using negative reinforcement has some disadvantages. Tantrums, attempts to flee, or destruction of materials are examples of escape and avoidance behaviors. They may occur particularly if the individual is unskilled at more subtle or socially acceptable forms of escape (Iwata, 1987). Apparently these behaviors are especially likely to happen when difficult demands or tasks are placed on students with limited behavioral repertoires. Aggressive or self-injurious behavior may be an avenue of escape from the demands because their intensity or topography can be alarming to a teacher (Carr & Durand, 1985; Weeks & Gaylord-Ross, 1981).

Alberto, Troutman, and Briggs (1983) employed negative reinforcement for initial response conditioning of a student with profound disabilities. Following an exhaustive reinforcer sampling, the only response made by the student was to pull his hand away from an ice cube. During instruction he was taught to turn toward a source of blowing air (a fan) by simultaneously guiding his head and removing ice from the palm of his hand. He was negatively reinforced by the removal of the ice for performing the desired behavior. Riordan, Iwata, Finney, Wohl, and Stanley (1984) used negative reinforcement with one of four students in a treatment of chronic food refusal. When the student refused food, a favorite toy was removed from her sight. When she permitted food to be placed in her mouth, the toy was returned. The negative reinforcer was the condition of the absence of the toy. That condition was removed when the target behavior was performed. Wacker et al. (1990) determined that escape from grooming activities (negative reinforcement) was maintaining the self-injurious biting of two young children. In other words, when the children bit themselves, efforts to comb their hair, for example, were abandoned. Intervention involved substituting a more appropriate means of indicating the desire for an activity to cease. Brief escape from grooming was made contingent upon a behavior incompatible with self-biting—pressing a microswitch to activate a prerecorded message of "stop." Iwata (1987) has made the point that it is often difficult to distinguish between negative reinforcement and positive reinforcement. We agree completely. One could certainly argue that the student was positively reinforced by the return of the toy or even punished by its removal. To make the distinction the teacher must consider the sequence of events and the prior environmental conditions. In some cases the real functional relationship may be very difficult to determine. Frankly, for a classroom teacher, it may not matter as long as the intervention is working. One of our colleagues has suggested that the finer distinctions among positive reinforcement, negative reinforcement, and punishment may be of interest primarily to researchers late at night during conferences of the Association for Behavior Analysis.

Teachers often inadvertently use negative reinforcement. When a student whines over an assignment and the teacher removes it, that student learns that whining will result in the termination of an aversive stimulus (schoolwork); so the child whines more often to escape again. Parents and teachers who give in to children's temper tantrums or whining find that the child has tantrums or whines with increased frequency.

Aversive stimuli may lead to aggressive reactions.

The use of aversive stimuli in the classroom should be minimized. As we will discuss in greater detail in Chapter 7, such stimuli may lead to aggressive reactions. The child who is confined to his room until he gets "every last doll and dinosaur *off* the floor" is likely to kick the unfortunate cat who comes to investigate the clattering and banging. Escape and avoidance behavior may not be limited to the aversive stimulus but may result in a student's escaping (running out of the room) or avoiding the entire school setting (playing truant). Mild aversive stimuli may sometimes be justified, but positive reinforcement is the procedure of choice for increasing or maintaining behavior. For a discussion of the theoretical and applied concerns relating to negative reinforcement, see Iwata (1987).

NATURAL REINFORCEMENT

As we wrote at the beginning of this chapter, reinforcement is a naturally occurring process. A structured reinforcement system in the classroom has at least four purposes. The first is simply to manage behavior. Second, for some students, the imposition of "artificial" high-intensity reinforcing stimuli provides highly visible connections between their behavior and its consequences. This allows them to learn a cause-and-effect relationship. Third, a classroom reinforcement system provides in microcosm a learning laboratory for how reinforcement works in the everyday world. The fourth purpose is to teach students to value a more general and natural pool of reinforcers. Students should be taught to be motivated by reinforcers that naturally occur in a situation; that is, those that will ordinarily result from their behavior in their school, home, and community settings.

Whether a reinforcer is natural depends on the situation, the setting, and the ages of the individuals. Almost any reinforcer can be natural. Most students in regular classes earn privileges for appropriate academic and social behavior—from being a lunch monitor in kindergarten to being excused from final exams in high school. Adults earn privileges as well—from a special parking place for the custodial employee of the month to access to the executive washroom. Activities are also often earned naturally, from an extra five minutes of recess for a hard-working kindergarten class to a trip to Bermuda for the salesman of the year. Everyone works for tokens—gold stars for kindergarteners and big bucks for some successful professionals (fortunately most teachers like gold stars). Finally, when everyone remembers his or her manners, social reinforcers abound in the natural environment. Reinforcers that are natural outcomes for a specific behavior are more effective than unrelated reinforcers (Litt & Schreibman, 1981; Williams, Koegel, & Egel, 1981). In addition, behavior reinforced naturally has an increased probability of being maintained and generalized (Haring, Roger, Lee, Breen, & Gaylord-Ross, 1986; Stokes and Baer, 1977). As students learn to anticipate and accept natural reinforcers, they are exposed to naturally occurring schedules of reinforcement. They learn that behavior in some situations results in immediate and frequent reinforcement, while in others it results in delayed and infrequent reinforcement.

Professor Grundy Teaches About Reinforcement

Professor Grundy's graduate class had turned in their observation assignments, muttering and grumbling all the while. After collecting the papers, Professor Grundy launched into his lecture on reinforcement (remarkably similar . . .). One of the students came up to the podium at the end of the lecture. Beaming, she said, "It's about time, Professor. I took this course to learn how to manage a classroom. For weeks, all we've talked about is history, theory, and all that technical junk. It was worth living through that just to hear tonight's lecture. I was going to drop the course, but now I won't miss a week."

"Why," asked Professor Grundy, lighting his pipe to hide the grin on his face, "do you think I wait to talk about reinforcement until *after* we're done with all that technical junk?"

SUMMARY

This chapter described procedures to increase or maintain appropriate academic or social behaviors. Positive reinforcement, the preferred approach, is the presentation of a stimulus contingent on appropriate behavior. Positive reinforcers may be either primary or secondary, and the best reinforcers are natual. Negative reinforcement is the removal of an aversive stimulus contingent on the performance of the target behavior. We suggested specific ways in which students' behavior can be changed using these procedures. We hope we have also positively reinforced your reading behavior and that you are now prepared to continue.

DISCUSSION QUESTIONS

1. Provide an example of how positive reinforcement (and/or negative reinforcement) naturally occurs in (a) the school in which you work, (b) your college experience, or (c) your daily life.

2. For a given class of preschoolers (or elementary, or secondary) select 8 or 10 backup reinforcers for a token system. Assign and justify point values for each.

3. Is anything always a positive reinforcer?

4. What reinforcement schedule has your local sports team had its fans on during the past month?

5. The team with the most points at the end of each week for complete and accurate homework assignments turned in gets to select how to fill Fun Friday. Kevin the Bully makes sure his team members do all their homework (and his) but he and his team pick the Friday activity every time they win, which they almost always do. The other teams are rapidly losing interest in the competition. What can Kevin's teacher do to make her system work better?

REFERENCES

Alberto, P., Jobes, N., Sizemore, A., & Doran, D. 1980. A comparison of individual and group instruction across response tasks. *The Journal of the Association for the Severely Handicapped, 5*, 285–293.

Alberto, P., Troutman, A., & Briggs, T. 1983. The use of negative reinforcement to condition a response in a deaf-blind student. *Education of the Visually Handicapped, 15*, 43–50.

Allison, M.G., & Ayllon, T. 1980. Behavioral coaching in the development of skills in football, gymnastics, and tennis. *Journal of Applied Behavior Analysis, 13*, 297–314.

Ayllon, T., & Azrin, N. 1968. *The token economy: A motivational system for therapy and rehabilitation.* New York: Appleton-Century-Crofts.

Baer, R., Blount, R., Detrich, R., & Stokes, T. 1987. Using intermittent reinforcement to program maintenance of verbal/nonverbal correspondence. *Journal of Applied Behavior Analysis, 20*, 179–184.

Balsam, P.D., & Bondy, A.S. 1983. The negative side effects of reward. *Journal of Applied Behavior Analysis, 16*, 283–296.

Barrish, H.H., Saunders, M., & Wolf, M.M. 1969. Good behavior game: Effects of individual contingencies for group consequences on disruptive behavior in a classroom. *Journal of Applied Behavior Analysis, 2*, 119–124.

Bauer, A., Shea, T., & Keppler, R. 1986. Levels systems: A framework for the individualization of behavior management. *Behavioral Disorders, 12*, 28–35.

Birnbrauer, J.S., Wolf, M.M., Kidder, J.D., & Tague, C.E. 1965. Classroom behavior of retarded pupils with token reinforcement. *Journal of Experimental Child Psychology, 2*, 219–235.

Brophy, J. 1981. Teacher praise: A functional analysis. *Review of Educational Research, 51*, 5–32.

Carr, E.G., Binkoff, J.A., Kologinsky, E., & Eddy, M. 1978. Acquisition of sign language by autistic children. I: Expressive labelling. *Journal of Applied Behavior Analysis, 11*, 489–501.

Carr, E., & Durand, M. 1985. Reducing behavior problems through functional communication training. *Journal of Applied Behavior Analysis, 18*, 111–126.

Clinton, L., & Boyce, K. 1975. Acquisition of simple motor imitative behavior in mentally retarded and near mentally retarded children. *American Journal of Mental Deficiency, 79*, 695–700.

Cohen, H., & Filipczak, J. 1971. *A new learning environment.* San Francisco: Jossey Bass.

Cronin, K.A., & Cuvo, A.J. 1979. Teaching mending skills to mentally retarded adolescents. *Journal of Applied Behavior Analysis, 12*, 401–406.

Dahlquist, L., & Gil, K. 1986. Using parents to maintain improved dental flossing skills in children. *Journal of Applied Behavior Analysis, 19*, 255–260.

Daly, M., Jacob, S., King, D., & Cheramie, G. 1984. The accuracy of teacher predictions of student reward preferences. *Psychology in the Schools, 21*, 520–524.

Datilo, J. 1986. Computerized assessment of preference for severely handicapped individuals. *Journal of Applied Behavior Analysis, 19*, 445–448.

Dewson, M., & Whiteley, J. 1987. Sensory reinforcement of head turning with nonambulatory, profoundly mentally retarded persons. *Research in Developmental Disabilities, 8*, 413–426.

Dunlap, G., Koegel, R., Johnson, J., & O'Neill, R. 1987. Maintaining performance of autistic clients in community settings with delayed contingencies. *Journal of Applied Behavior Analysis, 20*, 185–191.

Durand, V.M. 1990. *Severe behavior problems.* New York: Guilford Press.

Durand, V.M., & Crimmins, D. 1988. Identifying the variables maintaining self-injurious behavior. *Journal of Autism and Developmental Disorders, 18*, 99–117.

Egel, A. 1981. Reinforcer variation: Implications for motivating developmentally disabled children. *Journal of Applied Behavior Analysis, 14*, 345–350.

Fabry, B., Mayhew, G., & Hanson, A. 1984. Incidental teaching of mentally retarded students within a token system. *American Journal of Mental Deficiency, 89*, 29–36.

Favell, J., McGimsey, J., & Schell, R. 1982. Treatment of self-injury by providing alternate sensory activities. *Analysis and Intervention in Developmental Disabilities, 2*, 83–104.

Fehr, M., Wacker, D., Trezise, J., Lennon, R., & Meyerson, L. 1979. Visual, auditory, and vibratory stimulation as reinforcers for profoundly retarded children. *Rehabilitation Psychology, 26*, 201–209.

Ferster, C., & Culbertson, S. 1982. *Behavior principles* (3rd ed.). Englewood Cliffs, N.J.: Prentice-Hall.

Ferster, C.B., & Skinner, B.F. 1957. *Schedules of reinforcement.* New York: Appleton-Century-Crofts.

Goldstein, H., & Wickstrom, S. 1986. Peer intervention effects on communicative interaction among handicapped and nonhandicapped preschoolers. *Journal of Applied Behavior Analysis, 19*, 209–214.

Green, C., Reid, D., Canipe, V., & Gardner, S. 1991. A comprehensive evaluation of reinforcer identification processes for persons with profound multiple handicaps. *Journal of Applied Behavior Analysis, 24*, 537–552.

Green, C., Reid, D., White, L., Halford, R., Brittain, D., & Gardner, S. 1988. Identifying reinforcers for persons with profound handicaps: Staff opinion vs. systematic assessment of preferences. *Journal of Applied Behavior Analysis, 21*, 31–43.

Guevremont, D., Osnes, P., & Stokes, T. 1986. Programming maintenance after correspondence training interventions with children. *Journal of Applied Behavior Analysis, 19*, 215–219.

Gutierrez-Griep, R. 1984. Student preference of sensory reinforcers. *Education and Training of the Mentally Retarded, 19*, 108–113.

Hall, C., Sheldon-Wildgen, J., & Sherman, J.A. 1980. Teaching job interview skills to retarded clients. *Journal of Applied Behavior Analysis, 13*, 433–442.

Hall, R.V., & Hall, M.C. 1980. *How to select reinforcers.* Lawrence, Kan.: H&H Enterprises.

Haring, T., Roger, B., Lee, M., Breen, C., & Gaylord-Ross, R. 1986. Teaching social language to moderately handicapped students. *Journal of Applied Behavior Analysis, 19*, 159–171.

Heward, W.L., & Eachus, H.T. 1979. Acquisition of adjectives and adverbs in sentences written by hearing impaired and aphasic children. *Journal of Applied Behavior Analysis, 12*, 391–400.

Homme, L., Csanyi, A., Gonzales, M., & Rechs, J. 1970. *How to use contingency contracting in the classroom.* Champaign, Ill.: Research Press.

Iwata, B. 1987. Negative reinforcement in applied behavior analysis: An emerging technology. *Journal of Applied Behavior Analysis, 20*, 361–378.

Jens, K.G., & Shores, R.E. 1969. Behavioral graphs as reinforcers for work behavior of mentally retarded adolescents. *Education and Training of the Mentally Retarded, 4*, 21–28.

Kaplan, P., Kohfeldt, J., & Sturla, K. 1974. *It's positively fun: Techniques for managing learning environments*. Denver: Love Publishing.

Kazdin, A.E. 1975. *Behavior modification in applied settings*. Homewood, Ill.: Dorsey Press.

Kazdin, A.E. 1977. *The token economy: A review and evaluation*. New York: Plenum Press.

Kazdin, A.E., & Bootzin, R.R. 1972. The token economy: An evaluative review. *Journal of Applied Behavior Analysis, 5*, 343–372.

Kazdin, A.E., & Polster, R. 1973. Intermittent token reinforcement and response maintenance in extinction. *Behavior Therapy, 4*, 386–391.

Keller, F., & Sherman, J. 1974. *The Keller plan handbook*. Menlo Park, Calif.: W.A. Benjamin.

Kincaid, M., & Weisberg, P. 1978. Alphabet letters as tokens: Training preschool children in letter recognition and labeling during a token exchange period. *Journal of Applied Behavior Analysis, 11*, 199.

Kirby, K., & Holborn, S. 1986. Trained, generalized, and collateral behavior changes of preschool children receiving gross-motor skills training. *Journal of Applied Behavior Analysis, 19*, 283–288.

Kulik, J., Kulik, C., & Carmichael, K. 1974. The Keller plan in science teaching. *Science, 183*, 379–383.

Litow, L., & Pumroy, D.K. 1975. A brief review of classroom group-oriented contingencies. *Journal of Applied Behavior Analysis, 8*, 341–347.

Litt, M., & Schreibman, L. 1981. Stimulus-specific reinforcement in the acquisition of receptive labels by autistic children. *Analysis and Intervention in Developmental Disabilities, 1*, 171–186.

Lovaas, O.I. 1977. *The autistic child: Language development through behavior modification*. New York: Irvington.

Magrab, P.R., & Papadopoulou, Z.L. 1977. The effect of a token economy on dietary compliance for children on hemodialysis. *Journal of Applied Behavior Analysis, 10*, 573–578.

Maher, G. 1989. Punch out: A behavior management technique. *Teaching Exceptional Children, 21*, 74.

Martens, B., Muir, K., & Meller, P. 1988. Rewards common to the classroom setting: A comparison of regular and self-contained room student ratings. *Behavior Disorders, 13*, 169–174.

Martin, G., Pallotta-Cornick, A., Johnstone, G., & Goyos, A.C. 1980. A supervisory strategy to improve work performance for lower functioning retarded clients in a sheltered workshop. *Journal of Applied Behavior Analysis, 13*, 183–190.

Mason, S., McGee, G., Farmer-Dougan, V., & Risley, T. 1989. A practical strategy for ongoing reinforcer assessment. *Journal of Applied Behavior Analysis, 22*, 171–179.

Mastropieri, M., Jenne, T., & Scruggs, T. 1988. A level system for managing problem behaviors in a high school resource program. *Behavioral Disorders, 13*, 202–208.

McCarty, T., Griffin, S., Apolloni, T., & Shores, R. 1977. Increased peer-teaching with group-oriented contingencies for arithmetic performance in behavior-disordered adolescents. *Journal of Applied Behavior Analysis, 10*, 313.

Nelson, G.L. & Cone, J.D. 1979. Multiple-baseline analysis of a token economy for psychiatric inpatients. *Journal of Applied Behavior Analysis, 12*, 255–271.

Newsom, C.D., & Simon, K.M. 1977. A simultaneous discrimination procedure for the measurement of vision in nonverbal children. *Journal of Applied Behavior Analysis, 10*, 633–644.

Nutter, D., & Reid, D.H. 1978. Teaching retarded women a clothing selection skill using community norms. *Journal of Applied Behavior Analysis, 11*, 475–487.

Odom, S., & Strain, P. 1986. A comparison of peer-initiation and teacher-antecedent interventions for promoting reciprocal social interaction of autistic preschoolers. *Journal of Applied Behavior Analysis, 19*, 59–71.

O'Leary, K.D., & Becker, W.C. 1967. Behavior modification of an adjustment class. *Exceptional Children, 33*, 637–642.

O'Leary, K.D. Becker, W.C., Evans, M.B., & Saudargas, R.A. 1969. A token reinforcement program in a public school: A replication and systematic analysis. *Journal of Applied Behavior Analysis, 2*, 3–13.

O'Leary, K.D., & O'Leary, S.G. (Eds.). 1977. *Classroom management: The successful use of behavior modification* (2nd ed.). New York: Pergamon Press.

Olenick, D.L., & Pear, J.J. 1980. Differential reinforcement of correct responses to probes and prompts in picture-name training with severely retarded children. _Journal of Applied Behavior Analysis, 13_, 77–89.

Pace, G., Ivancic, M., Edwards, G., Iwata, B., & Paget, T. 1985. Assessment of stimulus preference and reinforcer value with profoundly retarded individuals. _Journal of Applied Behavior Analysis, 18_, 249–255.

Parrish, J., Cataldo, M., Kolko, D., Neef, N., & Engel, A. 1986. Experimental analysis of response covariation among compliant and inappropriate behaviors. _Journal of Applied Behavior Analysis, 19_, 241–254.

Peterson, N. 1982. Feedback is not a new principle of behavior. _Behavior Analyst, 5_, 101–102.

Pigott, H.E., Fantuzzo, J., & Clement, P. 1986. The effects of reciprocal peer tutoring and group contingencies on the academic performance of elementary school children. _Journal of Applied Behavior Analysis, 19_, 93–98.

Polirstok, S.R., & Greer, R.D. 1977. Remediation of mutually aversive interactions between a problem student and four teachers by training the student in reinforcement techniques. _Journal of Applied Behavior Analysis, 10_, 707–716.

Polloway, E., & Polloway, C. 1979. Auctions: Vitalizing the token economy. _Journal for Special Educators, 15_, 121–123.

Premack, D. 1959. Toward empirical behavior laws: I. Positive reinforcement. _Psychological Review, 66_, 219–233.

Raschke, D. 1981. Designing reinforcement surveys: Let the student choose the reward. _Teaching Exceptional Children, 14_, 92–96.

Reynolds, G.S. 1975. _A primer of operant conditioning._ Glenview, Ill.: Scott, Foresman.

Rincover, A., Cook, R., Peoples, A., & Packard, D. 1979. Sensory extinction and sensory reinforcement principles for programming multiple adaptive behavior change. _Journal of Applied Behavior Analysis, 12_, 221–233.

Rincover, A., Newsom, C., Lovaas, O., & Koegel, R. 1977. Some motivational properties of sensory reinforcement in psychotic children. _Journal of Experimental Child Psychology, 24_, 312–323.

Riordan, M., Iwata, B., Finney, J., Wohl., M., & Stanley, A. 1984. Behavioral assessment and treatment of chronic food refusal in handicapped children. _Journal of Applied Behavior Analysis, 17_, 327–341.

Roberts, R., Nelson, R., & Olson, T. 1987. Self-instruction: An analysis of the differential effects of instruction and reinforcement. _Journal of applied Behavior Analysis, 20_, 235–242.

Russo, D.C., & Koegel, R.L. 1977. A method for integrating an autistic child into a normal public-school classroom. _Journal of Applied Behavior Analysis, 10_, 579–590.

Saigh, P., & Umar, A. 1983. The effects of a good behavior game on the disruptive behavior of Sudanese elementary school students. _Journal of Applied Behavior Analysis, 16_, 339–344.

Sainato, D., Maheady, L., & Shook, G. 1986. The effects of a classroom manager role on the social interaction patterns and social status of withdrawn kindergarten students. _Journal of Applied Behavior Analysis, 19_, 187–195.

Schumaker, J.B., Hovell, M.F., & Sherman, J.A. 1977. An analysis of daily report cards and parent-managed privileges in the improvement of adolescents' classroom performance. _Journal of Applied Behavior Analysis, 10_, 449–464.

Schwartz, G.J. 1977. College students as contingency managers for adolescents in a program to develop reading skills. _Journal of Applied Behavior Analysis, 10_, 645–655.

Sigueland, E. 1968. Reinforcement patterns and extinction in human newborns. _Journal of Experimental Child Psychology, 6_, 431–442.

Skinner, B.F. 1953. _Science and human behavior._ New York: Macmillan.

Stainback, W., Payne, J., Stainback, S., & Payne, R. 1973. _Establishing a token economy in the classroom._ Columbus, Ohio: Merrill.

Stern, G., Fowlers, S., & Kohler, F. 1988. A comparison of two intervention roles: Peer monitor and point-earner. _Journal of Applied Behavior Analysis, 21_, 103–109.

Stevenson, J., & Clayton, F. 1970. A response duration schedule: Effects of training, extinction, and deprivation. _Journal of the Experimental Analysis of Behavior, 13_, 359–367.

Stevenson, H., & Odom, R. 1964. Visual reinforcement with children. _Journal of Experimental Child Psychology, 1_, 248–255.

Stokes, T., & Baer, D. 1977. An implicit technology of generalization. _Journal of Applied Behavior Analysis, 10_, 349–367.

Trant, L. 1977. Pictorial token card (communication). *Journal of Applied Behavior Analysis, 10*, 548.

Trovato, J., & Bucher, B. 1980. Peer tutoring with or without home-based reinforcement, for reading remediation. *Journal of Applied Behavior Analysis, 13*, 129–141.

Valcante, G., Roberson, W., Reid, W., & Wolking, W. 1989. Effects of wait-time and intertrial interval durations on learning by children with multiple handicaps. *Journal of Applied Behavior Analysis, 22*, 43–55.

Van Hasselt, V., Hersen, M., Egan, B., McKelvey, J., & Sisson, L. 1989. Increasing social interactions in deaf-blind severely handicapped young adults. *Behavior Modification, 13*, 257–272.

Wacker, D., Berg, W., Wiggins, B., Muldoon, M., & Cavanaugh, J. 1985. Evaluation of reinforcer preferences for profoundly handicapped students. *Journal of Applied Behavior Analysis, 18*, 173–178.

Wacker, D., Cigrand, K., Berg, W., Novak, C., Reimers, T., Sasso, G., & DeRaad, A. 1990. Use of negative reinforcement in the treatment of self-injurious behavior. *Journal of Applied Behavior Analysis, 23*, 459–467.

Weeks, M., & Gaylord-Ross, R. 1981. Task difficulty and aberrant behavior in severely handicapped students. *Journal of Applied Behavior Analysis, 14*, 449–463.

Welch, M.W., & Gist, J.W. 1974. *The open token economy system: A handbook for a behavioral approach to rehabilitation*. Springfield, Ill.: Charles C. Thomas.

Williams, J., Koegel, R., & Egel, A. 1981. Response-reinforcement relationships and improved learning in autistic children. *Journal of Applied Behavior Analysis, 14*, 53–60.

Wood, R. & Flynn, J.M. 1978. A self-evaluation token system *versus* an external evaluation token system alone in a residential setting with predelinquent youth. *Journal of Applied Behavior Analysis, 11*, 503–512.

CHAPTER 7

Differential Reinforcement: Stimulus Control and Shaping

Did you know that . . .

- Not all discrimination is the concern of the Equal Employment Opportunity Commission?
- Not all prompters work in the theater?
- Applied behavior analysts shape up behavior rather than shipping out students?
- You can teach anybody anything?

In Chapter 6 we described some ways to increase appropriate behavior. That solved a number of problems having to do with behavioral deficits. Not all problems, however, can be solved simply by increasing the frequency of behaviors. Many behaviors are defined as appropriate or inappropriate based not on their frequency but on the circumstances under which they occur. Running, for example, may be viewed very differently by the track coach and the teacher with hall duty. What makes running appropriate or not depends not on how often or how fast someone runs, but on the circumstances under which someone runs. It's very appropriate to run on the track during practice, but very inappropriate to run in the halls of the school. Yelling is perfectly acceptable, even admirable, when the team scores a touchdown, but considered a problem behavior when it occurs in the cafeteria. Many academic skills are acquired when a student learns, for example, to say a word he knows in response to printed letters—we call that reading—or to write a numeral he knows how to write on a worksheet with examples like "2 + 2"—we call that math. Bringing responses the learner already knows under the control of the appropriate cue or signal is called *stimulus control*.

When people learn about reinforcement procedures they often protest that the behavior they are looking for can't be reinforced because it never occurs. How can one increase something that doesn't exist? How does a teacher reinforce talking when a student never talks? sitting when a student never sits? or anything at all when a student appears to do absolutely nothing? One way of teaching students to do new things is by **shaping**. The teacher literally molds or shapes an existing response into the desired behavior.

Stimulus control and shaping are often used together to teach students academic and social behaviors. For that reason, and because both make use of differential reinforcement procedures, they are both described in this chapter. The first part of the chapter describes in detail the phenomenon of stimulus control and stimulus control procedures for use in the classroom.

DIFFERENTIAL REINFORCEMENT FOR STIMULUS CONTROL

In Chapter 6, when we talked about arranging consequences to increase behavior, we were concerned with what happens after a behavior is performed—with the effects of behavior on the environment. In this chapter, we address another component of behavior change: the environmental conditions or events that precede the behavior. Our concern will be with what happens before the behavior is performed—with the effects of the environment on behavior.

Operant and respondent conditioning are contrasted on page 32.

When describing events that affect operant behavior, it is important to remember the distinction between operant and respondent behavior described in Chapter 1. Respondent conditioning involves stimuli that elicit reflex behavior—for example, the puff of air (unconditioned stimulus) that results automatically in an eye blink (response). This automaticity is absent in operant behavior; the relationship between antecedent events and behavior is learned rather than reflexive. Although antecedent events do not elicit operant behavior, they do exert considerable influence over such behavior.

Principles of Discrimination

Students learn to discriminate as a result of differential reinforcement.

The basis for antecedent control of operant behavior is discrimination learning (Terrace, 1966). Discrimination is simply the ability to tell the difference between environmental events or stimuli. Discrimination develops as a result of differential reinforcement. A certain response results in positive reinforcement (S^{R+}) in the presence of a given stimulus or group of stimuli that are said to be discriminative stimuli (S^D) for the response. The same response is not reinforced in the presence of a second stimulus or group of stimuli, referred to as **S-deltas** (S^Δ). After a period of time, the response will occur reliably in the presence of S^D and infrequently, if at all, in the presence of S^Δ. The S^D is then said to occasion the response (Holland & Skinner, 1961). This relationship between the S^D and the response is different from that between the unconditioned stimulus and response in respondent conditioning. The S^D does not elicit the response; it just sets the occasion for it, or to use the technical terminology, it *occasions* it. The response that occurs in the presence of S^D, but not in its absence, is said to be under stimulus control. A behavior under stimulus control will continue to occur in the presence of the S^D even when reinforcement is infrequent. Michael (1982) suggested care be taken to avoid saying an event is an S^D for reinforcement—it is the behavior that is occasioned, not its reinforcement. The development of discrimination is an important factor in much human learning. A baby learns that saying "mama" is reinforced in the presence of the adult with the glasses and the curly hair, but usually results in the disappearance of the adult with the beard. Glasses and curly hair are an S^D for the response "mama;" a beard is an S^Δ. The first-grader learns that saying "went" in the presence of a flashcard with the letters *w-e-n-t* (S^D) results in praise, but that the same response to a flashcard with the letters *c-a-m-e* (S^Δ) does not. A group of junior-high students learns that obscene language and disruptive behavior get their math teacher's (S^D) attention, but that the social studies teacher (S^Δ) attends only to raised hands and completed assignments.

Much of the everyday behavior of adults is a result of discrimination learning. We answer telephones when they ring, not when they are silent; we drive through intersections when lights are green, not when they are red. Discriminations based on relatively informal or imprecise patterns of reinforcement develop slowly and are often imperfect. For example, babies may, for a while, call all men with beards "daddy." First-graders may say "went" when they see a flashcard with the letters *w-a-n-t* or *w-e-t*. Junior-high students may occasionally raise their hands in math class or utter obscenities in social studies class. Adults sometimes pick up the phone when the doorbell rings. The imperfect stimulus control exerted by traffic signals provides employment for numerous police officers, tow-truck drivers, and ambulance attendants.

Discrimination Training

Teaching students to respond appropriately to specific stimuli is the teacher's basic job. As teachers, we want our students to obey rules, follow instructions, and perform specified academic or functional skills at the appropriate time, in the appropriate place, and in response to specified instructions or other cues. A major part of the task of teaching is establishing specific times, places, instructions, and other antecedent events as discriminative stimuli for various student behaviors. In order to accomplish this, the teacher must

1. identify the target behavior
2. identify the stimulus to be established as the S^D
3. plan a reinforcement strategy

We are simply taking a behavior already in the student's repertoire (but not emitted under specified conditions) and establishing the desired conditions as discriminative for performance of the behavior. For example, a student may use the word "went" in conversation but not say "went" when shown a flashcard with the letters *w-e-n-t* and asked, "What is this word?" The teacher wants to bring saying "went" under stimulus control of the letters *w-e-n-t*. The accompanying chart illustrates the teaching process.

Stimulus	Response	Result
went (S^D)	"went"	"right"
go (S^Δ)	"went"	no praise (extinction)

In this example, the teacher establishes the letters *w-e-n-t* as the S^D for the response "went" through the process of differential reinforcement. The response is reinforced in the presence of *w-e-n-t* (S^D) and not in the presence of *g-o* (S^Δ). With sufficient repetition, the student should reliably respond correctly and could then be said to have formed a discrimination. Notice that *g-o*, which functions as S^Δ in this example, will be the S^D for responding with "go." The definition, as always, depends on the function. To state with any degree of confidence that the response "went" is under stimulus control, the teacher will have to establish that no other combination of letters occasions the response, including combinations such as *w-a-n-t* and *w-e-t*, whose shape and spelling (topography) closely resemble that of the S^D. The teacher

The teacher tells the student what the word is before asking for the discrimination to be made. This kind of prompting will be discussed later in the chapter.

will also want to determine that *w-e-n-t* is a reliable S[D] for "went" when it is written in places other than on the original flashcard.

One first-grade teacher thought she had finally taught one of her students to read the word "come" only to learn that the real S[D] was a smudge on the flashcard. This example illustrates that it is important to establish that the student is responding to the salient features of the stimulus. Many beginning readers identify words by their first letters alone. This strategy works well as long as "went" is the only word in the reader that starts with *w*. When the word "what" is introduced, however, the student can no longer discriminate reliably. The student is responding either to some totally irrelevant stimulus, like the smudge on the flashcard, or to only one aspect of the stimulus, like the first letter of a word. This **stimulus overselectivity** (Lovaas, Schreibman, Koegel, & Rhen, 1971) is often a characteristic of students with disabilities. A student may identify his or her classroom by the scratch in the door without attending to other factors—that it is the third door down the hall or that it is opposite the water fountain. If, over the weekend, the door is painted, it is no longer an S[D] for entering the room. The student gets lost and the teacher complains again that some students never remember anything. The simple examples in this section illustrate how a discrimination is established by differential reinforcement so that an antecedent stimulus reliably occasions the appropriate response. The response is then under stimulus control. The following sections offer more complex variations of discrimination training.

Discriminations Involving Multiple Stimuli

The preceding section described the process of bringing a single response under the control of an antecedent stimulus using differential reinforcement: the response in the presence of S[D] was positively reinforced; the same response in the presence of S[Δ] received no reinforcement or was extinguished. In many instances, a teacher may want to establish two or more antecedent stimuli as S[D]s for different responses. For example, teachers ask students to identify several letters of the alphabet, numerals, colors, words, and so on. In such cases, a number of different antecedent stimuli are established as S[D]s for an equal number of different responses and as S[Δ]s for all the others. The following chart shows an example using letters of the alphabet as a stimulus.

Stimulus	Response	Result
A	"A"	"Good"
B	"A"	Silence
B	"B"	"Good"
A	"B"	Silence

The vocal response of naming the letters of the alphabet must be brought under stimulus control, again by a process of differential reinforcement. Much of the activity taking place in classrooms involves just this type of discrimination training. Both the teacher of students with severe disabilities, who wants students to respond differently to the instructions "Find your spoon" and "Hang up your coat," and the regular classroom teacher, who asks students to classify plays as comedies or tragedies, are bringing responses under stimulus control.

Concept Formation

Students who are asked to make discriminations based on many different S^{D}s, all of which should occasion the same response, must form an abstraction (Ferster, Culbertson, & Boren, 1975) or a concept (Becker, Engelmann, & Thomas, 1975a). To classify words as parts of speech, for example, requires such an abstraction. (See the accompanying chart.)

Stimulus	Response	Result
The player made a home *run*.	"Noun"	"Right"
Put it on the *table*.	"Noun"	"Right"
Run over here.	"Noun"	Silence

In the examples shown in the chart, the student must discriminate based on specific characteristics common to a large number of stimuli. Such training may be accomplished by providing many samples of positive and negative instances of the concept or abstraction and reinforcing correct responses. Using such a procedure, Herrnstein and Loveland (1964) were able to teach pigeons to respond differently to pictures that included people and to pictures that did not. They simply reinforced responding only when the pictures contained people. Basic concepts, according to Engelmann and Carnine (1982), must be taught in almost the same way to people. The authors define a basic concept as "one that cannot be fully described with other words (other than synonyms)" (p. 10).

Try to think of a way to teach a 3-year-old child the concept "red" by describing it. Obviously, it's impossible. What most parents do is provide many examples of red things, label them, and provide strong reinforcement when the child points and says "red" appropriately or when the child responds correctly to the instruction "Give me the red block." Most children learn thousands of basic concepts in this informal manner before ever entering school. Children who don't must be taught them systematically. For these children, we don't wait for casual opportunities to introduce "red" into the conversation. We get some red objects and some not-red objects and proceed to label, instruct, and ask for responses until the student demonstrates mastery of the concept.

Although teaching such an abstraction as humanness can also be accomplished successfully in this way, such abstractions or concepts may often be taught more quickly by using some additional antecedent stimuli. It may be more efficient to provide a set of rules for identifying instances. Concepts do not need to be taught using only differential reinforcement. Most students, unlike pigeons, have some verbal skills that enable a teacher to use sets of rules as shortcuts in teaching them concepts or abstractions. The use of prompts is discussed in detail in the following section.

Prompts

A **prompt** is an additional stimulus that increases the probability that the S^D will occasion the desired response. Prompts are offered after an S^D has been presented and has failed to occasion the response. Most people are familiar with the use of prompts in the theater. An actor who fails to respond to his cues (the preceding lines, for example) is prompted from the wings. The use of the word prompt in applied behavior analysis has a similar meaning. Students who fail to respond to S^Ds are prompted. Prompts may be presented verbally, visually, or physically. The desired response may also be demonstrated or modeled. The reading teacher who holds up a flashcard with the letters *w-e-n-t* and says, "Not came, but . . ." is providing a verbal prompt. The kindergarten teacher who puts photographs as well as name tags on her students' lockers is providing a visual prompt. The mother who says to her child, "Wave bye-bye to Granny," while vigorously flapping the infant's hand, is furnishing a physical prompt. Each hopes that control will eventually be attached to the S^D "went," the student's name, or "wave bye-bye." The prompt is a crutch to be dropped as soon as the need for it no longer exists. Prompts increase teaching efficiency. Rather than waiting for the student to emit the desired behavior, the teacher uses extra cues to increase the number of correct responses. The more correct responses that occur, the more there are to be reinforced, and the faster the behavior will be learned. When prompting is used, a reinforcer is usually delivered just as if the student had not needed prompting.

Rules as Verbal Prompts

The English teacher who wants students to identify nouns and verbs correctly will probably not simply give students numerous chances to respond with "noun" or "verb" when they read sentences with the S^D underlined. Because most people have the ability to use verbal rules or definitions to form concepts, the English teacher might define noun, then present students with sentences and ask, "Is the underlined word a noun?" (S^D). "Is it the name of a person, place, or thing? Then it's a noun" (prompt). "Right, John, it's a noun" (S^{R+}). Prompting using rules or definitions is not confined to academic tasks. By defining honesty, politeness, kindness, or any other concept related to social behavior, a teacher can prompt students until they are able to identify instances of each behavior. This, of course, does not ensure that students will engage in the behaviors, merely that they can label them. Engelmann (1969) provides an extended discussion of concept teaching that is applicable to both academic and social behavior.

Instructions as Verbal Prompts

It's not easy to give instructions.

Instructions are often a means of prompting behavior. If, when the teacher says, "Get ready for reading," the children do not move, the teacher will probably add, "Put your materials away and go to the reading circle." If the S^D does not occasion correct responding, the teacher may provide step-by-step instructions. The teacher who uses instructions as prompts is making two assumptions. The first is that the instructions offered are accurate. It isn't easy to give clear, verbal instructions for a complex task. If people who ask you for directions to get from one place to another by car usually become hopelessly lost, do not be surprised if students fail to follow your instructions. The second assumption is that the student's behavior is under stimulus control of the general S^D, "Follow instructions." Many students do not follow instructions, as any experienced teacher will attest. Before depending on instructions as prompts, the wise teacher will determine that students do indeed follow them. It may be necessary to bring this response under stimulus control first. Becker, Engelmann, and Thomas (1975a) suggest that teachers reinforce following instructions to the most specific detail. Practice in this skill can be provided by specifying details arbitrarily: for example, telling students to line up with their toes on a crack in the floor or to perform activities in a specified order even though no specific order is required. This kind of practice can become a game. The traditional Simon Says game provides practice in following instructions.

Hints as Verbal Prompts

Many verbal prompts are less elaborate and more informal than rules or instructions. A reading teacher might prompt the correct response to the S^D, dog, by saying, "This is an animal that says 'bow-wow.'" When a teacher tells the class to line up, then adds, "Quietly," this too is a prompt. Such reminders, or hints, increase the probability that the correct response will be emitted, thus supplying an opportunity for reinforcement.

Visual Prompts

Many teaching strategies involve some form of visual prompting. The illustrations in most beginning readers are designed to aid students in identifying the printed word. Teachers may give examples of correctly completed math problems to prompt students. Picture prompts have been used to help teach a wide variety of behaviors to learners with disabilities, particularly complex daily living and vocational tasks (Wacker & Berg, 1983). Martin, Rusch, James, Decker, and Trtol (1974) taught learners with moderate and severe disabilities to prepare meals independently by using sequenced picture prompts. Wacker and Berg taught high-school students with moderate and severe retardation complex vocational tasks. They provided the students with books of pictures illustrating the successive steps in performing a complex assembly task and trained them to use the books, that is, to turn a page after each step and to match the correct object to its illustration. The authors found that the books greatly improved students' performance. The students were able to learn new tasks using picture prompts more quickly than they learned the initial task. Students were able to perform tasks without the books after training had been completed.

One advantage of this procedure is the enormous saving of teacher time. Bulletin boards in classrooms can easily be used to provide picture prompts. Line drawings or photographs of the correct procedure for accomplishing some task, or a picture of the way desks should look before leaving the room, or a photograph of the class in a nice straight line on the way to the cafeteria posted just inside the doorway could all be used to prompt correct responding.

Other visual prompts are provided in written form. Classroom schedules and rules are often posted to serve as reminders or cues. Many students are easily prompted to do complex new tasks by written instructions. Think of all the tasks you do that depend on written instructions and think of how important it is that the instructions are clear and accurate. Anyone who has tried to assemble children's toys late at night before a holiday can attest to the importance of clarity and accuracy. Of course, written instructions are technically verbal prompts, since the written word is a form of verbal (not vocal) communication. Since they are processed visually, however, it seems logical to consider them here.

Teachers often provide such prompts for themselves as well as for their students. A road map may help the itinerant resource teacher who is given the S^D, "Go to Oakhaven School." Some teachers post reminders to themselves to help them remember to reinforce certain student behaviors.

Modeling

"Watch me, I'll show you," says the teacher. This teacher is using yet another kind of prompt. When verbal instructions or visual cues are insufficient, many teachers demonstrate, or model, the desired behavior. In many cases, demonstration may be the procedure of choice from the start. A home economics teacher attempting to tell the class how to thread a sewing machine is a convincing example of the superiority of demonstration.

The majority of students, including those who have mild disabilities, respond by imitating the behavior of a model. Many explanations of this phenomenon have been offered (see Bandura, 1969, for a complete discussion), but the simplest is that most students' history of reinforcement includes considerable reinforcement of imitative behavior, resulting in a generalized imitation response. In other words, "Do it like this" has become an S^D for imitation in virtually any setting.

Origin of the generalized imitation response.

Several studies have established that individuals reinforced for imitating various responses will eventually also imitate unreinforced responses (Baer, Peterson, & Sherman, 1967; Brigham & Sherman, 1968; Lovaas, Berberich, Perloff, & Schaeffer, 1966). Anyone observing a parent interacting with an infant has seen examples of positive reinforcement of imitation. Such reinforcement occurs throughout the preschool years so that most children come to school already accustomed to responding to the S^D, "Do it like this" or "Do it like Mary." Of course, children are as likely to imitate inappropriate behavior as appropriate behavior. Many a parent has at some point been startled at how quickly children imitate less admirable parental habits.

Students also imitate the behavior of their classmates. Kindergarten students spontaneously play Follow the Leader. Nonacademic behaviors, such as speech patterns, are frequently imitated. It is amazing how quickly a new student with a distinctive regional accent begins to sound exactly like his or her peers. The tendency to imitate peers perhaps reaches its zenith in the secondary school. Adolescents tend to dress alike, talk alike, and engage in the same activities.

Furnishing appropriate models for students with disabilities is one of the primary goals of the current trend toward placement of such students in settings with as many typical students as possible. It is hypothesized that the students with disabilities will imitate and thus learn from their nondisabled peers.

In using demonstration techniques to prompt behavior, a teacher may choose to model the behavior personally, to allow another student to be a model, or to bring in someone from outside the group. The choice of a model is important, as certain characteristics increase models' effectiveness. Students are most likely to imitate models who

1. have high status, particularly celebrities (Hovland, Janis, & Kelley, 1953; Lefkowitz, Blake, & Mouton, 1955)

2. have demonstrated competence (Gelfand, 1962; Rosenbaum & Tucker, 1962)

3. are similar to themselves (Bandura, 1969), particularly of the same sex (Goldstein, Heller, & Schrest, 1966)

4. are reinforced for the modeled behavior (Bandura, 1969; Mayer, Rohen, & Whitley, 1969)

Modeling may be used to prompt simple or more complex behaviors. A teacher may use modeling to prompt speech in a student with severe disabilities. A math teacher may ask a competent student to demonstrate a problem on the board before other students are expected to work similar problems on their own. A physical education teacher may demonstrate a complex gymnastic performance. Hunter (1984) describes a procedure that combines verbal and physical modeling. She suggests that the teacher first perform the skill while describing the actions involved, then perform the skill while the students provide the verbal prompts, then ask students to perform it while the teacher provides verbal guidance. Students are then asked to perform the skill on their own. This is an excellent way to teach many skills, although some students may require more than one repetition of any or all of the steps involved.

Modeling can be an effective prompting procedure, but it does have limitations. Some behaviors are difficult to imitate. Some students, particularly those who have severe disabilities, have not acquired a generalized imitation response. Although it is possible to teach students to respond to modeled prompts by reinforcing imitation (Baer, Peterson, & Sherman, 1967; Lovaas et al., 1966), another form of prompting may also be required. Many teaching procedures involve combining various kinds of prompts. The following anecdote illustrates a procedure combining modeling with verbal instructions.

The Students Learn to Polka

Self-instruction is discussed in Chapter 12.

Some children with poor gross-motor skills were enrolled in an after-school program designed to improve motor coordination. Their teacher decided that, because the students had mastered skipping and hopping, they would enjoy learning to polka. "Let's polka!" said the teacher. "Watch what I do. Step-together-step-hop! Now you do it. Step-together-step-hop." Soon, when the teacher said, "Let's polka!" the students produced the desired movement. Many of them, incidentally, continued to whisper "step-together-step-hop" as they danced.

Physical Guidance

The teacher puts his or her hand on the student's hand and pulls it up.

When students fail to respond to less stringent forms of prompting, they may be physically prompted. Such a procedure, often called *putting-through*, is useful for teaching many motor behaviors and some vocal behaviors that may be manually guided (Karen, 1974). Physical prompting may be a first step in the development of a generalized imitation response. Baer and his colleagues (1967) prompted imitation with physical guidance and ultimately brought imitation under stimulus control. Streifel and Wetherby (1973) taught a student with severe retardation to follow instructions, such as "Raise your hand," by using a physical guidance procedure. The teacher first gave the verbal instruction, then guided the student so that the instruction was followed. Eventually, the student's behavior was under the control of the instructions. The implications of bringing the behavior of students with severe disabilities under stimulus control of imitation and instructions are enormous. Students who will imitate a model and follow instructions can be taught many things. Physical guidance procedures are by no means limited to use with students with disabilities. Most teachers routinely use such procedures when teaching beginning handwriting skills, for example. Music teachers may guide their students' fingering. Many athletic skills are most easily taught using physical guidance. It is difficult to imagine any other way of teaching anyone to change gears in a car with a four-speed manual transmission. When using physical guidance, teachers need to be sure that the student is cooperative. Such a procedure will be unpleasant (possibly to both parties) if it is performed with a resisting student. Even cooperative students may have a tendency to tighten up when physically prompted. Sulzer-Azaroff and Mayer (1977) suggest relaxation training for students who resist physical guidance because of tension.

Fading

A prompted response is not under stimulus control. Prompts must be withdrawn, and the response must be occasioned by the S^D alone. Too abrupt removal of prompts, however, may result in termination of the desired behavior. Gradual removal of prompts is referred to as **fading**. Any prompt may be gradually faded so that the response occurs and is reinforced when the S^D alone is presented. Considerable skill is involved in determining the optimum rate of fading: too fast, and the behavior will not occur; too slow, and students may become permanently dependent on the prompt. Prompts can be faded in a number of different ways. Billingsley and Romer (1983) reviewed systems for fading prompts and suggest four major categories: decreasing assistance, graduated guidance, time delay, and increasing assistance.

Decreasing Assistance

In decreasing assistance, the teacher begins with whatever level of prompting is necessary for the student to perform the desired behavior. The amount of assistance is then systematically reduced as the student becomes more competent. This procedure can be used to fade a wide variety of prompts. The English teacher using rules to help her students discriminate nouns might start with the S^D, "Is this a noun?" and the prompt, "If it's the name of a person, place, or thing, it's a noun." When her students respond reliably she might say:

Is this a noun?—(S^D)
Is it the name of a person, place, or thing?—(prompt)
then
Is this a noun?—(S^D)
Remember, person, place, or thing.—(prompt)
then
Is this a noun?—(S^D)
Remember your rule.—(prompt)

and finally

Is this a noun?—(S^D, no prompt)

The math teacher using the decreasing-prompts procedure to fade a visual prompt might allow students a complete multiplication matrix to help them work problems and systematically remove easier combinations as they are mastered. The teacher who fades a modeling prompt may demonstrate less of the behavior, perhaps fading from full demonstration to only partial demonstration of the response (Wilcox & Bellamy, 1982), and finally providing only a gesture. The following anecdote illustrates such a fading procedure.

The Children Learn to Hula Hoop

Coach Townsend was an elementary-school physical education teacher. He decided to teach the first-graders to hula hoop, so they could perform at open house. He began by demonstrating. "Watch me!" he said and proceeded to show the students how to do it. When the giggles died down, he handed each first-grader a hula hoop. "Ready," he said, "hoop!" Twenty-six hoops hit the floor clattering and banging. The children looked discouraged. The coach took a hoop from one student. "Okay," he said, "start it like this." He pushed his hoop with his hands. "Now do this." He rotated his hips. When the giggles died down, he said, "Again, just like this!" Coach Townsend gave the hoop back to the student and just demonstrated the movements. He eventually faded the hand movement to a flick of the wrist and the hip movements to a mere twitch. Before long, the cry, "Ready, hoop!" was enough. The great day finally arrived. Twenty-six first-graders equipped with hula hoops stood in the gym. Their parents sat in the bleachers. Coach Townsend started the music and said, "Ready, hoop!" He stood to one side of the group. The children did him great credit, but he heard suppressed giggling from the audience. The coach finally realized that, in his enthusiasm, he had gone back to modeling the necessary hip movements.

The system of decreasing prompts when using a physical guidance procedure was illustrated by Csapo (1981) in teaching students with severe disabilities a discrimination task. The verbal instruction was initially followed by a full physical prompt, then by a partial prompt, and then by a gesture.

The system of decreasing prompts may also be used when combinations of prompts are used. If teachers initially provide students learning a new math skill with a demonstration, a sample problem, and step-by-step instructions, these prompts may be removed one by one until the students are responding simply to the incomplete example.

Graduated Guidance

Graduated guidance is used in fading physical prompts (Foxx & Azrin, 1972). The teacher begins with as much physical assistance as necessary and gradually reduces pressure. The focus of the guidance may be moved from the part of the body concerned (spatial fading), or a shadowing procedure may be substituted in which the teacher's hand does not touch the student but follows his movement throughout the performance of the behavior (Foxx & Azrin, 1973). Juan learns by a graduated guidance procedure in the following vignette.

Juan Learns to Eat with a Spoon

Juan was a student in Ms. Baker's class for students with severe mental retardation. He could feed himself with his fingers but had not learned to manage with a spoon. Ms. Baker decided that the time had come. She equipped herself with a bowl of vanilla pudding and a spoon, hoping that the pudding, which Juan loved, would be a positive reinforcer for eating using the spoon and that vanilla would make a less visible mess than chocolate on Juan, herself, the table, and the floor. (Teachers have to think of everything!) Ms. Baker sat next to Juan, put her hand over his right hand, and guided it to the spoon. She helped him scoop up some pudding and guided his hand toward his mouth. When the spoon reached his mouth, he eagerly ate the pudding. Ms. Baker then removed Juan's left hand from the pudding dish and wiped it off with the damp cloth that she had thoughtfully provided. She repeated this procedure a number of times, praising and patting Juan whenever the spoon reached its goal. As she felt Juan making more of the necessary movements on his own, she gradually reduced the pressure of her hand until it was merely resting on Juan's. She then moved her hand away from his—to his wrist, to his elbow, and finally to his shoulder. Eventually, she removed her hand entirely. Juan was using the spoon on his own.

Time Delay

Time delay differs from other fading formats in that the form of the prompt itself is not changed, just its timing. Rather than presenting the prompt immediately, the teacher waits, thus allowing the student to respond before prompting. Delays are usually only a few seconds. Time delays can be constant (the delay remains the same length) or progressive (the interval before the prompt becomes longer as the student gains competence) (Kleinert & Gast, 1982). Time delay procedures can also be used with a variety of prompting formats. Many teachers use them instinctively. Let's go back to our English teacher. She asks, "Is this a noun?" waits a few seconds, finds no response forthcoming, and prompts, "If it's the name of a person, place, or thing, it's a noun." Luciano (1986) used a systematic variation of this informal procedure to teach children with mental retardation to produce the appropriate verbal responses.

Time delay can also be used to fade visual prompts. A teacher working on sight vocabulary might cover up the picture on the flashcard and wait a few seconds to allow students to identify the word without seeing the picture. If they fail to respond within the latency the teacher has established, the picture is uncovered. Stevens and Schuster (1987) used a similar procedure to teach 15 spelling words to a learning disabled student.

Touchette and Howard (1984) used a progressive time delay to fade a modeled prompt. Students were asked to point to a specific letter or word printed on one of four cards. Initially, the teacher pointed to the correct card immediately on presentation of the verbal S^D. The teacher's pointing was gradually delayed to provide an opportunity for the student to respond without prompting. Touchette and Howard's results also indicated that responding to the S^D alone was learned somewhat more efficiently when responses made before the prompt were reinforced more heavily than responses occurring after the prompt. Time delay is easily implemented when using a physical prompt. A teacher working with a student on dressing skill might say, "Pull up your pants," and then wait for the student to perform the behavior without assistance before providing it.

Increasing Assistance

Billingsley and Romer (1983) describe increasing assistance as "similar to the reverse application of the decreasing assistance approach" (p. 6). Increasing assistance is also referred to as the system of least prompts. When using this procedure, the teacher starts with the S^D, moves to the least intrusive prompt in her repertoire, and gives students an opportunity to respond. Bear with us for one more visit to the English teacher. She says, "Is it a noun?" and gets no response. She prompts, "Remember your rule," and gets no response. She says, "Remember person, place, or thing," and gets no response. She prompts, "Is it the name of a person, place, or thing?" and gets no response. She whimpers, "If it's the name of a person, place, or thing, then it's a noun." It is sometimes difficult to implement an increasing assistance procedure without sounding either strident or frustrated.

An increasing prompts procedure can be used to fade a visual prompt. A beginning reading teacher using a set of flashcards might first show a card with just the word boy and then a card with a stick figure, finally moving to a card with a representational drawing of a boy. To use the procedure with modeling, one could first provide a gesture and move toward a full demonstration. To use increasing prompts with physical guidance, one would also start with a gesture and then move toward a full putting-through procedure.

Increasing prompts may also be implemented with combinations of prompt modalities. Van Etten, Arkell, and Van Etten (1980) describe a procedure for teaching a student to drink out of a cup. The teacher starts with a verbal prompt, moves to a partial physical prompt, and finally uses a full physical prompt.

Effectiveness of Methods for Fading Prompts

The majority of the literature on fading prompts has examined the efficacy of their use with students who have severe and profound disabilities (cf.

Billingsley & Romer, 1983). Caution should be observed in generalizing the result to other populations. It appears that all methods may be used effectively but that "decreasing assistance training may be more effective than increasing assistance training at least for severely handicapped subjects in the acquisition phase of learning, and that progressive time delay procedures are no less effective, and may in some cases be more effective, than increasing assistance methods" (p. 7). It is interesting in the light of these tentative conclusions that increasing assistance procedures, according to our observations, are almost routinely used by teachers of average students and those with mild disabilities. It would be interesting to see the results of systematic study of increasing assistance and other prompting procedures with these populations.

Procedures for establishing and maintaining stimulus control are powerful tools. Once all prompts have been withdrawn and behaviors are under stimulus control, they will continue to occur, sometimes for years, without any reinforcement except that naturally available in the environment, and even when the person knows no reinforcement will be forthcoming. Have you ever sat at a red light at 3 A.M. at a deserted intersection and waited for the light to change? If you have, you have some idea of the power of stimulus control.

It appears that stimulus control procedures have great promise in facilitating not only the acquisition of behaviors, but also their generalization and maintenance. Stimulus control has recently emerged as one of the most powerful potential tools for programming generalization—for assuring that the skills acquired by students are performed in settings other than that in which they were taught and that the skills will continue to be performed long after the original programmer is gone (Halle, 1989; Halle & Holt, 1991; Schussler & Spradlin, 1991). Generalization and maintenance, and their relationship with stimulus control, are discussed at length in Chapter 11.

In the following anecdote Professor Grundy illustrates the power of stimulus control in maintaining behaviors—be they appropriate or not.

A Smoke Free Environment

Ms. Cadwallader, who had been a university departmental secretary for over 20 years, returned from a campus-wide clerical staff meeting with her arms full of signs and a smile on her face. "They didn't believe the memos and announcements," she chortled to herself, "but these they'll believe." As she entered the department the atmosphere of pipe and cigarette smoke assailed her nostrils. "Whew," she said aloud, "I'll be glad to be rid of this." She busied herself removing ashtrays from the public areas and posting signs on all the outside doors and inside walls—big, shiny signs with the international symbol for forbidden behavior and the legend "THIS IS A SMOKE FREE BUILDING."

An hour or so later she looked up from her desk and observed Professor Grundy standing outside the glass front door of the building, holding his smoking pipe and staring fixedly at the new sign. She kept her head down over her computer terminal and watched from the corner of her eye as he shrugged and deposited the smoking mess from his pipe into the ashtray she had thoughtfully placed outside the building. "Good," she thought, "stimulus control gets even professors. He's minding the sign."

She greeted the professor cheerily, "Good morning, Professor, I hope the new policy is not going to be a problem for you."

"Certainly not," growled Grundy, "do you think a professor has habits he can't control?" Grundy picked up his mail and phone messages and proceeded to his office. He settled in his chair, put his pipe in the tray on his desk, and prepared to go about his business. He read the first phone message and reached for the phone. As he finished dialing the number, his hand automatically reached for the pipe. He quickly withdrew the hand, completed the call, and began to read his mail. As he opened a large envelope containing an eagerly awaited research report, he settled back in his chair, put his feet up, and automatically reached for the pipe.

"This," he admitted to himself, "may be a little more difficult than I had anticipated. It appears that many of the routine actions that I perform have become S^{D}s for smoking." By noon he had identified a number of other stimuli—advising students, conferring with colleagues, making last-minute preparations for class—that occasioned the reaching response. He determined that he needed a substitute response and stopped at a local market during his lunch break for a supply of candy.

During the afternoon he happily reached for a piece of candy instead of the pipe. As he left for the day, he cheerfully assured Ms. Cadwallader that for Professors who understood applied behavior analysis, control of even their own behavior was no problem.

Errorless Learning

Stimulus shaping should not be confused with the shaping procedures described later in this chapter.

Any procedure using prompts to help establish stimulus control is designed to enable students to learn as rapidly as possible without making an excessive number of mistakes. Incorrect responses, once made, tend to be repeated (Bereiter & Englemann, 1966). In some cases, students may practice errors to the extent that such wrong responses become well established. It is possible, however, to develop programs in which prompts are so effective and faded so slowly that virtually **errorless learning** occurs. It is possible to use any of the systems described in this section to program for errorless learning, but that term has been used most often to describe a slightly different procedure. In the systems described above, the S^D itself remained constant and prompts were added to elicit the response. Such prompts are often called **response prompts**. Many procedures termed errorless learning use alterations within the stimuli (SDs or SDEs) to prompt correct responses. These prompts are often called **stimulus prompts** and the procedure itself is sometimes called *stimulus shaping*. To enable the student to make a discrimination more easily, some features of the S^D, the S$^\Delta$, or both are changed. Whaley and Malott (1971) taught Betty, a student with severe mental retardation, to discriminate her name from another by pasting the name *Betty* in white letters on a black card and the name *Susan* in white letters on a white background. Reinforcing the choice of *Betty* established the correct card as the S^D. The background color on the *Susan* card was gradually darkened until both names were printed in white on black. The student made a minimal number of incorrect choices and eventually made the discrimination based on the relevant stimulus properties.

Haupt, Van Kirk, and Terraciano (1975) used two fading procedures to teach math facts. In one procedure, the student was asked to give the answer to subtraction facts on flashcards. At first, the answers were visible, but they were gradually covered with colored cellophane. Eventually, there were 32 pieces of cellophane over the answer. The student learned and remembered the facts. The second procedure required written answers to multiplication facts. Successive thicknesses of tracing paper covered the initially visible answers. This procedure, too, was successful.

Another example was described by Ayllon (1977). A teacher was trying to teach a group of young children to discriminate their right from their left hands. On the first day of training, each child's right hand was labeled with an *x* made by a felt-tipped marker. This enabled the students to discriminate the S^D (right hand) from the S^Δ (left hand) when asked to raise their hands. On the second day, the plan was again to mark right hands, but because of the permanence of the marker (or the personal habits of the children), each child still had a visible mark. As the training proceeded during the week, each child's mark gradually faded, and by week's end, each child consistently raised his or her right hand when asked. Mosk and Bucher (1984) used a combination of prompting and stimulus alteration to teach students with moderate and severe mental retardation to hang toothbrushes and washcloths on the correct peg. At the beginning of instruction, only one peg was on the board. Distractor pegs were introduced, one at a time. At first, each distractor peg was too short to hang the item on; longer pegs were gradually introduced. This procedure was more effective than a procedure using prompting alone.

Evidence indicates (Schreibman & Charlop, 1981; Stella & Etzel, 1978) that errorless learning is most efficient if only the features of the S^D are altered, and the S^Δ is held constant. Some researchers suggest that time delay may be a more efficient and economical alternative (Bradley-Johnson, Johnson, & Sunderman, 1983; Touchette & Howard, 1984); others (Etzel & LeBlanc, 1979) disagree. This lack of agreement need not overly concern the classroom teacher. "Each has been shown to produce errorless learning under some circumstances and each should be considered as an alternative when the other fails" (Touchette & Howard, 1984, p. 187).

Fading for errorless learning provides for development of stimulus control without practicing incorrect responses. Such a procedure, however, has its disadvantages. Providing a completely error-free learning environment is not necessarily desirable. Spooner and Spooner (1984) suggest that optimal learning may occur when initially high error rates decrease quickly and correct responding accelerates rapidly. Terrace (1966) points out that a lack of frustration tolerance may result from errorless training. In the real world some errors are inevitable, and students must learn to handle mistakes. Krumboltz and Krumboltz (1972) suggest gradually programming students to persist after errors. Rodewald (1979) suggests that intermittent reinforcement during training may mitigate possible negative effects of errorless learning. Such intermittent reinforcement may help develop a tolerance for nonreinforcement of responses.

Effective Prompting

The effective use of prompts to facilitate development of stimulus control requires the teacher's attention to several influences:

Guidelines for using prompts

1. Prompts should focus students' attention on the S^D, not distract from it. Prompts that are spatially or otherwise distant from the stimulus may be ineffective (Schreibman, 1975). Cheney and Stein (1974) point out that using prompts unrelated to the stimulus may be less effective than using no prompts or trial-and-error learning. The well-meaning teacher who encourages beginning readers to use the illustrations in the preprimer as clues to the words on the page may find that overemphasis on such prompts may result in some children's developing an overdependence on the illustrations at the expense of the written word. For some students, such dependence may be so well developed as to require the use of reading materials without illustrations in order to focus attention on the relevant S^D.

2. Prompts should be as weak as possible. The use of strong prompts when weak ones will do is inefficient and may delay the development of stimulus control. In general, the best prompt is the weakest one that will result in the desired behavior. Strong prompts are often intrusive. They intrude on the environmental antecedent, the S^D, and drastically change the circumstances or conditions under which the response is to be performed. Every effort should be made to use the least intrusive prompt possible. Although there is little empirical validation on which to base a hierarchy of prompts (Wilcox & Bellamy, 1982), Figure 7–1 presents a tentative hierarchy, arranged from least to most intrusive. Visual and verbal prompts are, on the whole, less intrusive than modeling, and all are less intrusive than physical guidance. This may not always be the case. A gentle push on the hand to help a young child slide in a recalcitrant puzzle piece is probably less intrusive than yelling "Push it the other way." Inefficiency is not the only undesirable effect of prompts that are stronger than necessary. Many students react negatively to strong or unnecessary prompts (Krumboltz & Krumboltz, 1972). When students say, "Don't give me a hint. I'll figure it out myself!" the wise teacher listens.

3. Prompts should be faded as rapidly as possible. Continuing to prompt longer than necessary may result in failure of the S^D to acquire control.

FIGURE 7–1
Hierarchy of
prompts.

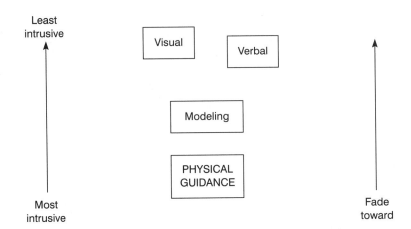

The efficient teacher uses prompts only as long as necessary and fades them quickly, thus avoiding students' becoming dependent on prompts rather than S^Ds. Students who are allowed to use a matrix of multiplication facts for extended periods may never learn their multiplication tables.

4. Unplanned prompts should be avoided. Anyone who has observed a large number of teachers has seen students watch the teacher carefully for clues to the correct answer. A teacher may be completely unaware that students are being prompted by a facial expression or vocal inflection. Neither is an inappropriate prompt when used intentionally. But the teacher who asks, while shaking her head, "Did Johnny really want to go to the park in the story?" in such a tone that all the children answer "no" is fooling herself if she thinks that the students necessarily comprehended the story.

TEACHING COMPLEX BEHAVIORS

So far we have discussed bringing behavior under stimulus control as if all behaviors consist of simple, discrete actions that may be occasioned by a discriminative stimulus and reinforced. Much of what we want students to learn involves many such discrete behaviors, to be performed in sequence on presentation of the S^D. Most functional, academic, and social skills are of this complex nature. Before even considering teaching such sequences of behaviors, the exact nature of the complex task must be analyzed.

Task Analysis

The most exacting task facing the teacher who wants students to acquire complex behavioral chains is determining exactly what steps, links, or components must be included and their sequence. Breaking complex behavior into its component parts is called **task analysis**. Task analysis requires considerable practice but can be applied to behaviors ranging from eating with a spoon to writing a term paper. It is perhaps easier, in general, to analyze motor tasks than those related to academic and social behavior, but the analysis is equally important for teaching all complex behaviors. Task analysis was originally used by teachers to break down basic skills in order to teach them step by step to learners with severe and profound disabilities. It proved such a valuable tool that it has been used not only for this population but to help teachers of all kinds of students to analyze all kinds of tasks.

To task analyze, pinpoint the terminal behavior, list necessary prerequisite skills, list component skills in sequence.

To acquire a general idea of what is involved in task analysis, take a simple task, such as putting on a jacket, and list its component parts in the correct sequence. Then read your steps, in order, to a tolerant friend while she or he does exactly what you have written. Don't worry, you'll do better next time. One of the authors assigns this task as part of a midterm exam. Fs are given only to task analyses that result in feet being placed through armholes.

Task analysis is the basis for programs teaching complex vocational skills to people who have severe and profound disabilities. It is theoretically possible, by breaking a task into sufficiently small components, to teach anybody anything. Time limitations, however, make it impractical to teach some students some things. The technology nevertheless exists. Teachers can even teach students to perform behaviors that those teachers cannot perform, so long as the teachers can recognize and reinforce the terminal behavior and its components (Karen, 1974). One is reminded of the middle-aged, somewhat overweight gymnastics coach cheering on his adolescent charges as they perform incredible feats of agility—feats that he has taught them but that it is laughable to picture him performing.

Moyer and Dardig (1978) provide a basic framework for analyzing tasks. The first step is always to determine what skills or concepts the learner must already have in order to learn the task at hand. These are known as the prerequisites for learning the skill. Anyone who has tried to teach a child who doesn't know how to hold a pencil to print her letters, or a child who doesn't know basic multiplication facts to find the least common multiple is aware of the folly of these endeavors. When analyzing any new task it is important to ask, "What does the learner already need to know in order to learn this?" If more teachers asked themselves that simple question before beginning a lesson, fewer children would be chronic failures in school. Although it is wise to attempt to list prerequisite skills before beginning a task analysis, many teachers find that one of the most valuable aspects of the analysis itself is that additional prerequisites are identified as they go through the process.

Before analyzing the task the teacher also lists any materials that will be required to perform it. Again, others may show up as necessary as the analysis progresses. Finally, the analyst must list all the components of the task in the order in which they must be performed. Although it is possible to do this simply from experience, many people find that watching someone competent perform the task (Moyer & Dardig, 1978) is helpful. It may be valuable to ask the "master" to list the steps verbally as he performs them.

Ms. Cadwallader Analyzes a Task

The consultant from Computer Services stood in Ms. Cadwallader's office waiting to get her attention. "Excuse, me, er, Ma'am," he said diffidently, "I'm here to install your new computer."

"Yes, indeed," answered Ms. Cadwallader cheerfully, "I can hardly wait." The consultant looked dubious; his experience had been that most clerical workers were attached to their current systems and highly resistant to new technology. He had not met Ms. Cadwallader.

As the young man unplugged and plugged, he muttered continuously about microprocessors, memory, bits, chips, viruses, spreadsheets, interfaces, buffers, and other esoteric lore. Ms. Cadwallader ignored him and continued working. Soon he happily announced that her system was "up" and prepared to leave.

"One moment, young man," said Ms. Cadwallader firmly, removing a pencil from her bun and a notebook from her pocket, "while you may safely assume that I have the necessary prerequisite skills to operate this system, I will need for you to show me exactly what steps to take in order to activate and operate the word processing program. Please be good enough to describe exactly what you are doing at each step. You may begin now."

"But, lady," protested the consultant, "this is a state-of-the-art system; you can access the mainframe and download updates . . ." The expression on Ms. Cadwallader's face silenced the consultant. "Step one?" she prompted. As the consultant listed and performed the steps in order (Ms. Cadwallader had noticed before that most computer programmers were quite good at this if pressed), Ms. Cadwallader carefully wrote them down. She knew that this task analysis would be useful not only for herself but for teaching the professors in the department how to use their new computers. As she thanked the somewhat chastened young man, she sighed quietly.

"As I expected," she thought, "nothing much to it. Most of my professors will pick it up quickly with a little coaching. After all, most of them have been using less efficient word processors for years. But, oh my, wait until Professor Grundy finds out that there's no more typing from longhand and he really has to learn word processing at last."

We suggest that you begin acquiring the skill of task analysis by breaking down simple, motor tasks into their prerequisites and components. A number of examples are provided below when we discuss teaching behavioral chains. For those who are accomplished cooks, many recipes provide models of task analysis. An understanding of the importance of prerequisite concepts and skills is easily understood by those of us less accomplished. When confronted by a recipe beginning, "First, bone a small hen," we have questions about concepts: "Bone? It looks pretty bony already. Small? How small? How big do hens get? Hen? How the heck would I know?" When informed that "to bone" to the well informed means to remove the bones, a serious question about prerequisite skills arises. The task of removing the bones from a chicken (of either sex) is one that itself requires analysis. However, the analysis is not enough. Simply reading the steps or even watching Julia Child (certainly a master of the skill) perform them is not sufficient. We, at least, will have to be taught. Someone will have to help us learn each component and perform them all in sequence. Only then can we incorporate that task into the even more complex task that will produce the delicious chicken cassoulet. We may send out for pizza instead—a task the components of which we have thoroughly mastered.

Chaining

The components of a task analysis form what behaviorists call a *behavioral chain*. The acquisition of such sequences of behaviors may require a more complex teaching procedure than differential reinforcement and prompting. Consider, for example, a classroom teacher who gives the instruction, "Get ready for math practice." The result is vague shuffling and furtive looking around among the students. Some students locate their math workbooks; others imitate them. "Come on," prompts (nags?) the teacher, "hurry up now." One or two students locate pencils; some students still appear completely confused. The process of getting ready for math practice is actually a series of behaviors performed in a sequence.

A behavioral chain

1. Clear desk of other materials.
2. Locate math workbook.
3. Locate pencil.
4. Wait quietly for instructions.

The students in this class may be able to perform each of these behaviors, but the behaviors are not under the control of the S^D presented ("Get ready for . . ."). The teacher must establish a series or chain of behaviors that will occur when the instruction is given. The teacher might proceed by giving each instruction separately and reinforcing compliance, always starting with "Get ready for math practice." Soon two steps could be combined, and reinforcement would follow only after completion of the two-part chain. Finally, the teacher would have to provide only the S^D. The students would have acquired a behavioral chain.

A behavioral chain is a sequence of behaviors all of which must be performed to earn a reinforcer. Many complex human behaviors consist of such chains—often with dozens or even hundreds of component steps. Usually, reinforcement occurs only when the final component is performed. The instructional procedure of reinforcing individual responses for occurring in sequence to form a complex behavior is called **chaining**.

To understand the process involved in the development of behavioral chains, first recall that any stimulus must be defined in terms of its function and that identical stimuli may have different functions. Similarly, behaviors included in chains may simultaneously serve multiple functions. Consider the behaviors in the get-ready-for-math-practice chain. When the chain is fully established, reinforcement occurs only after the last link. The last link in the chain, however, is paired with the reinforcer and thus becomes a conditioned reinforcer, increasing the probability of occurrence of the preceding link. Each link is subsequently paired with its preceding one: each link serves as a conditioned reinforcer for the link immediately preceding it.

We can also look at the behavior chain from another perspective: each link also serves as an S^D for the link immediately following it. Consider again the getting-ready-for-math-practice chain:

1. Clear desk of other materials (S^D for 2).
2. Locate math workbook (S^{R+} for 1; S^D for 3).
3. Locate pencil (S^{R+} for 2; S^D for 4).
4. Wait quietly for instructions (S^{R+} for 3).

Each link increases the probability of the one it follows and specifies, or cues, the one it precedes (Ferster, Culbertson, & Boren, 1975; Staats & Staats, 1963). On another level, each of the component links of a chain, as in our example, can in turn be described as a chain; that is, clearing one's desk includes picking up books and papers, opening the desk, and putting books in the desk. Picking up books is also a chain of behaviors—raising the arm, extending it, opening the hand, grasping the books, and raising the arm. Grasping books, in fact, is still another chain, including placing the thumb . . . but wait. We can go on this way in both directions—toward increasing specificity in behaviors and toward increasing complexity. Later in the school year, the teacher in our example may say, "Boys and girls, for math practice I want you to do the first 10 problems on page 142," whereupon the students promptly

1. get ready for math practice
2. open their books
3. pick up their pencils
4. complete the assignment

The original chain has now become merely a link in a more complex chain. The process of chaining simple behaviors into longer and more complicated sequences results in production of the most elaborate and sophisticated forms of human behavior. There are several chaining procedures. Those most commonly used are backward chaining, forward chaining, and total task presentation. For many students, behavioral chains can be acquired by having each step in the chain verbally prompted or demonstrated. The prompts can then be faded and the links combined (Becker, Engelmann, & Thomas, 1975b). For other students, some or all of the separate steps of the chain may have to be taught using more elaborate prompting procedures as the chain is developed.

Backward Chaining

When backward chaining is used, the components of the chain are acquired in reverse order. The last component is taught first, and other components are added one at a time. Delbert and Harmon (1972) describe an elegant backward chaining procedure for teaching a child to undress himself. The child is given the instruction, "Timmy, take your shirt off," and his shirt is pulled over his head until his arms are free and the neckband is caught just above his eyes. If the child does not automatically pull the shirt off, he is physically guided to do so. Primary and social reinforcers are then given. During the next training session, the neckband is left at his neck; in subsequent sessions, one arm, then both arms are left in the sleeves. The S^D, "Timmy, take your shirt off," is always presented and reinforcers given only when the task has been completed. The removal of each garment is taught in this manner; then the component steps are combined until the instruction, "Take your shirt off," has acquired stimulus control.

Many self-care skills, such as toileting, grooming, and eating, may be taught using backward chaining. Many academic and functional skills may also be efficiently taught using this procedure. Espich and Williams (1967) provided a model of a math program using backward chaining. At first, steps until the final one are provided, and the last step is prompted. Each frame of the program prompts one less step until students are on their own. We suggest you work through the program, reproduced in Figure 7–2, to see how effectively backward chaining can be applied to academic subjects.

Forward Chaining

When forward chaining is used, the teacher starts with the first link in the chain, teaches it until it is mastered, and then goes on to the next link. The student may be required to perform all the steps previously mastered each time (Banks & Baer, 1966), or each step may be separately taught to the criterion and then the links made (Patterson, Panyon, Wyatt, & Morales, 1974). To use forward chaining to teach undressing skills, the teacher would start with the student fully dressed and deliver the instruction, "Timmy, take your shirt off," and then provide whatever prompting was required to get Timmy to cross his arms and grab the bottom of his T-shirt. When Timmy reliably performed this behavior, she would add the next step until Timmy's shirt was off. Many academic applications of forward chaining come to mind. The first-grade teacher who wants students to print the letters of the alphabet in sequence may start with *A* and add a letter a day until the children can print all 26 capital letters in sequence. The chemistry teacher who wants students to know the elements on the periodic table in order starts with a few at a time and adds a few each day. A teacher who wants students to recite a poem may have them recite the first line until it is mastered and then add a line at a time until they can recite the entire poem. A conscientious teacher who requires students to write a report (an extremely complex chain) teaches them to find refer-

FIGURE 7–2
Backward chaining academic program.

This is not a test. It is a program.

It is designed to *teach you something* by making you apply the knowledge you already have plus new information that this program will supply.

Do whatever the program asks. If you come to a blank (_____), put the correct word, number, symbol, or whatever, in the blank.

When a response is required, you will find the correct response on the lower part of the page. Check your answer, then go on to the next bit of information.

Program page 1

---

1. To find the square of a two-digit number ending in 5:
   A. Multiply the first digit by the next higher consecutive number.
   B. Write 25 to the right of the result.

   NO RESPONSE REQUIRED

   Program page 2

---

2. To find the square of 35:
   A. Multiply the first digit (3) by the next higher consecutive
      number (4).   12
   B. Write 25 to the right of the result (12).   12   25
   C. The square of 35 is <u>1225</u>.

   NO RESPONSE REQUIRED

   Program page 3

---

3. To find the square of 25:
   A. Multiply the first digit (2) by the next higher consecutive
      number (3).   6
   B. Write 25 to the right of the result.   6   25
   C. The square of 25 is ____.

   $2 \times 3 = 6$

   C. The square of 25 is <u>625.</u>

   Program page 4

---

ences, then take notes, then outline, then prepare a rough draft, and then turn in a final copy.

Total Task Presentation

When using total task presentation, the teacher requires the student to perform all the steps in sequence until the entire chain is mastered. Total task

4. To find the square of 75:
    A. Multiply the first digit (7) by the next higher consecutive number.
    B. Write ____ to the ____ of the result.
    C. The square of 75 is ____.

    $7 \times 8 = 56$
    B. Write <u>25</u> to the <u>right</u> of the result.
    C. The square of 75 is <u>5625.</u>

    Program page 5

5. To find the square of 15:
    A. Multiply ____ by ____.
    B. Write ____ to the ____ of ____.
    C. The square of 15 is ____.

    A. Multiply <u>1</u> by <u>2</u>.
    B. Write <u>25</u> to the <u>right</u> of <u>2</u>.
    C. The square of 15 is <u>225.</u>

    Program page 6

6. What is the square of:
    A. 65? ____
    B. 95? ____

    A. <u>4225</u>
    B. <u>9025</u>

    The End

    Program page 7

Note: From Developing programmed instructional materials, by J. E. Espich & B. Williams. Copyright © 1967 by Fearon Publishers. Reprinted by permission of Pitman Learning, Inc., Belmont, CA 94002

presentation may be particularly appropriate when the student has already mastered some or all the components of a task but has not performed them in sequence. It is also possible, however, to teach completely novel chains in this manner (Spooner, 1981; Spooner & Spooner, 1983; Walls, Zane, & Ellis, 1981). The following anecdote illustrates teaching a skill using total task presentation. Notice Mr. Grist's use of various prompting strategies. Can you label each one?

Combining verbal instructions, modeling, and chaining

Carole Learns to Go Through the Lunch Line

It was Carole's first day in a regular school. She had previously attended a center for individuals with moderate retardation but was now placed in a self-contained class in a regular elementary school. Her teacher, Mr. Grist, knew that meals at the center were served family-style and that the self-service line in the school cafeteria might be confusing to Carole. He put her in line behind Linda and walked beside the girls, saying, "Look, Carole, Linda took a fork. Now you take a fork." If necessary, he added a gesture or a physical prompt. He repeated this strategy for each of the required steps. When Carole reached the table safely, he praised her. He repeated this strategy daily, waiting to see whether she needed prompting before he offered it. By the end of the week, Carole was managing nicely.

Many academic chains are forged using a total task presentation. The arithmetic teacher working on long division usually requires her students to solve an entire problem, with whatever coaching is required, until they have mastered the process. Students practice the entire process of finding the longitude and latitude of a given location in geography until it is mastered, as do biology students learning to operate a microscope. As with prompting techniques, the jury is still out as to which chaining technique is most effective, although there is some indication (Spooner & Spooner, 1984) that total task presentation may be the most effective in teaching complex assembly tasks to individuals with mental retardation. Classroom teachers are again advised to try what seems, in their professional judgment, to be the best procedure, and if that doesn't work, to try something else. This may be a good place to say again that a teacher must regularly read the professional literature. New conclusions about effective management and instructional techniques are published constantly.

DIFFERENTIAL REINFORCEMENT FOR SHAPING

The behavioral procedures described in this chapter assume that students are able to perform with some degree of prompting the components of the target behavior. The emphasis has been on differential reinforcement to bring the desired behavior under the control of a specified stimulus. Many behaviors that teachers want students to perform are not a part of the students' behavioral repertoire. For such behaviors, a different approach, called **shaping**, is required. Shaping is defined as differential reinforcement of successive approximations to a specified target behavior. Becker, Engelmann, & Thomas (1975b) list two essential elements of shaping: differential reinforcement and a shifting criterion for reinforcement. Differential reinforcement, in this case, requires that responses that meet a certain criterion are reinforced, while those that do not meet the criterion are not. The criterion for reinforcement shifts ever closer to the target behavior.

Although the term differential reinforcement is used in both stimulus control and shaping, the usage is somewhat different. In developing stimulus control, a response in the presence of the S^D is reinforced; the same response in the presence of S^{Δ} is not reinforced. The differentiation of reinforcement depends on the antecedent stimulus. In shaping procedures, differential reinforcement is applied to responses that successively approximate (or become increasingly closer to) the target behavior. It is easy to confuse shaping with fading, because both involve differential reinforcement and gradual change. The following guidelines should clarify the differences:

1. Fading is used to bring an already learned behavior under the control of a different stimulus; shaping is used to teach a new behavior.
2. The behavior itself does not change when fading is used; only the antecedent stimulus varies. In shaping, the behavior itself is changed.
3. In fading, the teacher manipulates antecedents; in shaping, consequences are manipulated. Shaping is not a stimulus control procedure; it is included in this chapter because it is an integral part of many teaching strategies that combine elements of stimulus control, prompting, fading, and chaining.

Suppose his teacher wants Harold to remain in his seat for an entire 20-minute work period. She has observed that Harold has never remained in his seat longer than 5 minutes, with an average of 2 minutes. A program in which Harold earns a reinforcer for remaining in his seat for 20 minutes is doomed—Harold will never come into contact with the reinforcer. Instead, the teacher defines her target behavior as Harold's remaining in his seat for the full 20 minutes but sets up a graduated sequence of criteria.

1. Harold remains in his seat for 3 minutes.
2. Harold remains in his seat for 5 minutes.
3. Harold remains in his seat for 10 minutes.
4. Harold remains in his seat for 15 minutes.
5. Harold remains in his seat for 20 minutes.

Each step in the sequence will be reinforced until established; then the criterion for reinforcement will be shifted to the next step. Shaping procedures may be used to establish many new behaviors, from verbal behavior in students with severe disabilities to study behaviors in college students.

Shaping appears deceptively simple. Its efficient use, however, requires great skill on the part of the teacher. Particularly important is the precise definition of the target behavior. A teacher who does not know exactly where he or she is going will have great difficulty in defining carefully graded steps toward getting there. The second skill required in planning a shaping program is the ability to choose a place to start. The teacher must select a behavior that the student already performs and that can be shaped. A further consideration is the size of the steps toward the goal. If the steps are too small, the procedure is needlessly time-consuming and inefficient. If the steps are too large, the student's responses will not be reinforced and the behavior will be extinguished (Reese, 1966). Finally, the teacher must consider how long to remain at each plateau—just long enough to establish the behavior solidly, but not so long that the student becomes stuck at that level.

"I wonder how he'll react when he finds out about our class behavior-shaping project."

It is not always possible to make all these decisions before beginning a program. For example, Harold's teacher might find that even after Harold has consistently remained in his seat for 5 minutes for a full week, he fails to meet the criterion of sitting for 10 minutes. The teacher would then have to drop back to 5 (or even 4) minutes and gradually work back up to 10, using smaller increments this time. The ability to evaluate and adjust ongoing programs is vital to the success of shaping procedures. In shaping Harold's behavior, the teacher was able to define rather simply a criterion for reinforcement at each level. Such simplicity is not always possible. When shaping such behaviors as vocalizing, the teacher must carefully judge whether a criterion has been met. A shaping procedure for teaching vocal imitation to a child with severe disabilities involves presenting the S^D—"ah," for example—and reinforcing successive approximations to correct imitation. The teacher might reinforce any vocalization at first, then only vowellike sounds, then only close approximations to "ah." In the heat of a language-training session with a child with autism, it is frequently difficult to determine whether a given vocal utterance is closer to the target behavior than the preceding one. Only extended practice, supervised by an instructor who shapes the teacher's behavior, will result in the development of such a skill.

Shaping is an extremely useful teaching tool. It provides a means of developing new behaviors in students with all levels of ability. It is by no means always the procedure of choice, however. Shaping should be used only when no combination of reinforcement, prompting, or chaining will result in the desired behavior. One of the authors, as a college supervisor, once observed a student teacher in a regular second-grade classroom who was, she said, shaping a child's behavior toward the objective of sitting in a chair. She was currently reinforcing his behavior of standing within five feet of his chair. The estimated time of arrival of his bottom on the chair using this technique was the end of her student teaching assignment, six weeks later. Having observed the child sitting for 30 minutes in the cafeteria, the college supervisor offered expert consultation. The student teacher, with great trepidation, gently led the student to his chair and issued the instruction, "Sit down, Mike." Mike sat. A program much like Harold's kept him sitting.

Save shaping for when it's necessary. Common sense and applied behavior analysis are not mutually incompatible.

Sam Develops Work Habits

Sam was a 9-year-old third-grader who spent an hour a day in a resource class for children with learning disabilities. He was able to keep up academically with his classmates due to the resource teacher's help, but his regular class teacher, Ms. Walker, complained that he had poor work habits. Mr. Finch, the resource teacher, determined that Sam's poor work habits included failing to bring pencils and paper, failing to complete class and homework assignments, and keeping a messy desk. The two teachers defined the target behavior as developing good work habits—bringing materials, completing assignments, and keeping a tidy desk. The successive approximations to the goal were defined as follows:

1. Sam brings at least one pencil to school.
2. Sam still has a pencil at noon.
3. Sam still has a pencil at 3:00.
4. Sam meets criterion 3 and also has a notebook containing at least 10 sheets of clean paper in the morning.
5. Sam meets criterion 4 and still has paper at noon.
6. Sam meets criterion 5 and still has paper at 3:00.
7. Sam meets criterion 6 and completes at least 1/2 of his class assignments.
8. Sam meets criterion 6 and completes at least 3/4 of his class assignments.
9. Sam meets criterion 6 and completes all class assignments.
10. Sam meets criterion 9 and has no more than three extraneous items (trash, toys, etc.) in his desk during a daily spot check.

11. Sam meets criterion 9 and has no more than two extraneous items in his desk.

12. Sam meets criterion 9 and has no more than one extraneous item in his desk. (The teachers agreed to stop here—everyone is entitled to one extraneous item.)

13. Sam meets criterion 12 and has books, notebook, and folders neatly stacked in his desk.

14. Sam meets criterion 13 and shows Ms. Walker his list of homework assignments at 3:00.

15. Sam meets criterion 14 and turns in at least 1/2 of his homework.

16. Sam meets criterion 14 and turns in at least 3/4 of his homework.

17. Sam meets criterion 14 and turns in all of his homework.

Mr. Finch had some difficulty persuading Ms. Walker that it was necessary to reward Sam for doing less than other students did (as she saw it) without rewards. She also stated that good work habits had to be learned at home and that students who had not developed them by the third grade were unlikely ever to do so. She agreed to try, however.

Mr. Finch provided a checklist and Ms. Walker recorded Sam's behavior. Sam was to earn the privilege of helping Mr. Finch clean the resource room from 3:00 to 3:15 each day that he met a criterion.

In spite of Ms. Walker's skepticism, the program was successful. It took Sam only a few days to begin bringing (and keeping) pencils and paper. He earned his privilege for five days just by having materials but, to Ms. Walker's surprise, completed all of his class assignments on two of those days. (It is much easier to complete assignments when you have pencil and paper.) The teachers agreed to drop step 7 and require Sam to complete 3/4 of his class assignments. Ms. Walker wanted to require the completion of all classwork, but Mr. Finch argued that this was expecting too much and that Sam might be unable to reach that criterion. "Let's not blow it now," he suggested, "he's doing so well." This criterion was maintained for a week. Then reinforcement was made contingent on completing all his classwork.

At this point, the teachers agreed that homework had a higher priority than a neat desk and went straight to step 14. Anyway, reported Ms. Walker, since Sam was completing his assignments, the number of paper airplanes, doodles, and other junk in his desk had diminished drastically, to within normal limits for third-graders. The greatest surprise in the entire program was that when Sam was required to write down his assignments in order to earn his privilege, he immediately began bringing all his homework. No further shaping was required; Sam had good work habits. When last observed, Ms. Walker, with a strange gleam in her eye, was muttering, "I'll bet I could shape up his sloppy handwriting too, and Melanie's tardiness, and Jack's loud voice, and . . ." Mr. Finch, meanwhile, praised Ms. Walker's cooperative attitude to the principal at a faculty meeting and decided that the next step in her shaping program was for her to design and reproduce her own checklist.

As we stated earlier, shaping and fading are often used in combination. The following example illustrates a combined procedure.

Ms. Wallace's Class Learns to Print the Letter A

Ms. Wallace was trying to teach her students to print the letter *A*. At first she just told them, "Make a capital *A*." They did not respond to this S^D. "Look at the one on the chart," she said. "Make it just like this one." Some of the students responded to this visual prompt by producing a creditable *A*. But,

"Does this look like the one on the chart, Harold?" asked Ms. Wallace. She then tried some verbal instructions: "Make two slanted lines that look like a teepee; then make another line across the middle." This verbal prompt resulted in success for some students. But,

"Ralph, your teepee is a little flat," sighed Ms. Wallace. In desperation, Ms. Wallace walked around the room guiding her students' hands through the correct movements. Physical prompting resulted in success for many students. But,

"Melissa, relax your hand, for heaven's sake. I'm only trying to HELP you," wailed Ms. Wallace.

    In the teachers' lounge that afternoon, Ms. Wallace sobbed, "I can't go through this 25 more times." An unkind colleague pointed out that she had forgotten the lowercase letters, making 51 more to go. Before Ms. Wallace became completely hysterical, an experienced first-grade teacher showed her a worksheet like this:

"You see," said Ms. Weatherby, "you just reinforce successive approximations to the terminal behavior of writing an A independently, tracing with fewer and fewer cues until the prompt just fades away."

In this chapter you have learned a variety of skills that will help you to teach students to perform behaviors, simple and complex. See how many of the strategies we discussed are described in the following anecdote.

The Computerized Professor

Ms. Cadwallader looked up from her computer screen to see Professor Grundy, pale and shaken, standing in front of her desk.

"What," he asked in a barely controlled tone, "is that THING doing in my office?"

"Why, Professor," chirped Ms. Cadwallader, "that's your new computer. As I'm sure you've noticed, we have sent several memos about the new policy. We secretaries will no longer be doing all your typing—you can do that yourself now. You're even hooked up to a printer, and a modem, and a fax . . ."

"Memos!" snorted the Professor, "Never read them. Waste of time. Get it out."

"Certainly, Professor, if that's what you want," answered the secretary, "but it will take several days. Do remember, however, that I will not be able to type any manuscripts for you."

During the next several days Ms. Cadwallader firmly refused to take several crumpled and stained handfuls of yellow paper from the professor. (The next chapter will explain why he did not approach her again after being rebuffed several times.) She cheerfully offered each time to show him how to use the computer, but it was another few days before he capitulated.

"Very well, Ms. Cadwallader," he said humbly, "if you will show me how to turn the thing on, I'll give it a try."

"Certainly," answered the secretary, mentally adding a few steps to the beginning of the task analysis provided by the computer consultant.

"Now, Professor," she began, "First, we boot the system. It's a little more complicated than turning it on, but I'm sure once you're used to it you will wonder how you managed with those yellow tablets."

"No, no, professor, that's not the way to boot the word processing program."

Ms. Cadwallader patiently demonstrated each step, describing her actions as she performed them. She then coached the professor through the process of creating, saving, and printing a short document, praising him profusely whenever he performed a step. She left him happily pecking away, referring only occasionally to the written instructions she had thoughtfully copied for each professor.

As she returned to her desk, Ms. Cadwallader pondered a statement she had heard the Professor make many times. "He's right," she thought, "if you break it down small enough and teach it well enough, you CAN teach anybody anything. Even professors."

In this chapter we have discussed the process of differential reinforcement for bringing students' behavior under stimulus control and the process for bringing simple and complex behaviors under the control of antecedent stimuli. Verbal, visual, modeling, and physical prompts have been discussed, as well as systematic procedures for fading these prompts. Task analysis, backward chaining, forward chaining, and total task presentation have been described. Finally, procedures for shaping behaviors that students cannot initially perform were suggested.

DISCUSSION QUESTIONS

1. Describe stimuli in your environment that evoke certain appropriate and inappropriate behaviors in you.

2. Anything can be taught to anybody if it is broken into small enough tasks. True or false? Explain.

3. Design a plan for teaching a complex task using shaping, fading, and chaining.

4. Design a series of prompts to facilitate acquisition of a concept.

5. As a group design a task analysis for an everyday task. Give your analysis to another group and see if they can perform it. Determine whether any difficulties they have require improvement to the task analysis or one of the teaching procedures described in this chapter.

REFERENCES

Ayllon, T. 1977. Personal communication.

Baer, D.M., Peterson, R.F., & Sherman, J.A. 1967. The development of imitation by reinforcing behavioral similarity to a model. *Journal of the Experimental Analysis of Behavior, 10*, 405–416.

Bandura, A. 1969. *Principles of behavior modification.* New York: Holt, Rinehart & Winston.

Banks, M.E., & Baer, D.M. 1966. Chaining in human learning. Working paper #138. Unpublished manuscript. Parsons Research Center.

Becker, W.C., Engelmann, S., & Thomas, D.R. 1975a. *Teaching 1: Classroom management.* Chicago: Science Research Associates.

Becker, W.C., Engelmann, S., & Thomas, D.R. 1975b. *Teaching 2: Cognitive learning and instruction.* Chicago: Science Research Associates.

Bereiter, C., & Engelmann, S. 1966. *Teaching disadvantaged children in the preschool.* Englewood Cliffs, N.J.: Prentice-Hall.

Billingsley, F.F., & Romer, L.T. 1983. Response prompting and the transfer of stimulus control: Methods, research, and a conceptual framework. *Journal of the Association for Persons with Severe Handicaps, 8*, 3–12.

Bradley-Johnson, S., Johnson, C., & Sunderman, P. 1983. Comparison of delayed prompting and fading for teaching preschoolers easily confused letters & numbers. *Journal of School Psychology, 21*, 327–335.

Brigham, T.A., & Sherman, J.A. 1968. An experimental analysis of verbal imitation in preschool children. *Journal of Applied Behavior Analysis, 1*, 151–158.

Cheney, T., & Stein, N. 1974. Fading procedures and oddity learning in kindergarten children. *Journal of Experimental Child Psychology, 17*, 313–321.

Csapo, M. 1981. Comparison of two prompting procedures to increase response fluency among severely handicapped learners. *Journal of the Association for the Severely Handicapped, 6*, 39–47.

Delbert, A.N., & Harmon, A.S. 1972. *New tools for changing behavior.* Champaign, Ill.: Research Press.

Engelmann, S. 1969. *Conceptual learning.* Sioux Falls, S.D.: Adapt Press.

Engelmann, S., & Carnine, D. 1982. *Theory of instruction: Principles and applications.* New York: Irvington.

Espich, J.E., & Williams, B. 1967. *Developing programmed instructional materials.* Palo Alto, Calif.: Fearon Publishers.

Etzel, B.C., & Leblanc, J.M. 1979. The simplest treatment alternative: The law of parsimony applied to choosing appropriate instructional control and errorless-learning procedures for the difficult-to-teach child. *Journal of Autism and Developmental Disorders, 9*, 361–382.

Ferster, C.B., Culbertson, S., & Boren, M.C.P. 1975. *Behavior principles* (2nd ed.). Englewood Cliffs, N.J.: Prentice-Hall.

Foxx, R.M., & Azrin, N.H. 1972. Restitution: A method of eliminating aggressive-disruptive behavior of retarded and brain damaged patients. *Behavior Research and Therapy, 10*, 15–27.

Foxx, R.M., & Azrin, N.H. 1973. *Toilet training the retarded.* Champaign, Ill.: Research Press.

Gelfand, D.M. 1962. The influence of self-esteem on rate of verbal conditioning and social matching behavior. *Journal of Abnormal and Social Psychology, 65*, 259–265.

Goldstein, A.P., Heller, K., & Schrest, L.G. 1966. *Psychotherapy and the psychology of behavior change.* New York: Wiley.

Halle, J.W. 1989. Identifying stimuli in the natural environment that control verbal responses. *Journal of Speech and Hearing Disorders, 54*, 500–504.

Halle, J.W., & Holt, B. 1991. Assessing stimulus control in natural settings: An analysis of stimuli that acquire control during training. *Journal of Applied Behavior Analysis, 24*, 579–589.

Haupt, E.J., Van Kirk, M.J., & Terraciano, T. 1975. An inexpensive fading procedure to decrease errors and increase retention of number facts. In E. Ramp & G. Semb (Eds.), *Behavior analysis: Areas of research and application.* Englewood Cliffs, N.J.: Prentice-Hall.

Herrnstein, B.J., & Loveland, D.H. 1964. Complex visual concept in the pigeon. *Science, 146*, 549–550.

Holland, J.G., & Skinner, B.F. 1961. *The analysis of behavior.* New York: McGraw-Hill.

Hovland, C.I., Janis, I.C., & Kelley, H.H. 1953. *Communication and persuasion.* New Haven, Conn.: Yale University Press.

Hunter, M. 1984. Knowing, teaching, and supervising. In P. Hosford (Ed.), *Using what we know about teaching.* Alexandria, Va.: Association for Supervision and Curriculum Development.

Karen, R.L. 1974. *An introduction to behavior theory and its applications.* New York: Harper & Row.

Kleinert, H.L., & Gast, D.L. 1982. Teaching a multi-handicapped adult manual signs using a constant time delay procedure. *Journal of the Association of the Severely Handicapped, 6*(4), 25–32.

Krumboltz, J.D., & Krumboltz, H.D. 1972. *Changing children's behavior.* Englewood Cliffs, N.J.: Prentice-Hall.

Lefkowitz, M.M., Blake, R.R., & Mouton, J.S. 1955. Status factors in pedestrian violation of traffic signals. *Journal of Abnormal and Social Psychology, 51*, 704–706.

Lovaas, O.I., Berberich, J.P., Perloff, B.F., & Schaeffer, B. 1966. Acquisition of imitative speech by schizophrenic children. *Science, 151*, 705–707.

Lovaas, O.I., Schreibman, L., Koegel, R.L., & Rhen, R. 1971. Selective responding by autistic children to multiple sensory input. *Journal of Abnormal Psychology, 77*, 211–222.

Luciano, M.C. 1986. Acquisition, maintenance, and generalization of productive intraverbal behavior through transfer of stimulus control procedures. *Applied Research in Mental Retardation, 7*, 1–20.

Martin, J., Rusch, F., James, V., Decker, P., & Trtol, K. 1974. The use of picture cues to establish self-control in the preparation of complex meals by mentally retarded adults. *Applied Research in Mental Retardation, 3*, 105–119.

Mayer, G.R., Rohen, T.H., & Whitley, A.D. 1969. Group counseling with children: A cognitive behavioral approach. *Journal of Counseling Psychology, 16*, 142–149.

Michael, J. 1982. Distinguishing between discriminative and motivational functions of stimulus. *Journal of the Experimental Analysis of Behavior, 37*, 149–155.

Mosk, M.D., & Bucher, B. 1984. Prompting and stimulus shaping procedures for teaching visual-motor skills to retarded children. *Journal of Applied Behavior Analysis, 17*, 23–34.

Moyer, J.R., & Dardig, J.C. 1978. Practical task analysis for educators. *Teaching Exceptional Children, 11*, 16–18.

Patterson, E.T., Panyon, M.C., Wyatt, S., & Morales, E. September 1974. Forward vs. backward chaining in the teaching of vocational skills to the mentally retarded: An empirical analysis. Paper presented at the 82nd Annual Meeting of the American Psychological Association, New Orleans.

Reese, E.P. 1966. *The analysis of human operant behavior*. Dubuque, Iowa: William C. Brown.

Rodewald, H.K. 1979. *Stimulus control of behavior*. Baltimore: University Park Press.

Rosenbaum, M.E., & Tucker, I.F. 1962. The competence of the model and the learning of imitation and nonimitation. *Journal of Experimental Psychology, 63*, 183–198.

Schreibman, L. 1975. Effects of within-stimulus and extra-stimulus prompting on discrimination learning in autistic children. *Journal of Applied Behavior Analysis, 8*, 91–112.

Schreibman, L., & Charlop, M.H. 1981. S$^+$ versus S$^-$ fading in prompting procedures with autistic children. *Journal of Experimental Child Psychology, 34*, 508–520.

Schussler, N.G, & Spradlin, J.E. 1991. Assessment of stimuli controlling the requests of students with severe mental retardation during a snack routine. *Journal of Applied Behavior Analysis, 24*, 791–797.

Spooner, F. 1981. An operant analysis of the effects of backward chaining and total task presentation. Dissertation Abstracts International, 41, 3992A (University Microfilms No. 8105615).

Spooner, F., & Spooner, D. 1983. Variability: An aid in the assessment of training procedures. *Journal of Precision Teaching 4*(1), 5–13.

Spooner, F., & Spooner, D. 1984. A review of chaining techniques: Implications for future research and practice. *Education and Training of the Mentally Retarded, 19*, 114–124.

Staats, A.W., & Staats, C.K. 1963. *Complex human behavior*. New York: Holt, Rinehart & Winston.

Stella, M.E., & Etzel, B.C. 1978. *Procedural variables in errorless discrimination learning: Order of S$^+$ and S$^-$ manipulation*. Toronto, Canada: American Psychological Association.

Stevens, K.B., & Schuster, J.W. 1987. Effects of a constant time delay procedure on the written spelling performance of a learning disabled student. *Learning Disability Quarterly, 10*, 9–16.

Striefel, S., & Wetherby, B. 1973. Instruction-following behavior of a retarded child and its controlling stimuli. *Journal of Applied Behavior Analysis, 6*, 663–670.

Sulzer-Azaroff, B., & Mayer, G.R. 1977. *Applying behavior-analysis procedures with children and youth*. New York: Holt, Rinehart & Winston.

Terrace, H.S. 1966. Stimulus control. In W.K. Honig (Ed.), *Operant behavior: Areas of research and application*. New York: Appleton-Century-Crofts.

Touchette, P.E., & Howard, J.S. 1984. Errorless learning: Reinforcement contingencies and stimulus control transfer in delayed prompting. *Journal of Applied Behavior Analysis, 17*, 175–188.

Van Etten, G., Arkell, C., & Van Etten, C. 1980. *The severely and profoundly handicapped: Programs, methods, and materials*. St. Louis: C.V. Mosby.

Wacker, D.P., & Berg, W.K. 1983. Effects of picture prompts on the acquisition of complex vocational tasks by mentally retarded adolescents. *Journal of Applied Behavior Analysis, 16*, 417–433.

Walls, R.T., Zane, T., & Ellis, W.D. 1981. Forward chaining, backward chaining, and whole task methods for training assembly tasks. *Behavior Modification, 5*, 61–74.

Whaley, D.C., & Malott, R.W. 1971. *Elementary principles of behavior.* New York: Appleton-Century-Crofts.

Wilcox, B., & Bellamy, G.T. 1982. *Design of high school programs for severely handicapped students.* Baltimore: Paul H. Brookes.

CHAPTER 8

Arranging Consequences That Decrease Behavior

Did you know that . . .

- You can use positive reinforcement to get students to stop doing inappropriate things?
- It is easier to give than to implement advice to "ignore it and it will go away"?
- Students who are sent out in the hall often thoroughly enjoy themselves?
- Spanking can be positive reinforcement?
- The teacher who told you to "chew that gum until you are sick of it" was using a form of behavior modification?

When teachers complain about a student's misbehavior, other teachers usually offer sympathy and advice. Their suggestions often emphasize punishment, defined in their terms as applying an aversive stimulus following the inappropriate behavior—for example, a rap on the back of the head, reading the riot act, a ruler across the knuckles, or a prolonged visit to the principal where the student "will learn how this school is run." The use of punishment can become a reflex, because in terms of simply and immediately stopping the behavior, it works! Using punishment is thus negatively reinforcing to teachers. Using reinforcement, however, may make teachers lose sight of the side effects or reactions that may accompany the use of such procedures.

This chapter describes a broad range of behaviorally based alternatives to punishment that will have the same effect of reducing the occurrence of inappropriate behavior(s). These alternatives are presented as a sequenced hierarchy. The sequence moves from the most positive approaches for behavior reduction (those that use reinforcement strategies) to the most aversive approaches. To be sure, the use of aversive consequences is included within this hierarchy. However, due to professional considerations and awareness of the undesirable side effects that aversive stimuli produce, these approaches are at the bottom of the hierarchy. Indeed, in our hierarchy three levels of options are presented before aversive consequences are even mentioned. These alternatives, with their individual constraints, are presented as viable alternatives to punishment, as they too have the desired effect of reducing the occurrence of inappropriate behavior.

Certain principles should guide the selection of a procedure for behavior reduction. The first is the principle of the least intrusive alternative. This principle can be interpreted to mean that when selecting a procedure the teacher should determine, based on a hierarchy of procedures from the least intrusive to the most intrusive (or aversive), an effective procedure that is highest on the hierarchy. For example, if a Level I procedure, as shown in Figure 8–1 will accomplish the behavior change, it is neither necessary nor ethical to use a Level IV (or more aversive) procedure. In addition, Gast and Wolery (1987) suggest that "if the choice of treatments is between procedures that are equally effective, then the least aversive (intrusive) should be selected. If the choice is between a less intrusive but ineffective procedure and more aversive but effective procedure, then the effective procedure should be selected" (p. 194).

The second principle is the principle of the functional alternative, meaning that when any behavior is to be reduced or eliminated by any means, a functional, appropriate alternative should be simultaneously taught to take its place. A behavior is a functional alternative if it successfully serves the same function as the original behavior. For example, if the student's inappropriate behavior is a way of getting the teacher's attention, or of escaping from a difficult or confusing task, the behavior taught to take its place must be one that also gets the teacher's attention or results in escape from the difficult or confusing aspect of the task. So, instead of screaming, talking to a neighbor, or ripping up a worksheet, the student is taught to raise her hand,

FIGURE 8–1
Hierarchy of procedural alternatives for behavior reduction

Procedure of choice

Level I   Strategies of differential reinforcement

a. Differential reinforcement of low rates of behavior (DRL)
b. Differential reinforcement of other behavior(s) (DRO)
c. Differential reinforcement of incompatible behavior (DRI)
d. Differential reinforcement of alternative behavior(s) (DRA)

Level II   Extinction (terminating reinforcement)

Level III Removal of desirable stimuli

a. Response-cost procedures
b. Time-out procedures

Level IV Presentation of aversive stimuli

a. Unconditioned aversive stimuli
b. Conditioned aversive stimuli
c. Overcorrection procedures

or to come quietly to the teacher's desk. The new functional alternative behavior must result in at least the same amount of reinforcement.

Several requirements must be met in implementing procedures for behavior reduction. The first requirement is that movement along the hierarchy must be data-based. That is, before deciding that a currently employed procedure is not effective and that an alternative, possibly more intrusive, procedure should be used, the data collected during the intervention must substantiate the ineffectiveness of the procedure. The second requirement is that a point of consultation and permission must be established. That is, at some point along the hierarchy it is agreed that the teacher must consult with her supervisor, the student's parent, and/or a behavior management committee for review of the progress of the current intervention and agreement on a further plan of action. It is advisable to be sure that any aversive or intrusive procedure is described clearly and accurately in a disabled student's IEP, along with time limitations on its use and alternatives in case problems arise.

PROCEDURAL ALTERNATIVES FOR BEHAVIOR REDUCTION

The hierarchy outlined in Figure 8–1 has four levels of options for reducing inappropriate behaviors. Level I is the first choice to consider, while Level IV is, in most instances, the choice of last resort.

Level I offers four strategies using differential reinforcement: differential reinforcement of low rates of behavior, differential reinforcement of other behaviors, differential reinforcement of incompatible behaviors, and differential reinforcement of alternative behaviors. These are options of first choice, because, by selecting them, the teacher is employing a positive (reinforcement) approach to behavior reduction.

Level II refers to extinction procedures. Using extinction means withdrawing or no longer delivering the reinforcers that maintain some behavior.

Level III contains the first set of options using what will be defined as a punishing consequence. However, these options—such as response-cost and timeout procedures—still do not require the application of an aversive stimulus. The administration of these options may be seen as a mirror image of negative reinforcement. In the use of negative reinforcement, an aversive stimulus is contingently removed in order to increase a behavior. Level III options require removal of a desirable stimulus in order to decrease a behavior.

The options in Level IV of the hierarchy are to be selected after unsuccessful attempts at the first three levels have been documented or when the continuation of some behavior presents an imminent danger to the student or to others. The options at this level include the application of unconditioned or conditioned aversive stimuli or the use of an overcorrection procedure. Administration of these options may be seen as the mirror image of a reinforcement procedure.

Positive reinforcement: Stimulus is contingently *presented* to *increase* a behavior.

Presentation of aversive stimuli: *Aversive* stimulus is *presented* to *decrease* a behavior.

The following sections discuss procedures at each level in greater detail.

LEVEL I: STRATEGIES OF DIFFERENTIAL REINFORCEMENT
Differential Reinforcement of Lower Rates of Behavior

DRL schedules may be used when shaping behavior (see Chapter 7).

Differential reinforcement of lower rates of behavior (DRL) is the application of a specific schedule of reinforcement, used to decrease the rate of behaviors that, while tolerable or even desirable in low rates, are inappropriate when they occur too often or too rapidly. For example, contributing to a class discussion is a desirable behavior; dominating a class discussion is not. Doing math problems is appropriate; doing them so rapidly that careless errors occur is not. Burping occasionally, while hardly elegant, is tolerable; burping 25 times an hour is neither. For behaviors whose reduction is desirable, DRL schedules may be used to gradually decrease the rate of the behavior.

In the initial laboratory version of DRL, a reinforcer was delivered contingent on a response, provided that a minimum period of time had elapsed since the previous reinforced response. To decrease the total number of occurrences within a total time period, it is necessary only to increase the minimum period of time that must pass before another response will be reinforced. This format is referred to as *interresponse-time DRL* or *spaced-responding DRL*. This procedure was used by Singh, Dawson, and Manning (1981) to reduce stereotypic behaviors (rocking, mouthing, complex movements) of three adolescent girls who were profoundly retarded. The time required between occurrences was increased from 12 seconds to 180 seconds. The average percent of intervals of occurrence for the three girls went from 92.5% to 13%.

The DRL format more commonly used in the classroom provides for reinforcement delivery "when the number of responses in a specified period of time is less than, or equal to, a prescribed limit" (Deitz & Repp, 1973, p. 457). This DRL has two variations: full-session DRL and interval DRL.

Full-session DRL compares the total number of responses in an entire session with a present criterion. A reinforcer is delivered if occurrences are at or below that criterion. For example, baseline data indicate that Jenny interrupts on the average of nine times per 30-minute lesson. While not wanting to totally extinguish this behavior, the teacher wants it reduced to no more than two such interruptions per lesson. Jenny is told that she is allowed two interruptions; and if she keeps her interruptions to that level, she will be awarded an extra token for good behavior that day. If she keeps interruptions at or below two occurrences, the reinforcer is delivered. Interval DRL involves dividing a session into smaller intervals (for example, dividing the 30-minute session into six 5-minute intervals) and delivering reinforcement at the end of each interval in which responding is below or equal to a specified limit. This format may be used if the teacher believes that a more gradual approach will be more successful. If the maximum number of interruptions that can be tolerated is two per session, that number is initially allowed during each 5-minute interval. Once the behavior has stabilized, the length of the interval is increased, so that the student may interrupt, for example, only twice per 10-minute interval if she is to earn a reinforcer. The contingency might then be that to earn a reinforcer the student may interrupt twice in each of two 15-minute intervals. Finally, the student would be allowed only two interruptions during the full 30-minute session. These forms of the DRL procedure have been used to reduce a variety of behaviors, including talking-out (Deitz & Repp, 1974; Hall et al., 1971), out-of-seat behaviors (Harris & Sherman, 1973), self-stimulatory behavior (Rotholz & Luce, 1983), and eating rate (Lennox, Miltenberger, & Donnelly, 1987).

Finally, DRL may be arranged in a manner analogous to using a changing criterion design. If baseline levels of the target behavior are high, the teacher may successively lower DRL limits to bring the rate into an acceptable range. For example, if a student's baseline rate of out-of-seat behavior averaged 12 occurrences, he would be told that if during a lesson he got out of his seat no more than 9 times he would be allowed to select the day's free time activity.

Recall the changing criterion design discussed in Chapter 5.

Once he had stabilized at 9 occurrences, the contingency would be changed to no more than 6 times, then no more than 3 times. When using this approach the teacher must bear in mind when she tells a student he can do something 9 times, he will (and she must congratulate him!).

In their initial experiments in the use of DRL, Deitz and Repp (1973) employed both criterion-setting strategies. In the first, an 11-year-old boy with moderate retardation had a baseline of talkouts within a 50-minute session that averaged 5.7, with a range of 4 to 10 talk-outs per session. He was told that if he talked-out 3 or fewer times in a 50-minute session, he would be allowed 5 minutes of free playtime at the end of the day. During this intervention, he averaged 0.93 talk-outs per session with a range of 0 to 2.

In the second experiment, 10 students with moderate retardation had an average of 32.7 talk-outs with a range of 10 to 45. The students were told that if the group talked-out 5 or fewer times in a session, each person would get two pieces of candy. This intervention yielded an average of 3.13 talk-outs per session with a range of 1 to 6. In the third experiment, 15 high-school girls in a regular class demonstrated a baseline level of 6.6 instances of inappropriate social discussion during a 50-minute class period. The intervention was planned in four phases: 6 or fewer inappropriate discussions, 3 or fewer, 2 or fewer, and then a zero rate in order to earn a free period on Friday.

As a guide in the use of DRL scheduling, Repp and Deitz (1979, pp. 223–224) suggest the following:

1. Baseline must be recorded in order to determine the average number of responses per full session or session intervals. This average occurrence may then serve as the initial DRL limit.

2. Reasonably spaced criteria should be established when using successively decreasing DRL limits to avoid too frequent reinforcement and ratio strain, and so that the program can be faded out.

3. A decision must be made as to whether or not to provide feedback to the student(s) concerning the cumulative number of responses during the session.

See Chapter 6 for a discussion of the merits of reinforcement strategies.

The primary advantage of DRL scheduling is its peculiar ability to reduce the occurrence of the behavior through delivery of reinforcement. It therefore offers the same advantages of reinforcement in general. In addition, the approach is progressive, because it allows the student to adjust, in reasonable increments, to successively lower rates rather than making a drastic behavioral change. The limits chosen should be within the student's abilities and acceptable to the teacher. DRL is not a rapid means of changing behavior and therefore is inappropriate for use with violent or dangerous behavior.

Ms. Sinclair Teaches Stacy to Be Self-confident

Stacy was a student in Ms. Sinclair's second-grade class. Stacy had excellent academic skills but raised her hand constantly to ask, "Is this right?" or to say "I can't do this." If Ms. Sinclair had not been a behaviorist, she would have said that Stacy lacked self-confidence.

One morning, Ms. Sinclair called Stacy to her desk. She remembered that Stacy always volunteered to clean the blackboards after lunch. She told Stacy that she wanted her to learn to do her work herself.

"If you really need help," she assured Stacy, "I'll help you. But I think three times in one morning is enough. If you raise your hand for help three times or less this morning, you may clean the blackboards when we get back from lunch."

Stacy agreed to try. Within a few days, she was raising her hand only once or twice during the morning. Ms. Sinclair praised her enthusiastically for being so independent. The teacher noticed that Stacy often made comments like "I did this all by myself, Ms. Sinclair. I didn't need help once." If Ms. Sinclair had not been a behaviorist, she would have said that Stacy was developing self-confidence.

Differential Reinforcement of Other Behaviors

When using the procedure called **differential reinforcement of other behaviors (DRO)**, a reinforcing stimulus is delivered contingent on the target behavior's not being emitted for a specified period of time (Reynolds, 1961). Whereas DRL reinforces gradual behavior reduction, DRO reinforces only zero occurrences. In fact, DRO is sometimes referred to as *differential reinforcement of zero rates of behavior*, or *differential reinforcement of the omission of behavior*. In Chapter 6, reinforcement was defined as the delivery of a reinforcing stimulus contingent on the occurrence of a desired behavior. DRO involves the presentation of a reinforcing stimulus contingent on the nonoccurrence of a behavior.

DRO may have at least three administrative variations, similar to those used with DRL procedures:

1. Reinforcement contingent on the nonoccurrence of a behavior throughout a specified time period. For example, reinforcement is delivered only if talking-out does not occur for an entire 40-minute period (DRO 40 minutes). The student is told, "If you do not talk-out during this reading period (40 minutes long), then you may be one of the captains in the gym this afternoon." If the student meets this contingency she receives the reinforcer. Scheduling reinforcement delivery only after no instances of the behavior occur during an entire session is called full-session DRO.

2. Reinforcement contingent on the nonoccurrence of a behavior within a time period that has been divided into smaller intervals. This procedure is used when a more gradual reduction of inappropriate behavior is more practical or realistic. In some cases of very high rates of inappropriate behavior, implementation of a full-session DRO would mean that the student would never earn a reinforcer. A 40-minute session may be divided into 5-minute intervals and reinforcement delivered at the end of each 5-

minute interval in which the student has not talked-out. This breaking down of the time period provides the student an increased number of opportunities for reinforcement, an increased amount of feedback, and an increased number of opportunities for success. The intervals may be of equal length or they may be of different lengths (that is, on the average of every 5 minutes, as is done in variable-interval scheduling). Once the student can control his behavior for these smaller intervals, the teacher increases the length of the intervals. For example, the schedule of eight 5-minute intervals is changed to four 10-minute intervals. This process continues to the point that the contingency can be met for the entire 40 minutes, the equivalent of a full-session DRO. If the teacher is having difficulty establishing the initial length of intervals, Deitz and Repp (1983) suggest using the average length of the target behavior (interresponse interval). For example, if during 100 minutes of baseline (five 20-minute sessions) Luke got out of his chair 25 times, the teacher would begin with intervals of 4 minutes or less (100 divided by 25). As an alternative, the initial interval may be set equal to the average amount of time between behaviors during baseline sessions (Repp, Felce, & Barton, 1991).

3. DRO may be used with permanent-product data. For example, the teacher may draw a happy face on every paper that does not contain doodles.

Three important factors should be considered before a teacher implements a DRO procedure. First, a "pure" DRO requires that reinforcement be delivered if the student does not perform the target behavior, no matter what else he does. In effect, the student may be positively reinforced for performing a wide range of inappropriate behaviors, as long as he doesn't perform the target behavior. Some students will take advantage of this loophole. They may not walk around the room but may instead, throw spitballs, something they have never done before. Technically, they would still be entitled to reinforcers. For practical classroom management this cannot be allowed to happen. For this reason, DRO procedures are sometimes used in conjunction with other reduction procedures for such interfering behaviors. Sometimes, also, occurrences of the target behavior may be followed by some consequence rather than ignored as in the traditional procedure (Vollmer & Iwata, 1992).

Second, DRO reinforces the absence of a behavior. The student earns the reinforcer if the target behavior does not occur during the specified time period. For students who do not have a large repertoire of appropriate behaviors, the teacher may be creating a behavior vacuum. If a behavior is not identified to replace the targeted one, the student may soon fill that vacuum with the only behavior he knows, the one the teacher tried to reduce. It is practical and ethical to identify an appropriate behavior to replace the inappropriate one and to positively reinforce its occurrence.

Third, the effectiveness of a DRO procedure may depend on the reinforcer selected (Repp, Felce, & Barton, 1991). The stimulus used to reinforce the student for not engaging in the inappropriate behavior must be of at least equal strength or motivating value as that which is currently maintaining the behavior. When one is teaching a student a new skill there is probably not a reinforcer in place that is working against his learning the new skill. However, when one is trying to reduce a student's inappropriate behavior there is, whether it can easily be identified or not, some reinforcer maintaining the inappropriate behavior. If the stimulus offered the student for not engaging in a behavior for a specific period of time is not as strong or motivating as the one maintaining it, the procedure will be ineffective. For example, if the student is clowning around during math class he may be getting reinforcement from the laughs of his peers and their attention during lunch. If you set a DRO contingency so that he may earn five minutes at the computer for not clowning this may not be as powerful as the reinforcement he gets from his peers.

DRO has been used with a variety of behaviors, such as self-injurious behavior (Repp, Deitz, & Speir, 1974; Rose, 1979), pinching (Friman, Bernard, Altman, & Wolf, 1986), exhibitionism (Lutzker, 1974), disruptions (Repp, Deitz, & Deitz, 1976), stereotypic behavior (Barrett, Matson, Shapiro, & Ollendick, 1981; Barton, Brulle, & Repp, 1986), and off-task and out-of-seat behaviors (Repp, Barton, & Brulle, 1983). Repp, Deitz, and Speir (1974) used DRO procedures with three individuals with severe retardation. The individuals were a 12-year-old girl whose target behavior was flapping her lips with her fingers, a 22-year-old woman whose target behavior was rocking, and a 23-year-old man whose target behavior was waving a hand in front of his eyes. A kitchen timer was set to a prescheduled number of minutes (the DRO interval). The student who did not emit the target stereotypic response during the interval was hugged and praised by the teacher when the bell rang. If the target stereotypic behavior occurred, the teacher said "no" and reset the timer. Very short intervals (40 seconds) were used initially. As the rates of behavior decreased, the intervals lengthened. All the subjects showed greatly decreased rates of stereotypic behaviors.

As a guide to the use of DRO scheduling, Repp and Deitz (1979, pp. 222–223) suggest:

1. Baseline must be recorded not only to measure the inappropriate behavior, but also to schedule the DRO procedure properly. Because the size of the initial DRO interval can be crucial, it should be based on data rather than set arbitrarily. From the baseline an average interresponse time (time between responses) should be determined, and a slightly smaller interval should be designated as the initial DRO interval.

2. Criteria must be established for increasing the length of the DRO interval. The basic idea is

   a. to start at a small enough interval that the student can earn more reinforcers for not responding than he could earn for responding, and

   b. to lengthen that interval over time. The decision to lengthen should be based on the success of the student at each interval length.

3. Possible occurrence of the undesirable behavior necessitates two additional decisions:

   a. whether to reset the DRO interval following a response occurrence or merely to wait for the next scheduled interval, and

   b. whether to consequate a response occurrence in any other way or just to ignore it.

4. Reinforcement should not be delivered immediately following a grossly inappropriate behavior even if the DRO interval has expired without the target response having occurred.

Clarence Learns Not to Hit People

Clarence was a student in Mr. Byrd's resource class. He often hit other students in the class, usually because someone had touched some possession of his. Having observed that Clarence hit someone an average of 12 times during the 90-minute resource period, for an average interresponse time of 7.5 minutes, Mr. Byrd chose an interval of 7 minutes. He told Clarence that he could earn a card worth 5 minutes to work on an art project for each 7 minutes that elapsed without hitting. When Clarence hit someone, Mr. Byrd reset the timer. He did this rather than simply not delivering the reinforcer at the end of the interval, because he was afraid that once Clarence had "blown it," he would engage in a veritable orgy of hitting until the end of the interval.

Within a few days, Clarence's hitting rate was much lower, so Mr. Byrd lengthened the intervals to 8 minutes, then 10, then 15. Soon he was able to reinforce the absence of hitting at the end of the period and still maintain a zero rate.

Differential Reinforcement of Incompatible Behaviors and Alternative Behaviors

One excellent way to prevent creating a behavior vacuum using DRO is to use **differential reinforcement of incompatible behavior (DRI)** or **differential reinforcement of alternative behavior (DRA)**. This automatically introduces the **functional alternative** described above. DRI is a procedure that involves reinforcing a topographically incompatible behavior with the behavior targeted for reduction. For example, if out-of-seat behavior is targeted for reduction, in-seat behavior is reinforced because these two behaviors cannot occur simultaneously. Mutually exclusive responses are chosen so that an appropriate response makes it physically impossible for the student to engage in the inappropriate behavior. This allows for increasing the strength and/or rate of the desirable behavior and decreasing the probability of the undesirable behavior. Reinforcing a child's play with a particular toy, and her play skills in general, decreases the opportunity and probability of her engaging in stereotypic hand movements (Favell, 1973).

When her hands are appropriately occupied, she cannot engage in the inappropriate behavior.

As with DRI, DRA reinforces the occurrence of a behavior that is an alternative to the behavior targeted for reduction (Deitz & Repp, 1983). With this procedure, however, the alternative behavior and the inappropriate behavior are topographically dissimilar, but not necessarily physically incompatible (Vollmer & Iwata, 1992). Each time the student attempts the inappropriate behavior she is redirected to performance of the alternative behavior, which is then reinforced. For example, each time Anne begins to talk-out to get her teacher's attention she is redirected to raise her hand; she is reinforced by being called on and receiving praise from the teacher. In some instances the DRA (or DRI) is combined with a mild punisher (for example, a mild reprimand or the loss of a token) for the continued use of the inappropriate behavior (Luiselli, 1980).

Certain criteria should be considered when selecting an incompatible or alternative behavior.

1. The efficiency of replacement is enhanced if a behavior already in the student's repertoire is selected (Deitz & Repp, 1983). If the student already knows how to perform the behavior, she is not simultaneously engaged in learning a new behavior and learning to replace an inappropriate behavior. Finding a behavior already in the student's repertoire is difficult with students whose existing repertoire of appropriate behaviors is limited, but the attempt should be made.

2. The teacher should analyze the inappropriate behavior to determine if it serves an environmentally relevant function for the student. If it does, then the behavior to replace it should be a more standard or appropriate behavior that fulfills that function. For example, instances of self-injurious and other aggressive behaviors have been found to serve a communicative function. If this is determined, then a communicative behavior to indicate the desire for attention or some object should be substituted (Durand & Carr, 1987; Durand & Kishi, 1987).

3. The behavior selected as the alternative should access the relevant reinforcer frequently, consistently, with less effort, and with as short a delay as did the original behavior. It should eventually be maintained by natural reinforcers (Carr, Robinson, & Palumbo, 1990; Matlock, Billingsley, & Thompson, 1985).

Differential reinforcement of incompatible and alternative behaviors has been employed to modify a variety of behaviors: sleeping in class (Repp, Deitz, & Deitz, 1976), classroom disruption (Ayllon, Layman, & Burke, 1972), hyperactivity (Patterson, 1965; Twardosz & Sajwaj, 1972), inappropriate speech (Barton, 1970), stereotypic behaviors (Baumeister & Forehand, 1971; Favell, 1973; Weisberg, Passman, & Russell, 1973), aggressive behavior (Vukelich & Hake, 1971), and self-injurious behavior (Tarpley & Schroeder, 1979).

Ayllon and Roberts (1974) used differential reinforcement to bring the disruptive (out-of-seat, talking, hitting) behaviors of five fifth-grade boys under control by reinforcing their academic performance. Points for daily and weekly exchange were made contingent on the percentage of correct answers in their reading workbooks during daily 15-minute sessions. This time period was selected because it was impossible to accurately complete the assignment (thus gaining access to the list of highly desirable back-up reinforcers) and engage in disruptive behaviors. During baseline, the mean percentages for both disruptive behavior and academic accuracy were in the 40% to 50% range. After intervention, disruptive behavior had decreased to an average of 5% of the intervals and average academic accuracy had increased to 85%.

As a guide to the use of DRI scheduling, Repp and Deitz (1979, p. 224) suggest:

1. A behavior that is incompatible to the undesirable behavior must be chosen. If there is no appropriate behavior that is opposite to the inappropriate behavior, then a behavior that is beneficial to the student should be selected and should be reinforced.
2. Baseline should be recorded to determine
   a. how often the inappropriate behavior occurs, and
   b. how often the chosen incompatible behavior occurs.
3. The schedule of reinforcement must be determined. In addition, a program for carefully thinning the schedule should be written so that the program can be phased out and the student's behaviors can come under control of natural contingencies in the environment.

Figure 8–2 summarizes and compares various options for differential reinforcement.

Ms. Elliott in the Community

Toni and Jake's mothers asked that trips to stores be included in their community-based instruction. When they took their children to stores the children would take items from shelves and throw them on the floor or themselves drop to the floor and scream. During her first trip with the two students Ms. Elliott found that this indeed occurred. She understood the parents' frustration and embarrassment. As alternative behaviors, Ms. Elliott decided to reinforce Toni for holding onto the shopping cart while pushing it down the aisles, and to reinforce Jake for holding a basket on his lap as he sat in his wheelchair. As she came to various items she would give the students opportunities to identify the correct item from two she held up, asking them to choose the "red" box or the "bottle" or the "little one" and then guiding them into placing the items in either the cart or the

FIGURE 8–2

Summary of differential reinforcement procedures

	Purpose	Formats	Management	Provides for reinforcement of alternative behavior	Objective
DRL[1]	Reduce behavior to acceptable level	Full-session Interval Changing criterion Spaced-responding	Focus on reducing number of occurrences	No	Tom will talk-out no more than 3 times in 40 minutes.
DRO[2]	Reduce behavior to zero occurrences	Full-session Interval Permanent product	Focus on increasing time of nonoccurrence	No	Tom will have no occurrence of talking-out in a 40-minute period.
DRI[3] DRA[4]	Reinforce a functional alternative behavior	Concurrent reduction and strengthening programming	Focus on developing functional alternative behavior	Yes	Tom will press a buzzer to indicate he wants the attention of an adult instead of engaging in yelling and face-slapping.

[1]Differential reinforcement of lower rates of behavior
[2]Differential reinforcement of other behaviors (or of zero rates of behavior, or of omission of behavior)
[3]Differential reinforcement of incompatible behavior
[4]Differential reinforcement of alternative behavior

basket. Once the students' behavior was consistently appropriate, Toni's mother was invited to come on a shopping trip to see how the procedure was done. Jake's mother, who was unavailable during school hours, received a video tape made during one of the shopping trips.

LEVEL II: EXTINCTION

In contrast to Level I, which focuses on providing reinforcement, Level II, **extinction**, reduces behavior by abruptly withdrawing or terminating the positive reinforcer that maintains an inappropriate target behavior. As mentioned in Chapter 6, this abrupt withdrawal results in the cessation or extinction of behavior. When the behavior being maintained is an appropriate one, preventing extinction is the goal. Many inappropriate behaviors, however, are also maintained by positive reinforcement. A parent who gives children cookies or candy when they cry may be positively reinforcing crying. If the cookies are withdrawn, crying should diminish.

Extinction is most often used in the classroom to decrease behaviors that are being maintained by teacher attention. Teachers often pay attention to students who are behaving inappropriately, and many students find such attention positively reinforcing. This may be true even if the attention takes the form of criticism, correction, or threats. Some students' behavior may be positively reinforced by even such extreme measures as yelling and spanking.

It is often difficult for teachers to determine when their attention is positively reinforcing inappropriate behavior. Thus, a teacher may find it helpful to have someone else observe the teacher-student interaction. Once the relationship between the teacher's attention and the student's behavior is verified by this method, extinction in the classroom most often takes the form of ignoring inappropriate behavior. The teacher withholds the previously given positive reinforcer (attention), and the inappropriate behavior extinguishes or dies out.

Extinction procedures have been used with a variety of behaviors: for example, disruptive classroom behavior (Zimmerman & Zimmerman, 1962), aggressive behavior (Brown & Elliott, 1965), tantrums (Carlson, Arnold, Becker, & Madsen, 1968), nonstudy behavior (Hall, Lund, & Jackson, 1968), and delusional speech (Liberman, Teigen, Patterson, & Baker, 1973).

Extinction is most often used in conjunction with reinforcing other more appropriate behaviors. Combining procedures this way appears to speed extinction (Scott, Burton, & Yarrow, 1967; Wilson & Hopkins, 1973). When extinction is used independently, "there is little or no evidence of constructive learning. What is learned is that a certain behavior no longer provides an expected reward; the net effect is a reduction in the repertoire of behavior" (Gilbert, 1975, p. 28). If attention is given to appropriate behavior, this indicates to the student that the teacher's attention (S^{R+}) is still available, but that it is selectively available. It is not the student who is being ignored, just the inappropriate behavior.

"Just ignore it and it will go away. He's only doing it for attention." This statement is one of the most common suggestions given to teachers. In truth, extinction is much easier to discuss than to implement. It *will* go away, all right, but not necessarily rapidly or smoothly. Whatever "it" is, the teacher who decides to implement an extinction procedure should give careful consideration to the following points.

Delayed Reaction

Problems with extinction

The effects of extinction are not usually immediate. The extinction procedure may take considerable time to produce reduction in behavior. Once reinforcement is withheld, behavior continues for an indeterminate amount of time (Skinner, 1953). This characteristic, known as *resistance to extinction*, is particularly marked when behaviors have been maintained on intermittent reinforcement schedules. The student continues to seek the reinforcer that a history of reinforcement has taught her or him will be the result. In an initial extinction phase to reduce aggressive behavior toward peers in a preschooler, Pinkston, Reese, LeBlanc, and Baer (1973) found it took eight days to reduce the rate of behavior from 28% of total peer interactions to 6% of interactions. In a study of the effects of self-injurious behavior, Lovaas and Simmons (1969) report that "John hit himself almost 9,000 times before he quit" (p. 146).

Increased Rate

The teacher should expect an increase in the rate and/or intensity of the behavior before significant reduction occurs (Watson, 1967). It's going to get worse, in other words, before it gets better. In comments on one subject, Lovaas and Simmons (1969) state, "Rick eventually did stop hitting himself under this arrangement (i.e., extinction) but the reduction in self-destruction was not immediate, and even took a turn for the worse when the extinction was first initiated" (p. 146). About John and Gregg, two other subjects, they acknowledge that "the self-destructive behavior showed a very gradual drop over time, being particularly vicious in the early stages of extinction" (p. 147). Figure 8–3 displays this phenomenon in graphic data from Lovaas and Simmons (1969) and Pinkston et al. (1973).

A common pattern is that of the teacher who decides to ignore some inappropriate behavior such as calling out. When a student finds a previously reinforced response is no longer effective, the student then begins to call out louder and faster. If, after a period of time, the teacher says, "Oh, all right, Ward, what do you want?" the teacher has reinforced the behavior at its new level of intensity and may find that it remains at this level. Once an extinction procedure has been implemented, the teacher absolutely must continue ignoring whatever escalation of the behavior occurs.

Controlling Attention

It is ridiculous to say to a student, "Can't you see I'm ignoring you?" Of course, what the student *can* see is that the teacher is *not* ignoring her. Even nonverbal indications that the teacher is aware of the misbehavior may be sufficient to prevent extinction. The teacher who stands rigidly with teeth and fists clenched is communicating continued attention to the student's behavior. It takes a great deal of practice to hit just the right note. We have found that it helps to have something else to do.

FIGURE 8–3
Data from studies using extinction procedures for behavior reduction

Note (top): From "Manipulation of self-destruction in three retarded children," by O. I. Lovaas & J. Q. Simmons, Journal of Applied Behavior Analysis, 1969. Copyright 1969 by the Society for the Experimental Analysis of Behavior, Inc. Reprinted by permission.

Note (bottom): From "Independent control of a preschool child's aggression and peer interaction by contingent teacher attention," by E. M. Pinkston, N. M. Reese, J. M. LeBlanc, & D. M. Baer, Journal of Applied Behavior Analysis, 1973. Copyright 1973 by the Society for the Experimental Analysis of Behavior, Inc. Reprinted by permission.

1. Become *very* involved with another student—perhaps praising the absence of the target behavior in her—"I like the way you raised your hand, Lou; that's the *right* way to get my attention."
2. Read something or write busily.
3. Recite epic poetry subvocally.
4. Carry a worry rock or beads.
5. Stand outside the classroom door and kick the wall for a minute.

Extinction-Induced Aggression

The last suggestion in the preceding section is related to another phenomenon that may occur: extinction-induced aggression by the student in the early stages of extinction procedures (Azrin, Hutchinson, & Hake, 1966). In search of the previously available reinforcer, the student says, in effect, "You only think you can ignore me. Watch this trick." The pattern of escalation and aggression that occurs in the early stages of extinction is illustrated by a typical interaction between a hungry customer and a defective vending machine. The customer puts two quarters in the machine (a previously reinforced response) and pushes the appropriate button. When no reinforcer is forthcoming, the customer pushes the button again . . . and again . . . and faster . . . and harder. Before her response is extinguished, she is likely to deliver a sharp rap or swift kick to the unreinforcing machine.

Spontaneous Recovery

Teachers can also expect the possible reappearance of an extinguished behavior. This phenomenon is known as *spontaneous recovery* (Skinner, 1953) and may occur after the behavior has been extinguished for some time. The student tries once again to see if the extinction rule is still in effect. Such reemergence of the behavior can be quickly terminated by ignoring it. Failure to ignore it, however, may result in rapid relearning on the part of the student.

Imitation or Reinforcement by Others

The behavior the teacher is ignoring may spread to other class members. If other students see a particular student getting away with a misbehavior, that he is not being punished for it, they may imitate the behavior (Bandura, 1965). This may serve to reinforce the behavior. It may also result in a number of students' performing a misbehavior instead of just one, making the behavior that much harder to ignore. The use of an extinction procedure relies on the teacher's ability to terminate the reinforcing stimulus for the inappropriate behavior. This is one of the hardest aspects of conducting an extinction procedure. In a classroom setting, the best bet is that the behavior is being reinforced by attention from the teacher (yelling) or from the classmates (laughing). To determine the reinforcing stimulus, the teacher may have to test several suspicions systematically, attempting to eliminate one potential reinforcer at a time.

It is frequently difficult to control the reinforcing consequences delivered by peers. Successful approaches to this problem have been used by Patterson (1965), who reinforced peers for withholding attention when the target student was out-of-seat, talking, or hitting others; by Solomon and Wahler (1973), who selected five high-status peers and trained them in the use of extinction and reinforcement of appropriate behavior; and by Pinkston et al. (1973), who attended to the peer being aggressed against while the aggressor was ignored.

Limited Generalizability

Although extinction is effective, it appears to have limited generalizability. That is, the behavior may occur just as frequently in settings where extinction is not in effect. Liberman and his colleagues (1973) reported no generalization of treatment to routine interchanges with staff on the ward. Lovaas and Simmons (1969) reported that behavior in other settings is unaffected when extinction is used only in one setting. Extinction may be required in all necessary environmental settings.

Benoit and Mayer (1974) suggest six considerations before making a decision to use extinction, here stated as questions to guide teachers' decision making:

Questions to ask yourself before implementing an extinction procedure

1. Can the behavior be tolerated temporarily based on its topography (for example, is it aggressive?) and on its current rate of occurrence?
2. Can an increase in the behavior be tolerated?
3. Is the behavior likely to be imitated?
4. Are the reinforcers known?
5. Can reinforcement be withheld?
6. Have alternative behaviors been identified for reinforcement?

A social consequence such as teacher attention is not always the maintaining consequence of a behavior. "Some persons do things not for attention or praise, but simply because it feels good or is fun to do" (Rincover, 1981, p. 1). In such instances sensory consequences rather than teacher consequences may be maintaining the behavior. This seems to be particularly true of certain stereotypic or self-injurious behaviors. A student's stereotypic hand flapping may be maintained by the visual input resulting from the behavior. A student's self-injurious, self-scratching may be maintained by the tactile input resulting from the behavior. When sensory consequences can be identified as the reinforcer of a behavior, the form of extinction known as *sensory extinction* may be employed (Rincover, 1981). Sensory extinction attempts to remove the naturally occurring sensory consequence of the behavior rather than directly preventing the behavior itself. The hand flapping may be reduced by placing weights on the student's arm, thereby making hand flapping more work, reducing its frequency, and fading the reinforcer (Rincover, 1981; Van Houten, 1993). Self-scratching may be reduced by covering the area with heavy petroleum jelly, thereby eliminating the tactile consequence of the behavior. Difficulties arise in using sensory extinction with precision due to difficulty identifying the sensory consequence (if there is one) and the difficulty eliminating "all the sensory consequences inherent in many commonly occurring stereotypic responses, such as rocking or clapping" (Aiken & Salzberg, 1984, p. 298).

Mr. Medlock Extinguishes Arguing

Judy was a student in Mr. Medlock's fourth-grade class. Whenever Mr. Medlock told Judy to do something, she argued with him. Mr. Medlock had found himself having conversations like this:

"Judy, get to work."

"I am working, Mr. Medlock."

"No you're not, Judy. You're wasting time."

"I'm getting ready to work."

"I don't want you to get ready. I want you to do it."

"How do you expect me to work if I don't get ready?"

He realized one day that he was having childish arguments with a 9-year-old and that his behavior was reinforcing Judy's arguing. He decided to put this behavior on extinction. The next day he said, "Judy, get to work." When Judy began to argue that she was working, he walked away.

Judy muttered to herself for a while and then said loudly, "I ain't gonna do this dumb work, and you can't make me." Mr. Medlock held on and continued to ignore her comments.

Emily raised her hand. "Mr. Medlock," she simpered, "Judy says she's not going to do her work."

"Emily," said Mr. Medlock quietly, "take care of yourself."

"But, Mr. Medlock, she said you can't make her," countered Emily.

Mr. Medlock realized that his only hope was to ignore Emily's behavior too. He got up and began to walk around the room, praising students who were working and reminding them of the math game they were going to play when the work was finished. Soon Emily went back to her work. Judy, however, began to tap her pencil ostentatiously on her desk. Mr. Medlock continued to interact with other students. Judy finally shrugged and began to do her assignment. When she had been working for several minutes, Mr. Medlock walked casually over to her and said, "Good job, Judy. You've already got the first two right. Keep it up."

It occurred to Mr. Medlock that Judy's delay in starting to do her work was probably reinforced by his nagging and that if he ignored her procrastination as well, Judy would probably begin to work more quickly.

A group of investigators has examined the use of extinction through manipulation of what is known about reinforcement schedules. In Chapter 6 we noted that once new behaviors are well-established we move from continuous to intermittent schedules of reinforcement so that behaviors become more resistant to extinction (Ferster & Skinner, 1957). The investigators wondered if inappropriate behaviors being maintained by occasional (intermittent) reinforcement would become easier to extinguish if reinforcement temporarily was delivered continuously. Many inappropriate behaviors may be maintained by teachers or parents who reinforce the behavior during occasional moments of weakness.

Ms. Troutman's Moment of Weakness

Ms. Troutman, a teacher and parent, picked her children up at day care after her work at school was done. Her 2-year-old son always asked for a p-bo-jelly as soon as they got home. She explained that it was too close to dinner time for peanut butter and jelly sandwiches. He fell to the floor and screamed. She ignored him. This pattern was repeated daily, often several times. One afternoon her 7-year-old daughter, over the sound of screaming, explained that when Ms. Troutman had an especially hard day at school, she occasionally went ahead and fixed him a sandwich in order to avoid the tantrums and that's why he kept asking and screaming. Ms. Troutman, albeit not graciously, was forced to acknowledge the correctness of the fledgling behaviorist's analysis.

Neisworth, Hunt, Gallop, and Nadle (1985) investigated the efficacy of this procedure with two 19-year-old students with severe mental retardation. One student engaged in stereotypic hand flapping and one in finger flicking. "During the CRF phase of treatment, the trainer delivered a reinforcer each time the participant emitted the target behavior. During the EXT phase of treatment, the reinforcer was, of course, no longer available to the participant" (p. 105). For both students the stereotypic behaviors were reduced to near zero levels. This remained so for one of the students at a two-week follow-up, while the other student's behavior returned to baseline levels. As noted by the authors, though the effects on behaviors "run close to textbook illustrations and laboratory demonstrations" (p. 111), this is a preliminary study. In addition, the necessity to increase a behavior's rate makes the selection of an appropriate target behavior an ethical question. (This study was replicated with laboratory animals by Wylie & Grossman in 1988).

PUNISHMENT

The two remaining levels of the hierarchy, Levels III and IV, contain options for behavior reduction that may be termed *punishment*. As is the case with the term **reinforcer**, we use a functional definition of the term **punisher**. A punisher is a consequent stimulus (S^P) that

1. decreases the future rate and/or probability of occurrence of behavior.

2. is administered contingently on the production of the undesired or inappropriate behavior.

3. is administered immediately following the production of the undesired or inappropriate behavior.

It must be clearly understood that the terms *punishment* and *punisher* as used in this context are defined functionally. Any stimulus can be labeled a punisher if its contingent application results in a reduction of the target behavior. *A punisher, like a reinforcer, can be identified only by its effect on behavior—not on the nature of the consequent stimulus.* For example, if a father paddles his son for throwing toys, and the son stops throwing toys, then the paddling *was* a punisher. If the son continues to throw toys, then the paddling *was not* a punisher. If each time a student talks-out, her teacher reduces her free playtime by one minute or takes tokens away and this results in the reduction or cessation of the talking-out, then the consequence was a punisher. If the behavior continues, the consequence was not a punisher. Again, this is a definition of the term *punisher* from a functional perspective.

Punishers, like reinforcers, may also be naturally occurring phenomena. Punishers are not simply techniques devised by malevolent behaviorists to work their will on students. Consider the examples and label the punishers:

Jeannie toddles into the kitchen while her father is cooking dinner. As her father's back is turned, Jeannie reaches up and touches the saucepan on the front burner. She jerks her hand away crying and thereafter avoids touching the stove.

Theresa has finished her math assignment quickly. Proudly, she raises her hand and announces this fact to her teacher. The teacher assigns her 10 additional problems to work. The next day Theresa works more slowly and fails to finish her assignment before the end of math class.

Gary is mainstreamed. On the first day that he attends Mr. Johnston's fourth-grade reading class, he stumbles through the oral reading passage. The other students ridicule him and he subsequently refuses to leave the special class to attend the fourth grade.

Mrs. Brice, a first-year teacher, decides to use praise with her junior-high social studies class. She greets each student who arrives on time with effusive compliments and a happy face sticker. The next day no students arrive on time.

LEVEL III: REMOVAL OF DESIRABLE STIMULI
Response-Cost Procedures

Response cost attempts to reduce behavior through removal of a reinforcer. The procedure itself may be defined as the withdrawal of specific amounts of reinforcer contingent on inappropriate behavior. As implied by this definition, "some level of positive reinforcement must be made available in order to provide the opportunity for . . . withdrawing that reinforcement" (Azrin & Holz, 1966, p. 392). If the use of a response-cost procedure empirically results in the desired behavior reduction, withdrawal of the reinforcement functions as a punisher.

Response-cost may be seen as a system of leveling fines, a familiar event. A city government has, as a means of behavior control and fund raising, a whole system of fines for predefined, inappropriate behavior. We, the citizens, have possession of the pool of reinforcers—the dollar bills we have earned. The city administration withdraws specific amounts of these reinforcing stimuli contingent on such inappropriate behaviors as littering, staying too long at a parking meter, and speeding. Similarly, McSweeny (1978) reported the number of directory assistance phone calls made in Cincinnati decreased significantly when a charge for these calls was instituted. Marholin and Gray (1976) found that when cash shortages were subtracted from employees' salaries the size of shortages was sharply reduced.

A token system can incorporate response-cost procedures. If a teacher informs students they will earn one token for each of 10 math problems they solve correctly, that teacher is employing a token reinforcement system. If, on the other hand, the teacher hands out 10 tokens to each student and informs them that, for each problem they solve incorrectly, one token will be "repossessed," that teacher is employing a response-cost procedure. In practice, a response-cost procedure is most often (Kazdin & Bootzin, 1972) and effectively (Phillips, Phillips, Fixsen, & Wolf, 1971) used in combination with a token reinforcement system. In such a combined format, the students concurrently earn the pool of reinforcers and lose the reinforcers as fines for misbehavior. The students have ongoing access to future reinforcers.

In classrooms, response-cost procedures have been shown to have great versatility, without the undesirable side effects usually associated with punishment (Kazdin, 1972). They have been used in modifying social behaviors such as rule violation, off-task behavior, and hyperactivity (DuPaul, Guevremont, & Barkley, 1992; Rapport, Murphy, & Bailey, 1982; Salend, 1988); aggressive behavior (Dougherty, Fowler, & Paine, 1985; Walker, Hops, & Fiegenbaum, 1976); disruptive classroom behaviors (Proctor & Morgan, 1991); disruptive and obscene vocalizations (Trice & Parker, 1983); and food scavenging (Smith, Piersel, Filbeck, & Gross, 1983). They have also been used to improve academic performance like completion of math problems (Iwata & Bailey, 1974) and vocational training activities in community settings (Rusch, Connis, & Sowers, 1978). The response-cost contingency has been enforced by both adults and peers (Dougherty, Fowler, & Paine, 1985). This procedure has been used to manage groups of students, as well as individuals (Mowrer & Conley, 1987; Salend & Kovalich, 1981). Salend and Lamb (1986) divided a class of students with learning disabilities into two groups during their reading periods. At the beginning of each period each group was given a preset number of tokens. Each time a group member made an inappropriate verbalization, a token was removed from the group's pool. Within a reversal design, the number of inappropriate verbalizations decreased from a mean of 50 during baseline, to a mean of 4.2 during the first intervention period, and from a mean of 34.8 to a mean of 2.9 during the second intervention period.

Problems with response cost

There are a number of practical cautions in the use of a response-cost procedure. First, the teacher must have the ability to withdraw the reinforcer once given. It is probably unwise to attempt to use response-cost procedures with edible primary reinforcers. The student who has at his desk a cup of candies that are to be contingently withdrawn is apt immediately to eat all the candy as his first inappropriate behavior. The slight young teacher in the secondary classroom who walks over to the football tackle and announces that he is to return five tokens may find that the student answers, "In a pig's eye" (or something to that effect). It is best in such an instance to use points, which can be withdrawn without being physically repossessed.

Careful consideration must also be given to the magnitude of the penalties—the number of tokens or points being withdrawn. Research has produced mixed recommendations. For example, Burchard and Barrera (1972) used severe fines, whereas Siegel, Lenske, and Broen (1969) used mild fines; both got good results. An important point to remember is that exacting large fines may make tokens worthless. If students learn an entire day's work can be wiped out by a fine, they are unlikely to work very hard.

Another problem may occur when all the reinforcers have been withdrawn. Then what happens? Consider, for example, the substitute teacher who is assigned to a ninth-grade remedial class for the day. One of the thoughts uppermost in her mind, in addition to the educational welfare of her temporary charges, is making it in one piece to lunchtime. When the students enter the room, she announces that if they cooperate and work hard during the morning hours, she will permit them 30 minutes of free time. If she fines them five minutes whenever anyone misbehaves, by 10 o'clock the students may have very little free time left. Once the reinforcement system has become debased to this extent, the student energy involved in being good far outweighs the remaining amount of the reinforcer.

When using response-cost, as with all management systems, students must clearly understand the rules of behavior and the penalties for infractions. Clear understanding will avoid lengthy conversations at the time of misbehavior, when the teacher should simply have to describe the infraction and exact the fine.

Before selecting a response-cost procedure, the teacher should answer the following questions:

Guide to setting up a response-cost procedure

1. Have more positive procedures, such as differential reinforcement strategies, been considered?
2. Does the student currently have, or have access to, a pool of reinforcers?
3. Have the rules of appropriate behavior and the results (fines) for infractions been clearly explained and understood?
4. Has the ratio of the size of the fine to each instance of misbehavior been thought out?
5. Can the reinforcers be retrieved?

6. Will appropriate behavior be reinforced in conjunction with the use of response-cost?

Response-Cost Coupons

In order to make a response-cost system more concrete for her class of six- and seven-year-olds, Ms. Calabash decided to use pictorial coupons as tokens. Before leaving the classroom and entering the community, the four children were given five coupons each to keep in their waist-packs. Four of the coupons had a picture of an item they could acquire while on their trip (i.e., a soft drink, a yogurt cone, a picture of a bus seat meaning they could choose who to sit next to, and a picture of the store where they could buy something). The fifth coupon had a picture of an activity they could choose when they got back to class (e.g., puzzle, record player). If they misbehaved while on the trip the teacher removed one of the coupons.

Time-Out Procedures

Time-out procedures serve as punishment by denying a student, for a fixed period of time, the opportunity to receive reinforcement. **Time-out** is a shortened form of the term *time-out from positive reinforcement*. Before using time-out procedures, the teacher must be sure that reinforcing consequences for appropriate behavior are available in the classroom. These consequences might be a formal reinforcement system or simply activities that the students enjoy. Identification of available reinforcers may be relatively simple when the students in a classroom are working for a specific item, such as tokens. The specific reinforcers in many classrooms where this is not the case are more difficult to identify. In some classrooms, reinforcers are infrequent, thus limiting the effectiveness of time-out procedures. Some classrooms may be so unpleasant that students are delighted to be excluded from them.

Time-out procedures may be categorized according to the method of denying access to reinforcers. While the student is still within the classroom, the teacher may make an environmental rearrangement. These procedures may be termed **nonseclusionary time-out**. For more disruptive behaviors, the student may be denied access to reinforcers by being taken outside the classroom or activity area. This procedure is called **exclusionary time-out**. If a time-out room is used, the procedure is referred to as **seclusionary time-out**.

Nonseclusionary Time-out Procedures

In *nonseclusionary time-out* procedures, the student is not removed from the instructional setting; instead, the teacher denies the student access to rein-

"I don't understand it, Professor—time-out just isn't working anymore."

forcers through a temporary manipulation of the environment. Teachers use this procedure in its most common form when faced with a generalized, minor disturbance. They may tell the students to put their heads on their desks, or they may turn out the room lights (Baron, Kaufman, & Rakavskas, 1967) to eliminate the mutual reinforcers of talking and laughing with one another. If during instruction, a student or students begin to act inappropriately, the teacher may remove the materials (for example, eating utensils, counting chips, frog and dissection kit), herself, and her attention for a brief period contingent on the inappropriate behavior. Similarly, time-out may be accomplished by turning off a record player during free time when jocularity gets out of hand, or turning off the radio on the school bus when students are out of their seats (Ritchl, Mongrella, & Presbie, 1972).

A frequently reported form of nonseclusionary time-out is use of the time-out ribbon model. This procedure has been used with individual students (Fee, Matson, & Manikam, 1990; Huguenin & Mulick, 1981; McKeegan, Estill, & Campbell, 1984; Salend & Maragulia, 1983) and with groups of students (Foxx & Shapiro, 1978; Salend & Gordon, 1987). During a group lesson, Foxx and Shapiro had students wear a ribbon-tie while behaving in a socially appropriate manner. A student's ribbon was removed for any instance of misbehavior. This removal signaled an end to teacher attention and an end to the student's participation in activities and access to reinforcers for three minutes. Various time-out "ribbons" have been used, including actual ribbons, badges, leather shoelaces in belt loops, and wristbands with smiling face stickers. In a study by Adams, Martin, and Popelka (1971), a misbehavior prompted the teacher to turn on a recorded tone. While the tone was audible, access to reinforcers was denied to the student.

In classrooms where token systems are in effect, simply taking a student's point card for a specified number of minutes provides a period of time-out from reinforcement.

Another form of nonseclusionary time-out is *contingent observation* (May, McAllister, Risley, Twardosz, & Cox, 1974). Contingent observation involves moving a student to the edge of an activity so that she or he can still observe other students' behavior being reinforced. In one study (Porterfield, Herbert-Jackson, & Risley, 1976), the teacher told the student what he should have done, moved him to the periphery of the activity, and told him to watch how the other students performed. After one minute, he was asked if he had learned how to behave appropriately. If he answered "yes," he was returned to the group activity. If he said "no," he remained in time-out for an additional minute. Barton, Brulle, and Repp (1987) used contingent observation with two elementary students with severe disabilities. When the students misbehaved they were moved slightly away from the group but were allowed to observe the classroom activities. Not every instance of the behavior resulted in contingent observation. A certain, prespecified number of occurrences was permitted within given time intervals. Time-out was used only when instances of misbehavior exceeded this maximum. Such scheduling is similar to that used for DRL procedures.

A type of nonseclusionary time-out that has been used with more severe behavior problems is known as facial or visual screening. Facial screening procedures have been successfully used with stereotypic behaviors (Jordan, Singh, & Repp, 1989; McGonigle & Rojahn, 1989; Singh, Landrum, Ellis, & Donatelli, 1993), pica (Singh & Winton, 1984), self-injury (Singh, 1980; Singh, Watson, & Winton, 1986; Watson, Singh, & Winton, 1986; Winton, Singh, & Dawson, 1984), disruptive meantime behavior (Horton, 1987), and trichotillomania (compulsive hair-pulling) (Baumann & Vitali, 1982). This procedure involves occluding the student's eyes with a terry-cloth bib or the teacher's hand usually for a period of three seconds (though data by Singh, Beale, and Dawson [1981] suggest that a one-minute duration is the most effective) following cessation of the behavior without removing him from the instructional setting. Once the bib or hand is removed, the ongoing lesson is immediately resumed. For older children a T-shirt or sweatshirt, slit up the sides, would be more age-appropriate. McGonigle, Duncan, Cordisco, and Barrett (1982) used visual screening with four students engaged in various stereotypic and self-injurious behaviors. Their procedure had the "teacher placing one hand over the child's eyes so as to preclude any source of visual input, while holding the back of the child's head with the other hand. Duration of the visual screening treatment was a minimum of 5 seconds for each child. Criterion for release from visual screening was contingent upon nondisruptive behavior following expiration of the minimum time requirement" (p. 463).

Exclusionary Time-out Procedures

Exclusionary time-out involves removing the student from an activity as a means of denying access to reinforcement. It is not always necessary to remove the student from the classroom completely. Exclusion (May et al., 1974) may be accomplished simply by removing the student from the immediate activity area to another part of the room. Observation and subsequent modeling of reinforced behavior (as with contingent observation) are not components of this procedure. The student is removed to a chair facing a corner or placed in a screened-off area of the room. Mace, Page, Ivancic, and O'Brien (1986) and Roberts (1988) used chairs in the back of the room facing away from the class. In the first study, time-out was used for a range of aggressive and disruptive behaviors in preschoolers and an adolescent; in the second, for noncompliant behaviors in preschoolers. A variation of such exclusion was employed by Baer, Rowbury, and Baer (1973). When a student misbehaved during an activity for which she was earning tokens, she was placed in the middle of the room out of reach of the work activity, and thereby denied access to earning tokens. In another variation, Matthews, Friman, Barone, Ross, and Christophersen (1987) used a playpen as a time-out location for young students who displayed potentially dangerous behaviors.

Seclusionary Time-out Procedures

In most instances, time-out is a procedure associated with the use of a time-out room (Birnbrauer, Wolf, Kidder, & Tague, 1965; Lahey, McNees, & McNees, 1973; MacPherson, Candee, & Hohman, 1974). The procedure involves removing the student from the classroom itself to a room identified for total social isolation, contingent on a misbehavior. In such a room, access is denied to all potential reinforcers from the teacher, classmates, or the classroom. Such a procedure is sometimes termed *seclusionary time-out*. This procedure is usually reserved for behaviors such as physical aggression, verbal aggression, and destruction of property (Zabel, 1986).

Unfortunately, time-out rooms have been seriously misused or mismanaged in many instances. This procedure has therefore been the subject of negative publicity and even considered and regulated in litigation (Morales v. Turman, 1973; Wyatt v. Stickney, 1972). Various states and school districts now have procedural regulations for the use of time-out rooms (May et al., 1974). Concern has arisen basically because of two aspects of the use of time-out rooms: duration of time in the room and physical features of the room. Gast and Nelson (1977b, p. 463) address both these concerns:

The duration of each time-out period should be brief. One to 5 minutes generally is sufficient. It is doubtful that time-out periods exceeding 15 minutes serve the purpose for which they are intended. If a seclusion time-out is to be employed, the time-out room should:

1. Be at least 6 by 6 feet in size.
2. Be properly lighted (preferably recessed, with the switch outside the room).
3. Be properly ventilated.
4. Be free of objects and fixtures with which children can harm themselves.
5. Provide the means by which an adult can continuously monitor, visually and auditorily, the student's behavior.

6. Not be locked. A latch on the door should be used only as needed, and only with careful monitoring.

A teacher should work through the following sequence of steps while using any form of time-out.

1. Before beginning to use time-out as a management procedure, identify the behavior(s) that will result in use of a time-out procedure. Be sure the students understand the behavior. Explain the behavior expected of students while they are in time-out. Tell them how long the time-out period will last.

Guidelines for seclusionary time-out

2. When the misbehavior occurs, reidentify it. Tell the student in a calm manner, "That is fighting. Go to time-out for . . . minutes." No other conversation should ensue. Ignore any statements the student may make as an excuse for misbehavior or relating to feelings about time-out. If necessary, lead the student to the time-out area. If the student resists, Hall and Hall (1980, p. 11) suggest that the teacher

   a. gently but firmly lead the student to time-out.

   b. be prepared to add time to time-out if the student refuses to go or yells, screams, kicks, or turns over furniture.

   c. require the student to clean up any mess resulting from resistance to time-out before the student may return to classroom activities.

   d. be prepared to use a back-up consequence for students who refuse time-out.

3. Once a student enters the time-out area, the time begins. Check your watch or set a timer. Gast and Nelson (1977a) review three formats for contingent release from time-out rooms:

   a. release contingent on a specified period of appropriate behavior (for example, two minutes).

   b. release contingent on a minimum duration of time-out, with an extension until all inappropriate behavior has terminated.

   c. release contingent on a minimum duration of time-out, with a specified extension (such as 15 seconds) during which no inappropriate responses are exhibited. Mace, Page, Ivancic, and O'Brien (1986) found this delayed release procedure effective.

4. Once the time interval has ended, return the student to the previous appropriate activity. Do not comment on how well the student behaved while in time-out. A student should be returned to the activity he or she was engaged in before time-out to avoid negatively reinforcing an escape from that activity.

To monitor the effects of time-out and to substantiate proper and ethical use of the procedure, records should be kept of each time-out occasion, especially when a time-out room is used. Records should include at least the following information (Gast & Nelson, 1977b):

Monitoring time-out

1. The student's name
2. The episode resulting in the student's placement in time-out (behavior, activity, other students involved, staff person, and so on)
3. The time of day the student was placed in time-out
4. The time of day the student was released from time-out
5. The total time in time-out
6. The type of time-out (contingent observation, exclusion, or seclusion)
7. The student's behavior in time-out

Before selecting a time-out procedure, the teacher should consider the following questions concerning its use:

Questions to ask before using time-out

1. Have more positive procedures—for example, differential reinforcement strategies—been considered?
2. Have both nonseclusionary and seclusionary time-out procedures been considered?
3. Can time-out be implemented with minimal student resistance? Can the teacher handle the possible resistance?
4. Have the rules of appropriate behavior and the results for misbehavior been clearly explained and understood?
5. Have the rules of behavior while in time-out been clearly explained and understood?
6. Have district regulations concerning the use of time-out procedures been reviewed and complied with?
7. Will appropriate behavior be reinforced in conjunction with the use of time-out?

The following vignette is an example of what might happen should a teacher fail to consider questions like these.

Ms. Sutton Tries Time-out

Ms. Sutton, a second-grade teacher, read about time-out. She decided that she would use it to teach Aaron not to hit other students. She did not have access to a time-out room, but concluded that putting Aaron in the hall outside the classroom would be just as good.

The next time Aaron hit someone, Ms. Sutton told him, "Aaron, you hit somebody. You have to go to time-out."

She sat him in a chair in the hall and went back to teaching reading. At the end of the period, about an hour later, she went to get him. He came back into the room and hit Elaine before he even got to his seat. Once again, he went to the hall. This pattern was repeated throughout the morning.

Aaron spent most of the time in the hall and the rest of the time hitting people. Ms. Sutton concluded that time-out was an ineffective procedure. Later that day, she heard Aaron say to Elaine, "Hey, I got this all figured out. If I hit you, I get to go sit in the hall. I don't have to do my work, and I get to talk to all the people in the hall. The principal even came by and asked me what I did. Boy, did I tell him!"

Factors that may make time-out ineffective

Time-out will not be effective if positive reinforcement is not available in the classroom, if students escape tasks while in time-out, or if reinforcing consequences are available during time-out.

LEVEL IV: PRESENTATION OF AVERSIVE STIMULI

What makes the presentation of aversive consequences so appealing to parents and teachers?

The presentation of an aversive stimulus as a consequence of an inappropriate behavior is, in popular usage, identified with the term *punishment*. As indicated earlier in this chapter, teachers turn to this form of punishment almost by reflex. Perhaps because many people have been disciplined at home and at school by being yelled at or hit, they learn to handle other people's inappropriate behavior by yelling and hitting, especially when their opponent is physically smaller. From a more functional perspective, this form of punishment is often used because it has three powerful advantages.

Usefulness of Aversive Stimuli

Reread the story on page 46 of Chapter 2. Was the presentation of an aversive stimulus justified in this instance?

First and foremost, the use of an aversive stimulus rapidly stops the occurrence of a behavior and has some long-term effects (Azrin, 1960). A child throwing a tantrum who is suddenly hit across the backside will probably stop immediately; a pair of students gossiping in the back of the room will stop when the teacher screams at them. Second, the use of aversive stimuli facilitates learning by providing a clear discrimination between acceptable and unacceptable behavior or between safe and dangerous behavior (Marshall, 1965). The student who is slapped for spitting, subjected to mild shocks on the arm for self-injurious behavior, or hit by a car while dashing across the street clearly and immediately sees the inappropriateness of the behavior. Third, the aversive consequence following a student's inappropriate behavior vividly illustrates to other students the results of engaging in that behavior and, therefore, tends to lessen the probability that those others will engage in the behavior (Bandura, 1965).

In listing these advantages, *we are not recommending the use of aversive consequences* (especially involving physical contact) as a routine management procedure in the classroom, in homes, or in institutions. We merely acknowledge the behavioral effects resulting from their use. Physical or other strong aversive consequences are justified only under the most extreme instances of inappropriate behavior. They are appropriate only when safety is jeopardized or in instances of long-standing serious behavior problems. Aversive consequences should be used only after considering appropriate safety and procedural guidelines. It is suggested that guidelines should minimally include

1. *Demonstrated* and *documented* failure of alternative nonaversive procedures to modify the target behavior.
2. Informed written consent of the student's parents or legal guardians, through due process procedures and assurance of their right to withdraw such consent at any time (Rimm & Masters, 1979).
3. The decision to implement an aversive procedure made by a designated body of qualified professionals.
4. A prearranged timetable for review of the effectiveness of the procedure and discontinuance of the procedure as soon as possible.
5. Periodic observation to ensure the staff member's consistent and reliable administration of the procedure.
6. Documentation of the effectiveness of the procedure as well as evidence of increased accessibility to instruction.
7. Administration of the procedure by only designated staff member(s). (The staff member should have had instruction in the procedure, have reviewed published studies in the use of the procedure, and be familiar with procedure-specific guidelines and possible negative effects.)
8. Positive reinforcement of incompatible behavior, whenever possible, as a part of any program using aversive stimuli.

Krasner (1976) pointed out an important distinction between effectiveness and acceptability. It is not the effectiveness of aversive procedures that is in question, but their acceptability to parents, the public, and many professionals. Techniques involving aversive consequences understandably cause concern to many people. Although their use may be acceptable in cases such as self-injurious behavior if proper safeguards are implemented, it is doubtful that such drastic measures could or even should become accepted as routine classroom management procedures.

Types of Aversive Stimuli

Aversive stimuli may be categorized into two groups: unconditioned aversive stimuli and conditioned aversive stimuli. **Unconditioned aversive stimuli** result in physical pain or discomfort to the student. Examples of such stimuli are slapping, biting, or pinching. This class of stimuli includes anything that causes pain—naturally occurring consequences, such as contact with a hot stove, or contrived consequences, such as the application of electric shock. Because these stimuli immediately produce a behavior change without the need for any previous experience, they may also be termed *universal, natural,* or *unlearned punishers.*

Unconditioned aversive stimuli also include consequences that may be described as *mild* aversives (McGonigle, et al., 1982; Singh, 1979; Zegiob, Jenkins, Becker, & Bristow, 1976). Rather than causing pain, these noxious stimuli result in annoyance, discomfort, or irritation (Dorsey, Iwata, Ong, & McSween, 1980; Singh, 1980; Zegiob, Alford, & House, 1978). These mild aversive consequences include the administration of substances and the use of physical control.

Substances used as aversive consequences of inappropriate behavior include water, lemon juice, and aromatic ammonia. Directing a fine mist of tap water toward a subject's face contingent on the occurrence of a targeted behavior has been employed with behaviors ranging from mouthing objects (resulting in vomiting or hand biting for some subjects), to head banging and tearing of flesh from lips and forearms (Dorsey et al., 1980; Gross, Berler, & Drabman, 1982), to other forms of self-injury and stereotypic behaviors (Bailey, Pokrzywinski, & Bryant, 1983; Fehr & Beckwith, 1989; Singh, Watson, & Winton, 1986), to pica—eating nonfood items (Rojahn, McGonigle, Curcio, & Dixon, 1987). Putting lemon juice into the subject's mouth has been used to suppress rumination—regurgitation of swallowed food (Apolito & Sulzer-Azaroff, 1981; Becker, Turner, & Sajwaj, 1978; Sajwaj, Libet, & Agras, 1974)—and self-injurious behavior (Mayhew & Harris, 1979). The strongest, and most extreme, of the substance consequences has been the use of aromatic ammonia. Aromatic ammonia in the form of capsules of smelling salts crushed and held under the subject's nose has been used to reduce self-injurious behavior (Altman & Haavik, 1978; Baumeister & Baumeister, 1978; Singh, 1979; Tanner & Zeiler, 1975), aggression toward others (Doke, Wolery, & Sumberg, 1983), and pica (Rojahn et al., 1987).

Physical control refers to procedures requiring direct, physical intervention in order to suppress a targeted behavior. Two such procedures are contingent exercise and immobilization or physical restraint. Contingent exercise requires the student to engage in unrelated physical activity such as push-ups or deep knee bends as a consequence for a targeted behavior. This procedure has been used with self-injurious, stereotypic, self-stimulatory, and aggressive behaviors (DeCatanzaro & Baldwin, 1978; Kern, Koegel, & Dunlap, 1984; Kern, Koegel, Dyer, Blew, & Fenton, 1982; Rolider & Van Houten, 1985; Singh, Watson, & Winton, 1986), as well as behaviors of military recruits that annoy drill sergeants.

Physical restraint has been used primarily with stereotypic behaviors (Reid, Tombaugh, & Van den Heuvel, 1981) and self-injurious behaviors (Hamad, Isley, & Lowry, 1983; Luiselli, 1986; Matson & Keyes, 1988; Pace, Iwata, Edwards, & McCosh, 1986), and pica (Singh & Bakker, 1984; Winton & Singh, 1983). Schloss and Smith (1987) suggest certain limitations to the use of physical restraint.

1. Restraint does not involve the reinforcement of an alternative behavior.
2. The inappropriate behavior may be reinforced by manual restraint, thereby increasing the probability of future occurrences.
3. Once the student learns that he will be physically blocked from performing the response, he is likely to increase his efforts to perform it.
4. Implementation may result in harm to the student or the teacher.

Given these cautions, Schloss and Smith suggest the following guidelines:

1. Manual restraint should be used only to prevent the learner from causing harm to himself, others, or objects.
2. Manual restraint should not be used to force a student to perform an appropriate behavior, but only to stop performing an inappropriate one. In other words, Schloss and Smith would not recommend physically guiding a student through a restitution exercise like returning something stolen from another student.
3. Every opportunity should be provided for the student to control his own behavior before physical management is implemented.
4. Extreme care should be taken to provide for the safety and comfort of the student during the restraint procedure.
5. Teachers should maintain a neutral affect throughout the physical management process. That is, they should not show anger, fear, tension, or, much worse, glee. The most effective attitude, in our opinion, is to appear not to notice that one is restraining a student and to go about business as usual.
6. A written report of the physical management episode that describes the antecedents, specific aggressive responses, and outcomes or consequences should be made immediately following each incident.

The potentially harmful nature of these aversive consequences clearly points to the need for any teacher, parent, or consulting behavior management committee to have read thoroughly the professional literature on a procedure before recommending and implementing its use. A clear understanding of the procedure-specific guidelines such as duration and schedule of administration of the consequence and, of special concern, the potential behavioral and physical negative effects must be shared by all parties before implementation.

Although these consequences are included in the category of unconditioned aversive stimuli, they are not necessarily universal punishers. Some students may find the procedure reinforcing rather than punishing. A student may indeed like the taste of lemon juice, may find it fun to have water sprayed in his or her face, or enjoy physical contact with the teacher. Access to restraint has actually been used as a positive reinforcer (Favell, McGimsey, & Jones, 1978; Favell, McGimsey, Jones, & Cannon, 1981).

Conditioned aversive stimuli are stimuli a person learns to experience as aversive as a result of pairing with an unconditioned aversive stimulus. This class includes consequences such as words and warnings, vocal tones, or gestures. A child, for example, may have experienced being yelled at, paired with being spanked. Yelling may thus have become a conditioned aversive stimulus, as experience has proven to the student that yelling is associated with pain. The pain associated with a conditioned aversive stimulus may also be psychological or social pain or discomfort, usually in the form of embarrassment or ridicule from peers.

Verbal reprimands (shouting or scolding) are the most common form of conditioned aversive stimuli used in the classroom (Heller & White, 1975; Thomas, Presland, Grant, & Glynn, 1978; White, 1975). A series of studies was conducted to identify factors that influence the effectiveness of reprimands (Van Houten et al., 1982). Three such factors were identified: (1) verbal reprimands were more effective delivered in conjunction with "nonverbal aspects of reprimands such as eye contact and a firm grasp"; (2) "reprimands were more effective when delivered from nearby the student than when delivered from across the room"; and (3) "the delivery of reprimands to one student reduced the disruptive behavior of an adjacent peer" (p. 81).

If unconditioned or conditioned aversive stimuli are to be used as consequences in a behavior-reduction program, they should be used as effectively as possible. As indicated in the functional definition, the teacher must be consistent and immediate in applying the consequences (Azrin, Holz, & Hake, 1963). The rules of behavior must be clearly associated with a contingency that has been previously stated: the "if . . . , then . . ." statement of cause and effect. The student must understand that the aversive consequence is not being arbitrarily applied. The immediacy of application convinces the student of the veracity of the contingency and underlines the connection between a particular behavior and its consequence.

In addition to ensuring consistency and immediacy, the teacher should avoid extended episodes of punishment. Consequences should be quick and directly to the point. Sometimes teachers become so involved in analyzing behavior and arranging consequences that they forget that sometimes, for some children, a polite request to "Please stop doing that," is all that's required. If words are a punisher for a student, a few words—such as, "Don't run in the hall"—may be far more effective than a 15-minute lecture, most of which the student tunes out.

Punishment is far less effective when the intensity of the aversive stimulus is increased gradually instead of being initially introduced at its full intensity (Azrin & Holz, 1966). With a gradual increase in intensity, the student has the opportunity to become habituated or desensitized to the intensity of the previous application. Such gradual habituation may eventually lead the teacher to administer an intensity level far above what was originally considered necessary to terminate the student's misbehavior.

A desire or actual attempt to escape from an aversive condition is a natural response. If punishment is to be effective in changing undesirable student behavior, the teacher will have to arrange the environment to prevent students' escaping punishment (Azrin, Hake, Holz, & Hutchinson, 1965; Bandura, 1969).

The most important element of any program that includes punishment of inappropriate behavior is to be sure that any punishment is always used *in association with reinforcement* for appropriate behavior. Punishment involves very little learning by the student. In effect, all the student learns is what behavior should not be engaged in. Reinforcing appropriate behavior instructs the student on appropriate or expected behaviors and provides an opportunity for successful or reinforced experiences.

Disadvantages of Aversive Stimuli

The disadvantages of aversive consequences far outweigh the advantages of their immediate effect. The following limitations of such procedures should make teachers stop and consider very carefully before choosing to use aversives:

1. In the face of aggressive punishers, the student has three behavior options:

   a. The student may strike back (for example, yell at the teacher or even become physically aggressive). A reaction may be triggered that will result in escalation of the situation.

   b. The student may become withdrawn, may tune out the punisher, and remain tuned out for the rest of the day, thus learning nothing.

   c. The student may engage in an escape and avoidance behavior. Once a student has run out of the room, a punisher in the classroom can have no immediate effect.

2. We know that a most basic and powerful form of instruction and learning takes place through modeling or imitation. Because a teacher is a figure of respect and authority, his or her behavior is closely observed by students. A teacher's reactions become a model of adult behavior for various situations. The teacher who yells or hits is, in effect, saying to the students this is how an adult reacts and copes with undesirable behaviors in the environment. Students may, through such a model, learn an inappropriate, aggressive form of behavior. As noted by Sobsey (1990) this punishment-induced aggression results in more inappropriate behavior, and can result in harm to both the individual and to her targets of aggression.

3. Unless students are taught to understand what behavior is being punished, they may come to fear and avoid the teacher or the entire setting in which the punishment occurred. Consider

   a. the fourth-grade teacher whose students flinch when she walks up and down between the rows of desks. She is a slapper.

b. the little girl in an institution who suddenly would not sleep in her room at night. She cried and screamed until she was taken out in the hall. It was discovered that an attendant had been taking her into her room and paddling her for bad behaviors during the day.

4. Many interactions that teachers consider punishers function as positive reinforcers instead. A child may find making an adult lose control and look ridiculous very reinforcing.

A final disadvantage of punishment is illustrated by the following vignette.

Professor Grundy Teaches Dennis a Thing or Two

Professor Grundy's 5-year-old nephew, Dennis, was spending the week at the professor's house. One of Dennis's more unpleasant habits was jumping on the bed. Mrs. Grundy had asked Dennis not to do it, but this had been completely ineffective.

Professor Grundy was sitting in his easy chair, smoking his pipe, and reading a professional journal. He heard the unmistakable "crunch, crunch, crunch" of the bedsprings directly overhead in the guest bedroom. "Minerva," he said, "the time has come for drastic action. Where is the flyswatter?"

"Oliver, you're not going to beat the child, are you?" asked Minerva.

"Certainly not, dear," replied the professor. "I shall merely apply an unconditioned aversive stimulus, contingently, at a maximum intensity."

"Oliver, let's first try offering him a treat if he doesn't jump on the bed."

The professor took the flyswatter in hand and tiptoed up the carpeted steps in his stockinged feet. He continued to tiptoe into the bedroom, where he observed Dennis happily jumping on the bed. Dennis did not observe the professor; his back was to the door. Grundy applied the immediate, contingent, and intense aversive stimulus saying, firmly, "Do not jump on the bed." Dennis howled.

"That, I think," said the professor to Mrs. Grundy, "will teach Dennis a thing or two." In fact, Dennis did not jump on the bed all weekend. Professor Grundy was at home all the time and knew he would have heard the springs.

On Monday, when the professor arrived home from the university, Minerva met him at the door. "Oliver," she said, "I don't know which thing or two you planned to teach Dennis, but the one he learned was not to jump on the bed when you were home. He's been at it all day."

Like Dennis, what students learn most often from punishment using aversive stimuli is not to perform the behavior when the person who applied the punishment is present. They learn not to get caught! They don't learn to behave appropriately.

Concern about inappropriate and excessive use of aversive interventions has resulted in position statements about their use from various advocacy and professional organizations. Several of these statements appear in the Appendix.

Overcorrection

Overcorrection was developed as a behavior-reduction procedure that includes training in appropriate behaviors. Overcorrection procedures are therefore considered educative (Azrin & Foxx, 1971). The purpose of overcorrection is to teach students to take responsibility for their inappropriate acts and to teach them appropriate behaviors. Correct behavior is taught through an exaggeration of experience. The exaggeration of experience characteristic of overcorrection contrasts with a simple correction procedure in which a student rectifies an error of behavior, but is not necessarily required to follow that with exaggerated or extended practice of the appropriate behavior.

There are two basic types of overcorrection procedures. *Restitutional overcorrection* is used when a setting has been disturbed by a student's misbehavior. The student must overcorrect the setting she or he has disturbed. *Positive-practice overcorrection* is used when the form of a behavior is inappropriate. In this procedure, the student practices an exaggerated correct form of an appropriate behavior (Foxx & Azrin, 1973).

Overcorrection procedures should have the following characteristics (Foxx & Bechtel, 1982, p. 231):

1. The consequence (behavior) required of the student should be directly related to the misbehavior. This should reduce the likelihood of use in a punitive or arbitrary fashion and should prevent the inappropriate response from occurring.

2. The student should directly experience the effort normally required of others to correct the results of the misbehavior.

3. Overcorrection should be instituted immediately following the misbehavior.

4. The student performing the overcorrection should act rapidly so that consequences constitute an inhibitory effort requirement.

5. The student is instructed and manually guided through the required acts, with the amount of guidance adjusted on a moment-to-moment basis according to the degree to which he/she is voluntarily performing the act.

Successful use of overcorrection has been demonstrated using various durations. Overcorrection periods may last anywhere from 30 seconds (Azrin, Kaplan, & Foxx, 1973) or 1 minute (Freeman, Graham, & Ritvo, 1975) to as long as two hours (Foxx, 1976), depending on the behavior involved. Successful reduction of stereotypic hand movements has been reported after requiring a student to engage in an overcorrection procedure for 2.5 minutes (Epstein, Doke, Sajwaj, Sorrell, & Rimmer, 1974) as well as 5 minutes (Foxx & Azrin, 1973). Carey and Bucher (1985) noted that shorter durations result in fewer instances of negative side effects such as aggression.

Restitutional Overcorrection

A restitutional overcorrection procedure requires that the student restore or correct an environment that he or she has disturbed not only to its original condition, but beyond that. For example, when the teacher catches a student throwing a spitball, she is employing simple correction when she says, "Michael, pick that up and throw it in the trash." She is employing restitutional overcorrection when she says, "Michael, pick that up and throw it in the trash, and now pick up all the other papers on the floor."

This form of environmental restoration was used by Azrin and Foxx (1971) as part of their toilet-training program. When a child had an accident, she or he had to undress, wash the clothes, hang them to dry, shower, obtain clean clothing, dress, and then clean the soiled area of the lavatory. A variation was employed by Azrin and Wesolowski (1974) when, in order to eliminate stealing, they required the thief to return not only a stolen item but also an additional identical item to the person who had been robbed.

A review of studies by Rusch and Close (1976) shows restitutional overcorrection techniques used to reduce various classes of disruptive behavior:

1. In cases where objects were disturbed or rearranged, all objects (such as furniture) within the immediate area where a disruption occurred were straightened, not merely the originally disturbed objects.

2. In cases where someone annoyed or frightened others, all persons present were to be apologized to, not just those annoyed or frightened.

3. In cases of self-inflicted oral infection, a thorough cleansing of the mouth with an oral antiseptic followed unhygienic oral contacts such as biting people or chewing inedible objects.

4. In cases of agitation, a period of absolute quiet was imposed following commotions such as shrieking and screaming.

Positive-Practice Overcorrection

With positive-practice overcorrection, the student, who has engaged in an inappropriate behavior is required to engage in exaggerated or overly correct practice of the appropriate behavior. For example, if a class runs to line up for recess, the teacher who makes everyone sit back down and line up again is using simple correction. The teacher who makes everyone sit back down and then practice getting in line several times while reciting the rules for doing it the right way is using positive-practice overcorrection.

Positive-practice overcorrection of behavior that is autisticlike is sometimes called autism reversal.

To ensure the educative nature intended by this procedure, the practice should be of an alternative appropriate behavior topographically similar to the inappropriate behavior. Foxx and Azrin (1973) and Azrin, Kaplan, and Foxx (1973) used this procedure to reverse the stereotypic behavior of autistic children. As shown in Figure 8–4, the researchers identified and then required the students to practice exaggerations of appropriate postures for extended periods of time. Azrin and Foxx (1971) used positive-practice procedures in their toilet-training program by artificially increasing the frequency of urinations through offering the students large quantities of appealing liquids. This technique increased the opportunity for practice and reinforcement. Azrin and Wesolowski (1975) eliminated floor sprawling by requiring the student to practice sitting on several chairs (one at a time, of course) for an extended time. Classroom disturbances have been overcorrected by requiring students to practice reciting correct classroom procedures to the teacher during periods such as recess (Azrin, Azrin, & Armstrong, 1977; Azrin & Powers, 1975; Bornstein, Hamilton, & Quevillon, 1977).

In addition to its use for these and other inappropriate behaviors such as stereotypic behavior (Denny, 1980; Doke & Epstein, 1975), aggression (Luiselli & Rice, 1983), and self-injury (Gibbs & Luyben, 1985; Wesolowski & Zawlocki, 1982), positive-practice has been successful with various academic behaviors (Lenz, Singh, & Hewett, 1991). To improve oral reading performance students who made an error were instructed to listen to the teacher read the word correctly while the student pointed to the word in the book. The student then said the word correctly five times and reread the sentence (Singh, 1987; Singh & Singh, 1986, 1988; Singh, Singh, & Winton, 1984). To correct spelling errors students were instructed to listen to the word pronounced, pronounce the word correctly, say each letter aloud, and write the word correctly (Matson, Esveldt-Dawson, & Kazdin, 1982; Ollendick, Matson, Esveldt-Dawson, & Shapiro, 1980; Stewart & Singh, 1986). Positive-practice has also been used with cursive writing (Mabee, 1988; Trap, Milner-Davis, Joseph, & Cooper, 1978) and manual communication (Hinerman, Jenson, Walker, & Peterson, 1982; Linton & Singh, 1984). In their review of academic remediation and the use of overcorrection, Lenz et al., (1991) suggest that overcorrection procedures used for academic remediation be called "directed rehearsal" because they found that the procedures did not totally meet the criteria set by Foxx and

FIGURE 8–4
Positive-practice overcorrection in reducing stereotypic behaviors

Note (top): From "The elimination of autistic self-stimulatory behavior by overcorrection," by R. Foxx & N. Azrin, Journal of Applied Behavior Analysis, 1973. Copyright 1973 by The Society for the Experimental Analysis of Behavior, Inc. Reprinted by permission.

Note (bottom): From "Autism reversal: Eliminating stereotyped self-stimulation of retarded individuals," by N. H. Azrin, S. J. Kaplan & R. M. Foxx. American Journal on Mental Deficiency, 1973. Copyright 1973 by the Society for the Experimental Analysis of Behavior, Inc. Reprinted by permission.

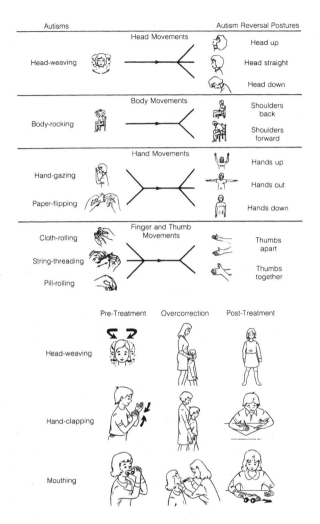

Bechtel (1982) (for example, use of manual guidance or prompt administration) and that their major components were rehearsal and attention directed to the learning task.

Overcorrection procedures should not themselves be allowed to become positively reinforcing. Indeed, a quality of aversiveness is involved in their use. Restitutional or positive-practice overcorrection procedures usually include the following components (Epstein et al., 1974; Rusch & Close, 1976):

1. Telling the student she or he behaved inappropriately

2. Stopping the student's ongoing activity

3. Providing systematic verbal instructions for the overcorrection activity in which the student is to engage

Guidelines for using overcorrection

4. Forcing the practice of correctional behavior (manually guiding the desired movements, using as much bodily pressure as necessary, but reducing such pressure immediately as the person begins to perform the movement with verbal instruction alone)

5. Returning the student to the ongoing activity

Before using an overcorrection procedure, teachers should consider the following management concerns:

1. Implementation of overcorrection requires the full attention of the teacher. She must be physically close to the student to ensure that he complies with the overcorrection instruction and be ready to intervene with physical guidance, if necessary.

2. Overcorrection procedures tend to be time-consuming, sometimes lasting 5 to 15 minutes and possibly longer (Foxx & Azrin, 1973; Ollendick & Matson, 1976; Sumner, Meuser, Hsu, & Morales, 1974). Recent studies suggest, however, that short-duration implementation may be at least as effective as longer durations in facilitating behavior changes, especially when appropriate alternative behavior is being taught emphasizing the educative rather than punishment potential of the procedure (Carey & Bucher, 1983; Conley & Wolery, 1980).

3. Because physical contact with the student is involved in the use of overcorrection, the teacher should be aware of the possibility of aggression by the student (Carey & Bucher, 1983; Rollings, Baumeister, & Baumeister, 1977) or attempts to escape and avoid the aversive situation.

4. During long periods of overcorrection the student may become so disruptive that the teacher cannot guide him through the overcorrection procedure (Matson & Stephens, 1977).

5. Because overcorrection often involves physical guidance for extended periods, it may be a very aversive procedure to the adults implementing it (Repp, 1983).

6. If students are reinforced for correct responses during positive-practice they may misbehave in order to perform the procedure and receive reinforcers (Foxx & Bechtel, 1982). This probably will not happen often and using reinforcement is generally the better course. In comparing positive-practice with and without reinforcing correct responses, Carey & Bucher (1986) found that use without reinforcement "showed no advantages over the reinforced variation, and resulted in a greater incidence of undesirable side effects such as aggression and emotionality" (p. 85).

Overcorrection may provide an alternative to aversive consequences in the classroom. It is important to remember that overcorrection procedures, although they have some aversive features, are to be used not as retaliative but as educative tools. The teacher's tone and manner make a difference in the way the procedures will be received by students. A teacher who uses an angry or haranguing tone of voice or unnecessary force when guiding students through overcorrection procedures may increase the probability of resistance. Firmness without aggression is the aim here.

Occasionally, two procedures that result in behavior reduction may be misidentified as a form of overcorrection or confused with those procedures. These other approaches are *negative practice* and *stimulus satiation*. The confusion may occur because, as in overcorrection, these procedures involve providing an exaggeration of experience.

Negative practice (Dunlap, 1928, 1930, 1932) may be confused with positive practice. Negative practice requires that the student repeatedly perform the *inappropriate* behavior. There is no pretense that the procedure is educative. The procedure is based on the assumption that repeated performance will result in response fatigue or satiation. For example, if a certain student's inappropriate behavior is getting up and running around the room during a lesson, positive-practice might involve extended time periods sitting in various chairs, whereas negative practice might involve requiring the student to run and run and run and run.

Negative practice has been used to reduce small motor behaviors (Dunlap, 1928, 1930). A limited number of studies report the use of this procedure. Those that have been published have dealt with tics (Walton, 1961; Yates, 1958), smoking (De Lahunt & Curran, 1976), grimacing and unusual body movements made by children with cerebral palsy when speaking (Rutherford, 1940), self-injurious behavior (Mogel & Schiff, 1967), and teeth grinding (Vasta & Wortman, 1988).

Negative practice depends on response fatigue or satiation. **Stimulus satiation**, on the other hand, depends on the student's becoming satiated with the antecedent to the behavior. Ayllon (1963) used stimulus satiation with an individual who hoarded large numbers of towels and stored them in her room in a psychiatric hospital. In order to reduce this hoarding behavior, nurses took towels to the woman when she was in her room and simply handed them to her without comment. The first week she was given an average of 7 towels daily; by the third week, the number was increased to 60 towels. When the number of towels kept in her room reached 625, she started to take a few out. Thereafter, no more towels were given to her. During the next 12 months, the average number of towels found in her room was 1 to 5 per week, compared with the baseline range of 13 to 29.

SUMMARY

This chapter reviewed a number of procedures to decrease or eliminate inappropriate or maladaptive behaviors: differential reinforcement, reinforcement of incompatible behaviors, extinction, punishment, and overcorrection. These procedures are most usefully and constructively viewed as a hierarchy of approaches, from those emphasizing reinforcement to those having aversive features. (See again Figure 8–1).

We stressed throughout the chapter that procedures to decrease behaviors should be chosen only when the behaviors in question are clearly interfering with a student's ability to learn or are presenting a danger to the student or to other people. Positive reinforcement of appropriate behavior should always be combined with any procedure to decrease or eliminate behavior.

DISCUSSION QUESTIONS

1. Design an in-school behavior management committee. Include at least the following points: (a) statement of purpose, (b) membership, (c) decision-making requirements and procedures, and (d) members' follow-up responsibilities.

2. Draft a statement that sets guidelines for use of punishment procedures (including aversives) for your school district.

3. For each of the following examples outline one approach for behavior reduction based on a differential reinforcement strategy and one approach based on a punishment strategy.

   a. Janice comes up to the teacher to ask basically frivolous questions on an average of 16 times per day.

   b. Max was caught writing racy limericks on the wall in the girls' bathroom.

   c. Simon takes 45 minutes to complete a math practice sheet that should take 20 minutes.

   d. While the teacher is lecturing, Kevin and Robert continually talk to each other.

   e. Whenever Louise is reprimanded by the teacher, she runs out of the room.

   f. When working on group projects, Jeremy pinches and threatens students next to him.

   g. After lunch period, Sara vomits.

   h. At least four times a day, Jeff runs around the room throwing over desks.

   i. While moving from class to class, Susan spits in the hallways.

   j. William returns his homework assignment each morning ripped into tiny pieces.

   k. Whenever the teacher calls on Steven to answer in class, he tells her to bug off.

   l. Mark, about 6 years old, throws toys and objects handed to him instead of engaging in appropriate use or even just calmly putting them down.

REFERENCES

Adams, N., Martin, R., & Popelka, G. 1971. The influence of timeout on stutterers and their dysfluency. *Behavior Therapy, 2*, 334–339.

Aiken, J., & Salzberg, C. 1984. The effects of a sensory extinction procedure on stereotypic sounds of two autistic children. *Journal of Autism and Developmental Disorders, 14*, 291–299.

Altman, K., & Haavik, S. 1978. Punishment of self-injurious behavior in natural settings using contingent aromatic ammonia. *Behavior Research and Therapy, 16*, 85–96.

Apolito, P., & Sulzer-Azaroff, B. 1981. Lemon-juice therapy: The control of chronic vomiting in a twelve-year-old profoundly retarded female. *Education and Treatment of Children, 4*, 339–347.

Ayllon, T. 1963. Intensive treatment of psychotic behavior by stimulus satiation and food reinforcement. *Behavior Research and Therapy, 1*, 53–61.

Ayllon, T., Layman, D., & Burke, S. 1972. Disruptive behavior and reinforcement of academic performance. *Psychological Record, 22*, 315–323.

Ayllon, T., & Roberts, M.D. 1974. Eliminating discipline problems by strengthening academic performance. *Journal of Applied Behavior Analysis, 7*, 71–76.

Azrin, N.H. 1960. Effects of punishment intensity during variable-interval reinforcement. *Journal of the Experimental Analysis of Behavior, 3*, 128–142.

Azrin, V., Azrin, N.H., & Armstrong, P. 1977. The student-oriented classroom: A method of improving student conduct and satisfaction. *Behavior Therapy, 8*, 193–204.

Azrin, N.H., & Foxx, R.M. 1971. A rapid method of toilet training the institutionalized retarded. *Journal of Applied Behavior Analysis, 4*, 89–99.

Azrin, N.H., Hake, D.G., Holz, W.C., & Hutchinson, R.R. 1965. Motivational aspects of escape from punishment. *Journal of the Experimental Analysis of Behavior, 8*, 31–44.

Azrin, N.H., & Holz, W.C. 1966. Punishment. In W.A. Honig (Ed.), *Operant behavior: Areas of research and application*. New York: Appleton-Century-Crofts.

Azrin, N.H., Holz, W.C., & Hake, D.F. 1963. Fixed-ratio punishment. *Journal of the Experimental Analysis of Behavior, 6*, 141–148.

Azrin, N.H., Hutchinson, R.R., & Hake, D.J. 1966. Extinction-induced aggression. *Journal of the Experimental Analysis of Behavior, 9*, 191–204.

Azrin, N.H., Kaplan, S.J., & Foxx, R.M. 1973. Autism reversal: Eliminating stereotyped self-stimulation of retarded individuals. *American Journal on Mental Deficiency, 78*, 241–248.

Azrin, N.H., & Powers, M. 1975. Eliminating classroom disturbances of emotionally disturbed children by positive practice procedures. *Behavior Therapy, 6*, 525–534.

Azrin, N.H., & Wesolowski, M.D. 1974. Theft reversal: An overcorrection procedure for eliminating stealing by retarded persons. *Journal of Applied Behavior Analysis, 7*, 577–581.

Azrin, N.H., & Wesolowski, M.D. 1975. The use of positive practice to eliminate persistent floor sprawling by profoundly retarded persons. *Behavior Therapy, 6*, 627–631.

Baer, A.M., Rowbury, T., & Baer, D.M. 1973. The development of instructional control over classroom activities of deviant preschool children. *Journal of Applied Behavior Analysis, 6*, 289–298.

Bailey, S., Pokrzywinski, J., & Bryant, L. 1983. Using water mist to reduce self-injurious and stereotypic behavior. *Applied Research in Mental Retardation, 4*, 229–241.

Bandura, A. 1965. Influence of models' reinforcement contingencies on the acquisition of imitative responses. *Journal of Personality and Social Psychology, 1*, 589–595.

Bandura, A. 1969. *Principles of behavior modification*. New York: Holt, Rinehart & Winston.

Baron, A., Kaufman, A., & Rakavskas, I. 1967. Ineffectiveness of "time out" punishment in suppressing human operant behavior. *Psychonomic Science, 8*, 329–330.

Barrett, R., Matson, J., Shapiro, E., & Ollendick, T. 1981. A comparison of punishment and DRO procedures for treating stereotypic behavior of mentally retarded children. *Applied Research in Mental Retardation, 2*, 247–256.

Barton, E.S. 1970. Inappropriate speech in a severely retarded child: A case study in language conditioning and generalization. *Journal of Applied Behavior Analysis, 3*, 299–307.

Barton, L., Brulle, A., & Repp, A.C. 1986. Maintenance of therapeutic change by momentary DRO. *Journal of Applied Behavior Analysis, 19,* 277–282.

Barton, L., Brulle, A., & Repp, A.C. 1987. Effects of differential scheduling of timeout to reduce maladaptive responding. *Exceptional Children, 53,* 351–356.

Baumann, B., & Vitali, D. 1982. Facial screening to eliminate trichotillomania in developmentally disabled persons. *Behavior Therapy, 13,* 735–742.

Baumeister, A., & Baumeister, A. 1978. Suppression of repetitive self-injurious behavior by contingent inhalation of aromatic ammonia. *Journal of Autism and Childhood Schizophrenia, 8,* 71–77.

Becker, J., Turner, S., & Sajwaj, T. 1978. Multiple behavioral effects of the use of lemon juice with a ruminating toddler-age child. *Behavior Modification, 2,* 267–278.

Benoit, R.B., & Mayer, G.R. 1974. Extinction: Guidelines for its selection and use. *The Personnel and Guidance Journal, 52,* 290–295.

Birnbrauer, J.S., Wolf, M.M., Kidder, J.D., & Tague, C.E. 1965. Classroom behavior of retarded pupils with token reinforcement. *Journal of Experimental Child Psychology, 2,* 219–235.

Bornstein, P., Hamilton, S., & Quevillon, R. 1977. Behavior modification by long-distance: Demonstration of functional control over disruptive behavior in a rural classroom setting. *Behavior Modification, 1,* 369–380.

Brown, P., & Elliott, R. 1965. The control of aggression in a nursery school class. *Journal of Experimental Child Psychology, 2,* 102–107.

Burchard, J.D., & Barrera, F. 1972. An analysis of timeout and response cost in a programmed environment. *Journal of Applied Behavior Analysis, 5,* 271–282.

Carey, R., & Bucher, B. 1983. Positive practice overcorrection: The effects of duration of positive practice on acquisition and response duration. *Journal of Applied Behavior Analysis, 16,* 101–109.

Carey, R., & Bucher, B. 1986. Positive practice overcorrection: Effects of reinforcing correct performance. *Behavior Modification, 10,* 73–92.

Carlson, C.S., Arnold, D.R., Becker, W.C., & Madsen, G.H. 1968. The elimination of tantrum behavior of a child in an elementary classroom. *Behavior Research and Therapy, 6,* 117–120.

Carr, E., Robinson, S., & Palumbo, 1. 1990. The wrong issue: Aversive versus nonaversive treatment. The right issue: Functional versus nonfunctional treatment. In A. Repp & N. Singh (Eds.), *Perspectives on the use of nonaversive and aversive interventions for persons with developmental disabilities.* Sycamore, Ill: Sycamore Publishing.

Conley, O., & Wolery, M. 1980. Treatment by overcorrection of self-injurious eye gouging in preschool blind children. *Journal of Behavior Therapy and Experimental Psychiatry, 11,* 121–125.

Decatanzaro, D., & Baldwin, G. 1978. Effective treatment of self-injurious behavior through a forced arm exercise. *Journal of Applied Behavior Analysis, 11,* 433–439.

Deitz, D.E.D., & Repp, A.C. 1983. Reducing behavior through reinforcement. *Exceptional Education Quarterly, 3,* 34–46.

Deitz, S.M., & Repp, A.C. 1973. Decreasing classroom misbehavior through the use of DRL schedules of reinforcement. *Journal of Applied Behavior Analysis, 6,* 457–463.

Deitz, S.M., & Repp, A.C. 1974. Differentially reinforcing low rates of misbehavior with normal elementary school children. *Journal of Applied Behavior Analysis, 7,* 622.

De Lahunt, J., & Curran, J.P. 1976. Effectiveness of negative practice and self-control techniques in the reduction of smoking behavior. *Journal of Consulting and Clinical Psychology, 44,* 1002–1007.

Denny, M. 1980. Reducing self-stimulatory behavior of mentally retarded persons by alternative positive practice. *American Journal of Mental Deficiency, 84,* 610–615.

Doke, L., & Epstein, L. 1975. Oral overcorrection: Side effects and extended applications. *Journal of Experimental Child Psychology, 20,* 496–511.

Doke, L., Wolery, M., & Sumberg, C. 1983. Treating chronic aggression. *Behavior Modification, 7, 531–556.*

Dorsey, M.F., Iwata, B.A., Ong, P., & Mcsween, T.E. 1980. Treatment of self-injurious behavior using a water mist: Initial response suppression and generalization. *Journal of Applied Behavior Analysis, 13,* 343–353.

Dougherty, S., Fowler, S., & Paine, S. 1985. The use of peer monitors to reduce negative interaction during recess. *Journal of Applied Behavior Analysis, 18,* 141–153.

Dunlap, K. 1928. A revision of the fundamental law of habit formation. *Science, 67*, 360–362.

Dunlap, K. 1930. Repetition in breaking of habits. *The Scientific Monthly, 30*, 66–70.

Dunlap, K. 1932. *Habits, their making and unmaking.* New York: Liverright.

Dupaul, G., Guevremont, D., & Barkley, R. 1992. Behavioral treatment of attention-deficit hyperactivity disorder in the classroom. *Behavior Modification, 16*, 204–225.

Durand, V.M., & Carr, E. 1987. Social influences on self-stimulatory behavior: Analysis and treatment application. *Journal of Applied Behavior Analysis, 20*, 119–132.

Durand, V.M., & Kishi, G. 1987. Reducing severe behavior problems among persons with dual sensory impairments. *Journal of the Association for Persons with Severe Handicaps, 12*, 2–10.

Epstein, L.H., Doke, L.A., Sajwaj, T.E., Sorrell, S., & Rimmer, B. 1974. Generality and side effects of overcorrection. *Journal of Applied Behavior Analysis, 7*, 385–390.

Favell, J. 1973. Reduction of stereotypes by reinforcement of toy play. *Mental Retardation, 11*, 21–23.

Favell, J.E., Mcgimsey, J.F., & Jones, M.L. 1978. The use of physical restraint in the treatment of self-injury and as positive reinforcement. *Journal of Applied Behavior Analysis, 11*, 225–241.

Favell, J., Mcgimsey, J., Jones, M., & Cannon, P. 1981. Physical restraint as positive reinforcement. *American Journal of Mental Deficiency, 85*, 425–432.

Fee, V., Matson, J., & Manikam, R. 1990. A control group outcome study of a nonexclusionary time-out package to improve social skills with preschoolers. *Exceptionality, 1*, 107–121.

Fehr, A., & Beckwith, B. 1989. Water misting: Treating self-injurious behavior in a multiply handicapped, visually impaired child. *Journal of Visual Impairment & Blindness, 83*, 245–248.

Ferster, C., & Skinner, B.F. 1957. *Schedules of reinforcement.* New York: Appleton-Century-Crofts.

Foxx, R.M. 1976. Increasing a mildly retarded woman's attendance at self-help classes by overcorrection and instruction. *Behavior Therapy, 7*, 390–396.

Foxx, R.M., & Azrin, N.H. 1973. The elimination of autistic self-stimulatory behavior by overcorrection. *Journal of Applied Behavior Analysis, 6*, 1–14.

Foxx, R., & Bechtel, D. 1982. Overcorrection. In M. Hersen, R. Eisler, & P. Miller (Eds.), *Progress in behavior modification* (Vol. 13, pp. 227–288). New York: Academic.

Foxx, R.M., & Shapiro, S.T. 1978. The timeout ribbon: A nonseclusionary timeout procedure. *Journal of Applied Behavior Analysis, 11*, 125–136.

Freeman, B., Graham, V., & Ritvo, E. 1975. Reduction of self-destructive behavior by overcorrection. *Psychological Reports, 37*, 446.

Friman, P., Barnard, J., Altman, K., & Wolf, T. 1986. Parent and teacher use of DRO and DRI to reduce aggressive behavior. *Analysis and Intervention in Developmental Disabilities, 6*, 319–330.

Gast, D., & Nelson, C.M. 1977a. Legal and ethical considerations for the use of timeout in special education settings. *The Journal of Special Education, 11*, 457–467.

Gast, D., & Nelson, C.M. 1977b. Time out in the classroom: Implications for special education. *Exceptional Children, 43*, 461–464.

Gast, D., & Wolery, M. 1987. Severe maladaptive behaviors. In M.E. Snell (Ed.), *Systematic instruction of people with severe handicaps* (3rd ed.). Columbus, Ohio: Merrill.

Gibbs, J., & Luyben, P. 1985. Treatment of self-injurious behavior: Contingent versus noncontingent positive practice overcorrection. *Behavior Modification, 9*, 3–21.

Gilbert, G. 1975. Extinction procedures: Proceed with caution. *Mental Retardation, 13*, 25–29.

Gross, A., Berler, E., & Drabman, R. 1982. Reduction of aggressive behavior in a retarded boy using a water squirt. *Journal of Behavior Therapy and Experimental Psychiatry, 13*, 95–98.

Hall, R.V., Fox, R., Willard, D., Goldsmith, L., Emerson, M., Owen, M., Davis, F., & Porcia, E. 1971. The teacher as observer and experimenter in the modification of disputing and talking-out behaviors. *Journal of Applied Behavior Analysis, 4*, 141–149.

Hall, R.B., & Hall, M. 1980. *How to use time out.* Lawrence, Kan.: H&H Enterprises.

Hall, R.V., Lund, D., & Jackson, D. 1968. Effects of teacher attention on study behavior. *Journal of Applied Behavior Analysis, 1*, 1–12.

Hamad, C., Isley, E., & Lowry, M. 1983. The use of mechanical restraint and response incompatibility to modify self-injurious behavior: A case study. *Mental Retardation, 21*, 213–217.

Harris, V.W., & Herman, J.A. 1973. Use and analysis of the "Good Behavior Game" to reduce disruptive classroom behavior. *Journal of Applied Behavior Analysis, 6*, 405–417.

Heller, M., & White, M. 1975. Rates of teacher approval and disapproval to higher and lower ability classes. *Journal of Educational Psychology, 67*, 796–800.

Hinerman, P., Jenson, W., Walker, G., & Peterson, P. 1982. Positive practice overcorrection combined with additional procedures to teach signed words to an autistic child. *Journal of Autism and Developmental Disorders, 12*, 253–263.

Horton, S. 1987. Reduction of disruptive mealtime behavior by facial screening. *Behavior Modification, 11*, 53–64.

Huguenin, N., & Mulick, J. 1981. Nonexclusionary timeout: Maintenance of appropriate behavior across settings. *Applied Research in Mental Retardation, 2*, 55–67.

Iwata, B.A., & Bailey, J.S. 1974. Reward versus cost token systems: An analysis of the effects on students and teacher. *Journal of Applied Behavior Analysis, 7*, 567–576.

Jordan, J., Singh, N., & Repp, A.C. 1989. An evaluation of gentle teaching and visual screening in the reduction of stereotypy. *Journal of Applied Behavior Analysis, 22*, 9–22.

Kazdin, A.E. 1972. Response cost: The removal of conditioned reinforcers for therapeutic change. *Behavior Therapy, 3*, 533–546.

Kazdin, A.E, & Bootzin, R.R. 1972. The token economy: An evaluative review. *Journal of Applied Behavior Analysis, 5*, 343–372.

Kern, L., Koegel, R., & Dunlap, G. 1984. The influence of vigorous versus mild exercise on autistic stereotyped behaviors. *Journal of Autism and Developmental Disorders, 14*, 57–67.

Kern, L., Koegel, R., Dyer, K., Blew, P., & Fenton, L. 1982. The effects of physical exercise on self-stimulation and appropriate responding in autistic children.

Journal of Autism and Developmental Disorders, 12, 399–419.

Krasner, L. 1976. Behavioral modification: Ethical issues and future trends. In H. Leitenberg (Ed.), *Handbook of behavior modification and behavior therapy* (pp. 627–649). Englewood Cliffs, N.J.: Prentice-Hall.

Lahey, B.B., Mcnees, M.P., & Mcnees, M.C. 1973. Control of an obscene "verbal tic" through timeout in an elementary school classroom. *Journal of Applied Behavior Analysis, 6*, 101–104.

Lennox, D., Miltenberger, R., & Donnelly, D. 1987. Response interruption and DRL for the reduction of rapid eating. *Journal of Applied Behavior Analysis, 20*, 279–284.

Lenz, M., Singh, N., & Hewett, A. 1991. Overcorrection as an academic remediation procedure. *Behavior Modification, 15*, 64–73.

Liberman, R.P., Teigen, J., Patterson, R., & Baker, V. 1973. Reducing delusional speech in chronic, paranoid schizophrenics. *Journal of Applied Behavior Analysis, 6*, 57–64.

Linton, J., & Singh, N. 1984. Acquisition of sign language using positive practice overcorrection. *Behavior Modification, 8*, 553–566.

Lovaas, O.I., & Simmons, J.Q. 1969. Manipulation of self-destruction in three retarded children. *Journal of Applied Behavior Analysis, 2*, 143–157.

Luiselli, J. 1980. Controlling disruptive behaviors of an autistic child: Parent-mediated contingency management in the home setting. *Education and Treatment of Children, 3*, 195–203.

Luiselli, J. 1986. Modification of self-injurious behavior: An analysis of the use of contingently applied protective equipment. *Behavior Modification, 10*, 191–203.

Luiselli, J., & Rice, D. 1983. Brief positive practice with a handicapped child: An assessment of suppressive and re-educative effects. *Education and Treatment of Children, 6*, 241–250.

Lutzker, J. 1974. Social reinforcement control of exhibitionism in a profoundly retarded adult. *Mental Retardation, 12*, 46–47.

Mabee, W. 1988. The effects of academic positive practice on cursive letter writing. *Education and Treatment of Children, 11*, 143–148.

Mace, F., Page, T., Ivancic, M., & O'Brien, S. 1986. Effectiveness of brief time-out with and without contingent delay: A comparative analysis. *Journal of Applied Behavior Analysis, 19,* 79–86.

Macpherson, E.M., Candee, B.L., & Hohman, R.J. 1974. A comparison of three methods for eliminating disruptive lunchroom behavior. *Journal of Applied Behavior Analysis, 7,* 287–297.

Marholin, D., II, & Gray, D. 1976. Effects of group response-cost procedures on cash shortages in a small business. *Journal of Applied Behavior Analysis, 9,* 25–30.

Marshall, H. 1965. The effect of punishment on children. A review of the literature and a suggested hypothesis. *Journal of Genetic Psychology, 106,* 23–33.

Matlock, B., Billingsley, F., & Thompson, M. 1985. Response competition and generalization. In N. Haring, K. Liberty, F. Billingsley, V. Lynch, J. Kayser, & F. McCarty (Eds.), *Investigating the problems of skill generalization* (3rd ed.) (pp. 80–87). Seattle: Washington Research Organization.

Matson, J., Esveldt-Dawson, K., & Kazdin, A.E. 1982. Treatment of spelling deficits in mentally retarded children. *Mental Retardation, 20,* 76–81.

Matson, J., & Keyes, J. 1988. Contingent reinforcement and contingent restraint to treat severe aggression and self-injury in mentally retarded and autistic adults. *Journal of the Multihandicapped Person, 1,* 141–148.

Matson, J., & Stephens, R. 1977. Overcorrection of aggressive behavior in a chronic psychiatric patient. *Behavior Modification, 1,* 559–564.

Matthews, J., Friman, P., Barone, V., Ross, L., & Christophersen, E. 1987. Decreasing dangerous infant behaviors through parent instruction. *Journal of Applied Behavior Analysis, 20,* 165–169.

May, J., Mcallister, J., Risley, T. Twardosz, S., & Cox, C. 1974. *Florida guidelines for the use of behavioral procedures in state programs for the retarded.* Tallahassee: Florida Division of Retardation.

Mayhew, G., & Harris, F. 1979. Decreasing self-injurious behavior: Punishment with citric acid and reinforcement of alternative behaviors. *Behavior Modification, 3,* 322–336.

McGonigle, J., Duncan, D. Cordisco, L., & Barrett, R. 1982. Visual screening: An alternative method for reducing stereotypic behaviors. *Journal of Applied Behavior Analysis, 15,* 461–467.

McGonigle, J., & Rojahn, J. 1989. An experimental analysis of visual screening and DRO for stereotyped behavior in young children with developmental disabilities. *Journal of the Multihandicapped Person, 2,* 251–270.

McKeegan, G., Estill, K., & Campbell, B. 1984. Use of nonseclusionary timeout for the elimination of stereotypic behavior. *Journal of Behavior Therapy and Experimental Psychiatry, 15,* 261–264.

McSweeny, A.J. 1978. Effects of response cost on the behavior of a million persons: Charging for directory assistance in Cincinnati. *Journal of Applied Behavior Analysis, 11,* 47–51.

Mogel, S., & Schiff, W. 1967. Extinction of a head-bumping symptom of eight years' duration in two minutes: A case report. *Behavior Research and Therapy, 5,* 131–132.

Morales v. Turman. 364 Supp., 166 (E.D. Tex., 1973).

Mowrer, D., & Conley, D. 1987. Effect of peer administered consequences upon articulatory responses of speech defective children. *Journal of Communication Disorders, 20,* 319–326.

Neisworth, J., Hunt, F., Gallop, H., & Nadle, R. 1985. Reinforcer displacement: A preliminary study of the clinical application of CRF/EXT effect. *Behavior Modification, 9,* 103–115.

Ollendick, T., & Matson, J. 1976. An initial investigation into the parameters of overcorrection. *Psychological Reports, 39,* 1139–1142.

Ollendick, T., Matson, J., Esveldt-Dawson, K., & Shapiro, E. 1980. Increasing spelling achievement: An analysis of treatment procedures utilizing an alternating treatments design. *Journal of Applied Behavior Analysis, 13,* 645–654.

Pace, G., Iwata, B., Edwards, G., & Mccosh, K. 1986. Stimulus fading and transfer in the treatment of self-restraint and self-injurious behavior. *Journal of Applied Behavior Analysis, 19,* 381–389.

Patterson, G.R. 1965. An application of conditioning techniques to the control of a hyperactive child. In L.P. Ullmann & L. Krasner (Eds.), *Case studies in behavior modification* (pp. 370–375). New York: Holt, Rinehart & Winston.

Phillips, E.L., Phillips, E.A., Fixsen, D.L., & Wolf, M.M. 1971. Achievement Place: Modification of the behaviors of pre-delinquent boys within a token economy. *Journal of Applied Behavior Analysis, 4,* 45–59.

Pinkston, E.M., Reese, N.M., Leblanc, J.M., & Baer, D.M. 1973. Independent control of a preschool child's aggression and peer interaction by contingent teacher attention. *Journal of Applied Behavior Analysis, 6,* 115–124.

Porterfield, J.K., Herbert-Jackson, E., & Risley, T.R. 1976. Contingent observation: An effective and acceptable procedure for reducing disruptive behavior of young children in a group setting. *Journal of Applied Behavior Analysis, 9,* 55–64.

Proctor, M., & Morgan, D. 1991. Effectiveness of a response cost raffle procedure on the disruptive classroom behavior of adolescents with behavior problems. *School Psychology Review, 20,* 97–109.

Rapport, M., Murphy, A., & Bailey, J. 1982. Ritalin vs. response cost in the control of hyperactive children: A within-subject comparison. *Journal of Applied Behavior Analysis, 15,* 205–216.

Reid, J., Tombaugh, T., & Van Den Heuvel, K. 1981. Application of contingent physical restraint to suppress stereotyped body rocking of profoundly retarded persons. *American Journal of Mental Deficiency, 86,* 78–85.

Repp, A.C. 1983. *Teaching the mentally retarded child.* Englewood Cliffs, N.J.: Prentice-Hall.

Repp, A.C., Barton, L., & Brulle, A. 1983. A comparison of two procedures for programming the differential reinforcement of other behavior. *Journal of Applied Behavior Analysis, 16,* 435–445.

Repp, A.C., & Deitz, D.E.D. 1979. Reinforcement-based reductive procedures: Training and monitoring performance of institutional staff. *Mental Retardation, 17,* 221–226.

Repp, A.C., Deitz, S.M., & Deitz, D.E.D. 1976. Reducing inappropriate behaviors in classrooms and in individual session through DRO schedules of reinforcement. *Mental Retardation, 14,* 11–15.

Repp, A.C., Deitz, S.M., & Speir, N.C. 1974. Reducing stereotypic responding of retarded persons by the differential reinforcement of other behavior. *American Journal of Mental Deficiency, 79,* 279–284.

Repp, A., Felce, D., & Barton, L. 1991. The effects of initial interval size on the efficacy of DRO schedules of reinforcement. *Exceptional Children, 58,* 417–425.

Reynolds, G.S. 1961. Behavioral contrast. *Journal of the Experimental Analysis of Behavior, 4,* 57–71.

Rimm, D.C., & Masters, J.C. 1979. *Behavior therapy: Techniques and empirical findings.* New York: Academic Press.

Rincover, A. 1981. *How to use sensory extinction.* Lawrence, Kan.: H&H Enterprises.

Ritschl, C., Mongrella, J., & Presbie, R. 1972. Group time out from rock and roll music and out-of-seat behavior of handicapped children while riding a school bus. *Psychological Reports, 31,* 967–973.

Roberts, M. 1988. Enforcing chair timeouts with room timeouts. *Behavior Modification, 12,* 353–370.

Rojahn, J., McGonigle, J., Curcio, C., & Dixon, J. 1987. Suppression of pica by water mist and aromatic ammonia. *Behavior Modification, 11,* 65–74.

Rolider, A., & Van Houten, R. 1985. Movement suppression in time-out for undesirable behavior in psychotic and severely developmentally delayed children. *Journal of Applied Behavior Analysis, 18,* 275–288.

Rollings, J., Baumeister, A., & Baumeister, A. 1977. The use of overcorrection procedures to eliminate the stereotyped behaviors of retarded individuals: An analysis of collateral behaviors and generalization of suppressive effects. *Behavior Modification, 1,* 29–46.

Rose, T. 1979. Reducing self-injurious behavior by differentially reinforcing other behaviors. *AAESPH Review, 4,* 179–186.

Rotholz, O., & Luce, S. 1983. Alternative reinforcement strategies for the reduction of self-stimulatory behavior in autistic youth. *Education and Treatment of Children, 6,* 363–377.

Rusch, F., & Close, D. 1976. Overcorrection: A procedural evaluation. *AAESPH Review, 1,* 32–45.

Rusch, F., Connis, R., & Sowers, J. 1978. The modification and maintenance of time spent attending to task using social reinforcement, token reinforcement and response cost in an applied restaurant setting. *Journal of Special Education Technology, 2,* 18–26.

Rutherford, B. 1940. The use of negative practice in speech therapy with children handicapped by cerebral palsy, athetoid type. *Journal of Speech Disorders, 5,* 259–264.

Sajwaj, T., Libet, J., & Agras, S. 1974. Lemon-juice therapy: The control of life-threatening rumination in a six-month-old infant. *Journal of Applied Behavior Analysis, 7,* 557–563.

Salend, S. 1988. Effects of a student-managed response cost system on the behavior of two mainstreamed students. *Elementary School Journal, 89*, 89–97.

Salend, S., & Gordon, B. 1987. A group-oriented timeout ribbon procedure. *Behavioral Disorders, 12*, 131–137.

Salend, S., & Kovalich, B. 1981. A group response cost system mediated by free tokens. *American Journal of Mental Deficiency, 86*, 184–187.

Salend, S., & Lamb, E. 1986. Effectiveness of a group-managed interdependent contingency system. *Learning Disability Quarterly, 9*, 268–273.

Salend, S., & Maragulia, D. 1983. The timeout ribbon: A procedure for the least restrictive environment. *Journal for Special Educators, 20*, 9–15.

Schloss, P., & Smith, M. 1987. Guidelines for ethical use of manual restraint in public school settings for behaviorally disordered students. *Behavioral Disorders, 12*, 207–213.

Scott, P.M., Burton, R.V., & Yarrow, M.R., 1967. Social reinforcement under natural conditions. *Child Development, 38*, 53–63.

Siegel, G.M., Lenske, J., & Broen, P. 1969. Suppression of normal speech disfluencies through response cost. *Journal of Applied Behavior Analysis, 2*, 265–276.

Singh, N. 1979. Aversive control of breath-holding. *Journal of Behavior Therapy and Experimental Psychiatry, 10*, 147–149.

Singh, N. 1980. The effects of facial screening on infant self-injury. *Journal of Behavior Therapy and Experimental Psychiatry, 11*, 131–134.

Singh, N. 1987. Overcorrection of oral reading errors. *Behavior Modification, 11*, 165–181.

Singh, N., & Bakker, L. 1984. Suppression of pica by overcorrection and physical restraint: A comparative analysis. *Journal of Autism and Developmental Disorders, 14*, 331–340.

Singh, N., Beale, I., & Dawson, M. 1981. Duration of facial screening and suppression of self injurious behavior: Analysis using an alternative treatments design. *Behavioral Assessment, 3*, 411–420.

Singh, N., Dawson, M., & Manning, P. 1981. Effects of spaced responding DRL on the stereotyped behavior of profoundly retarded persons. *Journal of Applied Behavior Analysis, 14*, 521–526.

Singh, N., Landrum, T., Ellis, C., & Donatelli, L. 1993. Effects of thioridazine and visual screening on stereotypy and social behavior in individuals with mental retardation. *Research in Developmental Disabilities, 14*, 163–177.

Singh, N., & Singh, J. 1986. Increasing oral reading proficiency: A comparative analysis of drill and positive practice overcorrection procedures. *Behavior Modification, 10*, 115–130.

Singh, N., & Singh, J. 1988. Increasing oral reading proficiency through overcorrection and phonic analysis. *American Journal of Mental Retardation, 93*, 312–319.

Singh, N., Singh, J., & Winton, A. 1984. Positive practice overcorrection of oral reading errors. *Behavior Modification, 8*, 23–37.

Singh, N., Watson, J., & Winton, A. 1986. Treating self-injury: Water mist spray versus facial screening or forced arm exercise. *Journal of Applied Behavior Analysis, 19*, 403–410.

Singh, N., & Winton, A. 1984. Effects of a screening procedure on pica and collateral behaviors. *Journal of Behavior Therapy and Experimental Psychiatry, 15*, 59–65.

Skinner, B.F. 1953. *Science and human behavior*. New York: Macmillan.

Smith, A., Piersel, W., Filbeck, R., & Gross, E. 1983. The elimination of mealtime food stealing and scavenging behavior in an institutionalized severely mentally retarded adult. *Mental Retardation, 21*, 255–259.

Sobsey, D. 1990. Modifying the behavior of behavior modifiers. In A. Repp & N. Singh (Eds.), *Perspectives on the use of nonaversive and aversive interventions for persons with developmental disabilities* (pp. 421–433). Sycamore, Ill.: Sycamore Publishing.

Solomon, R.W., & Wahler, R.G. 1973. Peer reinforcement control of classroom problem behavior. *Journal of Applied Behavior Analysis, 6*, 49–56.

Stewart, C., & Singh, N. 1986. Overcorrection of spelling deficits in mentally retarded persons. *Behavior Modification, 10*, 355–365.

Sumner, J., Meuser, S., Hsu, L., & Morales, R. 1974. Overcorrection treatment of radical reduction of aggressive-disruptive behavior in institutionalized mental patients. *Psychological Reports, 35*, 655–662.

Tanner, B.A., & Zeiler, M. 1975. Punishment of self-injurious behavior using aromatic ammonia as the aversive stimulus. *Journal of Applied Behavior Analysis, 8*, 53–57.

Thomas, J.D., Presland, I.E., Grant, M.D., & Glynn, T.L. 1978. Natural rates of teacher approval and disapproval in grade-7 classrooms. *Journal of Applied Behavior Analysis, 11*, 91–94.

Trice, A., & Parker, F. 1983. Decreasing adolescent swearing in an instructional setting. *Education and Treatment of Children, 6*, 29–35.

Van Houten, R. 1993. The use of wrist weights to reduce self-injury maintained by sensory reinforcement. *Journal of Applied Behavior Analysis, 26*, 197–203.

Van Houten, R., Nau, P., Mackenzie-Keating, S., Sameoto, D., & Colavecchia, B. 1982. An analysis of some variables influencing the effectiveness of reprimands. *Journal of Applied Behavior Analysis, 15*, 65–83.

Vasta, R., & Wortman, H. 1988. Nocturnal bruxism treated by massed negative practice. *Behavior Modification, 12*, 618–626.

Vollmer, T., & Iwata, B. 1992. Differential reinforcement as treatment for behavior disorder: Procedural and functional variations. *Research in Developmental Disabilities, 13*, 393–417.

Walker, H., Hops, H., & Fiegenbaum, E. 1976. Deviant classroom behavior as a function of combinations of social and token reinforcement and cost contingency. *Behavior Therapy, 7*, 76–88.

Walton, D. 1961. Experimental psychology and the treatment of a tiqueur. *Journal of Child Psychology and Psychiatry, 2*, 148–155.

Watson, J., Singh, N., & Winton, A. 1986. Suppressive effects of visual and facial screening on self-injurious finger-sucking. *American Journal of Mental Deficiency, 90*, 526–534.

Watson, L.S. 1967. Application of operant conditioning techniques to institutionalized severely and profoundly retarded children. *Mental Retardation Abstracts, 4*, 1–18.

Wesolowski, M., & Zawlocki, R., 1982. The differential effects of procedures to eliminate an injurious self-stimulatory behavior (digito-ocular sign) in blind retarded twins. *Behavior Therapy, 13*, 334–345.

White, M.A., 1975. Natural rates of teacher approval and disapproval in the classroom. *Journal of Applied Behavior Analysis, 8*, 367–372.

Wilson, C.W., & Hopkins, B.L. 1973. The effects of contingent music on the intensity of noise in junior high home economics classes. *Journal of Applied Behavior Analysis, 6*, 269–275.

Winton, A., & Singh, N. 1983. Suppression of pica using brief-duration physical restraint. *Journal of Mental Deficiency Research, 27*, 93–103.

Winton, A., Singh, N., & Dawson, M. 1984. Effects of facial screening and blindfold on self-injurious behavior. *Applied Research in Mental Retardation, 5*, 29–42

Wyatt v. Stickney, 344 F. Supp. 373; 344 F. Supp. 387 (M.D. Ala., 1972) affirmed sub nom. *Wyatt v. Aderholt*, 503 F. 2nd 1305 (5th Cir., 1974).

Wylie, A., & Grossman, J. 1988. Response reduction through superimposition of continuous reinforcement: A systematic replication. *Journal of Applied Behavior Analysis, 21*, 201–206.

Yates, A.J. 1958. Symptoms and symptom substitution. *Psychological Review, 65*, 371–374.

Zabel, M. 1986. Timeout use with behaviorally disordered students. *Behavioral Disorders, 11*, 15–20.

Zegiob, L., Alford, G.L., & House, A. 1978. Response suppressive and generalization effects of facial screening on multiple self-injurious behavior in a retarded boy. *Behavior Therapy, 9*, 688.

Zegiob, L., Jenkins, J., Becker, J., & Bristow, A. 1976. Facial screening: Effects on appropriate and inappropriate behaviors. *Journal of Behavior Therapy and Experimental Psychiatry, 7*, 355–357.

Zimmerman, E.H., & Zimmerman, J. 1962. The alteration of behavior in a special classroom situation. *Journal of the Experimental Analysis of Behavior, 5*, 59–60.

9

Functional Assessment and Analysis

Did you know that . . .
- Nothing works every time.
- Nothing works for everything.
- Nothing works on everyone.
- Nothing works forever.

THE NEED FOR ANOTHER STRATEGY

The procedures described in this text thus far have proven successful in many cases, for many students, in many settings, and for many different types of behavior. It is unfortunately true, however, that an occasional inappropriate behavior is resistant to change or that changing it appears to create new problems. Consider the following examples:

> At Whittier Middle School the certain consequence for fighting is 3 days in-school suspension. During such suspension, students must labor all day at written work in study carrels adjacent to the principal's office, where they are not allowed to talk or socialize. Until now, fighting has been a very infrequent behavior. Suddenly, in the last few weeks of school, Ms. Phelps, the principal, is dealing with several fights a day. Repeated interviews with the participants have provided little information. "He just came up and hit me—I don't hardly know the dude." Ms. Phelps has narrowed the instigators down to two or three students but can pin down no apparent reason for their behavior. She wonders if the heat (the classrooms are not air-conditioned and severe winter weather has extended the school year well into June) is causing aggression. Whatever the cause, in-school suspension, even increased to 4 days, has lost its effectiveness for some students.

> Angela is a new student in Mr. Wilkins's self-contained class for young children with developmental delays. Angela screams. Mr. Wilkins decides to use time-out to decrease Angela's screaming. Sure enough, Angela stops screaming but starts hitting adults and other children, apparently at random. Mr. Wilkins, not easily discouraged, begins to put Angela in time-out for hitting. Soon he observes that Angela has begun banging her head on the floor. Since he obviously cannot allow her to injure herself by banging her head on the floor in time-out, he does become discouraged. He abandons time-out and Angela gradually returns to screaming.

In both the anecdotes above, educators are dealing with apparently random behavior and with students who cannot or will not provide information about what antecedents or consequences are controlling it. Attempts are made to interfere with the behaviors with techniques that have been effective in the past, but these attempts have been unsuccessful. The behavior has a familiar form or topography—it looks like behavior we have seen before. The problem may be that in our preoccupation with the behavior's form we fail to determine its function. In other words, informal analysis fails to provide us with an accurate assessment of what purpose the behavior serves for the student. In such cases a more complex procedure known as functional assessment/analysis (Skinner, 1953) may provide additional guidance.

Throughout this text we have stressed using the least complex possible strategy when planning an intervention. The suggestions in this chapter, without a doubt, are the most complicated and time-consuming that we have described. These procedures, however, will often enable teachers and parents to change behavior that has proved resistant to simpler techniques, and to do so without using aversive interventions. After describing some of the functions that behavior may serve, we will examine functional assessment and analysis in two stages. The first stage, functional assessment, includes procedures to develop hypotheses about a behavior's function for an individual. The second stage, functional analysis, involves manipulation of variables to verify these hypotheses.

STAGE ONE: FUNCTIONAL ASSESSMENT
Discovering the Function a Behavior Serves

Questions that can be answered using functional assessment/analysis

When applied behavior analysts ask "Why does she do that?" they are really wondering what function the behavior serves.

Functional assessment/analysis attempts to answer one of the following questions (Lennox & Miltenberger, 1989):

1. What antecedent is occasioning the behavior?
2. What consequence is maintaining the behavior?
3. Can the student be taught an alternative, appropriate behavior to accomplish the same function as the inappropriate behavior?

The physical characteristics (form or topography) of behavior are what we observe. We develop an operational definition of the behavior based on our observation. A quantitative measure of topography (for example, frequency, duration, or percentage of intervals during which the behavior occurs) is typically the dependent variable when we seek to change a behavior (Pyles & Bailey, 1990, p. 381). In some cases, however, it may be necessary for us to know what purpose the behavior serves—why the student engages in it. It may be that some naturally occurring antecedent or consequent events maintaining the behavior are more powerful than those arranged by the teacher to interfere with it. Interventions like token economies, time-out, and overcorrection are often implemented without thoroughly assessing the variables that occasion or maintain the inappropriate behavior they are expected to reduce. These procedures will be effective only to the extent that they successfully compete with existing contingencies that support inappropriate behavior (Mace, Lalli, & Lalli, 1991).

Even if an intervention is effective it may be so only in the short term unless a new behavior fulfills the same purpose as the inappropriate one. Teachers often find that an intervention will eliminate an inappropriate behavior for a short time but that the behavior (or an equally inappropriate one serving the same function) reappears as soon as the novelty of a procedure is gone. It may well be that the failure to consider a behavior's function is the basis for the assumption that the suppression of inappropriate behavior inevitably results in "symptom substitution" or the appearance of new inappropriate behavior based on some underlying disturbance. (See the description of Professor Grundy's presentation in Chapter 2 for a description of this phenomenon.) A need for functional analysis does not assume some internal motive for a student's behavior but focuses on the purpose of that

It's neither fair nor ethical to punish functional behavior.

behavior (or a substitute for it) as defined by environmental events that occasion or maintain it. Attempts to eliminate behaviors, even if effective, may be unethical.

Although it is possible to eliminate behaviors using aversive consequences, it is unethical to do so if the individual lacks an alternative means to serve the behaviors' functions (Pyles & Bailey, 1990). If a student with a communication deficit uses tantrums to get attention or a student who can't read throws his book to escape embarrassment or ridicule, it is hardly fair to punish these behaviors unless we provide the students with other ways to accomplish their purpose.

Focusing on a behavior's topography may provide little information about factors responsible for the behavior. The same behavior exhibited by two different students may be maintained by entirely different stimuli. One student's aggressive behavior may be a function of teacher or peer attention (positive reinforcement). Another student may be negatively reinforced by escape from an academic or vocational task, social interaction, or other event the student finds aversive. It is unlikely that any single intervention will have the same effect on behaviors serving such different functions (Iwata, Vollmer, & Zarcone, 1990).

By neglecting to conduct a functional analysis, we may fail to see that topographically unrelated behaviors, such as signing "ketchup," pointing to a ketchup bottle, or banging one's head on the table, may serve the same function by controlling a particular outcome—getting ketchup (Remington, 1991). The purpose of functional assessment/analysis is to give equal attention to the function of behavior as to its form. An analysis of a problem behavior's function in terms of its antecedents and consequences is necessary for the selection of the most effective treatment procedures (Crawford, Brockel, Schauss, & Miltenberger, 1992).

Reviews and models in the literature (Mace et al., 1991; O'Neill, Horner, Albin, Storey, & Sprague, 1990; Pyles & Bailey, 1990) and our classroom experience yield agreement on some of the antecedents of which behaviors may be a function and some of the functions inappropriate behaviors serve for students. A summary of these antecedents is presented in Figure 9–1.

Antecedent Conditions Functionally Related to Inappropriate Behavior

In discussing antecedents leading to inappropriate behavior we often use words not usually associated with applied behavior analysis. Rest assured that we have not suddenly become preoccupied with internal causation and emotional states. When we talk about frustration, embarrassment, boredom, and the like, we will provide operational definitions for each.

Even adults sometimes lash out when they are frustrated.

Frustration, operationally defined as the inability to perform a task resulting in natural or arranged reinforcement, may cause a student to behave inappropriately. A student with a severe disability who lacks a functional

FIGURE 9–1
Examples of some antecedents to behavior and their functions

I. ANTECEDENTS TO INAPPROPRIATE BEHAVIOR

    A. Frustration due to:

        1. Response ignorance

        2. Complex materials, lacking in appropriate adaptations

        3. Lack of functional vocabulary to communicate (verbal or on augmentative/alternative communication system)

        4. Goal or performance interruption

    B. Understimulation: Boredom

        1. Being ignored

        2. Meaningless repetition beyond criterion

        3. Nonfunctional activity

        4. Pacing too slow

    C. Overstimulation

        1. Environment: For example, number of students, noise

        2. Rate of physical prompting or verbalizations

        3. Pace of activity

    D. Environmental expectation or models

II. FUNCTIONS SERVED BY INAPPROPRIATE BEHAVIOR

    A. Attention Seeking

        1. A communication attempt to indicate needs and wants (for example, to indicate need/want for person [for environmental change or social/emotional feedback], object, event)

        2. Historical/current pattern of positive reinforcement resulting in a means to access people (positive or negative attention), object, event

        3. Inconsistent pattern of reinforcement or punishment

    B. Means of escape/avoidance (negative reinforcement)

        1. Internal stimuli: ear ache, sinus pain, skin irritation, hunger, constipation, fatigue

        2. External stimuli: touching, difficult task (demand), change in routine, setting, physical discomfort (position in wheelchair), environmental discomfort (heat, noise), social embarrassment (due to age-inappropriate tasks, materials, dress)

    C. Sensory feedback/stimulation

        1. To obtain reinforcement from internal stimulation, for example, visual, auditory, vestibular, gustatory, or tactual stimulation

    D. Nature of current reinforcement: desirability, quantity, intensity, scheduling vocabulary or an augmentative or alternative communication system may be unable to accomplish tasks as simple as requesting a drink when she is thirsty or a change of clothing when she is uncomfortable. If quiet vocalizations or body movements do not result in reinforcement, she may scream or bang her head on the table. A student who is unable to read cannot possibly earn the sticker offered to every student who correctly answers the comprehension questions in the workbook. He may throw his book on the floor, curse at his teacher, or pick a fight with another student. Frustration may occur when instructional materials are cognitively or physically too complex or when appropriate adaptations are not made.

If we implement a differential reinforcement procedure with discriminative stimuli that are not sufficiently clear to the student, his crying, or screaming, or hitting may be intended to communicate, "I don't know what you want me to do!" Students may become frustrated because they cannot perform an action that they see others do easily. A student who has seen a peer pour juice from a pitcher and drink (natural reinforcer) or do math problems correctly and receive teacher praise, but who can't pour juice or do math problems correctly becomes frustrated. Students who experience frustration are apt to express this frustration in the form of inappropriate behavior. Interruption of a task may also result in frustration. A student engaged in a task she has often successfully completed and been reinforced for may scream, throw materials, or refuse to engage in the next activity if the teacher removes the materials because it is time to move on to another activity.

Students have learned that teasing from peers results from certain behaviors.

Embarrassment, operationally defined as the anticipation of ridicule, may also occasion inappropriate behavior. The use of age-inappropriate materials (for example, giving a teenager toddlers' toys or a high school resource student a Dr. Seuss book to practice reading from) may result in refusal to participate in the activity. If pressed, the student may escalate the inappropriate behavior and have a tantrum or storm from the room.

Instructional procedures that result in periods of time when students have nothing to do provide an opportunity, especially for students with limited functional repertoires, to fill these periods with inappropriate behavior. We often use the term "bored" to describe people who have too little stimulation. When a lesson is paced so slowly that students' attention wanders, or when there are so many students in a learning group that interaction with each student is infrequent, misbehavior often results. Another route to student boredom is repetition of a task that has been mastered rather than progression to generalization across materials and settings or to a new task. Needless repetition resulting in boredom may also occur when the teacher, needing time for other students, gives a student something to do that he has done over and over and over before. The old aphorism that the devil finds work for idle hands certainly was a response to this phenomenon.

Inappropriate behavior may result from overstimulation in the environment. In classes or community environments where there are many people or a high noise level, students may become agitated. A student may be overstimulated during instruction by the amount of physical touching during a prompting strategy, or by the teacher's rapid delivery of physical or verbal prompts.

Sometimes inappropriate behavior occurs because students are in environments in which others provide antecedents or models for what a teacher may see as misbehavior. In the gym, in a mall during community instruction, and even in school halls during class changes, peers and adults may behave in ways that are inappropriate.

Once the antecedent occasioning inappropriate behavior is identified, the teacher may remove it from the environment (Carr, Newsom, & Binkoff, 1980), or teach the student an alternative behavior that is more acceptable.

Obscure Consequences Functionally Related to Behavior

Some inappropriate behaviors may be maintained by reinforcers not easily identified. Sometimes simple observation may enable us to identify a functional relationship that is obvious. For example, Daniel's teacher lets him stop working and play with blocks every time he cries over his math assignment. Sometimes, however, the relationship is much more difficult to identify and requires more complex assessment procedures. In either event, once a relationship is established, it may be possible to remove access to the reinforcers (Horner, 1980). In the example at the beginning of this chapter, functional assessment finally resulted in the insight that students at Whittier Middle School were picking fights in order to spend 3 days in a cool environment—the principal's suite was air-conditioned while the rest of the school was not.

Typical toddlers sometimes have tantrums when they can't make someone understand what they want.

What parents or teachers describe as inappropriate behavior may serve a communicative function for students. The behavior results in some environmental outcome that is reinforcing to the student. A student without a standard form of communication may attempt to indicate that he wants someone's attention in order to accomplish some environmental change. A student might scream and hit himself because he is not able to ask, "Please change my position in my wheelchair; I'm very uncomfortable." To refer to an earlier example, a student may bang her head on the table to indicate "Please pass the ketchup," because she lacks the ability to sign "ketchup" or has not learned that she may obtain it by pointing. A student who has not been taught an acceptable way to indicate that he needs to use the bathroom may display what appears to be simply inappropriate restlessness and agitation. Functional analysis enabled Mr. Wilkins, Angela's teacher in the anecdote at the beginning of this chapter, to determine that Angela used screaming to communicate a variety of needs and that when screaming became ineffective she turned to hitting and head-banging. Providing her with an augmentative communication device and the training to use it gradually reduced her screaming.

Things that inappropriate behaviors might serve to communicate

Donnellan, Mirenda, Mesaros, & Fassbender (1984) suggest focus on identifying the communicative function of an inappropriate behavior. They suggest that these functions may include interactive functions such as requests (for attention, social interaction, assistance, objects), negations (protest, refusal, or cessation), declarations/comments (about events, objects, persons, errors, greetings), or non-interactive functions such as self-control, rehearsal, or relaxation. Once the function is identified, the student may be taught a more appropriate form of behavior that serves the same communicative purpose (Carr & Durand, 1985; Durand & Carr, 1987). Inappropriate behavior with a communicative function is often maintained by positive reinforcement (either consistently or inconsistently administered). For example, a student whose self-injury or disruptive behavior has a communicative function may have the need met—the frustrated teacher repositions the student, hands her ketchup, or takes her to the restroom—perhaps as one of a number of attempts to placate her—and thus positively reinforces the inappropriate, but sometimes successful, communicative behavior.

A second possible function served by an inappropriate behavior may be escape from an aversive condition. To calm a screaming student, the teacher may remove something the student doesn't like—long division, circle time, reading aloud, being placed in time-out. The inappropriate behavior thus results in avoidance, delay, or reduction of the aversive condition—negative reinforcement, which, as you remember from Chapter 6, results in increased future probability of the behavior. O'Neill et al. (1990) divide stimuli from which students may want to escape into internal stimuli and external stimuli (see Figure 9–1 again).

Internal stimulation is a third possible function. A student may engage in inappropriate behavior in order to gain visual stimulation (finger flicking), auditory stimulation (ear rubbing or vocalizations), vestibular stimulation (body rocking), gustatory stimulation (mouthing objects), or tactile stimulation (self-scratching). Inappropriate behavior may be telling us that our activity does not provide sufficient competing reinforcers for those available naturally. The student may be asking us, "Why would I want to listen to music when I can make those great noises all by myself?" Even if the reinforcer is potentially effective, the student may be telling us that he needs a lot more potato chips a lot more often, or louder or softer or different music.

STAGE TWO: FUNCTIONAL ANALYSIS (MANIPULATION OF VARIABLES)

The following selection procedures are used to gather information in order to form a hypothesis as to variables occasioning or maintaining a behavior. Information may be gathered from an informant or by direct observation. Based on the results of this **functional assessment** the teacher may then manipulate the identified variables to verify their effect on the behavior. This is known as **functional analysis**. Table 9–1 presents a list of these procedures.

Informant Assessment

Informant (or indirect) assessment procedures involve questioning a person familiar with the student (teacher, parent, paraprofessional, related service professional) about the behavior and the circumstances surrounding its occurrence. Because this questioning necessarily takes place after the behav-

Functional Assessment Procedures: Information Gathering

A. Informant Assessment (Indirect Assessment)

 1. Behavioral Interview

 2. Behavioral Scales and Questionnaires

B. Descriptive Assessment (Direct Observation Assessment)

 1. Scatter Plot

 2. A-B-C Assessment

Functional Analysis: Variable Manipulation

A. Within-Session Manipulation

B. Use of Reversal Design

C. Use of Multielement Design

ior has occurred it is limited by the informant's memory, presence during the behavior, distraction by other events, potential bias, and ability to verbalize what was seen (Kazdin, 1980; Mace et al., 1991).

Behavioral Interview

The purpose of a behavioral or functional interview is to get as complete a picture as possible of the problem behavior and the environmental conditions and events surrounding it. A teacher may interview a parent about a behavior occurring at home; a special education teacher may interview a regular class teacher. A baffled teacher may ask a colleague or supervisor to interview *him*. The interview provides preliminary information to help form a hypothesis about what may be occasioning or maintaining the behavior and may be used to structure direct observation and data collection for further analysis. The interviewer wants to know, for example:

Things that can be learned by interviewing

- the topography of the behavior—to pinpoint exactly what is happening
- how often it is occurring
- at what times of the day the behavior is occurring
- in what setting the behavior occurs
- what medication the student takes
- what consequences of the behavior the informant noticed
- what the informant noticed immediately before the behavior (antecedents)
- what the student does right after the behavior
- what other people do right after the behavior
- what materials or tools are involved
- what efforts have already been made to reduce the behavior

In some instances the interview may be the only source of information available before forming a hypothesis and making suggestions. However, it is preferable that it be just the first in a series of steps.

Behavioral Rating Checklists, Scales, and Questionnaires

The use of checklists and questionnaires is a more structured method of obtaining functional assessment information from an informant. Their purpose is generally to determine the function a behavior is serving.

Wolery, Bailey, and Sugai (1988, p. 360) have suggested an instrument with questions concerning:

*   instructional dimension of the environment (the nature of materials, activity, and instruction)
*   physical dimension of the environment (lighting, noise, heat, physical arrangement, time of day)
*   social dimension of the environment (number of students, adults, proximity)
*   changes in the environment (changes in schedule, physical arrangement, and changes at home).

Evans and Meyer (1985) suggest a checklist of 15 open-ended questions to ask about excess behavior. They include questions such as: Is the behavior very rhythmic or cyclical? In what settings is the behavior most prevalent? What general instructional factors elicit the behavior (demands, frustrating situations, adult or peer interactions)?

The Motivation Assessment Scale (MAS) (Durand, 1990; Durand & Crimmins, 1988) is an example of a more structured questionnaire instrument developed to assess the function of problem behavior. Informants are asked to rate the likelihood of a behavior's occurring in different antecedent conditions. The data are then analyzed in order to identify the maintaining variables. The MAS contains 16 brief descriptions of behavior in the form of questions. For example: Does the behavior occur following a request to perform a difficult task? Does the behavior seem to occur in response to your talking to other persons in the room? Does the behavior ever occur to get a toy, food, or activity that this person has been told that he or she can't have? Does it appear to you that this person enjoys performing the behavior (it feels, tastes, looks, smells, and/or sounds pleasing)? Does the behavior stop occurring shortly after you give this person the toy, food, or activity he or she has requested? Does the behavior stop occurring shortly (1 to 5 minutes) after you stop working or making demands of this person? (Durand, 1990, pp. 176–178). The informant responds to each description as having occurred on a continuum from never occurring to always occurring. Responses are scored to determine if the behavior is being reinforced by sensory stimulation, escape from an undesirable situation, attention, or some tangible reinforcer.

Mrs. Grundy Uses a Questionnaire

Professor Grundy was having an absolutely rotten day. He was finding the university's smoke-free policy to be very difficult to live with. He had reached for his pipe a dozen times during a departmental meeting and expressed his frustration with a loud expression of "Tchah!" when he remembered the new rules. His colleagues had begun to look at him quizzically as he repeatedly reached into the pocket of his tweed jacket and snorted "Tchah!" He thought he overheard the word "tic" as two of his colleagues muttered together.

Later, as he stood outside the building, huddling under the portico for some protection from the rain, a student asked an innocuous question and Grundy, cold, damp, and embarrassed to be hanging around the front door like a derelict, snapped rudely at the student.

Upon arriving home, he began to share his feelings with Mrs. Grundy, who had been after him for years to give up what she referred to as "that filthy habit."

She surprised him by sympathizing. "You know," suggested Mrs. Grundy, "I came across something while I was straightening your study. An article (Axelrod, 1991) in one of those grey magazines that are all over the place said that you can use something called functional analysis to figure out *why* you smoke. Then you'll know how to stop."

She showed him the questionnaire (see Table 9–2). He read it carefully and replied, "But my dear, how does it help to know that I smoke for *all* these reasons?" In spite of his skepticism, Professor Grundy began to wonder if he could use the change in his environment to change his behavior rather than developing a whole new pattern of behavior in a different environment.

TABLE 9–2
Functional analysis questions for smokers

Why Do You Smoke?

True or False: I smoke
1. because I light up automatically and don't know I'm doing it.
2. because it's relaxing.
3. because I like handling cigarettes, matches, and lighters.
4. to help deal with anger.
5. to keep from slowing down.
6. because it's unbearable not to.
7. because I enjoy watching the smoke as I exhale it.
8. to take my mind off my troubles.
9. because I really enjoy it.
10. because I feel uncomfortable without a cigarette in my hand.
11. to give myself a lift.
12. without planning to—it's just part of my routine.

Results: "True" answers to 5 and 11 indicate that you smoke for stimulation; to 3 and 7, that the pleasure of handling is important; to 2 and 9, that you seek relaxation; to 4 and 8, that you need a tension-reducing crutch; to 6 and 10, that you have a physiological addiction; to 1 and 12, that you smoke from habit. No doubt you smoke for a combination of these reasons.

Direct Observation Assessment

Direct observation is more reliable than informant assessment. Someone who observes the problem behavior directly will derive a more accurate measure of potential antecedent and consequent stimuli maintaining the behavior. Two types of direct observation include the use of scatter plot assessment and anecdotal recording of antecedent-behavior-consequence (A-B-C assessment).

Scatter Plot Assessment

Scatter plot procedure is helpful in identifying a relationship between an environmental condition and behavior that is frequent, seemingly random,

FIGURE 9–2
A grid for scatter plot assessment

Source: From "A scatter plot for identifying stimulus control of problem behavior," by P. Touchette, R. MacDonald, and S. Langer. Journal of Applied Behavior Analysis, 18, 1985. Copyright 1985 by The Society for the Experimental Analysis of Behavior, Inc. Reprinted by permission.

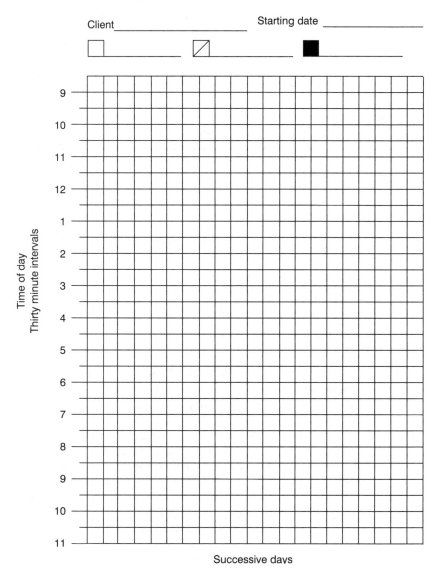

but steady throughout long periods of time. For such behaviors, informal observations often do not suggest correspondence with particular stimuli. It is easier to isolate a particular antecedent for behavior that occurs in bursts or isolated incidents (Touchette, MacDonald, & Langer, 1985, p. 343).

For scatter plot assessment, the teacher prepares a grid as seen in Figure 9–2. Time is plotted along the ordinate. Time may be divided into hours, half hours, quarter hours, etc., depending on the amount of time to be observed and/or how close a representation of the behavior is wanted. Successive days or observation periods are plotted along the abscissa. When scoring the behavior, a cell is left blank if the behavior did not occur during the interval. A low rate of occurrence during the interval can be differentiated from a high rate of occurrence by putting a slash through the cell rather than filling it in completely. As the scatter grid is filled in, each time cell contains a designation indicating whether the behavior occurred at a high, low, or zero rate. A more precise representation may be obtained by inserting numbers to represent the exact number of occurrences in the cell (Axelrod, 1987).

A scatter plot may reveal temporal patterns.

In analyzing a completed grid, Touchette et al. (1985) suggest that problem behavior may be found to correlate a time of day, the presence or absence of certain people, a social setting, certain types of activities, a reinforcement contingency, a physical environment, and/or combinations of variables. They suggest that such plotting helps offer "insights into patterns of responding not readily available from graphs of daily or weekly frequency" (p. 351). Axelrod (1987) notes that a scatter plot will detect only environmental conditions that are related to behavior on a time-cyclical basis. Some events affect behavior in a noncyclical manner. For example, a student may become disruptive whenever a classmate is given a special privilege or she feels she was treated unfairly or "cheated." He suggests that it might be helpful to write comments on the data sheet to document such events. The scatter plot strategy does not specifically identify potential controlling variables. It provides only a rough representation of rate, but it narrows the field of analysis so that closer assessment (for example, A-B-C) can be conducted more efficiently (Lennox & Miltenberger, 1989).

A-B-C Assessment

A-B-C assessment attempts to describe and evaluate the stimuli surrounding a behavior through direct observation. A-B-C assessment is conducted by directly observing the student and recording anecdotal data over several observation periods. The data in the report are then structured by identifying each problem behavior and the events right before the behavior (antecedents) and events right after the behavior (consequences). Formatting the information as seen in Figure 4–2 allows the teacher to identify a pattern among the behaviors, antecedents, and consequences that indicates a possible functional relationship. (This process is described in Chapter 4.)

This kind of ABC assessment is more detailed than that described in Chapter 4.

As noted in Chapter 4, Wright (1960) provided some suggested guidelines for writing anecdotal reports. Cooper, Heron, and Heward (1987, p. 40) made additional suggestions:

- Use any kind of shorthand or abbreviations to make recording more efficient. Notes can be expanded immediately after the observation session.
- Report only behavior that is seen or heard, not interpretations of that behavior.
- Record the temporal relationship of each behavior noted. Write down what happened just before (antecedent) and just after (consequence) each response of the student.
- Record the estimated duration of each instance of the student's behavior. Note the beginning and ending time of each behavior recorded.
- Try to be as unobtrusive as possible. Most students behave differently when they see someone with a pencil and clipboard staring at them.
- Carry out the observations over a period of several days so that the novelty of having someone observe the student will lessen, and the repeated observations can produce a truer picture of day-to-day behavior.

Repp, Felce, and Barton (1988) demonstrated that interventions based on hypotheses derived from an A-B-C analysis were more effective than those that were not. However, a relationship noted as a result of A-B-C assessment is correlational, not causal, since this is a descriptive process that does not manipulate any of the variables (Lennox & Miltenberger, 1989). Once the relationship leads to a hypothesis concerning what is occasioning and/or maintaining the behavior, structured data collection and manipulation of the variables are possible.

Functional Analysis Procedures

The following procedures involve taking a hypothesized relationship and manipulating the variables thought to occasion or maintain the behavior in order to verify this relationship. This manipulation is called functional analysis since the purpose is to see if the behavior changes as a function of the presence, absence, heightening, or lessening of the variable (Axelrod, 1987; Iwata, Dorsey, Slifer, Bauman, & Richman, 1982). Conducting a functional analysis involves establishing at least one condition in which the variable of interest is present (for example, contingent teacher attention for inappropriate behavior) and another condition in which the variable is absent (for example, no attention, noncontingent attention, DRO) (Iwata et al., 1990).

Functional analysis can be done directly in the school or community setting where the behavior and surrounding events, people, and contingencies are in effect, or in an analogue setting. An analogue setting is an environment where controlled presentation of the variables can be conducted—often an unused classroom. Analogue sessions are conducted before attempting to alter the behavior in the natural environment. It is possible that in the controlled analogue setting the behavior may not be exposed to the same variables responsible for the behavior in the natural environment (Evans & Meyer, 1985). Using an analogue setting may also raise concern about generalization of the hypothesis or treatment. The setting is not naturalistic. Other things may affect the behavior in the natural settings where it originally occurred (Iwata et al., 1982). However, the precision that may result from precise manipulation of variables in a controlled environment may make using an analogue setting more efficient in the long run.

Three approaches to functional analysis have been reported. Within-session manipulation of variables (O'Neill et al., 1990; Vollmer, Iwata, Zarcone, Smith, & Mazaleskki, 1993), use of the reversal design (Durand & Carr, 1987, 1991; Wacker et al., 1990), and use of the multi-element design (another name for the alternating treatments design discussed in Chapter 5). It is referred to as a multi-element design since the presence or absence of stimuli thought to occasion or maintain the behavior, rather than treatments or interventions, are being compared (Chapman, Fisher, Piazza, & Kurtz, 1993; Iwata et al., 1982; Iwata, Pace, Kalsher, Cowdery, & Cataldo, 1990; Mace, Page, Ivancic, & O'Brien, 1986).

Within-Session Manipulation

O'Neill et al. (1990) used a within-session format for structured exposure to variables with a young worker in a community vocational program. She pounded her work station and pinched and slapped staff members. Interview and observation data suggested that the behavior served either as a means of escape or as a means of obtaining attention from staff. The analysis focused on attempting to determine whether the behaviors were serving a single function or multiple functions. During the sessions presented in the first four sections of the graph in Figure 9–3, Karen received attention (brief descriptive praise) from a staff member approximately every 30 seconds. She was asked to complete either a difficult or easy (previously mastered) task. Different tasks did not appear to have much effect on the number of disruptive behaviors that she exhibited. During the last four sessions, staff members presented the same tasks used in the high demand/difficult condition—but varied the level of attention. Under the high-attention condition Karen received brief descriptive praise approximately every 15 seconds. Under the low-attention condition she received similar praise approximately every 3 minutes. Karen's rate of disruptive behavior was significantly elevated in the low-attention condition. These manipulations demonstrated that pounding and slapping primarily served an attention-getting function for her.

Vollmer, Iwata, Zarcone, Smith, and Mazaleski (1993) state that within-session analysis can identify "behavioral sensitivity" to specific contingencies during a functional analysis procedure. They suggest that for assessing behavior function, this format involves analyzing within-session trends and fluctuations in rate for each minute of a session with exposure to a condition for 10 to 15 minutes.

Reversal Design

Durand and Carr (1991) assessed the hypothesis that the self-injurious and disruptive behaviors of three students with developmental disorders (moderate and severe mental retardation and autism), aged 9 to 12 years, were maintained by escape. Previous attempts at behavior management, which included differential reinforcement of other behavior (DRO), time-out, overcorrection, restraint, and medical interventions resulted in improvement for only a few weeks. The Motivation Assessment Scale, the structured questionnaire described above, was com-

FIGURE 9–3
Graph of a within-sessions analysis of the function of inappropriate behavior

Note: From Functional Analysis of Problem Behavior: A Practical Assessment Guide, by R.E. O'Neill, R.H. Horner, R.W. Albin, K. Storey, and J.R. Sprague. Copyright © 1990 by Sycamore Publishing Co. Reprinted by permission of Brooks/Cole Publishing Company, a division of International Thompson Publishing Inc., Pacific Grove, CA 93950.

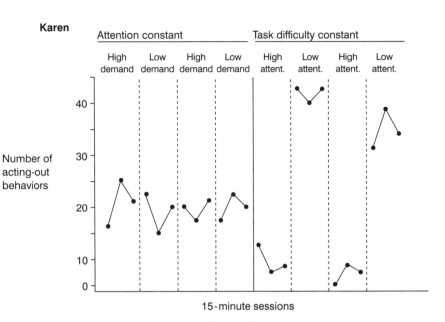

pleted by the teacher and assistant teacher. For two students, behaviors received the highest scores in the escape category. The third student's behavior was rated high on both escape and attention. To validate these hypotheses, an experimental analysis of the roles of escape and attention was conducted in their classroom. Within a reversal design (see Figure 9–4) tasks that each student was regularly asked to do were selected individually. For each student an easy group and a difficult group of tasks was selected. The student could respond correctly 100% of the time to the easy group of tasks (for example, last step in a backward chain for dressing, relaying personal information), and approximately 25% of the time to the difficult group (for example, last three steps in a backward chain, relaying personal information). The tasks alternated, 5 minutes each, within each 10-minute session. During baseline, students were given easy tasks and lots of attention and praise. During escape phases, hard tasks were presented with attention, praise, and correction. Figure 9–4 illustrates the results of the functional analysis. The data supported the results obtained from the MAS. The inappropriate behaviors of all three students increased when difficult tasks were introduced, suggesting that escape from tasks was maintaining these behaviors. Following this analysis, an intervention was designed based on its results. Each student was taught to request assistance with tasks. They were taught to say, for example, "I don't understand" or "help me," through use of verbal prompts faded over time. Inappropriate behavior was reduced for each student following functional communication training. The reduction was maintained in several classes and for three school years. The inappropriate behaviors occurred at the following percentages of their original frequency in the third year: Tim, 0%; Hal, 5.5%; and Ben, 3%.

FIGURE 9–4
Use of a reversal design for functional analysis

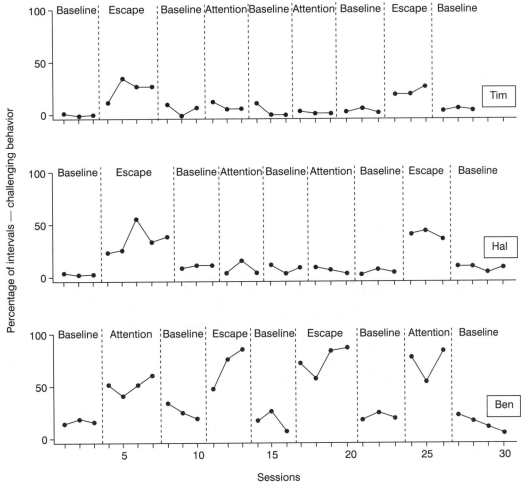

Note: From "Functional Communication Training to Reduce Challenging Behavior," by V.M. Durand and E. Carr. *Journal of Applied Behavior Analysis, 24, p.127, 1991. Copyright 1991 by The Society for the Experimental Analysis of Behavior, Inc. Reprinted by permission.*

Multi-element Design

Mace et al. (1986) conducted a functional analysis with Amy, a 3-year-old with developmental disabilities. Her disruptive behavior was defined as throwing objects, standing on furniture, spitting, damaging objects, knocking over furniture, undressing inappropriately, and urinating in her clothes. The analysis was conducted in an analogue training room with age-appropriate toys. Amy was exposed to a series of separate experimental conditions within a multielement design. One to four 15-minute sessions were conducted daily. Four conditions were selected on the basis of information supplied by Amy's parents and preliminary observations of situations associated with high and low levels of the behavior. These conditions were:

1. *Social disapproval.* Disruptive behavior was followed by a disapproving comment, for example, "Stop that, Amy, you know you shouldn't throw toys." In this condition appropriate behavior was positively reinforced by contingent adult attention.

2. *Divided attention.* Amy was told that the experimenter and another adult had some things to talk about, "You can play with the toys while we talk." In this condition appropriate behavior was again positively reinforced by adult attention.

3. *Demand.* Amy was given several things to do that were difficult for her and that she rarely completed. This condition was analogous to situations in which her disruptive behavior allowed her to escape from certain tasks.

4. *Play.* This served as a control condition in which the experimenter and Amy engaged in unstructured toy play. No instructions or tasks were presented and disruptive behavior was ignored.

The functional analysis of Amy's behavior suggested that contingent social disapproval maintained high rates of disruptive behavior (see Figure 9–5). The analysis further suggested that an important component of an effective intervention would be withdrawal of social disapproval. A time-out procedure was chosen to remove adult attention and other sources of reinforcement following disruptive behavior. (The authors report that Amy's parents had tried planned ignoring in the past and found it very difficult to avoid becoming angry and eventually providing social disapproval.) Time-out was effective in both the social disapproval and divided attention conditions.

Multiple procedures may be necessary in order to determine a behavior's function (Crawford et al., 1992; Mace et al., 1991). If, for example, the results of a multielement design do not clearly identify the function of a student's behavior, function can sometimes be clarified by using a traditional reversal design (Vollmer, Iwata, Duncan, & Lerman, 1993). Lennox and Miltenberger (1989) tried several assessment and analysis procedures for a 22-year-old man who slapped his face and bit himself on the wrist. The sequence began with interviews of staff members who identified episodes occurring in spurts throughout the day. The researchers administered the MAS to the workshop supervisor and staff members and taught them to scatter plot assessment to determine temporal patterns. The assessment confirmed the behaviors occurred most often during individual training sessions. Staff members then used anecdotal recording to perform an A-B-C assessment. Only after this extended functional assessment was it possible to design a strategy to perform a functional analysis. The young man was then exposed to three randomly sequenced conditions that commonly occurred

FIGURE 9–5
Use of a multi-ele-ment design for functional analysis

Note: From "Analysis of Environmental Determinants of Aggression and Disruption in Mentally Retarded Children," by F. Mace, T. Page, M. Ivancic, and S. O'Brien. Applied Research in Mental Retardation, 7, 1986. Copyright 1986 by Pergamon Journals Inc. Reprinted by permission.

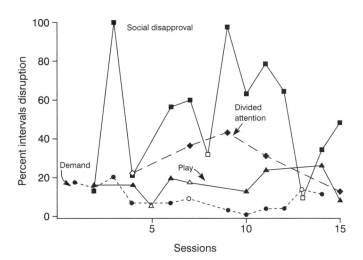

during the work day (escape from demand, contingent social attention, alone condition). All of these assessment procedures consistently indicated that the client's self-injury was motivated by his desire to terminate new demand tasks (negative reinforcement). The intervention designed "included two critical components: one to teach a new communication skill that was functionally equivalent to self-injury . . . and a second component to eliminate the negative reinforcement for the self-injury" (p. 309). He was taught to sign "break" following presentation of a new task trial and given a short break as a consequence. The intervention also included the extinction of the self-injurious behavior because staff members physically guided him to complete any task during which he injured himself. The behavior no longer resulted in escape from the task.

Axelrod (1987) notes that a disadvantage of functional analysis is the complexity of the technology involved. This is especially true when using scatter plots and analogue conditions. When easily observable evidence strongly suggests a relationship, an informal analysis (as described in Chapter 4) might be sufficient. Remember that we always suggest that you use the simplest procedure possible.

Functional Equivalency Training

The process of (a) conducting a functional assessment/analysis to identify the stimuli that occasion and maintain a problem behavior, and (b) teaching a socially appropriate behavior to replace it (which will be under control of the same antecedent and consequence as the problem behavior) is known as functional equivalence training (Baer, Wolf, & Risley, 1968; Bijou & Baer, 1978; Horner & Day, 1991). Such training takes a long-term, educational view of behavior enhancement, rather than a short-term, crisis management view for immediate reduction of behavior (Carr, Robinson, & Palumbo, 1990).

New behaviors must be at least as efficient at recruiting reinforcers or providing escape as the inappropriate behavior they are designed to replace. A problem behavior may be replaced by a more efficient behavior when a less efficient alternative behavior proves ineffective (Horner & Day, 1991). Behaviors that require less effort or that result in quicker and more consistent reinforcement are more likely to be performed (O'Neill et al., 1990). At least three variables affect the efficiency of a response: (1) the physical effort required to perform the response, (2) the schedule of reinforcement, and (3) the delay between presentation of the discriminative stimulus for the target response and delivery of the reinforcer for that response (Horner & Day, 1991).

SUMMARY

When teachers pay as much attention to behavior's function as to its form, it is often possible to design changes in the environment that eliminate the necessity for aversive techniques. This is in keeping with the Principle of the Least Intrusive Alternative. Aversive intervention should never even be considered until environmental, instructional, and curricular factors have been carefully evaluated using functional assessment and analysis. We must always attempt to teach students a functional equivalent of any behavior identified as being communicative.

In this chapter we have described procedures that, though elaborate and time-consuming, may sometimes be necessary when the stimuli occasioning or maintaining inappropriate behavior are difficult to identify. The following sequence of procedures should be included in every functional assessment/analysis:

1. Pinpoint and operationalize the behavior.
2. Screen for medical explanations, sensory impairments, or a specific learning disability.
3. a. Conduct a form of indirect functional assessment (that is, behavior interview or use of a questionnaire).

   b. Follow the indirect assessment, if possible, by direct observation of the behavior (that is, scatter plot and/or A-B-C assessment).

   c. Test hypothesis concerning occasioning or maintaining behavior through on-site or analogue functional analysis.
4. Plan and implement. Team planning and implementation of environmental, instructional, or curricular rearrangement, and/or program of differential reinforcement of functionally equivalent behavior.
5. Evaluate data. If program is not successful, evaluate the efficiency of the equivalent behavior chosen and teach a more efficient behavior.
6. If successful, maintain and generalize in school, home, and community settings.

DISCUSSION QUESTIONS

1. How might a functional analysis have been conducted to determine antecedent or consequent stimuli related to the inappropriate behaviors described in the short anecdotes at the beginning of this chapter?

2. Many teachers of typical students and those with mild disabilities attempt to functionally analyze their students' behaviors by interviewing the students. They repeatedly ask students "why" they perform certain behaviors. Why is this unlikely to be effective?

REFERENCES

Axelrod, S. 1987. Functional and structural analyses of behavior: Approaches leading to reduced use of punishment procedures? *Research in Developmental Disabilities, 8*, 165–178.

Axelrod, S. 1991. Smoking cessation through functional analysis. *Journal of Applied Behavior Analysis, 24*, 717–718.

Baer, D., Wolf, M., & Risley, T. 1968. Some current dimensions of applied behavior analysis. *Journal of Applied Behavior Analysis, 1*, 91–97.

Bijou, S., & Baer, D. 1978. *Behavior analysis of child development*. Englewood Cliffs, NJ: Prentice-Hall.

Carr, E., & Durand, V.M. 1985. Reducing behavior problems through functional communication training. *Journal of Applied Behavior Analysis, 18*, 111–126.

Carr, E., Newsom, C., & Binkoff, J. 1980. Escape as a factor in the aggressive behavior of two retarded children. *Journal of Applied Behavior Analysis, 13*, 101–117.

Carr, E., Robinson, S., & Palumbo, L. 1990. The wrong issue: Aversive versus nonaversive treatment. The right issue: Functional versus nonfunctional treatment. In A. Repp & N. Singh (Eds.), *Current perspectives in the use of nonaversive and aversive interventions with developmentally disabled persons* (pp. 361–380). Sycamore, IL: Sycamore Press.

Chapman, S., Fisher, W., Piazza, C., & Kurtz, P. 1993. Functional assessment and treatment of life-threatening drug ingestion in a dually diagnosed youth. *Journal of Applied Behavior Analysis, 26*, 255–256.

Cooper, J., Heron, T., & Heward, W. 1987. *Applied behavior analysis*. Columbus, OH: Merrill.

Crawford, J., Brockel, B., Schauss, S., & Miltenberger, R. 1992. A comparison of methods for the functional assessment of stereotypic behavior. *Journal of the Association for Persons with Severe Handicaps, 17*, 77–86.

Donnellan, A., Mirenda, P., Mesaros, R., & Fassbender, L. 1984. Analyzing the communicative functions of aberrant behavior. *The Journal of the Association for Persons with Severe Handicaps, 9*, 201–212.

Durand, V.M. 1987. "Look Homeward Angel": a call to return to our (functional) roots. *Behavior Analyst, 10*, 229–302.

Durand, V.M. 1990. *Severe behavior problems: A functional communication training approach*. New York: Guilford Press.

Durand, V.M., & Carr, E. 1987. Social influences on "self-stimulatory" behavior. *Journal of Applied Behavior Analysis, 20*, 119–132.

Durand, V.M., & Carr, E. 1991. Functional communication training to reduce challenging behavior: Maintenance and application in new settings. *Journal of Applied Behavior Analysis, 24*, 251–264.

Durand, V.M., & Crimmins, D. 1988. Identifying variables maintaining self-injurious behavior. *Journal of Autism and Developmental Disorders, 18*, 99–117.

Evans, I., & Meyer, L. 1985. *An educative approach to problem behaviors: A practical decision model for interventions with severely handicapped learners*. Baltimore: Paul H. Brookes

Gadow, K. 1986. *Children on medication, Vol. II*. San Diego, College-Hill Press.

Horner, R. 1980. The effects of an environmental enrichment program on the behavior of institutionalized profoundly retarded children. *Journal of Applied Behavior Analysis, 13*, 473–491.

Horner, R., & Day, H.M. 1991. The effects of response efficiency on functionally equivalent competing behaviors. *Journal of Applied Behavior Analysis, 24*, 719–732.

Iwata, B., Dorsey, M., Slifer, K., Bauman, K., & Richman, G. 1982. Toward a functional analysis of self-injury. *Analysis and Intervention in Developmental Disabilities, 2*, 3–20.

Iwata, B., Pace, G., Kalsher, M., Cowdery, G., & Cataldo, M. 1990. Experimental analysis and extinction of self-injurious escape behavior. *Journal of Applied Behavior Analysis, 23*, 11–27.

Iwata, B., Vollmer, T., & Zarcone, J. 1990. The experimental (functional) analysis of behavior disorders: Methodology, applications, and limitations. In A. Repp & N. Singh, (Eds.), *Perspectives on the use of nonaversive and aversive interventions for persons with developmental disabilities* (pp. 301–330). Sycamore, IL: Sycamore Press.

Kazdin, A. 1980. *Behavior modification in applied settings.* Homewood, IL: Dorsey Press.

Lennox, D., & Miltenberger, R. 1989. Conducting a functional assessment of problem behavior in applied settings. *Journal of the Association for Persons with Severe Handicaps, 14*, 304–31.

Mace, F., Lalli, J., & Lalli, E. 1991. Functional analysis and treatment of aberrant behavior. *Research in Developmental Disabilities, 12*, 155–180.

Mace, F.C., Page, T., Ivancic, M., & O'Brien, S. 1986. Analysis of environmental determinants of aggression and disruption in mentally retarded children. *Applied Research in Mental Retardation, 7*, 203–221.

O'Neill, R., Horner, R., Albin, R., Storey, K., & Sprague, J. 1990. *Functional analysis of problem behavior.* Sycamore, IL: Sycamore Press.

Pyles, D., & Bailey, J. 1990. Diagnosing severe behavior problems. In A. Repp & N. Singh, (Eds.), *Perspectives on the use of nonaversive and aversive interventions for persons with developmental disabilities* (pp. 381–401). Sycamore, IL: Sycamore Press.

Remington, B. 1991. *The challenge of severe mental handicap: A behavior analytic approach.* New York: Wiley & Sons, Ltd.

Repp, A., Felce, D., & Barton, L. 1988. Basing the treatment of stereotypic and self-injurious behavior on hypotheses of their causes. *Journal of Applied Behavior Analysis, 21*, 281–290.

Sasso, G., & Reimers, T. 1988. Assessing the functional properties of behavior: Implications and applications for the classroom. *Focus on Autistic Behavior, 3*, 1–15.

Skinner, B.F. 1953. *Science and human behavior.* New York: Macmillan.

Touchette, P., Macdonald, R., & Langer, S. 1985. A scatter plot for identifying stimulus control of problem behavior. *Journal of Applied Behavior Analysis, 18*, 343–351.

Vollmer, T., Iwata, B., Duncan, B., & Lerman, D. 1993. Extensions of multielement functional analyses using reversal-type designs. *Journal of Developmental and Physical Disabilities, 5*, 311–325.

Vollmer, T., Iwata, B., Zarcone, J., Smith R., & Mazaleski, J. 1993. Within-session patterns of self-injury as indicators of behavioral function. *Research in Developmental Disabilities, 14*, 479–492.

Wacker, D., Steege, M., Northup, J., Sasso, G., Berg, W., Reimers, T., Cooper, L., Cigrand, K., & Donn, L. 1990. A component analysis of functional communication training across three topographies of severe behavior problems. *Journal of Applied Behavior Analysis, 23*, 417–429.

Wolery, M., Bailey, D., & Sugai, G. 1988. *Effective teaching: Principles and procedures of applied behavior analysis with exceptional students.* Boston: Allyn and Bacon, Inc.

Wright, H. 1960. Observational study. In P. H. Mussen (Ed.), *Handbook of research methods in child development.* New York: Wiley.

CHAPTER **Chapter 10**
Putting It All Together

In previous chapters we have discussed a great many principles, cited numerous research studies, and provided dozens of examples of how procedures can be implemented in classrooms. In this chapter we will try to show how teachers put all the principles, research studies, and procedures together to provide classrooms in which students learn efficiently and effectively. We also want to stress ways in which school and learning can provide enjoyment for both teachers and students. If it is not, for the most part, fun, no one will want to keep doing it. Surely no one goes into teaching for the money. First we will describe practical implementation of various principles; then we will describe several classrooms in some detail. Throughout the chapter, we will point out with marginal notes which behavioral principles are being used.

The most important part of running an efficient classroom takes place before the students arrive. Careful planning can ensure that all students successfully acquire knowledge and learn skills and that few disruptive or inappropriate behaviors occur. Being prepared for students who have trouble mastering knowledge and skills or who behave inappropriately despite preventive planning enables the teacher to react quickly and to solve problems as soon as possible. It is, however, impossible to anticipate every potential problem. One thing that makes teaching so challenging and so much fun is that students are not completely predictable. At this very moment, somewhere in the world, a teacher is asking an assistant, "Have you ever seen one do *that* before?"

STIMULUS CONTROL

Students whose academic or social behavior is inappropriate or maladaptive present a special challenge. These students may or may not be classified as disabled or at risk. Many such students respond to the entire school environment as an S^D for either acting-out behavior or complete withdrawal. To design a classroom environment to alter such behaviors, teachers must simultaneously avoid presenting old S^Ds and concentrate on establishing certain elements of the classroom as discriminative stimuli for appropriate behavior. This process may be thought of as providing appropriate classroom structure. We will describe several kinds of structure, including the physical arrangement of the room; time, instructional, and verbal structure; and teacher characteristics.

Physical Arrangement

The physical arrangement of the classroom provides discriminative stimuli for students. Some of the behaviors occasioned by these stimuli may be undesirable. For some students, proximity to other students (or a particular classmate) may be an S^D for off-task talking or physical abuse. Sitting in a chair may be an S^D for tilting it. The teacher may need to arrange the classroom in a way that interferes with such behaviors before more appropriate behavior can be taught. Gallagher (1979), Haring and Phillips (1962), Hewett and Taylor (1980), and Stephens, Hartman, and Lucas (1978) have all described the relationship between classroom arrangement and student behavior. Specific suggestions from these sources include

1. Provision for easy teacher observation of all students.
2. Sufficient physical separation of students to minimize inappropriate behaviors.
3. Careful delineation of areas in which only work behaviors are reinforced from those in which more informal behavior is permitted.
4. Availability of study carrels for students so distractible that virtually any stimulus is an S^D for off-task behavior.

It's not interior decoration; it's stimulus control.

The specific arrangement of the classroom will depend on what instruction is being delivered, the students in the class, and, of course, the constraints of the space itself. (If you're in the boiler room, you'll have to work around the furnace.) If most instruction is to be one-on-one, then either there must be several comfortable work areas where the teacher and a student can sit comfortably and see necessary materials or, better yet, each student must have a workstation large enough to accommodate another chair and an adult. We do not recommend leaning over or squatting when moving from station to station to provide instruction—in a very few years either the back gives way or the knees do. In addition, students react badly to an adult's looming over or crowding them. One creative teacher we know uses a typist's chair and wheels herself from desk to desk in her classroom. If there is to be a great deal of group instruction, there must be an area where students are oriented toward the teacher and the chalkboard or other visual aids. Perhaps this seems painfully obvious but we have seen many teachers talking to groups half of whom have their backs to the teacher or showing transparencies on an overhead projector screen that many students must turn around to see. Not only does this not make for good instruction, it creates opportunities for inappropriate behavior. Small groups require a table and chairs or a large enough floor area for all to sit comfortably. A kidney-shaped table is excellent because it enables the teacher to be close to all students at once. Many teachers who use the floor for instruction mark individual spaces with tape and require students to stay within their squares. This minimizes pushing and squirming. Carpet samples taped to the floor can serve the same function. (Inexpensive carpet samples are available or they often can be obtained for free if a sufficiently moving request is made at a carpet store. Some teachers take along photographs of their most attractive children.)

It is also important that the classroom be attractive. Brightly colored bulletin board displays, plants, aquariums, and student projects all contribute to a friendly, welcoming atmosphere. Displays of charts, graphs, visual prompts, and goals send a message that this classroom is a place where serious business is conducted. Although a "sterile classroom" (Haring & Phillips,

1962) in which walls are painted gray, windows covered, and all materials stored where they are not visible to students has not proved necessary, it is important to remember that many students are distractible and that excessively busy decorations should be avoided. Students should have work areas in which it is easy to assure that the task to which they are supposed to pay attention is the most attention-getting item in sight.

When we begin to talk about the importance of neatness in the classroom, students who have visited our offices invariably giggle. We maintain, like Professor Grundy, that it is easier for middle-aged college teachers to adapt to working in cluttered surroundings than it is for most children and adolescents. A messy classroom may even be dangerous, especially for students with mobility problems. It certainly contributes to inefficient instruction. A teacher who must search her desk, a bookcase, and two cabinets to find teaching materials hidden under piles of paper wastes valuable time. She also provides a poor model for students. Students whose desks are covered with extraneous items may find it impossible to attend to the task at hand. It is worth the sometimes Herculean effort to keep things neat.

The physical classroom itself can and will become a complex S^D for appropriate student behavior. It is important to be consistent about what behaviors are reinforced and about room arrangement. Allowing students with behavior problems to play in the work area on a rainy day may result in a weakening of the stimulus control of that area. Suddenly changing the room arrangement may also create problems for these students. In a study examining the establishment of stimulus control in an animal laboratory, Rodewald (1979) found that even cleaning pigeons' cages disrupted stimulus control. Subtle changes in the classroom may have similar effects on students.

Time Structure

When we say "It's time to . . ." we're using stimulus control.

The time of day functions as an S^D for many human behaviors. At certain times, certain behaviors are reinforced. A predictable schedule for the classroom will maximize the controlling aspects of time. Gallagher (1979) suggests prompting students by posting pictures of clock faces showing the time for scheduled activities near the classroom clock. Other time aspects should also be considered. There is evidence (Van Houten, Hill, & Parsons, 1975; Van Houten & Thompson, 1976) that students work more quickly when their performance is timed. Apparently, being timed is an S^D for working rapidly.

A simple, relatively inexpensive kitchen timer can be of enormous help in structuring classroom time. A timer that produces a ticking noise and a single, clear bell-tone is available in department or discount stores and may be used in many ways. Individual students may be assigned a timer during individual work periods and instructed to "beat the clock." The timer may also be used to delineate segments of the class day. Students may be taught that when the timer is ticking, no talking or moving around is allowed. The ticking thus becomes an S^D for working independently and quietly. The ring becomes an

S^D for stopping work and waiting for further instructions or for beginning another activity. Teachers who have no assistant and who work with small groups in the classroom, may teach students that a person who is not in the group receiving instruction may not talk to the teacher except in case of dire emergency (the fire is out of control, or there is more than a quart of blood on the floor). It appears that the S^D, "no talking to the teacher while the timer is set," is prompted by the ticking sound. People of all ages and ability levels can be taught to attend to a timer. As a matter of fact, my timer was ticking as I wrote this—it is an S^D for writing, as well as an S$^\Delta$ for interruptions by colleagues, who, by the way, were much harder to train than preschool children. The ring is a conditioned reinforcer—coffee-break time.

Before leaving the topic of time, we must address the issue of wasting it. Unfortunately, many activities that can be observed in classrooms seem to have little or no purpose beyond that of keeping students busy, sometimes, even more unfortunately, while teachers and assistants chat among themselves, do paperwork, or engage in other nonteaching activities. Sometimes students appear not to be engaged in any activity beyond that of waiting for something to happen. Particularly for at-risk students or those with disabilities, there is no time to waste. Every effort must be made to keep every student actively learning for as much of the school day as possible. We know a first-grade teacher who requires her students to give the answer to an addition fact on a flashcard to gain admittance to the restroom during the traditional routine of lining-up in the hall for the morning break. We think this is perhaps a trifle extreme, but we applaud the determination to use every available minute to teach.

Instructional Structure

Prompting is discussed at length in Chapter 7.

Good instructional structure begins with planning and planning begins with goals and objectives. Chapter 3 describes at great length the process of deriving and writing appropriate goals and objectives. Once long- and short-term objectives have been established for a class or written on an IEP for a student with disabilities, daily objectives can be written. We do not agree with the statement that for an individual with disabilities the IEP is the lesson plan, especially if that IEP is stored in a locked file cabinet in the school office. Teachers need to plan daily objectives that lead toward established goals, as well as specific activities that will help students master those objectives. A minimal lesson plan must include, in addition to the objective(s), a statement of what the teacher will do, what students will do, what materials will be required, and how mastery of the objective will be tested. If there is more than one teacher, the plan should also state who will be responsible for delivering instruction. (Chapter 13 addresses the issue of finding and working with classroom helpers.) If, as we suggested earlier, the classroom has a written daily and weekly schedule, lesson-plan forms can be duplicated and daily activities written quickly and efficiently. Previous chapters detail research-based ways to design verbal and visual stimuli, to use prompts effectively, and to reinforce student responses. These methods should be the basis of daily lessons. We remind you again that applied behavior analysis is a teaching method, not just a way to control students. In addition to assuring that instruction is goal-oriented and efficient, a written daily plan is a prompt for most teachers to "get on with it." It makes it much more difficult to decide just to extend the free play period until lunch and forget about math for today.

The way instruction is delivered is also important. If the teacher is bored and indifferent, the students will be bored and indifferent as well. It may be difficult to seem enthusiastic when teaching the concept "bigger" for the hundredth time but it is absolutely necessary. Instruction that moves along briskly is much more likely to occasion student response than instruction that is delivered at a lethargic pace. Finally, all teaching must include provision for student responses. Talking is not teaching; the teacher must continually seek responses from students that indicate that they are learning. Asking students if they understand something, by the way, is absolutely useless. Many students think they understand something when they don't; many will nod their heads enthusiastically simply so instruction will stop. Rather than simply explaining what "bigger" means, the effective teacher repeatedly asks students to tell which one is bigger, show which one is bigger, find a bigger one, draw a bigger one, build a bigger one. The teacher will also positively reinforce correct responses and correct those that are wrong.

Stimulus control can work against teachers.

The teaching materials used with students also generate responses. The teacher hopes these responses will be in the form of correct oral and written answers. For many students with learning and behavior problems, however, traditional materials such as textbooks, workbooks, and ditto sheets may be S^{D}s for inappropriate behaviors. Often the best materials to use with such children are those that look most different from what they have seen in the past. Even tearing pages out of workbooks (Gallagher, 1979) or presenting only a part of a page that has been cut into several pieces (Hewett & Taylor, 1980) may provide enough difference so that inappropriate responses will not occur. Doing academic work more traditionally may gradually be shaped. A great deal of creativity is required to provide some students with assignments that cause appropriate responding. It is well worth being creative—a group of students doing long division as fast as they can is bound to be less disruptive than a group doing nothing.

Verbal Structure

All classrooms have rules. Whether or not expectations for student behavior are made explicit, they exist. Wise teachers share their expectations for classroom behavior with students—it is difficult for students to follow rules if they don't know what the rules are. Many students follow rules; for them, rules have become S^{D}s for compliance (because of their history of reinforcement).

The students whose behavior upsets the teacher are those who do not follow the rules, who are disruptive, or who fail to complete assigned tasks. For such students, merely specifying what is expected has little effect on behavior (Madsen, Becker, & Thomas, 1968); for them, complying with rules is not under stimulus control. These students must be taught to follow rules. Adherence to the following rules about rules will facilitate this process.

1. Be very specific about what is expected (specificity).
2. Make as few rules as possible (economy).
3. Be explicit about the relationship between rules and consequences (consequences).

Specificity

Effective rules describe observable behavior. An unequivocal decision can be made about whether or not an effective rule has been followed. Some teachers, in an effort to anticipate every situation, make rules that are so vague as to be useless. It can be very difficult to decide whether a student has been a good citizen, has respected others' rights, or has done unto others as he would have others do unto him. Following such rules is also difficult—what does a good citizen do? What are others' rights? Had I not better do unto him before he does unto me? Teachers must decide what behaviors are important in their classrooms and describe these behaviors in a set of rules. If being a good citizen means "complete assignments" or "don't hit people," those should be the rules, not "be a good citizen." In general, it is preferable to specify which behaviors are desired rather than which are forbidden. Some teachers, however, in an effort to be completely positive, invent convoluted rules that are not at all clear. "Keep your hands to yourself" is a poor substitute for "don't hit people," if such a rule is needed. A teacher once asked for help in phrasing a rule. She had been told that all rules must be stated positively and needed a rule about spitting. We concluded that "keep your saliva in your mouth" lacked the impact and pellucid clarity of "don't spit." Sometimes it's all right to tell students what not to do.

Economy

It's also hard (even for the teacher) to remember all those rules.

Making too many rules is inefficient. Neither the teacher nor the students can remember a large number of rules. Teachers who make 88 rules in an effort to anticipate every possible situation may find that students are challenged to find the 89th inappropriate behavior. "But there's no rule against it." This is the primary disadvantage of allowing students to make the rules. They always seem to want to make dozens (and to invoke the death penalty for noncompliance).

Sometimes, unnecessary rules can even give students ideas. If on the first day of school a teacher announces to his seventh-graders, "Do not bring straws back from the cafeteria. I will not have students in my classroom dampening the ends of the paper covers and blowing them upward so they stick to the ceiling," he can expect them to do just that. They might never have thought of it themselves. For this reason, rules about hitting (especially about hitting the teacher) and other drastic forms of misbehavior should not be made unless there is incontrovertible evidence that they are necessary.

Furthermore, enforcing unnecessary rules is time-consuming. It would be interesting to collect data on the amount of time spent dealing with the "problem" of chewing gum in the average classroom. Many of us have heard (or participated in) interchanges like this:

Teacher: "Are you chewing gum?"

Student (swallowing rapidly): "Who me?"

or

Teacher: "Are you chewing gum?"

Student: "No, Ms. Franklin.

Teacher: "Open your mouth. Let me see! You are chewing gum! Spit it out this minute! I want to see it in the trash can!"

Many students find exchanges like this reinforcing. They chew gum to avoid or escape instruction and to have their teacher's undivided attention for a few minutes. Classroom rules, therefore, should concentrate on behaviors necessary for efficient instruction. Making rules into effective S^{D}s is often quite difficult. Why do it unless the rule is necessary?

It is usually necessary to teach students rules just as we teach them other things. If one of the rules is "raise your hand before you speak," the teacher may model appropriate hand raising, ask students to provide examples, and be sure that students understand the usually unstated (because it makes the rule cumbersome) but necessary behavior of waiting for the teacher to see and respond to the raised hand before asking or answering a question or offering a comment. Practice sessions with lots of praise and other reinforcement will help students learn the rule.

Consequences

For students whose behavior is not under the control of rules, systematic efforts must be made to establish a relationship between following rules and positive reinforcement or punishment. Prompts may be needed. The teacher may

1. Post the rules on a bulletin board in either written or pictorial form, thus providing a visual prompt.

2. State the rules at the beginning of each class period or ask a student to read them, thus providing a verbal prompt.

3. Draw attention to a student who is following rules, thus providing a model.

4. Less frequently, point out to a student that she is not following a rule.

When the rules have been learned and are in force, the teacher must continue to provide consistent reinforcement for following them. Systematic efforts like these to bring rule following under stimulus control will succeed even if students do not comply with rules in other settings, either at school or at home. This teacher and this classroom will become S^Ds for following rules.

Teacher Characteristics

Almost everyone—certainly, almost everyone who wants to be a teacher—remembers a special teacher. When we ask our students to tell us what made the teacher so special they talk about warmth, caring, personal interest, a sense of humor, sensitivity, and many other similar characteristics. Being applied behavior analysts, of course, we are not satisfied with such vague descriptions. When we pinpointed them, we found that what those teachers did was to make themselves conditioned positive reinforcers. By delivering large amounts of positive reinforcement, usually social, they acquired reinforcing characteristics by just being around. Many uninformed people believe that teachers who systematically use applied behavior analysis procedures must be cold, mechanical, and impersonal. In fact, the opposite is true.

All classrooms provide consequences for behavior. There are some in which virtually all students are motivated to work hard in order to learn and to earn good grades. In such classrooms, good instruction and an occasional word of praise or gentle admonition are the only management techniques necessary. In other classrooms, students have had so little experience with success and so much reinforcement for inappropriate behavior that no instruction is possible unless their behavior can be brought under control. Virtually all such students will respond positively to one of the token systems described in Chapter 6; a few may make it necessary to use procedures to decrease behavior. In yet other classrooms, students respond best to a combination of primary and social reinforcement, again with occasional procedures to decrease inappropriate behaviors. The teacher who is familiar with the tools of applied behavior analysis is equipped to design an appropriate management system for any classroom.

A LOOK INTO CLASSROOMS

Now we will visit several teachers, all applied behavior analysts, teaching in several rather different classrooms. We will look at everything from their room arrangement to their daily schedules to see how they implement the principles they have read about and observed.

Remember Miss Harper?

Remember Ms. Harper? Her second teaching placement is in an integrated preschool setting. Since she is seeking a minor in early childhood special education, Professor Grundy feels that this will be perfect for her. Ms. Harper is not so sure. She has been informed that about one-fourth of her prospective students are "developmentally delayed," and she knows that could mean almost anything.

Ms. Harper tentatively approaches the classroom for her first day in this placement. As she walks through the open door into a large, airy room she is struck by the appearance of the classroom. There are a few tables with tiny little chairs but most of the room is divided into large areas containing various collections of what she characterizes as toys—blocks, both sand and water tables with buckets and other utensils, colorful construction materials, dolls and furniture, and a miniature collection of kitchen and other household furniture. She also observes easels and paints, displays of children's art, and modeling clay, along with numerous riding toys, smaller toy vehicles, and what appears to be a huge number of very young children. As she attempts to identify those "developmentally delayed" ones she is approached by a smiling young woman wearing a split skirt and tennis shoes, whom Ms. Harper assumes must be an assistant.

"Miss Harper?" she inquires, "I'm Amy Storey, the lead teacher. Welcome to our class." She looks dubiously at Ms. Harper's tailored suit, mid-heel pumps, and wary expression, but continues, "Come on over and meet the other teachers; we're really looking forward to working with you.

"Michael," she states firmly to a tot whizzing in front of her in a tiny electric wheelchair, "look where you're going, kiddo."

As they make their way through the mass of children, Ms. Harper spots two children with Down syndrome and two more with braces. They appear to be engaged in playing with other children. As they approach the other teachers, Ms. Amy asks, "What's your first name, Miss Harper? We're very informal, here."

"Michelle," gasps Ms. Harper, as she is introduced to four other adults. No distinction is made as to status, but Barry, Lisa, Bonnie, and Lucille apparently have responsibility with Ms. Amy for the 25 (could there really be only 25?) 3- and 4-year-olds in the classroom.

Lisa takes charge of Ms. Harper, "We've already done circle this morning and the children are getting ready to work in the centers." Her pitying look at Ms. Harper's outfit is undisguised. "Perhaps you'd like just to observe for a while." She guides Ms. Harper to an adult-sized chair at a work table and hurries away to take a shovel away from a child at the sand table.

Positive social reinforcement

"Sand," she states firmly, "is for building, not throwing." She sinks to the floor at the sand table and begins asking the children about their activities. She encourages the children to work together and praises a student who gets a dump truck in order to move the sand more efficiently.

As Ms. Harper watches the activities in the room, a pattern begins to emerge. Small groups of children are playing—working, she remembers—at the various centers. She decides to watch one center for a while to zero in on what's going on. She picks the block center. Four children are building a city series of struc-

*Barry prompts Dejohn,
then Charlie.*

tures and chattering about their activities. One child sits by himself. Barry is seated on the floor nearby.

"Mr. Barry," insists one of the children, "Charlie's hogging the big blocks." Indeed, Charlie appears to be simply collecting the largest blocks and keeping himself between them and the other children.

"Maybe you should ask him to share, Dejohn," suggests Barry.

"No way, man," states Dejohn, "he'll hit me." Ms. Harper begins to suspect that Charlie, too, may be "developmentally delayed."

"Charlie," suggests Barry quietly, "I think Dejohn doesn't know how hard we've been working on sharing. Remember, you earn computer time. Go on," he adds more loudly, "Dejohn, ask, you remember how."

"Charlie," says Dejohn, "we need some big blocks. Come over and help us." With a glance at Barry, Charlie pushes several blocks from his hoard toward Dejohn and moves slightly toward the group. Barry quietly slips a token into Charlie's pocket. "Good job, Charlie; you too, Dejohn." Ms. Harper is very impressed; she makes a note to ask how Dejohn learned to ask so appropriately.

Ms. Harper turns her attention to the area where students are playing—working, working—with water. Both Ms. Bonnie and Ms. Lucille are there with six children. One of them is Maria, the child with Down syndrome. The children are pouring water from smaller into larger containers, and yes, from larger into smaller containers. Ms. Harper admires both the ingenious design of the table and the presence of two adults. Both adults converse with all the children. Ms. Harper notices that Maria answers with monosyllables when a teacher asks a question but does not initiate interaction. The other students talk among themselves but ignore Maria. She begins, however, to pick up a pattern. Casually, Ms. Lucille suggests, "Melanie, ask Maria to hand you that yellow cup, please. Good job saying thank you, Melanie."

A few minutes later, Ms. Bonnie says, "Kyung, would you ask Maria if she would like to be a cleanup helper? You can be the leader." She is impressed that the teachers are encouraging the typical students to interact with their peers with disabilities. She realizes that a setting using developmentally appropriate practices can adapt those practices to a wide variety of developmental levels, even those considered "delayed."

By the end of the day Ms. Harper, having observed indoor work, outdoor work, lunchroom work, and quiet-time work, is convinced that this is exactly the right placement for her. She leaves the preschool headed for the mall. She needs a split skirt and a pair of tennis shoes. What else would Miss Michelle wear?

Ms. Mitchell's Self-contained Class

Ms. Mitchell teaches eight 6- to 9-year-olds. All have severe developmental disabilities. Three students use wheelchairs; one student has braces and crutches. Some of the students have no verbal skills; others are able to talk fairly well. Ms. Mitchell shares a two-room suite with a resource teacher. She has a full-time assistant and works with a speech and language therapist, a physical therapist, and an occupational therapist, all of whom work in several schools. Her room is arranged so that her students with wheelchairs and crutches can move about easily and safely. There is a table where all the children and several adults can sit, areas where students can sit or lie on the floor, and a number of adapted seating and standing devices designed for specific children. There is also a screened area where students' clothing can be changed when necessary.

Ms. Mitchell's daily and weekly schedules are quite complex. She must arrange the schedules to take maximum advantage of the professional and paraprofessional help available and to see that all students have opportunities to be with their nondisabled and less disabled peers. Perhaps the best way to show how Ms. Mitchell puts it all together in her classroom is to spend an entire day with her class.

All Ms. Mitchell's students ride buses to school. Either she or Ms. Post, her assistant, meets each bus to help the driver get the students off and to help the students get to the classroom. Several volunteers from regular classrooms also meet their "buddies" and provide assistance. As little assistance as necessary is provided; indeed, the teachers have recently started just shadowing Malcolm as he makes his own way to the classroom. Since the buses arrive at considerable intervals, there is plenty of time to spend with individual students as they arrive in the classroom. Part of what makes Ms. Mitchell's planning so complex is that in getting coats and boots off and hung up she must constantly remember that, for example, Malcolm is working on colors, Trish is working on counting objects, and Steven is working on responding to his name. As they arrive in the classroom, each student is prompted as necessary to go to his or her own coat hook. Students' names and pictures are posted by each hook. "Take off your coat, Trish. That's good, Malcolm, you took off your coat. Now hang it up. Good, Malcolm. Take off your coat, Trish." Ms. Mitchell puts her hand over Trish's and helps her through the unbuttoning process. "How many buttons, Trish? Let's count. One, two, three; three buttons. Take off your coat." As Trish begins to comply, Ms. Mitchell says, "Is your shirt red, Malcolm?" Malcolm nods. "Speak up, Malcolm, say 'yes.' Good, Malcolm. Good girl, Trish, you took off your coat. How many coats this morning? Good job, Trish, three coats. Steven!" As Steven turns his head, he is rewarded with a tickle and "Good, Steven, let's go to the circle."

Ms. Mitchell likes to start the day with a variation of "show and tell" as in regular primary classes. The speech and language therapist is here on Monday mornings so today she leads the session, asking each student to respond verbally or with a communication device.

Bringing responses under stimulus control   "Tell me something you did yesterday. Malcolm, what did you do yesterday? Did you watch TV? Tell me, 'I watched TV.' Good, Malcolm. Hannah, did you watch TV? Good, Hannah (when Hannah points to the TV on her communication board). What did you watch, Trish? Disney? I watched that, too." Ms. Mitchell moves among the children, prompting responses and patting students who respond on the shoulder. Steven, who has the fewest language skills, responds to "TV" by laughing. Ms. Post, who is standing behind him, provides another tickle and says, "Do you like TV, Steven?"

After the circle activity, it is time for Malcolm to change to go to PE with the second grade. Ms. Post works on his dressing skills, helping him take off his red shirt and put on his blue shorts, while Ms. Mitchell and the speech and language therapist engage the other students in rearranging and putting things on and under the bookshelf, asking Trish to count the books, and occasionally attracting Steven's attention.

A second-grader comes to get Malcolm, who returns in 45 minutes. He tells Ms. Mitchell all about kickball (it was a red ball) while he changes into his regular clothes. Several of the children help Ms. Post prepare the morning snack. Malcolm gets the cups and hands the red one, the yellow one, and the blue one to Ms. Post. Trish counts two cookies for each student. After the snack has been cleaned up (surely, by now you can guess who washes the red cup and who counts the cups to be sure they were all washed), six of the children and Ms. Post join the resource class for a math activity; and Ms. Mitchell, Hannah, and Trish put on coats and go for a walk. Most of Hannah's neighbors walk to school and Ms. Mitchell's goal is for Hannah to learn to cross streets safely so she can join them. Trish lives too far away to walk, but is also ready to learn the skills. Ms. Mitchell talks with the girls as they walk, identifying things they see and asking them to do the same. She asks Trish to count several things during the walk. They walk to Hannah's house and back, looking both ways even after the light is green.

Several of the students eat lunch with regular classes, each with a lunch buddy to be sure that all goes well. Ms. Post takes several others, who still need a little more help and supervision, to the cafeteria as a group. Ms. Mitchell helps Steven in the classroom; he becomes very excited and displays some self-injurious behavior if he has to cope with the cafeteria. Ms. Mitchell plans to start taking him by himself in few weeks.

Teachers need positive reinforcement, too.

After lunch, as in most primary classrooms, there is a quiet story and music listening time. Ms. Post and Ms. Mitchell each take charge of half the time so the other can eat lunch peacefully in the teachers' lounge. Ms. Mitchell times her lunch so she can eat with a friend and, for a change, have somebody tell her that *she's* doing a good job.

After the quiet time, Malcolm goes to the resource room for reading readiness activities. Ms. Post, Ms. Mitchell, and the physical therapist help the others change for PE. The physical therapist has helped develop a plan for gross motor activities for each student and also helps implement it. By the time the children have finished PE, it's time to start getting ready for the buses.

Ms. Mitchell used to be frustrated at the amount of time spent in her classroom on routines, until she realized how much she could teach during those routines.

Ms. Washington's Resource Room

Ms. Washington is a resource teacher in a large, suburban middle school. She works with about 30 fifth- and sixth-grade students who have learning disabilities or mild mental retardation, or whose behavior problems have earned them the label "seriously emotionally disturbed." Being a behaviorist, she doesn't worry too much about their disturbed emotions but concentrates on their academic and social behavior. All Ms. Washington's students spend at least half their day in a regular classroom. Some are with her for as much as three hours every day, others come only when they encounter a problem in the regular classroom. Ms. Washington is responsible, with a multidisciplinary team, for developing an IEP for each of her students and for coordinating the implementation of that IEP with regular classroom teachers. She has a half-time assistant who comes in the afternoons.

Another kind of prompt

It usually takes Ms. Washington several weeks to get her weekly and daily schedule coordinated. She has to work around art, music, physical education, and lunch schedules for many classes; she must also be sure that her students do not, for example, miss math, which they're good at, to come to her for reading, which they're not good at, meanwhile sitting in a reading class in which they're totally lost. If that sounds very confusing, think how Ms. Washington feels. She does not try to schedule her students by grade level or type of disability but tries to schedule students who are working at about the same level in a subject area at the same time. She often has several subclasses in her room at a given time; for example, five students working on reading and one needing help with math. She does what all teachers do: she provides independent work for some students while she works with others. She schedules her largest groups and her most difficult students in the afternoon when the assistant will be available to monitor and help with independent work. This year she has two boys who spend all morning with her; she is responsible for their instruction in reading, math, and social studies. She has scheduled an additional five students for each hour of the morning, thus having seven students in her room at any given time. Three students spend 2 hours each afternoon and Ms. Washington schedules five others during each of those 2 hours. She eats lunch from 11:30 to 12:00 and keeps the hour from 12:00 to 1:00 for observations and conferences. She has found that many working parents prefer to have meetings during the lunch hour. She requires students to be in their seats at their scheduled time and provides a small clock face with the time they need to leave the regular class for those students who need a prompt.

Ms. Washington uses a formal token system in her classroom. Each student has a point card and earns points for being on time, completing assignments, and behaving appropriately. Many students also bring less elaborate point cards from their regular teachers and earn additional points for having behaved appropriately in the regular classroom. She provides what her students call the "store" on Fridays; students may trade filled cards for food items, school supplies, and small toys. Ms. Washington, like many teachers, buys the items for her store herself. She maintains that it is cheaper than the psychiatric treatment that she would require without the token system. She also has a time-out area where disruptive students can be separated from the group.

All instruction in Ms. Washington's classroom is individualized. Contrary to what some teachers apparently believe, this means neither that all instruction is one-on-one nor that each student has his own personal packet of dittos that he works on without interaction with the teacher. It means that each student's lesson for each day is designed to help her master the goals and objectives written in her IEP. Some children may have the same goals; they can often receive instruction as a group. Ms. Washington posts the daily schedule with what each child will be doing on a bulletin board that is convenient to her and her assistant.

Ms. Washington has arranged her room so that she has two teaching and work areas as far apart as possible. Most of the students sit at tables instead of desks. She provides separate desks for a few students to prevent them from bothering other students. Two of her students do some of their work at a study carrel that she has created with a bookcase.

We will visit Ms. Washington first thing Monday morning.

At 8:30 on the dot, having said the Pledge of Allegiance and paid for lunch in the regular classroom, Alvin and Tyrone, the two children who stay all morning, along with Melanie, Michael, Donna, Charlie, and Harold, have picked up their point cards and are sitting in their assigned seats. Ms. Washington greets them only after they are seated.

Tokens are always paired with praise.

"Good morning, Alvin; it's good to see your smile on this rainy Monday. You're right on time; you've already earned 10 points for that and 2 bonus ones for getting started on your order task" (Hewett & Taylor, 1980). Each student's place has a simple paper and pencil task that reinforces following instructions. Each student is greeted and given points.

As the students finish their order tasks (usually in less than 5 minutes), Ms. Washington puts a large *A* on each one, gives more points, and continues: "Alvin, we're going to be doing reading first. While I get the others started, you get three red books and bring them here." She gets four of the students started on a written reading comprehension activity based on a story they read yesterday, reminds them that they can raise their red (cardboard) flag if they need help, and sits down at the table with Alvin, Tyrone, and Harold.

Praise is always specific.

"Alvin, thank you for bringing our books. You did a great job—no talking and fooling around on the way. That's worth another 3 bonus points. Now I'm going to put the title of the story we're going to read today on the board. I'll bet somebody can read it easily because it has a lot of the clusters we've been working on." She prints the title "The Fantastic Voyage" on the board and, sure enough, all three students are eager to read it.

"Marvin, you try." Marvin reads the title as "The Fantastic Voyeur." Suppressing a giggle, Ms. Washington prompts, "What sound do the letters *a-g-e* make? Right! Now try it. Great! Harold, what does fantastic mean? It's a word we might use about science fiction. Right! It means strange or hard to believe. Very good!"

Ms. Washington continues to present vocabulary words, prompting correct responses and heavily reinforcing them. She avoids getting sidetracked or slowing down, but keeps the group on task and her pace brisk. She starts the group silently reading the first paragraph and goes to check the students working independently. No one has raised a flag, but Melanie has not started. She is staring out the window.

"Melanie, take your work into the carrel, please. It will be easier for you to concentrate. I expect that work to be finished before it's time for you to read."

Designing a token system so that partial credit can be earned is always a good idea.

Ms. Washington's reading lesson is finished in about 20 minutes. She gives the boys an assignment and points for paying attention and participating. She then checks the work of the other students, gives more points and asks Charlie to get the blue books for his group. She determines that Melanie (who is a group unto herself) is working and spends about 2 minutes going over her work while Charlie distributes the blue books. She also gives Melanie fewer points than she could have earned "because you had a little trouble getting started today." The reading lesson has the same format as the first group's. As the group starts to review vocabulary, Alvin, who should be working independently, leans over and says something to Tyrone, who tries to ignore him.

"Excuse me for interrupting our lesson, Group. Alvin, you need to do your own work and leave Tyrone alone, please."

When this group is finished, Ms. Washington spends 10 uninterrupted minutes with Melanie, who is still having trouble with the short vowel sounds. She is frustrated that she has so little time to spend with each child, but she tries very hard to make the independent work meaningful and to make every minute of instruction count. She spends the last 5 minutes of the hour helping each student total his or her points and decide what kind of day he or she had. She dismisses the students and reminds them pleasantly that their teachers expect them back right on time.

Ms. Washington repeats the cycle four more times. During the afternoon, with the help of her assistant, she is able to give her undivided attention to each instructional group. For that reason, she tries to schedule most of the children with the most serious learning problems and all of the children with serious behavior problems in the afternoon.

Who Needs Behavior Mod?

Ms. Samples is a 30-year veteran fifth-grade teacher at the middle school where Ms. Washington teaches students with mild disabilities. She is somewhat of a legend—never sends children to the office and only reluctantly sends them to the resource room. At the beginning of the year she listened doubtfully to Ms. Washington's explanation of her token system.

"Good heavens," she declared, "you young teachers with your new-fangled notions. All those points and charts. Coddling them with bribes. I've been tough as nails for 30 years and that's what works for me."

Is Ms. Samples being punished for being a good teacher?

Mr. Jackson, the principal, is somewhat in awe of Ms. Samples. Her tough talk worries him but the children seem happy and parents clamor to get their children in her class. In spite of the fact that she ridicules each successive wave of reform in curriculum and methodology, her students do well on standardized tests and are well-prepared for sixth grade. Mr. Jackson generally leaves Ms. Samples alone and guiltily tends to assign her more than her share of children with learning and behavior problems. Tyrone, Harold, and Melanie are all members of her class, along with several other children who attend the resource class.

Ms. Samples accosted Ms. Washington in the teacher's lounge one Monday morning. "Listen," she said, "I really need to keep all the kids all this week. I've got important stuff to teach and if they miss parts of it they'll get behind." Ms. Washington, having recently attended a seminar on inclusion, agreed to this temporary arrangement. She asked with some trepidation if she could observe how her children functioned under this arrangement.

"Come any time," said Ms. Samples. "I've got nothing to hide. Just don't expect to see any of your individualized education or whatever it is . . . not any of your foolish behavior mod either."

Ms. Washington rearranged her schedule to free up a full hour Friday afternoon. She approached the door of Ms. Samples' class, firmly closed as usual, and quietly entered. To her immense surprise, the children were not seated quietly at their desks watching Ms. Samples at the board. She did not, in fact, see Ms. Samples right away because the teacher was sitting on the floor surrounded by a group of children engaged in attaching curtain hooks to a 6-foot length of burlap with brightly colored pieces of felt glued to it. Other groups of children were occupied framing printed documents and arguing about the distance between cup hooks on a long piece of wood. Desks and tables were pushed aside or arranged in clusters with several children working on other apparently nonacademic tasks. Ms. Washington sat down at an empty desk and tried to make some sense of the seemingly chaotic activity. Tyrone approached her and asked what she was doing. When she stated that she had wanted to see him and the others working in their "other" classroom, he gloated, "Oh, we haven't done any work all week. We all worked hard last 6 weeks and brought the class report card average up a whole letter grade so we've just been making our tapestry about the American Revolution." Tyrone explained that he had been on the team that researched the battle of Bunker Hill and decided what scene to cut from felt and glue on the wall hanging.

"It was fun," he stated, "Amanda helped with the hard words, and I even got to measure the felt."

Ms. Washington immediately realized that Ms. Samples' teaching methods, whatever her statements about new-fangled notions, were right up to date. When Tyrone went back to his group she examined the classroom carefully. One bulletin board was labeled CLASSROOM POLICIES. Children's work was posted on another. She asked a student about it and was told that it wasn't really work, just copies of the best short reports about the Revolution that were being framed to accompany the mural.

Positive reinforcement in action

"It's awesome to have your work on that board," she said. "It has to be like totally perfect. I rewrote mine three times and got help from my spelling partner before it was good enough." She proudly pointed out her essay. Ms. Washington was interested to see Melanie's essay, right next to it, much shorter, but neatly written and bearing the same big, red $A+$. The heading attributed the essay to Melanie, as told to Lee Anne.

Ms. Samples had gotten up from the floor. "Thanks, guys" she said to two boys who had each given her a hand, "it's nice to know that you apply our class policy on helping others to me, too." She began to move around the room.

Sometimes punishment is necessary.

"Melanie," she asked, "have you finished cutting the mats? Remember, your group depends on you. Mike, watch Harold carefully—he's really an expert framer." Harold grinned hugely. A stranger to Ms. Washington muttered, "That retard's an expert?" to a friend, who snickered. Ms. Samples took each boy's arm, marched them to an unoccupied area of the room and quietly, but with steel in her voice, reminded them that another class policy was respect for others and that each of them was to copy that policy from the board and write an essay on how it makes others feel when you call them names.

Suddenly there was a commotion at one end of the room. Tyrone pushed a chair over and cocked his fist at another student. Ms. Samples had both his arms by the elbow before he could carry out the act.

Stimulus control.

"Tyrone, that is totally unacceptable. Hitting is not the solution to any problem. You will have to sit out for 15 minutes." Tyrone sullenly but obediently went to a chair behind a file cabinet and sat down. Ms. Washington noticed while Tyrone was "sitting out" Ms. Samples spoke with the other boy, reminding him that Tyrone was sometimes volatile and that the kind of teasing other children take in stride was apt to make him blow.

Ms. Samples rang a bell sitting on her desk. There was instant silence and all eyes turned to her.

"We have only 30 minutes left, boys and girls," she said to accompaniment of groans, which she ignored, "We'll have to finish up next week. Let's clean up now so our room will be a pleasure to enter on Monday. Think how proud we're all going to be when the students, teachers, and parents see our tapestry in the cafeteria. I can't wait, and I'll bet you can't either."

As the students began very efficiently to put away supplies and restore order to the room, Ms. Washington reflected that for a real tough teacher who didn't believe in behavior mod Ms. Samples certainly seemed to understand clearly the benefits of applying learning principles. She also decided to talk with her about placing some of her students with mild disabilities in her class on a full-time basis.

Mr. Boyd's Math Classes

Mr. Boyd teaches math in a large, urban high school. He has a homeroom, three sections of ninth-grade arithmetic, and two sections of tenth-grade consumer math. Most of his students score below grade level on achievement tests, and each of his sections contains several students who have been classified as having special education needs. His class sizes range from 22 to 25. At the beginning of the year Mr. Boyd, using the diagnostic tests provided with the textbooks issued to the students, divided each class into four teams. He composed teams carefully so that each has a mixture of more and less competent students. One year he tried forming teams each week based on the past week's performance but found that to be a logistical nightmare. He now keeps the teams intact for a 6-week grading period. Each team has a captain, who is in charge of overall management, and an accountant, who is in charge of recordkeeping. These jobs rotate weekly. Each team is allowed to choose a name.

Group token systems are described in Chapter 6.

Mr. Boyd follows the same weekly schedule as much as possible because he has found that things run more smoothly when he does. When the schedule will not be followed, he tries to let the students know in advance. On Mondays and Wednesdays he presents new concepts using large-group instruction. Tuesdays and Thursdays are team days. The students work together on assignments, helping one another as necessary. Mr. Boyd circulates, being sure that peer tutors are providing correct information and working with individuals and small groups when necessary. Fridays are test and reward days. Students receive grades for individual work but all activities also earn points for their team. Teams receive points when members are present and on time, have necessary materials, complete homework and class assignments, perform well on tests and other activities, and behave appropriately. Teams lose points when members are disruptive or noncompliant. Expectations are explained at the beginning of the school year and each student has a copy of the class rules and procedures in a required notebook. Every team can be a winner every week if enough points are earned. Each team's scores are posted on a bulletin board and the team with the highest score is named Team of the Week. Mr. Boyd was afraid that high-school students might find this system too childish, but the students seem to enjoy the camaraderie. There is a good bit of friendly competition and lots of encouragement to bring supplies, be on time, behave appropriately, and learn the material. Let's look at a typical Monday in Mr. Boyd's first period arithmetic class.

Effusive praise can serve as a punisher for many adolescent students.

Mr. Boyd stands in the doorway as the students enter. He greets each one by name, with a positive comment about appearance, or at least with a smile and eye contact. Because many of his students are athletes, he attends many games and keeps track of all of them. He often offers a word of congratulation or commiseration. He also remembers birthdays and writes them on his lesson plans so he can acknowledge them—quietly, of course, because he knows adolescents are easily embarrassed. This greeting routine also allows him to determine if any students are obviously intoxicated or under the influence of drugs and to be forewarned about any student whose body language clearly indicates that she or he is angry or upset.

As students enter the room they go immediately to their assigned seats, which are arranged in rows so that all can see the chalkboard. There are several review problems on the board and all students except the accountants begin work immediately. The accountants, who are excused from the review activity (they get plenty of math practice keeping up with all those points), move down their team's row with a clipboard and a data sheet on which they record whether students have supplies. Mr. Boyd ignores team members' surreptitiously lending one another supplies; that's what teamwork is all about.

As soon as the bell rings, Mr. Boyd takes roll by referring to his seating chart. Each team captain also notes absences; captains are encouraged to find out why their team members are not at school. Although teams are not penalized for excused absences, a member who is not present can't earn bonus points. Within 5 minutes, the students have completed the review activity. Team members check one another's work, and the papers are passed to the front and collected.

Mr. Boyd begins the lesson on equivalent fractions by donning a pizza deliverer's hat and asking how many students would like to order a pizza. All raise their hands eagerly, and Mr. Boyd passes out photo copies of a pizza he has drawn and cut into pieces. There is some good-natured muttering about the inedibility of this pizza and the pitifulness of Mr. Boyd's drawing, a standing joke.

Mr. Boyd raises his hand in his established signal for quiet and the students stop talking. He asks, "How many pieces do you have? Marvin? Sara? Hey, that's not fair, Marvin has eight pieces and Sara has only four! Marvin, you'll have to give Sara some of yours." When Marvin protests that Sara's pieces are bigger than his, Mr. Boyd is well launched into his lesson. He uses larger cardboard pizzas to illustrate that 1/2, 2/4, 4/8 all represent the same amount of pizza.

"What about 500,000/1,000,000?" he asks, writing it on the board. Marvin quips, "You're gonna have to eat that pizza with a spoon." There is general laughter. Mr. Boyd laughs, too, but soon raises his hand again. All students become quiet except two who are repeating the joke. Mr. Boyd says matter-of-factly, "Rappers just lost two points," and continues his lesson. The other members of the team glare at the malefactors and the room is again quiet.

Mr. Boyd models the procedure for determining equivalency, brings students to the board to work problems, and assigns a short written lesson to be sure students understand the concept and can do the computation. He moves constantly about the room as students work independently, providing frequent positive comments, pointing out errors, reteaching when necessary. He notes students who are having difficulty to be sure that they are assigned a peer tutor tomorrow.

Ten minutes before the end of the period, Mr. Boyd has students exchange papers again and goes over the correct answers. He reminds them not to panic if they're having trouble because they will get help tomorrow. He announces the number of points earned by each team and congratulates them. When the bell rings, Mr. Boyd dismisses this class and gets ready to do it all again with the next one.

On Tuesday the first-period class rearranges the room into clusters of desks for each team. The procedure for doing this quickly and quietly was taught at the beginning of the year. Mr. Boyd gives each team captain his team's papers from yesterday, and the captains themselves work out how to assure that each team member learns the material. Some captains assign individual tutors; some assign several students to one tutor; one looks at her team's papers and tells Mr. Boyd that they all need help. He makes sure all the teams are functioning efficiently and sits down to work with the "trouble team." He reminds himself to distribute the members of this team differently during the next grading period. The two strongest members of the original team have moved and their replacements are weak. The in-class assignment for today will earn a grade for each student as well as points for the team.

After working with the weak group for several minutes, he tells them to continue working on the assignment and monitors the class to be sure that team members are working together but not doing one another's work. He answers questions, makes suggestions to tutors, and provides an enrichment activity for bonus points to one team whose members have all completed the assignment correctly. Several times the "busy hum" of the classroom approaches a roar. Mr. Boyd raises his hand and, because all the students are not facing him, snaps his fingers twice. Team members shush one another and the noise never becomes a serious problem.

Ten minutes before the end of the period, Mr. Boyd asks the class to turn around and look at him. He collects the papers of students who are finished, reminds those who are not finished that their work must be turned in tomorrow, and gives a short homework assignment. He announces points earned for appropriate behavior, reminds the students that he will announce points for the in-class assignment when it has been graded, and allows students to begin their homework assignment. The chairs remain as they are until sixth period when that class rearranges them in rows. Mr. Boyd at one time thought it might be more efficient to do two days of group work in a row to avoid all the furniture moving but was quickly informed by the building engineer that it is impossible to clean any room whose desks are not in rows.

Ms. Michaels Has It in the Bag

Ms. Michaels teaches a group of students with moderate to severe disabilities. Her students range in age from 17 through 20. She shares responsibility for twenty-four students with another licensed teacher and two paraprofessionals. Her job has changed dramatically over the years. She started her career in a state-run residential institution and is now working with a similar population of students located at a regular suburban high school. Her students spend a great deal of time outside school learning skills they will need as adults.

Today she plans to take three of her students into the community for several hours. This requires a great deal of advance planning. She and her colleagues determine that the other teacher and one assistant will work on domestic skills, simulated shopping skills, and prevocational skills, with most of the students remaining at school. The classroom contains a fully equipped kitchen and laundry room and the students will prepare lunch for themselves, wash and fold towels from the school gym, and prepare brochures from a local health club for mailing. In return, the health club has agreed to allow class members to use the facility. The classroom also has an area that can simulate a grocery, drug, or convenience store so that students can practice shopping using lists or picture cues. Four highly verbal students will accompany the assistant to the resource room where the teacher is working on appropriate social skills on the job. They will eat lunch with some of the resource students and return to their classroom for the shopping simulation.

The students who are to be in the community will work at a job site for an hour, eat lunch at a cafeteria, and shop for clothing at a local discount department store. The students accompanying Ms. Michaels today are Sam, 17 years old with good verbal skills and excellent behavior, Kimberly, 18, who uses a communication board and behaves well unless frustrated or confused, and Ricardo, 19, who has some verbal skills but is prone to violent outbursts.

Ms. Michaels checks first thing to see that all three students are present and feeling well, then spends some time previewing the trip, using pictures. Sam and Kimberly are old hands at the grocery store where they are learning job skills. They have also eaten at the cafeteria and shopped at the department store several times. Ricardo has less experience at the grocery store but has eaten and been shopping alone with a teacher. This will be his first group experience at these sites. Ms. Michaels has specific objectives for each student at each site. After the preview, which serves as a language lesson, Ms. Michaels checks to see that everyone has their identification, that everyone has used the restroom, that Kimberly has the right sheets for her communication board, and that she, herself, has everything she needs. (She occasionally indulges in a sigh of nostalgia for the simplicity of her work at the residential institution.) Everyone makes fun of the large satchel she carries into the community, but she has learned to be prepared. She picks up the bag, as she calls it, as she leaves the room.

The bus stop is right outside the school. While waiting for the bus each student counts out the correct change from his or her coin purse—they've been riding the bus since elementary school. The bus is right on time and the students put their coins in the container and greet the bus driver. Ricardo begins humming with excitement but subsides immediately when Kimberly touches him on the shoulder and shakes her head. Ms. Michaels decides that Ricardo is going to need support today from the token system that they are trying to phase out. She pulls some chips from her bag and puts them in her pocket. She will give them throughout the trip on a random interval schedule contingent on good behavior. Ricardo is familiar with the tokens, their value, and the expected behaviors, so no explanation will be required. Ricardo can keep the chips in his pocket until they return to school. Ms. Michaels will try to keep the process as unobtrusive as possible.

After an uneventful ride—Sam takes charge of watching for the approach of the right stop and pulling on the cord—the students and Ms. Michaels exit at the stop near the supermarket. Sam and Kimberly immediately go to the time clock, followed by Ricardo after a reminder from Ms. Michaels. All three don red aprons with nametags. Kimberly makes her way independently to the deli, greets Ms. Phelps, her supervisor, with a smile and is greeted in return. Today she will be filling containers with the various dips and spreads made in the deli. Ms. Phelps puts a poster from Ms. Michaels' bag showing pictures of each step of the task on the wall over the work area. She has asked for extras of the various posters Kimberly and other students use. She believes they will help many of her nondisabled employees. Ms. Phelps gives Kimberly instructions, watches her go through this new task several times as she would with any employee, and shows her where she can get more containers from the storeroom if she runs out. She has agreed to keep track of the number of times Kimberly either gets new materials or asks for assistance rather than whining or shouting in frustration.

Ms. Michaels accompanies Sam and Ricardo to the check-out area where they will be bagging groceries. Sam will also accompany customers to their cars and unload groceries. On his next visit he will begin learning to stock shelves and replenish the produce counters. This particular chain of grocery stores has an excellent history of hiring persons with disabilities and Sam will have a summer job this year with the possibility of permanent employment when he finishes school. He greets his friend Stan, an older individual with retardation, who is employed full-time at the store. They chat as they bag groceries quickly and efficiently. At one point they become excited about an upcoming sports event and are reminded by the checkout clerk to "Keep it down, guys." They comply immediately.

Ms. Michaels meanwhile works directly with Ricardo and the assistant manager who trains the bag persons. They work on correctly loading sacks and being careful with fragile items. The students all take a break and get a soft drink from the machine in the break room. They interact with other employees, disabled and nondisabled, and groan like the others when the break is over. Sam and Kimberly can read the passage of 15 minutes on the clock. Ricardo carries a small timer that he is learning to set for various spans of time. Ms. Michaels observes and records on a small clipboard from her bag the number of times Sam appropriately interacts with a coworker, her main objective for him on this part of the trip.

After about an hour the students remove their aprons and clock out. Calling and waving their farewells, they leave the supermarket. The cafeteria is within walking distance and Ms. Michaels has planned the excursion so that the hour is early enough that the restaurant will not be crowded. Sam asks for what he wants; Kimberly points or shows pictures. Ms. Michaels stays close to Ricardo, who is showing signs of agitation. Recognizing a potential crisis, Ms. Michaels decides to abandon education for expedience, and begins positively reinforcing any semblance of OK behavior. She pulls from her bag Ricardo's list (made during the rehearsal this morning of what he wants for lunch). "Ricardo," she says cheerfully, "I like the way you're walking." She pops a token in his pocket.

"Fish," mutters Ricardo as she orders for him.

"*Good* talking quietly Ricardo," she says quickly, popping another token. Ricardo begins to appear less agitated.

"Would you like to order your tea? Tell the lady 'I want tea, please.'" Ricardo complies.

Task analysis is discussed in Chapter 7.

"*Good* ordering, Ricardo," she says, hoping the danger of Ricardo's blowing it has passed. "Can you carry your tray?" Ricardo picks up the tray and follows Sam. Ms. Michaels picks up his check—she isn't about to remind him at this point—along with hers. She is disappointed because she had planned to collect data on his independent accomplishment of getting through the line, a task that she has, of course, analyzed.

Ms. Michaels has done a very quick functional analysis, discussed in Chapter 9.

The students make it to an empty table without mishap and unload their trays. Ricardo suddenly announces loudly that he has to "GO." Ms. Michaels reminds him to announce that quietly in the future and directs him to the men's room. (She feels that she knows the location of every public restroom in the city.) She also reminds herself that she and her colleagues need to work on getting

Ricardo to communicate his needs before they become urgent and thus cause him to become agitated.

After a lunch spent discussing the upcoming shopping trip, the students prepare to pay for their meals. Each reads the number on the bottom of the ticket and gets out one more dollar. They hand their ticket and the money to the clerk and hold out their hands for change. Ms. Michaels jots down that Sam, for the first time, responds, "Thanks, you too," to the clerk, who encouraged him to "Have a nice afternoon." She is really pleased with Sam's social skills.

After another bus ride, they arrive at the department store. All three students need to buy sweats to wear to the health club they will begin using next week. The unisex sweats are in large bins. Kimberly finds the "M" bin, Sam finds the "L" bin, and Ms. Michaels helps Ricardo find the "S" bin. He wants red sweats but sees only black in his bin. He begins to shout and wave his arms. Ms. Michaels instructs Sam and Kimberly to "Come with me, please," and (thankful that Ricardo is "S") hustles him into the gardening equipment area at the back of the store, which she knows from previous trips will be virtually unpopulated. She instructs Ricardo to "Settle down," meanwhile holding him firmly against a wall to prevent his flailing. An elderly lady, looking horrified, says, "Young lady, you're abusing that poor, afflicted child. I'm going to report this." Ms. Michaels says, through her teeth, "Kimberly, give the lady a blue card, please." Kimberly, who is holding the bag, reaches into a side pocket and hands the woman an official looking card explaining who Ms. Michaels is and why she is in the community. The card invites anyone who has concerns to call Ms. Michaels' supervisor and provides the telephone number. Ricardo, meanwhile, does settle down and apparently no one else has noticed the episode. They return to the shopping floor, pick out sweats (the red are in the *other* "S" bin), check the label for the correct letter, pay for them, and exit.

Ms. Michaels is delighted that she had earlier decided to put off until later in the week her students' prewashing the sweats at a local group home while they worked on kitchen cleaning. Breathing a sigh of relief, she arrives with her charges at the bus stop. Her sense of relief begins to wane when several minutes pass without the bus's arrival. Even Sam begins to shift restlessly on the bench and demand, "Where's the bus?" Ms. Michaels reaches into her bag and offers each student a choice of a magazine or a hand-held video game. They sit quietly for the remaining 20 minutes of their wait.

SUMMARY

In this chapter we have described how teachers implement the principles and procedures of applied behavior analysis in actual classrooms. We have discussed the importance of structure, planning, consistency, and consequences. We have described the operation of several hypothetical learning environments. Although none of these will be exactly like yours, we believe that visiting them will help you put it all together.

DISCUSSION QUESTIONS

1. What data should each of the hypothetical teachers be keeping? How could each keep them most efficiently?

2. Identify additional elements of stimulus control, positive reinforcement, and punishment for each of the vignettes.

3. In which one of the six classrooms would you prefer to teach? Why?

4. Give two original examples of each kind of structure described.

REFERENCES

Gallagher, P.A. 1979. Teaching students with behavior disorders: Techniques for classroom instruction. Denver: Love Publishing.

Haring, N.G., & Phillips, E.L. 1962. Educating emotionally disturbed children. New York: McGraw-Hill.

Hewett, F.M., & Taylor, F.D. 1980. The emotionally disturbed child in the classroom: The orchestration of success. Boston: Allyn & Bacon.

Madsen, C.H., Becker, W.C., & Thomas, D.R. 1968. Rules, praise and ignoring: Elements of elementary classroom control. *Journal of Applied Behavior Analysis, 1*, 139–150.

Rodewald, H.K. 1979. Stimulus control of behavior. Baltimore: University Park Press.

Stephens, T.M., Hartman, A.C., & Lucas, V.H. 1978. Teaching children basic skills: A curriculum handbook. Columbus, Ohio: Merrill.

Van Houten, R., Hill, S., & Parsons, M. 1975. An analysis of a performance feedback system: The effects of timing and feedback, public posting, and praise upon academic performance and peer interaction. *Journal of Applied Behavior Analysis, 8*, 435–448.

Van Houten, R., & Thompson, C. 1976. The effects of explicit timing on math performance. *Journal of Applied Behavior Analysis, 9*, 227–230.

Section Four

Maintaining Behavior Change

Providing for Generalization of Behavior Change

It takes a long time and a lot of hard work to decide which of a student's behaviors to change.

- Planning a program to change those behaviors takes a lot of research and considerable creativity.
- Carrying out that program is time-consuming and demanding.

Behavior change that doesn't last is useless.

Imagine then how frustrated teachers become if, as soon as the program has been completed and the contingencies withdrawn, the student goes right back to behaving the way he did before the program was started. The potential for this kind of disappointment emphasizes the importance of programming for generalization and the importance of this chapter.

Preceding chapters described principles and procedures related to strengthening appropriate behaviors, reducing or eliminating maladaptive behaviors, and teaching new behaviors. The technology of behavior change presented in these earlier chapters has been thoroughly investigated and its efficacy demonstrated beyond doubt. Applied behavior analysts have not, however, been as thorough in demonstrating that behaviors changed using their technology are changed permanently or, indeed, that the changed behaviors are displayed in any setting except that in which training programs are executed. It is meaningless to change behavior unless the change can be made to last and unless behavior will occur in settings other than the original training site and in the absence of the original trainer.

Ways that behavior change can generalize.

Many of the criticisms of applied behavior analysis that we discussed in Chapter 2 have resulted from the short-lived results of many behavior-change programs. Fortunately, these criticisms have resulted in a radical increase in concern for documenting generalization of behavior change. To program meaningful behavior change, teachers must use the behavioral principle of generality. Baer, Wolf, and Risley (1968) stated: "A behavioral change may be said to have generality if it proves durable over time, if it appears in a wide variety of possible environments, or if it spreads to a wide variety of related behaviors" (p. 96). Baer and his colleagues describe three ways a behavior may show generality: over time, across settings, and across behaviors. Each of these types of generalization will be discussed in more detail later in this chapter. The following examples illustrate behavior changes that do not have generality:

> The students at the Foxwood Youth Center have a very structured program both during the school day and in their dormitories. Most of them have been referred because of serious behavioral problems that have brought them in contact with the judicial system, but under the point and level system of the center they display very few problems. When discharged, however, many of them go right back to the same behaviors that caused them to be referred. A significant percentage of the discharged students are back at Foxwood or in another correctional facility within a few months.

> Ms. Kitchens is a resource teacher for children with learning disabilities. Her students spend approximately 2 hours a day in her classroom and the remainder of their time in regular classes. Ms. Kitchens has noticed that, although her students do very well in the resource room, when they are in the regular classroom they do not perform academic tasks that she knows they can do.

> Mr. Foote's first-graders have learned to recognize a large number of words using flashcards and a look-say approach. When confronted with an unfamiliar word, however, the students just guess. They have not learned to decode new words based on relationships between symbols and sounds.

The preceding examples describe situations in which some academic or social behavior has been successfully changed. The change, however, was accomplished only for as long as the contingencies were in effect, or only in the setting where training took place, or only for very specific behaviors that were trained. There is no question that applied behavior analysis procedures often cause situation-specific behavior changes. Indeed, several of the research designs described in Chapter 5 depend on this phenomenon (Hartmann & Atkinson, 1973). The classic **ABAB** (reversal) **design** demonstrates functional relationships between behavior and consequences by successfully applying and withdrawing such consequences and demonstrating that the dependent variable (the behavior) changes according to the condition. If the behavior failed to return to its baseline rate under one of these designs, the experimenter would have failed to demonstrate a functional relationship.

The multiple baseline design enables an experimenter to demonstrate functional relationships by successfully applying contingencies to several different behaviors, to behavior in several different settings, or to the same behavior displayed by different students. Again, a functional relationship is shown only when the behaviors are not changed until contingencies are implemented. Baer, Wolf, and Risley (1968) stated that "generalization should be programmed rather than expected or lamented" (p. 97). The experimenter attempting to establish functional relationships between procedures and behavior may, indeed, lament the occurrence of generalization. The classroom teacher is more likely to expect it and to lament its absence. With few exceptions (Kifer, Lewis, Green, & Phillips, 1974; Patterson, 1965), it is the professional expecting generalization who is disappointed. Because generalization does not automatically result when behavior is changed (Axelrod, 1977; Kazdin, 1977; Stokes & Baer, 1977), are applied behavior analysis procedures useless? If you have stuck with us this far, you know that we don't think so. To most behavior analysts, the lack of automatic generalization simply indicates the need for developing a technology of generalization as efficient as the technology of behavior change. Such a technology need not interfere with the necessity for demonstrating functional relationships; it may be applied after these relationships have been established (Kallman, Hersen, & O'Toole, 1975).

As Baer, Wolf, and Risley (1968) suggested, generalization must be programmed. This chapter describes the principles of generalization that are the foundation of this programming and suggests specific ways that teachers can increase the odds that the behaviors their students learn will be maintained even when all the charts and graphs have been discarded.

GENERALIZATION

How to write objectives for generalization and maintenance

In Chapter 3 we described a response hierarchy for designing objectives. It included response levels of acquisition, fluency, maintenance, and generalization. It is important that the IEP for each student with a disability include objectives for the levels of maintenance and generalization (Billingsley, 1984). Haring and Liberty (1990) suggest that maintenance and generalization objectives differ from acquisition objectives in two ways: the conditions under which the behavior is to be performed and the criteria defined for performance. The conditions specified should be those that exist in the setting or settings in which the behavior will ultimately be performed. For example, if our generalization objective for a student is that he or she will order food at a fast food restaurant we might begin instruction in the classroom under simulated conditions. Numerous prompts and reinforcers would probably be provided. However, in a real restaurant the student will have to function with only a prompt such as "May I help you?" or "Help you?" or "What do you want?", or, conceivably, "Would you like to try our roasted buffalo burger special today?" Neither the order taker nor other customers is likely to say "Good ordering," "Nice waiting," or "Good getting your money out," or to provide hugs, tokens, or points as a consequence. These prompts and reinforcers may be perfectly appropriate during the acquisition phase but the conditions specified in a generalization objective should reflect conditions in the real-life environment.

Criteria specified in a generalization objective should reflect performance that is good enough, a phrase that occurs frequently in popular self-help literature. Can the student, for example, wash, dry, and fold towels at the laundromat well enough that the towels can be stored in the linen closet at the group home? During the acquisition phase the instructor may insist that towels be folded with corners exactly square and stacked precisely. If that same instructor, however, were to permit us a peek at his linen closet we might find that he, too, settles for "good enough" performance in towel-folding.

The evaluation of generalization objectives is also critical (Billingsley, 1987). We must consider both where the behavior is to be evaluated and who is to do the evaluation. If we want George to be able to get a soft drink from any machine he encounters, we might begin instruction on the vending machine in the community center where he goes swimming twice a week. It is important to be aware that even though we may pat ourselves on the back because we are conducting instruction in the community, this skill is no more likely to generalize than if we brought a vending machine into the classroom (Haring, 1988). After we have taught George to use various vending machines in various locations we can assess generalization. It is obviously impossible to take George to every vending machine in his community, so we conduct *probes*. We select several vending machines in different locations and check to see whether George gets a soft drink—without prompts and with no reinforcer except the soda. If we really want to be certain that George has a generalized skill it will be important that his teacher and another adult he knows not be standing near him with a clipboard. Generalization probes are best taken by someone unfamiliar to the student or at least someone who would normally be in the environment.

There are several kinds of generalization.

Before suggesting guidelines for facilitating generalization, we need to differentiate several types. The first of these occurs when a response that has been trained in a specific setting with a specific instructor occurs in a different setting or with a different instructor. This phenomenon, called simply *generalization* (Koegel & Rincover, 1977), *transfer of training* (Kazdin, 1977), or *stimulus generalization* (Barton & Ascione, 1979), should be distinguished from *response maintenance* (Kazdin, 1977), which refers to the tendency of a learned behavior to occur after programmed contingencies have been withdrawn. Response maintenance may also be labeled *maintenance* (Koegel & Rincover, 1977), *resistance to extinction, durability*, or *behavioral persistence* (Atthowe, 1973). Finally, the term *response generalization* is used when referring to unprogrammed changes in similar behaviors when a target behavior is modified (Twardosz & Sajwaj, 1972). This phenomenon may also be termed *concomitant* or *concurrent behavior change* (Kazdin, 1973). It is easy to see why some confusion may result from varying terminology or from researchers' failure to differentiate among the varieties of generalization. In this chapter, the term *generalization* will refer to any of the three types and the terms *stimulus generalization, maintenance*, and *response generalization* will be used when distinctions are made among them. Table 11–1 illustrates the relationships among the terms used to describe generality of behavior change.

Stimulus Generalization

Chapter 7 discussed the development of discrimination. You will recall that discrimination training involves bringing a response under stimulus control so that, for example, a student reads "went" only when the stimulus *w-e-n-t* is presented and not when the teacher shows a flashcard with *w-a-n-t* or or *w-e-t*. The student whose reading behavior is under faulty stimulus control is demonstrating stimulus generalization. Such faulty stimulus control is also demonstrated when young children call all four-legged animals "doggie" or when the "big man on campus" calls the president of the Women's Studies program "baby."

Not all generalization is a good thing.

Stimulus generalization occurs when responses that have been reinforced in the presence of a specific stimulus (S^D) occur in the presence of different but similar stimuli (Guttman & Kalish, 1956). A group of stimuli that should occasion the same response may be considered members of a stimulus class. In general, the more similar the stimuli, the more likely stimulus generalization will occur. As the stimuli become increasingly different from S^D, the likelihood decreases that the response will be emitted in their pres-

TABLE 11–1
Terminology used to describe types of generalization

	Generalization		
	Stimulus Generalization	**Maintenance**	**Response Generalization**
Synonyms	Generalization Transfer of training	Response maintenance Resistance to extinction Durability Behavioral persistence	Concomitant behavior change Current behavior change

ence. The pattern of decreased responding as stimuli become less similar to the S^D has been called a *generalization gradient*. Figure 11–1 illustrates a hypothetical generalization gradient for a student who is learning to identify the letter *b*. Responding with "*b*" to letters similar to *b* is more frequent than responding to letters whose configuration is quite different. In this example, stimulus generalization is working against the teacher, so efforts must be directed at tightening stimulus control.

On the other hand, we could illustrate a very similar generalization gradient using the letter *b* as originally presented and the letter *b* in different sizes, typefaces, colors, and contexts. In this instance, the teacher wants to promote stimulus generalization, not prevent it. Unfortunately, the same teaching process that facilitates appropriate discrimination may result in too fine a discrimination for practical purposes. The students described at the beginning of this chapter who performed differently in the resource room and the regular classroom illustrate this problem. Those students formed a discrimination that resulted in responses that were too situation-specific. The resource room had become an S^D for appropriate behavior; the regular classroom, an S^Δ. To return to an example we used earlier in the chapter, a student who has been carefully taught to respond appropriately only to the stimulus "May I help you?" when ordering fast food, may become completely befuddled when an order taker says something else. It is paradoxical that teachers must expend so much effort to bring students' behavior under stimulus control but must also work toward avoiding too great a degree of the same control.

Maintenance

If you were unable to remember this, perhaps your behavior, when no longer reinforced by passing tests, has undergone extinction.

Most behaviors that teachers want students to perform should occur even after systematic applied behavior analysis procedures have been withdrawn. Teachers want their students to read accurately in class and also to continue reading accurately after they are no longer in school. Math problems in school are merely a means to an end—we want students eventually to balance checkbooks, fill out income tax forms, or multiply measurements in recipes. Appropriate social behaviors, too, while adaptive in the classroom, are also necessary when a specific program for their systematic reinforcement no longer exists. Chapter 8 detailed what happens when positive reinforcement is abruptly withdrawn from a behavior that previously has been reinforced on a continuous schedule: the behavior decelerates and is eventually extinguished. Extinction may be a very useful phenomenon when a teacher withdraws attention from a maladaptive behavior. On the other hand, it may be frustrating when the teacher has systematically developed some appropriate behavior only to see that it has disappeared when the student is observed a year later.

Assuring that behavior will be maintained is an important part of teaching. It is impossible for the teacher to follow students around forever, reinforcing them with cereal or a smile and praise. Behaviors that extinguish rapidly when the artificial contingencies used to develop them are with-

FIGURE 11–1
Hypothetical generalization gradient for a student learning the letter b

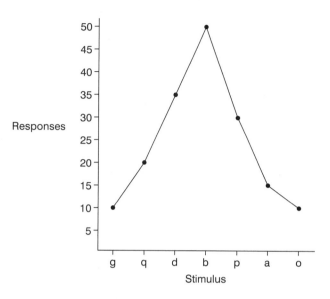

drawn can hardly be considered learned in any meaningful sense. Most experimental evidence indicates that extinction occurs unless specific measures are taken to prevent it (Kazdin, 1977; Kazdin & Bootzin, 1972; Rincover & Koegel, 1975; Stokes, Baer, & Jackson, 1974).

Response Generalization

Sometimes changing one behavior will result in changes in other similar behaviors. Such similar behaviors are often referred to as a *response class*, and changes in untrained members of the response class, as **response generalization**. For example, if students receive reinforcers for completing multiplication problems and subsequently increase their rates of completing both multiplication and division problems, response generalization has occurred to untrained members of the response class: completion of arithmetic problems. Unfortunately, this kind of generalization does not happen often. Usually only the specific behavior being reinforced will change. "Behavior, unlike the flower, does not naturally bloom" (Baer & Wolf, 1970, p. 320).

TRAINING GENERALIZATION

Assuring the generality of behavior change is particularly important to the teacher of students with disabilities. Since legislation requires that all such students be educated in the least restrictive environment, large numbers of students with mild disabilities are in special classes only temporarily or for only part of the school day. The special educator cannot count on being able to apply systematic applied behavior analysis procedures for extended periods of time or even for the entire school day. Even the teacher of students with more pervasive disabilities must be aware that these students, too, will be living, learning, and working in an environment that is least restrictive—that is, one that as much as possible resembles that of their nondisabled peers. Special educators must prepare their students to perform in situations where systematic contingency management programs may not be available.

The regular educator also must be aware of techniques for promoting generalization. Regular teachers will teach large numbers of students with mild disabilities who have been taught appropriate academic and social behaviors using applied behavior analysis procedures. To help these students perform optimally in the regular classroom, regular teachers must be aware not only of the techniques used to teach these students but also of techniques that will encourage generalization to less-structured settings. The current emphasis on increasing integration of students with disabilities in the regular programs makes awareness of this technology more important for all teachers.

The procedures for promoting generalization described in the following sections include some that would not meet more stringent or technical definitions of generalization of behavior change (see Johnston, 1979; Keller & Schoenfeld, 1950; Skinner, 1953). Traditionally, generalization has been noted only when behavior occurs spontaneously in circumstances where no contingencies are in effect. For practical purposes, we shall also consider behavior changes that can be facilitated by relatively minor changes in the setting in which generalization is desired. If such changes can be made fairly effortlessly and if gains made in the training setting can be maintained, for all practical purposes the behavior has generalized. Haring and Liberty (1990) suggest a number of questions that instructors should ask in order to make decisions about programming for generalization. In simplified form, questions that a teacher might ask when assessing and programming for generalization include:

1. Has the skill been acquired? Unless the student can perform the skill accurately and reliably in an instructional setting, it is useless to hope that she will perform it in any other setting.

2. Can the student acquire reinforcers (natural or otherwise) without performing the skill? If when George stands helplessly in front of a soft drink vending machine at the local miniature golf course, nondisabled peers impatiently take his change and get him a drink, he is unlikely to be motivated to get it for himself.

3. Does the student perform part of the skill? When the student performs part of a skill in a generalization setting, the teacher's job is to go back to his task analysis, assess the antecedent and consequent stimuli for the missing or nonperformed component, provide more effective ones during retraining, and identify potentially effective stimuli in the generalization environment.

 Stokes and Baer (1977, p. 350) reviewed the literature on generalization assessment and training in applied behavior analysis and categorized the techniques for assessing or programming generalization as follows:

Train and hope.

Sequentially modify.

Introduce to natural maintaining contingencies.

Train sufficient exemplars.

Train loosely.

Use indiscriminable contingencies.

Program common stimuli.

Mediate generalization.

Train to generalize.

The following sections review relevant research on each of the techniques described by Stokes and Baer and provide examples illustrating possible classroom uses.

Train and Hope

Unplanned generalization does sometimes happen. It may be likely to happen in cases where the skill trained is particularly useful to the student or where the skill becomes reinforcing in itself. For example, Patterson (1965) used a DRO procedure to eliminate aggressive/disruptive classroom behavior in a boy who behaved hyperactively. The inappropriate behavior was reduced on the playground and at home (where no formal contingencies were in operation), as well as in the classroom. Other researchers have reported that students who are given token reinforcers for appropriate behavior during some part of the school day may show changes in that behavior during other parts of the day or even in other classrooms (Walker, Mattsen, & Buckley, 1971).

Appropriate behaviors may also last after programs are withdrawn. Hewett, Taylor, and Artuso (1969) used a structured classroom design including token reinforcement for academic and social behavior. They reported maintenance of high rates of academic behavior and low rates of disruption even after the tokens were withdrawn. Many behaviors taught to typical children and those with mild disabilities do generalize. Students who learn to read in school delight their parents (and sometimes drive them to distraction) by reading street signs. This spontaneous generalization, however, is much less likely to occur with students with more severe disabilities (Horner, McDonnell, & Bellamy, undated).

Remember that changes in children's behavior may change adults' behavior, too.

In spite of reported evidence that some behaviors are automatically generalized, it is important to remember that most are not. When they are, we do not usually know why (Kazdin, 1977). It has been suggested that some aspect of the generalization setting may have acquired conditioned reinforcing characteristics (Baer & Wolf, 1970; Bijou, Peterson, Harris, Allen, & Johnston, 1969; Chadwick & Day, 1971; Medland & Stachnik, 1972). Another possibility is that the behavior of teachers or parents has been permanently altered by the implementation of the applied behavior analysis procedure and that reinforcing consequences, though no longer formally programmed, may still occur more frequently than before intervention (Greenwood, Sloane, & Baskin, 1974; Kazdin, 1977).

Although there is hope that behaviors acquired or strengthened through formal contingency management programs may generalize, there is no certainty. Hoping will not make generalization happen. The teacher who expects it should be prepared to monitor students' behavior closely and to instigate more effective procedures immediately on learning that early hopes have been dashed. The following example illustrates a behavior that generalized for no discernible reason.

Ms. Andrews Works a Miracle

Ms. Andrews, who did private tutoring at home to supplement her income, was asked to work with Brandon, who had completed the first semester of the seventh grade with 2 Cs, 2 Ds, and an F. Because Brandon had previously been an excellent student, his parents were frantic. Ms. Andrews tested Brandon, found no learning problem, and decided that Brandon simply had a particularly bad case of seventh-grade slump. He was not doing homework or classwork, and he didn't study for tests. He seemed to have efficient study skills—he just wasn't using them. Ms. Andrews suggested that once-a-week tutoring was not the answer and urged the parents to implement some contingency management. She explained the low probability that study behavior would generalize beyond her living room. They insisted on tutoring and implemented no program.

For two weeks, Ms. Andrews worked with Brandon on grade-level materials—not the books he was using at school because he naturally forgot to bring them. She provided very high rates of verbal praise for reading, studying, and completing math problems, as well as access to a gamelike vocabulary development program if Brandon completed other tasks.

During the third week, Brandon's mother called. Three of his teachers had written notes indicating that Brandon's work in their classes had improved dramatically. Tests and papers from all classes were As and Bs. Ms. Andrews, said Brandon's mother, had worked a miracle. Agreeing modestly before hanging up, Ms. Andrews spent the next few minutes staring into space and wondering, "Did he just coincidentally decide to kick into gear, or was it really something I did?"

Sequentially Modify

Review Chapter 5 for an extended discussion of the multiple baseline design.

A procedure that allows stimulus generalization or transfer of training across settings is *sequential modification*. In this procedure, generalization (in the practical sense) is promoted by applying the same techniques that successfully changed behavior in one setting to all settings where the target behavior is desirable. Exactly the same process is undertaken when using a multiple-baseline-across-settings design to demonstrate a functional relationship between independent and dependent variables. For example, for a student who learned to behave appropriately and complete academic tasks in a resource room but did not perform in any regular classrooms, the teachers involved might set up a reinforcement system similar to that used in the resource class in each regular classroom. A similar procedure to promote maintenance would necessitate training those responsible for the student's education and care after the student has been dismissed from a special training program. Teachers, parents, or other caregivers would be trained to carry out the same applied behavior analysis procedures employed in the training situation. In some cases, it may be unrealistic to program exactly the same contingencies in the generalization setting. For example, a regular classroom teacher may not be able to monitor disruptive behavior as closely, or deliver reinforcers as often, as a special-class teacher. Similarly, parents may be unable or unwilling to structure programs as closely as may be done in institutional settings. In such cases, modified versions of programs may still provide enough environmental control to maintain the target behaviors at rates close to those established during training.

Homes may be harder to structure than schools or other institutions.

Examination of any published study using a multiple-baseline-across-settings experimental design provides an example of sequential modification. Hall, Cristler, Cranston, and Tucker (1970) changed the behavior of a group of fifth-grade students who were consistently late after three different recesses during the school day. A contingency applied to the students' being in their seats within 4 minutes of the end of the noon recess resulted in decreased tardiness in coming back from that recess but no change in the tardiness in returning from the other two. The contingency was then applied to return from the morning recess as well, whereupon tardiness diminished for that situation but not for the afternoon recess. Not until reinforcement depended on rapid return from all three recesses did the tardiness rates decline for all.

Long and Williams (1973) reinforced appropriate behavior in a junior-high class using contingent free time. Behavior was monitored during math and geography classes. No behavior change occurred in the second class when the program was implemented in the first, but when contingent free time was used in both classes, appropriate behavior occurred at high rates in both.

Walker and Buckley (1968) changed the behavior of a 9-year-old child in a special class for children labeled behaviorally disturbed. The student received points for attending to academic tasks while in the special class and displayed high rates of attention in that class. When the student was returned to the regular classroom, a similar point system was employed and attending behavior remained at a high level for both settings.

A study by Lovaas, Koegel, Simmons, and Long (1973) demonstrated the effectiveness of applying sequential modification in assuring both transfer and maintenance. Parents whose children with autism had acquired basic communication, self-care, and social skills in a special program were trained to reinforce these skills with their children. On a 1- to 4-year follow-up, children who had remained at home and whose parents had continued to reinforce appropriate behavior had maintained the gains made in the special program and in some cases had made additional progress. Those children who had been institutionalized where personnel were not trained in applied behavior analysis procedures had lost all the gains made in the special program.

Using peers to modify behavior is discussed in Chapter 13.

It is not always necessary to employ identical procedures to obtain stimulus generalization or maintenance. Walker and Buckley (1972) studied the effects of several ways of promoting maintenance in students whose behavior was changed in a special class setting using a token economy. After 2 months in the special class, the students were divided into four groups and sent back to regular classes. For one group, the authors used a procedure they referred to as *peer reprogramming*. Each experimental subject had the opportunity to earn points for appropriate behavior during two 30-minute periods a week. The points could be exchanged for prizes such as field trips, which were then awarded to the entire class. An interesting double contingency was in effect, because the target student had to earn the right to the 30-minute reinforcement period by appropriate behavior during the rest of the week. A rather elaborate electronic signaling system involving lights and buzzers was used during the reinforcement period to indicate to the subject and classmates that points were or were not accumulating. The authors theorized that, because the student's peers were being rewarded for appropriate behavior, the peers would reinforce such behavior rather than disruption or inattentiveness.

The procedure described by Walker and Buckley (1972) for the second group was more closely related to exact sequential modification. This procedure used a duplication of many conditions in the special class. The same curriculum materials, systematic social reinforcement, and token economy were implemented in the regular class. The only procedural difference was the absence of time-out and response-cost contingencies, which the authors feared might be used punitively by inexperienced teachers. An adapted rating system was used when the students were in classes other than their homeroom, and points based on ratings were awarded by the homeroom teacher.

For the third group, the classroom teachers in whose classes the target students were to be placed received systematic training in applied behavior analysis. The teachers' implementation of the procedures in their classrooms was monitored, and course credit and free tuition for graduate credit for the teachers was contingent on correct implementation (another double contingency). A final group of students was simply returned to the regular class.

The authors reported that peer reprogramming and similar reinforcement procedures maintained the students' appropriate behavior at over 70% of the rate shown in the special class. The teacher-training and no-treatment procedures were less effective, though still maintaining over 60% of the gains. A reanalysis of the data by Cone (1973) showed smaller percentages of maintenance and no clear difference among the three treatment procedures, which were, however, all more effective than simply training and hoping—the no-treatment procedure. In addition, students who received the programmed maintenance procedures continued to show more appropriate behavior 4 months after all modifications were withdrawn.

Martin, Burkholder, Rosenthal, Tharp, and Thorne (1968) used systematic sequential modification in an educational program at a community mental health center in changing the behavior of adolescents whose behavior was severely disruptive. A four-phase system was used, beginning with full-time special-class placement, token reinforcement, and home-based reinforcement, and eventually moving to full-time attendance in regular classes with very small amounts of tangible reinforcement based on grades and attendance. The students maintained high rates of academic performance and low rates of disruptive behavior. Drabman (1973), working with students in a state hospital classroom, used feedback in the form of ratings given by either a teacher or a peer to maintain low levels of disruptive behavior after reinforcement was withdrawn.

Anderson-Inman, Walker, and Purcell (1984) used a procedure they call *transenvironmental programming* to increase generalization from resource rooms to regular classrooms. Transenvironmental programming involves assessing the target environment, providing students in the resource room with skills identified as critical in the regular classroom, using techniques to promote transfer of the skills acquired, and evaluating student performance in the regular classroom. Specific techniques for facilitating transfer included reinforcing the newly acquired skills in the regular classroom.

Browning (1983) used taped reminders of appropriate behavior to maintain the improved behavior of six adolescents with autism. Their inappropriate verbalizations and angry outbursts were brought under control in a highly structured setting using time-out and response cost. When the students were integrated into a less restrictive setting, they heard 10- to 30-second messages reminding them of appropriate verbal behavior and giving them directions for coping with anger or difficult situations. The program was effective for all the students.

The transfer and maintenance of behaviors by sequential modification may not technically qualify as generalization, as we discussed earlier. The provision of identical or similar applied behavior analysis procedures in alternate settings, however, is practical and frequently successful. Even if the alterations are necessary for extended periods, their effectiveness may make their implementation well worth the trouble. The following vignette illustrates the use of sequential modification.

Connie Learns to Do Her Work

Connie was a second-grade student in Ms. Gray's resource room for children with learning disabilities. Connie performed very well in the resource room, where she earned points exchangeable for free time when she completed academic tasks, but did no work in the regular classroom, where she spent most of the school day. Instead, she wandered around the classroom bothering other students.

After conferring with the regular classroom teacher, Ms. Gray provided her with slips of paper preprinted with Connie's name, a place for the date, and several options to check regarding Connie's academic work and classroom behavior (see Figure 11–2). Ms. Gray then awarded Connie bonus points for her work in the regular classroom. Although Connie continued to be less productive in the

FIGURE 11–2
Connie's chart

Connie	Date: _____
Assignments complete:	Behavior:
Yes _____	Good _____
No _____	Fair _____
Partly _____	Poor _____
	_____ Initials

regular classroom than in the resource room, her behavior was acceptable, and the amount of academic work completed was comparable to that of most students in the class. The regular classroom teacher was so impressed with the procedure that she made several rating slips for several of her problem students and awarded them special privileges when they completed their work and behaved properly.

Whose behavior has generalized here?

Introduce to Natural Maintaining Contingencies

An ideal applied behavior analysis program seeks to change behaviors that receive reinforcement in the student's natural environment. In other words, as a result of the program the student would behave appropriately for the same reasons that motivate students who had never been referred because of inappropriate behavior. The student would work hard at academic tasks to earn good grades, behave well in the classroom to receive the approval of the teacher, or perform a job for money. It may be possible to accelerate the process of making the natural reinforcers more powerful (Horcones, 1992). If a teacher points out how a student's hard work on a math paper resulted in a big red "A+," or how proud a resource student's regular teacher has been of his good behavior, or how terrific it is to be able to spend money one earns by working hard, these natural reinforcers become more noticeable. For example, although fairly complicated procedures—including shaping, chaining, and graduated guidance—may be necessary to teach students with severe disabilities to feed themselves, feeding themselves may generalize to other settings and be durable after training is withdrawn (Browning, 1980). Such a skill has a built-in positive reinforcer in that children who feed themselves efficiently can control their own intake of food. Toilet training of persons with mental retardation (Azrin, Sneed, & Foxx, 1973) and nondisabled young children (Foxx & Azrin, 1973) may be maintained after contingencies are withdrawn because discomfort is avoided. Similarly, students who are taught such skills as reading or math may maintain these skills without programmed generalization because the skills are useful. Some social behaviors may also generalize.

*We try to teach func-
tional skills—those that
are useful to the student.*

An increasing emphasis in the education of persons with severe disabilities has been on training functional skills; that is, skills useful to the individual in his environment—school or workplace and community (Brown, Nietupski, & Hamre-Nietupski, 1976). Rather than teach these students meaningless school skills like sorting blocks by color, we teach them skills they need for maximum independence—riding the bus, using the laundromat, cooking a meal, even using an automated bank teller machine (Shafer, Inge, & Hill, 1986). These skills by their nature are more prone to be maintained by the natural environment. Choosing behaviors to change that will be maintained by the natural environment applies the Relevance of Behavior Rule. This rule was first described by Ayllon and Azrin (1968). Baer and Wolf (1970) conceptualize the Relevance of Behavior Rule as a form of *trapping*. They assert that if applied behavior analysts can generate behaviors that are reinforced by the natural environment, a situation analogous to catching a mouse in a trap will be created. The mechanism of trapping works this way:

> Consider, for example, that very familiar model, the mouse trap. A mouse trap is an environment designed to accomplish massive behavior modification in a mouse. Note that this modification has thorough generality: The change in behavior accomplished by the trap will be uniform across all environments, it will extend to all of the mouse's behaviors, and it will last indefinitely into the future. Furthermore, a mouse trap allows a great amount of behavioral change to be accomplished by a relatively slight amount of behavioral control. A householder without a trap can, of course, still kill a mouse: He can wait patiently outside the mouse's hole, grab the mouse faster than the mouse can avoid him, and then apply various forms of force to the unfortunate animal to accomplish the behavioral change desired. But this performance requires a great deal of competence: vast patience, supercoordination, extreme manual dexterity, and a well-suppressed squeamishness. By contrast, a householder with a trap needs very few accomplishments: If he can merely apply the cheese and then leave the loaded trap where the mouse is likely to smell that cheese, in effect he has guaranteed general change in the mouse's future behavior. The essence of a trap, in behavioral terms, is that only a relatively simple response is necessary to enter the trap, yet once entered, the trap cannot be resisted in creating general behavioral change. For the mouse, the entry response is merely to smell the cheese. Everything proceeds from there almost automatically. The householder need have no more control over the mouse's behavior than to get him to smell the cheese, yet he accomplishes thorough changes in behavior. (Baer & Wolf, 1970, p. 321)

Some behaviors do lend themselves to trapping. If behaviors can be generated that result in increased peer reinforcement, they are particularly likely to be maintained in the natural environment. Social and communication skills, grooming skills, and even assertiveness may need only to be generated to be maintained (Bourbeau, Sowers, & Close, 1986). The network of reinforcement available for such behaviors may form an irresistible environmental trap that, like the mouse trap, once entered is inescapable. Unfortunately, it is often difficult to pinpoint behaviors that will be reinforced by the natural environment (Kazdin, 1977). Most natural environments seem to ignore appropriate behavior and concentrate attention on inappropriate behavior. Few drivers are stopped by policemen for compliments; workers are seldom praised for getting to work on time and attending regularly. Even in the classroom, teachers tend to pay little or no attention to students who are doing well but instead correct students whose behavior is disruptive or inattentive. It is unwise for the applied behavior analyst to assume that any behavior will be maintained by the student's natural environment. We can say, however, that the maintenance or transfer of behaviors to reinforcement contingencies in the natural environment may be facilitated by:

1. Observing the student's environment. What parents, teachers, or other adults describe as desirable behavior for the student may or may not be what they reinforce.

2. Choosing behaviors that are subject to trapping as determined by observation. For example, if teachers in a given school heavily reinforce pretty handwriting, students may be taught pretty handwriting by a resource teacher, even if it would not otherwise be a priority.

3. Teaching students to recruit reinforcers from the environment (Seymour & Stokes, 1976). Students can be taught to call adults' attention to appropriate behavior and thus to receive praise or other reinforcers.

Ways to promote generalization

4. Teaching students to recognize reinforcement when it is delivered. It has been the authors' experience that many students who have difficulty in the regular classroom may not recognize more subtle forms of social reinforcement. This may be a function of what Bryan and Bryan (1978) call a lack of social perception. Some students cannot pick up subtleties of nonverbal communication that may be the only reinforcers available. Teaching students to recognize such subtleties may increase the reinforcing potential of the natural environment.

The teacher who wants the natural environment to take over reinforcement should be aware that this is by no means an automatic process. Careful monitoring should take place to assess the natural environment and to determine how well the behavior change is being maintained. The first vignette illustrates a behavior that is maintained because it receives naturally occurring reinforcers. The second anecdote illustrates a failure of the environment to provide sufficient reinforcers.

Alvin Learns to Read

Alvin was an adjudicated juvenile delinquent in Mr. Daniel's class at the detention center. He was a virtual nonreader when he came into the class, but with a systematic phonic reading method using token reinforcement for correct responses, Mr. Daniel taught Alvin to read phonetically regular one- and two-syllable words. Mr. Daniel wondered whether Alvin would ever read after being released from the center, for the boy certainly showed little enthusiasm for any of the high-interest, low-vocabulary books available in the classroom for recreational reading. Alvin appeared to read only when the token condition was in effect. About a year after Alvin's release, however, Mr. Daniel happened to meet him emerging from an adult bookstore. He had several paperback books under his arm, one open in his hands, and a look of intense concentration on his face.

Marvin Fails the Sixth Grade

Not all teachers believe in praising children.

Mr. Cohen, a resource teacher, had worked with Marvin for two years, while he was attending regular fourth- and fifth-grade classes. Marvin had done well in his regular classes because his teachers had used high rates of verbal praise and free time contingent on completion of work. Marvin was dismissed from the resource room at the end of fifth grade. Mr. Cohen had not even considered that Marvin might have trouble in the sixth grade, but the sixth-grade teacher, Ms. Roach, was, to put it bluntly, hard-nosed. She did not believe in praising students for good behavior or in providing any consequence for academic work except grades. As she put it, "That's why they come to school. I don't believe in coddling them." Marvin went back to the behaviors that had resulted in his original referral: he disrupted the classroom, did not complete assignments, and ultimately failed the sixth grade. Mr. Cohen felt he had learned two things at Marvin's expense: never assume that the same conditions exist in all classrooms and always follow up students whose behavior appears to have been permanently changed.

Train Sufficient Exemplars

Most academic and social behaviors that we want to teach our students to perform are members of various response classes. That is, there is seldom a single behavior that is always performed in exactly the same way in exactly the same place. For example, when we teach a student to read we expect that she will eventually apply her reading skills to decoding and comprehending material she has never read. We would certainly not, however, expect her to do that after learning one or two words with the same beginning sound or after one example of how to use the context to derive the meaning of an unfamiliar word. We would provide lots of examples and lots of lessons; we would provide sufficient exemplars. Similarly, we would not expect a student with severe disabilities to use any vending machine in the city after learning to use only the one in the community center, or a student who had learned to greet his teacher in the morning to greet any adult. Again, we would train sufficient exemplars.

General Case Programming

General case programming promotes generalization by training sufficient exemplars. It was developed to teach language, academic, and social skills to young children at risk (Becker & Engelmann, 1978). General case programming emphasizes using sufficient members of a class of stimuli to ensure that students will be able to perform the task on any member of the class of stimuli. If we want a child to identify red objects, we do not have to expose him to *every* red object in the world to ensure that he can perform this task. We just have to expose him to enough red objects having enough variety in their redness, and he will reliably identify any red object as red. For many children it is not necessary to be very systematic in picking the red objects—we just label whatever objects come our way. With learners who have disabilities, however, careful attention must be given to selecting objects that will facilitate their acquisition of this skill.

Engelmann and Carnine (1982) state that examples used to train the general case must teach *sameness*—the characteristics of a stimulus that are the same for all members of a class—and *difference*—the range of variability within the members of a class. In other words, what do all red things have in common and how different can things be and still be red? The selection of the training stimuli is the critical factor in general case programming. If all the stimuli used in training sessions are red plastic objects of the same shade, the student asked to fetch the red book from the teacher's desk (it's her copy of Engelmann and Carnine's *Theory of Instruction*) may very well fail to do so because the book is an orangish-red, not the pinkish-red of the training stimuli. General case programming has been very successful in teaching academic behaviors to students with and without disabilities. It has also been used to teach appropriate social behaviors (Engelmann & Colvin, 1983).

General case programming (though not usually labeled as such) has also been used to teach prelanguage and language skills to learners with severe disabilities. The study discussed in Chapter 7 in which students were taught a generalized imitation response is an example. You will remember that the students, systematically taught to imitate movements made by the trainer, also imitated movements whose imitation was never reinforced. Similar training (Garcia, Baer, & Firestone, 1971) has resulted in generalized correct use of many verbal responses including plurals (Guess, Sailor, Rutherford, & Baer, 1968), present and past tense (Schumaker & Sherman, 1970), and appropriate syntax (Garcia, Guess, & Byrnes, 1973).

It would be wise to prepare students for vending machines that talk, which can startle even those of us without serious disabilities.

Recent applications of general case programming emphasize teaching functional skills to learners with severe disabilities (Wilcox & Bellamy, 1982). If, for example, a teacher wanted to teach a student to use any vending machine in a section of a city, the teacher would have to determine what variations in vending machines existed (where coins are put, how the machine is activated, and so on) and provide training on machines having all these variations (Sprague & Horner, 1984). The procedure has been equally successful in teaching telephone skills (Horner, Williams, & Stevely, 1984), street crossing (Horner, Jones, & Williams, 1985), using different soap dispensers in handwashing (Pancsofar & Bates, 1985), sorting mail by zip code (Woolcock & Lengel, 1987), bussing cafeteria tables (Horner, Eberhard, & Sheehan, 1986), and many other skills.

Training in Multiple Settings

Another approach to using sufficient exemplars is to train the behavior in a number of settings or with several different trainers. Such a practice often results in generalization of the behavior change into settings where no training has taken place. Considerable evidence exists to indicate that training novel responses under a wide variety of stimulus conditions increases the probability of generalization under conditions where no previous training has occurred. This procedure differs from sequential modification in that change is targeted and assessed in settings (or behaviors) in which no intervention has taken place. For example, Stokes, Baer, and Jackson (1974) determined that a greeting response occurred only in the presence of the trainer who had systematically reinforced the response. The introduction of a second trainer resulted in the generalization of the response to 14 staff members.

Emshoff, Redd, and Davidson (1976) trained adolescent students who were delinquent to use positive interpersonal comments. Students trained under multiple conditions (activities, trainers, locations) showed greater generalization in a nontreatment setting than did those trained under constant conditions.

See Chapter 8 for a discussion of generalization after punishment.

Many studies have demonstrated that the effects of suppressing deviant behaviors in individuals with severe disabilities are situation- and experimenter-specific unless trained across several conditions (e.g., Birnbrauer, 1968; Corte, Wolf, & Locke, 1971; Garcia, 1974; Lovaas & Simmons, 1969; Risley, 1968). The effects of punishment contingencies are apparently even less likely to generalize than behavior changes resulting from positive reinforcement.

The training of sufficient exemplars is a productive area for teachers concerned with increasing generalization. It is not necessary to teach students to perform appropriate behaviors in every setting or in the presence of every potential teacher or other adult. The teacher need train only enough to ensure that a generalized response has been learned. Nor is it necessary to teach every example of a response class that we want students to perform. Imagine the difficulty of teaching students to read if this were so. We expect students to generalize letter or syllable sounds and thus to decode words they have never read before. Most teaching of academic skills is based on the assumption that students will be able to use these skills to solve novel problems or to perform a variety of tasks. The following examples show how teachers may use training a number of exemplars to program response generalization, as well as generalization across trainers and across settings.

Carol Learns to Use Plurals

Carol was a 5-year-old student with a language delay in Ms. Sims's preschool special education class. Carol had learned the names of many common objects but did not differentiate the singular from the plural forms. Ms. Sims made a point of labeling single and multiple examples of objects frequently during the school day: "Look, Carol, *coat*" (as Carol took hers off); "Carol, *coats*" (as she ran her hand over all the students' coats in the cloakroom); "Say *coat*" (as Carol hung up hers). "Say *coats*" (as she moved Carol's hand along all the coats). Using a discrimination training procedure, she brought Carol's verbal responses under stimulus control of the correct form of a number of singular and plural pairs:

cow	cows
shoe	shoes
dog	dogs
bird	birds
plane	planes

She then tested for generalization. She showed Carol a new set of pictures:

chair	chairs

This is the same phenomenon that causes a typical city 2-year-old to call the first cow she sees a "doggie."

Carol responded correctly. Her response using singular and plural forms had generalized to an untrained example. Carol used singular and plural forms correctly in a variety of untrained examples. Her response generalization was so broad that when the principal and superintendent visited the class, Ms. Sims heard Carol say to another student, "Mans come." Ms. Sims restrained herself from tearing her hair out by remembering that such overgeneralization is not uncommon among young children and that she would just have to teach irregular plurals as a separate response class.

Ms. Almond Has a Student Teacher

After much effort, Ms. Almond had taught her junior-high remedial English class to behave appropriately and to complete the assignments she gave them. She had used a point system but now depended primarily on social reinforcement and free time on Friday, awarded if the class had had what she rather loosely called "a good week." They almost always earned their free time, because their behavior was generally very good. At the beginning of the winter quarter, Ms. Almond was assigned a student teacher. To her horror, although the students behaved appropriately as long as Ms. Almond remained in the room, they went wild when only the student teacher was there. She concluded that her students had formed a discrimination—that she was an S^D for appropriate behavior, but that teachers in general were not. Ms. Almond reinstituted the token system that she had used at the beginning of the year and made certain that her student teacher was as involved in giving points and awarding free time as she was. The students maintained their appropriate behavior for either teacher, and the point system was subsequently phased out with little loss of behavior change.

Soon after the student teacher departed, Ms. Almond became ill and a substitute was hired. Ms. Almond returned to school after a week, fully expecting the usual horror stories from her principal and colleagues about the misbehavior of her students during her absence. To her surprise, the students had behaved beautifully. Apparently generalization had taken place. Teaching the students to behave appropriately in English class in the presence of two different teachers resulted in their behaving in English class in the presence of any teacher.

Ms. Almond's Pupils Become Model Students

Ms. Almond was so intrigued with her students' generalized appropriate behavior that she asked Mr. Rich, the math teacher, about their behavior in his class. She was disappointed to learn that in his class they were as disruptive and inattentive as ever. Mr. Rich, however, was so impressed by Ms. Almond's story that he decided to start a point system of his own and soon found that the students behaved well and completed assignments. Soon after, Ms. Almond met the eighth-grade social studies teacher in the lounge and was pleased to hear her say that although she had not done anything differently, the students were behaving much better in her class. The science and health teachers told the same story. Training the desired behavior in two settings had resulted in generalization into settings where training had never occurred.

Train Loosely

Sometimes too much structure interferes with generalization.

Teaching techniques based on principles of behavior have usually emphasized tight control of many teaching factors (Becker, Engelmann, & Thomas, 1975; Stephens, 1976; White & Haring, 1980). Teaching procedures for students with disabilities are often rigidly standardized: adhering to the same format, presenting items in a predetermined sequence, and requiring mastery of one skill before training on another has begun. Although this may be an efficient means of instruction, and although it is the way that most special educators were taught to teach, especially those training to work with populations having more severe disabilities, there is increasing evidence that it is not the best way to assure that skills will be generalized. As you will see in the studies described below, what began in the early 1970s as an investigation of alternating or rotating various stimuli or responses in highly structured training sessions has resulted in a major change in the instruction of individuals with disabilities in the 1990s. Schroeder and Baer (1972) found that vocal imitation skills were better generalized to untaught members of the response class when the training stimuli were varied within sessions rather than when each skill was taught to mastery before instruction on another was begun. Rather than tightly restricting the vocal skills being taught (serial training), the researchers allowed a number of different imitations to be taught within a single session (concurrent training).

In an example of response alternation, Panyan and Hall (1978) investigated the effects of concurrent as opposed to serial training in the acquisition, maintenance, and generalization of two different response classes: tracing and vocal imitation. The serial training procedure required mastery of one response class (tracing) before instruction began on a second response class (vocal imitation). In the concurrent training procedure, training on the two different response classes was alternated in a single training session before either task was mastered. The procedure used did not affect the time required for acquisition or maintenance of the response trained, but generalization to untrained responses was greater under the concurrent training condition. These studies have definite implications for the teacher. Apparently, it adds no efficiency to train students to master one skill before beginning instruction on another, unless of course the first skill is prerequisite to the second. Alternating teaching within sessions not only does not interfere with learning, on the contrary, it leads to greater generalization. Thus, statements like "I can't worry about Harold's math until I get him reading on grade level" may not be justified.

Recent investigations of "loose training" have showed great promise in a wide variety of settings and for many behaviors. Variously termed *incidental teaching, naturalistic teaching, nonintensive teaching,* or *minimal intervention*, strategies that incorporate instruction for individuals with disabilities into less structured activities have been successful in promoting acquisition of behaviors and even more successful in promoting generalization.

Campbell and Stremel-Campbell (1982) taught two boys with moderate to severe disabilities to use various statements and questions while they were being taught academic and self-help skills. The target verbal skills were reinforced when they were emitted spontaneously or when their use was prompted. Both boys acquired the verbal skills along with the academic and self-help skills, and generalization also occurred. Using a procedure they called nonintensive, Inglesfield and Crisp (1985) compared the effects of teaching dressing skills 10 times a day for 3 days (an approach many special educators might choose for initial skill acquisition) to the effects of teaching the same skills twice a day for 15 days (an approach that would occur in the natural environment). They found the twice-daily procedure more effective for both initial learning and generalization.

Several other studies have indicated that less intensive, more natural instructions promote generalization with little or no loss of efficiency in acquisition. Success has been demonstrated in teaching receptive object labels (McGee, Krantz, Mason, & McClannahan, 1983), expressive language (Koegel, O'Dell, & Koegel, 1987; Woods, 1984), sign language (Carr & Kologinsky, 1983), and reading (McGee, Krantz, & McClannahan, 1986).

As we have stated, the use of naturalistic or loose training represents a departure from tradition in special education teaching. Its success suggests again the importance of teachers' maintaining their skills and keeping up with current research.

Use Indiscriminable Contingencies

As we described in Chapter 6, resistance to extinction or maintenance of behavior is greatly prolonged by intermittent reinforcement schedules. Intermittent reinforcement may be used to maintain behaviors at a high rate, or it may be a step toward eliminating reinforcement entirely. It is possible to thin a reinforcement schedule to such a degree that few reinforcers are used. If reinforcement is then withdrawn altogether, the behavior will continue. This resistance to extinction is not permanent, because behavior, if unreinforced, will eventually be extinguished. It may be possible, however, that eventually resistance will be so far in the future as to make no practical difference. The behavior will be maintained as long as necessary.

Considerable evidence indicates that intermittent reinforcement schedules lead to increased maintenance of behavior change (Kale, Kaye, Whelan, & Hopkins, 1968; Kazdin & Polster, 1973; Phillips, Phillips, Fixsen, & Wolf, 1971). Teachers should consider this evidence when planning and implementing behavior change strategies. Even if intermittent reinforcement must be continued indefinitely, if schedules are very lean, this may be a fairly efficient and economical means of providing for maintenance.

Other procedures besides intermittent reinforcement make it difficult for students to discriminate which responses will be reinforced. One strategy that may lead to generalization across settings is delaying the delivery of reinforcers. Schwarz and Hawkins (1970) videotaped the behavior of a student during math and spelling classes. After the end of the school day, the student was shown the videotape, and appropriate behaviors in math class were reinforced. In the next days, a behavior change was evident in spelling class as well as math class. The authors hypothesized that the generalization across settings was due to the delayed reinforcement, which made it more difficult for the student to determine when contingencies were in effect.

Fowler and Baer (1981) used a delayed reinforcement procedure to modify various behaviors of preschool children. The children received tokens exchangeable for toys either immediately after the period during which they earned them, or at the end of the day, after other periods during which no contingency was in effect had intervened. The children generalized the appropriate behavior; that is, they behaved better all day when the reinforcer was not given until the end of the day. Similarly, Dunlap, Koegel, Johnson, and O'Neill (1987) used delayed reinforcement to maintain the work performance of students with autism in community settings.

Another way of delivering reinforcers that resulted in decreased discriminability of contingencies was demonstrated by Koegel and Rincover (1977). The authors taught children with autism to perform simple nonverbal imitations or to follow simple instructions. After the behavior was learned (using continuous reinforcement), schedules were thinned. Once training was concluded, the children were observed in order for the researchers to assess maintenance of behavior change. The behaviors were ultimately extinguished. (The thinner the schedule during training, the more responses occurred before extinction.) The use of noncontingent rewards after extinction, however, resulted in recovery of the behavior. At random intervals, the children were given candy identical to that earned in the original training setting—whether their responses were correct or not. The noncontingent rewards delayed extinction considerably. Apparently, the reinforcer had acquired the properties of a discriminative stimulus. It served as a cue to the students that, in this setting, reinforcement was available. The students were unable to discriminate which responses would be reinforced, so they produced larger numbers of the correct (previously reinforced) responses before extinction.

Very thin intermittent reinforcement schedules are the most frequently used means of making reinforcement contingencies indiscriminable. Evidence indicates, however, that any procedure that makes it difficult for students to determine when contingencies are in effect is likely to result in greater durability of behavior change, either in the original training setting or in other settings. The following examples illustrate procedures that make it difficult for students to make such determinations.

Suzie Learns to Comply with an Instruction

Suzie was a 4-year-old student in Mr. Wethered's class for preschool children with developmental delays. Suzie was very active, and Mr. Wethered was concerned because she responded neither to her name nor to "Come here." He was afraid that she would run into the street while waiting for the bus or playing on the playground.

To teach Suzie to come when called, Mr. Wethered started by issuing the instruction, "Suzie, come here," while Suzie was only a few steps from him. He physically prompted Suzie by pulling gently on her hand. He gradually faded the prompt and then began increasing the distance that Suzie had to move. Throughout the initial training procedure, Suzie received a small bite of cookie whenever she responded correctly.

Once the behavior was well established, Mr. Wethered thinned the schedule of reinforcement: Suzie got a bite of cookie on a VR5, then VR10, then VR20, and so on. As time passed, Mr. Wethered was able to keep the behavior occurring at a high rate by very occasionally giving Suzie a bite of cookie when she complied with his instruction. He felt that he could depend on her to come when called and that occasional reinforcement of the response could be kept up indefinitely without disrupting the classroom. After Suzie's mother began calling Suzie occasionally to come get a cookie, she found that Suzie consistently came when called at home as well as at school.

Ms. Bell's Class Learns to Complete Assignments

In the morning group in her intermediate-level resource room, Ms. Bell's students with mild retardation consistently failed to complete their assignments. Each student was expected independently to complete a reading comprehension, a math, and a spelling activity, while Ms. Bell worked with small groups on other academic skills. Ms. Bell began giving her students tokens worth 5 minutes of free time to be exchanged at the end of the morning for each assignment completed. This resulted in almost 100% completion of assignments. Ms. Bell then announced that tokens would not be given until the end of the morning and that only two assignments could earn tokens. She put the words reading, spelling, and math on slips of paper and allowed a student to draw two slips. The students did not know until the end of the morning which two assignments would earn free time but continued to complete their assignments. Ms. Bell, who wanted to move to a very lean reinforcement schedule, then announced that there would be the possibility of two drawings daily: one for a "yes/no" card, which would determine whether reinforcement would be available, and a second if the "yes" card was drawn. The second drawing would determine which assignment would earn free time. At first, one "yes" and one "no" card were available. She then gradually added "no" cards to the pool until there was only a 20% probability that free time would be available. The students continued to complete their assignments in all three subject areas and seemed to enjoy the suspense of never knowing when free time would be available or for which specific behavior.

Program Common Stimuli

Walker and Buckley (1972) assert that "intra-subject behavioral similarity across different settings is probably a function, in part, of the amount of stimulus similarity which exists between such settings" (p. 209). Kirby and Bickel (1988) suggest that stimulus similarity, and thus stimulus control, is the major factor in any generalization. A possible method of achieving either maintenance or stimulus generalization is deliberate programming of similar stimuli in the training setting and in the setting in which generalization is desired. This may be accomplished by either increasing the similarity of the training situation to the natural environment or by introducing elements of the training situation into the natural environment.

Several studies have investigated the effects of introducing elements of the natural environment into the training situation in order to increase the probability of generalization. For example, Ayllon and Kelly (1974) restored speech in a girl who was electively mute. After speech occurred frequently in the training situation (a counselor's office), elements similar to those present in the classroom were introduced. Other children, a blackboard, and desks were installed in the room; and the trainer began to function more as a traditional teacher by standing in the front of the room, lecturing, and asking questions. Training was also continued in the classroom. Increases in speech occurred in the classroom, and a follow-up one year later indicated that speech was maintained in several novel settings. Although the specific effects of the increase in similarity between training and natural settings are difficult to assess because of the package of treatments employed, generalization to the classroom did occur and was maintained.

Jackson and Wallace (1974) used tokens to increase vocal loudness in an adolescent girl with retardation. After satisfactory levels of loudness were achieved within the training setting, procedures similar to those employed by Ayllon and Kelly (1974) were introduced. Generalization to the classroom setting occurred.

Koegel and Rincover (1974) trained children with autism to respond to instructions in a one-to-one situation. Generalization to a classroom setting was programmed by gradually introducing more children into the training situation, so that it resembled the classroom. Livi and Ford (1985) found that domestic skills generalized from a training site to each student's home much more efficiently when stimuli similar to those in each home were used. (Nowadays, every effort would be made to teach those skills *in the students'* homes.) In general, using discriminative stimuli during training that are similar to those in the setting where generalization is desired has proven to be a very effective technique (Stainback, Stainback, & Strathe, 1983). Woods (1987) has suggested that such a procedure is an adaptation of the naturalistic procedures discussed above, in that the stimuli in the generalization setting are natural ones.

Simulations may be more practical than always teaching every skill in the natural environment.

One way of attempting to introduce natural stimuli into training settings is through the use of simulations. For example, van den Pol et al. (1981) successfully used pictures of fast-food items to teach students with moderate retardation to use community fast-food establishments. Simulated instruction for students with more severe disabilities is generally less successful (Foxx, McMorrow, & Mennemeier, 1984; Marchetti, McCartney, Drain, Hooper, & Dix, 1983). Horner, McDonnell, and Bellamy (no date) suggest that simulations employing real rather than representational items from the environment may be more successful. When real telephones are used, for example, students learn a generalized telephone response (Horner, Williams, & Stevely, 1984). Simulations using real stimuli have been used to teach numerous generalized skills including comprehension of category labels (Hupp, 1986), video game use (Sedlack, Doyle, & Schloss, 1982), and menstrual care (Richman, Reiss, Bauman, & Bailey, 1984). They have in general proved more effective than procedures using pictures.

A limited number of studies have attempted to increase generalization by introducing elements of the training situation into the setting where generalization was desired. Rincover and Koegel (1975) taught children with autism to imitate nonverbal behaviors modeled by a therapist. When the children responded correctly on 20 consecutive trials without a prompt, a transfer test was made. For children who emitted no correct responses on the transfer test, an assessment of stimulus control was made. Stimuli from the training environment were introduced into the extratherapy setting, one at a time. If the child did not respond correctly in the presence of the first stimulus, that stimulus was removed and another one introduced. This process was continued until the stimulus controlling the behavior was identified, and the responses occurred in the extratherapy setting. It was found that each of the children was responding selectively to some incidental stimulus in the treatment room. When this stimulus was provided in the extratherapy setting, each child responded correctly. The amount of responding in the extratherapy situation was, however, consistently less than in the training situation.

A similar attempt to provide a discriminative stimulus present in the treatment situation in an extratherapy situation was reported by Bachrach,

Erwin, and Mohr (1965). A hospitalized girl with anorexia nervosa earned reinforcers for eating and gaining weight. All meals were eaten on a table covered with a purple tablecloth. The patient was discharged after gaining 33 pounds and was given the purple tablecloth and told to eat all meals at a table covered with it. It was postulated that the tablecloth had become an S^D for eating, because eating had been consistently reinforced in its presence. The patient continued to gain weight after discharge and maintained the gains after 2 years.

Troutman (1977) used an analogous procedure to program generalization from resource rooms to regular classrooms. Six students with learning disabilities showed high rates of academic task completion and low rates of disruptive behavior in the resource room but did not perform appropriately in the regular classroom. Each student was allowed to bring from home some object, such as a figurine, to decorate his or her desk in the resource room, where points were earned for completing academic tasks and for behaving appropriately. After a few weeks, the students were instructed to take their objects to the regular classroom. Suggestions indicated that the "object" would remind the students to work hard. Both academic task completion and appropriate behavior increased in the regular classroom.

Several researchers have investigated the use of students' peers as stimuli common to the training and generalization settings. Stokes and Baer (1976) taught word recognition to students with learning disabilities through a peer-tutoring procedure. The students did not display the skills in other settings until the peer tutor and pupil were brought together. Then both students showed increased generalization.

"If it worked on the bananas, it'll work on the keys. As soon as he leaves, it's back to the jungle for us."

Johnston and Johnston (1972) used a similar procedure to maintain and generalize correct articulation in two students. Each was trained to monitor and correct the other's speech, and monitoring was reinforced with tokens. The students consistently showed more correct speech when the monitor was present, even when monitoring no longer occurred.

A logical extension of programming common stimuli may change completely the approach to providing services for persons with severe and profound disabilities. The setting with the most stimuli common to the setting where generalization is desired is that setting itself. If we want behavior to occur in the classroom, why not teach it in the classroom rather than an isolated treatment room or corner (Horner & Budd, 1985)? If the behavior should occur in the community (Bourbeau, Sowers, & Close, 1986) or in an employment site (DeHaven, Corley, Hofeling, & Garcia, 1982), why not teach it there? Community-based programming for persons with disabilities is now accepted practice.

The potential effectiveness of stimulus control for stimulus generalization and maintenance is a factor that should be considered by all teachers. Relatively simple and economical measures can help ensure reliable generalization in many settings and help maintain gains long after training has been terminated.

The following vignettes illustrate generalization achieved by increasing stimulus similarity.

Ms. Statler's Students Get Ready for Supported Employment

Ms. Statler was a teacher of secondary students with moderate to severe retardation and other disabilities. Some of her students were receiving instruction that would enable them to gain independence in employment, others were preparing for employment in a more supportive environment. For these students supported employment in a local nursery greenhouse with a full-time job coach on site was the goal. Because of transportation and other logistical problems, it was possible to take the students to the nursery for instruction only about once a week.

Although Ms. Statler could teach relevant skills in the classroom, she was concerned that the environment was much less visually and aurally distracting than the nursery. To solve this problem she borrowed a number of props from the nursery, including a bench like the one at which the students would eventually work, and created a mini-environment in one corner of her classroom. She also made an audiotape of the nursery environment. While she played this tape she arranged for as many people as possible to visit her classroom for a minute or two and to walk through the mini-environment exchanging plants and communicating with the students.

Sammy Learns to Behave in the Second Grade

Sammy was a student in Mr. Reddy's class for students who were seriously emotionally disturbed. His academic work was superior, but he displayed bizarre behavior, like shouting gibberish and making strange movements with his hands and arms. This behavior was controlled in the special class by positive reinforcement on a DRO schedule, but Mr. Reddy had noticed that outside the special class Sammy continued to shout and gesture. Because the goal of the special program was to return students to the regular classroom, Mr. Reddy was concerned about Sammy's behavior outside the special class.

Mr. Reddy decided to borrow a second grader from the regular class. After getting parental permission, he invited Brad, a gifted student, to visit his class for half an hour three times a week. He taught Brad basic learning principles to help with a project Brad was doing for his enrichment class. He also allowed Brad to give reinforcers to Sammy during his observation periods. When Sammy began spending short periods of time in the regular class, Brad came to get him and brought him back. Sammy consistently behaved appropriately in the second-grade class, even though no reinforcers were ever given there.

Brad's presence had become an S^D for appropriate behavior for Sammy.

Mediate Generalization and Train to Generalize

We shall consider together these last two procedures for facilitating generalization: mediating generalization and training to generalize. It is possible to increase the probability of generalization by reinforcing generalization as a response class (Stokes & Baer, 1977). In other words, if students receive reinforcers specifically for displaying behavior in settings other than the training setting, performing learned behaviors in a novel setting may become a generalized response class. The students have thus been taught to generalize. It is particularly appropriate to explain the contingency to the student; that is, students may be told that if they perform a particular behavior in a new setting, reinforcement will be available (Mastropieri & Scruggs, 1984).

We can teach students to generalize some skills.

In *mediating generalization*, students are taught to monitor and report on their own generalization of appropriate behavior. Such a program involves self-control or self-management, possibly the most promising of all techniques for ensuring the generalization and maintenance of behavior change. Procedures for teaching students such skills are described in Chapter 12. For many students, the ultimate objective of the applied behavior analyst is to bring behavior under the control of self-monitoring, self-administered contingencies, and even self-selected goals and procedures.

Many procedures for promoting generalization have been described in this chapter. Decide for yourself which one results in a domestic problem for Professor Grundy in the following vignette.

Professor Grundy Takes Up Jogging

Professor Grundy looked at the chart above his bathroom scales. "Big bones or not," he muttered, "something's got to be done. Maybe I need to jog. Argh!" He began to listen to the large number of his colleagues who ran daily. (He learned that the correct term, for those in the know, was running, not jogging.) Professor Grundy read all about the benefits of running. He began to be a believer.

One Saturday morning, the professor visited his local sporting goods store. He purchased expensive shoes, a *T-shirt*, and a pair of extremely brief running shorts. Sunday morning he donned his outfit and presented himself to Mrs. Grundy.

"Well, Minerva, my dear," he asked, "how do I look?"

Ten minutes later, as Mrs. Grundy was still gasping for breath and wiping her eyes, he left the house and proceeded to run (albeit slowly and stiffly) around the block. He made it for an entire mile, before deciding that perhaps tennis. . . . Then he remembered the expense and decided to stick with it for a month. Three weeks later, he was hooked. He could hardly wait to hit the street. When he walked downstairs one morning about this time, Mrs. Grundy looked at him appraisingly. "Why, Oliver," she said thoughtfully, "you have very nice legs."

"I'm all right officer—just taking a break."

"Thank you, my dear," said Professor Grundy. That very morning several young ladies leaned out of a passing car and whistled at the professor. His dignity was somewhat offended, but still. . . . The next Saturday he wore his running shorts all day. He noticed admiring glances at the shopping center and at the public library (where he had gone to return several overdue books on running). He bought more shorts and wore them during all his leisure time. Mrs. Grundy balked, however, when he prepared to wear them on a visit to her mother. "Oliver," she said, "I think this is carrying generalization just a bit far!"

SUMMARY

In this chapter, we have investigated many techniques for promoting stimulus generalization, response generalization, and maintenance of behavior. In the first edition of this text, we stated that the technology of generalization was in its infancy. In the second edition, we suggested that it had reached the toddler stage. With increased emphasis on theoretical and practical analysis of generalization, there is reason to hope that the technology will continue to mature. Every year there is more emphasis on generalization in the literature. Its status, however, is still well described by Buchard and Harig (1976, pp. 428–429):

> Formulating questions about generalization is somewhat like a game that might go something like this: At the start, there are two things to worry about. Will the behavioral change be maintained in the natural environment or won't it? If it won't, then there are two more things to worry about. Does the lack of generalization reflect the type or level of the reinforcement schedule that produced the behavioral change in the first place, or did the behavior fail to generalize because of a lack of supporting contingencies in the community? If the problem pertains to the schedule, you have little to worry about. You go back to the treatment setting and strengthen the desirable behavior, preferably through a positive reinforcement schedule. However, if the problem is with the supporting contingencies in the natural environment, then you have two more things to worry about. Should you reprogram the natural environment to provide supporting contingencies through intermittent reinforcement, fading, or overlearning? And so on. . . .

Obviously the game is one in which these questions can be formulated ad infinitum. With generalization, the unfortunate part is that there will probably always be something to worry about; this is the nature of the beast! It's hard enough to try to determine whether or not behavior has changed, and if so why, let alone trying to determine whether or not the change also occurred in a completely different setting. Applied behavior analysts who are also teachers may never stop worrying about generalization. Given the techniques described in this chapter, however, there appears to be less and less excuse for mere worrying. If applied behavior analysis procedures are to become an accepted part of the repertoire of every teacher, it is time, as Baer, Wolf, and Risley (1968) suggested, "to stop lamenting and start programming."

DISCUSSION QUESTIONS

1. Part-time resource services for mildly handicapped students who spend most of their time in the regular classroom have not been as successful as most educators hoped. What have you learned about generalization that may explain this? Give some suggestions that might increase the success of resource programs.

2. Providing services to children and adults with severe disabilities in community settings seems to increase their successful functioning in those settings. How can you explain this? What are some advantages and disadvantages to this approach?

REFERENCES

Anderson-Inman, L., Walker, H.M., & Purcell, J. 1984. Promoting the transfer of skills across settings: Transenvironmental programming for handicapped students in the mainstream. In W. Heward, T.E. Heron, D.S. Hill, & J. Trap-Porter (Eds.), *Focus on behavior analysis in education*. Columbus, Ohio: Merrill.

Atthowe, J.M. 1973. Token economies come of age. *Behavior Therapy, 4,* 646–654.

Axelrod, S. 1977. *Behavior modification for the classroom teacher.* New York: McGraw-Hill.

Ayllon, T., & Azrin, N. 1968. *The token economy: A motivational system for therapy and rehabilitation.* New York: Appleton-Century-Crofts.

Ayllon, T., & Kelly, K. 1974. Reinstating verbal behavior in a functionally mute retardate. *Professional Psychology, 5,* 385–393.

Azrin, N.H., Sneed, T.J., & Foxx, R.M. 1973. Drybed: A rapid method of eliminating bedwetting (enuresis) of the retarded. *Behavior Research and Therapy, 11,* 427–434.

Bachrach, A.J., Erwin, W.J., & Mohr, J.P. 1965. The control of eating behavior in an anorexic by operant conditioning techniques. In L.P. Ullman & L. Krasner (Eds.), *Case studies in behavior modification* (pp. 153–163). New York: Holt, Rinehart & Winston.

Baer, D.M., & Wolf, M.M. 1970. The entry into natural communities of reinforcement. In R. Ulrich, T. Stachnik, & J. Mabry (Eds.), *Control of human behavior* (Vol. 2). Glenview, IL: Scott, Foresman.

Baer, D.M., Wolf, M.M., & Risley, T.R. 1968. Some current dimensions of applied behavior analysis. *Journal of Applied Behavior Analysis, 1,* 91–97.

Barton, E.J., & Ascione, F.R. 1979. Sharing in preschool children: Facilitation, stimulus generalization, response generalization, and maintenance. *Journal of Applied Behavior Analysis, 12,* 417–430.

Becker, W.C., & Engelmann, S.E. 1978. Systems for basic instruction: Theory and applications. In A. Cata-

nia & T. Brigham (Eds.), *Handbook of applied behavior analysis: Social and instructional processes* (pp. 57–92). Chicago: Science Research Associates.

Becker, W.C., Engelmann, S., & Thomas, D.R. 1975. *Teaching 2: Cognitive learning and instruction.* Chicago: Science Research Associates.

Bijou, S.W., Peterson, R.F., Harris, F.R., Allen, K.E., & Johnston, M.S. 1969. Methodology for experimental studies of young children in natural settings. *Psychological Record, 19,* 177–210.

Billingsley, F.F. 1987. Where are the generalized outcomes? (An examination of instructional objectives.) *Journal of the Association for Persons with Severe Handicaps, 11,* 176–181.

Birnbrauer, J.S. 1968. Generalization of punishment effects: A case study. *Journal of Applied Behavior Analysis, 1,* 201–211.

Bourbeau, P.E., Sowers, J., & Close, D.E. 1986. An experimental analysis of generalization of banking skills from classroom to bank settings in the community. *Education and Training of the Mentally Retarded, 21,* 98–107.

Brown, L., Nietupski, J., & Hamre-Nietupski, S. 1976. The criterion of ultimate functioning. In M.A. Thomas (Ed.), *Hey, don't forget about me!* (pp. 2–15). Reston, VA: CEC Information Center.

Browning, E.R. 1983. A memory pacer for improving stimulus generalization. *Journal of Autism and Developmental Disorders, 13,* 427–432.

Browning, R.M. 1980. *Teaching the severely handicapped child: Basic skills for the developmentally disabled.* Boston: Allyn & Bacon.

Bryan, T., & Bryan, J. 1978. *Understanding learning disabilities.* Sherman Oaks, CA: Alfred.

Buchard, J.D., & Harig, P.T. 1976. Behavior modification and juvenile delinquency. In H. Leitenberg (Ed.), *Handbook of behavior modification and behavior therapy.* Englewood Cliffs, NJ: Prentice-Hall.

Campbell, C.R., & Stremel-Campbell, K. 1982. Programming "loose training" as a strategy to facilitate language generalization. *Journal of Applied Behavior Analysis, 15*, 295–305.

Carr, E.G., & Kologinsky, E. 1983. Acquisition of sign language by autistic children: II. Spontaneity and generalization effects. *Journal of Applied Behavior Analysis, 16*, 297–314.

Chadwick, B.A., & Day, R.C. 1971. Systematic reinforcement: Academic performance of underachieving students. *Journal of Applied Behavior Analysis, 4*, 311–319.

Cone, J.D. 1973. Assessing the effectiveness of programmed generalization. *Journal of Applied Behavior Analysis, 6*, 713–718.

Corte, H.E., Wolf, M.M., & Locke, b.J. 1971. A comparison of procedures for eliminating self-injurious behavior of retarded adolescents. *Journal of Applied Behavior Analysis, 4*, 201–213.

Dehaven, E.D., Corley, M.J., Hofeling, D.V., & Garcia, E. 1982. Developing generative vocational behaviors in a business setting. *Analysis and Intervention in Developmental Disabilities, 2*, 345–356.

Drabman, R.S. 1973. Child versus teacher administered token programs in a psychiatric hospital school. *Journal of Abnormal Child Psychology, 1*, 68–87.

Dunlap, G., Koegel, R.L., Johnson, J., O'Neill, R.E. 1987. Maintaining performance of autistic clients in community settings with delayed contingencies. *Journal of Applied Behavior Analysis, 20*, 185–191.

Emshoff, J.G., Redd, W.H., & Davidson, W.S. 1976. Generalization training and the transfer of treatment effects with delinquent adolescents. *Journal of Behavior Therapy and Experimental Psychiatry, 7*, 141–144.

Engelmann, S., & Carnine, D. 1982. *Theory of instruction: Principles and applications*. New York: Irvington.

Engelmann, S., & Colvin, G. 1983. *Generalized compliance training: A direct-instruction program for managing severe behavior problems*. Austin, TX: Pro-Ed.

Fowler, S.A., & Baer, D.M. 1981. "Do I have to be good all day?": The timing of delayed reinforcement as a factor in generalization. *Journal of Applied Behavior Analysis, 14*, 13–24.

Foxx, R.M., & Azrin, N.H. 1973. *Toilet training the retarded: A rapid program for day and nighttime independent toileting*. Champaign, IL: Research Press.

Foxx, R.M., McMorrow, M.J., & Mennemeier, M. 1984. Teaching social/vocational skills to retarded adults with a modified table game: An analysis of generalization. *Journal of Applied Behavior Analysis, 17*, 343–352.

Garcia, E. 1974. The training and generalization of a conversational speech form in nonverbal retardates. *Journal of Applied Behavior Analysis, 7*, 137–149.

Garcia, E., Baer, D.M., & Firestone, I. 1971. The development of generalized imitation within topographically determined boundaries. *Journal of Applied Behavior Analysis, 4*, 101–112.

Garcia, E., Guess, D., & Byrnes, J. 1973. Development of syntax in a retarded girl using procedures of imitation, reinforcement, and modelling. *Journal of Applied Behavior Analysis, 6*, 299–310.

Greenwood, C.R., Sloane, N.H., JR., & Baskin, A. 1974. Training elementary aged peer-behavior managers to control small group programmed mathematics. *Journal of Applied Behavior Analysis, 7*, 103–114.

Guess, D., Sailor, W., Rutherford, G., & Baer, D.M. 1968. An experimental analysis of linguistic development: The productive use of the plural morpheme. *Journal of Applied Behavior Analysis, 1*, 297–306.

Guttman, N., & Kalish, H.I. 1956. Discriminability and stimulus generalization. *Journal of Experimental Psychology, 51*, 79–88.

Hall, R.V., Cristler, C., Cranston, S.S., & Tucker, B. 1970. Teachers and parents as researchers using multiple baseline designs. *Journal of Applied Behavior Analysis, 3*, 247–255.

Haring, N.G. 1988. *Investigating the problem of skill generalization: Literature review III*. Seattle, WA: Washington Research Organization.

Haring, N.G., & Liberty, K.A. 1990. Matching strategies with performance in facilitating generalization. *Focus on Exceptional Children, 22*(8), 1–16.

Hartmann, D.P., & Atkinson, D. 1973. Having your cake and eating it too: A note on some apparent contradictions between therapeutic achievements and design requirements in N-1/21 studies. *Behavior Therapy, 4*, 589–591.

Hewett, F.M., Taylor, F.D., & Artuso, A.A. 1969. The Santa Monica Project: Evaluation of an engineered classroom design with emotionally disturbed children. *Exceptional Children, 35*, 523–529.

Horcones. 1992. Natural reinforcements: A way to improve education. *Journal of Applied Behavior Analysis, 25,* 71–75.

Horner, R.H., & Budd, C.M. 1985. Acquisition of manual sign use: Collateral reduction of maladaptive behavior, and factors limiting generalization. *Education and Training of the Mentally Retarded, 20,* 39–47.

Horner, R.H., Eberhard, J.M., & Sheehan, M.R. 1986. Teaching generalized table bussing: The importance of negative teaching examples. *Behavior Modification, 10,* 457–471.

Horner, R.H., Jones, D., & Williams, J.A. 1985. A functional approach to teaching generalized street crossing. *Journal of the Association for Persons with Severe Handicaps, 13,* 71–78.

Horner, R.H., McDonnell, J.J., & Bellamy, G.T. Undated. *Teaching generalized skills: General case instruction in simulation and community settings* (Contract No. 300-82-0362). Unpublished manuscript, University of Oregon.

Horner, R.H., Williams, J.A., & Stevely, J.D. 1984. *Acquisition of generalized telephone use by students with severe mental retardation.* Unpublished manuscript.

Hupp, S.C. 1986. Effects of stimulus mode on the acquisition, transfer, and generalization of categories by severely mentally retarded children and adolescents. *American Journal of Mental Deficiency, 90,* 579–587.

Inglesfield, E., & Crisp, A. 1985. Teaching dressing skills to the severely mentally handicapped: A comparison of intensive and non-intensive strategies. *British Journal of Mental Subnormality, 31,* 46–53.

Jackson, D.A., & Wallace, R.F. 1974. The modification and generalization of voice loudness in a fifteen-year-old retarded girl. *Journal of Applied Behavior Analysis, 7,* 461–471.

Johnston, J.M. 1979. On the relation between generalization and generality. *The Behavior Analyst, 2,* 1–6.

Johnston, J.M., & Johnston, G.T. 1972. Modification of consonant speech-sound articulation in young children. *Journal of Applied Behavior Analysis, 5,* 233–246.

Kale, R.J., Kaye, J.H., Whelan, P.A., & Hopkins, B.L. 1968. The effects of reinforcement on the modification, maintenance, and generalization of social responses of mental patients. *Journal of Applied Behavior Analysis, 1,* 307–314.

Kallman, W.H., Hersen, M., & O'Toole, D.H. 1975. The use of social reinforcement in a case of conversion reaction. *Behavior Therapy, 6,* 411–413.

Kazdin, A.E. 1973. Methodological and assessment considerations in evaluating reinforcement programs in applied settings. *Journal of Applied Behavior Analysis, 6,* 517–531.

Kazdin, A.E. 1977. *The token economy: A review and evaluation.* New York: Plenum Press.

Kazdin, A.E., & Bootzin, R.R. 1972. The token economy: An evaluative review. *Journal of Applied Behavior Analysis, 5,* 343–372.

Kazdin, A.E., & Polster, R. 1973. Intermittent token reinforcement and response maintenance in extinction. *Behavior Therapy, 4,* 386–391.

Keller, F.S., & Schoenfeld, W.N. 1950. *The principles of psychology.* New York: Appleton-Century-Crofts.

Kifer, R.E., Lewis, M.A., Green, D.R., & Phillips, E.L. 1974. Training predelinquent youths and their parents to negotiate conflict situations. *Journal of Applied Behavior Analysis, 7,* 357–364.

Kirby, K.C., & Bickel, W.K. 1988. Toward an explicit analysis of generalization: a stimulus control interpretation. *The Behavior Analyst, 11,* 115–129.

Koegel, R.L., O'Dell, M.C., & Koegel, L.K. 1987. A natural language teaching paradigm for nonverbal autistic children. *Journal of Autism and Developmental Disorders, 17,* 187–200.

Koegel, R.L., & Rincover, A. 1974. Treatment of psychotic children in a classroom environment: I. Learning in a large group. *Journal of Applied Behavior Analysis, 7,* 45–59.

Koegel, R.L, & Rincover, A. 1977. Research on the difference between generalization and maintenance in extra-therapy responding. *Journal of Applied Behavior Analysis, 10,* 1–12.

Liberty, K.A. 1987. Behaver-control of stimulus events to facilitate generalization. In N. Haring (Principal Investigator), *Research in education of the severely handicapped: Washington Research Organization* (U. S. Department of Education, Contract No. 300-82-0364). Seattle: University of Washington Press.

Livi, J., & Ford, A. 1985. Skill transfer from a domestic training site to the actual homes of three moderately handicapped students. *Education and Training of the Mentally Retarded, 20,* 69–82.

Long, J.D., & Williams, R.L. 1973. The comparative effectiveness of group and individually contingent free time with inner-city junior high school students. *Journal of Applied Behavior Analysis, 6*, 465–474.

Lovaas, O.I., Koegel, R., Simmons, J.Q., & Long, J.S. 1973. Some generalization and follow-up measures on autistic children in behavior therapy. *Journal of Applied Behavior Analysis, 6*, 131–166.

Lovaas, O.I., & Simmons, J.Q. 1969. Manipulation of self-destruction in three retarded children. *Journal of Applied Behavior Analysis, 2*, 143–157.

Marchetti, A.G., McCartney, J.R., Drain, S., Hooper, M., & Dix, J. 1983. Pedestrian skills training for mentally retarded adults: Comparison of training in two settings. *Mental Retardation, 21*, 107–110.

Martin, M., Burkholder, R., Rosenthal, R., Tharp, R.G., & Thorne, G.L. 1968. Programming behavior change into school milieux of extreme adolescent deviates. *Behavior Research and Therapy, 6*, 371–383.

Mastropieri, M.A., & Scruggs, T.E. 1984. Generalization: Five effective strategies. *Academic Therapy, 19*, 427–431.

Medland, M.B., & Stachnik, T.J. 1972. Good-behavior game: A replication and systematic analysis. *Journal of Applied Behavior Analysis, 5*, 45–51.

McGee, G.G., Krantz, P.J., & McClannahan, L.E. 1986. An extension of incidental teaching procedures to reading instruction for autistic children. *Journal of Applied Behavior Analysis, 19*, 147–157.

McGee, G.G, Krantz, P.J., Mason, D., & McClannahan, L.E. 1983. A modified incidental-teaching procedure for autistic youth: Acquisition and generalization of receptive object labels. *Journal of Applied Behavior Analysis, 16*, 329–338.

Pancsofar, E.L., & Bates, P. 1985. The impact of the acquisition of successive training exemplars on generalization. *Journal of the Association for Persons with Severe Handicaps, 10*, 95–104.

Panyan, M.C., & Hall, R.V. 1978. Effects of serial versus concurrent task sequencing on acquisition, maintenance, and generalization. *Journal of Applied Behavior Analysis, 11*, 67–74.

Patterson, G.R. 1965. An application of conditioning techniques to the control of a hyperactive child. In L.P. Ullmann & L. Krasner (Eds.), *Case studies in behavior modification*. New York: Holt, Rinehart & Winston.

Phillips, E.L., Phillips, E.A., Fixsen, D.L., & Wolf, M.M. 1971. Achievement place: Modification of the behaviors of predelinquent boys within a token economy. *Journal of Applied Behavior Analysis, 4*, 45–59.

Richman, G.S., Reiss, M.L., Bauman, K.E., & Bailey, J.S. 1984. Teaching menstrual care to mentally retarded women: Acquisition, generalization, and maintenance. *Journal of Applied Behavior Analysis, 17*, 441–451.

Rincover, A., & Koegel, R.L. 1975. Setting generality and stimulus control in autistic children. *Journal of Applied Behavior Analysis, 8*, 235–246.

Risley, T.R. 1968. The effects and side effects of punishing the autistic behaviors of a deviant child. *Journal of Applied Behavior Analysis, 1*, 21–34.

Schroeder, G.L., & Baer, D.M. 1972. Effects of concurrent and serial training on generalized vocal imitation in retarded children. *Developmental Psychology, 6*, 293–301.

Schumaker, J., & Sherman, J.A. 1970. Training generative verb usage by imitation and reinforcement procedures. *Journal of Applied Behavior Analysis, 3*, 273–287.

Schwarz, M.L., & Hawkins, R.P. 1970. Application of delayed reinforcement procedures to the behavior of an elementary school child. *Journal of Applied Behavior Analysis, 3*, 85–96.

Sedlak, R.A., Doyle, M., & Schloss, P. 1982. Video games: A training and generalization demonstration with severely retarded adolescents. *Education and Training for the Mentally Retarded, 17*, 332–336.

Seymour, F.W., & Stokes, T.F. 1976. Self-recording in training girls to increase work and evoke staff praise in an institution for offenders. *Journal of Applied Behavior Analysis, 9*, 41–54.

Shafer, M.S., Inge, K.J., & Hill J. 1986. Acquisition, generalization, and maintenance of automated banking skills. *Education and Training of the Mentally Retarded, 21*, 265–272.

Skinner, B.F. 1953. *Science and human behavior*. New York: Macmillan.

Sprague, J.R., & Horner, R.H. 1984. The effects of single instance, multiple instance, and general case training on generalized vending machine use by moderately and severely handicapped students. *Journal of Applied Behavior Analysis, 17*, 273–278.

Stainback, W., Stainback, S., & Strathe, M. 1983. Generalization of positive social behavior by severely handicapped students: A review and analysis of research. *Education and Training of the Mentally Retarded, 18*, 293–299.

Stephens, T.M. 1976. *Directive teaching of children with learning and behavioral handicaps.* Columbus, Ohio: Merrill.

Stokes, T.F., & Baer, D.M. 1976. Preschool peers as mutual generalization-facilitating agents. *Behavior Therapy, 7*, 549–556.

Stokes, T. F., & Baer, D.M. 1977. An implicit technology of generalization. *Journal of Applied Behavior Analysis, 10*, 349–367.

Stokes, T.F., Baer, D.M., & Jackson, R.L. 1974. Programming the generalization of a greeting response in four retarded children. *Journal of Applied Behavior Analysis, 7*, 599–610.

Troutman, A.C. 1977. *Stimulus control: A procedure to facilitate generalization from resource rooms to regular classrooms.* Unpublished doctoral dissertation, Georgia State University.

Twardosz, S., & Sajwaj, T. 1972. Multiple effects of a procedure to increase sitting in a hyperactive, retarded boy. *Journal of Applied Behavior Analysis, 5*, 73–78.

Van Den Pol, R.A., Iwata, B.A., Ivancic, M.T., Page, T.J., Neef, N.A., & Whitley, F.P. 1981. Teaching the handicapped to eat in public places: Acquisition, generalization and maintenance of restaurant skills. *Journal of Applied Behavior Analysis, 14*, 61–69.

Walker, H.M., & Buckley, N.K. 1968. The use of positive reinforcement in conditioning attending behavior. *Journal of Applied Behavior Analysis, 1*, 245–250.

Walker, H.M., & Buckley, N.K. 1972. Programming generalization and maintenance of treatment effects across time and across settings. *Journal of Applied Behavior Analysis, 5*, 209–224.

Walker, H.M., Mattsen, R.H., & Buckley, N.K. 1971. The functional analysis of behavior within an experimental class setting. In W.C. Becker (Ed.), *An empirical basis for change in education.* Chicago: Science Research Associates.

White, O.R., & Haring, N.G. 1980. *Exceptional teaching* (2nd ed). Columbus, Ohio: Merrill.

Wilcox, B., & Bellamy, G.T. 1982. *Design of high school programs for severely handicapped students.* Baltimore: Paul H. Brookes.

Woods, T.S. 1984. Generality in the verbal tacting of autistic children as a function of "naturalness" in antecedent control. *Journal of Behavior Therapy and Experimental Psychiatry, 15*, 27–32.

Woods, T.S. 1987. Programming common antecedents: A practical strategy for enhancing the generality of learning. *Behavioural Psychotherapy, 15*, 158–180.

Woolcock, W.W., & Lengel, M.B. 1987. Use of general case instruction with visually impaired, multiply handicapped adults in the sorting of national zip codes. *Journal of Visual Impairment and Blindness, 81*, 110–114.

CHAPTER 12

Teaching Students to Manage Their Own Behavior

- Who is the only person who will be with a student through his or her entire educational experience, in school and out?
- Who is most tuned in to a student's day-to-day behavior and learning?
- Who knows best what kind of reinforcement a student desires at any one time?
- So who should learn to bear the primary responsibility for maintenance, monitoring, and reinforcement of behavioral programs?

That's right; the answer to all of the questions above is *the student*. The best person to manage a student's behavior is the student himself or herself. We call this kind of behavioral intervention *self-management*. Your grandmother called it self-control or self-discipline. Any person who is to function independently to any degree must learn it.

Throughout this book, we have described procedures for teachers to use in changing the behavior of their students. In Chapter 11, we discussed some ways of increasing the generalizability of behavior-change procedures and thus minimizing the necessity for continued teacher support. This chapter further examines techniques that enable teachers to make students less dependent on teachers' environmental manipulation. The procedures discussed in this chapter place the responsibility for change on the student. The focus in all the approaches is on self-management, on teaching students to become effective modifiers of their own behavior. John Dewey (1939) suggested that "the ideal aim of education is the creation of self control" (p. 75). Students who have self-control are able to learn and to behave appropriately even when adult supervision is not available. The better able students are to manage themselves, the more time teachers can spend designing effective learning environments.

Lovitt (1973) noted that "self-management behaviors are not systematically programmed [in the schools] which appears to be an educational paradox, for one of the expressed objectives of the educational system is to create individuals who are self-reliant and independent" (p. 139). If we, as teachers, agree that our goals include independence for our students, then we must make provisions for making students independent. One of our colleagues tells prospective special education teachers that they should always be trying to do themselves out of their jobs—to teach their students to manage without special education programs. Although total independence is not possible for all students, most can be taught to be more self-reliant. Kazdin (1975, pp. 189–190) offered several additional reasons for preferring self-management to that controlled by external change agents:

1. The use of external change agents sacrifices consistency, since teachers or others may "miss" certain instances of behavior.
2. Problems associated with communication between agents in different settings (such as teachers and parents) can also undermine the success of a program.
3. The change agents themselves can become an environmental cue for the performance or lack of performance of a behavior.
4. An individual's contribution to the development of a personal behavior-change program may increase performance.
5. External agents are not always available in the environment where the target behavior is occurring or should occur.

Both typical learners and those with disabilities can be taught to monitor and alter their own behavior. For the procedures to be used effectively, students must be trained in their use (as, for example, in O'Leary & Dubey, 1979; Rosenbaum & Drabman, 1979; Rueda, Rutherford, & Howell, 1980). Students are trained in self-management procedures much as they are in other behaviors—according to the principles of learning.

Any technique a teacher can use to change behavior can also be used by students to change their own behavior. Students can be taught self-management by instructing them to monitor their behavior through self-data recording, evaluate their behavior, and provide their own consequences through self-reinforcement and self-punishment. Students can also learn to manipulate behavioral antecedents by using self-instruction.

Self-management usually comes in packages.

Although each of these self-management techniques is reviewed separately in this chapter, in practice they have most often been employed in packages, where combinations of the procedures were put into effect—for example, self-recording with self-reinforcement or self-instruction with self-reinforcement. Examples of self-management packages are given later in this chapter.

A COMMON EXPERIENCE

Self-management procedures are as much a part of the natural environment as are all the behavioral procedures described in this book. Many people use self-recording, self-reinforcement, self-punishment, and self-instruction in managing their everyday behavior. Noted author Irving Wallace describes how he and other authors have practiced **self-recording** techniques. Of his own work habits, he relates:

> I maintained work charts while writing my first four published books. These charts showed the date I started each chapter, the date I finished it, and the number of pages written in that period. With my fifth book, I started keeping a more detailed chart, which also showed how many pages I had written by the end of every working day. I am not sure why I started keeping such records. I suspect that it was because, as a free-lance writer, entirely on my own, without employer or deadline, I wanted to create disciplines for myself, ones that were guilt-making when ignored. A chart on the wall served as such a discipline, its figures scolding me or encouraging me. (Wallace, 1977, p. 516).

Wallace then quotes from the autobiography of novelist Anthony Trollope, published in 1883:

> When I have commenced a new book, I have always prepared a diary, divided into weeks, and carried on for the period which I have allowed myself for the completion of the work. In this I have entered, day by day, the number of pages I have written, so that if at any time I have slipped into idleness for a day or two, the record of that idleness has been there, staring me in the face, and demanding of me increased labour, so that the deficiency might be supplied. According to the circumstances of the time—whether my other business might then be heavy or light, or whether the book I was writing was or was not wanted with speed,—I

have allotted myself so many pages a week. The average number has been about 40. It has been placed as low as 20, and has risen to 112. And as a page is an ambiguous term, my page has been made to contain 250 words; and as words, if not watched, will have a tendency to straggle, I have had *every* word counted as I went. . . . There has ever been the record before me, and a week passed with an insufficient number of pages has been a blister to my eye and a month so disgraced would have been a sorrow to my heart.

I have been told that such appliances are beneath the notice of a man of genius, I have never fancied myself to be a man of genius, but had I been so I think I might well have subjected myself to these trammels. Nothing surely is so potent as a law that may not be disobeyed. It has the force of the water-drop that hollows the stone. A small daily task, if it be really daily, will beat the labours of a spasmodic Hercules. (p. 518).

Finally, Wallace quotes from an article written about Ernest Hemingway by George Plimpton that appeared in the *Paris Review* in 1965:

He keeps track of his daily progress—"so as not to kid myself"—on a large chart made out of the side of a cardboard packing case and set up against the wall under the nose of a mounted gazelle head. The numbers on the chart showing the daily output of words differ from 450, 575, 462, 1250, back to 512, the higher figures on days Hemingway puts in extra work so he won't feel guilty spending the following day fishing on the gulf stream. (p. 518).

The use of **self-reinforcement** is probably familiar to most people. Consider the following teacher's internal monologue as she heads home from a day at school:

What a day!

Bus duty at 7:00 A.M. . . . Jenny Lind fell, sprained her ankle, screamed like a banshee . . . her mother says she's going to sue . . .

Clifford refused to believe that 6 times 4 was 24 today just because it was yesterday . . .

Two fights over whose turn it was to use the blue paint in art class. Pat ended up with the blue; Mark ended up blue . . .

The lunch money didn't balance . . .

Why does that Velma Johnson always sit next to me at lunch and talk my ear off?

I kept my temper all day though—I deserve a stop at Baskin Robbins!

If the same teacher also practices **self-punishment**, she may remember the three scoops of rocky road at lunchtime tomorrow and confine herself to two pieces of lettuce and a diet drink.

Many of us also practice **self-instruction**, providing ourselves with verbal prompts. We talk to ourselves, sometimes aloud, as we do complex or unfamiliar tasks. Many children also use such self-instruction naturally. For example, Kohlberg, Yaeger, and Hjertholm recorded the self-instruction processing of a 3½-year-old child during solitary play with a set of Tinker Toys.

> The wheels go here, the wheels go here. Oh, we need to start it all over again. We have to close it up. See, it closes up. We're starting it all over again. Do you know why we wanted to do that? Because I needed it to go a different way. Isn't it pretty clever, don't you think? But we have to cover up the motor just like a real car. (1968, p. 695).

Training students to manage their behavior is a mechanism for systematizing and making more powerful these naturally occurring phenomena. Some students may be effective self-managers without training, others unready to manage their own behavior to even a small extent. Diminished ability for self-regulation has been found in students with mental retardation (Whitman, 1990), learning disabilities (Baker, 1982; Short & Weissberg-Benchell, 1989), and emotional disturbance (Kern-Dunlap, Dunlap, Clarke, Childs, White, & Stewart, 1992). The wise teacher will remain alert for signs that students are ready to begin managing their own behaviors and will take advantage of this readiness. The strategies discussed in this chapter are often called cognitive training strategies (Hallahan, Kneedler, & Lloyd, 1983) or metacognitive strategies (Borkowski, 1992). Along with other strategies less closely related to applied behavior analysis, they are ways to help students think and solve problems more productively.

PREPARING STUDENTS TO MANAGE THEIR OWN BEHAVIOR

The teacher who uses some systematic behavior management program can try a number of techniques to increase students' potential for taking the responsibility for managing their own behavior.

1. When giving reinforcers, the teacher should explain to the student what behavior resulted in reinforcement. "Sammy, you did 10 math problems correctly. You get 10 points—1 for each problem."
2. The teacher may ask the student to relate part of the contingency. "Sammy, you get 10 points. Why do you get 10 points?" or "Sammy, you did 10 problems right. How many points have you earned?"
3. The teacher may ask the student to state the entire contingency. "Sammy, how many points? Why?"
4. The teacher may involve students in choosing reinforcers and in determining their cost in terms of behavior.

Students who have been exposed to such techniques will frequently volunteer statements about their behavior and its consequences. It is a small step from asking a student how many points he has earned and why, to allowing him to record the points himself with teacher supervision. Ultimately, Sammy may be allowed simply to count the number of problems he has done correctly and record his points on his card. Such self-recording is the foundation for many self-management procedures.

Self-Recording of Data

Chapter 4 describes techniques for data collection.

The purpose of data collection is to provide a record that reflects the occurrence of a behavior. If a student is taught self-recording procedures and asked to collect the data, that student is managing at least one part of her or his program for behavior change. Systems of data collection can be adapted so that the student simply records the occurrence or nonoccurrence of the target behavior. The student is thus asked to assess the quantity of a behavior. For example, a student may be asked to note each time she raises her hand before speaking in class or, conversely, each time she calls out without raising her hand. In addition, the student may be asked to assess the quality of her behavior. For example, she may be instructed to count and record each correctly solved arithmetic problem or each one of a series of assigned tasks.

Self-recorded data provide the student and teacher with concrete feedback regarding behavior. This information may be used to determine what reinforcers are available. In some cases, a student's collecting data on a behavior may have what is termed a reactive effect on the behavior. Simply as a function of the self-recording process, the behavior may change in the desired direction. In this capacity, self-recording functions as a behavior-change technique (Rosenbaum & Drabman, 1979). In some cases, it is as effective as an external cue or reminder (Hayes & Nelson, 1983). Consider the effect of a student's recording each instance of daydreaming while reading a chapter on self-management. In many cases, tallying each instance on a 3×5 card will reduce the rate of daydreaming. (If 3×5 cards are unavailable, just make a pencil mark in the margin.)

The reactive effect of self-recording may be only temporary.

As a self-management and behavior-change technique, self-recording, or self-monitoring, has been successfully used with a variety of behaviors. Increases have been noted in paying attention (Broden, Hall, & Mitts, 1971; DiGangi, Maag, & Rutherford, 1991; Kneedler & Hallahan, 1981), academic responses (Hundert & Bucher, 1978; James, Trap, & Cooper, 1977; Lovitt, 1973; Prater, Joy, Chilman, Temple, & Miller, 1991; Sagotsky, Patterson, & Lepper, 1978), class attendance (McKenzie & Rushall, 1974), appropriate verbalizations (Nelson, Lipinski, & Boykin, 1978), and vocational skills (Connis, 1979). Decreases have been recorded in talking-out in class (Broden, Hall, & Mitts, 1971; Lovitt, 1973), aggression (Lovitt, 1973), off-task behavior (Glynn, Thomas, & Shee, 1973; Sagotsky, Patterson, & Lepper, 1978), out-of-seat behavior (Sugai & Rowe, 1984), generally disruptive behavior (Stevenson & Fantuzzo, 1984), and overeating (Snoy & van Benten, 1978). Although self-recording may change behavior when first used, changes tend to dissipate over time unless supported with additional self-management procedures, such as self-reinforcement (Kanfer, 1975; McLaughlin, 1976; O'Leary & Dubey, 1979).

Although self-recording has been used for initial behavior-change programs, it appears to be most effective in maintaining behavior changes resulting from traditional, teacher-managed strategies (O'Leary & Dubey, 1979). Teaching students to use self-recording should include the following components:

1. Selecting a target behavior.
2. Operationally defining the behavior.
3. Selecting an appropriate system of data collection. (Successful data-collection systems include adaptations of event recording, time sampling, and permanent product recording; notation methods include tally sheets, wrist counters, graphs, and charts.)
4. Instructing the student in the use of the data-collection system selected.
5. Monitoring at least one practice data-recording session.
6. Students' employing self-recording independently.

Self-Recording Using Event Recording

Broden, Hall, and Mitts (1971) investigated the use of self-recording with two eighth-grade students. The first student, Liza, was earning a D– in history. Due to the lecture format of his class, the history teacher felt he could not participate in a suggested behavior-change program, because he could not consistently attend to Liza during the class period. Liza's counselor therefore decided to employ a self-recording procedure to increase the time Liza spent attending and studying. The counselor met with Liza and gave her a slip of paper that had three rows of 10 squares (see Figure 12–1). They discussed a definition of studying and examples of what constituted studying. Liza was instructed to take the slip of paper to class each day and, whenever she thought of it, to record a "+" in the square if she had been studying for the past few minutes and a "–" if she had not.

At a weekly conference, Liza and her counselor discussed the self-recording slips and the counselor praised Liza for studying. Before the self-recording strategy was used, Liza's study rate was 30% of the history class period despite two conferences with the counselor and promises from Liza that she would "really try." After self-recording was instituted, Liza's study behavior increased to 78% of the class period. After 30 days, when the teacher noted the change in Liza's study behavior, he agreed to praise Liza and give her increased attention when she studied. Liza continued to carry slips to class, sometimes filling them out and sometimes not. Her study time continued to increase and finally reached 88% of the class period.

The second eighth-grade student in the study, Stu, was referred by his math teacher who wanted to find "some means to shut Stu up" (Broden, Hall, & Mitts, 1971, p. 195). The teacher was asked to give Stu a slip of paper at the beginning of each of the two class periods (25 minutes before

FIGURE 12–1
Liza's self-record-ing data form

Note: From "The effect of self-recording on the class-room behavior of two eighth-grade students" by M. Broden, R.V. Hall, & B. Mitts. Journal of Applied Behavior Analysis, 1971, 4, 193. Copyright 1971 by Society for the Experimental Analysis of Behavior, Inc. Reprinted by permission.

Date

+	+	–	–	+	+	–	+	–	+

–	+	–							

At the top of the page are several rows of squares. At different times during the period (whenever you think of it but don't fill them all in at the same time) put down a "+" if you were studying, a "–" if you weren't. If, for example, you were ready to mark a square, you would ask yourself if for the last few minutes you had been studying and then you would put down a "+" if you had been or a "–" if you hadn't been studying.

lunch and 20 minutes after lunch). On each slip of paper was a 2 x 5-inch box, a place for his name and the date, and the statement, "make a mark every time you talk-out without permission" (see Figure 12–2). No further instructions or contingencies were given to Stu. During baseline, Stu talked-out on an average of 1.1 times per minute during the first period and 1.6 times a minute during second-period math. When self-recording was employed during both sessions, talk-outs were recorded 0.3 times per minute during the first period and 1.0 times per minute during the second period. When self-recording was reinstituted following a return to baseline conditions, the first period talk-outs returned to a low level but not the talk-outs during the period after lunch.

A similar self-recording procedure was used by Sagotsky, Patterson, and Lepper (1978) with fifth- and sixth-grade students working on math modules. The students were given a sheet with a space to mark the page and problem where they stopped working each day and a grid of 12 empty boxes. The students were told that during the math period each day, they should note from time to time whether or not they were actually working on their math units. If the student was not working, he or she was to put a tally mark in one of the boxes. It was suggested to the students that this might serve as a reminder to them to resume studying. The percentage of time spent studying increased.

Instead of tally sheets, such as those used by Liza and Stu, Nelson, Lipinski, and Boykin (1978) chose to use a mechanical adaptation. In a study employing self-recording of instances of appropriate classroom verbalizations, adolescents with mental retardation were given either handheld counters or ones worn on the belt to count the number of times they talked appropriately. Results were similar to those obtained in the other studies.

Self-recording using event recording has also been used to improve social skills in a student with a behavior disorder (Kiburz, Miller, & Morrow, 1984) and to modify the behavior of a child who was disruptive at home (O'Brien, Riner, & Budd, 1983).

Self-Recording Using Time Sampling

Glynn, Thomas, and Shee (1973) employed self-recording using time sampling to increase on-task behavior with a class of second-graders. In one condition, an audio tape was prerecorded so an audible tone sounded randomly. The 30-minute lesson was divided into intervals ranging from 1 to 5 minutes. One of the class members was selected and instructed to make marks on the chalkboard beside the names of any of three reading groups in which all members were on-task during the 10 seconds following every interval tone. In another condition, the taped signal was maintained, but each student in the class was given a 10×2 inch card with his or her name and five rows of 20 squares, one row for each day of the week. The students were instructed to place a check in one of the squares if they were on-task whenever the signal sounded. The students' rate of on-task behavior increased in both conditions.

Essentially the same procedure was used with three 7- to 10-year-old boys described as hyperactive (Barkley, Copeland, & Sivage, 1980). Each of the students had a card for self-recording. A poster of the rules for individual work time that they had assisted in developing was on a wall facing the boys. The rules were (1) stay in your seat, (2) work quietly, (3) don't bug others, (4) don't space out, and (5) raise your hand if you need help. A tape recorder signaled an opportunity for the students to record their on-task behavior. At randomly programmed intervals, a bell would sound on the

FIGURE 12–2
Stu's self-recording data form

Note: From "The effect of self-recording on the classroom behavior of two eighth-grade students" by M. Broden, R.V. Hall, & B. Mitts. Journal of Applied Behavior Analysis, 1971, 4, 196. Copyright 1971 by Society for the Experimental Analysis of Behavior, Inc. Reprinted by permission.

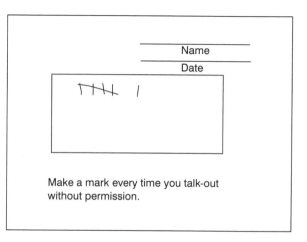

Make a mark every time you talk-out without permission.

tape player. At this signal, each boy was to ask himself if he had been on-task as determined by the rules on the poster. If so, he was to place a check mark on his card. For the first week, the bell rang at random intervals on an average of once every minute during a 30-minute work period. This was therefore a variable interval 1-minute schedule. For the second and third weeks, a VI 3-minute schedule was used. If a boy's tally agreed with an observer's record of his behavior, he earned extra points for accuracy (honesty). This procedure was successful in increasing study behavior.

Self-recording using time sampling has also been used to teach task attention to students with learning disabilities (Harris, 1986; Heins, Lloyd, & Hallahan, 1986), task attention and academic productivity of adolescents with multiple handicaps (Morrow, Burke, & Buell, 1985), and reduction of tongue protrusion of an adult with moderate retardation (Rudrud, Ziarnik, & Colman, 1984). These studies used some signal or cue to teach students to monitor their own behavior at intervals.

The following vignette shows how one teacher used time sampling combined with self-recording to help her students learn self-management.

Ms. Dietrich's Students Learn to Work Independently

Ms. Dietrich was a resource teacher for elementary students with learning problems. She arranged her schedule so that each group of students received direct instruction for the first 20 minutes of each scheduled resource hour. That group then worked independently while Ms. Dietrich taught another group. She was concerned that she could not give tokens to the groups working independently without disrupting the lesson she was teaching. She decided to teach the students self-recording. She acquired a child's noisemaker, a "cricket." At first, she observed the students working independently and clicked the cricket only if all of them appeared on-task. They awarded themselves a point when they heard the click. After a while, she just clicked randomly during her direct teaching and told the students to give themselves a point if they were working hard when they heard the sound. She found her procedure very effective. It was almost as good as being in two places at once.

Self-Recording Using Permanent Product Recording

James, Trap, and Cooper (1977) employed self-recording using a form of permanent product recording. Students copied letters from a model sheet and used a transparent overlay to correct their work. Pretraining for the accuracy of their self-recording included proper alignment of the overlay, using the overlay to determine which letter strokes were close enough to the model, and using practice sheets to self-record correct letter strokes. After completing each worksheet the students were given transparent overlays of the letters copied. Each letter they judged to conform to the letter on the transparent overlay was traced (dots connected) on the self-recording overlay to indicate those strokes they considered correct. They entered the total correct on the right edge of their self-recording sheets. The students received no feedback from the teacher on the accuracy of their self-recording, but their copying improved.

Connis (1979) used a form of permanent product self-recording with adults with mental retardation to sequence steps for food service vocational skills, such as dishwashing. The training stations were part of a public restaurant facility. Photographs representing assigned tasks were taped in correct sequence on a wall in the trainees' work area. Below each picture was taped a small, blank square of paper. The self-recording procedure required the trainees to (1) walk to the photographs, (2) look at the appropriate photograph in sequence, (3) mark an X on the square of paper beneath the photograph, and (4) begin the task represented in the photograph within a 40-second time limit. The students learned the sequence more rapidly with this self-recording system than with traditional procedures.

Similar monitoring or self-recording systems are used daily in the classroom and at home. For example, one teacher used a checklist similar to the one in Figure 12–3 for a language arts activity. In another example, a teacher who was also the mother of twin 7-year-old boys devised a self-recording checklist for morning tasks. The checklist was initiated because either she or the boys were late getting out of the house every morning. So she wouldn't have to remind the boys constantly of the tasks they needed to do first thing in the morning, the mother placed a checklist on the refrigerator (see Figure 12–4).

Two reasons for the success of self-recording procedures

Several suggestions have been made as to why self-recording changes behavior (Hayes & Nelson, 1983; Kanfer, 1975; Rachlin, 1974). All agree that self-recording forces students to monitor their behavior. Kanfer (1975) emphasizes self-reward and self-punishment, which, he states, inevitably accompany self-monitoring. Thus, a student who indicates on a chart that he has completed his daily tasks or reviews his tally of hand raising may, by his act of self-recording, be saying to himself, "I am a good boy" (Cautela, 1971). Rachlin (1974), Hayes and Nelson (1983), and Baer (1984) emphasize that self-monitoring provides environmental cues that increase the students' awareness of potential consequences. As the preceding examples show, self-recording must have some reinforcing qualities if there is a behavior change in the desired direction.

FIGURE 12–3
Self-recording checklist for a language arts activity

Name: _____	Date: _____

Check yourself off

Have I capitalized the correct letters?   _____

Have I put a period at the end of sentences?   _____

Have I spaced between words?   _____

Have I put my name on the paper before handing it in to the teacher?   _____

Have I answered all the questions?   _____

Have I checked my answers in the paragraphs I read?   _____

FIGURE 12–4
Self-recording checklist for home use

Have I?	Terry	Todd
1. Washed my face and hands?	_____	_____
2. Brushed my teeth?	_____	_____
3. Brushed my hair?	_____	_____
4. Picked up my dirty clothes?	_____	_____
5. Made my bed?	_____	_____
6. Put my lunch money in my pocket?	_____	_____
7. Gotten my homework and my books?	_____	_____

Self-recording does not always have reinforcing effects, however. Lovitt (1973) describes a procedure used with a second-grade boy who "had the irksome habit of hitting other children when he first arrived at school" (p. 144). The boy hit other children 10 to 15 times in the 5-minute period allowed for hanging up coats and settling in. The boy was told to record each time he hit someone by marking it on a tally sheet. At the end of each day, the teacher interviewed him regarding his record. His hitting behavior dropped to approximately five hits per 5-minute period. On the 13th day of the project, the boy tore up his tally sheet and announced he would no longer record his hits. For the 5 days following, during which the teacher continued to record data, the hit rate was zero. Lovitt notes: "Recording in most of the other instances appeared to be reinforcing, whereas in this instance self-recording was apparently a punishing event. His performance was far better when he was not self-recording than when he was" (p. 144). The improvement in behavior, however, did not occur until after the self-recording activity had taken place.

But won't they cheat?   An issue often raised when considering a self-recording procedure is the accuracy of students' records. The teacher may worry that students may be untruthful. Israel (1978) has indicated a higher correspondence between what a child says and then does, than between what a child does and then reports. If heightened awareness is an important factor in the success of self-recording procedures, however, accuracy may not matter. Indeed, Rosenbaum and Drabman (1979) state that self-recording does not have to be accurate to produce desirable changes in target behaviors. Nevertheless, researchers have reported high reliability of self-recording. Santogrossi, O'Leary, Romanczyk, and Kaufman (1973) reported 95% reliability of recording among adolescent boys in a psychiatric hospital. Broden, Hall, and Mitts (1971) reported that Liza's mean estimate of her study behavior was 81%, whereas the independent observer reported a mean estimate of 80% for her behavior. Bolstad and Johnson (1972) found that elementary-school children "were capable of self-observing their frequency of disruptive behavior with respectable accuracy" (p. 451). Glynn, Thomas, and Shee (1973) calculated mean percentages of on-task behavior, comparing the recording of eight of their second-graders and that of independent observers. Their data are presented in Figure 12–5. The general trend was that students were harder on themselves when judging the quality of their behavior than were the observers.

Increased student accuracy in self-recording has been successfully taught (Hundert & Bucher, 1978; Nelson, Lipinski, & Boykin, 1978; Wood & Flynn, 1978). Students received reinforcers contingent on matching their self-recording of behavior to records made by independent observers. Checking was then faded so it occurred only occasionally. Increased accuracy, however, did not necessarily lead to better performance (O'Leary & Dubey, 1979).

Self-Reinforcement

Contingencies students set themselves may be more effective than those set by teachers.

In most classrooms, teachers arrange contingencies. They specify what behaviors are expected and the consequences for performing those behaviors. Contingencies are stated in the form of "if . . . , then . . ." statements: "If you complete your composition, then you may have 5 minutes extra free time"; or "For each correct answer to the reading comprehension questions, you will earn one token." Students may be involved in contingency management in a number of ways. They may be allowed to choose reinforcers, to assist in determining the cost of the reinforcers in relation to behavior, or even to choose behaviors to be modified. The ultimate goal in allowing students to participate in contingency management is to encourage their use of the procedures they have been taught to manage their own behavior. As with self-recording, the transition from teacher-managed to student-managed programs must be gradual, and students must be explicitly taught to use self-reinforcement or self-punishment.

FIGURE 12–5
On-task behavior recorded by students and independent observers

		David	Clifford	Billy	Robbie	Dean	Deborah	Wayne	Chris
Mean percentages of on-task behavior recorded	Student Record	93	100	86	92	65	62	67	69
	Observer's Record	77	96	82	95	82	81	94	96

Note: From "Behavioral Self-Control of On-Task Behavior in an Elementary Classroom," by E.L. Glenn, J.D. Thomas, and S.M. Shee, 1973. 1973, Journal of Applied Behavior Analysis, 6, p. 110. Copyright 1973 by the Association for the Experimental Analysis of Behavior. Reprinted by permission.

It has been repeatedly demonstrated that self-determined contingencies and teacher-determined contingencies can be equally effective in producing behavior change. In fact, self-determined standards and reinforcers may sometimes be more effective than those externally determined (Hayes, Rosenfarb, Wulfert, Munt, Korn, & Zettle, 1985). Lovitt and Curtiss (1969, p. 51) compared the academic response rate of a 12-year-old student under a teacher-determined contingency for reinforcement with his rate under a self-determined contingency for reinforcement. The self-selected contingencies resulted in a 44% increase in academic response rate. The teacher-selected contingencies had been explained, written out, and attached to the student's desk. As he completed each academic assignment, the student was shown how many responses had been made and was asked to calculate the corresponding points he had earned. The teacher had set the following reinforcement value for each assignment:

Math:	10 problems	1 minute free time
Reading:		
(no errors)	1 page	2 minutes
(errors)	1 page	1 minute
Spelling:	18 words	1 minute
Writing:	20 letters	1 minute
Language arts:	10 answers	1 minute
Library book:	1 story	3 minutes
	3 questions	1 minute

Under the self-determined contingency for reinforcement, the student was asked to specify his own reinforcer in each area and to record his selections on a card that was then attached to his desk. The student selected the following reinforcers for each task:

Math:	10 problems	2 minutes free time
Reading:		
(no errors)	1 page	3 minutes
(errors)	1 page	2 minutes
Spelling:	5 words	1 minute
Writing:	10 letters	2 minutes
Language arts:	10 answers	2 minutes
Library book:	1 story	6 minutes
	3 questions	2 minutes

Rhode, Morgan, and Young (1983) used a self-reward system to generalize appropriate behavior from resource rooms to regular classrooms. Students were trained first to evaluate their own behavior in the resource room and then asked to do so in the regular classroom. O'Brien, Riner, and Budd (1983) successfully taught the parent of a disruptive child to implement a self-reward system and thus to teach her child to evaluate his own behavior.

When allowing students to select their own contingency for tasks to be completed, specific instructions should be given as to the procedure to be followed. The following set of instructions (Felixbrod & O'Leary, 1974, p. 846) has served as a model for many investigations of self-reinforcement:

1. When people work on a job, they get paid for what they do. I am going to pay you points which you can use to buy these prizes (pointing to prizes and point-exchange values). YOUR job is to answer these arithmetic questions. Answer the questions in order. In order to earn the points, only correct answers will count (repeated). You will have 20 minutes to do these. But you can stop before 20 minutes are up if you want to. . . .

2. I am going to let YOU decide how many points you want to get paid for each right answer. Take a look at the numbers on the next page (pointing to a separate page on which the subject is to choose a performance standard). I want YOU to decide how many points you want to get paid for each right answer. (Experimenter points to each possible choice in a list of 10 possible performance standards: "I want to get paid 1 point; 2 points . . . 10 points for each right answer.") After I leave the room, draw a circle around the number of points you want to get paid for each right answer.

Several studies conducted in classrooms (for example, Felixbrod & O'Leary, 1974; Fredericksen & Fredericksen, 1975) have shown that students tend to select more lenient performance standards than those selected by teachers. Because stringent standards—whether self-determined or teacher-determined—produce significantly better academic performance than do lenient standards, students should be taught to set fairly stringent standards for themselves. A prompt for selecting stringent standards can be used successfully if it is followed by social reinforcement. The following instructional prompt has been used to encourage students to select stringent standards:

If you pick 10 points per problem and you do 2 problems then you get 20 points. But, if you pick 2 points per problem and you get 10 problems correct you still get 20 points and the same good prize. So, if you pick a lower number you can get the same good prize just doing more problems. We would really like you to pick 1, 2, or 3 points per problem. Let's take a look at the prizes and I'll show you what I mean. (Starting with the lowest value prize describe to the child how much each prize is worth, and then concentrate on the highest.) Now, this prize costs 250 points. If you pick 1 point per problem then you have to do more than 12 pages of problems to win this prize. But, if you pick 2 points per problem then you only have to do 6 pages of problems to get the same prize. Do you understand? I'll leave the room and you circle one of these numbers. Remember, we would like you to pick 1, 2, or 3 points. (Brownell, Coletti, Ersner-Hershfield, Hershfield, & Wilson, 1977, p. 445)

Start with teacher-controlled contingencies.

Contingency management systems are most often implemented with the teacher controlling the selection and administration of reinforcers. A period of teacher-controlled contingency management should precede any effort to teach students self-reinforcement (O'Brien, Riner, & Budd, 1983). After the students become accustomed to the mechanics of the system, contingencies can be effectively managed by the students themselves. Drabman, Spitalnik, and O'Leary (1973) and Turkewitz, O'Leary, and Ironsmith (1975) used the following successive steps to transfer gradually both recording and reinforcement responsibilities from the teacher to the students in a token economy. Desired changes in behavior were maintained throughout the transfer process. In addition, behavior changes generalized to control periods in which token reinforcement was not in effect. Students initially recorded points awarded by the teacher and were awarded bonus points for matching teacher ratings. Matching was gradually faded and students ultimately rated their own behavior and determined their own reinforcement independently (Drabman, Spitalnik, & O'Leary, 1973, p. 11). Drabman and his colleagues suggested several factors that may have contributed to the maintenance of the desired changes in behavior. Continuous teacher praise for appropriate student behavior may have become more reinforcing over the course of the investigation. Peer reinforcement for appropriate behavior also increased. Accurate self-evaluation was praised by the teacher and may have acquired conditioned reinforcing properties, thereby strengthening appropriate behavior. Improved academic skills incompatible with inappropriate behavior were developed.

The following vignette illustrates a combined self-recording and self-reinforcing procedure.

DeWayne Passes Intro to Behavior Mod

DeWayne was panic-stricken. At midterm, his average in his behavior mod course was 67. If he failed, his grade point average would drop below the point where he would be retained in college. After listening to a lecture on self-reinforcement, he decided to try it on himself.

DeWayne acquired an inexpensive kitchen timer and a supply of 3 × 5 cards. He decided that he needed short-term and long-term reinforcers. He began setting the timer for an hour and making a check on a 3 × 5 card whenever he sat at his desk or in the library without getting up or talking to anyone for the entire hour. He then allowed himself a 10-minute break for talking to his roommate, making a cup of coffee, or taking care of bodily necessities. When he had four checks, he decided to allow himself to go out with his friends for pizza and a soft drink. He saved the cards and when he had accumulated five cards with at least four checks, he called his girlfriend and asked her to go to a movie. Although he was somewhat skeptical about the effectiveness of his plan, he found it worked. When he studied for an average of four hours a day, his grades began to

"What do you mean, you've got another date? I didn't know until just now if I'd have enough cards to go out tonight!"

improve. He finished the semester with a 3.0 grade point average and a conviction that applied behavior analysis was more than a gimmick for getting students to stay in their seats.

Self-Punishment

Self-reinforcement is more effective than self-punishment.

Most self-management procedures have emphasized self-reinforcement. Some investigations, however, have analyzed the effectiveness of teaching students to punish rather than reinforce behaviors. In classrooms, the form of self-punishment most often investigated has been the use of response cost in conjunction with token reinforcement systems (Humphrey, Karoly, & Kirschenbaum, 1978; Kaufman & O'Leary, 1972).

Humphrey and his colleagues (1978) worked in a second-grade reading class that was "initially a chaotic one as evidenced by the teacher's having referred 13 of 22 children to a special program for children with behavioral problems" (1978, p. 593). A self-reinforcement system and a self-punishment system were put in place to compare their relative effectiveness and also to assess potential side effects of self-punishment. The students using reinforcement placed tokens from banks into cups kept at their desks, contingent on accurate performance on reading assignments. The criteria for reinforcement were printed on the answer keys accompanying each reading paper. The teacher checked the work of six randomly selected students each day to minimize inaccuracy and cheating. The students using response cost began each morning with their cups filled with the maximum number of tokens that could be earned that day. They fined themselves for inaccurate work by referring to the response-cost criteria printed on the answer keys. Students also fined themselves for failing to complete the daily allotment of reading assignments. Under both self-management systems, the students did more reading assignments and maintained the accuracy of their work. In addition, disruptive behaviors, which were not under the contingencies, decreased slightly. Although self-punishment (response cost) was effective, self-reinforcement appeared to work better.

Several explanations for the relative superiority of self-reinforcement to self-punishment are possible (Humphrey, Karoly, & Kirschenbaum, 1978, p. 599). Self-response cost may have simply been more difficult to use because it required children to subtract rather than add. A second possible explanation is that concern about losing reinforcers may have caused a fear of failure. Response cost may maximize fear of failure. If response cost accentuated children's awareness of failure, the children may have evaluated their behavior more negatively. Negative self-evaluation or selective attention to failures or inadequacies can result in abandonment of behavior strategies.

In the following vignette, observe the combination of self-recording, self-reinforcement, and self-punishment.

Professor Grundy Completes a Book

Professor Grundy was panic-stricken. He had just received a telephone call from the editor in charge of production on his textbook manuscript (which, as you may remember, was considerably overdue). Because he had heard the words *breach of contract* and *by the end of the month* used in the same sentence, he concluded he had best accelerate his writing rate. He decided that he needed to write at least 10 pages every day and that he would need some motivation for doing so. He had bought a personal computer for word processing but had spent hours playing interactive games and communicating with others on bulletin boards and very little time processing words. He therefore provided himself with a supply of chocolate chip cookies, two styrofoam cups, and a number of marbles borrowed from his nephew Dennis. He figured out exactly how many bits of memory equaled a printed page. Before he sat down to work, he filled one styrofoam cup with marbles and set the other next to it. He also made a neat stack of 10 cookies. Mrs. Grundy agreed to cooperate by keeping his coffee cup constantly full. (She was motivated by the hope that her living room decor might eventually consist of something besides stacks of books, notecards, and crumpled yellow paper.)

Professor Grundy's preparations for writing had consumed almost an hour. He was tempted to take a break before beginning but restrained himself. He began putting words on the screen and at the end of each page ate 1 of the 10 cookies in his stack. Whenever he found his mind wandering, he transferred a marble from the full to the empty cup. He had decided he would have to write an extra page for each marble over 10 that accumulated in the previously empty cup.

Professor Grundy was very pleased with the effectiveness of his self-management system. "It's amazing," he thought to himself. "I've been using applied behavior analysis procedures on other people for years and even teaching students to do it. Why didn't I ever think to try it on myself?" He spent considerable time in self-congratulation and then, with a guilty start, transferred a marble and got back to work.

Self-Instruction

Self-instruction is a process of providing one's own verbal prompts. Prompting, as we discussed in Chapter 7, is necessary when discriminative stimuli are insufficient to set the occasion for the required response. Prompts are often supplied by others; self-instruction involves providing prompts for oneself. Many adults give themselves prompts when they engage in difficult or unfamiliar tasks. We talk ourselves through such activities as starting a new car or performing a complicated dance step. We use prompts like "*i before e except after c*" when we encounter a hurdle in letter writing. Some of us still sing the "ABC" jingle when looking for a name in the phone book. Teaching students to use self-instruction tactics enables them also to provide verbal prompts for themselves, rather than to remain dependent on others.

Self-instruction enables students to identify and guide themselves through the process necessary to solve problems. Training in self-instruction occurs before students are given problems to solve, questions to answer, or tasks to perform. Students who are taught self-instruction procedures may be able to generalize these strategies to other settings: for example, from one-to-one tutoring to the classroom (Bornstein & Quevillon, 1976). They may also be able to generalize across tasks: for example, from arithmetic or printing tasks to a phonics task not specifically trained but requiring similar process management for completion (Burgio, Whitman, & Johnson, 1980).

Teaching students self-instruction tactics has been effective in

1. Training children who are hyperactive and impulsive to increase their attending and on-task behaviors (Barkley, Copeland, & Sivage, 1980; Meichenbaum & Goodman, 1971; Peters & Davies, 1981).
2. Increasing students' ability to demonstrate academic skills (Borkowski, 1992; Bryant & Budd, 1982; Burgio, Whitman, & Johnson, 1980; Case, Harris, & Graham, 1992; Leon & Pepe, 1983).

3. Increasing appropriate social behaviors (Burron & Bucher, 1978; O'Leary, 1968).

4. Teaching a wide variety of skills to persons with moderate, severe, and profound disabilities (Browder & Shapiro, 1985; Lagomarcino, Hughes, & Rusch, 1989).

Most studies investigating self-instruction have used adaptations of a training sequence developed by Meichenbaum and Goodman (1971). A five-step training program for self-instruction successfully increased the self-control of second-graders who had been labeled hyperactive and thus increased their ability to attend to a task and to decrease errors. Students were taught individually using the following sequence (Meichenbaum & Goodman, 1971, p. 117):

1. An adult model performed a task while talking to himself out loud (cognitive modeling).

2. The student performed the same task under the direction of the model's instructions (overt, external guidance).

3. The student performed the task while instructing himself aloud (overt self-guidance).

4. The student whispered the instructions to himself as he went through the task (faded, overt self-guidance).

5. The student performed the task while guiding his performance via private speech (covert self-instruction).

Cognitive modeling

The cognitive model provided by the teacher and then rehearsed, overtly and covertly, by the student is shown in the following example for a task requiring the copying of line patterns:

Okay what is it I have to do? You want me to copy the picture with the different lines. I have to go slowly and carefully. Okay, draw the line down, down, good; then to the right, that's it; now down some more and to the left. Good. I'm doing fine so far. Remember, go slowly. Now back up again. No, I was supposed to go down. That's okay. Just erase the line carefully. . . . Good. Even if I make an error I can go on slowly and carefully. I have to go down now. Finished. I did it! (Meichenbaum & Goodman, 1971, p. 117).

For students to learn to imitate an effective and complete strategy, the teacher must include in the initial modeling several performance-relevant skills that guide the task process. These skills (Meichenbaum, 1977, p. 123) include

1. Problem definition ("What is it I have to do?")

2. Focusing attention and response guidance ("Carefully . . . draw the line down.")

3. Self-reinforcement ("Good, I'm doing fine.")

4. Self-evaluative coping skills and error-correction options ("That's okay. . . . Even if I make an error I can go on slowly.")

The same basic strategy has been used to teach kindergarten children with handwriting deficiencies to print the letters of the alphabet (Robin, Armel, & O'Leary, 1975), and fifth- and sixth-grade students with learning disabilities to solve word problems in arithmetic (Case, Harris, & Graham, 1992). Burgio, Whitman, and Johnson (1980) used a similar procedure to increase on-task behavior for students with mild retardation.

To train impulsive students to be more reflective and thus better able to finish a task, a teacher modeled the following strategy:

> Now let's see, what am I supposed to do? I have to find which of these (pointing to the six alternatives) goes into this space (pointing to the blank space in the rectangular figure). Good. Now I have to remember to go slowly and be sure to check each one of these carefully before I answer. Is this the one (pointing to the first alternative)? It's the same color but it looks different because the lines are thicker. Good, now I know it isn't this one. Now I have to check this next one (pointing to the second alternative). It looks different because there aren't any lines on it and this one (pointing to the standard) has lines on it. Good, now I know it isn't this one. Next I have to check this one (pointing to alternative three). It looks the same to me. The colors are the same and the lines are the same too. I think it might be this one but I have to check the other ones slowly and carefully before I choose . . . (continues to check remaining three alternatives one at a time). Good, I have checked them all and I have gone slowly and carefully. I think it is this one (points to the correct variant). (Peters & Davies, 1981, p. 379).

In a study to develop self-control for boys with chronic behavior problems during math and reading lessons, Barkley, Copeland, and Sivage (1980) added a group modeling process to self-instruction training. The teacher presented a problem and modeled its solution via self-instruction. She then divided the group of boys into smaller groups and presented a series of similar problems for each boy to solve using self-instruction techniques. Thus, the modeling of self-instruction was provided by both the teacher and the other boys in the group.

Four similar self-instruction steps were used in training 9-year-old boys who were under psychiatric care for hyperactive behavior (Palkes, Stewart, & Kahana, 1968). With these students, visual cues were added to encourage and remind them to use the self-instruction statements. These cues consisted of four 5×7 inch cards printed with instructions and self-directed commands (see Figure 12–6) and kept on the student's desk in front of him during task performance.

Factors influencing the effectiveness of self-instruction

Self-instruction can be a useful procedure for helping students become more independent and for maintaining and generalizing behavior change. Several factors (O'Leary & Dubey, 1979, paraphrased from pp. 450–451) appear to influence the effectiveness of self-instruction.

1. *Actual implementation of the procedure during task performance.* Roberts, Nelson, and Olson (1987), however, found no difference in performance between students who used self-instruction and those who had merely been taught a self-instructional strategy. They suggest that, at least in some cases,

FIGURE 12–6
Self-instruction
cuing cards

Note: From "Porteus maze performance of hyperactive boys after training in self-directed verbal commands," by H. Palkes, M. Stewart, & K. Kahana, 1968, Child Development, 39, p. 819. Copyright 1968 by Child Development. Reprinted by permission.

training in self-instruction to solve specific kinds of problems may simply be good academic instruction rather than a modification of cognitive processing.

2. *The ability of the students to perform the response in question.* Higa, Tharpe, and Calkins (1978) found that unless kindergarten and first-graders had practiced making a motor response, self-instructions actually interfered with performance. No amount of self-instruction will enable students to perform tasks not in their repertoire.

3. *Reinforcement for adhering to self-instructions.*

4. *Making the focus of instructions specific.* For example, Mishel and Patterson (1976) found nursery school children were better able to resist talking to a puppet if they specifically instructed themselves not to talk to the clown than if they reminded themselves with general instructions to work on their assigned tasks.

Results of self-instruction training have been somewhat inconsistent. Billings and Wasik (1985) recently failed to replicate the results of Bornstein and Quevillon's (1976) study cited earlier. Bornstein (1985) suggests that differential effects of the procedure may result from age, gender, intelligence, race, history, or attributional or cognitive style. Whitman (1987) suggests that self-instruction may be most successful with young children and persons with mental retardation who "have developed some language proficiency but have difficulty processing information given them by socialization agents and subsequently using this information in the absence of these socialization agents to regulate their behavior independently" (p. 216). Bornstein (1985) points out, "Quite simply, it appears that self-instructional programs can be effective, although obviously they are not always effective" (p. 70). As we have said before, "Nothing always works."

Most self-instructional procedures are taught in combination with self-monitoring and self-reinforcement. Thus, students provide for themselves both antecedents to behavior and consequences for correct performance.

SUMMARY

This chapter has described a number of techniques for transferring behavior management from teachers to students. Several advantages come with such transfer. Students become more independent. Their behavior may be maintained and generalized in settings where no intervention is in effect. The emphasis is changed from short-term intervention designed to change a single target behavior to the acquisition of strategies that may be used to change many behaviors over the long term. Discussion of self-management procedures may seem contradictory to the emphasis on overt, observable behavior throughout this book. Some of the processes described in this chapter, such as covert self-instruction, are not directly observable. It must be pointed out, however, that the emphasis, as always, is on changes in behaviors that are observable. For example, although we cannot observe students' covert self-instruction, we can observe that they perform academic tasks more rapidly and more accurately than before they were taught to use the procedure.

DISCUSSION QUESTIONS

1. Design a self-management program for yourself. Include self-recording, self-monitoring, and self-reinforcement.

2. Implement the program and see if you can change your own behavior. Describe the change process.

REFERENCES

Baer, D. M. 1984. Does research on self-control need more control? *Analysis and Intervention in Developmental Disabilities, 4*, 211–284.

Baker, L. 1982. An evaluation of the role of metacognitive deficits in learning disabilities. *Topics in Learning and Learning Disabilities, 2*(1), 27–35.

Barkley, R., Copeland, A., & Sivage, C. 1980. A self-control classroom for hyperactive children. *Journal of Autism and Developmental Disorders, 10*, 75–89.

Billings, D.C., & Wasik, B.H. 1985. Self-instructional training with preschoolers: An attempt to replicate. *Journal of Applied Behavior Analysis, 18*, 61–67.

Bolstad, O., & Johnson, S. 1972. Self-regulation in the modification of disruptive classroom behavior. *Journal of Applied Behavior Analysis, 5,* 443–454.

Borkowski, J.G. 1992. Metacognitive theory: A framework for teaching literacy, writing, and math skills. *Journal of Learning Disabilities, 25*(4), 253–257.

Bornstein, P.H. 1985. Self-instructional training: A commentary and state-of-the-art. *Journal of Applied Behavior Analysis, 18,* 69–72.

Bornstein, P.H., & Quevillon, R.P. 1976. The effects of a self-instructional package on overactive preschool boys. *Journal of Applied Behavior Analysis, 9,* 179–188.

Broden, M., Hall, R.V., & Mitts, B. 1971. The effect of self-recording on the classroom behavior of two eighth-grade students. *Journal of Applied Behavior Analysis, 4,* 191–199.

Browder, D.M., & Shapiro, E.S. 1985. Applications of self-management to individuals with severe handicaps: A review. *Journal of the Association for Persons with Severe Handicaps, 10,* 200–208.

Brownell, K.D., Coletti, G., Ersner-Hershfield, R., Hershfield, S.M., & Wilson, G.T. 1977. Self-control in school children: Stringency and leniency in self-determined and externally imposed performance standards. *Behavior Therapy, 8,* 442–455.

Bryant, L.E., & Budd, K.S. 1982. Self-instructional training to increase independent work performance in preschoolers. *Journal of Applied Behavior Analysis, 15,* 259–271.

Burgio, L.D., Whitman, T.L., & Johnson, M.R. 1980. A self-instructional package for increasing attending behavior in educable mentally retarded children. *Journal of Applied Behavior Analysis, 13,* 443–459.

Burron, D., & Bucher, B. 1978. Self-instructions as discriminative cues for rule-breaking or rule-following. *Journal of Experimental Child Psychology, 26,* 46–57.

Case, L.P., Harris, K.R., & Graham, S. 1992. Improving the mathematical problem-solving skills of students with learning disabilities. *Journal of Special Education, 26*(1), 1–19.

Cautela, J.R. 1971. Covert conditioning. In A. Jacobs & L.B. Sachs (Eds.), *The psychology of private events: Perspective on covert response systems.* New York: Academic Press.

Connis, R.T. 1979. The effects of sequential pictorial cues, self-recording, and praise on the job task

sequencing of retarded adults. *Journal of Applied Behavior Analysis, 12,* 355–361.

Dewey, J. 1939. *Experience and education.* New York: Macmillan.

Digangi, S.A., Maag, J.W., & Rutherford, R.B. 1991. Self-graphing of on-task behavior: Enhancing the reactive effects of self-monitoring on on-task behavior and academic performance. *Learning Disability Quarterly, 14*(3), 221–230.

Drabman, R.S., Spitalnik, R., & O'Leary, K.D. 1973. Teaching self-control to disruptive children. *Journal of Abnormal Psychology, 82,* 10–16.

Felixbrod, J.J., & O'Leary, K.D. 1974. Self-determination of academic standards by children: Toward freedom from external control. *Journal of Educational Psychology, 66,* 845–850.

Fredericksen, L.W., & Fredericksen, C.B. 1975. Teacher determined and self-determined token reinforcement in a special education classroom. *Behavior Therapy, 6,* 310–314.

Glynn, E.L., Thomas, J.D., & Shee, S.M. 1973. Behavioral self-control of on-task behavior in an elementary classroom. *Journal of Applied Behavior Analysis, 6,* 105–113.

Hallahan, D.P., Kneedler, R.D., & Lloyd, J.W. 1983. Cognitive behavior modification techniques for learning disabled children: Self-instruction and self-monitoring. In J.D. McKinney and L. Feagans (Eds.) *Current topics in learning disabilities* (vol. 1). Norwood, NJ: Ablex.

Harris, K.R. 1986. Self-monitoring of attentional behavior versus self-monitoring of productivity: Effects on on-task behavior and academic response rate among learning disabled children. *Journal of Applied Behavior Analysis, 19,* 417–423.

Hayes, S.C., & Nelson, R.O. 1983. Similar reactivity produced by external cues and self-monitoring. *Behavior Modification, 7,* 183–196.

Hayes, S.C., Rosenfarb, I., Wulfert, E., Munt, E.D., Korn, Z., & Zettle, R.D. 1985. Self-reinforcement effects: An artifact of social standard setting? *Journal of Applied Behavior Analysis, 18,* 201–214.

Heins, E.D., Lloyd, J.W., & Hallahan, D.P. 1986. Cued and noncued self-recording of attention to task. *Behavior Modification, 10,* 235–254.

Higa, W.R., Tharpe, R.G., & Calkins, R.P. 1978. Developmental verbal control of behavior: Implications for self-instructional training. *Journal of Experimental Child Psychology, 26,* 489–497.

Humphrey, L.L., Karoly, P., & Kirschenbaum, D.S. 1978. Self-management in the classroom: Self-imposed response cost versus self-reward. *Behavior Therapy, 9,* 592–601.

Hundert, J., & Bucher, B. 1978. Pupils' self-scored arithmetic performance: A practical procedure for maintaining accuracy. *Journal of Applied Behavior Analysis, 11,* 304.

Israel, A.C. 1978. Some thoughts on correspondence between saying and doing. *Journal of Applied Behavior Analysis, 11,* 271–276.

James, J.C., Trap, J., & Cooper, J.O. 1977. Technical report: Students' self-recording of manuscript letter strokes. *Journal of Applied Behavior Analysis, 10,* 509–514.

Kanfer, F. 1975. Self-management methods. In F. Kanfer & A. Goldstein (Eds.), *Helping people change: A textbook of methods.* New York: Pergamon Press.

Kaufman, K.F., & O'Leary, K.D. 1972. Reward, cost, and self-evaluation procedures for disruptive adolescents in a psychiatric hospital school. *Journal of Applied Behavior Analysis, 5,* 293–309.

Kazdin, A.E. 1975. *Behavior modification in applied settings.* Homewood, IL: Dorsey Press.

Kern-Dunlap, L., Dunlap, G., Clarke, S., Childs, K.E., White, R.L., & Stewart, M.P. 1992. Effects of a video tape feedback package on the peer interactions of children with serious behavioral and emotional challenges. *Journal of Applied Behavior Analysis,* 25, 355–364.

Kiburz, C.S., Miller, S.R., & Morrow, L.W. 1984. Structured learning using self-monitoring to promote maintenance and generalization of social skills across settings for a behaviorally disordered adolescent. *Behavior Disorders, 10,* 47–54.

Kneedler, R.D., & Hallahan, D.P. 1981. Self-monitoring of on-task behavior with learning-disabled children: Current studies and directions. *Exceptional Education Quarterly, 1,* 73–82.

Kohlberg, L., Yaeger, J., & Hjertholm, E. 1968. Private speech: Four studies and a review of theories. *Child Development, 39,* 691–736.

Lagomarcino, T.R., Hughes, C., & Rusch, F.R. 1989. Utilizing self-management to teach independence on the job. *Education and Training of the Mentally Retarded, 24*(2), 139–148.

Leon, J.A., & Pepe, H.J. 1983. Self-instructional training: Cognitive behavior modification for remediating arithmetic deficits. *Exceptional Children, 50,* 54–60.

Lovitt, T.C. 1973. Self-management projects with children with behavioral disabilities. *Journal of Learning Disabilities, 6,* 138–154.

Lovitt, T.C., & Curtiss, K.A. 1969. Academic response rate as a function of teacher- and self-imposed contingencies. *Journal of Applied Behavior Analysis, 2,* 49–53.

McKenzie, T.L., & Rushall, B.S. 1974. Effects of self-recording on attendance and performance in a competitive swimming training environment. *Journal of Applied Behavior Analysis, 7,* 199–206.

McLaughlin, T.F. 1976. Self-control in the classroom. *Review of Educational Research, 46,* 631–663.

Meichenbaum, D.H. 1977. *Cognitive-behavior modification: An integrative approach.* New York: Plenum Press.

Meichenbaum, D.H., & Goodman, J. 1971. Training impulsive children to talk to themselves: A means of developing self-control. *Journal of Abnormal Psychology, 77,* 115–126.

Mishel, W., & Patterson, C.J. 1976. Substantive and structural elements of effective plans for self-control. *Journal of Personality and Social Psychology, 34,* 942–950.

Morrow, L.W., Burke, J.G., & Buell, B.J. 1985. Effects of a self-recording procedure on the attending to task behavior and academic productivity of adolescents with multiple handicaps. *Mental Retardation, 23,* 137–141.

Nelson, R.O., Lipinski, D.P., & Boykin, R.A. 1978. The effects of self-recorders' training and the obtrusiveness of the self-recording device on the accuracy and reactivity of self-monitoring. *Behavior Therapy, 9,* 200–208.

O'Brien, T.P., Riner, L.S., & Budd, K.S. 1983. The effects of a child's self-evaluation program on compliance with parental instructions in the home. *Journal of Applied Behavior Analysis, 16,* 69–79.

O'Leary, K.D. 1968. The effects of self-instruction on immoral behavior. *Journal of Experimental Child Psychology, 6,* 297–301.

O'Leary, S.G., & Dubey, D.R. 1979. Applications of self-control procedures by children: A review. *Journal of Applied Behavior Analysis, 12,* 449–465.

Palkes, H., Stewart, M., & Kahana, K. 1968. Porteus maze performance of hyperactive boys after training in self-directed verbal commands. *Child Development, 39*, 817–826.

Peters, R., & Davies, K. 1981. Effects of self-instructional training on cognitive impulsivity of mentally retarded adolescents. *American Journal of Mental Deficiency, 85*, 377–382.

Prater, M.A., Joy, R., Chilman, B., Temple, J., & Miller, S.R. 1991. Self-monitoring of on-task behavior by adolescents with learning disabilities. *Learning Disability Quarterly, 14*(3), 164–177.

Rachlin, H. 1974. Self-control. *Behaviorism, 2*, 94–107.

Rhode, G., Morgan, D.P., & Young, K.R. 1983. Generalization and maintenance of treatment gains of behaviorally handicapped students from resource rooms to regular classrooms using self-evaluation procedures. *Journal of Applied Behavior Analysis, 16*, 171–188.

Roberts, R.N., Nelson, R.O., & Olson, T.W. 1987. Self-instruction: An analysis of the differential effects of instruction and reinforcement. *Journal of Applied Behavior Analysis, 20*, 235–242.

Robin, A.L., Armel, S., & O'Leary, K.D. 1975. The effects of self-instruction on writing deficiencies. *Behavior Therapy, 6*, 178–187.

Rosenbaum, M.S., & Drabman, R.S. 1979. Self-control training in the classroom: A review and critique. *Journal of Applied Behavior Analysis, 12*, 467–485.

Rudrud, E.H., Ziarnik, J.P., & Colman, G. 1984. Reduction of tongue protrusion of a 24-year-old woman with Down syndrome through self-monitoring. *American Journal of Mental Deficiency, 88*, 647–652.

Rueda, R., Rutherford, R., & Howell, K. 1980. Review of self-control research with behaviorally disordered and mentally retarded children. *Monograph in Behavioral Disorders* (pp. 188–197). Tempe, AZ: Teacher Educators for Children with Behavioral Disorders.

Sagotsky, G., Patterson, C.J., & Lepper, M.R. 1978. Training children's self-control: A field experiment in self-monitoring and goal-setting in the classroom. *Journal of Experimental Child Psychology, 25*, 242–253.

Santogrossi, D.A., O'Leary, K.D., Romanczyk, R.G., & Kaufman, K.F. 1973. Self-evaluation by adolescents in a psychiatric hospital school token program. *Journal of Applied Behavior Analysis, 6*, 277–287.

Short, E.J., & Weissberg-Benchell, J. 1989. The triple alliance for learning: Cognition, metacognition, and motivation. In C.B. McCormick, G.E. Miller, and M. Pressley (Eds.), *Cognitive strategy research: From basic research to educational applications* (pp. 33–63). New York: Springer-Verlag.

Snoy, M.T., & Van Benten, L. 1978. Self-modification technique for the control of eating behavior for the visually handicapped. *Education of the Visually Handicapped, 10*, 20–24.

Stevenson, H.C., & Fantuzzo, J.W. 1984. Application of the "generalization map" to a self-control intervention with school-aged children. *Journal of Applied Behavior Analysis, 17*, 203–212.

Sugai, G., & Rowe, P. 1984. The effect of self-recording on out-of-seat behavior of an EMR student. *Education and Training of the Mentally Retarded, 19*, 23–28.

Turkewitz, H., O'Leary, K.D., & Ironsmith, M. 1975. Generalization and maintenance of appropriate behavior through self-control. *Journal of Consulting and Clinical Psychology, 43*, 577–583.

Wallace, I. 1977. Self-control techniques of famous novelists. (Introduction by J.J. Pear.) *Journal of Applied Behavior Analysis, 10*, 515–525.

Whitman, T.L. 1987. Self-instruction, individual differences, and mental retardation. *American Journal of Mental Deficiency, 92*, 213–223.

Whitman, T.L. 1990. Self-regulation and mental retardation. *American Journal on Mental Retardation, 94*(4), 347–362.

Wood, R., & Flynn, J.M. 1978. A self-evaluation token system versus an external evaluation token system alone in a residential setting with predelinquent youths. *Journal of Applied Behavior Analysis, 11*, 503–512.

13

Teaching Behavior-Change Procedures to Others

- While Ms. Rose was using backward chaining to teach Cynthia to put on her sweater at school, Cynthia's mother was hurriedly dressing her daughter every day without giving the girl a chance to demonstrate or practice what she knew. The mother didn't know Cynthia had learned to dress herself at school.

- Jim, the part-time assistant in Ms. Rose's classroom, spent the early days of Cynthia's dressing program trying to get Cynthia to "start at the beginning" in putting on her sweater.

- Suzie, one of Cindy's classmates, decided on her own to help Cindy learn to put on her sweater like Mike was helping Ronnie learn to raise his hand before speaking. Suzie had been giving Cindy some of her own tokens every time she saw Cindy put on her sweater.

- Ms. Rose found a teacher's work in changing behavior does not stop with the students. Parents, assistants, and other students can be effective monitors of behavior-change programs, but they can also interfere with or obstruct those programs if they don't understand or haven't been informed.

We have stressed the rec-
iprocal nature of behav-
ior change throughout
the text.

This chapter gives some guidelines for working with many kinds of helpers. Teachers are significant agents of change in their students' lives. They are, however, by no means the only people who influence a particular student's behavior. Every person who comes in contact with a student affects the student's behavior in some way. The behavior of the student, in turn, changes the behavior of other people. The teacher who is determined to provide students with the best possible learning environment must be concerned with all these interactions.

The other people whose behavior a teacher is most often concerned with include parents, paraprofessionals such as teachers' assistants, and the students' peers. As you probably surmised from the opening example, these people's efforts to change behavior may either facilitate or hinder the teacher in helping students move toward academic and behavioral goals. A parent who inadvertently reinforces inappropriate behavior in the child may make such behavior virtually impervious to extinction at school. A parent's inability to manage a child with disabilities at home may sometimes lead to otherwise unnecessary institutionalization of the child.

Students' learning in school is influenced by classroom personnel other than teachers. In recent years, more schools have responded to the demand for increased individualization of instruction by hiring noncertified personnel to serve as assistants to teachers. Many teachers consider this a mixed blessing. Although almost always well-meaning, persons with little training may be unaware of the needs of students and may bring to the classroom preconceptions that prevent their being helpful to students. Peers are also very influential in determining patterns of behavior (Patterson, Littman, & Bricker, 1967; Solomon & Wahler, 1973). Their importance is significant even with younger children but becomes especially strong when students reach adolescence. It is wasteful not to harness this influence for good. Students affect not only the behavior of their peers but also that of adults. An understanding of the effects their behavior has on parents and teachers can enable students to be active managers of their environment.

The influence of parents, paraprofessionals, and peers can be positive as well as negative. Teachers can help these other change agents to be helpful by working with them. Sharing the principles and techniques of applied behavior analysis with others, the focus of this chapter, is one way to provide this help.

FAMILIES

Intervention for children
with disabilities must be
family centered.

Perhaps the most significant recent development in the provision of educational services to children with disabilities has been a change in attitudes toward the families of these children. Historically there has been a tendency either to view parents as the cause of their children's problems or as victims of their child's disability. Dunlap, Robbins, and Darrow (1994) report that educators are "becoming increasingly sensitive to an alternative perspective; namely that family systems are characterized often by great strengths that enable families to adapt and function successfully even in the presence of very serious challenges" (p. 211). Along with this changing perspective has come an emphasis on empowering parents and including them as collaborative partners in designing and delivering their child's education (Shea & Bauer, 1991). It is no longer considered sufficient simply to inform parents or to invite them to become involved as a courtesy. Services to children with disabilities must be family-centered (Raver & Kilgo, 1991) and must consider first, not as an afterthought, families' cultural norms, goals for all family members, resources, and desires. Making families a part of the educational process requires a good deal of effort, but it can result in much better progress for students. There is no question that parents can be effective teachers of their children (Turnbull & Turnbull, 1990). Not all parents, however, wish to teach their children at home what they believe the child should be learning at school. Sometimes teachers' well-meaning efforts to solicit parental assistance antagonize parents. Consider the very understandable reply to the following note received by a parent:

Dear Parent,

Virginia missed 10 problems on her math test. Please work on this at home.

REPLY:

Dear Teacher, Virginia left all her clothes on the bathroom floor again last night. Please work on this at school.

If the parent and teacher, after discussing Virginia's progress, had agreed that messiness contributed to Virginia's difficulty with math, each might determine ways to help Virginia become neater, thus making her more academically and socially successful. Because the emphasis in this text is on using applied behavior analysis techniques, we will stress helping families use these techniques to change behaviors of concern to family members. Parents report finding these techniques helpful (Dunlap, Robbins, & Darrow, 1994) and educators can assist families in learning and implementing them in several ways. Teachers may be consulted about parents' problems in managing behavior at home and may be asked to conduct training programs for parents concerned about behavior management.

Increasing concern with providing generalized behavior change is reflected in efforts to teach parents and others to use applied behavior analysis procedures consistently and correctly. Although these efforts have not always been successful (Forehand & Atkeson, 1977), perhaps it is time for professionals to concentrate on developing procedures that will enable parents to be effective behavior modifiers.

Planning with Parents

Parents of all young people in school should be aware of the teacher's plans for the year and, if possible, should be included in making these plans. Parent involvement in planning is mandated by law for children in special education programs, but it can be an asset for all students. It may be difficult to reach some parents even to inform them about what is planned, but teachers should make the effort.

Some educators state that many parents don't seem to care about their children. This is almost invariably an unjust assumption. Parents may not respond to efforts to communicate with them for any number of reasons, including a generalized avoidance reaction to schools because of aversive experiences during childhood. Many parents have demands on their time, energy, and abilities to cope that are difficult for teachers to understand. Some parents may place less value on the educational process than do teachers, but this should not be interpreted as a lack of interest in their child. After several years of listening to negative reports about their offspring, parents may develop—rather than a lack of concern about the child—a total lack of interest in discussing her or him with teachers and other school personnel. A quick review of the discussion of punishment in Chapter 8 will make the dynamics of this situation abundantly clear.

Advantages of including parents in planning

Including parents in the planning process has many advantages for the teacher. Parents who are familiar with educational goals, teaching procedures, and management techniques are much more likely to be supportive. For example, a special education teacher who uses time-out will receive fewer irate phone calls about shutting students in rooms by themselves if parents are familiar with the technique and its purpose. The regular classroom teacher who elects to make field trips contingent on appropriate behavior should make this clear to parents in advance. Any teacher who uses behavior-change procedures in the classroom, either formally or informally, should at least familiarize parents with behavioral principles.

Implementation with Parental Support

Many behaviors that teachers wish to change may persist because they are reinforced outside school, inadvertently or otherwise. Parents may be unaware they are reinforcing such behaviors as tantrums, whining, procrastination, or dependence. Such behaviors are often as maladaptive at home as at school. Many parents, once made aware of the problem and provided with suggestions for changing behavior, will be of enormous support to the teacher's efforts to help students.

A word of caution is in order. Modifying the behavior of one's own child may be more difficult than modifying the behavior of other people's children. This scientifically unverified principle is illustrated in the following vignette.

The Behavior Modifier's Child Has No Shoelaces

Bas's mother teaches behavior management courses to university students and offers in-service training to teachers on the same topic. Bas attends the campus school at his mother's university and reports to her office after school. For two years, he arrived almost every afternoon with his shoelaces untied. On several occasions, however, the shoelaces were missing entirely, having fallen out during math class while Bas was seated perfectly still at his desk. Bas's mother, being an expert "behavior modifier," employed several sophisticated techniques to rectify the situation. Among the most notable of these were nagging, yelling, begging, and smacking Bas with his sneakers, which, predictably, tended to fall off when he walked fast.

Recently, however, Bas's shoelaces have been tied every afternoon. Naturally, his mother stopped mentioning shoelaces under these circumstances, until Bas asked if she wanted to know why they were tied. It seems one of Mother's colleagues, whose office Bas must pass to reach hers, became aware of the problem—not being profoundly deaf—and suggested Bas might like to earn a balloon for having his shoes tied in the afternoon. Results were immediate, and the behavior has been maintained for several months on a VR10-day schedule of reinforcement.

"If LaDonna needs hair ribbons, let her use her own shoelaces."

When asking parents to use behavior-change procedures with their children, long-standing behavior patterns may have to be broken before success will occur. Professionals must be prepared to offer support and encouragement.

Consultation with Parents

Clue for advice-givers

Regularly scheduled conferences with parents, supplemented by those called to deal with specific problems, provide many opportunities to share information. Parents frequently ask teachers to make suggestions about management of their children at home. Most people who regularly work with parents have found it advisable to avoid superficial advice, offering quick and easy solutions to problems. People who ask for advice frequently want only sympathy or confirmation that they are doing the most possible under the circumstances. Jong (1977) has suggested, "Advice is what you ask for when you already know the answer but wish you didn't" (p. 55). A clue to the sensitive teacher is the motorboat syndrome, in which every suggestion is met with a protest: but, but, but, but, but. This should be a signal to stop making suggestions and listen for the real concern. Price and Marsh (1985) offer helpful suggestions for conducting parent conferences.

If conferences are viewed as an opportunity to share information rather than as a vehicle merely to inform parents from a vantage of superior knowledge and wisdom, the teacher may learn a great deal about management of the child. Parents have the advantage of having known their child considerably longer than the teacher and may therefore be able to offer helpful insights into conditions precipitating inappropriate behavior and consequences that are likely to be reinforcing. When specific suggestions about handling behavior appear to be appropriate, phrase such suggestions as nontechnically as possible. Although the language of applied behavior analysis offers a precise means of communication among professionals, there is a fine line between precision of language and jargon. The teacher who urges parents to consider the importance of stimulus generalization in facilitating transfer across settings, when he means the student needs a desk at home where she can do her homework, has probably crossed this line. It is possible to be precise without pedantry.

Formal Parent Training

Efforts to teach parents behavioral techniques for managing their children have been reported since 1959, when Williams documented the home-based modification of temper tantrums. A wide range of behaviors has been modified, from autistic-like and self-injurious behavior of students with severe disabilities (Allen & Harris, 1964; Risley, 1968) to what has been described as Brat Syndrome (Bernal, Duryee, Pruett, & Burns, 1968). Parents have been trained individually in conferences and by telephone, through home visits (Johnson & Katz, 1973; Risley, 1968; Wetzel, Baker, Roney, & Martin, 1966), and through complicated laboratory procedures involving electronic cueing (Wahler, Winkel, Peterson, & Morrison, 1965). Other programs have used group training procedures (Galloway & Galloway, 1971; Lindsley, 1978; Patterson, Shaw, & Ebner, 1969). Parents have even learned to teach their children self-management strategies (O'Brien, Riner, & Budd, 1983).

In general, the results of parent training procedures have been somewhat equivocal, at least partly because of a lack of methodological rigor in evaluating the programs (Hornby & Singh, 1983). As with many behavioral procedures, early efforts concentrated on providing assistance rather than determining the efficacy of the assistance in a scientific manner. It also appears that some families use behavioral techniques more successfully than others (Robbins, Dunlap, & Plienis, 1991) and that family characteristics should be taken into account when planning programs. Hornby and Singh (1983) suggest that future reports of group training for parents should provide a more careful description of the parents and children involved, more explicit details about program organization, the goals of the intervention, leaders' training and experience, the training procedures used, and the content of the intervention program. O'Dell (1974) reviewed the literature on parent training and concluded that such training could be successful only if attention were given to choosing optimal methods of training and to providing for generalization and maintenance of the skills learned. Several studies have addressed the issue of generalization and maintenance. Allen, Bryant, and Bailey (1986) suggest that both written instructions and direct intervention by professionals in the home are successful in increasing generalization, but that written instructions are more cost-effective. Singh and Kaushik (1982) suggest that a combination of specific instructions, demonstrations, and general instructions facilitates generalization. The parent training program outlined in this chapter addresses all these considerations. The following sections also discuss group organization, planning, and implementation.

ORGANIZING PARENT GROUPS

Steps in organizing a parents' group

The first step in organizing a group of parents interested in learning behavior-change procedures is choosing a group leader or leaders. Group leaders fill several roles in parent groups. They provide basic information in lecture, demonstration, discussion, and practice activities. They answer questions and provide feedback. They provide positive reinforcement for parents' efforts to learn applied behavior analysis principles and to change their children's behavior. In short, they are teachers.

Choosing group leaders

Ability to teach should not, however, be the only criterion for choosing leaders. Personal characteristics may be more important than impressive credentials. A parent who has successfully completed a training program and who is perceived as warm, caring, and sympathetic may be a more effective teacher than a clinical psychologist who lectures dryly and who may be perceived as cold, superior, and unsympathetic. Of course, the same would be true of a warm, caring psychologist and a cold, unsympathetic parent. Teachers are often called on as parent trainers and may have the advantage of familiarity with at least some of the parents and their children.

It is frequently advantageous to have two group leaders. Aside from the obvious considerations of not having to cancel sessions in case of illness or other unexpected events, two group leaders may complement one another in experience, personality, and point of view. The leaders may be a psychologist and teacher, parent and teacher, or any other combination of people who work well together. It is most important that the leaders agree on basic principles and techniques. If both group leaders are professionals, their credibility will be enormously enhanced if at least one of them is a parent as well. Parents are often understandably reluctant to accept suggestions about how to manage children at home from people who have never undertaken such a project.

Once group leaders have been chosen, the composition of the group can be considered. Parents should volunteer for membership; requiring parents to attend parent training programs to keep their children enrolled in a given program is difficult to enforce and may result in hostile, uncooperative groups. Advertisement may encourage parents to volunteer for the initial group. If the first group of parents finds the process helpful, word of mouth will encourage other parents to attend subsequent sessions. Considerable thought should be given to characteristics of the parents in a group and to the characteristics of their children. A mixed group can be successful, but we recommend "different groups for different troops" (Arnold, Rowe, & Tolbert, 1978, p. 124). There are advantages to achieving homogeneity along several criteria.

Severity of Disability

Parents of typical children, gifted children, and children with mild disabilities often have similar management problems. On the other hand, the needs of parents of children with moderate and severe disabilities may best be met in a group of parents whose children are more similar. Parents who take turns sitting up all night with a child with autism who seems never to sleep and who leaves the house and wanders onto the expressway if left unattended may react negatively to the concern of the parents of a child who won't go to bed on time because she wants to read the encyclopedia all night.

Age of Children

Management problems differ with children of different ages. It is almost impossible to deal specifically with everything from toilet training to the hazards of drug addiction and sexual promiscuity in one group. Separation into preschool, elementary, junior high or middle school, and secondary age groups may provide a more helpful setting.

Socioeconomic and Educational Level

Management of children is a problem for parents at all socioeconomic levels. Neither affluence nor an extensive educational background guarantees superior child-rearing skills. A group of parents from many sectors of the community may find surprising commonality in their concerns about their children, but there are also significant differences. Available solutions may also be different. If the majority of the group is, for example, from an affluent suburban area, a solitary member who is less well educated, less articulate, and noticeably less well dressed may feel very uncomfortable. The problems faced by parents who are poor or culturally different may be very different from those of the more affluent. The two best approaches may be to choose either a group with a number of members from various socioeconomic levels or one with members from similar communities.

Single Parents

The problems encountered by single parents are unique in some ways. Divorce, separation, or death of a parent often increases children's behavior problems (Gardner, 1978; Kessler, 1966). The single parent is also faced with the necessity of managing such behavior alone. Single parents may feel their problems are different from those of two-parent homes and the difficulties others have are minimized by the presence of two parents to handle them. This attitude may undermine group effectiveness. No group will ever have perfect homogeneity, whether of children or parents. We do, however, suggest considering the effects of the group's composition on its success.

The size of the group is also important. Lindsley (1978) suggested beginning with a large group, perhaps 30, anticipating some dropouts. It has been the authors' experience that sometimes a smaller group, of 10 or 12, results in more commitment and fewer dropouts. It is difficult however, to maintain a task-oriented relationship in a very small group. Although 6 to 10 participants are recommended for parent counseling (Dinkmeyer & Carlson, 1973), because the purpose of the groups we are describing is teaching rather than counseling, slightly larger groups are recommended.

PLANNING PARENT TRAINING SESSIONS

Good teaching is important for adults, too.

In planning for parent training, the group leaders should remember that principles that affect children's learning also affect adults' learning. The following aspects of good teaching are applicable when working with parents:

1. The arrangement of the physical environment affects behavior by providing cues for certain acts.   If parents found their school years aversive, they may react to meeting in a classroom by becoming withdrawn or hostile. In contrast, if meetings are held around the fire in someone's living room, behavior such as extraneous conversation more appropriate at social events may occur. A businesslike, comfortable location, like a conference room with tables and chairs, will provide an environment most conducive to a task-oriented discussion. It is always vital to remember the process under way is teaching, not counseling. Group therapy or counseling is a complex process for which teachers are not qualified. If parents need therapy or counseling, they should be referred to qualified professionals.

2. The group leaders' verbal and nonverbal behavior at the outset will set the tone for future group interaction.   A leader who is introduced as Dr. Jones, a well-known expert on child-rearing, may occasion different responses from one who is introduced as Charlie, whom some of you may remember as the "nerd" in the PTA program. This may be true even if both introductions refer to the same person. A leader dressed in jeans and sweatshirt should expect different responses from one wearing a fashionable designer suit. The wise leader will consider the custom of the community regarding both dress and manner of address and attempt to conform to some degree.

3. Teaching occurs only when a response is required.   Telling is not teaching with adults any more than with children. Participants must have the opportunity to apply the procedures discussed and to receive feedback.

4. Positive reinforcement accelerates learning for adults as well as for children.   Although changes in their children's behavior may provide some reinforcement, this may not be sufficient. Various incentives have been used—from reduced fees to trips to the hairdresser and steak dinners (Johnson & Katz, 1973). One of the authors once led a group that provided an evening's babysitting to each family that attended all sessions and completed all assignments. The sitters were high-school members of a Future Teachers of America club, who volunteered their time as part of their public-service commitment. The praise and encouragement of the group leaders and other group members are potential reinforcers. Positive reinforcement for group members should be directed toward increasing attendance, participation, record-keeping, and persistence in implementing difficult procedures, such as extinction, with their children.

General Format

Once leaders have been selected and the group formed, a decision must be made about how often and for how long the group will meet. There is no hard-and-fast rule about either decision. The authors have found that once-a-week sessions, lasting from 60 to 90 minutes and meeting for about 10 weeks, appear to work well. It is usually easier for parents to arrange to attend once a week than more frequently. Flexible time scheduling allows the leaders to complete the formal part of the session and to have time for individual questions parents may not feel comfortable raising in front of the group. A statement, such as "The group will meet from 7:30 to 8:30, but we [the leaders] will plan to be here until around 9:00 if some of you have questions," may encourage parents to bring up their individual concerns.

Each session follows the same general format:

1. Discussion of previous week's assignment
2. A teaching segment consisting of lecture, demonstration, or discussion
3. Practice activities
4. Assignment for the next week

The following sections follow this format in describing one possible 10-week course. To demonstrate the process parents may go through as they progress through the group, we shall apply each procedure to Woody, a student described in the following vignette.

Woody

Woody is an 8-year-old student who attends second grade at Parkview School. He spends most of his school day in the regular classroom and an hour in a resource room for children with learning and behavior problems. Woody is making excellent progress academically in the resource room. However, he frequently fails to complete tasks in the resource room and in the regular class. His work is invariably messy and disorganized. A recent conference with Woody's parents revealed they are having many problems with him at home. He often fails to come directly home from school and, on at least one occasion, was so late his mother called the police. He dawdles and procrastinates when getting ready for school, eating meals, doing homework, and performing any task he is asked to do. He consistently leaves his clothes and toys strewn from one end of the house to another. Woody's parents took the following 10-session parent training program.

Session 1

Session 1: Pinpointing Behavior

1. Discussion of previous week's assignment.   Because this is the first session, there will, of course, have been no assignment. Leaders should introduce themselves (after due consideration of the possible effects of such introductions) and ask parents to introduce themselves and to describe their child or children, including the children's ages and what general problems have brought the parents to the group. At this point, the advantage of the group leaders' having children may be demonstrated. The leaders may model the desired behavior before asking parents to perform. A leader who has children may describe some behavior of his or her child that causes concern and then carry out behavior-change projects along with the group members throughout the sessions.

2. Teaching segment.   The major goal of the first session is to help participants accurately describe behavior. After introductions, one of the leaders describes pinpointing, using several examples, in a 5- or 10-minute minilecture.

3. Practice activities.   Each parent is asked to refine the description of the child's problem given during the introduction. Parents should be reinforced for approximations until they have accomplished a behavioral description. It often takes considerable effort to get from

lack of respect	to	swears at mother
poor table manners	to	belches at the dinner table
irresponsibility	to	loses his lunchbox
easily frustrated	to	screams when expected to dress herself

Once participants are able to describe behavior in observable terms, they must choose a countable behavior they wish to increase. This requirement may produce a long moment of total silence; many parents, like teachers, tend to focus on behaviors they want to decrease. Again, modeling and demonstration by the group leaders are excellent teaching devices. Parents' approximations toward pinpointing should be positively reinforced to shape them toward the goal. Behaviors appropriate to event recording should be chosen. Although some behaviors parents want to increase may require time sampling (homework, staying in bed after bedtime) or latency recording (getting dressed, compliance), these procedures should not be introduced until later in the course.

4. Assignment for next week. Give each parent a chart similar to the one in Figure 13–1, which provides space for each day of the week. This simple chart may be used for behaviors that occur once a day (use a plus if, for example, the child gets up the first time she's called or a minus if she doesn't) or for more frequently occurring behaviors (put a tally mark every time the child complies with an instruction). Ask each parent to write the target behavior on the chart during the session so that no confusion will occur. The assignment is to observe, count, and chart the target behavior for at least five consecutive days and bring the chart back for Session 2. Provide the parents with written instructions for the assignment at this and all subsequent sessions. These written instructions can be kept in a looseleaf notebook and referred to long after the last session.

Session 2

Session 2: Positive Reinforcement

1. Discussion of previous week's assignment. Devote the beginning of this session to discussing the charts. The trainers, as in every session, begin by dis-

FIGURE 13–1
Chart for parents to record behavior

Name_____

Behavior_____

Day	M	T	W	T	F	S	S

FIGURE 13–2
Woody's chart

Name_____

Behavior_____

Day

M	T	W	T	F	S	S
+	–	–	+	–		

playing their charts. Congratulate parents for recording the behavior and for remembering to bring charts. Parents who are present but who failed to bring materials should not receive an undue share of the trainers' attention, as is likely to happen if elaborate explanations of the reasons for failure are allowed. Devote the majority of trainer time to those who followed instructions. Discuss and clear up any problems. Woody's chart is shown in Figure 13–2.

2. Teaching segment.   Discuss the principle of positive reinforcement in very simple terms. Use words such as reward or positive consequence if parents are likely to be resistant to the technical term. Reinforcers may be described as

a. Tangible (including money)
b. Activities
c. Praise

Although money is technically a token reinforcer, for this audience it may be grouped with tangibles. Encourage parents to choose either a tangible or an activity as a reinforcer of the target behavior, and urge them to pair it consistently with praise. The list in Table 13–1 may help parents identify a positive reinforcer. Urge parents to choose something that may be earned daily rather than weekly and that can be administered immediately. For example, Woody might be allowed to have a special snack (usually unavailable) on days when he gets home by 3:30. The major goal of this first assignment is to ensure that parents are reinforced for implementing the behavior-change project. This will occur only if the project works.

3. Practical activities.   Use demonstration and rehearsal until parents are able to

a. Describe the program clearly to the child: "Woody, it's important to me that you come straight home from school. On days when you do, you may have a Supercookie for a snack. The Supercookies are only for days when you are home before Power Rangers starts at 3:30."
b. Demonstrate positive social reinforcement: "Woody, you got home from school before 3:30. I'm proud of you. You can eat your Supercookie in the den while you watch Power Rangers."

TABLE 13-1
Suggested positive reinforcers (to be used by parents)

Preschool Children

Tangibles: any food the child likes that is limited because of concern about nutrition
                  or dental health
              small toys
              activity or coloring books
              pennies
              Underoos® (perfect for toilet training)

Activities: television time
              playing records
              excursions—to library, museum, zoo, department store
              helping parents with housework
              games

Elementary School-aged Children

Tangibles: food, otherwise unavailable
              records, tapes
              toys
              comic books
              magazines
              money

Activities: television time
              late bedtime
              reading in bed
              sleeping on the floor with a sleeping bag
              having a friend sleep over
              cooking
              picnics (eating peanut butter and jelly sandwich in the backyard)
              excursions

Adolescents

Tangibles: money
              clothing
              records, tapes
              something expensive and possibly unattractive (to parents) done to hair,
                  face, or body (e.g., frizzy perm)

Activities: access to car keys (may be earned in 15-minute increments)
              late curfew
              getting a part-time job

c. Demonstrate a verbal procedure to use when the child fails to perform the behavior: "Woody, it's 3:45. To get a Supercookie, you have to be home before 3:30, so no Supercookie today." Parents should also have the opportunity to rehearse each kind of statement for the behavior they are trying to change. Feedback and correction may be provided by the leaders and other participants.

4. Assignment for next week.   The assignment for the next week is to implement the reinforcement strategy and to continue to record the behavior on the chart, which should be brought to Session 3.

Session 3

Session 3: Token Systems

A "stroke" is a positive reinforcer.

1. Discussion of previous week's assignment.   The chances of 100% success on this first project are high. Everyone will be ready to try for more changes as quickly as possible. Some parents may not have been successful, however, and will need much encouragement. Every effort should be made to determine what went wrong and to rectify the situation. Lindsley (1978, p. 89) suggested the following reasons for parents' lack of success with behavior-change procedures:

a. *Projecting stroke preference*: Just because a father enjoyed playing Monopoly as a child does not mean that the opportunity to play Monopoly will be rewarding to his son. It may even be punishing! "The child knows best."

b. *Loopholes in the welfare system*: A child would have to be stupid to change his behavior to earn a cookie if he can raid the cookie jar any time he wishes regardless. Parents need to close all leaks in the system, including indulgent grandparents. If necessary, locks can be put on cupboard or refrigerator. The behavior manager (parent) needs to control the strokes.

c. *Reaching for the unreachable star*: Idealism may be an admirable philosophy but can be frustrating to a child and his parent. Behavior goals and the intermediate steps to be rewarded need to be realistic and attainable so the child and parent can experience success.

d. *Failing to grow with the child*: An initially challenging goal can become dull and aversive as the child masters it and girds for bigger and better goals. The behavior manager needs to keep pace with the child's progress.

e. *Trying too hard or wanting too much for the child*: The parent who continually reminds the child about the reward and what must be done to earn it is not allowing the behavior mod system to work. Among other things, such a parent is contaminating the reward with an aversive stimulus—nagging.

2. Teaching segment.   Once any problems have been discussed, the trainers will describe token reinforcement, relating the use of tokens to the modification of adult behavior with money.

FIGURE 13–3
A home token sys-
tem chart

Name_____   Dates_____

Behavior: Points:

Day	M	T	W	T	F	S	S
Total earned							
Total spent							
Saved							
Available							

Points for bank_____

3. Practice activities.   Parents can now choose two or three behaviors to use on a slightly more complex chart (see Figure 13–3). All should be behaviors to increase, which may or may not include the behavior from Figure 13–1. If that program is going well, it can be left as is. The process of pinpointing may need to be described, practiced, and reinforced again.

Once target behaviors have been selected, parents should specify what tokens they wish to use. Points are the easiest to manage, but some parents may prefer to use stars, happy faces, or some other symbol. Also specify some back-up reinforcers at the meeting. Although there are advantages to including the child in this process, they are outweighed by the danger of having parents make their reinforcer menu at home. Parents sometimes have a great deal of difficulty selecting back-up reinforcers that are cheap enough (from the child's point of view) to make the system work. It is impor-tant to avoid extremely long-term requirements and to make some items

FIGURE 13–4
A home token system sample reinforcer

	What Woody's Points Earn
1 point	gum
5 points	make popcorn choose dinner menu
10 points	15 minutes late bedtime skip bath (no more than 20 points may be spent in one night, but points may accumlate for later use)
25 points	3 comic books 50¢ for ice cream dinner at McDonald's
50 points	skating on Saturday Saturday afternoon movie
100 points	have a friend spend the night (only Friday or Saturday)

available at least daily. Figure 13–4 illustrates a sample reinforcer menu prepared by Woody's parents.

4. Assignment for next week.   The assignment for Session 4 is to bring the chart recording the implemented home token system.

Session 4

Session 4: Extinction

1. Discussion of previous week's assignment.   Handle any problem with the token system at the beginning of the meeting. Woody's chart is illustrated in Figure 13–5. Make changes in target behaviors, tokens received, and back-up reinforcers if necessary. For the time being, parents should make such changes only after consulting with the group leaders.

2. Teaching segment.   Describe the extinction principle in simple terms. Parents will probably agree that children do many inappropriate things "just to get attention." What it may be difficult to do is to convince them that the children will ultimately stop doing them if attention is not forthcoming. The trainers must make it clear that the behavior will escalate at first but persistence will pay off. Examples of behaviors frequently mentioned by parents are tantrums, crying, whining, begging, and interrupting phone conversations. Some of these behaviors are somewhat difficult to define precisely, but it can be done. Encourage parents to engage in some activity incompatible to attending to the behavior, such as counting to 100, reading a magazine, running the vacuum, engaging in a conversation with someone other than the child, listening to music with headphones, or, in extreme cases, standing

FIGURE 13–5
Woody's point chart

Name_____   Dates_____

Behavior: Points:
Ready to leave for school at 7:45   5
Clothes in hamper by 8:30 bedtime   5 (jeans, pants, shirt, 2 socks)
Toys in room by 8:30   5 (– 1 for each toy *not* in room)

Day	M	T	W	T	F	S	S
Ready for school	5	0	5	5	5		
Clothes	4	3	4	4	5	4	5
Toys	2	3	3	2	4	2	5
Total earned	11	6	12	11	14	8	10
Total spent	5	6	0	0	0	25	5
Saved	6	1	12	11	14	0	5
Available	6	7	19	30	44	27	33

Points for bank_____

under the shower. Parents should also reinforce themselves when they successfully ignore inappropriate behavior.

3. Practice activities.   It may be helpful to have parents role-play ignoring an escalating behavior. By now the members of the group will probably be familiar enough with one another to be comfortable doing this, particularly if the session leaders demonstrate first!

4. Assignment for next week.   The assignment is to continue the token program and to record the behavior to be decreased for three days before beginning extinction and for four days afterward. A chart similar to Figure 13–1 may be used.

Session 5: Factors of Time in Changing Behavior (Latency, Duration)

1. Discussion of previous week's assignment.   The discussion of the extinction procedure will almost certainly be lengthy. Reinforce persistence even if there has been no improvement. Parents should continue to record this behavior for another week.

2. Teaching segment.   Each participant should now identify a behavior in which time is a factor, such as obeying instructions promptly, finishing some task quickly, or persisting in some activity for a specified period of time. Specific examples might include obeying within 10 seconds (slow, subvocal count—one thousand one, one thousand two, and so on), getting dressed within 20 minutes of being awakened, finishing dinner in 25 minutes, reading a library book for 15 minutes, and working on homework for one hour. Although we are, in reality, considering aspects of latency and duration here, parents will continue to use event recording, simply counting the instances of occurrence of the time-related behavior. This behavior will be included in the existing token economy.

Using a kitchen timer is recommended for behaviors measured in minutes rather than seconds. For example, if his mother wants Woody to finish his dinner within 25 minutes, she will set the timer for 25 minutes when Woody sits down at the table. She will record points earned if he has finished before the timer rings.

3. Practice activities.   Rehearsal of instructions to the child and practicing pairing of praise with points will take place if there is time.

4. Assignment for next week.   The assignment includes adding the new (time-related) behavior to the chart already in use and continuing to record the results of the extinction procedure.

Session 6: Thinning Reinforcers

1. Discussion of previous week's assignment.   Use the beginning of this session for a general review of progress made so far, as well as for a discussion of the previous week's progress. Provide a recapitulation of what has been taught. Parents should assess the overall effectiveness of their own programs.

2. Teaching segment.   Parents may have begun to wonder whether they will have to continue to reinforce every instance of appropriate behavior forever. This is a good time to introduce the concept of intermittent reinforcement. Suggest that parents explain to their child that one behavior on the chart must be performed for two days in a row before points can be earned. This week, change the schedule for only one behavior.

3. Practice activities.   Parents may be asked to rehearse what they will say to their child about thinning the reinforcement schedule. Anticipate problems such as protests ("It's not fair") and practice responses.

4. Assignment for next week.   The assignment is to continue charting for the token economy. The recording of extinction may be dropped if success has been achieved.

Session 7

Session 7: Punishment

1. Discussion of previous week's assignment.   Discuss any problems that occurred with thinning the schedule at this time. Parents may choose to thin the reinforcement schedule for a second behavior.

2. Teaching segment.   Describe function of punishment. Parents may find it difficult to relate the loss of points to what they have previously attempted to use as punishers—spanking, loss of privileges, and so on. Few parents will have difficulty, however, selecting a behavior to decrease. Have them write the behavior at the bottom of the chart along with the contingency: for example, Woody loses five points *every* time he leaves his bedroom after 8:45 P.M. It is especially important to impress on parents that point loss is to occur only for the specific behavior described. Some parents become so taken with this procedure that they begin removing points whenever the child behaves in some way that annoys them.

Whose behavior generalizes when this happens?

3. Practical activities.   Have parents rehearse instructions and pairing verbal punishment with removal of points: "Woody, you are not to leave your room for any reason after 8:45. That costs you 5 points." Rehearsal should include anticipated problems, such as arguing and crying, and encourage parents to ignore such behavior.

4. Assignment for next week.   The assignment is to continue charting, to thin the reinforcement schedule for another behavior, and to implement the response-cost procedure.

Session 8: Time-out

Session 8

1. Discussion of previous week's assignment.   Review charts and answer any questions.

2. Teaching segment.   Parents often confuse time-out with sending children to their rooms. It is important to emphasize that no positive reinforcement should be available in a time-out room and most children's rooms contain a variety of potential reinforcers. An area such as a hallway that contains nothing but a chair should be used. Time-out is also different from parents' usual practice when sending a child to her or his room, because it is limited to short periods, with 15 minutes after the child stops protesting suggested as a maximum. After describing the procedure, ask parents to identify another behavior they want to decrease. Such behaviors as hitting and deliberate destructiveness are often suggested. Time-out should be reserved for one seriously inappropriate behavior at this point. Unfortunately, some people who never think to apply positive reinforcement to any except specified target behaviors generalize the use of punishment procedures without the slightest hesitation.

3. Practice activities.   Rehearsal should include pairing verbal punishment with time-out and effecting release from time-out. This practice should anticipate such problems as yelling and crying while in time-out. Refusal to go to time-out should result in physical removal; we do not suggest time-out procedures to parents whose children are so large or so aggressive as to make such physical removal impossible.

4. Assignment for next week.   The assignment, in addition to implementing time-out, includes continuing to thin reinforcement schedules. One behavior may be removed from the chart at this time. It may be replaced by another if parents still wish to increase a behavior.

Session 9

Session 9: Stimulus Control

1. Discussion of previous week's assignment.   Discuss any problems related to time-out and offer suggestions.

2. Teaching segment.   In describing stimulus control, focus on rules, modifications to the physical environment, and generalization. Relate the discussion of rules to the token charts. Parents have used rules when stating contingencies to their children. Parents have used rules in describing expected behavior before guests arrive, before entering a restaurant, and before making a telephone call. Tell parents that after compliance with instructions has been consistently reinforced over time, instructions will be effective even when following them is not reinforced. Their children will have learned to "do as they are told."

Other stimulus control procedures likely to be helpful to parents include modifying the physical environment and using stimulus control to promote generalization. For example, providing plenty of places to store possessions increases neatness, as does labeling storage areas for toys and clothing. Giving the child a desk at which to do homework will increase studying, if such behavior is reinforced at school.

3. Practice activities. Parents should be able to think of other examples where using stimulus control would improve behavior. They may also ask their child's teacher for suggestions on arranging events at home to encourage appropriate behavioral patterns taught at school.

4. Assignment for next week. The assignment is to continue charting and to try at least one environmental modification.

Session 10

Session 10: Evaluation

During this last session, parents have an opportunity to evaluate their progress in managing their children's behavior. The charts should provide tangible evidence of improvement. A single 10-week training program cannot be expected to change a child from a holy terror into a model person. Dramatic changes do sometimes occur, however, and some parents may feel able to cope without further consultation. For those who do not feel ready, several alternatives are available.

1. Parents may re-enroll in subsequent sessions. For parents whose children present major problems, continuous enrollment may be appropriate. The feedback and reinforcement provided by weekly meetings may help such parents persist in the effort to manage their children more effectively.
2. Individual follow-up may be provided. In any case, encourage parents who have completed training to communicate with the group leaders if problems arise. Such communication may be by telephone or individual conference. Parents who continue using the token economy should share information with their child's teacher. In this way, conferences between parents and teachers can provide continuous follow-up.
3. Some parents may need referral to agencies other than the school. If family problems are so serious as to require counseling or therapy, referral may be made at this time.
4. Parents who have kept their weekly instruction sheets have a resource to use indefinitely.
5. The leaders may also provide a list of books that may be useful to parents.

PARAPROFESSIONALS, AIDES, AND VOLUNTEERS

Many classroom teachers, faced with having to provide individualized instruction for as many as 35 children with a wide range of aptitudes, academic achievement, and social behaviors, feel another pair of hands in the form of an assistant would be the solution to all their problems. Although the advantages of such classroom help are obvious, unless classroom helpers are carefully chosen, trained, and supervised, their presence may prove more of a hindrance than a help.

Selection of Classroom Helpers

Characteristics to consider in classroom helpers

Often, the selection of classroom assistants is the responsibility of someone other than the teacher. The helper who is a paid paraprofessional will probably be hired through the school system's usual personnel procedures and presented to the teacher without prior consultation. If teachers have some choice in the matter, however, they will naturally be concerned with the prospective helper's general knowledge and specific skills. When selecting a person who will spend several hours a day in the room with the teacher and students, the teacher should consider several purely subjective questions:

1. Is the potential assistant a pleasant person with whom the teacher will enjoy interacting?
2. Does the candidate have mannerisms the teacher finds irritating?
3. Does the candidate show obvious signs of thinking he or she knows more about teaching than the teacher?

It may seem peculiar to emphasize personal characteristics in forming what is, after all, a professional relationship. Any teacher, however, who has spent six hours a day isolated from other adult contact with someone whose voice grates on the ear is aware of the devastating effect such a situation can have on the ability to teach. The teacher who has no paid helper may, with the approval of the school administration, explore various sources of possible volunteer aid. Wiederholt, Hammill, and Brown (1978) suggest community service organizations, such as the Junior League, Kiwanis, and Lions' Club. Brighton (1972) describes the use of older students as classroom volunteers. Parents may also be classroom assistants, either in their own child's class—if one goal is to increase generalization from school to home—or in classes other than their child's, as is most often appropriate. Some special education programs have extensive parent volunteer programs organized and coordinated by the parents themselves. High-school students can be recruited, trained, and placed for an hour a day in elementary classrooms if at least part of a staff member's time is devoted to coordinating such a program. Students from nearby universities may be required to spend time in classrooms as part of their training.

There are several kinds of helpers whose presence in classrooms, unless carefully managed, will do more harm than good. Unfortunately, such people seem often to be drawn to work with children, particularly children with disabilities. The following examples describe three "unhelpful" helpers who are familiar to the authors (and many other teachers).

The Lover of Children with Disabilities

Anyone who states that he or she just loves little handicapped children should be immediately suspect. Such a person may express love by positive reinforcement of inappropriate behavior. If a person thinks children's behaviors resulting from a disability are cute, for example, she may encourage dependency, immaturity, and helplessness and thus prevent the child from becoming less disabled. Bateman (1971) has described this attitude as comparable to that of a person who, confronted by a broken toaster, states there is nothing wrong with it; it is just different from other toasters in that it doesn't toast bread. "But it does lend a decorative touch to the kitchen and we should accept it and cherish it for what it does do" (p. 70). Of course we value every child, disabled or not; but the teacher's goal should always be to minimize the effects of the disability by setting goals that will help each student become the least disabled individual possible. The following vignette illustrates what may happen when an assistant reinforces dependent behavior.

Ms. Jackson Sets Things Straight

Mark is a fourth-grader identified as learning disabled who attends a special education resource room three times a week for instruction in mathematics. He is making excellent progress and has almost reached grade level in math skills. He participates enthusiastically in small-group instruction and particularly enjoys demonstrating a problem on the board and receiving his teacher's praise for doing it correctly. However, when he is expected to work independently while the teacher instructs another group, Mark sits and cries until the assistant, Ms. Jackson, sits next to him and helps him do the assignment. Mark almost never completes an assignment independently. The teacher has asked Ms. Jackson not to help Mark, explaining that her attention reinforces his crying and that Mark will never be able to function in the regular classroom unless he can work independently. Ms. Jackson's answer was that, although she might not understand all those charts and graphs, she did know the poor little thing needed love. Ms. Jackson insisted the teacher would understand things better if she had children of her own.

The Frustrated Therapist

The second variety of unhelpful helper is the one who really wants to be a psychiatrist or psychologist. Most often, this is a person who has recently acquired an undergraduate degree in psychology and has discovered its dubious usefulness as vocational training. This helper, too, may reinforce inappropriate behavior because he or she feels that students should "do their own thing" and not be required to meet standards set by other people.

The Disabled Helper

Occasionally, a teacher may be presented with an aide who is so intellectually limited or so emotionally disturbed as to make it very difficult for the person to be helpful. One teacher has described such a situation as very much like having one more IEP to write.

Even these three potentially harmful types of assistants can often be taught to be effective classroom helpers. Careful planning and explicit teaching are necessities, however, even with helpers whose entering skills are much better.

Role Description

Functions of classroom helpers

Effective use of classroom helpers depends to a great extent on the explicit description of expectations, clear statement of responsibilities, and precise description of the task to be undertaken. Not all components of teaching can or should be undertaken by nonprofessionals. Smith, Krouse, and Atkinson (1961) suggest that the diagnostic/prescriptive process, including selection of the content or skill to be taught, the materials to be used, and the evaluation of effectiveness, must remain the teacher's responsibility. A number of instructional and noninstructional roles, however, may be filled by classroom assistants. Appropriate assignments include but are not limited to

1. Direct instruction under the guidance of the teacher
2. Observation and recording of academic and social behavior
3. Preparation of instructional materials
4. Supervision of children as they work independently

The role definition of any particular classroom helper will depend on a number of factors, such as the characteristics of the students in the class and the special skills or talents of the assistant. The important thing is that the definition be explicit and known to all concerned.

Training Classroom Helpers

Helpers also need to know when for purposes of generalization, instructions, prompts, and cues should be varied.

Any person who is hired or who volunteers as a classroom assistant should receive some preservice training. Such training may be limited, because of time or economic considerations, but should include at least a description of the characteristics of the students to be served, the objectives of the program, the principles on which teaching techniques are based, and, of course, a description of the expectations the helper is to fulfill. A training program following the outline for parents presented earlier may be used, if time is available. When people will be working in the classroom, however, it is important to familiarize them with the vocabulary of applied behavior analysis and with any more elaborate observational procedures that may be used. Training should include emphasis on stimulus control, particularly in terms of all adults' providing students with the same instructions, cues, prompts, and so on.

Preservice training will almost certainly be carried out by someone other than the classroom teacher. The teacher's task is to take the assistant—with whatever personal characteristics, training, expectations, and goals he or she brings to the situation—and help that person become a productive member of the team responsible for meeting the educational needs of each student in the classroom.

The initial interaction between teacher and assistant is of paramount importance in establishing a good working relationship. In most cases, the teacher and the assistant will have some time before the students arrive, whether several days at the beginning of the school year or just a half-hour before the buses arrive. Use such time to familiarize the aide with the physical arrangement of the school and the classroom. Mundane considerations, such as expectations for signing in, storage locations for personal items during the day, dress regulations or conventions, and areas where eating and drinking are permitted, can be handled at this time. Also introduce the assistant to other faculty members and to such vital personnel as the school secretary and the maintenance staff. The assistant has the right to be treated as a colleague (Shank & McElroy, 1970), and elementary courtesy is a part of this right. The teacher's behavior during this first orientation will permanently affect future relations with the assistant. A common mistake made by teachers is that, in an effort to put a new assistant at ease, they fail to make clear that, although certainly a colleague, the assistant is expected to defer to the teacher's decisions regarding educational planning and procedures. Such well-meant statements as "Just do things your way" or "I'm sure you know more about some of these things than I do" may well come back to haunt the teacher who makes them. This may be particularly dangerous when it is the teacher who is new and the assistant or assistants who have been with the class for some time.

The teacher who follows the suggestions in Chapter 10 regarding structure and organization of the classroom will now reap yet another benefit of such preparation. It is much easier to orient a classroom helper to a classroom whose rules, schedules, expectations, and procedures are explicitly stated for the students. The teacher who manages a classroom using less explicitly stated procedures may have considerable difficulty teaching someone else to fit into the plan. The assistant should become familiar with the overall organization of the classroom and with the plan for each student. The more information assistants have, the more effective they will be.

Once the students arrive, the assistant should be introduced. Few teachers would advocate making a distinction as to authority in such introductions. It is, however, almost inevitable the students, unless severely disabled or very young, will know very soon who the real teacher is, just as they always seem to be aware—no matter how hard we try to fool them—which reading group is the top and which the bottom. This should cause no problem, as long as the adults are consistent in their expectations and support one another.

The teacher may use many of the same procedures in training the assistant as in teaching students. Specific techniques applicable in this situation are

1. *Modeling.* The assistant should have an opportunity to observe the teacher before being expected to perform most tasks. Such observation, combined with an explanation of the specific procedure, the reasons for its use, and its effect, provide an excellent teaching mechanism.

2. *Instructions.* The instructions the teacher gives to the assistant must be as clear as those given to students. The assistant who is asked to "help Harold with his math" may interpret this to mean anything from offering encouragement from across the room to doing the problems for Harold. If a helper is asked to check on Harry every five minutes and give him a bonus point for each problem done correctly, that helper knows exactly what to do. Written instructions may help the assistant remember and follow them, as well as provide a mechanism for evaluation and feedback.

3. *Feedback.* Assistants, like all other learners, need to know how they are doing. Feedback may take the form of positive reinforcement when the assistant has done something the teacher wants to see repeated, or correction when a mistake has been made. Correction should always be combined with a suggestion about how to handle the situation in the future and should always occur privately.

If, in spite of best efforts, a teacher finds it impossible to teach an assistant effectively, that person's presence has become a liability. The source of the difficulty, particularly if the assistant is older than the teacher, may be that the teacher finds it impossible to assert authority. If the assistant is an older person, she or he may be a discriminative stimulus for obedience to the young teacher. Teachers who find themselves in such situations may profit from assertiveness training. A simple introduction to the concept of assertiveness may be found in Alberti and Emmons (1970).

We have emphasized the negative aspects of having a helper in the classroom because most teachers are unprepared for possible problems. Most helpers are an asset. They give students an opportunity to learn from more than one adult, thus increasing the likelihood of generalization of new behavior patterns. They bring to the classroom new skills, abilities, and interests to be shared with teacher and students. They allow the teacher to be more flexible in planning so that, for example, a student may receive one-on-one attention if needed. Having an assistant may force a teacher to analyze and possibly improve teaching procedures. The teacher who is asked why he always ignores Harold's talking-out but always answers Tyrone may not even have been aware of the inconsistency. Finally, many things happen in a classroom that can be shared when two adults are present—the frustration when a student seems not to be making progress, the joy when he does, and humorous events that never seem quite so humorous when repeated to someone not involved. Having an assistant means never having to say, "I guess you had to be there."

TEACHING STUDENTS
TO MODIFY PEER BEHAVIOR

Young students can be applied behavior analysts, too.

The influence of students on the behavior of one another is recognized and often lamented by teachers. Indeed, much of the lamentation is justified: the behaviors most frequently reinforced by peers are those least desirable to teachers (Patterson, Littman, & Bricker, 1967; Solomon & Wahler, 1973). Some strategies for interfering with this process, such as modeling and the use of group contingencies, have been discussed in previous chapters. This section discusses the use of peers as direct change agents for one another.

That peers can observe, record, and reinforce behavior systematically has been well documented (Patterson, Shaw, & Ebner, 1969; Surratt, Ulrich, & Hawkins, 1969). Even elementary students can be effective behavior modifiers, dispensing tokens and praise contingent on appropriate academic and social behavior. Solomon and Wahler (1973) implemented a program combining social reinforcement and extinction. Sixth graders observed and recorded appropriate behavior of a peer and changed the peer's behavior using only differential attention. Axelrod, Hall, and Maxwell (1972), after failing to help a teacher reinforce appropriate academic behavior in a disruptive student, had great success by enlisting a peer. Strain, Shores, and Timm (1977) trained preschool children to modify the social behavior of their peers. Direct prompting and modeling strategies have shown promise in teaching typical children to modify the social behavior of their siblings with disabilities (James & Egal, 1982) and in teaching students with mild disabilities to modify the social behavior of children with autism (Shafer, Egal, & Neef, 1984).

The use of peer-managed behavior-change strategies is particularly useful to the regular classroom teacher who may identify only a few students whose behavior is not controlled by the usual contingencies, such as grades, social reinforcement, or activities. The behavior of such children may be managed using a token system administered by a peer and may require investment of very little time by the teacher once training has taken place. The choice of peers is crucial, however. They must be sufficiently responsible to undertake the project and to follow through, but care should be taken to avoid choosing Goody Two-Shoes as the behavior manager. Such a student may be resented by the target students.

The process of teaching students to manage their peers' behavior should be as simple as possible. Only the specific procedures to be used need to be explained. The teacher should be certain the peer manager can identify, count, and record the target behavior(s) and understands the contingency in effect. It is helpful if positive reinforcement for the manager can be built into the program; if not, some means of providing such reinforcement should be found. The following example illustrates a problem that might be solved using a peer-management procedure.

Tyrone

Tyrone's seventh-grade English teacher is about to refer him for special education services. Although he is clearly bright, he never completes an assignment;

seldom brings pencil, paper, or texts to class; is frequently late; and sometimes skips class altogether. He is failing English and appears interested only in the part of the class concerned with literature. He recently astounded his teacher by confiding that he and his friend Jake were rewriting a selection from the literature book as a play and planned to produce it as a neighborhood project. Jake is an excellent student who often bails Tyrone out with pencils, paper, and excuses. He has been heard admonishing Tyrone to "get his act together."

Tyrone's teacher might handle this situation by appointing Jake as behavior manager. Behaviors such as attending class, being on time, bringing materials, and completing assignments could earn points toward time in class to work on the play or even to present it. The teacher's role would be only to explain the program to Jake and Tyrone and to monitor it occasionally.

TEACHING STUDENTS TO MODIFY ADULTS' BEHAVIOR

Bandura (1975) points out the unilateral direction of most plans for behavior change: some people are identified as deviant, and systematic attempts to alter their behavior are made by those who are putatively normal. The actual situation is a little more complicated. In any given social system, *every* individual's behavior is subject to modification by others (Tharp & Wetzel, 1969). While teachers are modifying their students' behavior, students—whether they or their teachers are aware of it—are modifying the teachers' behavior. The same is true of the social system in the home; *everyone* modifies the behavior of *everyone* else. An understanding of the complexity of these interactions is central to understanding these complex social systems (Johnston & Zemitzsch, 1988).

Berberich (1971) systematically investigated the effects of students' behavior on their teachers and established that a simulated student's responses changed a teacher's administration of tangible and social reinforcers and punishers, as well as the teacher's motor behavior. Sherman and Cormier (1974) found that fifth graders could be taught to change their teacher's behavior in a positive direction. Even college professors' behavior can be modified by their students (Whaley & Malott, 1968).

In perhaps the most helpful study for teachers, Graubard, Rosenberg, and Miller (1974) trained junior-high students to identify teacher-pleasing behaviors, such as asking questions, nodding wisely, and complimenting teachers on their explanations. They demonstrated that students who had been labeled as deviant could significantly increase their classroom teachers' positive responses to them by emitting higher rates of teacher-pleasing behaviors. With the current emphasis on educating most students in regular classrooms, such skills can greatly increase the acceptability of some students with disabilities. Teachers who want to give students the most powerful possible tools for success will not omit training in behavior modification. Such teachers may even find that a student trained in this way will begin consciously and systematically reinforcing the teacher's behavior, particularly when the teacher is providing interesting instruction and high rates of positive social reinforcement. Thus, as teachers train class members to be better students, students train teachers to be better teachers.

SUMMARY

This chapter brings us full circle. Having already considered techniques for changing student behavior, we discussed ways to help other adults change children's behavior and ways to teach children to change adults' behavior. No teacher can expect to do everything for students. Each teacher must be prepared to teach others to help students and ultimately to help the students themselves become effective managers of their own environment.

Epilogue

As Professor Grundy began the second mile of his daily run, he began to think about the recently completed semester. On the whole, it hadn't been too bad: his book was finished, Ms. Harper had finally completed her student teaching, DeWayne had made the Dean's List, and he himself was in better shape than he had been in years, in spite of a drastically increased rate of cookie consumption. "I've learned a lot, too," he thought as he ran. "I think I finally understand what Professor Peltry was trying to tell me about applied behavior analysis when I was a student. It's not just something to think about using when someone's behavior annoys me. It's a way of looking at human behavior that helps me teach. I taught Ms. Harper to observe behavior, I taught DeWayne to write a behavioral objective, and I taught myself how to stop performing a self-destructive behavior and how to stick to a job until it was finished."

He entered his house in a state of high excitement. "Minerva," he panted, "I've finally figured out what applied behavior analysis is all about! It's not just M&Ms and tokens. It's not just a way to deal with behavior problems. When people understand applied behavior analysis, they can teach themselves and one another just about anything." Mrs. Grundy looked at him quizzically. "Is that so, Oliver?" she replied. "That's nice. When you've finished showering, I'd really like for you to come and help me move all these books out of the living room. If we can get it done quickly, I'll have time to make a chocolate mousse for dessert tonight."

DISCUSSION QUESTIONS

1. Mr. and Mrs. Macho have come to talk with you about Billy, a student in your self-contained special education class. Your concern is that Billy reacts to almost any interaction by hitting. When you express this concern to the Machos, Mr. M. states he has told Billy "not to take nothin' off nobody," and Billy should learn to take care of himself. How do you react?

2. Make a hypothetical schedule for a classroom of your choice (1) with no teacher assistant, (2) with a half-time teacher assistant, and (3) with a full-time teacher assistant.

3. Is it ethical to teach students the principles of applied behavior analysis? Will this not give them too much control over their parents, teachers, and employers?

REFERENCES

Alberti, R.E., & Emmons, M.L. 1970. *Your perfect right: A guide to assertive behavior*. San Luis Obispo, Calif.: Impact.

Allen, L.D., Bryant, M.C., & Bailey, J.S. 1986. Facilitating generalization: The effectiveness of improved parental report procedures. *Behavior Modification, 10*, 415–434.

Allen, K.E., & Harris, F.R. 1964. Elimination of a child's excessive scratching by training the mother in reinforcement procedures. *Behaviour Research and Therapy, 4*, 70–84.

Arnold, L.E., Rowe, M., & Tolbert, H.A. 1978. Parents' groups. In L.E. Arnold (Ed.), *Helping parents help their children*. New York: Brunner/Mazel.

Axelrod, S., Hall, R.V., & Maxwell, A. 1972. Use of peer attention to increase study behavior. *Behavior Therapy, 3*, 349–351.

Bandura, A. 1975. The ethics and social purposes of behavior modification. In C.M. Franks and G.T. Wilson (Eds.), *Annual review of behavior therapy, theory and practice* (vol. 3, pp. 13–20). New York: Brunner/Mazel.

Bateman, B.D. 1971. *The essentials of teaching*. Sioux Falls, S. Dak.: Adapt Press.

Berberich, J.P. 1971. Do the child's responses shape the teaching behavior of adults? *Journal of Experimental Research in Personality, 5*, 92–97.

Bernal, M.E., Duryee, J.S., Pruett, H.L., & Burns, B.J. 1968. Behavior modification and the Brat Syndrome. *Journal of Consulting and Clinical Psychology, 32*, 447–455.

Brighton, H. 1972. *Handbook for teacher aides*. Midland, Mich.: Pendell Publishing.

Dinkmeyer, D., & Carlson, J. 1973. *Consulting: Facilitating human potential and change processes*. Columbus, Ohio: Merrill.

Dunlap, G., Robbins, F. R., & Darrow, M. A. 1994. Parents' reports of their children's challenging behaviors: Results of a statewide survey. *Mental Retardation, 32*, 206–212.

Forehand, R., & Atkeson, B.M. 1977. Generality of treatment effects with parents as therapists: A review of assessment and implementation procedures. *Behavior Therapy, 8*, 575–593.

Galloway, C., & Galloway, K.C. 1971. Parent classes in precise behavior management. *Teaching Exceptional Children, 3*, 120–128.

Gardner, R.A. 1978. Guidance for separated and divorced parents. In L.E. Arnold (Ed.), *Helping parents help their children*. New York: Brunner/Mazel.

Graubard, P.S., Rosenberg, H., & Miller, M.B. 1974. Student applications of behavior modification to teachers and environments or ecological approaches to social deviancy. In R. Ulrich, T. Stacknick, & J. Mabry (Eds.), *Control of human behavior* (vol. 3). Glenview, Ill.: Scott, Foresman.

Hornby, G., & Singh, N.N. 1983. Group training for parents of mentally retarded children: A review and methodological analysis of behavioural studies. *Child-Care, Health and Development, 9*, 199–213.

James, S.D., & Egal, A.L. 1982. A direct prompting strategy for increasing reciprocal interactions between handicapped and nonhandicapped siblings. *Journal of Applied Behavior Analysis, 19*, 173–186.

Johnson, C.A., & Katz, R.C. 1973. Using parents as change agents for their children: A review. *Journal of Child Psychology and Psychiatry, 14*, 181–200.

Johnston, J. C., & Zemitzsch, A. 1988. Family power: An intervention beyond the classroom. *Behavioral Disorders, 14*, 69–79.

Jong, E. 1977. *How to save your own life*. New York: Signet.

Kessler, J.W. 1966. *Psychopathology of childhood*. Englewood Cliffs, N.J.: Prentice-Hall.

Lindsley, O. 1978. Teaching parents to modify their children's behavior. In L.E. Arnold (Ed.), *Helping parents help their children*. New York: Brunner/Mazel.

O'Brien, T.P., Riner, L.S., & Budd, K.S. 1983. The effects of a child's self-evaluation program on compliance with parental instructions in the home. *Journal of Applied Behavior Analysis, 16,* 69–79.

O'Dell, S. 1974. Training parents in behavior modification: A review. *Psychological Bulletin, 81,* 418–433.

Patterson, G.R., Littman, R., & Bricker, W. 1967. Assertive behavior in children: A preliminary outline of a theory of aggressive behavior. *Monographs of the Society for Research in Child Development, 32*(6) 1–43.

Patterson, G.R., Shaw, D.A., & Ebner, M.J. 1969. Teachers, peers and parents as agents of change in the classroom. In A.M. Benson (Ed.), *Modifying deviant social behaviors in various classroom settings.* Eugene: University of Oregon Press.

Price, B.J., & Marsh, G.E., II. 1985. Practical suggestions for planning and conducting parent conferences. *Teaching Exceptional Children, 17,* 274–278.

Raver, S.A., & Kilgo, J. 1991. Effective family-centered services: Supporting family choices and rights. *Infant-Toddler Intervention, 1,* 169–176.

Risley, T.R. 1968. The effects and side effects of punishing the autistic behaviors of a deviant child. *Journal of Applied Behavior Analysis, 1,* 21–34.

Robbins, F.R., Dunlap, G., Plienis, A.J. 1991. Family characteristics, family training, and the progress of young children with autism. *Journal of Early Intervention, 15,* 173–184.

Shafer, M.S., Egal, A.L., & Neef, N.A. 1984. Training mildly handicapped peers to facilitate changes in the social interaction skills of autistic children. *Education and Training of the Mentally Retarded, 17,* 461–476.

Shank, P.C., & McElroy, W. 1970. *The paraprofessional or teacher aide.* Midland, Mich.: Pendell Publishing.

Shea, T.M., & Bauer, A.M. 1991. *Parents and teachers of children with exceptionalities: A handbook for collaboration.* Boston: Allyn and Bacon.

Sherman, T.M., & Cormier, W.H. 1974. An investigation of the influence of student behavior on teacher behavior. *Journal of Applied Behavior Analysis, 7,* 11–21.

Singh, R., & Kaushik, S.S. 1982. Parent training techniques in acquisition and generalization of behavior modification skills to train the retardate. *Indian Journal of Clinical Psychology, 9,* 193–201.

Smith, E.W., Krouse, S.W., & Atkinson, M.M. 1961. *The educator's encyclopedia.* Englewood Cliffs, N.J.: Prentice-Hall.

Solomon, R.W., & Wahler, R.G. 1973. Peer reinforcement control of classroom problem behavior. *Journal of Applied Behavior Analysis, 6,* 49–56.

Strain, P.S., Shores, R.E., & Timm, M.A. 1977. Effects of peer social initiations on the behavior of withdrawn preschool children. *Journal of Applied Behavior Analysis, 10,* 289–298.

Surratt, P.R., Ulrich, R., & Hawkins, R.P. 1969. An elementary student as a behavioral engineer. *Journal of Applied Behavior Analysis, 2,* 85–92.

Tharp, R.G., & Wetzel, R.S. 1969. *Behavior modification in the natural environment.* New York: Academic Press.

Turnbull, A.P., & Turnbull, H.R. 1990. *Families, professionals, and exceptionality: A special partnership.* Columbus, Ohio: Merrill.

Wahler, R.C., Winkel, G.H., Peterson, R.F., & Morrison, D.C. 1965. Mothers as behavior therapists for their own children. *Behaviour Research and Therapy, 3,* 113–134.

Wetzel, R., Baker, J., Roney, M., & Martin, M. 1966. Outpatient treatment of autistic behavior. *Behaviour Research and Therapy, 4,* 169–177.

Whaley, D.L., & Malott, R.W. 1968. *Elementary principles of behavior.* Kalamazoo, Mich.: Behaviordelia.

Wiederholt, J.L., Hammill, D.D., & Brown, V. 1978. *The resource teacher: A guide to effective practices.* Boston: Allyn & Bacon.

Williams, C.D. 1959. The elimination of tantrum behavior by extinction procedures: Case report. *Journal of Abnormal and Social Psychology, 59,* 269.

Appendix
Professional Resolutions Regarding the Avoidance of Aversive Behavioral Intervention

Five major associations of professionals involved in education and the use of behavioral change procedures have adopted policies recommending that aversive behavioral intervention be avoided. Their statements follow.

THE ARC'S POSITION STATEMENT ON BEHAVIOR INTERVENTION: OCTOBER, 1989

Issue

Behavior intervention programs include a variety of techniques to develop and maintain skills that will enhance an individual's opportunities for learning and achieving independence. The Arc supports the development and use of positive behavior intervention programs in meeting individual needs, while prohibiting and preventing the use of procedures that may cause physical or psychological harm or are dehumanizing. Specifically, the use of aversive and deprivation procedures[1] is in direct conflict with the right of people with mental retardation to be free from harm. These procedures cause a loss of dignity and inhibit full participation in society.

Position

Prior to consideration of any behavior intervention program, the nature and extent of the perceived behavior problem and what the person is trying to communicate through this behavior must be determined. Contributing factors such as physical or medical conditions, social influences, living arrangements, work setting, and inappropriate programming must be reviewed and addressed prior to development of a behavior intervention program through a comprehensive functional analysis.[2]

For individuals with mental retardation, the Arc supports behavior intervention programs that are:

- designed and applied in a humane and caring manner with the ultimate goal of growth and development;
- based upon a formal functional analysis and thorough assessment of each individual's existing competencies and characteristics;
- based on procedures adequately documented in the clinical/educational research literature;
- intended to replace challenging behavior with adaptive and socially productive behavior;
- implemented in positive and socially supportive environments;
- carried out by staff who have been trained and are qualified to effectively apply positive, nonaversive approaches;
- monitored continuously and systematically to ensure that the approach is consistent with individual needs and successful in achieving established goals and changed in a timely fashion if success is not evident or occurring at an appropriate rate.

Further, The Arc calls for the elimination of any aversive interventions that withhold essential nutrition and hydration, inflict pain, use chemical restraints in lieu of programming, or impose techniques which produce physical or psychological pain, humiliation, or discomfort. All means of review processes, including human rights committees independent of service providers, should be used to monitor the quality of ongoing programs and make necessary adjustment. Extraordinary measures should be taken (if necessary) to ensure the success of positive interventions.

Adopted by Delegate Body, October 1989. Position of the Arc of the United States. (Used by permission)

---

[1]Aversive refers to noxious, painful, or intrusive stimuli or activities applied in response to challenging behavior, including, but not limited to, ammonia spray, contingent electric shock, water spray to the face, seclusion, etc. Deprivation refers to such actions as withholding, withdrawing, or delaying visitation or private communication with family and friends, adequate sleep, shelter, bedding, bathroom facilities, and food or drink.

[2]A functional analysis involves the observation of how a behavior is affected by both internal (e.g., illnesses) and external (e.g., social interactions) influences.

COUNCIL FOR EXCEPTIONAL CHILDREN POLICY ON PHYSICAL INTERVENTION: APRIL, 1993

The Council recognizes the right to the most effective educational strategies to be the basic educational right of each special education child. Furthermore, the Council believes that the least restrictive positive educational strategies should be used, as they relate to physical intervention, to respect the child's dignity and personal privacy. Additionally, the Council believes that such intervention shall assure the child's physical freedom, social interaction, and individual choice. The intervention must not include procedures which cause pain or trauma. Lastly, behavior intervention plans must be specifically described in the child's written educational plan with agreement from the education staff, the parent, and when appropriate, the child.

The Council recommends that physical intervention be used only if all the following requirements are met:

- The child's behavior is dangerous to herself/himself or others or the behavior is extremely detrimental to or interferes with the education or development of the child.
- Various positive reinforcement techniques have been implemented appropriately and the child has repeatedly failed to respond as documented in the child's records.
- It is evident that withholding physical intervention would significantly impede the child's educational progress as explicitly defined in his/her written educational plan.
- The physical intervention plan specifically will describe the intervention to be implemented, the staff to be responsible for the implementation, the process for documentation, the required training of the staff and supervision of staff as it relates to the intervention and when the intervention will be replaced.
- The physical intervention plan will become part of the written educational plan.
- The physical intervention plan shall encompass the following provisions:

    1. A comprehensive analysis of the child's environment including variables contributing to the inappropriate behavior;
    2. The plan to be developed by a team including professional and parent/guardians, as designated by state/provincial and federal law;
    3. The personnel implementing the plan shall receive specific training congruent with the contents of the plan and receive ongoing supervision from individuals who are trained and skilled in the techniques identified in the plan;
    4. The techniques identified in the physical intervention plan are approved by a physician to not be medially contraindicated for the child (a statement from the physician is necessary); and
    5. The impact of the plan on the child's behavior must be consistently evaluated, the results documented, and the plan modified when indicated.

The Council supports the following prohibitions:

- Any intervention that is designed to, or likely to cause physical pain;
- Releasing noxious, toxic or otherwise unpleasant sprays, mists, or substances in proximity to the child's face;
- Any intervention which denies adequate sleep, food, water, shelter, bedding, physical comfort, or access to bathroom facilities;
- Any intervention which is designed to subject, used to subject, or likely to subject the individual to verbal abuse, ridicule or humiliation, or which can be expected to cause excessive emotional trauma;
- Restrictive interventions which employ a device or material or objects that simultaneously immobilize all four extremities, including the procedure known as prone containment, except that containment may be used by trained personnel as a limited emergency intervention;
- Locked seclusion, unless under constant surveillance and observation;
- Any intervention that precludes adequate supervision of the child; and
- Any intervention which deprives the individual of one or more of his or her senses.

- The Council recognizes that emergency physical intervention may be implemented if the child's behavior poses imminent and significant threat to his/her physical well-being or the safety of others. The intervention must be documented and parents/guardians must be notified of the incident.

- However, emergency physical intervention shall not be used as a substitute for systematic behavioral intervention plans that are designed to change, replace, modify or eliminate a targeted behavior.

- Furthermore, the Council expects school districts and other educational agencies to establish policies and comply with state/provincial and federal law and regulations to ensure the protection of the rights of the child, the parent/guardians, the education staff, and the school and local educational agency when physical intervention is applied.

THE AMERICAN ASSOCIATION ON MENTAL RETARDATION (AAMR) POLICY ON AVERSIVE PROCEDURES: JANUARY 20, 1990

Some persons who have mental retardation or other developmental disabilities continue to be subjected to inhumane forms of aversive procedures as a means of behavior modification. The American Association on Mental Retardation (AAMR) condemns such practices and urges their immediate elimination. The aversive procedures to be eliminated have some or all of the following characteristics:

1. Obvious signs of physical pain experienced by the individual.
2. Potential or actual physical side-effects, including tissue damage, physical illness, severe stress, and/or death.

3. Dehumanization of the individual, through means such as social degradation, social isolation, verbal abuse, techniques inappropriate for the individual's age, and treatment out of proportion to the target behavior. Such dehumanization is equally unacceptable whether or not an individual has a disability.

This statement is intended to articulate important values and principles and to challenge the field of developmental disabilities to promote research activities leading to identification, testing, implementation, and dissemination of non-aversive alternatives to address severe behavioral disorders. Specific regulations regarding research, clinical practice, or individuals making professional judgements are the province of regulatory agencies, funders, and certifying bodies.

Eliminating inhumane aversive procedures is a reflection of a growing concern for reducing actions by professionals and others that compromise the lives of persons with mental retardation or other developmental disabilities and their families. Relationships between providers and consumers should foster empowerment of the consumer, enhance choice, and promote integration of persons with mental retardation or other developmental disabilities into community settings.

The AAMR urges continuing research into human methods of behavior management and support of existing programs and environments that successfully habilitate individuals with complex behaviors.

Used with permission.

ASSOCIATION FOR PERSONS WITH SEVERE HANDICAPS RESOLUTION ON THE CESSATION OF INTRUSIVE INTERVENTIONS: NOVEMBER 5, 1986[1]

WHEREAS, In order to realize the goals and objectives of the Association for Persons with Severe Handicaps, including the right of each person who has severe handicaps to grow, develop, and enjoy life in integrated and normalized community environments, the following resolution is adopted:

WHEREAS, Educational and other habilitative services must employ instructional and management strategies which are consistent with the right of each individual with severe handicaps to an effective treatment which does not compromise the equally important right to freedom from harm. This requires educational and habilitative procedures free from chemical restraint, aversive stimuli, environmental deprivation or exclusion from services;

THEREFORE, TASH calls for the cessation of the use of any treatment option which exhibits some or all of the following characteristics: (1) obvious signs of physical pain experienced by the individual; (2) potential or actual side effects such as tissue damage, physical illness, severe physical or emo-

---

[1]TASH resolution on the Cessation of Intrusive Interventions. (The Association for Persons with Severe Handicaps, adopted in October 1981, November 5, 1986, revised.)

tional stress, and/or death that would properly require the involvement of medical personnel; (3) dehumanization of persons with severe handicaps because the procedures are normally unacceptable for persons who do not have handicaps in community environment; (4) extreme ambivalence and discomfort by family, staff, and/or caregivers regarding the necessity of such extreme strategies or their own involvement in such interventions; and (5) obvious repulsion and/or stress felt by peers who do not have handicaps and community members who cannot reconcile extreme procedures with acceptable standard practice;

IT IS FURTHER RESOLVED THAT The Association for Persons with Severe Handicaps' resources and expertise be dedicated to he development, implementation, evaluation, dissemination, and advocacy of educational and management practices which are appropriate for use in integrated environments and which are consistent with the commitment to a high quality of life for individuals with severe handicaps.

NATIONAL ASSOCIATION OF SCHOOL PSYCHOLOGISTS RESOLUTION ON CORPORAL PUNISHMENT: APRIL 19, 1986[1]

As the purpose of the National Association of School Psychologists is to serve the mental health and educational needs of children and youth; and

The use of corporal punishment as a disciplinary procedure in the schools negatively affects the social, educational, and psychological development of students; and

The use of corporal punishment by educators reinforces the misconception that hitting is an appropriate and effective technique to discipline children; and

Corporal punishment as a disciplinary technique can be easily abused and thereby contribute to the cycle of child abuse; and

School psychologists are legally and ethically bound to protect the students they serve; and

Research indicates that punishment is ineffective in teaching new behaviors, that a variety of positive and effective alternatives are available to maintain school discipline, and that children learn more appropriate problem solving behaviors when provided with the necessary models;

Therefore it is resolved that the National Association of School Psychologists joins other organizations in opposing the use of corporal punishment in the schools and in other institutions where children are cared for or educated;

And will work actively with other organizations to influence public opinion and legislative bodies in recognizing the consequences of corporal punishment, in understanding and researching alternatives to corporal punishment, and in prohibiting the continued use of corporal punishment;

And will encourage state affiliate organization and individual members to adopt positions opposing corporal punishment, to promote understanding of and research on alternatives to corporal punishment including preventive initiatives, and to support abolition of corporal punishment at state and local levels.

Glossary

AB design A single-subject experimental design. The AB design has two phases: baseline (A) and treatment (B). This design cannot demonstrate a functional relationship between dependent and independent variables.

ABAB design An extension of the AB design in which the independent variable is withdrawn and then reapplied. This reversal design can demonstrate a functional relationship between dependent and independent variables.

ABC design See *changing conditions design*.

A-B-C assessment A form of information gathering for functional assessment through direct observation of behavior.

abscissa The horizontal or x-axis of a graph. The time dimension (sessions) is represented along the abscissa.

acquisition The basic level of student response competence. It implies the student's ability to perform a newly learned response to some criterion of accuracy.

activity reinforcement See *Premack principle*.

alternating conditions design See *alternating treatments design*.

alternating treatments design A single-subject experimental design that allows comparison of the effectiveness of two or more treatments. It differs from other single-subject designs in that treatments (sometimes including baseline) are alternated randomly rather than presented sequentially (also known as *multiple schedule design, multielement baseline design, alternating conditions design*).

anecdotal reports Written continuous data recording that provides as much information about the behavior and environmental surrounding as possible. The events contained in the report are then sequenced, identifying each behavior, its antecedent, and its consequence.

antecedent stimulus A stimulus that precedes a behavior. This stimulus may or may not serve as discriminative for a specific behavior.

aversive stimulus A stimulus that decreases the rate or probability of a behavior when presented as a consequence; as such, it is a type of punisher. Alternatively, an aversive stimulus may increase the rate or probability of a behavior when removed as a consequence; as such, it is a negative reinforcer.

back-up reinforcer An object or event received in exchange for a specific number of tokens, points, etc.

bar graph A graph that employs vertical bars rather than horizontal lines to indicate levels of performance (also called a *histogram*).

baseline data Data points that reflect an operant level of the target behavior. *Operant level* is the natural occurrence of the behavior before intervention. Baseline data serve a purpose similar to that from a pretest, to provide a level of behavior against which the results of an intervention procedure can be compared.

behavior Any observable and measurable act of an individual (also called a *response*).

behavioral objective A statement that communicates a proposed change in behavior. A behavioral objective must include statements concerning the learner, the behavior, the conditions under which the behavior will be performed, and the criteria for evaluation.

chaining An instructional procedure that reinforces individual responses in sequence, forming a complex behavior.

changing conditions design A single-subject experimental design that involves successively changing the conditions for response performance in order to evaluate comparative effects. This design does not demonstrate a functional relationship between variables. Also called *ABC design*.

changing criterion design   A single-subject experimental design that involves successively changing the criterion for reinforcement. The criterion is systematically increased or decreased in a stepwise manner.

conditioned aversive stimulus   A stimulus that has acquired secondary aversive qualities through pairing with an unconditioned aversive stimulus, such as pain or discomfort.

conditioned reinforcer   A stimulus that has acquired a reinforcing function through pairing with an unconditioned or natural reinforcer; includes most social, activity, and generalized reinforcers (see *secondary reinforcers*).

consequence   Any stimulus presented contingent on a particular response.

continuous behavior   A behavior with no clearly discriminable beginning and ending.

continuous schedule of reinforcement (CRF)   A schedule of reinforcer delivery that rewards each correct response. The ratio between responses and reinforcement is 1:1.

contracting   Placing contingencies for reinforcement (if . . . then . . . statements) into a written document. This creates a permanent product that can be referred to by teacher and student.

controlled presentations   A variation of *event recording*. A method of predetermining the number of opportunities to respond. This method often involves presenting a specific number of trials per instructional session.

cumulative graph   A graph on which the number of occurrences of behavior observed in a given session is added to the number of occurrences of previous sessions in order to derive the data points to be plotted.

dependent variable   The behavior to be changed through intervention.

deprivation state   A condition in which the student has not had access to a potential reinforcer.

differential reinforcement of alternative behavior (DRA)   Reinforcing a more appropriate form of a behavior than the one the student is currently engaged in. DRA is often used in conjunction with redirecting behavior.

differential reinforcement of incompatible behavior (DRI)   Reinforcing a response that is topographically incompatible with a behavior targeted for reduction.

differential reinforcement of lower rates of behavior (DRL)   Delivering reinforcement when the number of responses in a specified period of time is less than or equal to a prescribed limit. This maintains a behavior at a predetermined rate, lower than at its baseline or naturally occurring frequency.

differential reinforcement of other behaviors (DRO)   Delivering reinforcement when the target behavior is not emitted for a specified period of time. Reinforcement is contingent on the nonoccurrence of a behavior.

directionality   A distinctive ascending or descending trend of data plotted on a graph.

discrete behaviors   Behaviors with a clearly discriminable beginning and ending.

discrimination   The ability to differentiate among stimuli or environmental events.

discriminative stimulus (S^D)   See *stimulus control*.

duration recording   Recording the amount of time between the initiation of a response and its conclusion; an observational recording procedure.

educational goals   Statements providing the framework for planning an academic year or an entire unit of learning. It sets the estimated parameters of anticipated academic and social development for which educators are responsible (also called *long-term objectives*).

errorless learning   An instructional procedure that arranges S^Ds and prompts to evoke only correct responses.

event recording   Recording a tally or frequency count of behavior as it occurs within an observation period; an observational recording procedure.

exclusionary time-out   Denying access to reinforcement by removing a student from an ongoing activity.

extinction   Withholding reinforcement for a previously reinforced behavior to reduce the occurrence of the behavior.

fading   The gradual removal of prompts to allow the S^D to occasion a response independently.

fixed-interval schedule (FI)   See *interval schedules*.

fixed-ratio schedule (FR)   See *ratio schedules*.

fixed-response-duration schedule (FRD)   See *response-duration schedules.*

fluency   The second level (after acquisition) of student competence. Fluency describes the rate that students accurately perform a response.

frequency   The number of times a behavior occurs during an observation period.

functional alternative   A less inappropriate behavior that replaces and serves the same communicative or other purposes as a dangerous or maladaptive behavior.

functional analysis   Procedures (usually reversal design or multielement design) that test a hypothesized relationship by manipulating the variables thought to occasion or maintain a behavior in order to verify a functional relationship.

functional assessment   Gathering information in order to form a hypothesis as to variables occasioning or maintaining a behavior. May be done by interview, checklist, or direct observation.

functional equivalency training   The process of (a) conducting a functional assessment/analysis of a problem behavior, and (b) teaching a socially appropriate behavior to replace it.

functional relationship   A quasi-causative relationship between the dependent and independent variables. This relationship is said to exist if the dependent variable systematically changes in the desired direction as a result of the introduction and manipulation of the independent variable.

generalization   Expansion of a student's capability of performance beyond those conditions set for initial acquisition. *Stimulus generalization* refers to performance under conditions—that is, cues, materials, trainers, and environments—other than those present during acquisition. *Maintenance* refers to continued performance of learned behavior after contingencies have been withdrawn. *Response generalization* refers to changes in behaviors similar to those directly treated.

generalized conditioned reinforcer   A reinforcer associated with a variety of behaviors or with access to a variety of other primary or secondary reinforcers; may simply be called *generalized reinforcer.*

group designs   Experimental investigations that focus on data related to a number of individuals.

histogram   See *bar graph.*

independent variable   The treatment or intervention that the experimenter manipulates in order to change a behavior.

intermittent schedules   Schedules in which reinforcement follows some, but not all, correct or appropriate responses or follows when a period of appropriate behavior has elapsed. These schedules include *ratio, interval,* and *response-duration schedules.*

interobserver agreement   See *reliability.*

interval recording   An observational recording system in which an observation period is divided into a number of short intervals. The observer counts the number of intervals when the behavior occurs rather than instances of the behavior.

interval schedules   Schedules for the delivery of reinforcers contingent on the occurrence of a behavior following a specified period or interval of time. In a *fixed-interval (FI) schedule,* the interval of time is standard. For example, FI5 would reinforce the first occurrence of behavior following each 5-minute interval of the observation period. In a *variable-interval (VI) schedule,* the interval of time varies. For example, VI5 would reinforce the first response that occurs after intervals averaging 5 minutes.

latency recording   Recording the amount of time between the presentation of the S^D and the initiation of a response.

limited hold (LH)   A procedure used with interval schedules of reinforcement that restricts the time during which the reinforcer is available.

long-term objectives   See *educational goals.*

maintenance   The ability to perform a response over time, even after systematic applied behavior procedures have been withdrawn. See *generalization.*

modeling   Demonstrating a desired behavior in order to prompt an imitative response.

multielement baseline design   See *alternating treatments design.*

multiple baseline design   A single-subject experimental design in which a treatment is replicated across (1) two or more students, (2) two or more behaviors, or (3) two or more settings. Functional relationships may be demonstrated as changes in the dependent variables that occur with the systematic and sequenced introduction of the independent variable.

multiple schedule design   See *alternating treatments design.*

natural aversive stimulus   See *unconditioned aversive stimulus.*

natural reinforcers   See *primary reinforcers.*

negative practice   Massed or exaggerated practice of an inappropriate behavior. Decreased occurrence results from fatigue or satiation.

negative reinforcement   The contingent removal of an aversive stimulus immediately following a response. Negative reinforcement increases the future rate and/or probability of the response.

nonseclusionary time-out   A time-out procedure wherein the student is not removed from the instructional setting in which reinforcers are being dispensed. The teacher denies access to reinforcement and manipulates the environment to signal a period of time during which access is denied.

observational recording systems   Methods of data collection used to record aspects of behavior while it actually occurs (*event recording, interval recording, duration recording,* and *latency recording*).

operant conditioning   The arrangement of environmental variables to establish a functional relationship between a voluntary behavior and its consequences.

operational definition   Providing concrete examples of a target behavior. This minimizes disagreements among observers as to the behavior's occurrence.

ordinate   The vertical or y-axis of a graph. The amount or level of the target behavior is represented along the ordinate.

outcome recording   See *permanent product recording.*

overcorrection   A procedure used to reduce the occurrence of an inappropriate behavior. The student is taught the appropriate behavior through an exaggeration of experience. There are two forms of overcorrection. In *restitutional overcorrection* the student must restore or correct an environment he has disturbed to its condition before the disturbance. The student must then improve it beyond its original condition, thereby overcorrecting the environment. In *positive-practice overcorrection* the student, having behaved inappropriately, is required to engage in exaggerated practice of appropriate behaviors.

pairing   Simultaneous presentation of primary and secondary reinforcers to condition the secondary reinforcer. Once the association has been established, the secondary reinforcer takes over the rein-forcing function, and the primary reinforcer is no longer necessary.

permanent product recording   Recording tangible items or environmental effects that result from a behavior; for example, written academic work (also called *outcome recording*).

pinpointing   Specifying in measurable, observable terms a behavior targeted for change.

PLACHECK   A data recording system, similar to time-sampling, in which several students are observed at the end of each interval.

positive-practice overcorrection   See *overcorrection.*

positive reinforcement   The contingent presentation of a stimulus immediately following a response, which increases the future rate and/or probability of the response. Written as S^{R+}.

Premack principle   A principle stating that any high-probability activity may serve as a positive reinforcer for any low-probability activity (also called *activity reinforcement*).

primary reinforcers   Stimuli (such as food) that may have biological importance to an individual; such stimuli are innately motivating (also called *natural, unlearned, unconditioned reinforcers*).

prompt   An added stimulus that increases the probability that the S^D will occasion the desired response (also known as *supplementary antecedent stimulus*).

punisher   A consequent stimulus that decreases the future rate and/or probability of a behavior.

punishment   The contingent presentation of a stimulus immediately following a response, which decreases the future rate and/or probability of the response.

rate   The frequency of a behavior during a defined time period:

$$\text{Rate} = \frac{\text{Frequency}}{\text{Time}}$$

ratio graphs   Graphs on which all data are plotted at rate per minute.

ratio schedules   Schedules for the delivery of reinforcers contingent on the number of correct responses. In a *fixed-ratio (FR) schedule*, the number of appropriate responses required for reinforcement is held constant. For example, FR5 would reinforce every fifth appropriate response. In a *variable-ratio (VR) schedule*, the number of appropriate responses required for reinforcement varies. For example, VR5 would reinforce on the average of every fifth appropriate response.

ratio strain　A disruption of response performance that follows when the schedule of reinforcement has been thinned so quickly that the ratio between correct responding and reinforcement is too great to maintain an appropriate rate of responding.

reinforcer　A consequent stimulus (S^R) that increases or maintains the future rate and/or probability of occurrence of a behavior.

reinforcer sampling　Allowing students to come in contact with potential reinforcers. Reinforcer sampling allows teachers to determine which reinforcers are likely to be effective with individual students. It also allows students to become familiar with previously unknown potential reinforcers.

reliability　The consistency of data-collection reports among independent observers. The coefficient of reliability is determined by the formula

$$\frac{\text{Agreements}}{\text{Agreements} + \text{Disagreements}} \times 100$$

Also known as *interobserver agreement*.

respondent conditioning　The process of pairing stimuli so that an unconditioned stimulus elicits a response. Most such responses are reflexive; they are not under voluntary control.

response　See *behavior*.

response cost　Reducing inappropriate behavior through withdrawal of specific amounts of reinforcer contingent upon the behavior's occurrence.

response-duration schedules　Schedules for the delivery of reinforcers contingent on how long a student engages in a continuous behavior. In a *fixed-response-duration (FRD) schedule*, the duration of the behavior required for reinforcement is held constant. For example, FRD10 minutes would deliver reinforcement following each 10 minutes of appropriate behavior. In a *variable-response-duration (VRD) schedule*, the amount of time required for reinforcement varies. For example, VRD10 minutes would deliver reinforcement following an average of 10 minutes of appropriate behavior.

response generalization　Unprogrammed changes in similar behaviors when a target behavior is modified. See *generalization*.

response prompts　Teaching procedures in which a student is assisted to respond until the response is under stimulus control.

restitutional overcorrection　See *overcorrection*.

return to baseline　See *reversal design*.

reversal design　A single-subject experimental design that removes a treatment condition after intervention in order to verify the existence of a functional relationship. This design has four phases: baseline, imposition of treatment, removal of treatment (also known as *return to baseline*), and reimposition of treatment (also called *ABAB design*).

S^D　See *stimulus control*.

S-delta (S^Δ)　See *stimulus control*.

satiation　A condition that occurs when there no longer is a state of deprivation.

scatter plot assessment　A form of information gathering for functional assessment through direct observation of behavior.

schedules of reinforcement　The patterns of timing for delivery of reinforcers (see *intermittent schedules, interval schedules, ratio schedules*, and *response-duration schedules*).

seclusionary time-out　A time-out procedure that removes the student from the instructional setting as the means of denying access to reinforcement.

secondary reinforcers　Stimuli that are initially neutral but acquire reinforcing qualities through pairing with a primary reinforcer (also called *conditioned reinforcers*).

self-evaluation　See *self-recording*.

self-instruction　The process by which a student provides verbal prompts to himself or herself in order to direct or maintain a particular behavior.

self-monitoring　See *self-recording*.

self-observation　See *self-recording*.

self-recording　Data collection on one's own behavior (also called *self-observation, self-evaluation*, or *self-monitoring*).

self-reinforcement (self-punishment)　Administering consequences to oneself. Students may be taught to select reinforcers (or punishers), determine criteria for their delivery, and deliver the consequences to themselves.

shaping　Teaching new behaviors through differential reinforcement of successive approximations to a specified target behavior.

single-subject designs　Experimental investigations in which each individual serves as his own control. (See *AB design, alternating treatments* *design, changing conditions design, changing criterion design, multiple baseline design*, and *reversal design*).

social reinforcers   A category of secondary reinforcers that includes facial expressions, proximity, contact, privileges, words, and phrases.

stimulus control   The relationship in which an antecedent causes behavior or serves as a cue for the behavior to occur. Repeated occurrences of the behavior depend on its being reinforced. An antecedent that serves as an appropriate cue for occasioning a response and therefore results in reinforcement is known as a *discriminative stimulus* (S^D). An antecedent that does not serve as an appropriate cue for occasioning a response and therefore does not result in reinforcement is known as an S-delta (S^Δ).

stimulus generalization   *See generalization.*

stimulus overselectivity   A tendency to attend to only one or a few aspects of a stimulus rather than the stimulus as a whole.

stimulus prompt   An alteration of a stimulus to increase the probability of correct responding, often used in errorless learning procedures.

stimulus satiation   A condition that exists when an object or event that previously occasioned some response has been presented so frequently that the response no longer occurs in its presence.

supplementary antecedent stimulus   *See prompt.*

task analysis   The process of breaking down a complex behavior into its component parts.

thinning   Making reinforcement gradually available less often or contingent on greater amounts of appropriate behavior.

time-out   Reducing inappropriate behavior by denying the student access, for a fixed period of time, to the opportunity to receive reinforcement.

time sampling   An observational recording system in which an observation period is divided into equal intervals; the target behavior is observed at the end of each interval.

topography   The physical form or description of a motor behavior.

trend   A description of data represented on a graph. An ascending or descending trend is defined as three data points in a single direction.

trial   A discrete opportunity for occurrence of a behavior. A trial is operationally defined by its three behavioral components: an antecedent stimulus, a response, and a consequating stimulus. The delivery of the antecedent stimulus marks the beginning of the trial, and the delivery of the consequating stimulus signifies the termination of the trial.

unconditioned aversive stimulus   A stimulus that results in physical pain or discomfort to an individual (also called *universal, natural,* or *unlearned aversive stimulus*).

unconditioned reinforcers   *See primary reinforcers.*

universal aversive stimulus   *See unconditioned aversive stimulus.*

unlearned aversive stimulus   *See unconditioned aversive stimulus.*

unlearned reinforcers   *See primary reinforcers.*

variable   Attributes unique to the individual involved in the study or to conditions associated with the environment of the study.

variable-interval schedule (VI)   *See interval schedules.*

variable-ratio schedule (VR)   *See ratio schedules.*

variable-response-duration schedule (VRD)   *See response-duration schedules.*

Subject Index

Author Index